MEDICAL ASTROLOGY

Discovering the Psychology of Disease using TRIANGLES

Edition 2.

Leoni Hodgson

All rights reserved

Edition 1 published 2018

Edition 2 published January 2024

Copyright © Leoni Hodgson

No part of this publication may be reproduced, stored in a retrieval system, or transmitted in any form or by any means, electronic, mechanical, photocopying, recording or otherwise, without the prior written permission of the author.

ISBN: 978-0-6458868-1-8

Using triangles to find disease patterns in the astrology natal chart is ground-breaking work; this book Medical Astrology is essential reading for every medical astrologer.

About the Author

Born in New Zealand of English-Maori descent, Leoni Hodgson currently resides in Brisbane Australia. Leoni works professionally as a practitioner and teacher in several specialist areas in the esoteric arts - Astrology (DMNZAS - Diploma Member of the NZ Astrological Society 1982, and the PMAFA - Professional Member of the American Federation of Astrologers 1983), Esoteric Psychology (MA in Esoteric Psychology and Ph.D. in Esoteric Philosophy), Raja Yoga and Esoteric Healing (INEH Certificate).

About this Book

After years of studying medical astrology and books written on the subject by many excellent astrologers, I became really dissatisfied with the existing diagnosis methods because they were inconsistent. I could not find a reliable method that would accurately map disease in the chart.

So, I decided to start from the beginning and devise my own method. To do so I fell back on my esoteric training. Esotericism is a science based on the notion that we are souls having an earthly experience. Having studied and taught Esoteric Astrology, Esoteric Psychology, Esoteric Healing and Raja Yoga for years, I went back and searched in these texts until I settled on the triangle.

The Tibetan Master Djwhal Khul (the real author of the Alice A. Bailey books), said *"The triangle is the basic geometric form of manifestation and is seen (by those who have eyes to see) underlying the entire fabric of manifestation, whether it is the manifestation of a solar system.. cosmic triplicities or the tiny reflection of this divine triple whole which we call man"* [1] - or a disease, I thought. This set me on an investigative study of hundreds of charts, using a triangulated method of disease diagnosis.

Another point I wanted to highlight is the link between psychology and disease. In Bailey's Esoteric Healing book, the Tibetan said that most diseases on an individual level are directly attributable to our inner states, mainly our disturbed emotions. I had been using that premise for years in my astrological counselling work and found it very accurate.

The results of my research are presented in this book, *Medical Astrology: Discovering the Psychology of Disease using Triangles*. It is a combination of Traditional and Esoteric Astrology, Eastern teachings on the Seven Rays and Chakras and modern medical and psychological notions.

It is my belief that this book is just one step towards a future goal where the sciences of psychology, medicine, astrology and the chakras are combined in the treatment and healing of disease. This the Tibetan predicted.

The 2nd Edition, 2023.

After the book's first publishing in 2018, the author created a Facebook group and worked with the general online public to continue testing the diagnosis and Health Triangle concepts presented in the book. As a result, adjustments were made to Chakra, Body and Disease rulerships, and a rewrite was done of the Diagnosing of Disease chapter. Additionally, new sections were added - Remedial Advice, Counselling, and Health Readings. All changes were designed to help readers develop and improve their astrology medical and psychological skills.

Leoni Hodgson

---

1 Bailey, Alice A; Esoteric Astrology, 429.

Acknowledgements

This book is dedicated to the world service work of the Tibetan Master Djwhal Khul.

Loving thanks to my friends and co-workers - Jeanni Monks, Paula Villano and Janette Moore for their courage, strength and inspiring optimism in the face of major health challenges.

Appreciation to the online site www.astro.com for astrology chart data, for artwork from authors named in the book, and for free online clipart or photos. All other artwork by Hodgson.

MEDICAL ASTROLOGY

Discovering the Psychology of Disease using TRIANGLES

The use of a triangle is not accidental. It is "the basic geometric form of all manifestation and it is to be seen underlying the entire fabric of manifestation, whether it is the manifestation of a solar system, a man", or in this case disease.

- Djwhal Khul

Edition 2.

Leoni Hodgson

Foreword

It is a pleasure to be writing the Foreword to this ground-breaking book on medical astrology written by my colleague Leoni Hodgson. For some reason, there are very few books on the esoteric aspect of medical astrology despite the great interest in what is essentially an esoteric subject. Given the huge interest in disease and health, you would think that astrologers over the decades would have already explored more fully the esoteric side of astrology.

Leoni Hodgson has made an impressive contribution to filling this gap, at the same time as including well-known models and formulas associated with astrological/medical diagnosis. Of especial note is how she has prepared the student with detailed information on those areas which she sees as necessary pre-requisites for the central issue of astrological diagnosis. The book begins with a description of our subtle constitution, so that we can understand where the astrological energies including those from the signs and planets are received by our vehicles of mind, emotions and physical body.

The next detailed section features the characteristics of the seven rays which form the basis of the energies that flow through the signs and planets, including their association with bodily parts and various diseases. She sees the study of the seven rays as vital to understanding medical astrology and has written and taught on this subject herself over the years. Following this section of the book, the astrological signs receiving the ray forces are described and related to bodily parts and possible health problems. There is then a natural progression to examining the planets associated with each sign.

Many people would not be aware that the planets are understood to fall into three types of influence on a person, depending on whether the planets concerned are classed as exoteric or esoteric. This particular philosophy comes from the writings of Alice Bailey whose work has been deeply studied by the author of this book together with other esoteric sources of wisdom.

The author then presents the subject of the human chakra system which forms the reception of the energies flowing through the signs and planets and which are finally received by the endocrine glands, tissues and body organs.

> After this hierarchical progression of energies which condition our health and disease, we come to the unique contribution of the book – triangulation of three planets related to each disease process. One planet will represent the cause of the disease problem; another represents the organ concerned or reception point, and a third planet shows the effects or actual disease such as blindness. Then follows many case histories illustrating this formula.

This book will be appreciated by all astrological students interested in health and disease whether physical or psychological, lay people interested to understand astrology, and all esoteric students who study the meaning of life. Leoni Hodgson has written a detailed, comprehensive, and lucid account of those energies that condition our health and wellbeing.

Judy Jacka, BH.Sc. Post Grad.Dip. HRE, N.D.

Leoni is my spiritual mentor and a beloved soul friend who I have known since the early 2000's when I undertook to study her two year esoteric psychology course about the seven rays and raja yoga meditation which revolutionized my life at that time. I continue our spiritual work together by attending her monthly Full Moon meditations and the Brisbane Goodwill Meditation & Friendship Group which meets on a monthly basis.

Leoni has worked professionally for over 20 years as an astrologer and as a teacher of esoteric psychology, esoteric healing, the science of the Seven Rays, the science of the Chakras and Raja Yoga meditation.

In her new ground-breaking book on *"Medical Astrology: the Psychological Link to Disease"*, Leoni combines exoteric and esoteric astrology in an easy informative way that takes us right to the core of how dis-ease inherent in the natal birth chart can be activated at any time by major transits, progressions or solar arc dynamic techniques throughout our life cycle.

Leoni's sensitive and enlightening way of pinpointing a particular illness and relating it to the astrological indicators in a horoscope with its underlying psychosomatic causes, makes this a unique and revolutionary book that every medical astrologer and healer needs to have on their book shelf. It delves into the deepest crevices of the astro-medical realm of cause and effect which our medical world and humanity in general can benefit from, at this very important stage of our Earth's evolutionary process. It was, after all, Hippocrates who stated that "a physician without a knowledge of Astrology has no right to call himself a physician".

In her book, Leoni succinctly examines how the astrological signs related to the energies of the seven rays, can be associated with the parts of the body they rule and health problems. Her presentation of the human chakra system and the etheric body via the flowing of energy through the zodiac signs, their planets, their rays and then on to the endocrine glands and organs of the body, takes us to a new level of understanding of esoteric healing on a cellular soul level. From this angle, esoteric healers will also benefit from a study of the book.

> Leoni's unique approach to finding disease in the body uses triangles; three planets at least that are related to each step of the progression of disease: one planet represents the Cause of disease, another the Organ that is targeted by the disease, and a third the ultimate Effect of the disease. This process is vividly demonstrated in her book with many examples of case studies and clear diagrams, which makes this book a vital teaching tool in the study of medical astrology and the esoteric healing arts.

I personally feel that all of humanity will benefit from this book, especially Leoni's unique insights and contribution to understanding how health and disease from a physical, emotional, mental, spiritual and psychological energetic level are interrelated. Thank you my dearest friend for writing this book which is so needed at this time, as it creates a new paradigm of miraculous wellbeing possibility for healing ourselves and each other in the future.

> "Today any astrological investigation done in the field of medicine has relation to physical disease within the physical body. In the future, it will concentrate upon the condition of the etheric vehicle." [1]

Namaste & Blessings, Jeanni Monks

> Active committee member of QFA (Queensland Federation of Astrologers); APA (Association of Professional Astrologers) and an examiner on the FAA Examination Board. BA Psych.; Master of Science in Esoteric Psych.; Post Grad. Education/Counselling Dip; FAA Practitioner's Diploma.

---

[1] Bailey, Alice A; Esoteric Healing, 277.

Table of Contents

1. Spirit, Soul and Body 1

2. Forces & Energies 9

    2a. The Seven Rays 11
        Ray 1 of Will and Power 14
        Ray 2 of Love and Wisdom 16
        Ray 3 of Intelligent Activity 18
        Ray 4 of Harmony through Conflict 20
        Ray 5 of Concrete Mind 22
        Ray 6 of Devotion and Idealism 24
        Ray 7 of Ceremony, Order and Magic 26

    2b. Astrology Signs 29
        1. Aries 30
        2. Taurus 32
        3. Gemini 34
        4. Cancer 36
        5. Leo 38
        6. Virgo 40
        7. Libra 42
        8. Scorpio 44
        9. Sagittarius 46
        10. Capricorn 48
        11. Aquarius 50
        12. Pisces 52

    2c. Astrology Planets 55
        1. The Sun 56
        2. The Moon 58
        3. Mercury 60
        4. Venus 62
        5. Mars 64
        6. Jupiter 66
        7. Saturn 68
        8. Uranus 70
        9. Neptune 72
        10. Pluto 74
        11. The Earth 76
        12. Vulcan 76

    2d. The Etheric Web and Chakras 77
        1. The Crown (Sahasrara) Chakra 80
        2. The Brow (Ajna) Chakra 82
        3. The Throat (Vishuddha) Chakra 84
        4. The Heart (Anahata) Chakra 86
        5. The Solar Plexus (Manipura) Chakra 88
        6. The Sacral (Svadhisthana) Chakra 90
        7. The Base (Muladhara) Chakra 92

3. Disease, Diagnosing, Counselling. 97
    A. Disease and its cause - it is simply the misuse of energy 98
    B. Diagnosing Health and Disease in the Chart. 102
    C. Remedial Advice 116

4. Health Readings. 123
    Helpful charts 124
    A. Basic Health Reading, when Health is Good...128
    B. Health Readings when a Disease has been Diagnosed. 131
    C. Conversations with people diagnosed as terminally ill....................................138

5. Case Studies. 143
1. Crown Chakra Diseases 144
    1a. The Brain 144
    1b. The Brain - Dementia 150

2. Ajna Chakra Diseases 154
    2a. Ears 154
    2b. Eyes 156
    2c. The Nose 161
    2d. The Nervous System 162
    2e. The Pituitary Gland 167
    2f. 5th Ray Psychological Disorders 169

3. Throat Chakra Diseases 172
    3a. Breathing Problems...172
    3b. Thyroid Disorders 176
    3c. Cancer in Throat Chakra Organs 177
    3d. Intestinal, Bowel Trouble 181

4. Heart Chakra Diseases 183
    4a. Problems with the Blood..183
    4b. Problems with Blood vessels..187
    4c. Problems with the Heart 188
    4c. Immune System 190

5. Solar Plexus Chakra Diseases 192
    5a. Allergies 192
    5b. Gallbladder and Stomach...194
    5c. Liver...195
    5d. Pancreas 197
    5e. Cancer in the Solar Plexus Organs...199
    5f. Psychological-Emotional Disorders 201

6. Sacral Chakra Diseases...206
    6a. Genetic Diseases 206
    6b. Reproduction Problems 208
    6c. Sexually Transmitted Diseases (STD's) 211
    6d. Cancer in the Sacral Chakra Organs 212

7. Base Chakra Diseases...213
    7a. Adrenal Glands 213
    7b. Bladder, Kidney problems 214
    7c. Skeletal, Spine, Joint, Muscle Diseases...216
    7d. Skin and Hair 220
    7e. Cancer in the Base chakra Organs 223

    Appendix 227
    Glossary 227
    Bibliography 229
    Index 230

1. SPIRIT, SOUL AND BODY

The Triangle is the basic geometric form of God in manifestation - Spirit, Soul and Body; the Divine pattern on which man is modelled.

1. The Journey of the Soul - Evolution of Consciousness

This section answers questions like "who am I" and "why am I here?" This is important because disease is related to our struggle to understand the world and ourselves.

Esoteric teachings tell us that we are more than just a body, or emotions or a mind. These are our human parts that enable our true self - the Spiritual Soul or Buddhi, to manifest on earth. When describing the soul, most people say something like "the soul is the inner-self that is wise and loving" and they are correct. But it is more than that. It is our link with the Life ensouling the universe, known in different philosophies by names such as God or the Oversoul.

In a technical sense, God in manifestation is triune, appears as a three-fold energy influence commonly known as "Spirit-Soul-Body", "Father, Son, Holy Ghost" (Bible), or as "Atma, Buddhi, Manas" in esoteric literature. Human beings reflect this triune model as the following drawings show.

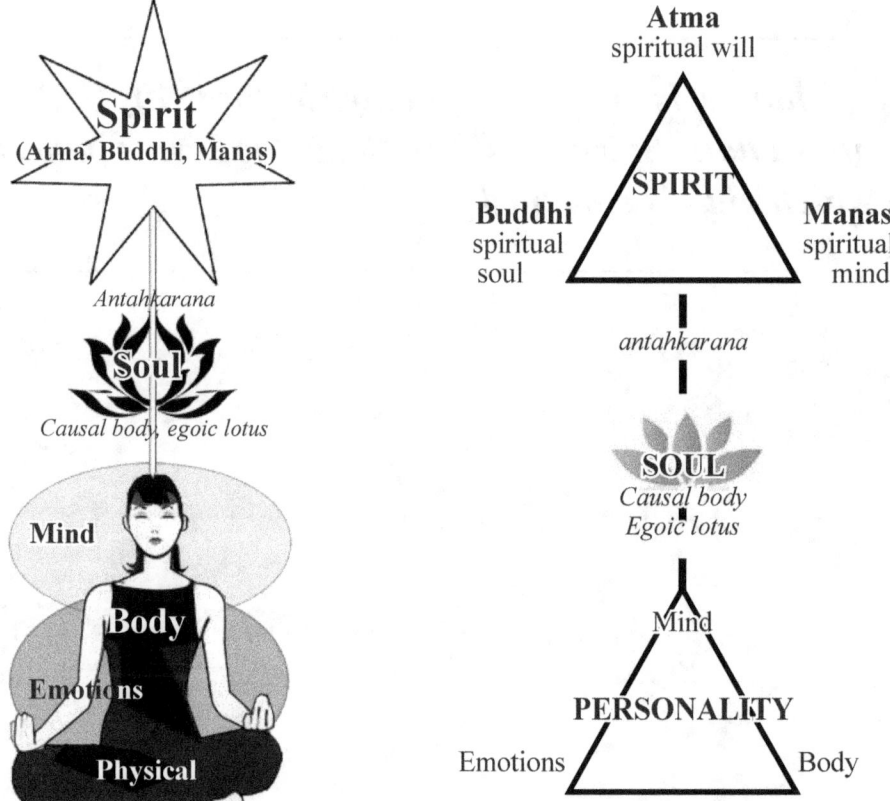

The soul - our human soul, is the bridge between our spiritual and human natures. It unfolds through experience on earth over many incarnations. A synonym of soul is "consciousness". As we acquire knowledge and apply it in our everyday lives, we learn to be more discerning and consequently our consciousness or soul expands. This proceeds across lives until union with Deity is achieved - in consciousness.

In the sketch, the dashed line from the mind to spirit, its Hindu name is "antahkarana." It represents a stream of lighted consciousness (between the brain and monad) that we must build to become spiritually aware and to reach the higher levels of existence. In most people, it has not been constructed. We build it through regular meditation, study of spiritual matters and by applying a holistic philosophy to the way we conduct our lives.

The "personality" consists of our human parts - the mind, emotions and the physical body. The soul uses the personality bodies to interact in the human world and to expand awareness and understanding.

"Who am I"?

If we are still identified with sexual desire, we might say "I am a passionate and sexual being". If we are still identified with intellectual cleverness, we might answer, "I am intelligent". Or, if we are identified with higher wisdom our response may be "I am a kind and loving soul". We express as much of the inner wisdom and love of the soul that we are able, and we answer the question differently depending upon our level of consciousness and the perspective from which we view life.

"Why am I here and where am I going?"

Our task is to live the most creative, fulfilling and productive life that we can manage. Across lives, this will take us through all the human departments in the world, from the very lowest to the highest.

Our task as a soul is to gain experience, to learn, to grow in character and expand our psychological understanding of the world. This will take us to the Spiritual Path. From that point on, our task is to climb to the heights of God wisdom, to become enlightened.

The term "enlightenment" as used in this book, refers to the stage when consciousness is filled with soul love and wisdom because all impediments that previously prevented this, have been removed. This occurs on the higher, Mental Plane. Here is a diagram to help explain things.

The Path and Consciousness

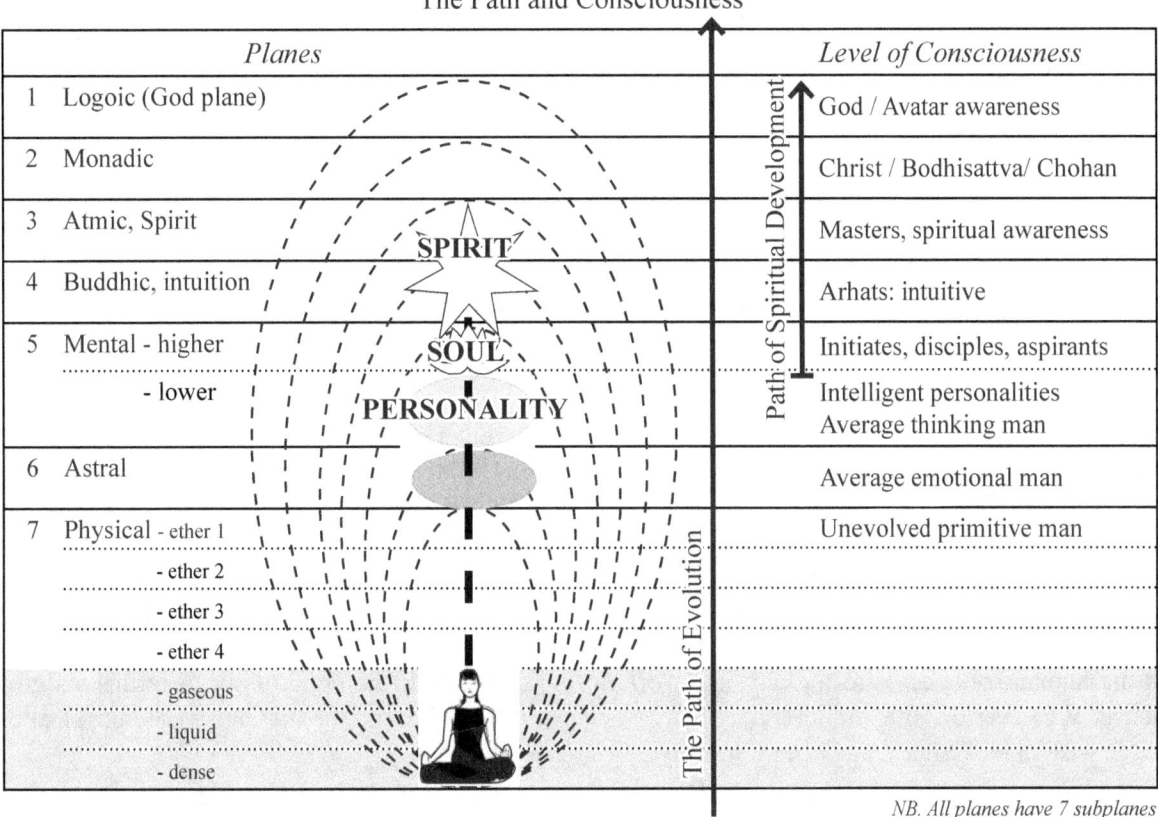

NB. All planes have 7 subplanes

The diagram depicts the 7 levels of consciousness in our solar system.

- The names of the planes or levels of consciousness are on the left-hand side. The lower 3 planes (5, 6, 7) are the human worlds. The higher four planes (1, 2, 3, 4) are the "spiritual worlds".
- Each of the 7 planes has 7 subplanes, but in the drawing they are shown only on the Physical Plane.
- On each plane, we have a seed-body which the soul uses when it has reached that plane.
- The names that are given to people who are stationed in consciousness on each plane are on the right-hand side of the chart.
- The Path of Spiritual Development, where we accelerate our progress, begins on the higher Mental Plane where the soul body (causal or egoic lotus) is located.
- The Monadic Plane is where our monads or the spiritual rays that connect us to God are located.
- A simple way to view the whole process - is like climbing a ladder.

    Each rung or plane symbolises both a plane of substance and a level of consciousness. When we move from one level to the next, it shows in our consciousness as increased wisdom and greater insight into ourselves, increased spiritual power and opportunity for service.

- Note that the arrow for the Path of Evolution goes off the chart at the top. There are six higher, equivalent universes above ours. We scale them all.

2. Consciousness ascends as our psychology expands

The whole emphasis of the evolutionary process is focused on the development of intelligent awareness and this is achieved on the Wheel of Rebirth, by incarnating through the astrological signs. We cycle round and round the zodiac through the twelve signs, all the time learning and expanding our psychological capabilities according to the sign we are travelling through. Each sign is responsible for developing and instilling certain positive qualities and values, though in the early stages, usually the negative traits are displayed.

Here is how Bailey describes the process.

> From point to point, stage to stage, and finally Cross to Cross, he fights for his spiritual life, in all the twelve houses and all the twelve constellations, subjected to countless combinations of forces and energies—ray, planetary, zodiacal and cosmic—until he is "made anew," becomes the "new man," is sensitive to the entire range of spiritual vibrations in our solar system and has achieved that detachment which will enable him to escape from the wheel of rebirth. [1]

Ascending the Ladder of Consciousness

As we evolve through the signs, gradually our consciousness ascends. "The Path and Consciousness" diagram on the previous page lays out in diagrammatic form, the levels through which consciousness rises. We start at the bottom, physical rung of the evolutionary ladder. Then, through the opportunities and growth challenges that incarnation provides, we gradually unfold our psychological faculties as we ascend or grow into the higher levels.

1. The etheric-Physical Plane and physical body

This is where our physical body is located. It has two levels - the etheric and dense, the latter consisting of the gaseous, liquid and dense subplanes. The etheric body is built from lighter etheric substance and is covered more fully in a later section. The dense body is built from heavier matter of the lower subplanes.

The consciousness of primeval man was focused in this body, at this level. He identified completely with the physical form, its instincts and physical survival instinct. The physical body is like a robot that does what its owner tells it to do. If we are emotional people, the body will be used to search for happiness. If we are ambitious, the body will be used to pursue wealth and power. If we seek enlightenment, the body will be used for that. The physical body gives the human soul access to the physical world, providing it with the opportunity to further its growth and experience. Whatever our life ambition may be, we achieve it only through the medium of the physical form. Therefore, it is wise to look after it and keep it healthy and strong.

Astrology: dense physical - Moon, Mars, Saturn. The sign on the ascendant, its ruler and the sign it is in, and planets in the first house; they colour the type of dense physical body we are born with and our appearance. The Moon represents all forms in nature, the physical containers that house the indwelling spiritual life, so it can be used to represent the physical form. Mars rules and controls the physical body when viewed as an animal form of blood and muscle. Saturn and Capricorn represent the dense skeletal structure and tissue of the body.

Astrology: The Etheric Body - Moon, Mercury, Uranus. Energy circulation through the etheric is governed by the Moon. [2] This means that any hard aspects to the Moon can be read as potential blockages in the etheric, the precursor to disease. Gemini (and Mercury), the custodian of conditioning energy and intermediary between soul and body is also related to the etheric. The 7th ray that Uranus carries, governs the etheric subplanes of the Physical Plane. The 3rd ray governs the etheric body as a whole, as it pervades the dense physical body. [3]

2. The Astral Plane and the astral/ emotional body - the Moon, Mars and Neptune

The Astral Plane is where our emotional body is located and where the consciousness of emotional people focus. The emotional-desire body gives expression to emotions ranging from love and compassion to fear and hate; and desires ranging from the most gross to the most sublime. The astral body is the most difficult vehicle to control and for many lives it keeps us trapped, swinging between the opposites of pleasure and pain.

---

1 Bailey, Alice A; Esoteric Astrology, 83.
2 Bailey, Alice A; Esoteric Healing, 143.
3 Bailey, Alice A; White Magic, 196.

Most people on the planet at this time are stationed at this level and are primarily emotional in their psychology. An unstable emotional body has the greatest negative effect upon our health. Toxic emotions produce toxic chemicals in the body, which result in disease. The development of a harmonious astral nature through the development of a serene mind, improves health.

Astrology: the Moon, Mars and Neptune govern our emotional life. The Moon is closely linked with our astral bodies [1] and its sign represents "the prison of the soul" pattern, a powerful negative core belief that controls consciousness.

Mars is the lower ruler of the Emotional Plane and governs the coarser emotions such as anger, annoyance, irritation, lust, rage, suspicion, hate, avoidance, disgust and loathing. It governs also the desire emotions such as passion, yearning, thirsting and higher emotions such as courage and aspiration.

Neptune is the higher ruler of the Emotional Plane. It refines our emotional life, instilling in us the softer emotions such as sadness, sorrow, grief, hurt, anguish, anxiety, guilt and acceptance; also admiration, joy, hope, serenity, ecstasy, bliss and devotion. Afflictions to these planets show troubled emotions.

3. The lower Mental Plane and the mind - Mercury, Venus and Uranus.
Mentally creative people have reached the lower Mental Plane.

People focused on the Mental Plane are definitely "mind" people and are not sometime thinkers who are dominantly astral. Due to widespread modern education, this is a fast growing group.

The mind is the individualizing principle that enables us to know that we exist, that we feel and know. It creates thoughtforms, concentrates, analyses, compares, deduces and memorises. It is not well organised in emotional people whose task is to develop the mind and mental discrimination. When this is achieved, when our psychology is firmly grounded on the Mental Plane, the soul (which is on the higher mental level) can begin to work through it.

Astrology: Mercury, Venus and their rays (4 and 5) influence the mind. Mercury's primary task is to unfold the discriminating and analytical powers of lower mind and to bring about its illumination. At a higher level, Mercury develops the intuition.

Venus carries the 5th ray of mind and works closely with Mercury to develop our mental powers. Its place in the chart shows where our thought life needs beautification and where we should endeavour to think and speak intelligently and with kindness.

Uranus is a representative of the scientific and abstract mind. Its place in the chart shows where we need to refresh the way we see life, shatter old concepts and develop new and freer ways of living.

4. The Personality - the Sun and Leo. When the mental body asserts itself, it integrates the forces of the emotions and physical body with itself into a composite entity called the "personality". This integration is a very important evolutionary advancement. Integrated personalities are powerful. They are the men and women who dominate the world and environment through the weight of their force, intelligence and power.

Astrology: our personality life is represented primarily by the Sun Sign. Aspects to the Sun show the level to which we have integrated our personality parts (mind, emotional, physical), and therefore the ability or inability of the personality to dominate the environment.

---

1 Bailey, Alice A; Esoteric Healing, 341.

Quotes from the Master Djwhal Khul

The Etheric Body
At present the etheric body is responsive to energies from:
1. The physical world.. the feeders and controllers of the animal appetites.
2. The astral world, determining the desires, emotions and aspirations which the man will express and go after upon the Physical Plane.
3. The lower Mental Plane, the lower mind, developing self-will, selfishness, separateness and the direction and trend of the life upon the Physical Plane.
4. The soul, the principle of individualism, the reflection in the microcosm of the divine intention. [1]

Opportunity of incarnation

For all of you this is an incarnation wherein the life focus becomes either irrevocably oriented toward the soul, as must be the case with newly accepted disciples, or powerfully expanded and inclusive as in the case of older disciples. [2]

---

1 Bailey, Alice, A: Telepathy and the Etheric Vehicle, 156.
2 Bailey, Alice, A: Discipleship in the New Age II, 546.

5. The Path of Spiritual Development on the higher Mental Plane

The Spiritual Path - sometimes just called "The Path", is the process that we embark upon when we begin the search for spiritual knowledge and illumination. This happens because at this level, the mind is coming under the illuminating effect of the soul.

In esoteric astrology, each sign functions at 3 levels to cater for the three levels of consciousness - personality, soul and spirit. Ordinary personality consciousness is represented by the *exoteric* planets, soul consciousness by the *esoteric* planets, and spiritual awareness by the *hierarchy* planets.

> **The presence of the soul in the chart is represented by the esoteric planets - the planets that rule each sign on the esoteric or soul level. They represent the purpose of the soul.**

The esoteric planet ruler of the ascendant sign is the "ruler of the chart" as far as the goals and ideals of the spiritual life are concerned. The Hierarchy rulers that develop spiritual awareness are not used in this book. They are not relevant to disease, except perhaps at a mass level. Here is a chart showing these rulerships. [1]

Chart 1: Planet rulers of the Signs

Signs	*Exoteric Ruler*	*Esoteric Ruler*	*Hierarchy ruler*
	Personality	**Soul**	**Spirit**
Aries	Mars	Mercury	Uranus
Taurus	Venus	Vulcan	Vulcan
Gemini	Mercury	Venus	Earth
Cancer	Moon v. Neptune	Neptune	Neptune
Leo	Sun	Sun v. Neptune	Sun v. Uranus
Virgo	Mercury	Moon v. Vulcan	Jupiter
Libra	Venus	Uranus	Saturn
Scorpio	Mars, Pluto	Mars	Mercury
Sagittarius	Jupiter	Earth	Mars
Aquarius	Uranus, Saturn	Jupiter	Moon v. Uranus
Capricorn	Saturn	Saturn	Venus
Pisces	Jupiter, Neptune	Pluto	Pluto

"v" Veiling forces from other planets.

The esoteric rulers start to influence us when we step onto the Path of Spiritual Development. So, for instance, a Cancer Sun person prior to the Path is ruled by the conflicted Moon; but on the Path is ruled by esoteric Neptune, which begins its refining process. Another example is Scorpio. Prior to soul influence we can be destructive (Pluto) and highly aggressive (Mars). On the Path, we come under higher Mars, where the soul urges us to fight for the higher good. The following quote defines esoteric and exoteric astrology.

> Exoteric astrology deals with the characteristics and qualities of the personality and of the form aspects, and also with the events, happenings, circumstances and the conditioning environment which appear in the personal horoscope... Esoteric astrology concerns itself primarily with the unfoldment of consciousness, with the impacts which awaken it to the peculiar "gifts" of any particular sign and ray endowment and with the reaction of the man and his consequent enrichment through his response to the influence of a sign, working through the esoteric planets from the angle of humanitarian awareness, of discipleship and of initiation. [2]

Higher Venus represents the human soul and the Solar Angel, our spiritual guide and mentor. When we establish conscious contact with our souls, our character begins to transform and gradually, values that are more inclusive are demonstrated such as intelligent love. These are higher Venus qualities.

---
1 Bailey, Alice A; Esoteric Astrology, 68.
2 Bailey, Alice A; Esoteric Astrology, 145-146.

Discipleship and the Path

Going back to the ladder diagram (remembering it portrays levels of consciousness), the Path of Spiritual Development starts on the higher mental and spans the top three subplanes. It takes three steps, three expansions of consciousness to cross this higher way on the upper Mental Plane and to become enlightened.

- The higher Mental Plane, subplane 3: the 1st step - Aspirants.

This is the first stage of the Path, sometimes called the Probationary Path. Aspirants whose minds have become infused a little with soul love and wisdom have reached this level in consciousness. The impact of this upon their psychology is like an electric shock. They feverishly run around looking for information, books, groups and teachers who can explain more about the wonderful world which they have contacted. Their task is to bring their physical appetites into balance and when successful they pass *the 1st initiation*. The word "initiation" simply refers to an expansion of consciousness and enhanced soul influence.

At this mystical stage of our development, the cause of illness and disease may change. Where before negative thoughts and emotions primarily caused disease, now the movement of energy from lower to higher chakras (with consequent energy disturbances and swings), cause the trouble.

Astrology: Vulcan and Pluto govern this stage. "The influence of Vulcan reaches to the very depths of his nature, whilst Pluto drags to the surface and destroys all that hinders in these lower regions." [1]

- The higher Mental Plane, subplane 2: the 2nd step - Disciples.

At this level are "older souls", those whose focus lies beyond the normal attractions of the human material world. On the ladder, consciousness has reached the top of the Mental Plane and is beginning to move into the Buddhic/Intuitional Plane, the world of inclusive love and wisdom.

Astrology: Disciples are becoming decentralised at a personality level, have found their chosen group and are working in a profession to help their fellow men. Their first task is to purify the emotional nature, a process governed by Venus, Jupiter and Neptune. When successful they pass the 2nd initiation. Here is a description of a disciple.

> For what is a disciple? He is one who seeks to learn a new rhythm, to enter a new field of experience, and to follow the steps of that advanced humanity who have trodden ahead of him the path, leading from darkness to light, from the unreal to the real. He has tasted the joys of life in the world of illusion and has learnt their powerlessness to satisfy and hold him. Now he is in a state of transition between the new and the old states of being .. His spiritual perception grows slowly and surely as the brain becomes capable of illumination from the soul, via the mind. As the intuition develops, the radius of awareness grows and new fields of knowledge unfold .. As he perseveres and struggles, surmounts his problems and brings his desires and thoughts under control .. the Master is found; his group of disciples is contacted; the plan for the immediate share of work he must assume is realized and gradually worked out on the Physical Plane. [2]

- The higher Mental Plane, subplane 1: the 3rd step - Initiates.

The battle taken up by the soul for complete domination of the personality is managed through Mars and most likely Uranus. It is a tremendous fight but success gives entry to the higher levels of spirituality. With the 3rd initiation complete, consciousness moves to the top of the Mental Plane and onto the Buddhic Plane. Later, towards the Atmic or Spiritual Plane. The Path continues ever upwards, or inwards perhaps is a more correct term. From the Buddhic to the Atmic, then to the Monadic where great consciousnesses like the Christ and Gautama Buddha are stationed. Then beyond to the Logoic, God-conscious level; and later, even further into higher planes of the universe.

Evolutionary progress takes its toll on the body. Every step forward we take, subjects the atoms of the physical body to forces of a higher and faster vibration than they were previously used to. This places stress on the system and the body causing disease.

---

1 Bailey, Alice A; Esoteric Astrology, 70.
2 Bailey, Alice A; Treatise on White Magic, 58-59.

2. FORCES & ENERGIES

2a. The 7 Rays

2b. Astrology Signs

2c. Astrology Planets

2d. The Etheric Web and Chakras

2a. The Seven Rays

From the One Life,
comes the Three - Spirit, Soul and Body;
From the Three come the Seven - the 7 Rays
- seven different energies, vibrations, colours and
characteristics that condition, shape and colour all that
is found in the universe.

Overview of the Seven Rays

According to Eastern Wisdom, the Seven Rays are the seven basic forces of the universe from which all things are made. They are seven different energies, vibrations, colours and characteristics that condition our human nature on all levels.

The Seven Rays are not used in traditional astrology, but all astrologers who wish to understand the link between psychology and disease should include them in their astrological work. This is because these fundamental forces, just as they determine our psychology, they also determine disease.

The 7 rays give rise to seven different psychological and disease groups. The diseases or disorders in each particular group display the energy traits of the parent ray.

Matching our psychology to a disease is made possible through the rays, which are the linking cause. For example, a violent 1st ray mind gives rise to a violent 1st ray disease such as a stroke; suppressed 6th ray emotions give rise to 6th ray psychological problems such as alcoholism or watery physical troubles such as oedema. We know which rays flow through the signs and planets making it easy to follow these streams of energy through the chart, linking planets, psychological states and disease. The rays knit together the various astrological forces we use, enabling us to study the arising of disease scientifically.

The 7 Rays in our System

The seven rays originate from the heart of our galaxy, reaching us via the signs and planets. Here is a simple diagram, depicting the ray flow through the signs, the planets, to earth and to us.

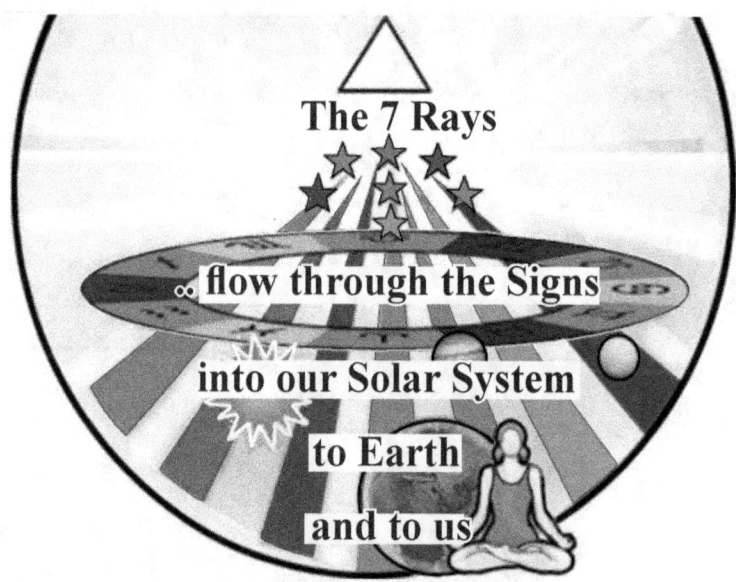

- Ray 1 of Will and Power (the red ray)
- Ray 2 of Love and Wisdom (the indigo blue ray)
- Ray 3 of Intelligent-Activity (the green ray)
- Ray 4 of Harmony through Conflict (the yellow ray)
- Ray 5 of Concrete Mind and Science (the orange ray)
- Ray 6 of Devotion and Idealism (the pale blue ray)
- Ray 7 of Ceremony, Order and Magic (the violet ray)

The rays form three groups

1. **Rays 1 and 7:** carry the will and power of God, give strength and will to our character.
2. **Rays 2, 4 and 6:** carry the love and wisdom of God, help us develop conscious wisdom.
3. **Rays 3 and 5:** carry the intelligence of God, they enhance our minds, our ability to think.

Chart 2: The Seven Rays and Astrology

The rays stream through space, through three constellations each and through one or two planets. The planets are the agents of the rays; each planet is a pure distillation of its ray's force. The chart shows how the rays connect to the body via the centres or chakras (wheels of force in the etheric body). This means that the signs and planets that carry each ray are also influential in the chakra and the organs the chakra rules. The drawing shows the rays that primarily govern each centre. But any ray can potentially flow through any chakra.

	Rays	Signs	Planets	Chakras
1	Will and Power	Aries, Leo, Capricorn	Pluto, Vulcan	Crown, Base
2	Love and Wisdom	Gemini, Virgo, Pisces	Sun, Jupiter	Heart
3	Intelligent Activity	Cancer, Libra, Capricorn	Saturn, Earth	Throat
4	Harmony through Conflict	Taurus, Scorpio, Sagittarius	Moon, Mercury	Ajna
5	Concrete Mind	Leo, Sagittarius, Aquarius	Venus	Ajna
6	Devotion and Idealism	Virgo, Sagittarius, Pisces	Mars, Neptune	Solar plexus
7	Ceremony, Order and Magic	Aries, Cancer, Capricorn	Uranus	Sacral

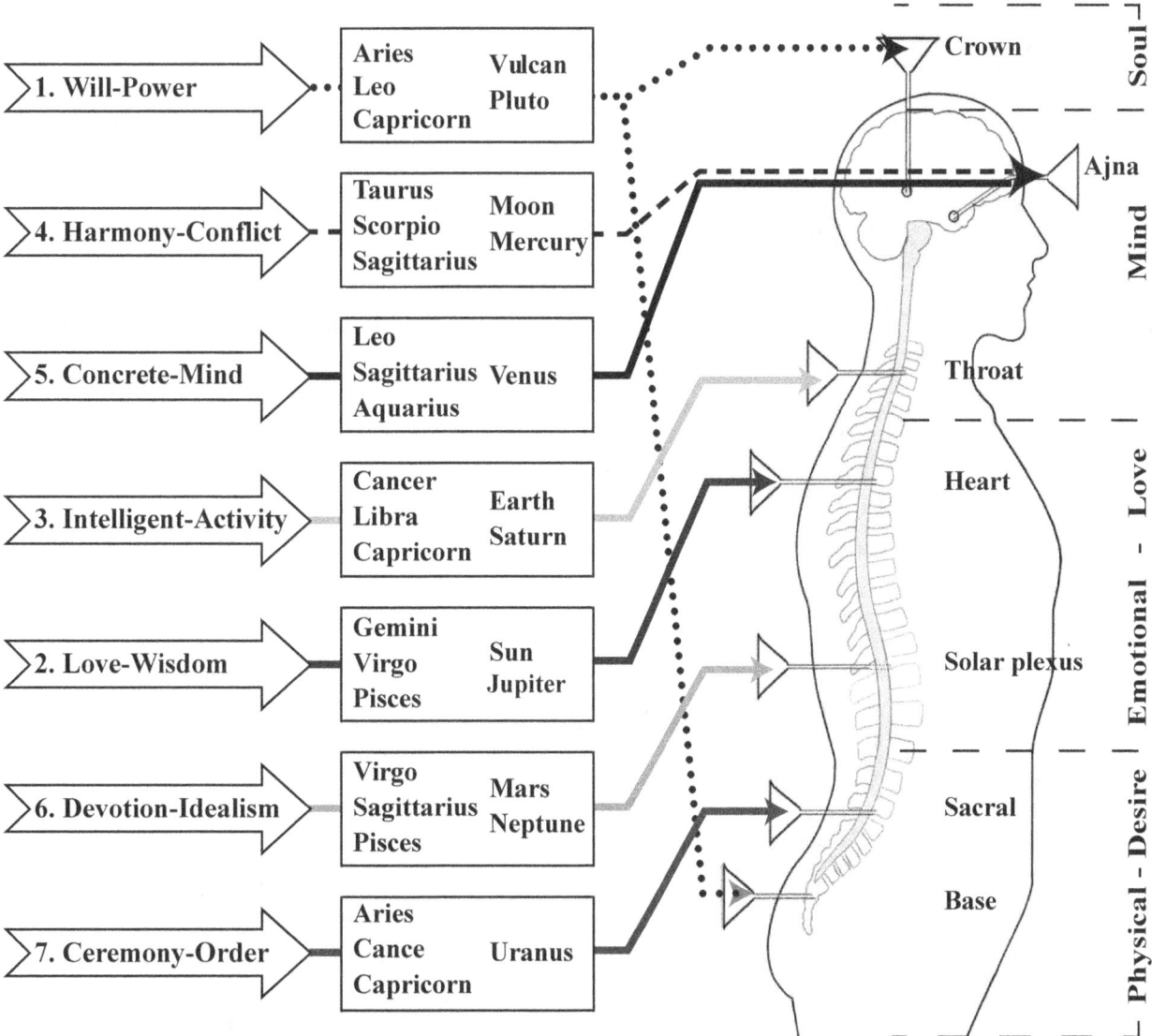

- **Chakra:**

  The Crown and the Base.

- **Planet agents:**

  Vulcan: higher spiritual will, power to purify and build.

  Pluto: power to destroy - for the higher good or for power and control.

  Saturn,[1] Uranus and Mars via Aries.

- **Sign agents:**

  Aries: power to lead and initiate for the greater good; or the arrogant use of power.

  Leo: power to rule for the greater good or arrogant displays of power. "I will because I can".

  Capricorn: executive power for the higher good or ruthless ambition.

  R1 virtues: strength, courage, steadfastness, truthfulness, fearlessness, power of ruling, capacity to grasp great questions, large-mindedness.

  Virtues to acquire: tenderness, humility, sympathy, tolerance, patience.[2]

---

1 Bailey, Alice A; Esoteric Astrology, 621.
2 Bailey, Alice A; Esoteric Psychology I, 201.

Ray 1 of Will and Power

"The will of God as it works through humanity"

The 1st Ray of Will and Power is the energy expression of the first aspect of God, the "spirit" aspect in the "Spirit-Soul-Body" trilogy. It is the most powerful force in the universe, ruling creation, life and death.

1. Ray 1 psychology

Ray 1 invests us with the will to be, to do and to survive. It is the energy in nature that governs death, birth and transformation. 1st ray types (the ascendant or Sun conjunct Pluto, Uranus or Saturn or located in Aries, Leo or Capricorn) are leaders, managers and organisers on all levels. For instance, kings, union bosses or the family matriarch who rules domestic life with a steely will.

The function of ray 1 people is to rule, to organise, to administer the law, to control the masses and ensure people follow the rules.

When the 1st ray expresses imperfectly, we see hard people who use power ruthlessly. Here are some 1st ray traits that may lead to problems and disease.

Anger, arrogance, pride.	Controlling, cruel, lacking pity.
Hard, insensitive, destructive.	Obstinate, wilful.
Ruthlessly ambitious.	Self-aggrandising.
Self-pity.	

2. Ray 1 in the Body

a. Crown and base chakras: the 1st ray works primarily through these centres.

b. Life-thread. The life of God reaches us through this thread of light (also known as the sutratma, the Monadic life stream, the silver cord). It connects our spirit aspect to the soul, then the soul to the body - anchoring in the pineal gland, in the heart and in the base chakras. From the brain, it connects to the ajna and the alta-major centre. Vital life energy flows through this thread into the heart, the bloodstream, the arteries and veins to vitalise every part of the organism. This enables the soul to hold the body coherently together during incarnation.

c. Respiration. The "breath" is related to spirit, the 1st aspect. The Bible tells us that God breathed life into man's nostrils and he became a living soul. Breath works via the throat chakra, whose organs manage breathing.

d. Sleep and death. The 1st ray governs these faculties. A good night's sleep is essential for good health - various body systems recuperate during sleep.

e. The will to live and to survive. The 1st ray gives these vital instinctual traits to the physical body via the base chakra and the adrenal glands.

f. The spinal column, bones, skeleton. Both rays 1 and 7 govern minerals, and the hardening, crystallising construction of the spine and skeleton.

3. Ray 1 in Disease

- Diseases that age, harden, dehydrate.
- Diseases that are relentless in their malevolent action.

Dictator-type ray 1 people use power and force to destroy people, launch a bullying and unrelenting onslaught to wear down all resistance. The same pattern occurs in ray 1 diseases, which wear down and destroy their hosts until death eventuates.

> *1st ray disease via Vulcan.* This fiery planet only becomes influential when we step onto the Path. At that level, it can represent brain trouble.

1st ray disease via Pluto. Pluto represents the destructive force of ray 1, that crystallises, hardens, represses, and brings death. It works through both the crown and base chakras and is very dangerous when it threatens health.

1st ray disease via Saturn. This planet also carries the 1st ray via its sign Capricorn. It represents the crystallising, repressive and hardening power of the 1st ray that works slowly but inexorably. Pluto's action is usually faster.

- Cancer (the disease). When the will is used continually to suppress emotion or desire in order to avoid emotional pain, the will-to-live force/ the survival instinct can run amok, infecting body cells so they become destructive. Suppression of emotion implicates the solar plexus as a major centre for cancer infection. The other ray involved is the primary building ray - Ray 2. To find cancer in the chart, look mainly to ray 1 planets Pluto and Saturn in hard aspect to planets representing the emotions. Jupiter for overbuilding.

Ray 1 in disease crystallises, hardens, restricts reduces, atrophies and ages. It is relentless and unstoppable, moving inexorably towards death, whether this is rapid or a long-term impairment. For ray 1 in disease, look for afflictions from Saturn and Pluto, and malefics in Aries, Leo and Capricorn.

▲ **R1 negative psychology.**
Egomania.
Megalomania.
Narcissism.
Obsessiveness.
Wilfulness.

▲ **Organs R1 rules, vitalises.**
Ageing.
Chemotherapy.
Electric fire.
Life and death.
Old age.
Radiation therapy.
Rigor mortis.

Crown
Melatonin.
Pineal gland.
Serotonin.
Sleep.

Heart
Life (1st aspect). [1]
Life-thread, sutratma, silver cord.

Throat
Breathing.
Respiration. [2]

Base
Adrenals.
Adrenaline.
Aldosterone.

---
1 Bailey, Alice: Esoteric Psychology I, 18.
2 Bailey, Alice: Esoteric Healing, 108.

Cortisol.
Fight - flight response.
Survival instinct.
Will to live, to exist.

▲ **R1 causing problems, disease.**
All diseases caused by ageing, blocking, destroying, hardening.
Abortion.
Addison's disease.
Aging unnaturally, progeria.
AIDS.
Alopecia.
ALS: amyotrophic lateral sclerosis, (Lou Gehrig's, motor neurone disease).
Alzheimer's.
Amputations.
Angina.
Arrested development.
Arteriosclerosis.
Arthritis.
Asphyxia.
Assassination.
Ataxia.
Atrophy.
Back pain, chronic.
Baldness.
Barrenness.
Blindness.

Blocking.
Blood clots.
Blood pressure high/ low: hypertension, hypotension.
Bones brittle, deformed.
Breaks, fractures.
Calcifying.
Cancer (a cause of).
Cardiomyopathy: chronic disease of the heart muscle.
Castration.
Cataracts.
Chronic diseases.
Cirrhosis, liver.
Clots.
Comas.
Concussion: head injuries.
Constipation.
Constricting.
Crippling.
Deafness.
Deep vein thrombosis.
Deformity.
Dementia.
Destroying.
Emaciation.
Fatigue: adrenal overload.
Gallstones.
Genocide.
Glaucoma.
Gout.
Hardening.

Head injuries.
Heart disease via ageing, hardening.
Huntington's disease.
Hypopituitarism.
Impotency.
Infertility.
Insanity, idiocy, lunacy - brain tissue cause.
Joints stiff.
Kidney disease via scarring, blocking.
Kidney stones.
Malnutrition.
Massacres.
Multiple sclerosis.
Murders.
Myopia.
Neuro-degenerative diseases.
Osteoarthritis.
Osteoporosis.
Paget's disease.
Pain, chronic.
Paralysis.
Paraplegia, quadriplegia.
Polio.
Possession.
Raynaud's disease.
Represses.
Scarring.
Scleroderma.
Sclerosis.
Senile decay.
Short sightedness.
SIDS: sudden death infant syndrome.
Simmond's disease.
Skull injuries.
Sleep apnoea.
Sleep disturbance.
Spinal arthritis.
Starvation.
Sterility.
Stiffening.
Stones.
Strangulation.
Stroke.
Stunting growth.
Suffocating.
Survival instinct over-reaction causing cancer.
Thrombosis.
Vertebrae degeneration.

- **Chakra:**

  The Heart and the Ajna.[1]

- **Planet agents:**

  Jupiter: it is the main distributor of ray 2. It fuses and expands, manifests as brotherly love or exaggeration and wastefulness.

  The Sun: it represents self-consciousness, the personality, which can radiate solar warmth and inclusiveness or egotistical selfishness.

- **Sign agents:**

  Ray 2 flowing through the signs manifests as:

  Gemini: a wise and loving messenger or an indiscriminate chatterer.

  Virgo: the wise server or an indiscriminate criticizer.

  Pisces: a wise and loving healer/ teacher or emotional naivety.

  R2 virtues: calm, strength, patience, love of truth, faithfulness, clear intelligence, serenity.
  Virtues to acquire: love, compassion, unselfishness, energy.[2]

---

1 Bailey, Alice A; Esoteric Healing, 210.
2 Bailey, Alice A; Esoteric Psychology I, 202.

Ray 2 of Love and Wisdom
"Christ-sensitivity as it works through man"

1. Ray 2 Psychology

Ray 2 is the energy expression of the "soul" aspect in the "Spirit-Soul-Body" trilogy, which means it deals with relationships, feelings and consciousness. Its job is to help us become sensitive, caring people - like our souls and like Christ.

The 2nd ray is the ray of consciousness, of sentiency. Under its influence, our senses are developed and refined, enabling us to become aware of ourselves as an "I", who we are as human beings and how we relate with others. "2" is the number of "relationships".

Through the cauldron of earthly experience, strife and striving, from our darkest and most shameful failures to our most amazing and self-sacrificing successes; Ray 2 helps us develop understanding and compassion for ourselves and for others. It is the ray of spiritual workers, teachers, healers and scholars.

There are two ray 2 types. "Love types" are more sensitive, feeling people. If they are advanced spiritually, they focus in the heart. If they are still working through their emotions they can be emotionally naive, fearful and impressionable. "Wisdom" types work through the ajna and negatively, they can be mentally cool. Below are some negative traits that may lead to 2nd ray type diseases.

Love, heart or solar plexus chakra types:
- Amorality (overactive thymus).
- Impressionable, oversensitive.
- Materialistic.
- Excessive, gluttonous, greedy.
- Love of comfort (excessive).
- Wasteful.

Wisdom, ajna, mind types:
- Cold, indifferent.
- Over-absorbed in study.
- Contempt of mental limitations in others.
- Self-love, extreme.

2. Ray 2 in the Body

a. Chakras. Ray 2 (primarily the love aspect of the ray), governs the heart centre and thymus gland. The wisdom/ consciousness aspect of ray 2 is related to the ajna, the centre of personality awareness.

b. The cardiovascular system, the heart. The 2nd ray flows through the Sun, the heart chakra, and the cardiovascular system is its Physical Plane means of distribution.

c. Vitality and vitalising of the body, prana. Prana is the vitalising energy of the cosmos that gives life to all living creatures. Prana that vitalises our bodies flows from the Sun. We receive solar prana from golden devas (intelligent angels of nature). Entering the body via the spleen, prana rises to the heart and merges with the life stream as it enters the blood; contributing to the overall vitalising of the body.

A balanced and unhindered flow of prana via the etheric web into the body is the basis of good physical health. If vitalisation does not reach a particular part of the body because there is damage to the etheric, congestion in a chakra or a diseased or destroyed gland; then that part of the body becomes diseased.

d. Consciousness utilises the nervous system. The 2nd ray is the energy that develops consciousness - of ourselves, of others and of the world around us. The "consciousness thread comes directly from the soul and anchors in the head (centre). There is the seat of consciousness".[1] From the crown, consciousness interacts with the human worlds via the ajna, the nervous system and sense organs.

---

1 Bailey, Alice: Education in the New Age, 146.

e. Sight and eyes. The Sun is the primary ruler of sight - the physical eye came into being in response to the light of the sun. [1] Sunlight is governed by the 2nd ray and so is sight.

f. Growth. The 2nd ray is the force behind our growth and development, physically and consciously. The Sun and Jupiter that carry this ray represent growth in the body.

3. Ray 2 in Disease

- Chronic overbuilding of cells.

Ray 2's task in the body is to build, grow and protect. During gestation it gathers atoms together, causes them to cohere so that a form or physical body is produced according to the plan of the soul. Prana/ life-force/ vitality, is drawn from the Sun to nourish and rebuild cell-life and to keep the body healthy, robust and resistant to disease.

> *Ray 2 via the Sun.* The Sun's primary task is to give life and vitality to the body and to protect it from disease. When its force is excessive, it inflames, burns, can overbuild. Problems occur in cell-life.
>
> *Ray 2 via Jupiter in disease.* This planet's main task is to foster growth. But when the building process goes awry there is over-stimulation. Too much energy is drawn in causing cell over-building.

Ray 2 in disease overstimulates. Excess energy pours in, more than the body can handle. The result is multiplication of atoms, inappropriate growths such as tumours, cancer, and extra body parts. Cancer is a ray 2 disease. For this ray's diseases, look for afflictions to Jupiter, the Sun and malefics in Gemini, Virgo and Pisces.

▲ **R2 negative psychology.**
Hypersensitive, oversensitive.

▲ **Organs R2 rules, vitalises.**
Expansion.
Growth.
Magnetism.
Prana.
Proteins, amino acids.
Tonifies.
Vitalises.

Crown
Consciousness thread (R2), [1] the antahkarana.

Ajna
Cognition.
Intelligent brain and nervous system activity.
Self-consciousness.
Sentiency.

1 Bailey, Alice: The Externalisation of the Hierarchy, 145.

Sight.
Vision.

Heart
Aorta.
Arterial blood.
Arteries.
Blood.
Blood cells.
Blood circulation, quality.
Bloodstream.
Capillaries.
Cardiovascular system.
Cell life.
Cholesterol.
Constitution.
Haemoglobin.
Heart organ.
Immune system.
Life breath.
Life-stream.
Oxygen, oxygenation.
Pulmonary circulation.
Recuperative power.
Spleen.

Thymus.
Veins.
Vena cava.
Venous system.

Solar plexus
Body fat (related to GI function).

▲ **R2 causing problems, disease.**
All diseases where there is 'too much.'
Acromegaly.
Amyloidosis.
Arteriosclerosis.
Bloating.
Blood cancer.
Blood pressure high.
Bone cancer.
Brain: cancer, tumour, abscess.
Cancer: breast, colon, liver, pancreatic, etc.
Cellulite.
Cholesterol (high).
Creation of too many body parts.
Cushing's syndrome.

Cysts.
Diseases caused by excess eating.
Extra body parts.
Fattening.
Fevers.
Fibroids, womb.
Flabbiness.
Gigantism.
Gluttony.
Goitre.
Grows abnormally.
Heatstroke.
High temperature.
Hypertension.
Inflammation.
Leukaemia.
Lymphomas.
Melanomas.
Metastasises.
Myeloma.
Obesity.
Overbuilds cells - cancers, tumours.
Overgrowth.
Over-vitalising.
Pituitary cancer, tumours.
Polyps.

Prostate cancer.
Raynaud's disease.
Sarcomas.
Sunburn.
Sunstroke.
Swellings.
Thickening.
Tumours.
Uterine fibroids.
Warts.
Weight gain.

---

1 Bailey, Alice A; Treatise on White Magic, 213.

Ray 3 of Intelligent Activity
"The ray of intelligent versatility and adaptability"

- **Chakra:**

The Throat; also the Sacral and Base.

- **Planet agents:**

Saturn: the responsible use of power or selfish manipulation.

The Earth: global experience that develops group skills, the ability to work cooperatively and intelligently with others.

Mercury [1] and the Moon

- **Sign agents:**

Cancer: intelligent nurturing or crafty dishonesty.

Libra: intelligent balance in relationships or superficiality.

Capricorn: intelligent action or devious ambition.

R3 virtues: wide views on abstract questions, sincerity of purpose, clear intellect.

Vices: intellectual pride, coldness, isolation, inaccuracy in details, dishonesty.

Virtues to acquire: sympathy, tolerance, devotion, accuracy, energy, common-sense. [2]

---

1 Bailey, Alice A; Esoteric Astrology, 280.

2 Bailey, Alice, A: Esoteric Psychology I, 204.

1. Ray 3 Psychology

The 3rd Ray of Intelligent Activity is the "body" aspect in the "Spirit-Soul-Body" trilogy. While ray 1 governs breathing and life and ray 2 governs consciousness; ray 3 generally governs digestion, reproduction and the physical body.

Ray 3 is the ray that is most closely associated with matter and form.

It represents the basic intelligence of all living forms whether this is the brilliance of an Einstein or the ability of an amoeba to survive and reproduce. Ray 3 rules creative intelligence and its highest expression is progressive development through experience. Ray 3 people (the ascendant or Sun conjunct Saturn or located in Cancer, Libra or Capricorn), are very intelligent in the ways of the material world. They use their wits to survive economically and are effective in business and finance.

When ray 3 intelligence is misused, people become predators, use their wits to manipulate and steal. Such as: white collar crimes, cyber-crimes, fraud and theft.

2. Ray 3 in the Body

a. Chakras and thyroid. Ray 3 works primarily through the throat, sacral and base chakras. The latter chakra generally rules the entire hard mainframe structure of the body.

b. Brain, central nervous system, 5 senses. They are created by the activity of the 3rd ray; [1] and are used by the thread of consciousness, of intelligence (R2).

c. Body intelligence. This force of Mother Nature, underlies the intelligent design of the body, giving it its instinctual ability to stay alive, reproduce and raise its young.

d. The endocrine and exocrine glands. The glands of the intelligent endocrine messaging system are ductless. They secrete their products (hormones), directly into the blood to balance and regulate health. The endocrine glands are the organs in which the chakras anchor. Exocrine glands secrete substances through ducts onto your body surfaces. Eg. sweat, tears, saliva, milk and digestive juices.

e. Breathing apparatus. The throat chakra, therefore ray 3, vitalises the respiratory organs. The 1st ray manifests through these organs - it is 'the breath'. The bronchial tract distributes air to the lungs.

f. Digestion, gastrointestinal tract (GI), and enteric NS. Ray 3 via the throat chakra governs digestion and the GI tract, and is related to the enteric nervous system.

g. The lymphatic system. This is governed by the throat chakra, ruled by ray 3.

h. The physical body and reproduction. The 3rd ray governs the physical form [2] and all physical organs. It also governs reproduction, which is an animal instinct. Cancer, the sign that rules the form and reproduction, carries the 3rd ray.

i. Body elimination of waste: kidneys, bladder, urinary tract, faeces, cell waste via lymph. The elimination of urine and faeces from the body.

j. Kundalini: Ray 3/ kundalini/ the fire of matter, is housed in the base chakra. It animates the atoms of the physical body and keeps the body warm.

3. Ray 3 in Disease

Ray 3 misused - the force of manipulation and deceit, it rebounds upon digestion, causing intestinal and gastric disorders via the solar plexus. Cancer, the sign most associated with digestion, carries the 3rd ray.

---

1 Bailey, Alice: Esoteric Psychology I, 251.

Being the force of intelligence in nature, ray 3 when malfunctioning can result in cross-wiring in the intelligent systems of the body - especially in the endocrine system and the organs and systems governed by the thyroid gland. Wrong hormonal messaging is given. While there may be excessive hormone distribution in one direction, there can be the lack of in another.

Ray 3 via Saturn. Saturn carries the 3rd ray. With this force via the throat chakra, Saturn assists the intelligent messaging of the endocrine system. Via the base chakra, Saturn represents the mainframe structure of the body, the protective frame for the soft inner organs. Overall, it represents body-intelligence.

Ray 3 via the Earth. The Earth can represent the throat chakra, its organs, functions and problems.

For ray 3 in disease look mainly for afflictions to Saturn, and malefics in Cancer, Libra and Capricorn.

The 3rd ray governs all parts of the physical form.

▲ **R3 negative psychology.**
ADD, ADHD: attention deficit hyperactivity disorder.
Deceit.
Dishonesty.
Manipulation.
Psychopath.

▲ **Organs R3 rules, vitalises.**
Atomic vitality. [1]
Body.
communication.
Body intelligence.
The dense physical body in its entirety.

Crown
Brain, brain cells, cerebral cortex, neocortex, skull.

Ajna
Endocrine system.
Face parts: eyes, ears, nose.
Homeostasis.
Nervous system. [2]

Throat
Brain, lower: alta-major centre, brainstem, cerebellum, medulla oblongata, pons, reptilian brain.
Breathing apparatus [3]: alveoli, bronchial tree, diaphragm, lungs, trachea, windpipe.
Carotid gland
Gastro-intestinal tract: palate, pharynx, salivary glands, uvula (is also related to the entire tract and digestive process including the intestines, rectum, anus.
Lymphatic system, adenoids, lymph nodes, peristalsis, sinuses, thoracic duct, tonsils.
Metabolic system.
Neck.
Speech, all organs: glottis, larynx, tongue, vocal cords.
Thyroid gland. parathyroids, parotid glands, thyroxine.
Tubes in the body.

Heart
Pericardium

Solar plexus
Enteric NS. [4]

Sacral
Locomotion, movement.
Reproduction, sex: breasts, cervix, clitoris, conception, Cowper's glands, egg ovum, embryo, epididymis, estrogen, genitals, fallopian tubes, fertility, gestation, menstruation, ovaries, penis, periods, placenta, pregnancy, procreation, progesterone, prostate gland, semen, testes, testosterone, uterus, vagina, vans deferens, womb.

Base
Body warmth.
Bone marrow.
Bones, ribs, vertebrae, flesh, tissue in the entire body.
Cells, of the physical body. [5]
Hair.
Kidneys, bladder, urea, ureters, urethra, urinary tract, urine, uric acid.
Skin.
Stem cells.

▲ **R3 causing problems, disease.**
Colic.
Congenital diseases, disorders.
Distorts.
Dyslexia.
Dyspepsia.
Endocrine dispensing wrong hormones.
Fatigue - thyroid.
Flatulence.
Gastric disorders.
Genital disorders, warts.
Hormonal trouble.
Hyperactivity.
Indigestion.
Learning difficulties.
Nausea.
Parasites, intestinal.
Social diseases,
Speech problems.
STD's. [6]
Stuttering.
Weight gain or loss, thyroid.
Worms.
Wrong messaging.

---
1 Bailey: Treatise on Cosmic Fire, 607.
2 Bailey; Esoteric Psychology I, 251.
3 Bailey; Esoteric Healing, 45.
4 Extends along the entire digestive tract – from esophagus to stomach, to intestines, to anus.
5 Bailey; Treatise on White Magic, 196. "R3"
6 Bailey, Alice A; Esoteric Healing 51.

- **Chakra:**

The Ajna and Throat via Mercury.
The Solar Plexus via the Moon.
The Base via the Moon, the ruler of form.

- **Planet agents:**

Moon: balanced emotional expression or a conflicted astral life ruled by the "prison of the soul" pattern.

Mercury: mental harmony and balance or a conflicted, agonising mind.

- **Sign agents:**

Taurus: aspiration or conflict and unregulated desire.

Scorpio: the internally centred warrior or inner war and conflict.

Sagittarius: the balanced archer or dominated by the lower appetites.

R4 virtues: strong affections, sympathy, physical courage, generosity, devotion, quickness of intellect and perception.

Virtues to acquire: serenity, confidence, self-control, purity, unselfishness, accuracy, mental and moral balance.[1]

---
1 Bailey, Alice, A: Esoteric Psychology I, 206.

Ray 4 of Harmony through Conflict
"The ray of music, dance and drama"

1. Ray 4 Psychology

The 4th Ray of Harmony through Conflict is aligned with the 2nd Ray of Love and Wisdom, which means it deals with relationships and their eventual harmonising after a period of conflict.

Ray 4 affects the mind and mental bodies on this ray are "right-brain", "feeling" minds - intuitive, artistic, picture making and colourful. Many artists and entertainers are on this ray. Affected intensely by discord they share what they feel through art, literature or music. Right-brain people have their brain cells coloured by Mercury since it carries the 4th ray.

Perhaps half the people on the planet have a 4th ray mind, which means that as a whole we are colourful and expressive people. Ray 4 is the bridging ray. It makes connections between people. First contact may be war and conflict, but in time this can lead to harmony as reconciliation and peace unfolds.

Ray 4 oscillates, it moves back and forth, shuttling between opposites. When it does this vertically in our psychology, between the mind and an unstable emotional body, it leads to mood swings. Such people reach the highs of exhilaration only to suddenly drop into the lows of depression. People who are susceptible have the Sun or ascendant in Taurus or Scorpio or a heavily afflicted Moon or Mercury. Here are some 4th ray negatives that may result in psychological problems or disease.

Agitation.	Continuous agonising.
The dramatic "I".	Emotional instability.
Extravagance.	Indolence.
Inner conflict, agitation.	Lack of moral courage.
Mood swings.	Self-absorbed in suffering.
Worrying, inner suffering.	

2. Ray 4 in the Body

Ray 4 is not a prime ruler of any chakra, but is clearly related when the two planets that carry its force are examined - the Moon and Mercury.

The 4th ray via Mercury. This planet is the main representative of our mental processes and the nervous system. Consequently, it is a natural ruler of the intelligent ajna chakra that carries out these functions.

Mercury is also a representative of the intelligent diagnosing and messaging function of the endocrine system. This system is very much related to the throat chakra and the thyroid gland, which has been called "the keystone of the endocrine system".[1] Thus, Mercury has rulership-rights over the throat chakra and its organs as well.

Likewise, the Moon is not given as the ruler of a chakra.

The 4th ray via the Moon. Its sign Cancer is the primary ruler of digestion, relating both the sign and planet to the solar plexus chakra that governs the digestive organs and functions.

The Moon is also given as the ruler of the form, and this relates it to the base chakra, which is responsible for the mainframe structure of the body and for vitalisation of its functional activities.

---
1 Bailey, Alice: The Soul and its Mechanism, 46.

a. Ajna chakra: Via its rulers Mercury and the Moon, this force affects mental perception and moods.

b. Pituitary gland. Primarily ruled by the 5th ray, the pituitary's intelligent distributing/ messaging function is influenced by Mercury - hence the 4th ray.

c. The central nervous system. The ajna rules this messaging system, bringing it under the corulership of Venus and the 5th ray, and Mercury and the 4th ray.

d. The endocrine system. The intelligent functioning of this system is tied together by the throat chakra and thyroid, bringing it under the rule of Saturn, Venus and Mercury - hence the 4th ray involvement.

3. Ray 4 in Disease

- Mental and nervous disorders based on mood swings.
- Ray 4 debilitation as a consequence of conflict.
- Chronic pain and suffering.
- Allergic reactions.

The 4th ray force of conflict and combat is innate in humanity as a whole. The fear, worry and stress this fosters leads to constant devitalisation in the race. This undermines immune resistance, opening the body up to all manner of fevers, infections and contagious diseases. This force is behind emotional swings, allergic reactions, mucous build up, epidemics and pandemics. Here is a quote from-- Esoteric Healing, page 301.

> Ray IV. [Constant] conflict leads to constant devitalisation. Where this is present, resistance to disease fades out and practically all forms of ill health and bodily ills become possible. Diffusion of energy leads to a constant lessening of this resistance. As a result, you have debility, quick and bad reaction to the disease indigenous in the planet itself, and a rapid taking on of infections and of contagious diseases. This energy lies behind epidemics, and influenza is one of its main expressions.

For ray 4 problems, look for afflictions to the Moon and Mercury, or malefics in Taurus and Scorpio.

The 4th ray via Mercury. When afflicted, it indicates mental conflict that can unduly affect the nervous system and its functions all through the body.

The 4th ray via the Moon. When afflicted, it indicates emotional conflict, emotional arguments, emotional mood swings and emotional congestion. This disturbance affects not only our moods, but congests body fluids. Where there is excess mucous or phlegm that causes lots of coughing and constricting of airways, the 4th ray via the Moon is likely involved.

▲ **R4 negative psychology.**
Agitation.
Anti-social.
Anxiety.
Bipolar.
Combativeness.
Depression.
Despair.
Fearfulness.
Fighting.
Inner conflict.
Insanities. [1]
Manic depression.
Mental instability.
Mood swings.
Opposing.
Panic attacks.
Phobias.
Postpartum blues.
Psychological trauma.
PTSD.

▲ **R4 causing problems, disease.**
Abscesses.
Agitation within systems.
Allergic reactions.
Asthma.
Bronchitis.
Buboes.
Candida.
Carcinogenic, unhealthy, tissue changes.
Catarrh.
Celiac disease.
Chronic fatigue.
Colds.
Contagions, contagious diseases.
Covid-19.
Croup.
Cystic fibrosis.
Debilitating.
Decaying.
Devitalising.
Epidemics, pandemics.
Fatigue.
Food allergies.
Fungal infections.
Hay fever.
Immunity low.
Immunosuppression.
Infections, infectious diseases.
Influenza.
Mucous, excessive.
Nasal congestion.
Organs not working well together.
Pandemics.
Phlegmy conditions.
Rejecting.
Thickens, toxifies body fluids - boils, mucous, pus.
Toxicity, toxic condition, toxifies.
Unhealthy conditions generally.
Vaginal candida, thrush.
Weakening. [2]

---
1 Bailey, Alice: Esoteric Healing, 51.

2 Bailey, Alice: Esoteric Healing, 301.

Ray 5 of Concrete Mind
"The Ray of Scientific Mind"

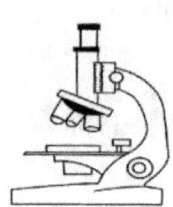

- **Chakras:**

The Ajna.

- **Planet agents:**

Venus: either the intelligent expression of love or a cold fact-finding mind.

- **Sign agents:**

Leo: an astute, intelligent leader or use of mental power to control people.

Sagittarius: an astute, intelligent director of men or an "I'm always right" expert

Aquarius: an astute and intelligent social reformer or the aloof and separative "expert".

Scientists and people who are purely mental and governed only by the [R5] mind.[1]

Ray 5 virtues: strictly accurate statements, justice based on facts, perseverance, common-sense, independence, keen intellect.

  Virtues to acquire: reverence, devotion, sympathy, love, wide-mindedness.[2]

---

1 Bailey, Alice, A: Discipleship in the New Age vol.1, xiii.
2 Bailey, Alice, A: Esoteric Psychology I, 207.

1. Ray 5 Psychology

The 5th ray is allied with Ray 3 of Intelligent Activity. It is the force of the lower concrete mind that is vital to our evolutionary development. This is because lower mind acquires knowledge about the world, helps us learn from our mistakes, thus teaching us discrimination. This intellectual movement towards improvement leads us from our own selfish truths and limited beliefs into wider and more inclusive understandings and eventually into the Mind of God.

People born with Ray 5 minds are "left-brain". They are logical and pragmatic, preferring a fact based and scientific approach to life. Consequently, scientists, researchers and technicians often have their mental bodies on this ray. Left-brain people have their brain cells coloured by Venus since it carries the 5th ray.

People are more likely to be of this type if the Sun, Mercury, Venus or ascendant are in Aquarius, which carries the 5th ray. In extreme cases we see "mind" people who are too mentally focused. Ultra-rational, their view of life is narrow. Lacking compassion or empathy, rigid in thought and belief, they are separative and judgemental.

> These traits - being *fixed-minded, judgemental* and *separative*, lie at the root of the many 5th ray modern psychological disorders that are appearing. They give rise to a psychological condition called "cleavage" and this in turn gives rise to a warped, very selfish, illusory or one-eyed way of viewing the world.

A cleavage can occur - within our emotional nature when there are competing desires, between the mind wanting something and the lower bodies yearning for something else, between the soul and the personality, or between a person and the environment. This latter problem is increasing rapidly - people feeling alienated and hostile towards anyone who looks or thinks differently to them. Here are a few ray 5 negatives that can lead to serious mental health issues.

Anti-social.	Austere and cruel.
Critical and judgemental.	Dogmatic.
Excessive mental activity.	Excessive objectivity.
Fixed, inflexible mind.	Lacking understanding, compassion.
Insensitive.	Mental, clinical coldness.
Misinterprets ideas.	Narrow, prejudiced in thought.
Over-analytical.	Over-detailed.
Sectarian.	Separative.
Socially awkward.	Ultra rational.

2. Ray 5 in the Body

Ray 5 influences primarily our mental life and the intellectual ajna centre. Although at first it may seem strange, Venus - which is commonly considered the Goddess of Love, carries the mental 5th ray. It is the custodian of the principle of Mind.[1]

> *The 5th ray via Venus*. The concrete mind is the thinking, analytical machine that we use to build thoughts and ideas. (Mercury). We spend many lives developing it. At first it is just a thinking-machine, like a computer. But when the soul begins to illumine the mind, it becomes wise, comprehensive and intelligently loving. This higher and beautified aspect of the mind is represented by Venus.

---

1 Bailey, Alice A. The Rays and the Initiations, 422.

Being able to think with love is the hallmark of a spiritually developed and inclusive person. The mind and heart have become unified. At this level, "Venus stands for the emergence of the love principle through the directing power of the mind." [1]

a. Ajna chakra: Ray 5 works primarily through this centre.

b. Pituitary gland. The endocrine function of the pituitary gland - particularly the creation of chemicals, is governed by this force. This gland is the body's chemist - ray 5 is the ray of pharmacologists.

The 5th ray force governs the concrete mind. Due to widespread modern education, humanity is rapidly becoming more mental in focus and less emotional - which means, problems affecting mental expression are increasing. Consequently, this force lies behind many modern psychological disorders. But even then, emotional disturbance still remains the root trouble. So, these disorders are a combination of the 5th and 6th emotional rays.

As mentioned previously in the psychology section for the 5th ray, "cleavage" is the root problem for this group of disorders. Here is text from Djwhal Khul in relation to this force and disease.

> Ray V. *"The Great One arose in His wrath and separated Himself... He produced cleavage on every hand, wrought with potent thought for separative action. He established barriers with joy. He brooked no understanding; He knew no unity, for He was cold, austere, ascetic and forever cruel... He widened all cleavages, erected barriers, and sought to make still wider gaps.*
>
> Cleavage is the outstanding characteristic—cleavage within the individual or between the individual and his group, rendering him anti-social. Other results are certain forms of insanities, brain lesions and those gaps in the relation of the physical body to the subtle bodies which show as imbecilities and psychological troubles. Another form of disease, emerging as a result of this fifth ray force is migraine, which is caused by a lack of relationship between the energy around the pineal gland and that around the pituitary body". [2]

3. Ray 5 in Disease

- Modern mental disorders due to a cleavage.
- Imbecilities: due to a total disconnection between the brain, the mind and the soul.
- Migraine: the esoteric cause is due to a cleavage between the energies of the pituitary and pineal glands. Hypothetically, this causes abnormal chemical activity in the head, which is thought to be the cause of headaches/migraine pain.
- Malfunction of the intelligence of the endocrine system as it relates to the pituitary gland. The over or under-prescribing of a particular hormone.

Ray 5 divides, separates, denies. This separative tendency affects brain-cell activity and is the force behind many modern psychological troubles. For ray 5 problems in psychology and in the body, look for afflictions to planets in Aquarius or to Venus in particular. For example, Saturn in Aquarius appears prominently in migraine sufferers.

▲ **R5 negative psychology.**
Antisocial.
Asperger's.
Autism.
Cleavage.
Dissociative disorders.
Fixed-minded.
Insanities.

Lower psychism. [1]
Many modern psychological troubles.
Narrow judgement.
Over-analytical.
Separateness.

▲ **Organs R5 rules, vitalises.**
Mastectomy.

---
1 Bailey, Alice: Esoteric Healing, 51.

Medicine, medical science: the many modern scientific advancements and treatments.
Prescription medicines, drugs.
Surgery.

▲ **R5 causing problems, disease.**
Brain cancer.

Brain lesions.
Diseases, troubles caused by wrong thinking.
Dividing and separating.
Endocrine trouble caused by a malfunction of the pituitary.
Frontal brain lobe trouble.
Headaches.

Migraines.
Pituitary cancers and tumours.
Pituitary diseases.

---
1 Bailey, Alice A. Esoteric Astrology, 126.
2 Bailey, Alice: Esoteric Healing, 302.

Ray 6 of Devotion and Idealism
"The force of human emotion"

The 6th Ray of Devotion and Idealism is closely aligned with the 2nd Ray of Love and Wisdom, which means it deals with relationships, emotions and consciousness.

1. Ray 6 Psychology

The 6th ray governs our emotions (ranging from love to fear and hate), and is the primary influencer of the astral/ emotional/ desire body.

In advanced spiritual man the astral body anchors in the heart centre, giving expression to higher feelings of spiritual love, inclusiveness, compassion, spiritual idealism, aspiration and devotional service. Spiritual servers, healers and carers are on this ray.

In the average person, the astral body anchors in the solar plexus centre, where it drives the physical body to satisfy its desire. Most people focus at this level. Desire is the sensuous grasping after objects that give pleasure. In man, desire can range from the grossest desires imaginable, up to an aspiration for spiritual union. Human love and desire without the inclusive influence of ray 2, is Mars-ruled, conditional, exclusive, intolerant and in extreme cases can be cruel and murderous. In the normal course of evolution, objects of desire change until ultimately the only desire remaining is a yearning to unite with the wholeness of Deity.

> **"Glamour" is a word used to describe how ray 6 distorts perception. Glamoured people refuse to see reality. They embellish situations with their hopes and wishes. Looking at life through rose coloured glasses, is a ray 6 phenomenon. Glamoured people live in delusion. They believe that the unreal is real, because they want life to be that way.**

Most people have a ray 6 emotional body, which means that Mars and Neptune rule the astral natures of most people on earth. Ray 6 influence increases in people who have the ascendant, Moon or Sun in Virgo, Sagittarius, Pisces, or conjunct Mars or Neptune. Here are some negative 6th ray traits that may lead to problems.

Addictive tendencies.	Cruelty, anger, vindictive, revengefulness.
Emotionalism, feelings of guilt.	Fanatic, sectarianism, separateness.
Self-deception, glamour.	Selfish, jealous love, envy.
Victim/ martyr consciousness.	Warped, narrow ideals.

2. Ray 6 in the Body

a. The solar plexus chakra: this centre is the entry point for ray 6 from the Astral Plane and from our astral nature.

b. The sympathetic nervous system. It is the apparatus of sensation. [1]

c. Body fluids and waterways. The water signs are related to the astral, water-plane and therefore to the 6th ray that governs it. Neptune that carries ray 6 rules Cancer and Pisces. Mars, the other carrier of ray 6, co-rules Scorpio.

Cancer rules white, pale fluids. With Neptune and Pisces, Cancer rules the lymphatic system, the watery drainage system of the body. Neptune rules the bloodstream. Scorpio via Mars, governs thicker body fluids such as menstrual blood and semen.

d. The 6th ray astral field. Most people on earth have their astral, emotional natures energised by this force. Devotional, idealistic, passionate and driven, such people are fiery, reactive, defensive and conditional in matters of love. As this field refines, finer expressions of emotion are seen.

---

[1] Bailey, Alice: Treatise on Cosmic Fire, 634; Treatise on White Magic, 284.

- **Chakra:**
The Solar Plexus and related to the Sacral.

- **Planet agents:**
Mars: the ardent devotee who fights for the higher good or the fanatical crusader who kills for his ideals.

Neptune: devotion to higher ideals or blinded by personal devotion and fantasy.

- **Sign agents:**
Virgo: the idealistic teacher devoted to healing and teaching, or devotion to the material world.

Sagittarius: the idealistic devotee, directing men and women to their higher good, or devotion to a hedonistic lifestyle.

Pisces: an idealistic and devoted server or a delusionary mystic, blinded by fanaticism.

R6 virtues: devotion, single-mindedness, love, tenderness, intuition, loyalty, reverence.

Virtues to acquire: strength, self-sacrifice, purity, truth, tolerance, serenity, balance and common sense. [1]

---

[1] Bailey, Alice, A: Esoteric Psychology I, 208.

3. Ray 6 in Disease

Emotional force lies behind most disorders and diseases today. [1] Ray 6 enters the body via the solar plexus (also influencing the sacral), but can contaminate any part of the body. Wrong desire results in the misuse of the sex function, trouble in that region, and in extreme cases, sexual violations.

6th ray via Mars. When virulent, this force attacks - is acidic, inflames and burns [2], causing trouble with the digestive organs and wrong-desire through the sacral. It governs "accidents." These are explosions of force generated by hatred, jealousy or vindictiveness (ray 6 traits), which are turned back upon those responsible like a boomerang. [3]

6th ray via Neptune. These diseases can be hard to see, find and treat. Neptune is the primary symbol of viruses, which are "infectious agents that enter the body via the life force, utilising the heart and bloodstream as a means of distribution". [4] They invade the body by masking their activities before the immune system discovers their presence.

For ray 6 problems, look for afflictions to Mars and Neptune and from malefics in Virgo, Sagittarius and Pisces.

▲ **R6 negative psychology.**

Solar Plexus
Addictions.
Alcoholism.
Anorexia.
Anxiety, worry.
Astral maniac.
Borderline personality disorder.
Bulimia.
Cruelty.
Cuts, cutting.
Delirium, delusory.
Depression.
Dreams, troubled.
Drug addiction.
Eating disorders.
Emotional problems.
Glamour.
Hallucination.
Hysteria.
Incest.
Masochism.
Neuroses.
Nervous trouble, root of all.
Obsessive compulsive.
OCD
Paedophilia.
Panic attacks.
Paranoia.
Perversions.
Phobias.
Promiscuity.
PTSD.
Rape.
Sadism.
Schizophrenia.
Self-harm/ injury.
Serial killer.
Sexual perversions.
Sleep-walking.
Sociopath.
Substance abuse.

▲ **Organs R6 rules, vitalises.**
Anaesthetics.

Solar plexus
Emotional life.
Sympathetic NS.

Sacral
Libido.
Puberty.
Sex life, desire, development.

▲ **R6 causing problems, disease (via Mars, Neptune).**
Abscesses.
Accidents.
Acid reflux.
Acidosis.
Acne.
AIDS.
Anal fissure.
Anaphylaxis shock.
Ankylosis spondylosis.
Appendicitis.
Attacks.
Autoimmune disease, immune attack.
Blood problems.
Boils.
Burns.
Candida.
Cerebral-spinal meningitis.
Chicken pox.
Chlamydia.
Colitis.
Common cold.
Conjunctivitis
Guillain-Barre syndrome.
Covid-19.
Crohn's disease.
Dengue fever.
Dermatitis.
Diabetes.
Diarrhea.
Digestion upsets.
Diverticulitis.
Dysentery.
Eczema.
Emphysema.
Encephalitis.
Epstein-Barr virus.
Eruptions.
Fever.
Flatulence.
Fractures.
Fungal problems.
Gastroenteritis.
Glandular fever.
Gonorrhea.
Grave's disease.
Hashimoto's disease.
Heartburn.
Hemorrhoids, piles.
Hepatitis.
Hydrocephalus.
Influenza.
Hyperuricaemia.
Impetigo.
Indigestion.
Inflammation.
Insomnia.
Intestinal gas, wind.
Irritable bowel syndrome.
Keratitis.
Laryngitis.
Liver trouble. [1]
Lumbago.
Lupus.
Measles.
Meniere's disease.
Misdiagnoses.
Murders.
Myasthenia gravis.
Myocarditis.
Narcolepsy.
Nausea.
Nerve pain.
Neuralgia.
Nightmares.
Obscure disorders.
Oedema.
Pain - acute, sharp.
Pancreatitis.
Perverts.
Pimples.
Pleurisy.
Poisons.
Rashes.
Reflux.
Scabies.
Sciatica.
Shingles.
Sinusitis.
Skin infection.
Sores, weeping
STD: sexually transmitted (social, venereal) diseases: genital warts/ herpes, pubic crabs, syphilis.
Thrush.
Tinea.
Ulcers, gastric.
Urinary tract infections.
Viral attacks.
Vomiting.

---
1 Bailey, Alice A; Esoteric Healing, 51

---
1 Bailey, Alice A; Esoteric Healing, 107.
2 Mars, the prime ruler of inflammation carries ray 6.
3 Bailey, Alice: Esoteric Psychology II, 547.
4 Bailey, Alice: Esoteric Healing, 321.

- **Chakra:**

The Sacral; also the Throat and the Base.

- **Planet agents:**

Uranus: the white magician, manifesting for the greater good or the evil black magician.

The Moon: the builder of "forms" and relationships that are harmonious and nurturing, or that create conflict and cause trouble.

- **Sign agents:**

Aries: the highly organised pioneer or the regimented fanatic.

Cancer: the highly organised nurturer and provider or the family dictator.

Capricorn: power and professional success used for the higher good, or for selfish profit and gain.

Ray 7 virtues: strength, courage, perseverance, courtesy, extreme care in details, self-reliance.
   Virtues to acquire: realisation of unity, wide-mindedness, tolerance, humility, gentleness and love. [1]

---

1 Bailey, Alice, A: Esoteric Psychology I, 210.

Ray 7 of Ceremony, Order and Magic

Ray 7 is the lower extension of ray 1 - it carries power. Its higher function is to unite spirit and matter and part of this task is to bring our bodies into alignment with the soul. This forces them to evolve so they become more sophisticated and useful vehicles for the soul's expanding powers and service work on earth.

1. Ray 7 Psychology

Ray 7 is the "manifesting" ray and all ray 7 people have the power to get things done and to bring their projects to fruition.

When the "order" aspect of this ray dominates (Sun or ascendant in Aries, Cancer or Capricorn), people have determined wills and managerial, organising and leadership skills. They use the will to control life.

But when egoism and self-will dominate, then we see the psychological negatives of this force play out through character. Examples of this type can demonstrate:

Bigotry.	Crystallisation.
Judging by appearances.	Materialism.
Narcissism.	Over-concern with rules.
Perfectionism.	Pride, over-weening.
Regimented (too).	Rigid, inflexibility.
Sectarianism.	Snobbishness.
Subservience to habit.	Superficiality.

Ceremony and magic types are Uranian, independent and freedom-loving. They shatter the past and bend rules and laws to create the world to their design. Some on this ray who misuse its power are:

Black magicians.	Creators of chaos.
Destructively wild and violent.	Selfish individualism, narcissism.

2. Ray 7 in the Body

a. Chakras: ray 7 is related to the sacral, throat and base chakras.

b. The ethers and the etheric body. Are ruled by ray 7 via the sacral chakra. Ray 7 governs predominantly upon the etheric levels. [1,2]

c. Sex and the foetus. Ray 7 brings together the opposites and "governs the sex relationship of all forms." [3] It governs marriage and problems such as sexual license, immorality and divorce. The 3rd aspect rules sex and reproduction at the animal level. Building the foetal body, "building of forms of expression" [4], comes under ray 7.

d. DNA (deoxyribonucleic acid). Physical body characteristics (DNA), are recorded in the 'physical permanent atom', a memory cell or atom located on the 1st etheric subplane of the Physical Plane. The 7th ray governs the ethers, which brings our genes under its rule and Uranus in particular, because it carries ray 7.

e. The ray 7 body type. Rays 3 and 7 govern the physical body. Ray 3 bodies are muscular, well-built, thick-boned and tough. Ray 7 bodies are delicate, smaller-boned and graceful. They like routine and though graceful, can be strong - the bodies of trained dancers such as ballerinas are usually on this ray. Graceful, dancing hands and the ability to move gracefully while walking and dancing are ray 7 expressions.

---

1 Bailey, Alice: A Treatise on White Magic, 373.
2 Bailey, Alice: Destiny of the Nations, 118.
3 Bailey, Alice: The Rays and the Initiations, 571.
4 Bailey, Alice A; Esoteric Psychology I, 261

3. Ray 7 in Disease

Ray 7 gives the ability to use spiritual power on earth - to build amazing structures and to organize and control people. When this power is misused, the rights of people are repressed, standardization is enforced, black magic is practiced.

> Ray IV. This energy is largely responsible for infections and contagious diseases. The keynote of the work of the seventh ray is to bring together life and matter upon the Physical Plane. [When imperfect], the result is activity of all germs and bacteria within the medium which will best nurture them. [1]

Through misuse, there can be wild and uncontrolled growth or the stunting of growth. Ray 7 is also related to bloodstream problems [2] and heart disease [3]. Its task is to establish beauty, balance and rhythm [4] but when this fails there is arrhythmia, seizures and spasms. Uranus carries ray 7.

- Ray 7 brings together life and matter upon the Physical Plane at an atomic, generic, DNA level. When this process breaks down, cells do not conform to the healthy design of nature resulting in cellular promiscuity, genetic mutations, abnormalities and aberrations. This ray (therefore Uranus), is responsible for the breeding of virulent germs and bacteria, for infectious and contagious diseases. This includes viruses.

For ray 7 problems, look for afflictions to Uranus and for malefics in Aries, Cancer and Capricorn.

▲ **R7 negative psychology.**
Immorality.
Incest.
Narcissism.
Paedophilia.
Promiscuity.
Sadism.
Selfish individualism.
Sexual license, perversions.

▲ **Organs R7 rules, vitalises.**
Catalysts, body.
Enzymes.
Minerals.
Sacral
Chromosomes, DNA.
Etheric body.
Genes, genetics.
Libido.
Physical permanent atom.
Sex life, sexual relations.

▲ **R7 causing problems, disease.**
Abnormalities.
Achondroplasia.
Anaemia.
Arrhythmia.
Astigmatism.
Atrial fibrillation.
Bacterial infections: buboes, cholera, cystitis, dental infections, enteritis, food poisoning, gonorrhea, impetigo, kidney infections, leprosy, lyme disease, periodontitis/ gingivitis/ pyorrhea, peritonitis, rheumatic fever, sepsis, skin infection, toothache/ decay, toxaemia, tuberculosis, typhoid fever, urinary tract infections.
Blood cancer.
Blood circulation problems.
Carpal tunnel syn.
Cerebral palsy.
Congenital abnormalities.
Conjunctivitis.
Contagious diseases.
Convulsions.
Cramps.
Electrification.
Endometriosis.
Epidemics.
Epilepsy.
Fistulas.
Foetal abnormalities.
Gene mutations.
Germs, toxic.
Growth extremes - dwarfism, gigantism.
Heart disease. [1]
Heart fibrillation.
Heart, congenital problems.
Hepatitis.
Hereditary diseases.
Imbalances in body organs, systems.
Labyrinthitis.
Leukaemia: blood cancer.
Miscarriage.
Palsy.
Parkinson's disease.
Pathogens.
Plagues.
Poisons.
Premature ejaculation.
Scabies.
Scoliosis.
Seizures.
Shocks.
Spasms, spasticity.
Spina bifida.
STD: sexually transmitted (social, venereal) diseases: chlamydia, genital herpes, gonorrhea, pubic crabs, syphilis.
Tics.
Tinnitus.
Tourette's syndrome.
Tremors.
Twitching.
Vertigo. [2]
Viruses, viral infections: AIDS, chicken pox, common cold, Covid-19, dengue fever, Epstein-Barr virus, glandular fever/ influenza, measles, mononucleosis, mumps, smallpox, yellow fever.

---

1 Bailey, Alice: Esoteric Healing, 51. "R7"

2 Under R7 balance is brought about. Bailey, Alice: Externalisation of the Hierarchy, 668.

---

1 Bailey, Alice A; Esoteric Healing, 304
2 Bailey, Alice A; Esoteric Healing, 128.
3 Ibid, 51.
4 Bailey, Alice A; Externalisation of the Hierarchy 668.

2b. Astrology Signs

Chart 3. Sign rulerships in the Body

Aries..................................head
Taurus................................throat
Gemini...............................lungs, arms, hands
Cancer...............................breasts
Leo....................................heart, spine.
Cancer...............................stomach
Libra..................................kidneys
Virgo.................................intestines
Scorpio..............................genitals
Sagittarius.........................hips   thighs
Capricorn..........................knees
Aquarius...........................ankles
Pisces................................feet

- **Rays:** 1,7 (6 via Mars, 4 via Mercury).

- **Chakra:**
The Crown and Ajna.

- **Planet rulers:**
Exoteric: Mars.
Esoteric: Mercury.
Hierarchy: Uranus.

- **Personality Keynote:**
Let form again be sought.

- **Soul Keynote:**
I come forth and from the plane of mind I rule.

Aries, at different points along the Path of Life forces the soul on to the burning ground and subjects it to a purifying process. Through the lesser fire of mind, the "jungles of experience are set on fire and dissolve in flames and then the Path stands clear and unobstructed vision is achieved." Old Commentary

The rays which are expressing themselves through Aries are curiously balanced, Rays 1 and 7 are the highest and the lowest, and therefore demand a point of balance upon the wheel which is provided in Libra. [1]

---

[1] Bailey, Alice A; Esoteric Astrology, 101.

1. Aries

CROWN CHAKRA

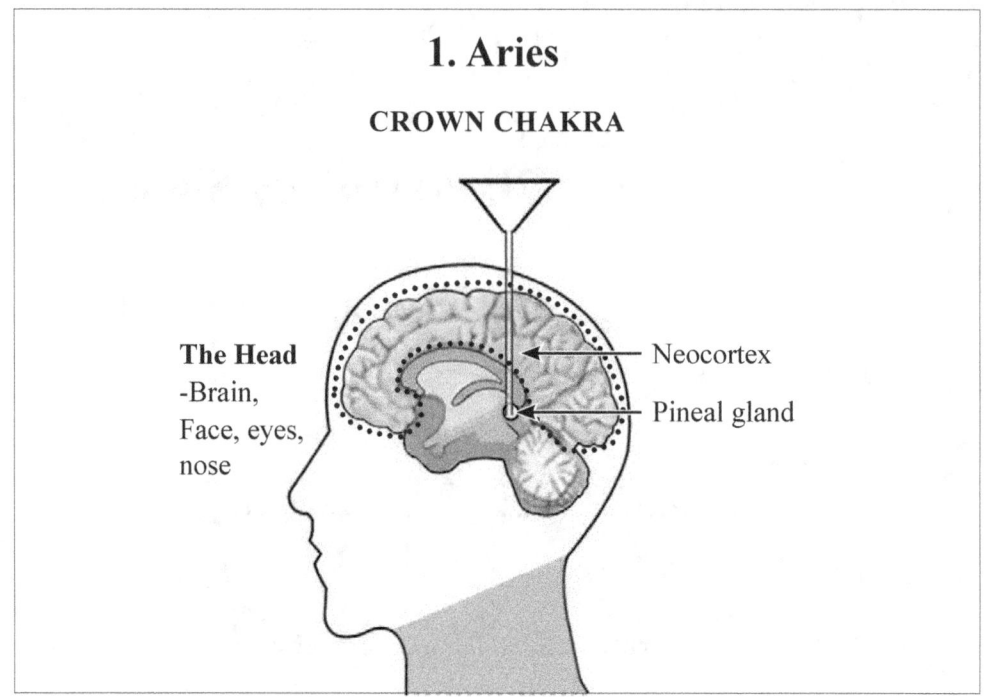

1. Psychology

The evolutionary task of Aries is to develop intelligent leaders who work for the higher good. Aries carries the two power rays to bring this about. The 1st Ray of Will-Power gives leadership skill and personal power and charisma. The 7th Ray of Ceremony and Order gives the ability to apply those skills in a practical and potent way to manage and lead people. It also gives the power to manifest.

The crown chakra enters the body at the top of the head, a region ruled by Aries. This centre is the portal for spirit. The exaltation of the Sun in Aries symbolises human consciousness that is a vessel for the radiance and glory of spirit.

However, the average Aries person focuses in the solar plexus or sacral chakras via Mars. At this level, Aries people are hot, ardent and tempestuous, traits that get them into trouble. Here are some negative Aries attitudes that may result in disease:

Aggression, anger.	Arrogance, violence.
Combativeness.	Emotionally impulsive.
Power hungry.	Prideful, wilful.
Ruthless ambition.	Self-pity, the dramatic "I".
Self-aggrandising.	Selfishness.

2. Body

a. Chakras, head, brain, skull, pineal gland, the cranium. The crown chakra enters through the top of the skull, anchoring in the pineal gland. The dividing line between Aries and Taurus is at the top of the neck. Some astrologers place it at the level of the mouth - the upper jaw and teeth going to Aries and Taurus ruling all below. But generally, Aries rules the head, Taurus the throat.

b. The "Triune Brain" and the neocortex. The Triune Brian theory was presented by American neuroscientist Paul D. MacLean in the 60's. It divides the brain into three parts based on evolutionary development - the *neocortex* or thinking brain, the *limbic* or emotional brain, and the *reptilian* or action brain. Aries, Taurus and Gemini are associated with each of these three parts.

- *The neocortex* is the latest part of the brain to evolve and is concerned with advanced cognition, language and planning. It is the seat of curiosity and asks, "What can I learn?" Aries, the sign that rules exploration and pioneering is the natural ruler of the neocortex.

- *The Limbic System or emotional brain (Taurus).* It emerged in the first mammals and in man is the seat of the desire nature. Taurus, the sign of desire rules this system. It asks, "What do I want and how do I get it?"
- *The Reptilian or instinctual brain (Gemini):* this is the brainstem and the cerebellum, the oldest part of the brain that dominated in reptiles. It controls breathing and balance, vital functions associated with Gemini. It constantly monitors the environment asking, "Am I safe?"

c. *The senses and the eyes, ears and nose.* Mars rules the five senses according to Bailey, [1] relating them to Aries, which Mars rules.

The Triune Brain

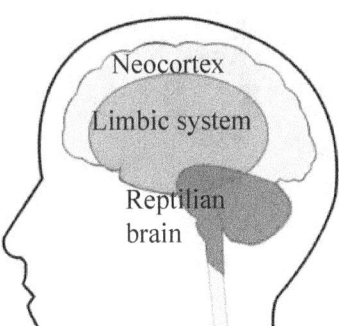

Though rejected by scientists today, this system fits the esoteric model of dividing all living organisms into 3 aspects that follow the spirit - soul - body model.

3. Disease

- Aries is the natural ruler of the head, so is associated with all disorders that involve the head or brain.

Aries is a cardinal-fire sign. Of all the elements, fire is most conducive to good health because it represents the life force of God and vitality. This is a huge benefit for people who have their Suns or ascendant in Aries, Leo and Sagittarius. But when Aries' fire turns rogue it results in inflammatory diseases that strike suddenly, without warning. This is emphasised because of the presence of the 1st ray in Aries, which is the most powerful and dynamic of all ray forces. Health problems associated with this type of force are strokes and head injuries.

Aries people fight their way through life, leading with their heads, opening themselves up to injuries or accidents to the head and its parts. They have powerful wills and when the will is too strong, in certain circumstances, overstimulation can occur with brain cells, causing brain trouble. Here is an interesting quote:

> Over-stimulation of the brain cells is necessarily one of the results of the merging, by an act of will, of the fires which circulate in the human body. Such stimulation can produce insanity and the breaking down of the cellular structure of the brain, and through the over-activity of the cell life can also induce that internal friction between them which will eventuate in brain tumours and abscesses. [2]

▲ **Aries negative psychology.**
Aggressive.
Egocentric.
Headstrong.
Impulsive.

▲ **Aries organs, functions.**
Crown
Brain: blood vessels, cells, tissue.
Cerebral cortex.
Cerebrum.
Cranium, skull.
Hair on the head.
Head.
Melatonin.
Neocortex.
Pineal and pituitary glands.
Serotonin.
Ajna
Face: brow, ears, eyes, facial bones, nose.
Jaw, upper.
Senses via Mars: sight, hearing, taste, touch, smell. [1]
Throat
Teeth, upper.

▲ **Problems affecting Aries organs.**
Acne.
Alopecia.
Alzheimer's.

[1] Bailey, Alice A; Esoteric Astrology, 215. "Mars rules the senses".

Astigmatism.
Baldness.
Blindness.
Blood pressure high, pineal cause.
Brain: abscesses, bacterial infections, cancer, congenital disorders, haemorrhages, inflammation, lesions, structural problems, tumours.
Broken nose.
Cataracts.
Cerebral palsy.
Cerebral-spinal meningitis.
Comas.
Concussion.
Conjunctivitis.

Dementia.
Ear infections.
Earache.
Encephalitis.
Epilepsy.
Glaucoma.
Head injuries.
Headaches.
Hearing loss.
Huntington's disease.
Hydrocephalus.
Insomnia.
Keratitis.
Lewy body dementia.
Memory loss.
Migraine.
Myopia.
Senile decay.
Short sightedness.
Skull injuries.

Stroke.
Vertigo.

▲ **Problems caused by Aries.**
Accidents caused through impulsive action.
Acute, fast rising diseases.
Concussions.
Fevers.
Inflammation.
Stroke.

---

[1] Bailey, Alice A; Esoteric Astrology, 215.
[2] Bailey, Alice: A Treatise on White Magic, 590.

- **Ray:** 4 (5 via Venus 1 via Vulcan).

- **Chakra:**
The Throat.

- **Planet rulers:**
Exoteric: Venus.
Esoteric: Vulcan.
Hierarchy: Vulcan.

- **Personality Keynote:**
Let struggle be undismayed.

- **Soul Keynote:**
I see, and when the eye is opened, all is illumined.

Carotid neck arteries and glands

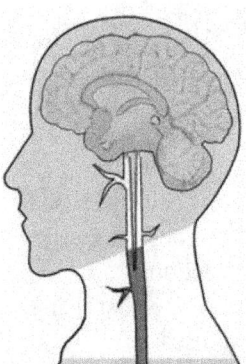

The mouth as the entry point of digestion.

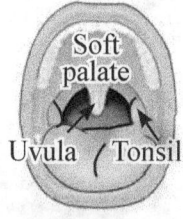

2. Taurus

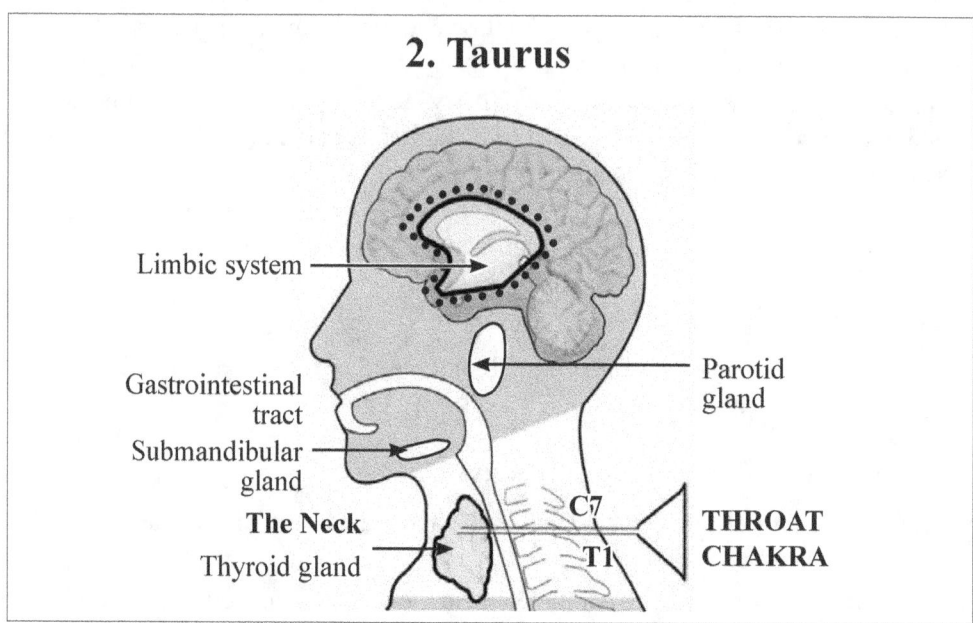

1. Psychology

Taurus and Scorpio are polar opposites and they both carry a single ray - the 4th of Harmony through Conflict. This makes them battleground signs. Taurus people often find themselves in conflict with others due to their powerful desires and wills. The evolutionary task of Taurus, is to teach us to "ride the bull" of desire rather than be ridden by it, to control our lower appetites rather than be ruled by them.

At the higher level, the 4th ray is the force of harmony and beauty and many great artists have Taurus in their make-up. It is likewise the force of diplomacy and negotiation and integrated Taurus people make fine diplomats and counsellors.

Taurus is a fixed earth sign and its people are notorious for their stubbornness. Over time, this blocks the physical systems in the body and when chronic can lead to crystallisation, hardening and atrophying of organs. It can also lead to insanity - mental inflexibility is a precursor to mental disorders. Here are some negative attitudes:

Bullheaded, stubbornness.	Continual conflict.
Emotional instability.	Gluttony, greed.
Sexual promiscuity.	Uncontrolled desire.

2. Body

a. Chakras. Taurus co-rules the throat centre with Gemini, which enters the body at the base of the neck on the borderline between the two signs. This centre is involved in both their functions - Taurus for food digestion and Gemini for breathing. Taurus is also related to the ajna chakra via Venus.

b. The thyroid gland. The throat chakra anchors in the thyroid gland. This gland uses iodine from food to make two main hormones: Triiodothyronine (T3) and thyroxine (T4). They regulate many functions including our metabolic rate, breathing, heart rate, muscle strength, menstrual cycles etc.

c. The neck, throat (also jaws, chin). Taurus is the traditional ruler of the neck, with Aries ruling the head and Gemini the shoulders.

d. The upper digestive tract: Taurus rules the neck and throat, all its organs and parts. This includes the upper gastrointestinal or digestive tract, the mouth as the organ for food intake, the palate, salivary glands, the hyoid bone, taste sense, etc.

e. Tonsils. They are part of the immune and lymphatic systems that fight infection. As the first line of defence, when they do their job and trap germs, we get a sore throat.

f. The limbic or emotional brain. This is the feel good recording part of the brain that asks "am I happy, am I appreciated, am I getting what I want, are my desires being satisfied?" Based on the answers it comes up with and records (it deals with memories), it influences our value judgements and future actions and behaviours. Every time we repeat a behaviour that brings us a reward we crave or cherish, the memory - behaviour - pay-off pattern is reinforced, and so is the urge to repeat the pattern to get the reward. The Limbic System influences our future choices, actions and habits and is at the root of any addictions we form. Here are its parts:

The Limbic System

- Hypothalamus and thalamus: connect the Limbic system with the rest of the brain, relaying information.
- Nucleus accumbens: the pleasure centre in the brain.
- Olfactory bulb: processes odours
- Amygdala: integrative center for emotions, emotional behaviour, and motivation.
- Hippocampus - memories

Whether we call this system *limbic* or the *reward-pleasure* centre, the seat of desire as far as it relates to the brain is centred in this region, linking it to Taurus and Venus.

3. Disease

- Diseases of the throat and thyroid gland, and of the sex organs via opposite sign Scorpio.

Attachment to desire is the cause of all sorrow according to Buddha. Gluttonous attachment to food and a hedonistic lifestyle are Taurus problems and its people often struggle with weight gain and associated diseases. Today scientists are claiming that our genes determine eating patterns, that DNA pre-programming causes us to eat in certain ways. This fits with the astrological theory that each sign invests our character with certain basic traits, qualities and behaviours. Taurus people - influenced by ruler Venus, like sweet or sugary foods and when laziness and a sedentary lifestyle is added it is a recipe for disease. One consequence is diabetes, a disease of wrong inner desires. [1]

▲ **Taurus negative psychology.**
Fixed-minded.
Powerful desires.
Stubbornness.

▲ **Taurus organs, functions.**

Ajna
Limbic system.
Nose.

Throat
Adam's apple.
Adenoids.
Alimentary canal/ digestive tract (upper).
Appetite.

Atlas axis.
Carotid arteries, carotid glands.
Cervical vertebrae.
Chin.
Esophagus (upper).
Glottis.
Gums.
Hyoid bone.
Jaw, lower.
Jugular vein.
Larynx.
Lips.
Mouth.
Neck, neck vertebrae.
Palate.
Parathyroids.
Parotid glands.

Pharynx.
Salivary glands.
Submandibular glands.
Taste.
Teeth, lower.
Throat.
Thyroid.
Thyroxine.
Tongue.
Tonsils.
Uvula.

Sacral
Sexual desire.

▲ **Problems affecting Taurus organs.**

Cancer in the throat, lower jaw.
Cervical osteoarthritis.
Croup.
Diphtheria.
Goitre.
Grave's disease.
Hyperthyroidism
Hypothyroidism
Herpes, oral.
Laryngitis.
Sore throat.
Strangulation.
Suffocation.
Weight problems, thyroid cause.

▲ **Problems caused by Taurus.**
Sugar addiction, cravings.
Myriad health problems through unregulated desire, gluttony.

---
1 Bailey, Alice A; Esoteric Healing, 311.

- **Ray:** 2 (4 via Mercury, 5 via Venus).

- **Chakra:**
The Ajna and Throat.

- **Planet rulers:**
Exoteric: Mercury.
Esoteric: Venus.
Hierarchy: Earth.

- **Personality Keynote:**
Let instability do its work.

- **Soul Keynote:**
I recognise my other self and in the waning of that self I grow and glow.

Nervous system, shoulders, arms, hands, fingers

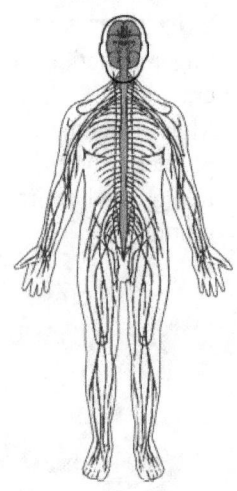

Bronchial tree

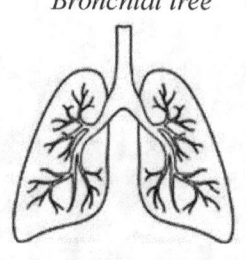

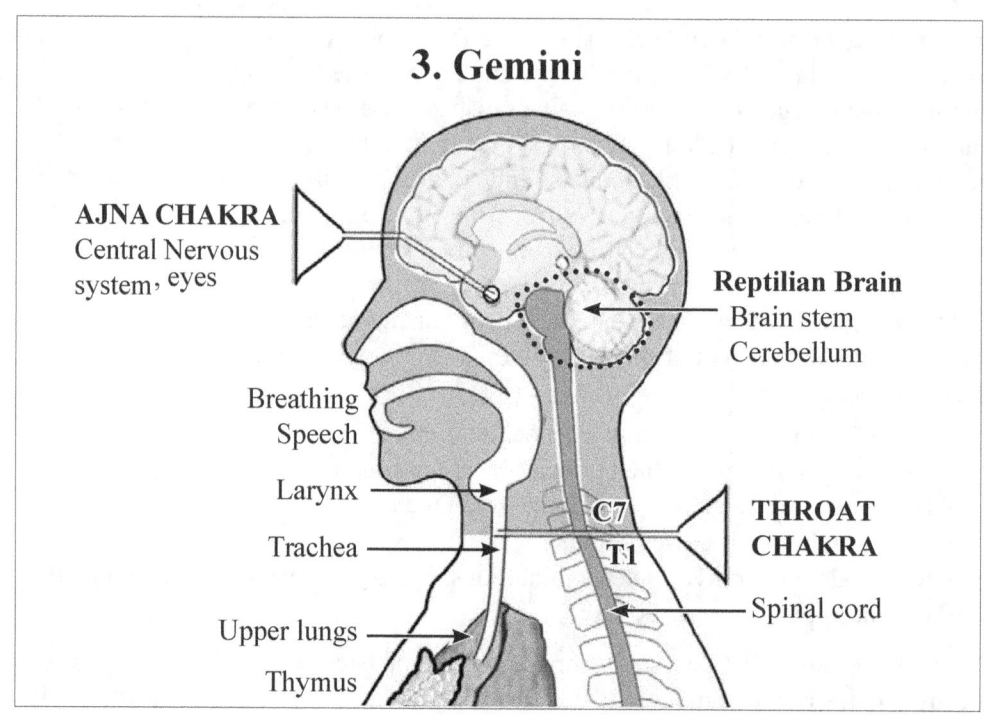

3. Gemini

1. Psychology

Gemini is an air sign whose task is to develop the powers of the mind and to teach us to communicate intelligently. For this purpose it carries a single ray - the 2nd Ray of Love and Wisdom, the "consciousness" ray. This is why Gemini people are curious, cerebral people, with minds that are continually reaching out for new information and knowledge. However, when the mind is unstable, Gemini's force produces flitting minds that cannot concentrate, which are restless and superficial. Here are some negative Gemini attitudes that may result in problems or disease:

Changeability.	Duality, unstable swings in consciousness.
Mental instability.	Shallowness, deceit, thievery.
Being "two-faced".	Superficial mental chit-chatter.

2. Body

a. The Chakras. Gemini is related to the intelligent ajna chakra via Mercury, and also to the throat chakra that enters the body between Taurus and Gemini around C7 and T1.

b. The pituitary gland and endocrine system. The pituitary is governed by the ajna - which is coruled by Mercury, relating this gland to Gemini. The pituitary is called the "master gland" because it controls the activity of most other endocrine glands, and their release of hormones to balance and regulate health.

c. The thymus: this gland is governed by the heart chakra. Normally it atrophies in adults, but Gemini [1] re-activates it in people who are spiritually advanced and who are expressing inclusiveness through an opened heart chakra. This strengthens the immune system and resistance to disease.

d. The Central Nervous System. Gemini rules the nervous system and governs the fluid reactions of the entire nervous organism.

e. Ears, eyes, hearing, speech and learning. Gemini and Mercury govern these vital functions, all ruled by the throat chakra. Mercury is the "Messenger of God".

f. Organs of respiration: Gemini governs the bronchial tract and oxygenation of blood.

---

[1] Bailey, Alice A; Esoteric Astrology, 367.

g. Tubes in the body. Gemini rules tubes that transport substances in the body from one place to another. For instance, the nervous system that enables nerve messages to flow around the body, digestive tubes that transport food, fallopian tubes that transport ova, and the urethra that transports urine and semen in men.

h. The Reptilian or Instinctual Brain: Gemini is related to the older parts of the brain, which we share with reptiles – the brainstem (pons, medulla oblongata) and cerebellum. They control Gemini-type functions such as breathing and balance.

i. Shoulders, arms and hands and upper body movement. Gemini traditionally rules these "grasping" and "balancing" parts of the body. Nerves that control these functions leave the spinal cord in the throat chakra region.

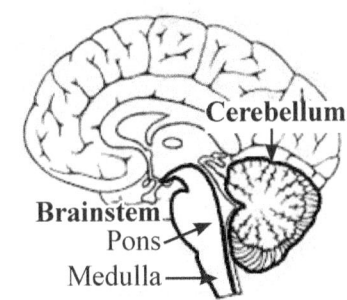

3. Disease

- Diseases of the nervous system and of breathing.
- Diseases and injuries that affect learning, speech and balance.

Ruler of Gemini, Mercury, carries the conflicted 4th ray. It creates turmoil in the lives of people who are mentally and emotionally unstable. This leads to debility and the easy taking on of germs. As an air sign, Gemini is related to the spread of air-borne pathogens and pollutants, resulting in breathing problems and epidemics such as influenza.

▲ Gemini negative psychology.
Mental instability.
Multiple personalities, possession.
Psychological troubles, insanities, imbecilities. Bipolar.

▲ Gemini organs, functions.

Crown
Antahkarana, the consciousness thread.

Ajna
Cerebellum.
Cognition.
Ears.
Eye nerves.
Hearing.
Hypothalamus
Intelligent self-consciousness.
Nerves, all:
CNS, peripheral, autonomic, enteric, motor, parasympathetic, sciatic, sympathetic, vagus.
Neurons.
Senses: sight, hearing, taste, touch, smell.
Spinal cord.
Synapses.
Thalamus.

Throat
Airways.
Alta-major centre.
Alveoli.
Arms, hands, shoulders, biceps, carpal/ metacarpal bones, clavicle, deltoid muscles, elbows, fingers, phalanges, hands, humerus, radius, scapula, wrists
Brainstem.
Breathing.
Bronchial tree.
Ears (rulership shared with the ajna).
Endocrine system.
Hearing.
Lungs.
Medulla oblongata.
Pons.
Reptilian brain.
Respiration.
Sinuses.
Speech.
Thalamus.
Tongue.
Trachea.
Tubes, body.
Vocal cords.
Voice box.
Windpipe.

Heart
Blood oxygenation.
Capillaries.
Oxygen
Pulmonary circulation.
Thymus gland.

Sacral
Etheric web (with Aquarius).

▲ Problems affecting Gemini organs.
ALS: amyotrophic lateral sclerosis/ Lou Gehrig's/motor neurone disease.
Aphasia.
Asphyxia.
Asthma.
Bells palsy.
Breathing allergies.
Bronchitis.
Carpal tunnel syndrome.
Catarrh.
Cerebral palsy.
Chronic obstructive pulmonary disease.
Colds.
Croup.
Diphtheria.
Dyslexia.
Emphysema.
Epilepsy.
Guillain-Barre syndrome.
Influenza.
Labyrinthitis.
Laryngitis.
Learning difficulties.
Locomotor ataxia.
Lung, breathing problems.
Meniere's disease.
Middle ear problems.
Myasthenia gravis.
Nasal congestion.
Nerve spasms.
Neuralgia.
Palsy.
Paralysis.
Paraplegia, quadriplegia.
Parkinson's disease.
Pleurisy.
Pneumonia.
Polio.
Pulmonary tuberculosis.
Scarlet fever.
Sciatica.
Seizures.
Shingles.
Smallpox.
Spasms, nerves.
Spasticity.
Speech impediment.
Stuttering.
Tinnitus.
Tourette's syndrome.
Tremors.
Tuberculosis.
Twitching, tics.

▲ Problems caused by Gemini.
Air-borne diseases.
Epidemics spread via the air, the breath, coughing.

- **Rays: 3 and 7** (4 via Moon, 6 via Neptune).

- **Chakra:**

The Solar Plexus and related to the Sacral for reproduction.

- **Planet rulers:**

Exoteric: Moon.
Esoteric: Neptune.
Hierarchy: Neptune.

- **Personality Keynote:**

Let isolation be the rule and yet the crowd exists.

- **Soul Keynote:**

I build a lighted house and therein dwell.

Motherhood, women and reproduction

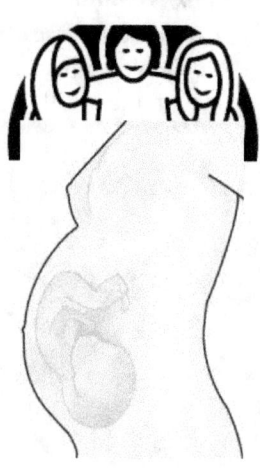

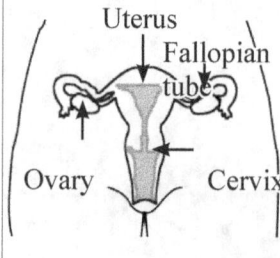

4. Cancer

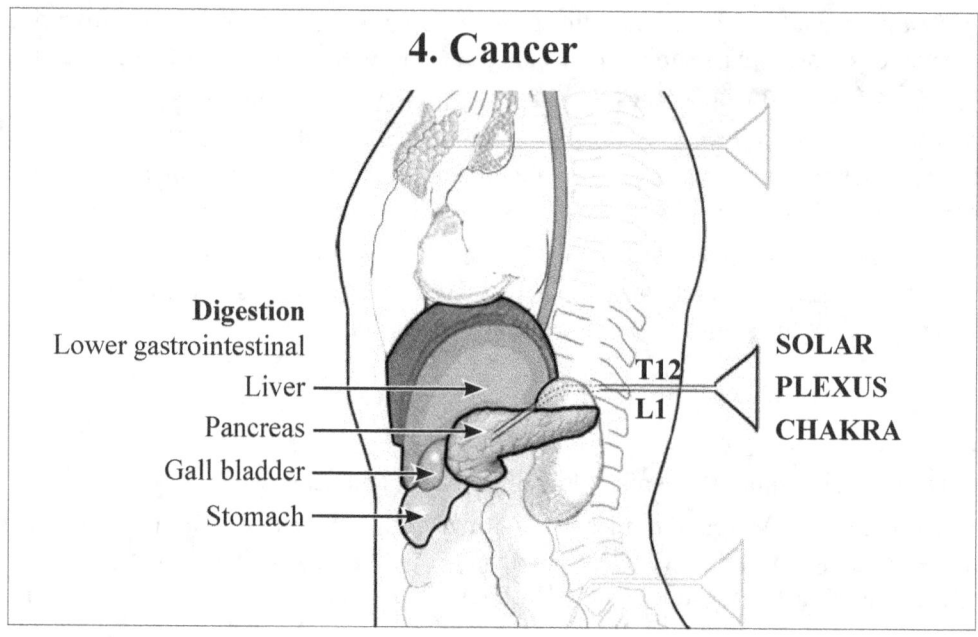

1. Psychology

Cancer is a water sign, the element ruling the emotional Astral Plane. Its evolutionary task is to develop the mind and use it to control and balance the emotions. Two rays help achieve this. Ray 3 of Intelligent Activity gives Cancer people intelligence (developed through their skilful feeding and housing of the family), and Ray 7 of Ceremony and Order, which gives them organising power. Here are some negative Cancer attitudes that can cause problems:

Addictive tendencies.	Emotionalism.
Moodiness.	Defensiveness, over-protective.
Glamour.	Hyper-sensitive.

2. Body

a. *Solar plexus chakra:* this centre enters the body in the Cancer-ruled region around T12 and L1, and anchors in the pancreas.

b. *Digestion, the stomach, pancreas, gallbladder and liver.* Ruled by Cancer.

c. *Reproduction, female organs and cycles.* Cancer rules women, childbearing, maternal matters, birth and babies. It has prime rulership over female reproduction.

d. *Body fluids, white blood cells and the lymphatic system.* Cancer rules white body fluids such as lymph and mucous. When these become toxic, the result is pus, phlegm and congestion. Cancer - the ruler of tidal activity on the planet, participates in the cleansing housework done by the lymphatic system.

The Crab, who clears the ocean of matter which flows around the soul of man.[1]

e. *The physical form, tissue and flesh.* Cancer and its opposite pole Capricorn rule the dense physical body via ray 3, the ruler of matter. Capricorn rules the dense skeletal structure, Cancer rules soft tissue such as bone marrow and brain matter.

f. *Containers.* Cancer's function in the body is to protect and nurture, to further the family's (the body as a whole) interests.

The protective quality of Cancer is seen in its rulership of all body "containers" that enfold organs such as the womb and provide the linings of tubes such as those for the thoracic duct.

---

1 Bailey, Alice A; Esoteric Astrology, 62.

3. Disease

- Psychological disorders caused through emotionalism.
- Diseases of the digestive system, reproduction organs, motherhood and body tissue.

The energy of Cancer is water-cardinal and just like its people can be weepy, moody and defensive, its diseases are seepy, watery, damp, lethargic and devitalising. Contaminated water is a breeding ground for germs and disease and so are the three water signs when there is emotional congestion. Of the water signs, Cancer is very susceptible to disease because it carries ray 7, which is related to the breeding of germs. Scorpio is more resistant to disease because ruler Mars carries heat which destroys them. Pisces is very susceptible to addictive type diseases, weight gain, and cancer through ray 2.

Cancer, being the sign that rules family life, also represents diseases we inherit genetically, through our family line or because we are part of the human kingdom.

Cancer (the disease). Emotional repression is the underlying psychological cause of cancer. This causes panic in the life-preservation forces in the body, which begin a cell-overbuilding process to compensate. Men born in Cancer often repress their feelings in order to present a more 'manly' front to the world. Now breast cancer rates are increasing amongst women, linking this to Cancer and the Moon, which rule the breasts. Professional women in particular, who compete in male-dominated fields are prone. The Moon carries the 4th ray and when people live in continual conflict, debilitating the immune system, they become susceptible to the indigenous diseases of the planet - syphilis, cancer, TB.

▲ **Cancer negative psychology.**
Anxiety, worry.
Bipolar.
Delirium, delusory.
Dreams, troubled.
Emotional problems, emotionalism.
Hallucination.
Hysteria.
Neuroses.
Panic attacks.
Past-life prison patterns - negative core beliefs.
Paranoia.
Phobias.
Postpartum blues.
PTSD.
Schizophrenia.

▲ **Cancer organs, functions.**
Body containers, sheaths.
Body fluids.
Bone marrow.
Child bearing, raising.
Flesh.
Membrane containers.
Mucous.
Nourishment.
Physical form.
Pregnancy.
Secretions.
Substance.
Tears.
Tissue.
Watery systems.

Throat
Lymphatic system.
Pleurae.
Thoracic duct.

Heart
Plasma.
Stem cells.
White blood cells.

Solar plexus
Abdomen.
Bile.
Chyle.
Digestion.
Gallbladder.
Liver.
Mammary glands.
Pancreas.
Peritoneum.
Stomach.

Sacral
Babies.
Birth.
Cervix.
Conception.
Egg ovum.
Embryo.
Estrogen.
Fallopian tubes.
Genes.
Gestation.
Lacteals, lactation.
Menstruation.
Ovaries.
Periods.
Placenta.
Pregnancy.
Procreation.
Progesterone.
Reproduction.
Uterus.
Womb.

Base
Epithelial tissue/ membranes: serous, mucous, synovial.
Physical form.
Soft tissue such as bone marrow.

▲ **Problems affecting Cancer organs.**
Acid reflux.
Anorexia.
Barrenness.
Bloating.
Breast cancer.
Bulimia.
Cirrhosis, liver.
Coeliac disease.
Dementia (disease in brain tissue).
Diabetes.
Dyspepsia.
Endometriosis.
Fibroids in womb.
Flatulence.
Food allergies.
Food poisoning.
Gallstones.
Gangrene.
Gastric disorders.
Heartburn.
Hodgkin's disease.
Hysterectomy.
Indigestion.
Infertility.
Lymphoma.
Miscarriage.
Nausea.
Obesity.
Pancreatitis.
Peptic ulcer.
Peritonitis.
Reflux.
Starvation.
Stomach cancer, ulcers.
Typhoid fever.
Uterine troubles.
Vomiting.

▲ **Problems caused by Cancer.**
Abscesses.
Allergic reactions.
Athlete's foot.
Bronchitis.
Candida.
Catarrh.
Congenital abnormalities.
Contagious infections.
Covid-19.
Cystic fibrosis.
Cysts.
Decay.
Dermatitis.
Epidemics.
Fungal infections.
Germs, breeding.
Hereditary diseases.
Influenza.
Mucous problems.
Oedema.
Phlegm.
Pus.
Ringworm.
Sinusitis.
Thrush.
Tinea.

- **Rays:** 1, 5
  (2 via the Sun).

- **Chakra:**
  The Heart.

- **Planet rulers:**
  Exoteric: the Sun.
  Esoteric: the Sun veiling Neptune.
  Hierarchy: the Sun veiling Uranus.

- **Personality Keynote:**
  Let other forms exist. I rule.

- **Soul Keynote:**
  I am That and That am I.

Vitality

Cardiovascular

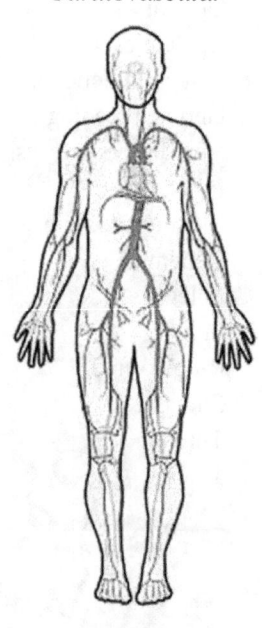

5. Leo

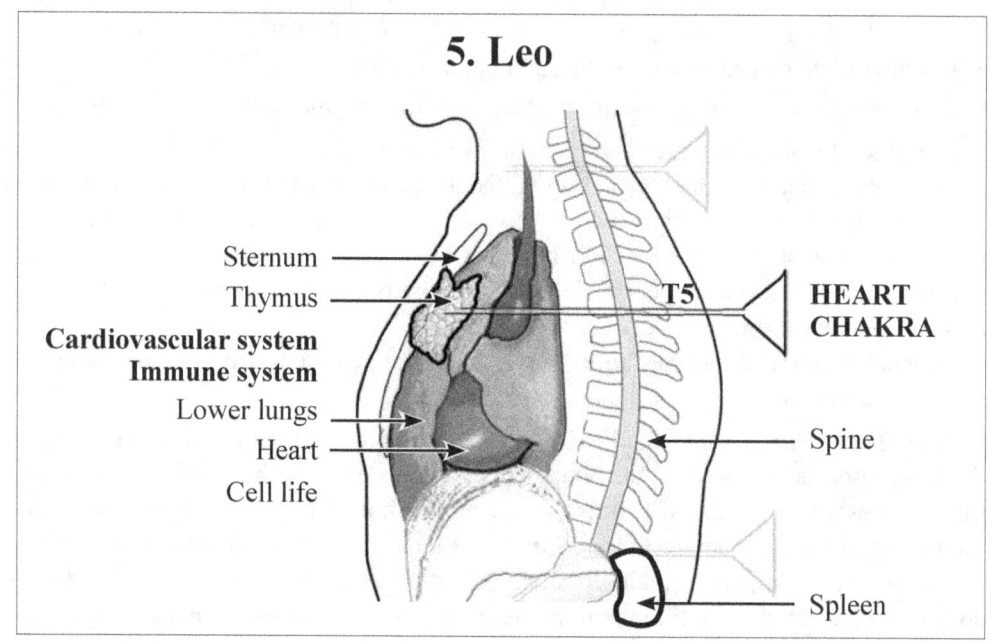

1. Psychology

Leo's evolutionary task is to produce a fully self-conscious, intelligent and integrated personality, who is fully aware of his individual and independent destiny. The 1st ray of Will and Power that flows through Leo helps to bring this about. At first such men and women are selfish and arrogant, serving only themselves and expecting all others to do so as well. Leo people are also exceedingly intelligent in the way they conduct their affairs, the gift of the 5th Ray of Scientific Mind. Both these forces are on the "will" line. If Leo people become wilfully hard-hearted and mentally rigid it leads to serious heart trouble. Here are some negative Leo attitudes that may result in disease.

Arrogance.	Cruel, pitiless.
Dogmatism.	Fixed minded.
Power hungry.	Pride.
Self-love, narcissism.	Self-pitying, the dramatic "I".
Self-aggrandising.	Selfish use of power.
Stubbornly self-willed.	Urge to control others.

2. Body

a. Heart chakra: this centre enters the body in the Leo-ruled region around vertebrae T5, and anchors in the thymus.

b. Sutratma, the life stream. Leo is related to the life of God the Father, and to the life aspect that reaches us via the sutratma. This stream of life energy emanates from the monad, flows through the crown and heart chakras and anchors in the heart organ. From there, life flows into the bloodstream vitalising the entire physical body. The soul utilises this thread and its force to hold the atoms of the body together during incarnation.

c. The cardiovascular system and pranic vitalisation. Leo and the Sun rule the heart, the powerhouse of the entire cardiovascular system. The life-stream flowing in from the soul via the sutratma, is the primary means of vitalisation. A second stream of vitality (prana) flows from the Sun. It enters the body via the spleen and flows to the heart where it merges with the life-stream as it flows into the cardiovascular system. Leo's opposite sign and partner Aquarius works with Leo to circulate blood. Together, these two signs rule the cardiovascular system.

d. The immune system and the thymus gland. Leo and the Sun govern the immune system, the body's natural vitality defence system to fight off disease. The heart chakra, ruled by the Sun, anchors in the thymus gland, which trains and develops T-lymphocytes (T cells), white blood cells that kill disease.

e. Spinal column and vertebrae. The Leo qualities of uprightness and erectness are apparent in the spine.

3. Disease

- Diseases of the cardiovascular system and spine.

Being hard hearted - or at the other end of the spectrum, being heart-centred and giving all that one has to others; these can cause heart/ cardiovascular trouble.

The energy of Leo is fiery-fixed. In disease, this manifests as inflammatory heart diseases and conditions that are slow forming and consequently become chronic and hard to heal. Because the heart organ is central to Physical Plane life, its diseases are dangerously life threatening.

▲ Leo negative psychology.
Arrogance.
Egoism.
Megalomania.
Self-pity.

▲ Leo organs, functions.

Heart
Aorta.
Arteries.
Body warmth.
Blood pressure.
Cardiovascular system.
Cell life.
Constitution.
Haemoglobin.
Heart.
Immune system and t-cells.
Leukocytes
Life-thread/ stream, sutratma, silver cord.
Prana.
Recuperative power.
Red blood cells.
Spleen.
Sternum, breast bone.
Thoracic vertebrae.

Thymus gland.
Vena cava.
Vitality.

Base
The spine.

▲ Problems affecting Leo organs.
AIDS.
Anaemia.
Aneurism.
Angina
Ankylosis spondylosis.
Arrhythmia
Atrial fibrillation.
Back pain.
Blood pressure high.
Cardiomyopathy
Congenital heart problems.
Heart attack, fibrillation, disease, problems.
Heart diseases caused by opening the heart chakra.
Hypertension.
Hypotension.
Myocarditis.
Scoliosis.

Spinal fractures.
Spinal meningitis.
Vertebrae degeneration.

▲ Problems caused by Leo.
Autoimmune diseases, immune attacks.
Burning.
Dizziness.
Fevers.
Heatstroke.
High temperatures.
Inflammation.
Over-vitalisation, over-heating.
Sunstroke.

The Cardiovascular System

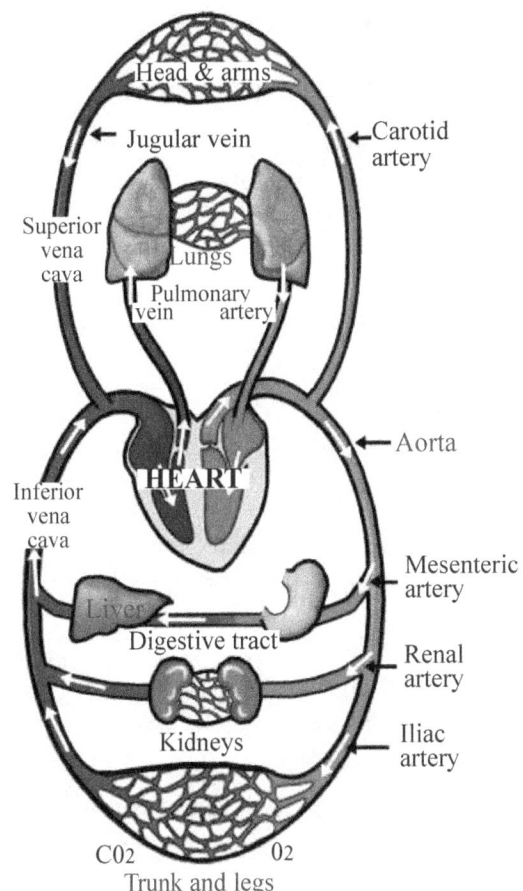

Spinal vertebrae

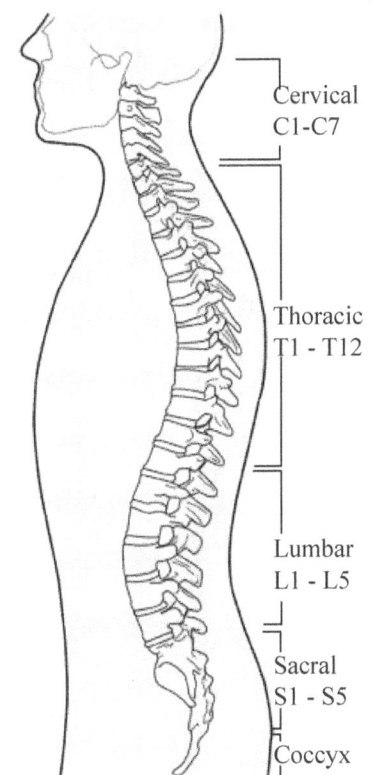

- **Rays: 2 and 6,** (4 via Mercury, 1 via Vulcan)

- **Chakra:**
  The Solar Plexus.

- **Planet rulers:**
  Exoteric: Mercury.
  Esoteric: the Moon veiling and Vulcan.
  Hierarchy: Jupiter.

- **Personality Keynote:**
  Let matter reign.

- **Soul Keynote:**
  I am the Mother and the Child. I, God, I matter am.

Virgo, represented by Eve, Isis and Mary, gives birth to the Christ child.

Eve, the symbol of the mind of man, took the apple of knowledge from the serpent of matter and started the long human undertaking of experiment, experience and expression. Eve has no child in her arms; the germ of the Christ life is as yet too small to make its presence felt. In Isis the quickening of that which is desired has taken place. Isis consequently stands in the ancient zodiacs for fertility, for motherhood and as the guardian of the child. Mary carries the process down to the Physical Plane, and there gives birth to the Christ child.[1]

---
1 Bailey, Alice A; Esoteric Astrology, 253.

6. Virgo

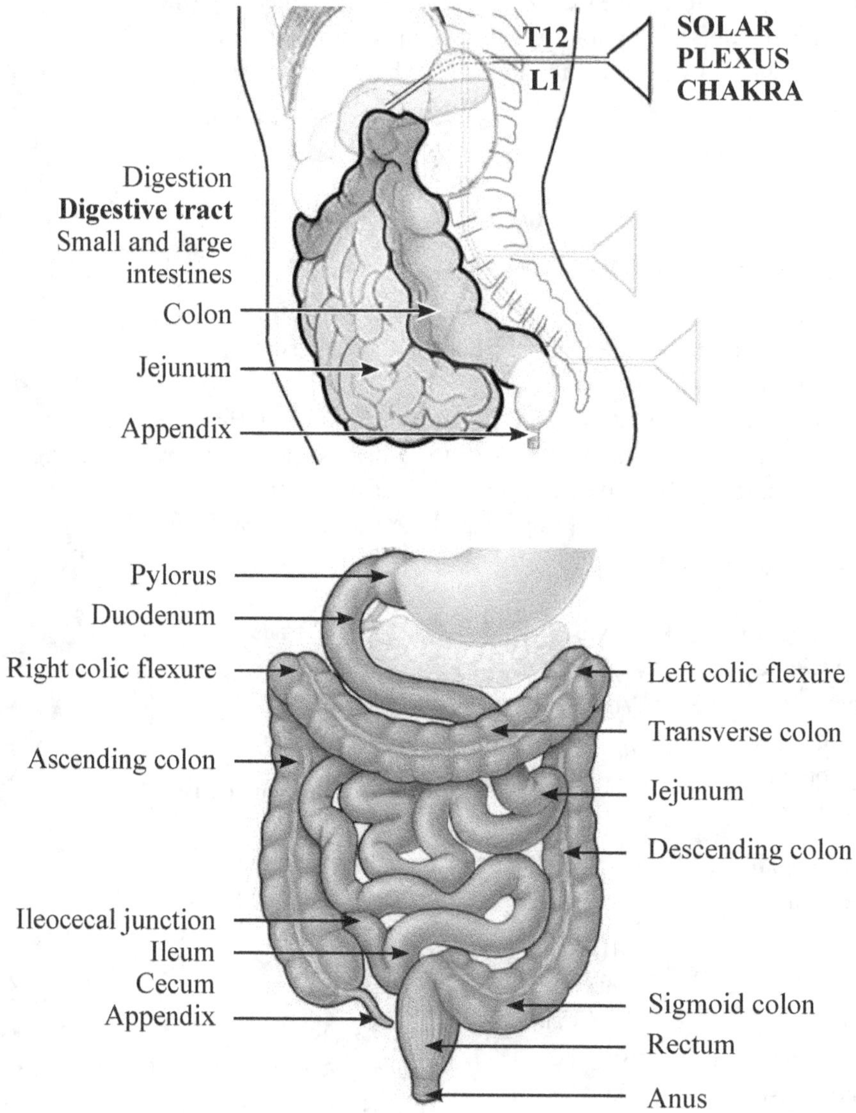

1. Psychology

In Virgo, we are taught to focus, to reason, to think, to discriminate and to purify the body through right diet and hygiene.

Further on the Path of Spiritual Development Virgo's task is to bring about the "birth of the Christ spirit in the heart". This is a 2nd ray occurrence, a deeply momentous event on the evolutionary path. Then, for the first time, the personality turns away from its materialistic focus and responds to the inner call to aspire to something higher and finer. Here is a mystical description of that event.

Later, upon the wheel of the disciple, the voice emerges from the Virgin Herself and she says: "I am the mother and the child. I, God, I, matter am." Ponder upon the beauty of this synthesis and teaching and know that you yourself have said the first word as the soul, descending into the womb of time and space in a far and distant past. The time has now come when you can, if you so choose, proclaim your identity with both divine aspects— matter and Spirit, the mother and the Christ.[1]

---
1 Bailey, Alice A; Esoteric Astrology, 284.

Signs in the earth element teach us to manage material life practically and pragmatically. In Taurus, the urge for material acquisition is powerful and its people avidly pursue their desires. In Virgo, we are taught to be more meticulous and discriminatory about possessions we acquire.

Ray 2 of Love and Wisdom flows through Virgo. Younger souls in Virgo love money and are engrossed with accumulating it. The love of money and the material comforts it can provide is a lower aspect of the 2nd ray. This is all as it should be in the normal course of evolution. But if the "love of money" should develop into avarice and an insatiable grasping after "things", it can lead to dense materialism. The keynote of lower Virgo warns us against this - and the Word said, "Let Matter reign." [1]

Virgo rules health and its people are particularly interested in diet and healthy lifestyle practices. Some become obsessed about health, which leads to hypochondria and other health complications. Health improves when Mercury loses its critical edge and when love infuses the mind and tongue. Here are some negative Virgo attitudes that may result in problems.

Picky criticism.	Being judgemental.
Materialism.	Extreme perfectionism.
Narrow view of life.	Nit picking.

2. Body

a. Throat chakra. This centre vitalises the gastro-intestinal tube, and therefore the intestines - the region of the body ruled by Virgo. For digestion, the throat and solar plexus chakras work together, the latter ruling the stomach, liver, gallbladder and pancreas.

b. Intestinal digestion. Digestion starts with Taurus and the consumption of food through the mouth, which then passes through the upper alimentary canal. Cancer represents the breaking down of food in the stomach, before chyme (gastric juices and partly digested food) is passed onto the intestines.

Then Virgo takes over. It rules the intestines and shares rulership of the bowel with Scorpio. The small intestine mixes food with digestive juices from the pancreas, liver and intestines, then Virgo decides which nutrients to absorb or to eliminate. Virgo's function in the body is to discriminate and assimilate. Nutrients are absorbed through the intestine walls into the bloodstream, delivering nourishment to the rest of the body. Finally, muscles push the remaining products into the large intestine, which absorbs any remaining nutrients before waste is eliminated.

c. The enteric nervous system. This system is one of the main divisions of the nervous system and consists of a mesh-like system of neurons that governs the function of the gastrointestinal tract. This relates it to Virgo.

3. Disease

- Diseases and problems of the intestines.

When emotionalism (via the 6th ray) is added to Virgo's perfectionist and nit-picking tendencies, this directly affects the intestines, digestion and bowel health. Examples of this type of trouble are Crohn's disease and diverticulitis. Virgo is a mutable, changeable sign and through ruler Mercury, its diseases are adaptive and infectious.

▲ Virgo negative psychology.
Hypercritical of self and others.
Hypochondria.

▲ Virgo organs, functions.
Appendix.
Chyle.
Colon.
Digestion.
Duodenum.
Enteric NS.
Ileum.
Intestines.
Jejunum.
Nutrition.
Pylorus.

▲ Problems affecting Virgo organs.
Appendicitis.
Bloating.
Cholera.
Celiac disease.
Colic.
Constipation.
Crohn's disease.
Diarrhea.
Diverticulitis.
Dysentery.
Enteritis.
Flatulence.
Gastric disorders.
Indigestion.
Irritable bowel syndrome.
Malnutrition.
Parasites, intestinal.
Peptic ulcer.
Peritonitis.
Tapeworm.
Typhoid fever.
Ulcers.
Worms.

▲ Problems caused by Virgo.
Any mental, emotional and physical problem caused by narrow, hypercritical, perfectionist attitudes.

---
[1] Bailey, Alice A; Esoteric Astrology, 284.

- **Ray: 3,** (5 via Venus and 7 via Uranus)

- **Chakra:**
The Base, also the Solar Plexus and Ajna.

- **Planet rulers:**
Exoteric: Venus.
Esoteric: Uranus.
Hierarchy: Saturn.

- **Personality Keynote:**
Let choice be made.

- **Soul Keynote:**
I choose the way that leads between the two great lines of force.

Libra occupies a unique place in the Great Wheel, for it is the energy coming from this constellation which controls the "hub of the wheel." This is that point in intermediate space where the twelve zodiacal energies meet and cross. Libra, therefore, controls the "moment of reversal of the wheel" in the life of every aspirant, for there comes a moment in the cycle of lives wherein a point of balance is reached and a relative equilibrium is attained, and over this event Libra presides. [1]

1 Bailey, Alice A; Esoteric Astrology, 183.

7. Libra

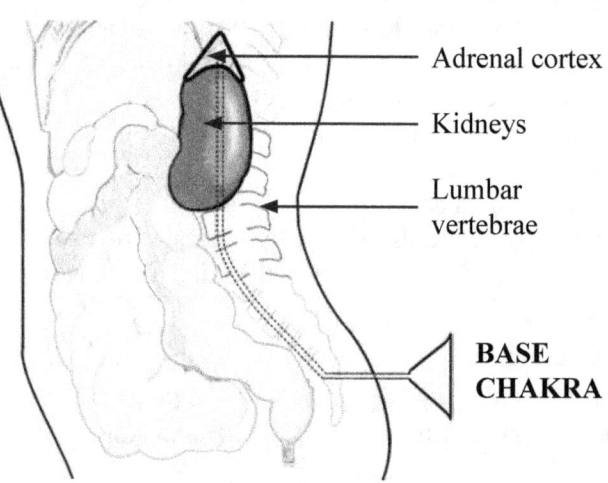

1. Psychology

In Libra, through Venus and the ajna chakra, we are taught judicious balance and discernment. We learn to weigh things carefully before making decisions and to be mentally dexterous and flexible. Wise King Solomon from the Bible story is an example of this higher type. Libran's are potentially very clever, because this sign is a channel for the two rays that govern the Mental Plane - ray 3 and ray 5 via Venus.

Negatively, Libran's procrastinate, find it hard to come to a definite conclusion or make a fuss because they do not want to make a mistake or upset people. This can weaken the body and cause imbalance. Libran's can also be manipulative via the 3rd ray and manoeuvre people to get what they want. This psychological trickery makes a negative impact in the gut, in gastric and intestinal disorders. Here are some Libra attitudes that may result in problems:

Fear of upsetting people.	Imbalance.
Indecisive.	Inaction to keep the peace.
Manipulation.	Procrastination.
Selfish and self-indulgent.	Superficiality.
Vain.	

2. Body

a. Chakras. Libra governs the belt area of the body, close to where the solar plexus enters the body. It supports the work of the solar plexus, sacral and base chakras, and is related to the ajna via Venus.

b. Homeostasis. Libra, the great sign of balance governs homeostasis. This is the body's natural ability to maintain internal balance of all its functions, bringing it naturally under Libra's rulership. Libra's function in the body is to balance, to regulate and to harmonise. The pituitary gland is the control centre for homeostasis, relating Libra to the ajna centre via Venus. If mental indecision becomes chronic, it upsets homeostasis. Energy follows thought, and self-doubt and other mental negatives can upset balance in the system.

> A point of equilibrium [is reached] in Libra, in which sign soul and personality achieve a balance of cooperation. [1]

1 Bailey, Alice; Esoteric Astrology, 93.

c. Glucose balancing, the pancreas gland and the Islets of Langerhans. Libra supports the work of the solar plexus chakra through the pancreatic endocrine glands. They secrete insulin to maintain blood sugar balance. The balancing function in the body is upset when people are excessive in their consumption of sugary foods and carbohydrates. A serious consequence of this is diabetes. Libra's ruler Venus represents the emotional craving for pleasure and love, which can manifest as a love of sweet foods if this desire is thwarted. Venus rules sugar, all sweet foods and carbohydrates. If we "comfort-eat", stuff ourselves with sweet or fatty food to try to alleviate feelings of emotional emptiness and upset, it is an indication that emotional neediness has hijacked the natural balancing systems in the body.

d. Adrenal cortex. Libra rules the adrenal cortex, the outer part of the adrenals, which are governed by the base chakra. This gland secretes hormones such as cortisol and aldosterone to help regulate metabolism and maintain the body's salt-water balance. The inner, combative part of the gland, the adrenal medulla, is linked to Scorpio.

e. The kidneys and urine: they are governed by Libra and the base chakra [1]. Through them, water levels are balanced and blood pressure and acid levels are regulated. The kidneys are the liquid waste-disposal system of the body, filtering toxins from the blood and producing urine, which is about 95% water and 5% waste. This function is assisted by Scorpio, which stores urine in the bladder and sees to its elimination.

f. Sex and female reproduction. These are sacral chakra functions. Libra rules sex from the point of view that it governs relationships and the balancing of the opposites. Libra via Venus is also related to the female reproductive system, co-ruling organs and functions such as menstruation, the ovaries, ovum, the vagina etc. Genital infections and sexually transmitted diseases caught through unbalanced sexual activities and promiscuity are related particularly to Venus and Mars. Here is a quote:

> It is because of this balancing quality in Libra that this constellation can be associated more specifically with the problem of sex than can any of the others. It is in Libra that the balancing of the pairs of opposites must take place and reach solution through the activity of the judicial mind and the establishing of a point of equilibrium between the male and the female principles. [2]

3. Disease

- Diseases of the kidneys, and the filtration of urine.

Libran moderation or right-balance in lifestyle and diet, is the key to good health. When this balance is upset, when for instance we eat too much and exercise too little; then trouble in the body appears. On mental levels, the indecisive and procrastinating traits of this sign, if they should become chronic, has a weakening effect.

> When afflicted (Libra) causes inharmony and want of tone by disturbances in the system. [3]

Libra and Venus rule poor muscle tone, including weak internal muscles, so that organs prolapse. There are many types of prolapse, which differ according to which organ is affected. For example, when the walls of the vagina become lax, the organs that they should be supporting bulge into the vagina. As an air-cardinal sign, Libra diseases are adaptive, infectious, acute and may strike suddenly and painfully, like cystitis.

▲ Libra negative psychology. Mental imbalance and manipulations. Procrastination. Promiscuity. ▲ Libra organs, functions. Balances,	regulates, filters. *Ajna* Balance/ vestibular system in inner ear. Homeostasis in the body generally. *Solar plexus* Insulin. Islets of	Langerhans. *Sacral* Sexual relations. *Base* Adrenal-cortex. Aldosterone. Cortisol. Kidneys. Lumbar. vertebrae. Urine.	Urinary tract. ▲ Problems affecting Libra organs. Addison's disease. Ataxia. Balance, all problems of. Cushing's syndrome.	Diabetes. Kidney filtration trouble. Kidney infection. Kidney stones. Lumbago. Nephritis. Yellow fever. ▲ Problems caused by Libra.	Imbalances in the various body systems and functions. Muscle weakness. Prolapses. STD's caused by licentious behaviour.

---

1 Bailey, Alice: Esoteric Healing,
2 Bailey, Alice; Esoteric Astrology, 233.
3 H. L. Cornell, Ency. of Medical Astrology, 449.

- **Ray:** 4 (6 via Mars, 1 via Pluto).

- **Chakra:**
The Sacral and Base.

- **Planet rulers:**
Exoteric: Mars, Pluto.
Esoteric: Mars.
Hierarchy: Mercury.

- **Personality Keynote:**
Let Maya flourish and let deception rule.

- **Soul Keynote:**
Warrior I am, and from the battle I emerge triumphant.

In Scorpio, the personality is humbled and brought to grips with the soul; in that sign the personality is "occultly killed and then resurrected into air and light," in order to become from that moment the servant of the soul.[1]

---

1 Bailey, Alice A; Esoteric Astrology, 145.

8. Scorpio

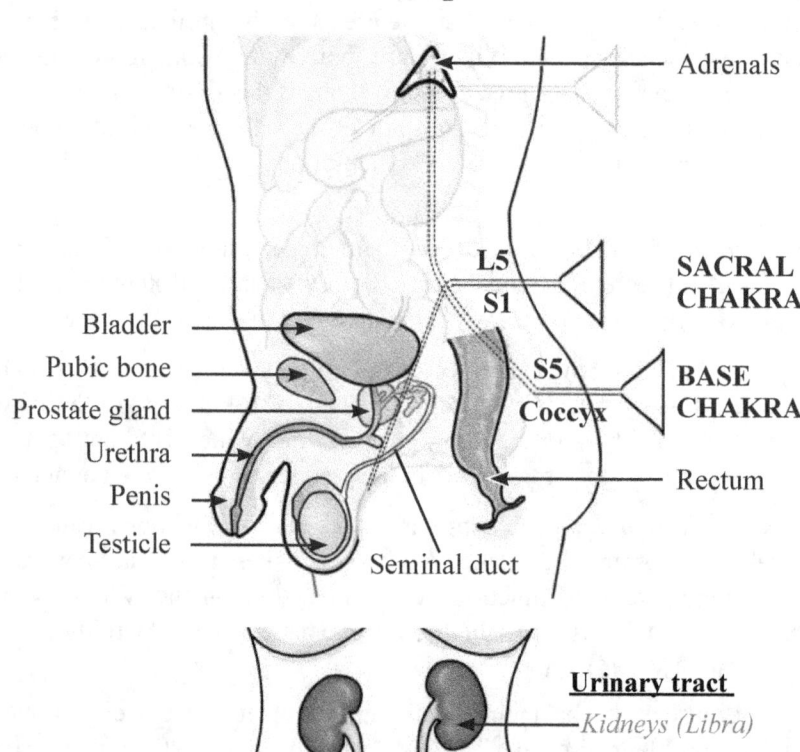

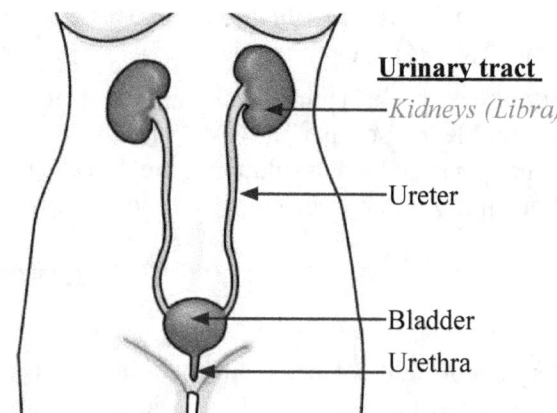

1. Psychology

Scorpio carries the 4th Ray of Harmony through Conflict, the force of warfare. In Scorpio we are trained to be warriors, because in this sign we are pitted against deadly astral delusion and lower desire. In Scorpio, we are forced to rise above delusion into the clear light of mind if we are to survive. There we learn to transmute desire into a higher form such as spiritual aspiration.

Hercules, the mythical warrior, portrayed this great test in his battle with the Lernean hydra. The beast had many heads, representing the fact that desire has many forms. Hercules defeated the hydra by lifting it up into the air. The message is to lift the mind up into the cool light of clear mind and from there assess a situation before acting or speaking. Otherwise, we get mired in the detritus of vindictive combat. Here are some negative Scorpio attitudes that may result in debility and disease:

Aggression, anger.	Continual conflict, combativeness.
Covetousness.	Hate.
Holding onto past grievances.	Jealousy, envy.
Maya, self-deceitfulness.	Revengefulness.
Vindictiveness.	Violent, violence.

2. Body

a. Sacral chakra: it enters the spine around L5 and S1, and is partially ruled by Sagittarius. Scorpio rules its reproductive/ sexual function.

b. Sex and reproduction. Scorpio's function in the body is reproductive and eliminative. It governs sex and the sex glands particularly the testes in men. Cancer and the Moon are the prime rulers of female reproductive organs.

c. Elimination of body waste, the urinary tract, bladder, rectum, anus. Scorpio is the traditional ruler of the excretory organs and of excretion - the elimination of waste from the body, both urine and solid waste. Libra presides over the production of urine, Scorpio assists its removal.

d. Adrenal medulla and the "fight or flight' reaction. The medulla, the inner part of the adrenal gland gives the urge to live and survive. This is a ray 1 attribute carried by Scorpio's rulers Pluto and Mars. It produces the hormone adrenaline, which enables us to respond quickly to perceived danger, physical or non-physical.

e. Death. Scorpio is the sign that rules death of the old and transformation into something new. Death can be physical, but in life has mostly to do with inner psychological change as a consequence of emotional trauma.

3. Disease

- Diseases of sexual performance, reproduction and excretion.

Promiscuity and licentiousness in early primitive man gave rise to sexually transmitted diseases and the syphilitic miasm is imprinted in our DNA. In some cases, this may emerge as dementia because there is a connection between the sex organs and the brain. Even if we have not contracted a syphilitic disease in this incarnation, given the right circumstances and because of karma, dementia could manifest due to this taint.

> The breaking down of brain tissue [many such diseases] are definitely syphilitic in origin.. the physical sex organs are a lower correspondence of the negative-positive relation existing in the brain between the two head centres and the pituitary and pineal glands.[1]

Scorpio is a fixed-water sign, bringing sluggish, damp conditions that are slow-moving and chronic. If we hold onto the past, old issues and hurts, the reflex action upon the body thickens body fluids causing phlegm and problems with other body fluids. If we harbour anger and vengeance, it poisons the blood, erupting as nasty skin conditions.

▲ **Scorpio negative psychology.**
Cruelty.
Cuts, cutting.
Masochism.
Murder, serial killer.
Sex: addiction, immorality, license, masochism promiscuity.
Sex violations: incest, paedophilia, perversions, rape, sadism.
Stalking.

▲ **Scorpio organs, functions.**

Solar plexus
Anal canal.
Anus.
Bowel, large.
Colon.
Defecation, excretion, faeces.
Rectum.

Sacral
Clitoris.
Conception.
Cowper's glands.
Epididymis.
Genitals.
Labia.
Libido.
Menstruation.
Penis.
Procreation.
Prostate gland.
Puberty.
Scrotum.
Semen.
Seminal vesicle.
Sigmoid flexure.
Sperm.
Testes.
Testosterone.
Vagina.
Vans deferens.
Vulva.

Base
Adrenal-medulla.
Adrenaline.
Bladder.
Cortisol.
Fight or flight.
response, survival instinct, will to live, to exist.
Urea, uric acid.
Ureters.
Urethra.
Urinary tract.

▲ **Diseases/ problems affecting Scorpio organs.**
Anal fissure.
Colitis.
Constipation.
Crohn's disease.
Cystitis.
Diarrhea.
Diverticulitis.
Dysentery.
Fatigue: adrenal overload.
Hemorrhoids, piles.
Impotency
Infertility.
Irritable bowel syn.
Pelvic organ prolapse.
Premature ejaculation.
Prostate trouble.
Sexual difficulties.
STD's: chlamydia, genital disorders/ warts/ herpes, gonorrhea, pubic, crabs, syphilis.
Sterility.

▲ **Problems caused by Scorpio.**
Abortion.
Asphyxia.
Castration.
Death, any cause.
Fistulas.
Hernias.
Miscarriage.
Mucous, excessive.
Murder.
Phlegmy conditions.
Ruptures.
STD's.
Strangulation.
Suffocating.
Suicide.

---
1 Bailey, Alice A; Esoteric Healing, 316.

46 ▲ Medical Astrology: Discovering the Psychology of Disease using Triangles

- **Rays:** 4, 5, 6 (2 via Jupiter, 3 via Earth).

- **Chakra:**
The Sacral and Base.

- **Planet rulers:**
Exoteric: Jupiter.
Esoteric: the Earth.
Hierarchy: Mars.

- **Personality Keynote:**
Let food be sought.

- **Soul Keynote:**
I see the goal. I reach the goal and see another.

Hips, thighs, buttocks

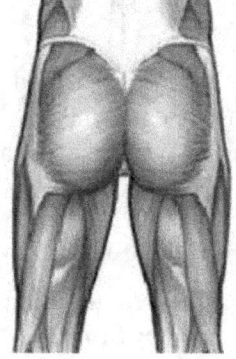

Sagittarius - the ordinary man demonstrates one-pointed selfishness. Though he may be friendly, kind, it is through a desire for popularity.

[On the higher cycle] This is now the sign of the one-pointed disciple. The arrow of the mind is projected unerringly towards the goal.[1]

---
1 Bailey, Alice A; Esoteric Astrology, 121.

9. Sagittarius

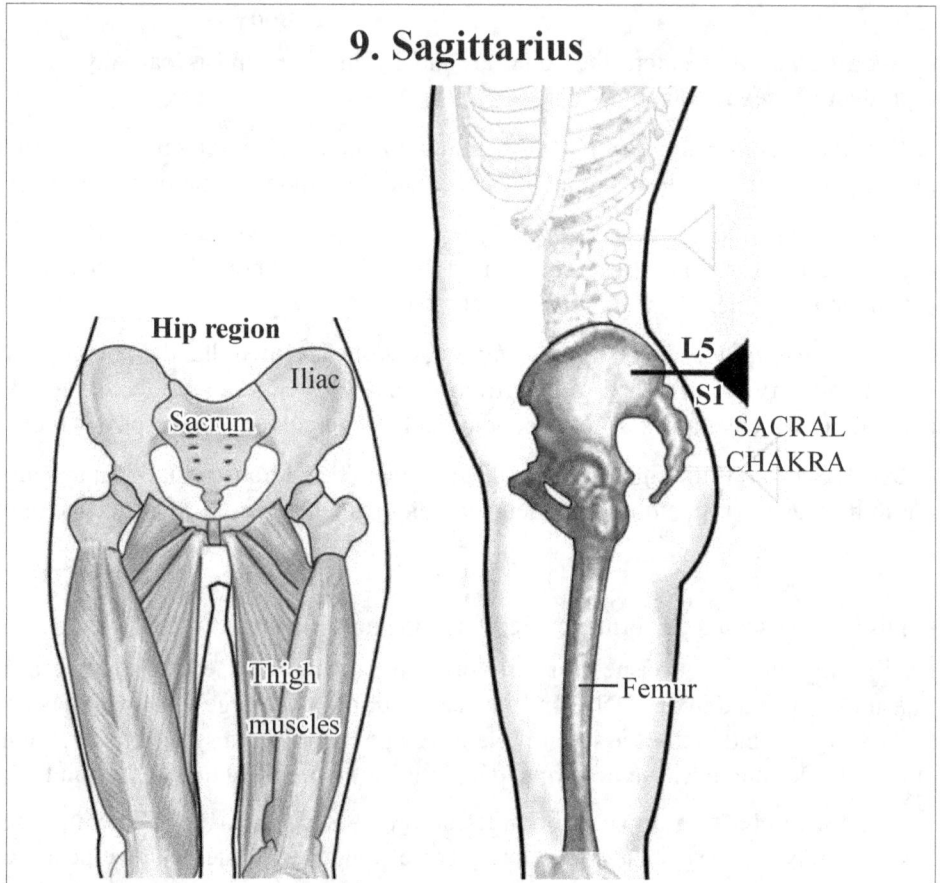

1. Psychology

Three rays flow through Sagittarius and the most powerful to influence the sign is the 6th Ray of Idealism and Devotion. It engenders a desire to find and follow one's highest ideals and consequently, Sagittarius people have an inner urge to "travel far" - physically, mentally or spiritually.

Ray 4 of Harmony and Ray 5 of Concrete Mind, also flow through Sagittarius. This accounts for the artistic ray 4 flair demonstrated by many in this sign, and their superb ray 5 intellects.

Sagittarius people are friendly and good humoured thanks to ruler Jupiter. But in its lower aspect, it represents their tendency to excess. Here are some negative Sagittarius attitudes that may result in problems or disease.

Exaggeration, extravagance, excess.	Gambling addiction.
Greed, hedonism.	Irresponsibility.
Pleasure seeking to excess.	Predatory behaviours.
Rash, recklessness.	Self-gratification (excessive).
Thoughtlessness.	Wastefulness.

The first eight signs govern the development of the human psyche or personality - then Sagittarius takes over. It is the sign of discipleship (a process started in Scorpio), and its evolutionary task is to direct those who have reached this level towards the higher spiritual way ruled by the final three signs.

|| *NB. Being born in Sagittarius does not mean we are spiritually advanced. We could be of course, but it takes many cycles around the zodiac, with several incarnations in each sign per cycle, to reach enlightenment. The final three signs represent the tests and trials required to achieve enlightenment, and all born in these signs receive an aspect of this training as a preparation.*

2. Body

In the physical body, Sagittarius marks a dividing point between the first eight signs, which rule the upper body organs found in the head and torso, and the final three signs - Capricorn, Aquarius and Pisces, which rule parts of the legs. With Sagittarius, these three signs are related to physical movement and locomotion. Esoterically, they symbolise moving forward in time and space, and climbing the Path of Spiritual Evolution. Sagittarius' function in the body is to promote body-power strength and movement.

Greek sculpture depicting movement

a. Chakras. The sacral centre is ruled by Sagittarius. It enters the spine around L5 and S1.

b. Physical power and sexual performance. A vital function of the sacral centre is to generate physical power and strength for locomotion and sex. Sexual desire is ruled by Scorpio, while Sagittarius generates the physical power that is required to see the sex act through. In this regard, these two signs work together. Sexual performance issues or problems in reproduction could indirectly be a Sagittarius or Jupiter problem. For example obesity, linked to excesses that are associated with this sign and its ruler Jupiter, has a degrading effect upon sexual performance, fertility, semen and egg ovum health.

c. Hips, thighs, buttocks and locomotion: these parts of the body when strong and healthy give us ease of movement.

3. Disease

- Diseases of excess.
- Diseases or problems with movement, mobility.

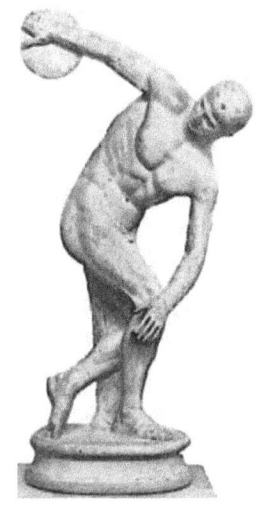

Ruler Jupiter continually wants to expand and include, which works positively via the heart chakra. But when it works through the solar plexus and sacral chakras, the lower appetites are stimulated. The keynote for average man struggling in this sign is "Let food be sought". This can manifest as gluttony at one end of the scale, to serious criminal, sexual abuse at the other. There is a predatory side to Sagittarius when its energy is misused, due to its association with the sacral chakra.

Afflictions to Jupiter or to planets in Sagittarius can represent problems with mobility. Psychologically, a fear of moving forward in life may contribute to impairment in movement. This sign also rules horses and horse riding, and horse-riding accidents come under Sagittarius.

Pegasus, mythical flying horse

▲ **Sagittarius negative psychology.**
Boastfulness.
Exaggeration.
Gambling addiction.
Irresponsibility.
Predatory behaviours.
Wastefulness.

▲ **Sagittarius organs, functions.**

Sacral
Locomotion, locomotor system.
Movement.
Physical/ sexual strength & power via the hips, thighs.
Sciatic nerve. [1]

Base
Buttocks.
Coccyx/ tailbone.
Femur.
Gluteus muscles.
Hamstrings.
Hips.
Ilium.
Ischium.
Pelvic girdle.
Pubis.
Quadriceps muscles.
Sacral vertebrae.
Sacroiliac joint.
Sacrum.
Thighs.

▲ **Problems affecting Sagittarius organs.**
ALS.
Crippling.
Dysplasia of the hip.
Gout.
Hip disease.
Hip, thigh injuries.
Limping.
Locomotive disorders - any injury, disease or problem that impairs mobility.
Locomotor ataxia.
Movement, impaired.
Parkinson's disease.
Polio.
Rheumatoid arthritis.
Sciatica.

▲ **Problems caused by Sagittarius.**
Arrow and gun-shot injuries.
Injuries caused through risk-taking, horse riding, running, physical activities generally, adventure sports.

A centaur archer

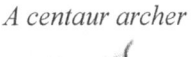

---

[1] The sciatic nerve drives motor function through the legs.

- **Rays:** 1, 3, 7.

- **Chakra:**
The Base.

- **Planet rulers:**
Exoteric: Saturn.
Esoteric: Saturn.
Hierarchy: Venus.

- **Personality Keynote:**
Let ambition rule and the door stand wide.

- **Soul Keynote:**
Lost am I in light supernal, yet on that light I turn my back.

Skeleton, knees

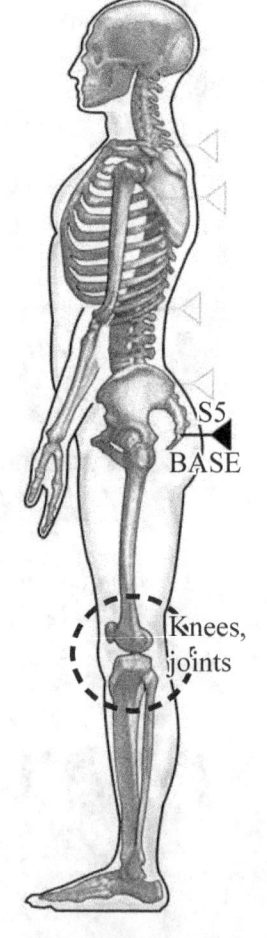

10. Capricorn

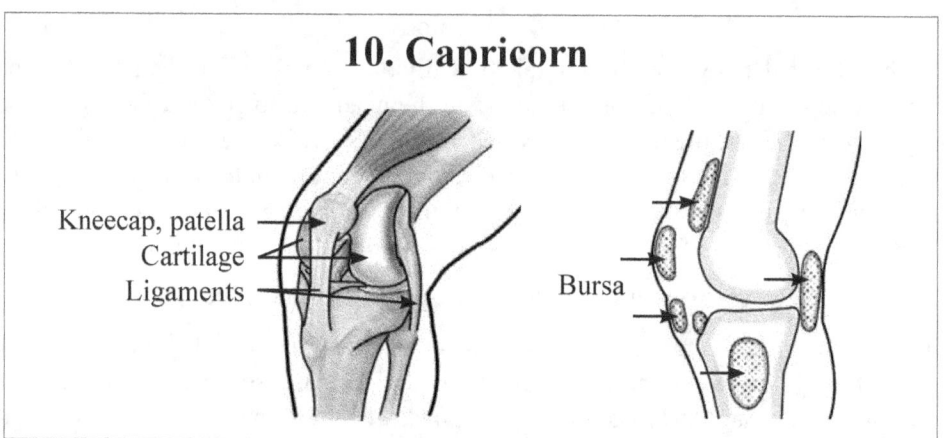

1. Psychology

Capricorn culminates the work of the previous two earth signs Taurus and Virgo. It teaches us to use desire (Taurus) and discrimination (Virgo), to realise ambition (Capricorn). In Capricorn, we acquire power and influence, then later we learn to handle power wisely and with humility.

Psychologically, integrated Capricorn people are very strong in character due to their rays. The two power rays 1 and 7 give a strong will, ambition and manifesting power. The 3rd ray gives intelligence and a native cunning, and through ruler Saturn, stability and an outlook of life that is prudent.

The lower man is ruled by the injunction "Let ambition rule and let the door stand wide". The 3rd ray tendency to manoeuvre and manipulate for profit and gain leads him straight through the doorway of deep materialism. Amongst all the twelve signs, the deepest venality is seen amongst people born in this sign. In some cases, this produces white collar criminals, people who are highly skilled at defrauding and cheating others. Here are some negative Capricorn attitudes that may result in trouble or physical disease:

Ambition that is ruthless.	Arrogance, wilfulness.
Avarice and greed.	Cruel, lacking pity.
Insensitive, cold, hard.	Manipulative, deviousness.
Overwhelming pride.	Power hungry.
Rigid orderliness.	Self-aggrandising.

In this sign, we climb the mountain of materiality, then very much later after many cycles around the zodiac we climb the mountain of spirituality. Capricorn is the sign of initiation and after having passed all the tests of karma, eventually we reach enlightenment where consciousness is fully illumined with soul love and light. This Jesus portrayed on the Mount of Transfiguration - mountains are ruled by Capricorn.

2. Body

a. The base chakra: it enters the spine between S5 and the top of the coccyx or tailbone. Capricorn's function in the body is to provide a structure for the dense body. It supports the base chakra's task of building and maintaining the entire dense physical body, supporting, protecting and holding in place all the vital organs.

b. Dense physical body, and ligaments that tie it together. Ray 3 governs the dense physical body, rays 1 and 7 govern the skeleton - and Capricorn carries these three rays. It governs the main-frame rigid skeleton and bony structure of the body, and the tendons, ligaments, cartilage and muscles that tie it together and give it its durability and strength.

Capricorn's specific area of rulership is the knee. When healthy, the knees give flexible rotation between the upper and lower leg. They are essential for ease in walking, running, sitting and standing. A stiff, unbending attitude (a negative Saturn attitude), will eventually manifest as stiffness in the knees and an inability to move without pain. A spiritual goal in Capricorn is to learn to kneel in humility.

> With his knees upon the rocky mountain top [his job is] to offer his heart and life to the soul and to human service. [1]

c. Skin, teeth and hair: Capricorn's rulership of the physical body includes the integumentary system - the teeth, skin, hair, nails and exocrine glands that protect the body from various kinds of external damage, wear and tear.

Knee muscles, tendons

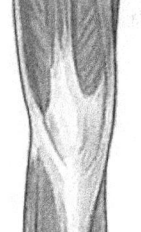

Arthritic knee

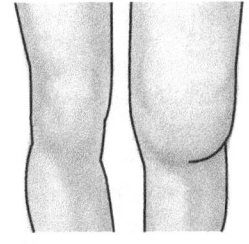

3. Disease

- Diseases of the body structure, the skin and knees.

Unbending pride, hard thoughts and attitudes lead to crystallisation, to a hardening in the body generally, to the atrophying of organs and joints. The body ages prematurely, organs shrivel, movement is restricted, bones dry out and the skin wrinkles. Any problems or diseases with the structure of the body and the parts that tie it together such as ligaments, membranes and skin are associated with Capricorn and Saturn.

Mean-spiritedness affects the heart, hardens its walls and causes failure of its function. Selfish manoeuvring and manipulating via ray 3, leads to gastric and intestinal disorders, certain brain disorders and low vitality.

▲ **Capricorn negative psychology.**
Avarice.
Coldness and calculation.
Miserliness.
Rigidity.

▲ **Capricorn organs, functions.**

Base
Birthmarks.
Bones.
Calcium.
Cartilage.
Collagen.
Connective tissue/ membranes.
Enamel.
Epidermis.
Flesh.
Hair.
Hard tissue (bones, teeth, enamel).
Integumentary system.

Joints.
Knees.
Ligaments.
Membranes.
Moles, skin.
Nails.
Patella.
Physical body.
Ribs.
Rigor mortis.
Sacroiliac joint.
Skeleton.
Skin.
Spine.
Substance.
Tendons.
Vertebrae, all.

▲ **Problems affecting Capricorn organs.**
Back pain.
Bone deformities.
Burns.
Bursitis.
Dermatitis.
Eczema.

Fractures, bones.
Impetigo.
Leprosy.
Melanoma.
Paget's disease.
Rashes.
Rheumatoid arthritis.
Rickets.
Ringworm.
Scabies.
Scleroderma.
Scoliosis.
Scurvy.
Skin eruptions.
Skin lesions.
Spinal meningitis.

▲ **Problems caused by Capricorn.**
Ageing prematurely.
Arthritis.
Attrition.
Calcification.
Chronic diseases.
Constrictions.

Crippling.
Deformities.
Geriatric conditions.
Gout.
Growth stunted.
Hardening.
Hypochondria.
Joints stiff.
Knee problems.
Neurodegenerative diseases.
Old age.
Osteoarthritis.
Osteoporosis.
Progeria.
Rheumatism.
Scleroderma.
Shrinking.
Stiffness.
Stones.
Vertebrae degeneration.
Warts.
Wasting away.
Wrinkles.

Capricorn crystallises.. it is an earth sign, and in it we the densest point of concrete materialisation of which the human soul is capable. When crystallisation has reached a certain "hardness," it is easily shattered and destroyed and man, born in Capricorn, then brings about his own destruction due to his fundamentally materialistic nature, plus the "blows of fate" which are the enactments of the law of karma.

Effort, strain, struggle, the fight with the forces native to the underworld, or the strenuous conditions entailed by the tests of discipleship or initiation—these are distinctive of experience in Capricorn. [1]

---
1 Bailey, Alice A; Esoteric Astrology, 158-9

---
1 Bailey, Alice A; Esoteric Astrology, 169.

- **Ray:** 5 (7 via Uranus, 2 via Jupiter).

- **Chakra:**
The Sacral and Base.

- **Planet rulers:**
Exoteric: Uranus.
Esoteric: Jupiter.
Hierarchy: Moon veiling Uranus.

- **Personality Keynote:**
Let desire in form be ruler.

- **Soul Keynote:**
Water of life am I, poured forth for thirsty men.

Lower legs and ankles

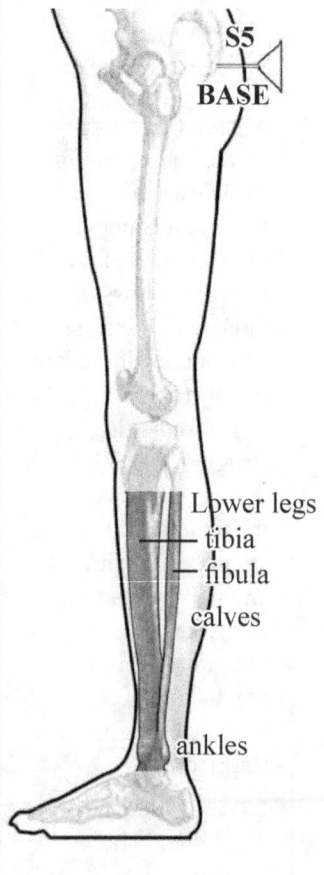

11. Aquarius

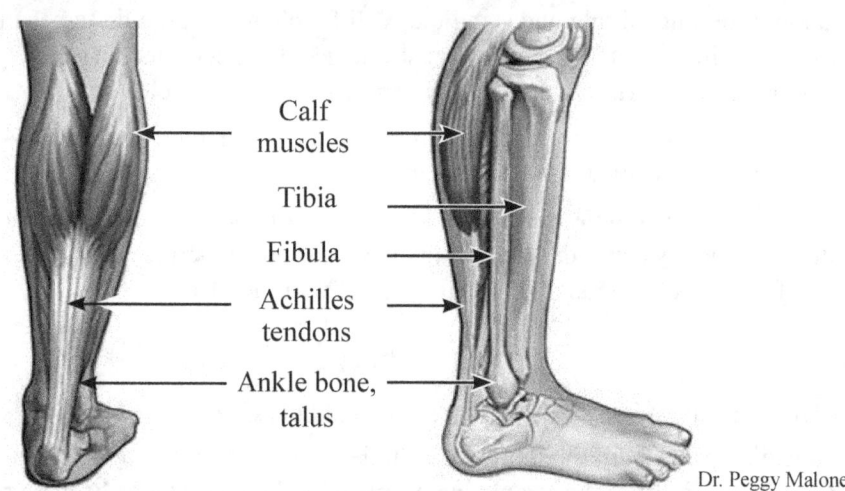

Dr. Peggy Malone

1. Psychology

The 5th Ray of Concrete Mind and Science flows through Aquarius. Its people are the purest examples of the developed concrete mind, the fact finding, knowledge gathering mind. People who have their Sun, ascendant, Mercury or Venus in this sign are often cerebral thinkers.

The higher evolutionary task of Aquarius, the Water-Bearer (another name for the Christ), is to teach us to combine the activities of the mind with the heart, to use the mind as a vessel for love and wisdom. When successful, we see great scientific and social reformers such as Abraham Lincoln who had an Aquarian Sun. On the negative side, Aquarius produces people who use their mental powers for their own personal and selfish gain. Here are some Aquarius attitudes that may result in disease:

Coldly unsympathetic.	Dogmatic.
Fixed, inflexible minded.	Ultra-critical.
Lacking emotional warmth.	Mentally aloof, isolated.
Narrow, closed mind.	Selfish individualism.
Sense of alienation.	Separativeness.

2. Body

a. Chakras. Aquarius is related to the heart centre via its opposite sign and partner Leo. It is also related to the base chakra, through its rulership of the lower legs and ankles.

b. Etheric body. Aquarius rules the ethers, and therefore is a ruler of the etheric body (with Gemini). Both the etheric body and Aquarius have as their goal the free distribution of energy: the etheric web is the medium that connects us into the whole, and Aquarius represents universal consciousness.

c. DNA (deoxyribonucleic acid). The basic energy pattern of the physical body is recorded in the physical permanent atom, which is etheric in nature and located on the 1st subplane of the Physical Plane. This pattern is replicated in our DNA, which science has proven to be the carrier of genetic information inherited from our forefathers - and from our own previous incarnations.

Aquarius is connected with the physical permanent atom, which is on the etheric level,[1] giving it rulership over DNA.

---
1 Bailey, Alice A; Esoteric Astrology, 303.

There is an obvious connection between DNA and karma. Karmic law brings forward our past imperfections for resolution in the present. Similarly, any physical body imperfections that we have to deal with are recorded in our DNA, and we have to sort these out in the current incarnation.

d. Blood circulation. Aquarius' function in the body is circulatory and distributive. It rules the circulation of blood and blood quality. When these are amiss, Aquarius and Uranus are often involved.

e. Nervous system. Aquarius - through the 5th ray, supports the work of the ajna chakra in its management of the nervous system. It is often implicated when there is nerve damage. Nervous disorders can involve Aquarius and Uranus in conflict with Mercury

f. Calves, ankles. Aquarius rules the calves and ankles, which enable stretching and bending. They also propel the body forward into space. This forward progress is a physical correlation with the forward progression of the spiritually mature Aquarian who is a world server – the Water Bearer.

DNA

3. Disease

- Diseases of blood circulation and quality, of the nervous system and lower legs.

The Aquarius trait that most often lies at the root of trouble is the habit of "living in an ivory tower". This refers to the tendency to separate off from others by dwelling singularly in a world of self-created thought. In such isolation, amongst the concepts and ideals they hold to be most worthy, it is easy to judge people for failing to measure up. This separation in thought is a cleavage problem, a lower 5th ray trait that underlies many modern "dissociative" disorders that occur today. Aquarius is not the only sign that generates this problem - anyone who has the discriminating 5th ray mind can succumb - if they do not love their fellow men. Cleavage also causes physical trouble Organs and systems that should work harmoniously together do not. For instance, the endocrine glands may start to send incorrect messages so that glands malfunction or release toxic chemicals. Another 5th ray problem is painful migraine, which is caused by a lack of harmony between the energies of the pineal and pituitary glands.

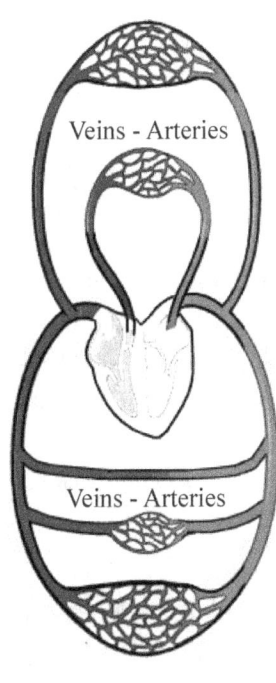

Blood Circulation

▲ **Aquarius negative psychology.**
Asperger's.
Autism.
Cleavages.
Dissociative disorders.

▲ **Aquarius organs, functions.**
Physical permanent atom.
Ajna
Nervous system.
Heart
Arteries.
Blood circulation.
Blood quality.
Blood transfusions.
Cardiovascular activity.
Valves - heart.
Sacral
Chromosome.
DNA.
Etheric web.
Genes, genetics.
Base
Ankles, calves.
Fibula, tibia.

▲ **Problems affecting Aquarius organs.**
Anaemia.
Angina.
Ankle problems.
Arteriosclerosis.
Artherosclerosis.
Blood cancer, disease, poisoning.
Blood circulation problems, poor quality.
Calf, lower leg problems.
Haemophilia.
Hyperuricaemia.
Leukaemia: blood cancer.
Nervous system abnormalities.
Sepsis.
Toxaemia.

▲ **Problems caused by Aquarius.**
Body electrical system malfunction.
Congenital abnormalities.
Genetic mutations, abnormalities.
Migraine (via R5).
Nervous system abnormalities.

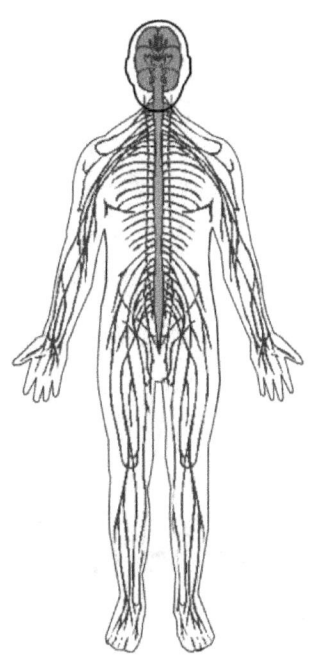

Nervous system

- **Rays:** 2 and 6 (1 via Pluto).

- **Chakra:**
The Base.

- **Planet rulers:**
Exoteric: Jupiter and Neptune.
Esoteric: Pluto.
Hierarchy: Pluto.

- **Personality Keynote:**
Go forth into matter.

- **Soul Keynote:**
I leave the Father's Home and turning back, I save.

Pisces rules the feet

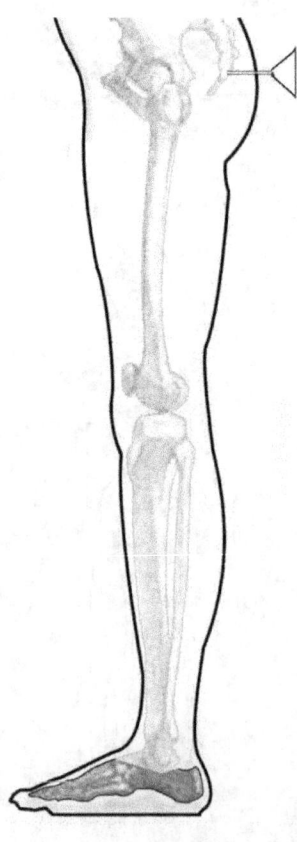

12. Pisces
Bones

1. Psychology

The average person born in a water sign is very susceptible to the psychological condition called glamour. This arises from the effects of the 6th Ray, the force of the Astral Plane, which Pisces happens to carry. The astral world is called the plane of delusion, because when its force dominates and discrimination has not been developed, its hazy or glamorous effect distorts perception. Those who are affected see and believe whatever they want to see and believe.

Pisces also carries the 2nd ray. In average man, it pours out through the solar plexus chakra as a boundless desire for feel-good experiences. This can lead to, uncontrolled drinking and all manner of over-indulging so that the body gets fat or unhealthy. Here are some negative Pisces attitudes that may contribute to disease:

Addictive susceptibility.	Emotionalism, glamour.
Escapism.	Fanaticism.
Hyper-sensitivity, impressionable.	Martyr complex.
Naive, guileless.	One-eyed (being).
Self-deception.	Victim consciousness.

The higher evolutionary task of Pisces is to transmute emotion into inclusive love, a 2nd Ray quality; then to radiate love-wisdom out into the world in service. This is the ultimate goal in this sign of the World Saviour.

2. Body

a. Chakras. Pisces is related to the base centre, which rules the feet, to the heart chakra via Neptune, which rules the bloodstream; and to the throat chakra, which rules the lymphatic system.

b. Sleep state. In the hours of sleep, consciousness slips away to the Astral Plane, which is ruled by Neptune. This relates the sleep state to Pisces.

c. Feet. Pisces rules the lowest part of the body, the feet and toes. Metaphorically, there is a parallel between world saviours and the feet. Just as the feet or Pisces carry the heavy load of the entire human body, world saviours carry the heavy load of human suffering and karma.

> Pisces governs the feet and hence the whole thought of progress, of attaining the goal, and the treading of the Path of Return has been the underlying spiritual revelation of the great cycle through which we are passing. [1]

d. Cyclic waterways, body fluids. Pisces' function in the body is fluidic, flushing and cleansing. With Neptune, it has general rulership over body fluids (with Cancer-Moon), and can represent problems like oedema or excess phlegm.

e. Lymphatic system. It is the body's sewerage system, and is governed by the throat chakra, which rules excretion generally as the end part of digestion. The

---
1 Bailey, Alice; Esoteric Astrology, 128.

lymphatic system includes the tonsils, adenoids, bone marrow, spleen, thymus, appendix, lymph nodes and vessels.

The lymphatic system cleanses dead cells and tissue waste from the body by washing clear watery fluid (lymph) through its tubes. Helped by valves and muscular contractions, this flow moves directionally always towards the heart. Interacting with blood circulation, plasma is drained from tissue and cells and interstitial fluid is returned to the blood via the subclavian veins. In the accompanying diagram, this connection is shown in the small circle at the base of the neck. The main central "drain" of this system is the thoracic duct. Cancer, Pisces, Neptune and the Moon rule the lymphatic system.

Immune system white blood cells, circulate through the lymphatic system. Some are stored in the lymph nodes and as lymph passes through, they attack and destroy any germs that may be present. Cancer and the Moon rule white blood cells and the lymphatic system in its cell-breeding and protective aspect.

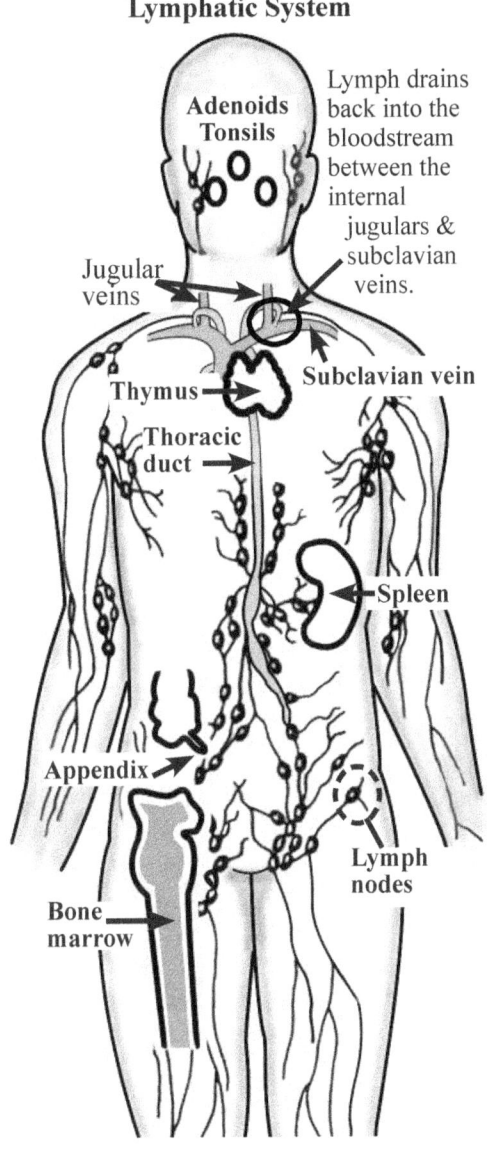

Lymphatic System

3. Disease

- Psychological troubles caused by emotionalism.
- Diseases of the feet and toes.
- Diseases of the lymphatic system and bloodstream.

Pisces rules the oceans via Neptune, which in our psychology represents the world of the emotions. Trying to escape emotional pain through mind-altering substances such as alcohol or drugs is prolific with Pisces people. If they play "the victim" and drown in self-pity, this leads to excess phlegm, colds, flu and problems with body fluids like oedema.

The 2nd ray flows through Pisces and when dysfunctional can cause overstimulation of cells so that they pile together and overbuild, resulting in fatness and more insidiously, tumours and cancer.

The deceiving action of ray 6 is implicated in carcinogenicity, which undermines cell life. Neurodegenerative diseases such as dementia and Alzheimer's that are due to brain fluid atrophy may be indicated by serious Neptune - Moon to Saturn afflictions.

▲ **Pisces negative psychology.**
Delirium, delusory.
Dreams, troubled.
Glamour.
Hallucination.
Hysteria.
Neurotics, neuroses.
Paranoia.
Phobias.
PTSD.

▲ **Pisces organs, functions.**
Anaesthetics.
Fluid waterways.

Throat
Lymph, nodes.

Lymphatic system.
Thoracic duct.

Heart
Bloodstream.

Base
Feet.
Metatarsal bones.
Tarsus bones.
Toes.

▲ **Problems affecting Pisces organs.**
Athlete's foot.
Bloodstream problems.
Buboes.
Bunions.

Feet problems.
Hodgkin's disease, lymphoma, lymphatic cancer.

▲ **Problems caused by Pisces**
Addictions.
Alcoholism.
Aneurysm.
Athlete's foot.
Cold, common.
Covid-19.
Cystic fibrosis.
Cysts.
Drowning.
Drug addiction.
Emotionalism,

that triggers food, alcoholic, drug addictions.
Epstein–Barr virus, glandular fever, mononucleosis.
Flabbiness.
Haemophilia.
Hallucinatory, recreational drugs.
Hiding, obscuring problems.
Hydrocephalus.
Misdiagnosis.
Mucous problems.
Narcolepsy.
Nightmares.
Oedema.

Phlegm.
Ringworm.
Self-harm, self-injury.
Substance abuse.
Swellings.
Viruses and viral attacks via Neptune.
Water retention.
Weakening, diluting.

2c. Astrology Planets

The planets are the transmitting agents of the Seven Rays.

- **Ray:** 2 (1 and 5 via Leo).

- **Chakra:**
The Heart.

- **Sign rulerships:**
Exoteric: Leo.
Esoteric: Leo.
Hierarchy: Leo.

Solar vitality

Cell life

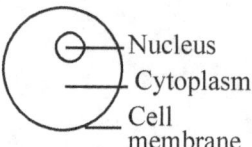

Immune System

Heart and cardiovascular system

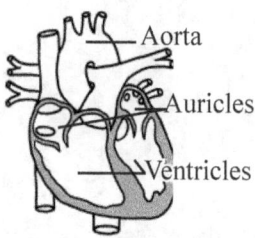

Spine, eyes

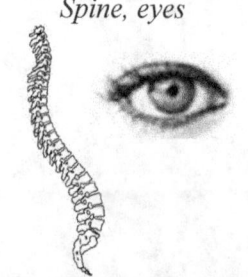

1. The Sun

1. Psychology

The Sun carries the 1st ray of assertiveness via Leo and the 2nd ray of Wisdom. Ray 2 is the "consciousness" or sentient ray that enables us to develop a sense of self, or "I-ness". At its highest, the Sun represents our spiritual aspect.

When the Sun is exalted and blazes forth in all its glory, the other lesser luminaries fade out. Just as the personality is lost sight of in the light of the soul, the solar Angel, so the soul itself disappears and its power and radiance fade out when the Presence, which it has hitherto veiled, appears and dominates the scene at the end of the greater world cycle. [1]

The Sun represents personality consciousness, the power of the individual "I" and its ability or inability to dominate the environment. Personality power hinges upon the level to which we have integrated our personality parts - mind, emotional, physical; and have brought them under the control of the central "I" self. When the personality is fully developed the soul fights to bring it under its control. When successful, the Sun then represents the expression of radiant soul love and wisdom.

Developing a strong and healthy ego is an important milestone on our spiritual journey. Prior to enlightenment, it is represented by the arrogant, proud and strutting lion, the symbol of Leo. Here are some negative attitudes that cause trouble:

Egoism, egomania.	Extreme self-will.
Pride.	Narcissism, extreme self-love.

2. Body

a. The heart chakra. It enters the body in the Leo-Sun ruled region of the body, anchoring in the thymus gland.

b. The thymus gland. Its main function is to support the immune system. To this end it develops T-lymphocytes, powerful killer immune cells.

c. Vitalising of the body and the immune system. Two major streams of energy vitalise the physical body. The first is the dynamic stream of life we receive from the soul via the sutratma that anchors in the heart. A smaller pranic stream from the Sun enters via the spleen where it rises to the heart and merges with the life stream as it enters the blood.

The Sun's energy is prophylactic - it kills all germs and frees from disease. This activity is reflected in the body by the immune system, which the Sun governs. It is a subset of the cardiovascular system and uses blood vessels to send out its army of white defender cells to fight infection.

d. The spleen, the organ of vitality. The spleen chakra and its physical counterpart the spleen organ are the primary receivers and distributors of pranic vitality. The spleen chakra receives vitality from the Sun, sends it to the spleen organ, which then sends it to the heart. A second important function of the spleen is to support the immune system by filtering dead cells and waste from the blood and storing white blood cells to fight disease. The spleen serves the physical form and is not included in the list of major seven chakras because it is not connected with the evolution of consciousness.

---

1 Bailey, Alice; Esoteric Astrology, 104.

e. Cardiovascular system: it includes the heart organ, arteries, capillaries, veins, blood and bloodstream. The heart plays a similar role in our physical system as the sun does in the solar system. It distributes life, vitality and nourishment to every cell in the body through blood circulation. When considered esoterically, the two types of blood channels (arteries and veins) are reflections in the body of the involutionary Path of Outgoing and the evolutionary Path of Return. All souls travel these paths, go out to explore desire on the red path and return to the Source on the blue path.

f. The eyes: we are able to see because of the light of the Sun. It is related to vision, to the eyes - particularly the right eye, and to eye health.

3. Disease

A well placed and well aspected Sun in the natal chart promotes a positive psychological outlook on life and is the most positive indicator of good health. It indicates a heart that has an excellent ability to absorb prana, thus vitalising cell life. Easy aspects to the Sun from Mars and Jupiter boost vitality. This is because the brute animal strength of Mars and the expansive power of Jupiter, support, promote and strengthen the Sun's power. Even hard aspects (square, semi-square, opposition, conjunction) are better than none. In this case, energy is available, though if misused can lead to burn-out.

The Sun's force when negative can burn, scald, overheat, produce fevers. Afflictions to the Sun indicate heart and circulation problems, depletion of vitality and lowered resistance to disease. The Sun sign often points to a part of the body that will suffer if vitality or immunity should falter. Sometimes solar function is potentially impaired if the Sun is in the sixth and twelfth houses, which govern illness and hospitalisation. This does not mean that illness naturally follows such placements; there may be other compensating factors in the chart. What it does mean is that attention should be given to diet, exercise and living a moderate lifestyle to help strengthen vitality and health.

In disease, the 2nd ray that flows through the Sun produces overstimulation and an over-production of atoms that show as growths, tumours, cancer, organs that are too big etc.

Interestingly, germs are living organisms that find their way into the human mechanism through the medium of the life force, which in its turn, uses the heart and the bloodstream as its agents of distribution.

▲ Sun negative psychology.
Arrested development.
Borderline personality disorder.
Egomania, egoism.
Megalomania.

▲ The Sun's organs, functions.
Energizing.
Grows, growth.
Nourishing, protecting and preserving. [1]
Tonifying.
Vitalising.

Ajna
Eyes.
Self-consciousness.
Sentiency.
Sight generally.
Sight, right eye.

Vision.

Heart
Aorta.
Arteries.
Blood.
Body warmth.
Cardiovascular, circulatory system - the heart chakra, which is ruled by the Sun, rules the blood and cardiovascular systems. [2]
Cell life.
Constitution.
Heart.
Immune system, t-cells.
Life-force.
Life-thread/ stream, sutratma, silver cord.
Metabolism.
Pericardium.

Prana.
Thoracic vertebrae.
Recuperative power.
Spleen.
Thymus.

Base
The spine.

▲ Problems affecting the Sun's organs.
Anaemia.
Aneurism.
Angina.
Ankylosis spondylosis.
Arrhythmia.
Arteriosclerosis.
Artherosclerosis.
Astigmatism.
Atrial fibrillation.
Back pain.
Blindness.
Blood cancer.
Blood circulation problems.

Cardiomyopathy.
Cataracts.
Congenital heart problems.
Eye trouble.
Glaucoma.
Heart: attack, disease, fibrillation, arrhythmia.
High blood pressure, hypertension.
Hypotension.
Keratitis.
Loss of consciousness.
Macular disease.
Myocarditis.
Myopia.
Palpitations.
Scoliosis.
Short sighted.
Spinal fractures.
Spinal meningitis.
Tiredness, fatigue, lethargy, debilitation due to low energy levels.
Vertebrae degeneration.

▲ Problems caused by the Sun
AIDS.
Burns.
Fevers.
Heart trouble.
Heat-stroke.
High temperatures.
Immune attacks.
Inflammation.
Lupus.
Over-growth (via R2), tumours, cancer.
Over-heating.
Spinal meningitis
Scalds.
Sunburn
Sunstrokes.

---

1 Bailey, Alice: A Treatise on Cosmic Fire, 924.

2 Bailey, Alice A; Esoteric Healing, 45.

- **Ray:** 4 (3 and 7 via Cancer).
- **Chakra:** The Solar Plexus; to the Sacral for reproduction; to the Base for the form.
- **Sign rulerships:**
  Exoteric: Cancer.
  Esoteric: Virgo.
  Hierarchy: Aquarius.

Motherhood, babies

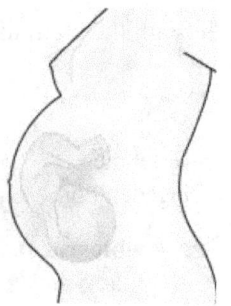

Ovaries, womb

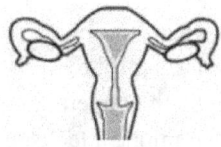

Body tissue

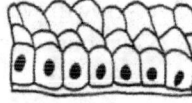

Body fluid

2. The Moon

Esoterically, the Moon is considered a dead planet. However, it retains a powerful influence over humanity because it orbits within the earth's atmosphere and continually sweeps its force over us affecting our astral nature and water/ tidal cycles. It carries the 4th ray and in the chart represents conflict, internal and with the environment.

1. Psychology

In our psychology, the Moon represents unresolved emotional baggage that we have brought from past lives into the new incarnation. These are hidden in the unconscious as negative core beliefs. They represent 'the prison of the soul pattern', because they stop the soul from moving forwards in its growth, keeping it bound to old 'dead" beliefs and modes of behaviour. These negative beliefs emerge automatically when we feel afraid, causing us to defend ourselves as we would if we were a child, in irrational and inappropriate ways. The most important task we can do in our personal development is to transform the Moon sign negatives. For this reason, always examine the Moon for potential emotional disturbances that could lead to a health issue. Here are some negative attitudes associated with the Moon that can lead to disease.

Agonising over issues.	Conflicted, torn within.
Anxiety, emotionalism.	Fear, deep and primeval.
Living always in the past.	Worry, agitation, inner suffering.

When the lunar pattern has been healed, then the Moon in the chart represents our ability to harmonise, to balance and to bring peace to troubled waters.

2. Body

a. The solar plexus chakra: this centre enters the body in the Cancer ruled region, relating the Moon to the function and organs ruled by this chakra.

b. The physical body, flesh and tissue. The Moon is the "mother of form" and with Cancer and ray 3, governs body substance and tissue generally. It governs brain substance and is often prominent when brain tissue breaks down. Cancer and the Moon also rule white blood cells.

c. Digestion. The Moon is related to digestion and all mid-region digestive organs, via Cancer (especially the stomach).

d. Women, female cycles, fertility, reproduction, motherhood. Cancer and the Moon rule women, the mother, home and family, babies, female organs (ovaries and womb/uterus), and functions such as menstruation, conception, pregnancy, gestation and breast-feeding. Lunar afflictions indicate problems in these organs and functions.

e. Body fluids, secretions, mucous. Traditionally, the Moon rules white or colourless body fluids such as mucous, lymph and plasma.

f. Lymphatic system, peristalsis. The Moon is gentle, co-governs the lymphatic system, using peristaltic waves of contraction to move lymph.

g. Circulation in the etheric body. The Moon governs body cycles, which includes circulation of energy through the etheric body.

3. Disease

The Moon's force when negative, tends to cause excess damp/ water, swellings, toxic thick liquids such as pus or excess mucous, problems with body and female cycles.

The Moon carries the 4th ray of Harmony through Conflict and in our psychology an afflicted Moon indicates conflict, anxiety, hysteria and stress. These traits debilitate, they wear down the immune system, rendering the body susceptible to infections such as influenza. The Moon also carries the 7th ray via Cancer, which is largely responsible for infections and contagious diseases. Consequently, the Moon and Cancer are often implicated in serious disease.

The Moon is the primary ruler of reproduction - especially female reproduction. So, its placement in the chart will indicate either ease or difficulty with reproduction. An afflicted Moon also shows susceptibility to the indigenous diseases (syphilis, cancer, TB) of the planet and of these, cancer is the most dangerous today.

Another important point to remember in conjunction with the Moon is that energy circulation through the etheric is governed by the Moon, which means that any hard aspects to the Moon can be read as potential blockages in the etheric and a lowering of vitalisation, the precursor to disease.

▲ Moon negative psychology
Anorexia.
Anxiety.
Bipolar.
Bulimia.
Delirium.
Delusion.
Depression.
Despair.
Emotionalism.
Fear.
Hallucination.
Hysteria.
Inner conflict.
Manic depression.
Mental conflict.
Mood swings.
Negative core beliefs.
Neuroses.
Panic attacks.
Paranoia.
Phobias.
Postpartum blues.
PTSD.
Schizophrenia.
Self-harm/ injury.
Suicidal thoughts, feelings.
Trauma.
Worry.

▲ The Moon's organs, functions.
Motherhood.

Crown
Brain mass/ tissue.

Throat
Lymphatic system, lymph fluid, lymph nodes.
Mucous membranes.
Pleurae.
Sinuses.
Tears.
Thoracic duct.

Heart
White blood cells.

Solar plexus
Abdomen.
Chyle.
Digestion.
Nutrition.
Pancreas.
Stomach.

Sacral
Babies.
Birth.
Breasts.
Cervix.
Conception.
Egg ovum.
Embryo.
Estrogen.
Etheric body.
Fallopian tubes.
Fertility.
Gestation.
Infancy.
Lacteals, lactation.
Maternal, maternity.
Menstruation.
Ovaries.
Periods.
Placenta.
Pregnancy.
Procreation.
Progesterone.
Reproduction.
Uterus.
Womb.

Base
All body containers, receptacles.
Bone marrow.
Epithelial tissue.
membranes: serous, mucous, synovial.
Flesh.
Physical body/ form.
Secretions, sweating.
Stem cells.
Substance.
The body/ form.
Tissue.
White fluids.

▲ Problems affecting the Moon's organs.
Abortion.
Acid reflux.
Blindness, left eye.
Bloating.
Brain haemorrhage.
Coeliac disease.
Dementia group of diseases in brain tissue.
Dyspepsia.
Eating disorders.
Flatulence.
Food allergies, poisoning.
Gastric disorders.
Indigestion.
Malnutrition.
Oedema.
Pancreatitis.
Peptic ulcer.
Peritonitis.
Reflux.
Reproduction (female) problems: barrenness, endometriosis, fibroids in womb, infertility, menstrual disorders, miscarriage, uterine troubles.
Starvation.
Typhoid fever.
Ulcers (stomach).
Vomiting.
Water retention.

▲ Problems caused by the Moon.
Abscess.
Allergic reactions.
Athlete's foot.
Bronchitis.
Buboes.
Candida.
Cataracts.
Catarrh.
Congenital abnormalities.
Contagious infections.
Contaminations
Covid-19.
Croup.
Cystic fibrosis.
Damp.
Decay.
Diseases caused by repressed or virulent emotions.
Emotionalism, triggering food, alcoholic, drug addictions.
Epidemics (via R4).
Fungal infections.
Hereditary diseases
Influenza.
Mucous excessive.
Myopia.
Nasal congestion.
Pandemics.
Phlegm.
Pneumonia.
Pus.
Putrefaction.
Reproduction problems.
Ringworm.
Short sightedness.
Sinusitis.
Spoiling food.
Thrush.
Tinea.
Tiredness due to emotional conflict.
Toxicity.
Weakening. [1]

---

[1] Bailey, Alice: Esoteric Healing, 301. "R4 weakens"

- **Ray: 4** (2 and 6 via Gemini and Virgo).

- **Chakra:**
Ajna, Throat, and Base for kundalini

- **Sign rulerships:**
Exoteric: Gemini and Virgo.
Esoteric: Aries.
Hierarchy: Scorpio.

Nervous system, arms, hands, fingers

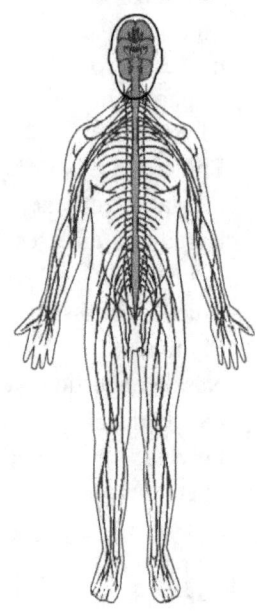

Speech, hearing

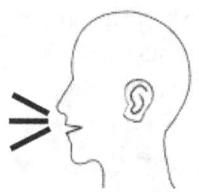

Respiration

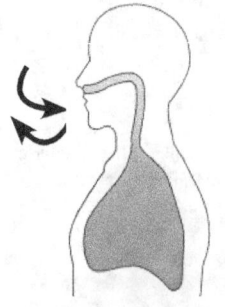

3. Mercury

1. Psychology

Mercury gives curiosity, an urge to know and understand. Through formal education and life experience it teaches us to think, unfolds our mental faculties.

Mercury is the "Messenger of the Gods", shuttling communications back and forth between opposites. This oscillating action is due to its force, ray 4, which makes connections between opposite poles. The negative effect of ray 4 causes conflict, mental and emotional. The troubled ray 4 mind is continually at war with itself and projects this disturbance onto others. Such people are always looking for someone to fight with, so they can play out in their external relationships, the conflict and drama being experienced within. Constant conflict devitalises the body, opening it up to disease and epidemics. Here are some Mercury negatives that can lead to disease.

Duality.	Flighty, instability.
Mind-chatter.	Shallow, superficiality.
Trickiness, theft.	Worry, agitation, agonising, inner suffering.

At a higher level Mercury represents the intuitive faculty, pure reason or instant knowing. It is called "the Star of the Intuition". [1]

2. Body

a. Ajna and throat chakras. Mercury governs the ajna with Venus and both planets represent "self-consciousness" which is achieved through these two centres. Mercury rules the antahkarana, [2] also called the consciousness thread. [3] Mercury is also related to the throat chakra, the "speech" centre.

b. Pituitary and thymus glands. After Venus, Mercury rules the pituitary gland. It is also related to the thymus via Gemini, which rules that gland in disciples and initiates.

c. The central nervous system, brain, spinal cord, senses. Mercury is the messenger and the nervous system is the messaging, signalling and communication system in the body that enables us to become aware and to know. Uranus and Venus are also related to the nervous system.

d. Respiration and airways. Mercury (and Gemini) govern the bronchial tree, upper lungs and blood oxygenation.

e. Sound, speech, hearing. Mercury represents the power of speech and governs the organs in the head and throat that are responsible for its production.

f. Intestines. Mercury rules the intestines via Virgo. From the food mass, the intestines discriminate - which nutrients to absorb and which to reject.

g. Tubes in the body. Gemini and Mercury govern transportation and rule tubes in the body that transport substances from one place to another. For example, the alimentary canal that transports food and the fallopian tubes that transport ova.

h. Shoulders, arms, hands, fingers. These upper body appendages and their movement are traditionally ruled by Gemini and Mercury.

---

1 Bailey, Alice A; Treatise on Cosmic Fire, 370
2 Bailey, Alice A; Esoteric Astrology, 281
3 Bailey, Alice A; The Rays and the Initiations, 449

3. Disease

A good mind is essential for mental health. If the emotional body is more powerful, if it regularly swamps consciousness with waves of emotion and discord, it leads to many mental-nervous disorders.

Mercury's force when negative makes wrong connections and misdirects messaging. Gemini is an air sign and Mercury's diseases primarily affect the airways, the lungs and breathing. Mercury carries the 4th ray, which rules epidemics. It fosters the rapid spread of air-borne germs, causing epidemics and is usually implicated in infectious disease outbreaks such as influenza.

▲ Mercury negative psychology.
ADD, AD(H)D: attention deficit (hyperactivity) disorder.
Asperger's.
Autism.
Bipolar.
White collar and cyber crime: fraud, scams, stealing, theft, identity theft, embezzlement.
Insanities due to disconnection of the consciousness thread.
Manic depression.
Mental conflict, instability.
Mood swings.
Multiple personalities.
Negative thinking.
Suicidal thoughts, feelings.

▲ Mercury's organs, functions.

Crown
Consciousness thread, the antahkarana.

Ajna
Cognition.
Ears.
Eye nerves, cornea.
Hearing.
Hypothalamus.
Intelligence.
Macular.
Nerves: all, primarily the CNS, the senses.
Brain as a data relay centre.
Neurons.
Pituitary gland.
Retina.
Self-consciousness.
Senses: sight, touch, smell.
Spinal cord.
Synapse, nerve.
Thalamus.
Vagus nerve.

Throat
Airways.
Alta-major centre.
Alveoli.
Arms, arm joints, elbows, hands, scapulas, shoulders, wrists.
Brainstem.
Breathing.
Bronchial tree.
Cerebellum.
Ears.
Endocrine system.
Glottis.
Intelligence.
Larynx.
Lungs, upper.
Medulla oblongata.
Oxygen, blood oxygenation.
Pulmonary circulation.
Pons.
Reptilian brain.
Respiration.
Speech.
Tongue.
Trachea.
Vocal cords.
Voice box.
Windpipe.

Heart
Capillaries.

Solar plexus
Appendix.
Duodenum.
Enteric NS (follows digestive tract from esophagus to anus).
Ileum.
Intestines.
Jejunum.
Pylorus.

Sacral
Sciatic nerve (etheric web and physical life energies flow through the sacral and the sciatic nerve, driving motor function through the legs).

▲ Problems affecting Mercury's organs.

Via Gemini:
All NS trouble.
ALS: amyotrophic lateral sclerosis/ Lou Gehrig's/ motor neurone disease.
Aphasia.
Arm fracture.
Asphyxia.
Bells Palsy.
Bronchitis.
Carpal tunnel syndrome.
Celiac disease.
Cerebral palsy.
Chronic obstructive pulmonary disease.
Colds.
Croup.
Deafness.
Diphtheria.
Dyslexia.
Emphysema.
Epilepsy.
Glaucoma.
Guillain-Barre syndrome.
Hay fever.
Influenza.
Labyrinthitis.
Laryngitis.
Learning difficulties.
Locomotor ataxia.
Meniere's disease.
Mental retardation.
Middle ear balance problems.
Multiple sclerosis.
Myasthenia gravis.
Nerve spasms, pain.
Neuralgia.
Paralysis.
Paraplegia, quadriplegia.
Parkinson's disease.
Pleurisy.
Pneumonia.
Polio.
Pulmonary tuberculosis.
Scarlet fever.
Sciatica.
Seizures.
Shingles.
Spasticity.
Speech impediments.
Stuttering.
Tinnitus.
Tourette's syndrome.
Tremors.
Twitching, tics.
Vertigo.

Via Virgo:
Appendicitis.
Cholera.
Colic.
Enteritis.
Flatulence, wind.
Parasites, intestinal.
Peptic ulcer.
Tapeworm.
Worms.

▲ Problems caused by Mercury.
Air-borne contagions, germs.
Contagious infections.
Debilitation, devitalisation, fatigue, lethargy caused by chronic mental-emotional conflict.
Epidemics.
Famine due to flying insect plagues.
Nervous system disorders.
Pandemics.
Pollen.
Wrong connections and wrong communications.

- **Ray:** 5 (4 via Taurus, 3 via Libra).

- **Chakra:**
The Ajna and Throat; Venus is also related to the Solar Plexus and Sacral chakras

- **Sign rulerships:**
Exoteric: Taurus and Libra.
Esoteric Gemini.
Hierarchy: Capricorn.

Nervous system

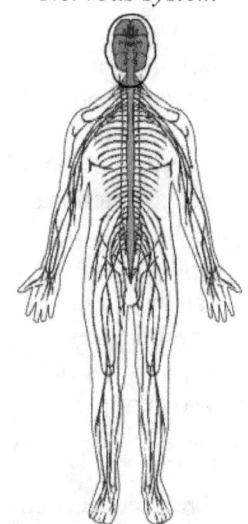

Throat, thyroid

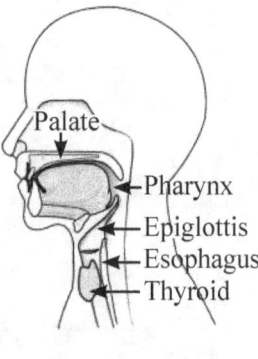

Kidneys, urine.

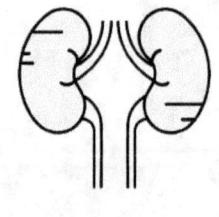

4. Venus

1. Psychology

Venus can be read on several levels, as can all the planets. In average emotional man it works primarily through the sacral chakra where it represents relationship intimacy and sex. It also represents the love of money and material benefit. Venus' force, the 5th Ray of Concrete Mind and Science, working through the ajna, trains us to think accurately and to reason logically. Venus sometimes acts as a substitute for concrete mind. It is involved in the higher mental faculties of comprehension and wise understanding and is a symbol for intelligence. On the highest level, Venus represents the Solar Angel, the guide and mentor of our human soul and of our spiritual development and values.

In the chart, Venus indicates where our thought life needs beautifying, where we should endeavour to think and speak with intelligent love and to radiate soul wisdom. On the negative side, here are some psychological attitudes associated with Venus that can lead to trouble or disease.

Greed, indolence, laziness.	A clinical and cold mentality. (R5)
Narcissism, extreme self-love.	Pleasure seeking to excess.
Unregulated desire.	Separativeness. (R5)

2. Body

a. The ajna and throat chakras. Venus rules the ajna chakra and its organs with Mercury. Through Taurus, it governs the throat chakra and its organs.

b. The pituitary and thyroid glands. Venus is the traditional ruler of the thyroid gland, which is the physical anchorage of the throat chakra, and Venus should be consulted for thyroid and throat problems.

c. Consciousness and the Nervous System. The ajna rules the nervous system, which in turn is ruled by Gemini and Mercury, and by Venus.[1] Venus is a representative of the nervous system[2] and of "consciousness".[3]

d. Venous system. Venus' colour is indigo blue. It rules the blue Path of Return, by which means, souls who have exhausted lower desire return to their spiritual source. This is reflected in the cardiovascular system. Venus rules the "blue" veins that return deoxygenated blood to the heart for re-oxygenation.

e. Digestion, glucose and insulin. Venus via Taurus rules the mouth as an organ of digestion and the Limbic System as an organ of desire.

Venus governs the endocrine part of the pancreas - the Islets of Langerhans that secrete insulin to extract glucose from the blood when blood sugar levels are low. Via Libra it represents the balancing of glucose levels. Venus rules sweet foods, sugar and body glucose. People who overload their diet with rich foods and carbohydrates may develop diabetes, a condition, where the insulin function is impaired and the pancreas loses its ability to balance (Libra) blood sugar. Diabetes is the karmic result of wrong inner desire. In this case, desire (Venus in its lowest aspect), is focused on comfort-eating and sweet foods to try to compensate for feelings of emotional emptiness.

---

1 Bailey, Alice A; Esoteric Healing, 143.
2 Bailey, Alice: Esoteric Healing, 143.
3 Bailey, Alice: Esoteric Astrology, 173.

f. Female cycles, sex and reproduction. Venus is related to the sex function through its rulership of Libra and the pituitary and its relation with the sacral chakra. The pituitary stimulates the sex processes in the ovaries and testes. With the Moon, Venus shares rulership over some female sex glands, organs and processes that involve reproduction.

g. Kidneys and urine: Venus rules the kidneys via Libra.

3. Disease

A positively placed Venus in the chart has many advantages, not least - if the outer life and actions confirm it, someone who is using the higher faculties of the concrete mind in a visionary and positive way to beautify the world around them.

> When the task of Saturn and of Mercury has been accomplished, then Venus, which is the union of heart and mind, will usher in the long hoped for era of love-wisdom, of brotherhood and of expressed brotherly relationships. [1]

Afflicted, Venus represents the opposite. It represents looseness in character, the misuse of "love" and of the sexual function.

Venus' 5th ray lies behind many of our modern mental troubles today. This is particularly so where feelings of alienation, of being excluded and isolated underlie the trouble. Positive Venus has a relaxing, soothing, fertile and nutritive affect. Misused Venus force weakens, loosens and debases. Prolapses for instance, which occur when organs move from their usual positions because of weak muscles, or the leakage of vital fluids because weakened valves or organs start to fail in their tasks. Mars and Venus represent the misuse of sex energy that results in sexually transmitted diseases.

▲ **Venus negative psychology.**

Immorality.
Promiscuity.
Psychological trouble due to a separative attitude, disassociation (via R5), limiting brain energy-flow routes: Eg. Asperger's, autism.

▲ **Venus' organs, functions.**

Ajna
Balance, equilibrium via pituitary.
Dopamine.
Intelligent self-consciousness.
Homeostasis via pituitary.
Hypothalamus.
Limbic system.
Nervous system.
Pituitary gland.
Thalamus.

Throat
Adam's apple.
Adenoids.
Appetite.
Atlas axis.
Carotid arteries.
Carotid gland.
Esophagus, upper.
Glottis.
Gums.
Hyoid bone.
Jugular vein.
Lips (via Taurus).
Mouth.
Neck.
Palate.
Parathyroids.
Parotid glands.
Pharynx.
Salivary glands.
Submandibular glands.
Taste.
Throat.
Thyroid.
Thyroxine.
Tongue.
Tonsils.
Uvula.

Heart
Veins.
Vena cava.
Venous system.

Solar plexus
Carbohydrates, glucose, sugar.
Insulin.
Islets of Langerhans.

Sacral
Clitoris.
Labia.
Libido.
Menstruation.
Periods.
Sex organs, female.
Sex relations.
Sex development, puberty in girls.
Vagina.
Vulva.

Base
Adrenal-cortex.
Aldosterone.
Cortisol.
Kidneys.
Lumbar vertebrae.
Urine.

▲ **Problems affecting Venus' organs.**
Acromegaly.
Addison's disease.
Balance problems via Libra.
Cushing's syndrome.
Deep vein thrombosis.
Diabetes.
Goitre.
Grave's disease.
Hashimoto's disease.
Hemorrhoids, piles.
Herpes, oral.
Hyperglycemia.
Hyperpituitarism.
Hyperthyroidism.
Hypoglycaemia.
Hypopituitarism.
Hypothyroidism.
Kidney infection.
Kidney stones.
Laryngitis.
Lumbago.
Menstrual heavy, painful.
Migraine.
Mumps.
Nephritis.
Pituitary growth hormone malfunction: dwarfism, gigantism.
Simmond's disease.
Snoring.
Thyroid imbalance.
Tonsillitis.
Varicose veins.
Vertigo.
Weight gain or loss, via thyroid.

▲ **Problems caused by Venus.**
Corruptions.
Kidney trouble.
Loosening, weakening of muscle, skin tone.
Migraine.
Prolapses.
Sugar addiction.

---
1 Bailey, Alice;, Esoteric Astrology, 149.

- **Ray:** 6 (1 via Aries, 4 via Scorpio).

- **Chakra:**
The Solar plexus, Sacral and Base for kundalini.

- **Sign rulerships:**
Exoteric: Aries and Scorpio.
Esoteric: Scorpio.
Hierarchy: Sagittarius.

Sex

Blood, red blood cells

Muscles

Adrenal Medulla

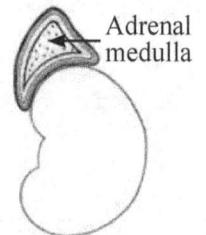

Energy, body warmth

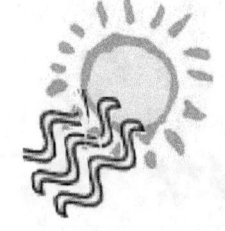

5. Mars

1. Psychology

Mars carries the 6th Ray of Devotion and Idealism, the force that rules the Astral Plane and the majority of human beings who are controlled by their emotions. Mars governs the fiery emotions such as anger, annoyance, irritation, rage, suspicion, hate, avoidance, disgust, loathing, passion, yearning, thirsting, courage and aspiration.

Mars is the primary representative of "desire" which plays out at all levels. For example, there is sacral chakra desire for sex and tangible rewards. Through the solar plexus, there is desire for love. Then there is higher aspiration, or desire on the Mental Plane associated with the ajna. "Desire" is the fuel we use to drive towards our goals and ideals. This makes Mars a very influential planet. Here are some Mars psychological negatives that can lead to trouble and disease.

Aggression, anger, hate.	Defensiveness, protective.
Fanaticism.	Glamour.
Jealousy, envy, covetousness.	One-eyed, blinkered perception.
Rampant desire.	Reactive emotionally.
Self-deceiving, self-deceit.	Vindictive, revengeful, cruel.
Violent, warlike.	Warped, partisan ideals.

2. Body

a. Chakras. Mars co-rules the sacral and solar plexus centres, and the following organs.

b. The brain, face and skull. Through Aries, Mars is related to the brain and head. Any sudden head or brain problem that creates brain eruptions and explosions or causes physical damage, is associated with Mars.

c. The sympathetic nervous system. Mars is related to the fight-flight function of this system.

d. Blood, haemoglobin, energy, vitalisation and purification. In the journey of the soul, Mars represents the prodigal son who, full of blood and life, leaves the father's house to experience the sensual pleasures of the material world. Mars' colour is red, the colour of sensuality, passion and desire - which Mars represents. In the body, Mars is the primary representative of blood. It governs haemoglobin, the oxygen-carrying protein in red blood cells that gives blood its red colour. Mars vitalises, purifies and stimulates all aspects and organisms in the body, via the blood.

e. Sex and reproduction. Mars governs sex generally and through the sacral chakra is the primary representative of sexuality, male sex organs and testosterone.

f. Adrenals and adrenaline. Mars co-rules the adrenals through Scorpio, especially the adrenal-medulla and adrenaline that is secreted when the fight-flight process is triggered. Mars represents this defensive instinct.

g. The dense physical body and kundalini. Mars rules and controls the physical body - the vital, living, muscled, blood filled, sexual, animal, physical form.

> Mars rules and controls the physical vehicle. [1]

Mars also represents kundalini fire that warms the physical body from the base chakra.

---

1 Bailey, Alice A; Esoteric Astrology, 210.

3. Disease

Toxic Mars/ violent emotions, these cause hot infectious diseases, poison the blood, bring fever, inflammation, ulcerated conditions, skin eruptions - and hot reactions that cause accidents. Mars rules the muscles and therefore is implicated in nerve - muscular disorders.

▲ **Mars negative psychology.**
ADD, ADHD: attention (hyperactivity) deficit disorder.
Addictions.
Alcoholism.
Astral maniac.
Cuts, cutting.
Delusion, glamour.
Murderous, violent thoughts and intentions.
Obsessive compulsive.
Promiscuity.
Rape.
Sadism.
Self-harm, self-injury.
Serial killer.
Sex crimes, perversions.
Sociopathic.
Substance abuse.
Suicidal thoughts.

▲ **Mars's organs, functions.**
Surgery.

Crown
Brain, head, cranium-skull (via Aries).

Ajna
Brow.
Motor nerves.
Nose.

Heart
Blood, blood pressure.
Energy, vitality.
Haemoglobin
Immune system.
Iron in the blood.
Recuperative power
Red blood cells.

Solar plexus
Bowel.
Colon.
Rectum.
Sigmoid flexure.
Sympathetic NS.

Sacral
Conception.
Cowper's glands.
Desire.
Fertility.
Genitals.
Libido.
Penis.
Physical power and strength.
Procreation.
Prostate gland.
Scrotum.
Semen.
Sex hormones, organs.
Sexual desire, power.
Sperm.
Testicles, testes, male gonads.
Testosterone.
Urethra.

Base
Adrenaline.
Adrenal-medulla.
Bladder.
Fight or flight.
Kundalini.
Muscles.
Physical body.
Survival instinct, will to live, to exist.
Urea, uric acid.
Urinary tract.

▲ **Problems affecting Mars organs/ parts.**
ALS: amyotrophic lateral sclerosis: Lou Gehrig's/ motor neurone disease.
Blood poisoned.
Broken nose.
Cardiomyopathy, hypertrophic.
Encephalitis.
Fatigue: adrenal overload.
Haemophilia.
Head injuries.
Impotency.
Muscle spasms, cramps.
Premature ejaculation.
Prostate cancer.
Sexual difficulties.
Skull injuries.
STD's.

▲ **Problems caused by Mars.**
Abortion.
Abscesses.
Accidents.
Acid reflux, heartburn.
Acidosis.
Acne.
Acute, fast acting diseases.
AIDS.
Allergic reactions.
Amputations.
Anal fissure.
Anaphylaxis.
Assassinations.
Attacks.
Autoimmune disease.
Blisters.
Blood poisoning.
Boils.
Brain haemorrhage.
Bruises.
Burns.
Castration.
Cholera.
Colitis.
Concussion.
Convulsions.
Crohn's disease.
Cuts.
Cystitis.
Dermatitis.
Diarrhea.
Diverticulitis.
Dysentery.
Eczema.
Eruptions.
Fevers.
Fistulas.
Genital disorders, genital herpes, gonorrhea, HIV, syphilis, venereal disease, etc.
Gunshot wounds.
Hay fever.
Haemorrhage.
Heatstroke.
Hemorrhoids.
Hepatitis.
Hernia.
High temperatures.
Hurts, harms, pains.
Hyperactivity.
Hypertension, high blood pressure.
Hyperuricaemia.
Impetigo.
Infection.
Inflammation.
Injuries.
Irritable bowel syndrome.
Irritations.
Itchiness.
Massacres.
Measles.
Meningitis.
Miscarriages.
Multiple sclerosis.
Murders.
Nephritis.
Nerve pain, neuralgia.
Overheating.
Parasites, intestinal.
Peptic ulcers.
Pimples.
Rashes.
Rheumatic fever.
Rheumatoid arthritis.
Ringworm.
Scabies.
Scalds.
Scarlet fever.
Scars.
Sciatica.
Scrapes.
Sepsis, septicaemia.
Sexual, reproduction troubles.
Shingles.
Skin eruptions.
Skull injuries.
Smallpox.
Sores.
Stabs.
STD's, all.
Strangulation.
Stroke.
Tears, rips.
Toothache
Typhoid fever.
Ulcers.
Urine burning.
Vomiting.
Wounds

- **Ray:** 2 (4,5,6 via Sagittarius and Pisces).

- **Chakra:**
The Heart: there is also a relationship to the Solar Plexus chakra

- **Sign rulerships:**
Exoteric: Pisces and Sagittarius.
Esoteric: Aquarius.
Hierarchy Virgo.

Hips and thighs

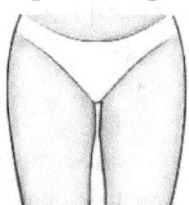

Movement

George G Anatomy Drawings

Liver

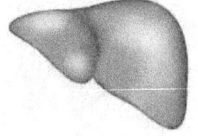

Arteries

6. Jupiter

The Lord of Love-Wisdom, Who is the embodiment of pure love, is as close to the heart of the Solar Logos as were the beloved disciples close to the heart of the Christ of Galilee. This Lord of Love expresses Himself primarily through the planet Jupiter, which is His body of manifestation. [1]

Jupiter represents this expansive Life. It is the attractive principle in nature, which gives us the ability to love, to desire, and the ability to attract to us all that the heart craves and desires.

1. Psychology

Traditionally Jupiter, which carries the expanding 2nd ray represents growth, success, rewards and good fortune. It assists the growth of consciousness, expanding it so that it becomes inclusive and group oriented.

> Leo and Aquarius, through the Sun and Jupiter, are related to Ray 2. Development of the individual consciousness into world consciousness. Thus a man becomes a world server. [2]

Jupiter also represents those larger than life, exaggerated behaviours such as excess, boastfulness and gambling. This is all due to the expanding and building 2nd ray. Here are some psychological attitudes associated with this side of Jupiter that can lead to disease or irresponsible behaviours.

Amorality (overactive thymus).	Boastfulness.
Exaggeration.	Gambling addiction.
Gluttony.	Greed.
Irresponsibility.	Excessive love of comfort.
Materialistic.	Pleasure seeking (excessive).
Wastefulness.	

2. Body

a. Heart chakra. Jupiter rules the heart centre in spiritually advanced people who have opened the chakra and are radiating inclusive love. In most people, its force flows through the solar plexus chakra. Jupiter represents "growth" in the body and along with the Sun, assists the growth and development of our physical bodies.

b. Cardiovascular system, the arteries and arterial blood. Jupiter, as a co-ruler of the heart chakra, closely supports the work of the Sun in vitalising the body. When Jupiter aspects the Sun it represents enhanced and expanded vitality.

Jupiter is the primary ruler of the arteries, the muscular-walled tubes through which oxygenated blood flows from the heart into the body to nourish cell life.

c. Liver: Jupiter supports the work of the solar plexus chakra in its rulership of the liver. This organ performs many functions. For digestion, it separates nutrients needed for the body from waste. It produces bile, routed via the gallbladder into the intestines to digest fatty foods and stores energy from sugar for later release. The liver is also an important participant in metabolism, changing amino acids in foods so that they can be used to produce energy.

---
1 Bailey, Alice A; Esoteric Psychology I, 23.
2 Bailey, Alice A; Esoteric Astrology, 67.

The liver also acts as the agent of Pisces, which rules the filtration and drainage systems of the body. After the digestive system has broken down food, the small particles enter the bloodstream and reach the liver. There, waste is filtered from nutrients and toxins are converted into less harmful products before being removed from the body.

d. The sciatic nerve, hips, thighs, strength, movement and locomotion. Jupiter via Sagittarius rules the hips and thighs. These regions of the body provide the physical power and strength that is required for heavy and stressful tasks. They also (via the sacral chakra) provide the energy required for sexual intercourse.

The hips, thighs and legs when healthy, give us freedom of movement, walking and running - assisted by the sciatic nerve that provides the motor function for leg movement. When mobility is impaired, Sagittarius and Jupiter are often implicated in a conflict pattern of some sort.

> Jupiter gives an inherent tendency to fusion which nothing can arrest. The achievement of ultimate synthesis is inevitable, and this Jupiter promotes.
> Bailey, Alice A; Esoteric Astrology, 139.

3. Disease

At all levels, Jupiter force when misused manifests as excess. There is too much energy. If desire is rampant - and in whichever direction it is being poured, the result is trouble and disease.

In average man, Jupiter's 2nd ray force pours out through the solar plexus chakra. This expands the desire for food, which can lead to uncontrolled drinking and eating so that the body gets fat and unhealthy. "Fatness" is particularly related to the misuse of Jupiter's expansive force.

At a cellular level, if Jupiter's building and magnetic force is out of control, cells run amok. Too many cells are attracted, over-building occurs resulting in growths, tumours, cancer, extra body parts, etc.

▲ **Jupiter negative psychology**

All attitudes involving excess, gluttony, that lead to social troubles such as gambling and greed.

▲ **Jupiter's organs, functions.**

Expansion.
Growth.
Nourishing, protecting and preserving.
Proteins, amino acids.
Tonifies.

Heart
Aorta.
Arteries.
Arterial blood.
Cholesterol.
Constitution
Heart.
Life-force.

Recuperative power.
Vitality.

Solar plexus
Liver

Sacral
Locomotion, movement.
Sciatic nerve
Sexual strength and power via the hips, thighs.

Base
Body fat.
Buttocks.
Coccyx - tailbone.
Femur.
Gluteus muscles.
Hamstrings.
Hips.
Ilium.
Ischium.
Locomotor system.
Pelvic girdle.
Pelvis.
Pubis.
Quadriceps muscles.

Sacroiliac joint.
Sacrum.
Thighs.

▲ **Problems affecting Jupiter's organs and functions.**

Aneurism.
Arrested development.
Arteriosclerosis.
Artherosclerosis.
Blood clots.
Cirrhosis, liver.
Crippling.
Gout.
Hepatitis.
High blood pressure.
Hips-thighs: disease, fractures, dysplasia, injuries.
Horse riding injuries, accidents.
Hypertension.
Jaundice.
Limping.

Liver: cancer, diseases.
Locomotion disorders.
Locomotor ataxia (cerebellum injury).
Paraplegia, quadriplegia.
Rheumatic fever.
Rheumatoid arthritis.
Sciatica.
Thigh injuries.

▲ **Problems caused by Jupiter.**

Acromegaly, gigantism.
Bad cholesterol.
Bloating.
Cancer, all types.
Cellulite, fatness.
Congestion.
Diseases caused by excess.
Extra body parts.
Fatness, obesity.
Flabbiness.
Gluttony.

Goitre.
Growths.
High blood pressure.
Locomotion, movement trouble.
Melanoma.
Metastases.
Obesity.
Overbuilding.
Over-eating.
Over-enlarging.
Overgrowth.
Polyps.
Swells, swollen, swellings.
Tumours.
Uterine fibroids.
Warts.
Weight gain.

- **Ray: 3** (1, 7 via Capricorn).

- **Chakra:**
The Throat and Base

- **Sign rulerships:**
Exoteric: Capricorn.
Esoteric: Capricorn.
Hierarchy: Libra.

Skeleton, bones, vertebrae, joints, knees, teeth

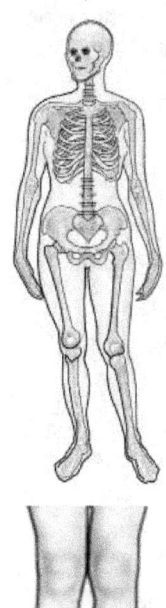

Endocrine system

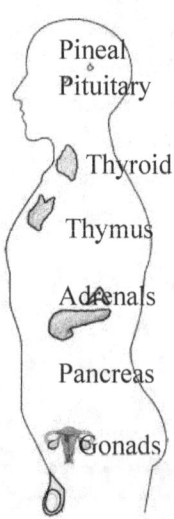

7. Saturn

1. Psychology

Saturn carries the 3rd Ray of Intelligent-Activity and its function is to teach us to act intelligently and responsibly, to make correct decisions and therefore to learn to use the Law of Karma to our advantage. This is the universal law of cause and effect, which teaches us that whatever we give out comes back to us; that evil attracts evil and good attracts good. Capricorn spiritually advances the man or woman who has learnt to kneel in humility and who offers his or her heart and life in service to the greater good.

People with a prominent Saturn are developing inner strength and fortitude. These qualities are required if we are to persevere through challenging karmic times every 7 years when transit Saturn makes hard aspects (conjunctions, squares, oppositions), to its natal position. In these adverse periods, life asks us to correct imbalances of the past and fulfil karmic obligations.

But human beings are disinclined to change so Saturn forces us to evolve through the application of retributive karma. It is the system's head-master who has the thankless task of making us comply with this law. It is a powerful agent of the 1st ray, which is related to karma. Here are some attitudes associated with Saturn that can lead to trouble or disease.

Avarice, greed.	Cold and clinical calculation.
Hard heartedness.	Manipulation, deviousness, dishonesty.
Rank materialism.	Ruthless ambition.

2. Body

a. Throat and base chakras: Saturn is related to the intelligent throat chakra, and co-rules the base chakra for body structure building and maintenance.

b. Thyroid gland, parathyroids. As ruler of the throat chakra, Saturn is related to the health of the thyroid gland and to the parathyroids that regulate calcium in the body. Saturn, the builder of the dense body structure rules calcium.

c. Endocrine system. The thyroid is the keystone gland of the endocrine system, locking it all together. Saturn's intelligent 3rd ray keeps this system operating efficiently, like clock-work.

d. Dense physical body, bones, skeletal structure and spine. Saturn is a ruler of the base chakra through which the third aspect, [1] the 3rd ray, is powerfully influential. This ray that flows through Saturn, Capricorn and Cancer, rules the dense physical body. Saturn and Capricorn govern the skeletal structure, the bones, spine, muscles, joints, tendons, ligaments and cartilage that tie it together and give it its durability and strength. Saturn is also related to the brain [2] mass.

Saturn/ Capricorn's specific area of rulership is the knee joint, formed by the shinbone, knee cap and lower part of the femur. This joint when healthy, gives the body flexibility in movement. Mental stiffness causes joint stiffness.

---

1 Bailey, Alice A; Esoteric Healing, 209.
2 Bailey, Alice A; Esoteric Astrology, 299.

e. Skin, hair, teeth. The outer structure of the body that Saturn rules includes the integumentary system (skin, hair, nails, exocrine glands), which protects the body from various kinds of external damage, wear and tear.

3. Disease

Saturn afflicted is a warning that we should avoid repressing our emotions and feelings, which blocks the flow of energy in the body. Since we know that the free and balanced flow of energy through the body underpins good health, it is easy to see how this sort of trouble represented by Saturn can lead to serious mental and physical health issues. Hardening at a psychological level, leads to hardening in the body.

Saturn carries the 1st ray as well as the 3rd, and is the primary representative of the repressing, hardening, crystallising, atrophying and ageing effect of 1st ray in the body. Pluto also carries the 1st ray, and is a back-up ruler for hardening and crystallising 1st ray diseases.

Saturn's sign points to a part of the body that may have a genetic or chronic weakness, which is underdeveloped or impaired in some way. So, for instance, Saturn in Cancer points to chronic digestion difficulties, while Saturn in Leo suggests the potential for chronic heart problems.

▲ **Saturn negative psychology.**
Avarice, greed.
Depression.
Hypochondria.

▲ **Saturn's organs, functions.**
Aging process, geriatrics.
Cadavers, corpses.
Dead things.
Death.
Medicine, orthodox, conservative.
Rigor mortis.

Crown
Brain mass.
Head bones, skull bones.

Throat
Cervical vertebrae.
Endocrine system.
Faeces, defecation.
Parathyroids.
Teeth.
Thyroid.
Thyroxine.

Heart
Thoracic vertebrae.

Solar plexus
Bile.
Gallbladder.
Lumbar vertebrae.
Ribs.

Base
Birthmarks

Body: bony, skeleton structure: including cartilage, tendons, ligaments, membranes and skin that brace it and hold it together.
Body intelligence.
Calcium.
Coccyx - tailbone.
Collagen.
Connective tissue/ membranes.
Enamel.
Integumentary system.
Joints.
Knees.
Moles, skin.
Nails.
Old age.
Patella.
Physical body.
Physical permanent atom.[1]
Spine, spinal column, backbone, vertebral column.
Substance.

▲ **Problems affecting Saturn's organs.**
Ankylosis spondylosis.
Back pain, chronic.
Bone cancer, deformities,

[1] Bailey, Alice: A Treatise on Cosmic Fire, 406.

fractures, disease.
Brain, spinal meningitis.
Bursitis.
Dental decay, gingivitis, pyorrhea.
Dermatitis.
Eczema.
Fractures, bones.
Impetigo.
Joint, knee problems.
Osteoarthritis.
Osteoporosis.
Otosclerosis.
Paget's disease.
Rashes.
Rheumatic fever.
Rheumatoid arthritis, rheumatism.
Rickets.
Scabies.
Scoliosis.
Scurvy.
Skin troubles, injuries, diseases.
Spina bifida.
Spinal fractures, a broken back.
Toothache.

▲ **Problems caused by Saturn.**
Achondroplasia, dwarfism.
Aging, premature.
Alopecia.
Alzheimer's.
Anorexia.
Arthritis.

Atrophy.
Bad breath, halitosis.
Barrenness.
Blood clots.
Bone troubles.
Bunions.
Calcification.
Cancer, all types initiated by emotional repression.
Chronic diseases, pain.
Chronic obstructive pulmonary disease.
Cirrhosis, liver.
Constrictions.
Crippling.
Crystallising.
Decaying.
Deforming.
Degeneration.
Dehydration.
Dementia.
Dental decay.
Fatigue.
Fibroids, uterine.
Frigidity.
Gallstones.
Gangrene.
Growth stunted.
Hardening, making brittle.
Huntington's disease.
Hypotension.
Impotency.
Joints stiff, joint trouble.
Karmic diseases.
Kidney stones.

Lead poisoning.
Malnutrition.
Neuro-degenerative diseases.
Obstructions, blockages in the body.
Osteoarthritis.
Osteoporosis.
Postpartum blues
Progeria.
Reducing.
Repressing.
Restricting.
Rheumatoid arthritis.
Scleroderma.
Sclerosis.
Senile decay.
Skin troubles.
Spine troubles.
Starvation.
Sterility.
Stiffening.
Stones.
Thyroid underactive.
Tiredness.
Underactive, undeveloped organs.
Vertebrae degeneration.
Warts.
Weight loss, thyroid cause.
Wrinkles.

- **Ray:** 7 (5 via Aquarius, 3 via Libra).

- **Chakra:**
The Sacral; also the ajna and crown

- **Sign rulerships:**
Exoteric: Aquarius
Esoteric: Libra.
Hierarchy: Aries.

Etheric body and Nervous system

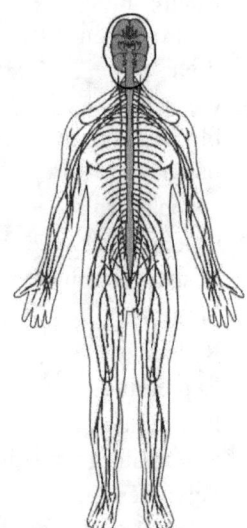

DNA

Calves, ankles

Enzymes

8. Uranus

1. Psychology

Uranus carries the 7th Ray of Ceremony, Order and Magic, the lower pole of the 1st ray. So, it carries power energy. Its task is to unite spirit and form, the personality with the soul. It represents the fire of spirit that drives us forward on the path of evolution.

Uranus is also related to the Mental Plane, representing higher powers of the concrete mind such as scientific analysis, experimentation and the abstract mind. It awakens us to new opportunities, urging us to let go of the past, to be free, to rebel, to experiment and to explore the new. It is the antithesis of Saturn, which represents stagnation. Very often, insurrections, rebellions and revolutions that are branded by some as terrorism are spiritually inspired uprisings by people fighting for a better way of life. However, when Uranus' force is seriously misused atrocities can occur. Here are some negative Uranus attitudes that may result in disease:

Creating chaos.	Destructive wildness.
Narcissism.	Promiscuity.
Repelling all conformity.	Selfish individualism.
Selfishness.	

2. Body

a. Chakras. Uranus rules the crown chakra in spiritually advanced people, and influences sexual attitudes via the sacral.

b. Etheric body. Uranus rules the sacral chakra and therefore is related to the etheric web that is vitalised by this centre. [1]

c. DNA (deoxyribonucleic acid). The basic energy pattern of the physical body is recorded in the physical permanent atom, which is located on the 1st subplane of the physical-etheric plane. This pattern is replicated in our DNA. Uranus, a ruler of the ethers via the 7th ray, is related to the permanent atom, genetics, DNA.

d. Sex and sex attitudes. Uranus represents our mental attitudes to sex. Its task via the incoming 7th ray and the Aquarian Age is to help us bring our sex life into line with universal law by transmuting whatever is aberrant and abnormal, so that the whole field of sex can be moved to a higher level of expression.

e. Germs and bacteria. The 7th ray (which Uranus carries), governs the atomic, cellular level of life and brings together life and matter to create form life on earth. When this process goes awry, aberrant and aborted cells become virulent germs, bacterial infections and contagious diseases. This makes Uranus and the Moon (which also carries ray 7 via Cancer), primary representatives of contagious diseases. The Moon doubly so because it carries the 4th ray which is responsible for epidemics.

f. Blood circulation and blood disorders. Aquarius and the 7th ray govern blood circulation and blood disorders often involve an afflicted Uranus.

g. Calves and ankles: Uranus rules the lower legs through Aquarius.

h. Nervous energy and synapses. Uranus' force is electrical. It governs nerve synapses, the exchange of nerve information from one nerve cell to the next and electrical signalling in the body generally. Everything we do involves electrical signals running through our bodies. When the central powerhouse of the brain tells the body to do

---
1 Bailey, Alice; Esoteric Healing, 45.

something, synapses fire, and electricity jumps from one cell to the next until it reaches its destination - resulting in body response. Any trouble in this process usually involves Uranus or Mercury, the primary rulers of this process.

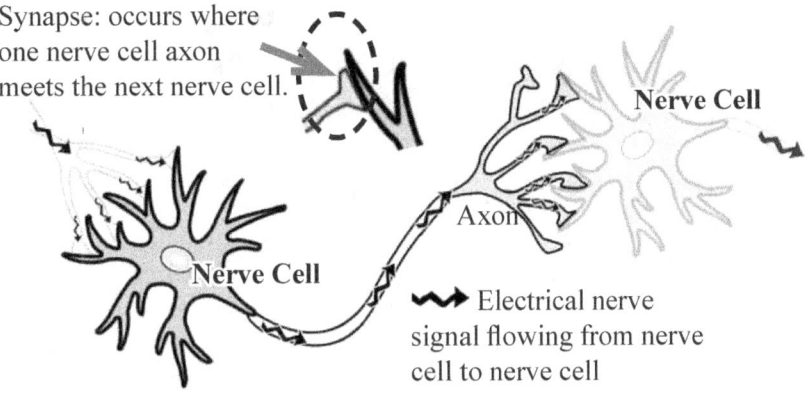

Synapse: occurs where one nerve cell axon meets the next nerve cell.

Nerve Cell

Axon

Nerve Cell

Electrical nerve signal flowing from nerve cell to nerve cell

3. Disease

In our psychology, negative Uranus represents uncontrolled behaviours, chaotic and wild desire that goes rampant so that behaviour is abnormal and bizarre. Similar things happen in the body. Uranus represents conditions and diseases that strike suddenly, which are arrhythmic and that no longer conform to nature's healthy design and pattern.

▲ **Uranus negative psychology.**
ADHD.
Bipolar.
Paedophilia.
Selfish individualism.
Sexual license.

▲ **Uranus' organs, functions.**
All nerves and electrical/ synapse signalling, in the body.
Anything modern or alternative, drugs, in medicine, surgery, in treatment such as chemotherapy.
Catalysts.
Chemicals, chemistry, chemical reactions.
Enzyme function.
Minerals.
Sexual attitudes, relations, alternative sexual preferences.

Crown
Pineal gland in initiates.

Ajna
Electrical nerve signalling.
Eye nerve signalling.
Neurons.
Retina.

Heart
Blood circulation.
Blood quality.
Heart valves.

Sacral
Chromosomes.
DNA.
Etheric body.
Genes, genetics.
Physical permanent atom.

Base
Ankles.
Calves.
Enzymes.
Fibula.
Lower legs.
Tibia.

▲ **Problems affecting Uranus' organs.**
ALS: amyotrophic lateral sclerosis, Lou Gehrig/ motor neurone disease.
Ankle problems.
Blood circulation problems, blood disorders, blood poisoning.
Calf problems.
Paraplegia, quadriplegia.

▲ **Problems caused by Uranus.**
Aberrations.
Abnormalities.
Achondroplasia - gene mutation.
Acromegaly, gigantism.
Anaemia.
Anaphylaxis shock.
Ankle troubles.
Arrhythmia.
Asymmetry.
Atrial fibrillation.
Bacterial infections.
Boils, carbuncles.
Bubonic plague.
Cerebral palsy.
Cholera.
Congenital abnormalities.
Conjunctivitis.
Epilepsy.
Contamination.
Convulsions.
Cramps.
Dental infections, gingivitis.
Dwarfism.
Electric shocks.
Epidemics.
Extremes (Eg. gigantism or dwarfism) caused by abnormal genes.
Fistulas.
Germs, antigens, pathogens.
Haemorrhages.
Heart fibrillation.
Hereditary diseases
Hyperactivity.
Impetigo.
Infections.
Leprosy.
Lesion, tissue.
Leukaemia: blood cancer.
Lower leg trouble.
Mineral poisoning.
Miscarriage.
Muscle spasms, cramps.
Nervous system abnormalities, spasms.
Palpitations.
Palsy, paralysis.
Pandemics.
Parkinson's disease.
Pathogens.
Polio.
Premature ejaculation.
Progeria.
Scarlet fever.
Seizures.
Sepsis.
Shocks.
Spasms.
Spasticity
STD's.
Streptococcus bacteria.
Tourette's syndrome.
Toxaemia.
Trauma.
Tremors.
Tuberculosis.
Twitching, tics.
Typhoid fever.
Urinary tract infections.
Vertigo.

- **Ray:** 6 (2 via Pisces, 4 via Cancer).

- **Chakra:**
The Solar Plexus: also the Heart chakra.

- **Sign rulerships:**
Exoteric: Pisces.
Esoteric: Cancer.
Hierarchy: Cancer.

Feet

Fluid systems, lymphatic and bloodstream.

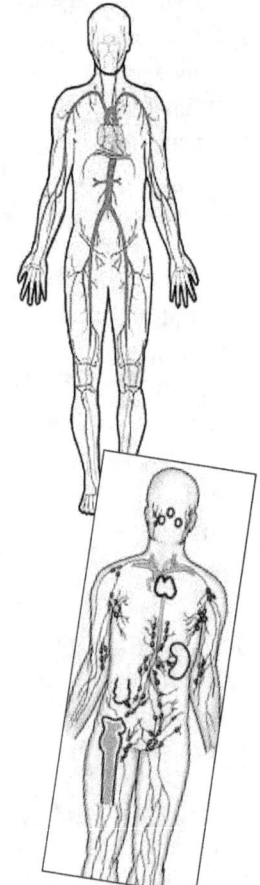

Sleep

9. Neptune

1. Psychology

Neptune carries the 6th Ray of Idealism and Devotion and is the agent of two water signs - Cancer esoterically, and Pisces traditionally. Neptune represents the action of the soul as it refines our emotional expression, softening it up and rendering it more sensitive so that it becomes a fit vessel to express soul love. It rules the higher levels of the Astral Plane and instils in us the finer emotions such as sadness, sorrow, grief, hurt, anguish, anxiety, joy, hope, serenity, ecstasy, bliss and devotion. As this refining process proceeds, consciousness, which was stationed in the solar plexus chakra gradually rises to become heart-centred. At this higher level, Neptune represents a heart connected to the "Heart of the Sun", the source of systemic love and wisdom. Neptune is also a representative of the heart chakra - in spiritually advanced people. Such people love inclusively not conditionally, the latter being a solar plexus chakra expression.

But Neptune has its dark side, as do all the planets. Here are some negative Neptune attitudes that may result in disease:

A martyr complex.	Addictive susceptibility.
Astralism, emotionalism.	Delusion, glamour.
Escapism.	Evil perversions.
Fanaticism.	Fearfulness.
Guilt inducing.	Naive, guileless.
Self-deception.	Ungrounded dreaminess.
Victim consciousness.	Warped, perverted ideals.

2. Body

a. Solar plexus chakra. Neptune refines the solar plexus expression of disciples.

b. Life. Esoterically, Neptune assists the vitalisation of the body. The "heart of the Sun employs Neptune as its agent," [1] and Neptune is a representative of the life aspect that is carried in the bloodstream.

c. Circular fluid waterways in the body. The water signs Cancer, Scorpio and Pisces are generally related to body secretions and liquids in the physical body. Neptune has general rulership over body fluids with the Moon, and may for instance show up in the chart for problems like oedema or excess phlegm. Pisces and Neptune have greater governance over the cyclic "waterways".

- Bloodstream. Neptune governs the bloodstream and is involved if blood flow is restricted through a blockage in the arteries, veins or capillaries.
- Lymphatic system. It is a cleansing, drainage system, keeping our bodies free of garbage by eliminating cellular waste.

d. Feet and toes. Neptune rules the lowest part of the body, the feet and toes via Pisces.

e. Sleep. We retire to the Astral Plane (which Mars and Neptune govern) in the hours of sleep. This relates Neptune (and potentially Mars), to sleeping, dreaming, nightmares and all strange things that may occur during sleep including activity on the Astral Plane.

---
1 Bailey, Alice A; Esoteric Astrology, 296.

3. Disease

As a ruler of the solar plexus chakra and of the Astral Plane, Neptune in the chart requires close scrutiny as a potential cause of disease. A study of charts from 1920 - 1943, when Neptune was in its detriment in Virgo, shows that it can be virulent. Now we have a new generation who have Neptune falling in Capricorn (1984 - 1998). In our psychology, this combination points to a tendency to repress subtle emotions, or potentially the selling out of higher dreams and ideals for materialistic purposes. Repression is more dangerous for physical health, the latter for our moral health. Generally, people in this group should cultivate ease of emotional expression.

Neptune's negative effect dilutes, weakens the body generally, causing for instance the weakening of artery walls so that an aneurysm occurs, or muscle tone so that a prolapse occurs. The deceiving action of ray 6 is implicated in carcinogenicity, which undermines cell life. Neurodegenerative diseases such as dementia and Alzheimer's that are due to brain fluid atrophy may be indicated by Neptune or Moon afflictions.

Viral infections. Viruses are of the nature of Neptune, subtle and stealthy, hiding until they replicate enormously prior to flooding the body with their poison.

Neptune, being the sign of the Deity of the waters, is related to the sixth ray which governs the astral or Emotional Plane of desire. Esoteric Astrology, 297.

Neptune is the God of the waters, and is esoterically related to Pisces. It should be noted that both Neptune and Jupiter are exalted in Cancer, the great sign wherein the desire for incarnation finds its fulfilment; the power of both is lessened in Virgo, wherein the first signs of the Christ consciousness are felt; both fall in Capricorn, when the Christ life and consciousness come to full fruition. Esoteric Astrology, 171.

The "heart of the Sun" employs Neptune as its agent. Esoteric Astrology, 296.

Neptune is "subjective and full of life." Esoteric Astrology, 217.

▲ **Neptune negative psychology.**
Addict, addiction.
Alcoholism.
Con-men.
Delirium, delusory.
Dreams, troubled.
Drug addiction.
Glamour.
Hallucination.
Hallucinatory drug addictions.
Hysteria.
Neurotic, neuroses.
Obscure diseases.
Online scammers.
Paranoia.
Perverts, perversions.
Phobias.
PTSD.
Sadism.
Schizophrenia.
Sleep-walking.
Substance abuse.

▲ **Neptune's organs, functions.**
Anaesthetics.
Fluid streams in the body.

Crown
Sleep.

Throat
Lymphatic nodes, system.
Thoracic duct.

Heart
Bloodstream.

Base
Feet, toes.

▲ **Problems affecting Neptune's organs.**
AIDS.
Bloodstream problems.
Buboes.
Bunions.
Feet and toes problems.
Hodgkin's disease, lymphoma, lymphatic cancer.
Insomnia.
Nightmares.
Sleep disturbance.
Water retention.

▲ **Problems caused by Neptune.**
Aneurysm.
Athlete's foot.
Blood poisoned, blood cell health perverted.
Cancer: perverts cell-life so tissue becomes carcinogenic.
Carcinomas.
Chicken pox.
Common cold.
Confuses.
Contagious diseases.
Contaminates.
Covid-19.
Cysts.
Cytokine storm.
Deceiving.
Dengue fever.
Diarrhea.
Diseases caused by emotionalism, that trigger food, alcoholic, drug addictions.
Drowns, drowning.
Epstein–Barr virus, glandular fever, mononucleosis.
Fungal infections.
Haemophilia.
Hepatitis.
Herpes.
Hidden, obscure disorders.
Hydrocephalus.
Impetigo.
Infections generally.
Influenza.
Leprosy.
Lymphatic sys. trouble.
Measles, rubella.
Meniere's disease.
Metastases.
Misdiagnosis.
Misrepresenting.
Mucous problems.
Narcolepsy.
Oedema.
Perverts.
Phlegm.
Pneumonia.
Poisons: plants, gas, drugs.
Pus.
Ringworm.
Sepsis.
Shingles.
Sluggish action of organs.
Smallpox.
Sores, weeping.
STD's.
Subverts.
Thrush.
Tinea.
Tissue, insidious changes.
Viruses, viral infections.
Warts.
Weakening.

- **Ray: 1** (4 via Scorpio).
- **Chakra:** The Crown and Base, also the Solar Plexus.
- **Sign rulerships:**
Exoteric: Scorpio.
Esoteric: Pisces.
Hierarchy: Pisces.

Colon, excretory

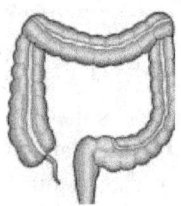

Kidneys, bladder, anus

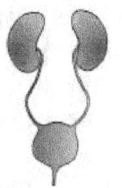

Sleep and Death

Adrenals, the will to live and to survive

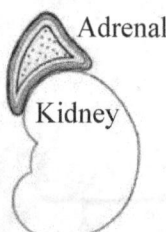

10. Pluto

Pluto is currently the most powerful distributor of 1st ray force on the planet, representing primarily its destructive side. It also represents nature's life and death processes governed by the 1st ray. Most people fear death. But in an evolutionary sense it is a compassionate and vital process that frees the soul from a worn out and often diseased body. In this regard, Pluto is a healer and liberator, assisting our spiritual journey towards enlightenment. This is not necessarily physical death. During the course of life, Pluto's force causes psychological transformation. It may be the death of an old way of life or the letting go of an old and limiting habit. But in either case the drastic change is engineered by Pluto (ray 1) through a life-changing event that forces us to move forward into a healthier future. Here is a powerful quote.

> Through Pluto [man comes] under the destroying power of death—death of desire, death of the personality and of all which holds him between the pairs of opposites, in order to achieve the final liberation. Pluto or death never destroys the consciousness aspect. [1]

The conscious soul lives on and will reincarnate in the future.

1. Psychology

In psychology, Pluto gives a powerful and selfish will. Power-hungry dictators, who refuse to move forward in their evolution, stay rooted strongly in the base chakra life after life. Since this is the chakra of matter, this potentially makes them dangerous because they are motivated by very selfish material values. Adolf Hitler had a powerful will and is an example of such a person. Here are some negative Pluto attitudes that may result in trouble or disease:

Arrogance.	Controlling.
Cruelty, lacking pity.	Extremely self-willed.
Insensitivity, coldness, hardness.	Power hungry.
Powerfully destructive.	Pure selfishness.
Ruthlessly ambitious.	Self-aggrandising.

As we evolve and integrate as personalities and develop the powers of the mind, our personal power and will increases. As we begin to align with the soul, selfish will transforms into the will-to-good, a force that flows through the crown chakra.

2. Body

a. Chakras - crown and base. Pluto governs the crown chakra in average man, where it presides over sleep and death. These two functions are related, because in both, consciousness vacates the physical body and moves onto the Astral Plane. At the end of sleep, the consciousness thread reconnects with the brain via the crown centre.

In death, the consciousness thread does not reconnect. The soul snaps the thread, an act represented by Pluto. It is the Lord of Death, the Arrow of God, which delivers death on one level or another.

b. Adrenals, the will-to-survive and the fight-or-flight syndrome. Pluto governs the base chakra, which anchors in the adrenals, giving it governance by default over the adrenals and survival instincts. The will-to-survive (Pluto) enables the physical

---
1 Bailey, Alice A; Esoteric Astrology, 127.

elemental - the nature spirit that rules the physical body, to react immediately and instinctively to protect itself. The will-to-survive is also associated with the urge to procreate, driving the animal urge to mate. Pluto's sign Scorpio and fellow ruler Mars, are associated with these instinctive functions.

c. Urinary tract. Pluto co-governs the urinary tract/ bladder, via Scorpio.

d. Physical atoms. The atoms in the physical body are energised by the third ray and therefore are related to Saturn, which carries this force. However, the power contained within an atom nucleus is a 1st ray, Plutonic phenomenon. Pluto was discovered in 1930, close to the time that Sir Ernest Rutherford split the atom in 1937. This resulted in the atom bomb. Pluto rules atomic fission, radiation poisoning as well as radiation therapy and chemotherapy used to kill off cancerous cells.

3. Disease

If Pluto is connected with the Moon, it indicates both emotional repression and explosions. Pluto's 1st ray in our psychology gives a very powerful will - for good or ill. When misused, people become dogmatic, they refuse to bend or be flexible and can be highly destructive in their words and actions. 1st ray diseases operate the same way. They are relentless and unstoppable. Any health issue we get under a hard Pluto aspect is a red-flag warning that a serious disease may be manifesting. In such a case, get a complete medical check-up.

|| *NB. We all receive hard Pluto aspects regularly and usually they work out as psychological stresses and radical life changes. Resisting healthy change and living in a toxic situation attracts the destructive force of Pluto, which will try to destroy that toxicity. Change is forced upon us, like it or not. If we adapt, adjust, make the requested transformation, then Pluto ushers us into a totally new situation, filled with new life and promise.*

▲ **Pluto negative psychology.**
Egomania.
Masochism.
Massacres.
Megalomania.
Murderous, violent thoughts and intentions.
Obsessive, compulsive.
Rape.
Sociopathic.
Stalking.
Terrorism.

▲ **Pluto's organs, functions.**
Atomic fission.
Chemotherapy.
Radiation therapy.

Crown
Death.
Sleep.

Solar plexus
Anus.
Bowel.
Colon.
Rectum.

Base
Adrenaline.
Fight or flight.
Survival instinct.
Will to live, to survive, to exist.

▲ **Problems affecting Pluto's organs.**
Anal fissure.
Colitis.
Crohn's disease.
Cystitis.
Diarrhea.
Diverticulitis.
Dysentery.
Fatigue: adrenal overload.
Irritable bowel syndrome.

▲ **Problems caused by Pluto.**
Abortion.
AIDS.
Asphyxia.
Assassinations.
Atrophying.
Cancer, all types due to the will-to-live running amok.
Carcinogenic.
Corruption of cells, of tissue.
Castration.
Dementia.
Destroys.
Hemorrhoids, piles.
Hyperuricaemia
Kills.
Malignant, malevolent in disease.
Massacres.
Melanoma.
Murders.
Neurodegenerative
diseases.
Parasitic infections, worms, tapeworm.
Poisoning, mineral, radiation.
Progressive, unstoppable diseases.
Rapes.
Repressing.
SIDS: sudden death infant syndrome.
STD's
Sterility.
Suffocation.
Terrorism.
Trauma.
Violations.

Through Pluto— under the destroying power of death— death of desire, death of the personality and of all which holds him between the pairs of opposites, in order to achieve the final liberation. Pluto or death never destroys the consciousness aspect. Bailey, Alice Esoteric Astrology, 127.

The arrow of God pierces the heart and death takes place." But in this connection it must be remembered that death is definitely brought about by the soul. It is the soul which shoots the arrow of death. Bailey, Alice Esoteric Astrology, 509.

The central opening at the top of the head .. is also the esoteric "door of departure" through which the soul withdraws the consciousness aspect in the hours of sleep and the consciousness aspect plus the life-thread at the moment of death. Bailey, Alice; Esoteric Psychology II, 609.

- **Ray:** 3.

- **Chakra:** Throat and the Base for form.

- **Sign rulerships:**

The earth does not influence consciousness at the exoteric level.

Esoteric: Gemini.

Hierarchy: Sagittarius.

11. The Earth

All people on earth are bathed continuously with nourishing planetary prana, the fluidic emanation of "Mother Nature". When absorbed through the skin and pores, planetary prana (flowing from the Sun to the planet then to us) is therapeutic. We all inherently recognise the wisdom in getting out of cities into nature, into the gentle and green embrace of Mother Earth. The 3rd ray, the green ray, flows through the Earth.

Once we are on the Path, the Earth begins to affect consciousness. It exerts a decentralising effect as a counterbalance to the ego represented by the Sun. The sign it is in - the sign opposite the Sun sign, helps us to become more inclusive.

Mother Earth offers us global experience and the opportunity to unfold our faculties, consciousness and group skills. Contact with different continents, races and cultures knocks off our selfish edges and renders us more inclusive and accepting of others.

As far as health goes, the Earth is related to the physical form, it corules the throat chakra and therefore is a ruler of the thyroid gland. Any afflictions to the Sun also afflict the Earth and these indicate difficulty with the absorption of planetary prana and consequent devitalisation.

- **Ray:** 1.

- **Chakra:** Crown

- **Sign rulerships:**

Vulcan does not influence consciousness at the exoteric level.

Esoteric: Taurus.

Hierarchy: Taurus and Virgo.

Vulcan's Hammer, beats common-sense into people

12. Vulcan

Vulcan only becomes influential when we begin our aspirational journey towards living a higher and finer type of life. At that point, under its influence, we start to apply purification disciplines to improve physical health such as eating the right food, exercising more, doing gym work, yoga, running, etc. We become more discerning in how we use our sexual energy and how we spend our money. When we start changing in this way, it is evidence that Vulcan is becoming influential and that we are on the Path. Vulcan's gift to us is the 1st Ray of Will-Power. It gives us the energy and determination to persist in our efforts to purify the nature and to strive towards greater spiritual understanding and improved life and living.

|| *NB. We do not have a credible ephemeris yet for Vulcan. Physically, it is said to be located between the Sun and Mercury, within 8 degrees of the Sun.*

Vulcan it is also influential through the Sun and Moon. In the charts of aspirants who are aspiring to that which is higher and finer; this refinement unveils Vulcan's purifying force - through the Sun (the personality) and the Moon (the unconscious). This means for instance, if the Sun is 5 degrees Cancer, then so is Vulcan; and can be read as such. If the Moon is at 7 degrees Libra, then so is Vulcan.

Vulcan rules the crown chakra in disciples and initiates. It is related to circulation in the etheric web.

2d. The Etheric Web and Chakras

The etheric body is a web of light energy, impulsed or motivated by the type or the quality of the energies to which it responds, from the angle of evolutionary development.[1]

---

[1] Bailey, Alice A; Discipleship in the New Age I, 699.

The Etheric Web and the Chakras

The etheric web is the fiery energy field upon which the physical body is constructed. Consequently, it is the media through which the various astrological and psychological energies must travel to reach the physical body. Disturbances of the mind or emotions (represented in the chart as afflictions to planets that rule those bodies), cause trouble in the chakras. If these troubles are brief, then there is no lasting harm. But if enduring habits set in so that thoughts or emotions are routinely troubled or unstable, then congestion and other troubles occur in the etheric. This is the fore-runner to disease.

Artistic impressions of the web and 7 major chakras

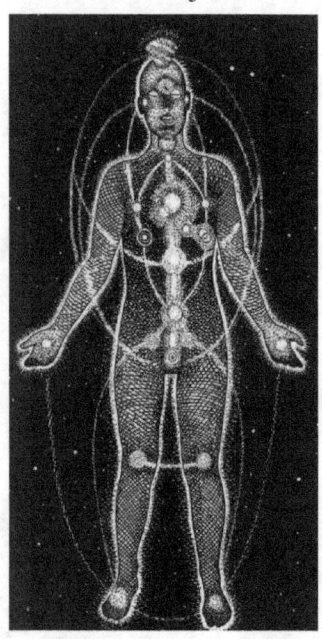

'A Thousand Points of Light',
Malvin Artley.

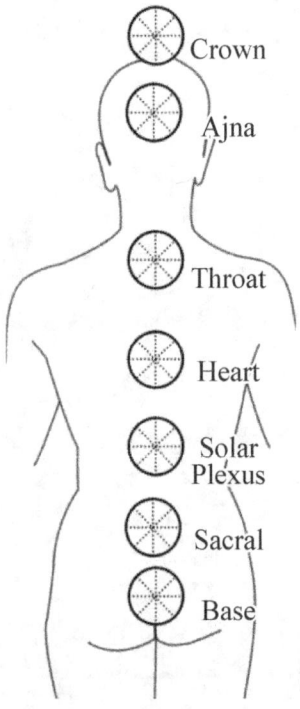

'Radionics and the Subtle Anatomy of Man' David Tansley.

1. The etheric web

The etheric web is a subtle level of the physical universe not normally visible to the naked eye. This golden network of very fine energy lines (nadis) stretches throughout space. All forces that play through the field of space pass through the etheric web to reach the Physical Plane and physical life. This is how astrology works. Far distant systems, stars and signs use the etheric highways to stream their forces to earth and man. Every form in the universe has its own individual etheric web, and each is a tiny link in the overall, universal mother-web. Here is how Bailey describes space in relation to the etheric.

> **The field of space is etheric in nature and its vital body is composed of the totality of etheric bodies of all constellations, solar systems and planets which are found therein. Throughout this cosmic golden web there is a constant circulation of energies and forces and this constitutes the scientific basis of the astrological theories.** [1]

The etheric web is the energy framework and blueprint upon which the dense physical body is constructed and with which it conforms. Underlying and interpenetrating the entire organism, the web gives the physical body quality, energy and life. The sketch top left is a clairvoyant impression.

Forces flowing into our web come from higher spiritual levels, from the soul, from the mind as mental force, and from the astral body as emotional force. On the Physical Plane, we receive solar prana, life-giving energy from the Sun that flows through the web to vitalise the physical body. We also pick up the energies of the particular environment we are in and from the people we mix with.

The state of our individual etheric web determines our health. A strong and robust etheric body is an excellent conductor for energy and gives us in return excellent health. A poorly strung together web with obstructions and impediments leaves us impoverished energetically and susceptible to disease and ill health.

It is interesting, but group ills and epidemics are able to sweep the planet because of "some condition in the etheric substance of the planet". [2] This means that the planetary etheric web in those places where people are more susceptible to epidemics, will have a weakness of some kind.

Gemini conditions the etheric body. [3] Aquarius is related [4] through its rulership of the ethers. Uranus, because it carries ray 7 that rules the ethers. The Moon is related to etheric circulation. Afflicted planets in Gemini may show potential etheric trouble.

If the connection with the body is very loose and the soul has difficulty keeping hold of it, possession of the body by a foreign entity can happen - it slips in and takes control. Neptune or Pluto afflictions could show this. Another problem that could arise is epilepsy and seizures - Uranus may be a causal factor.

---

1 Bailey, Alice A; Esoteric Astrology, 11.
2 Bailey, Alice: Esoteric Healing, 25.
3 Bailey, Alice A; Esoteric Astrology, 357.
4 Bailey, Alice A; ibid, 303.

2. The chakras

Where many nadis cross in the etheric web, energy vortexes form. These are the etheric reception and distribution centres for energy, the chakras. There are hundreds of chakras, mostly minor. Seven chakras are considered major because they are involved with the development of consciousness. The spleen chakra is not one of these. Five of these seven centres lie up the spine and two are in the head.

Often chakra drawings show the centres in the front of the body. These represent the consciousness of average man - the front of the body carries energy downwards, it is the involutionary route. But once we are on the Spiritual Path of Return, we are told to work and think with the spine and head, to visualise the chakras in the spinal column, which represents the upwards evolutionary route. Here is a chart that gives details of these chakras and their relation to the planets.

Chart 4: the 7 Major Chakras

Centre	Plane, origin	Petals	Gland	Astrology
Crown	Monadic/ Atmic Planes. Monad. Jewel in the lotus.	960	Pineal	Pluto, Vulcan (Uranus)
Ajna	Buddhic/ higher Mental Planes. Lotus sacrifice petals.	96	Pituitary	Venus (Mercury)
Throat	Mental plane/ body/ centres. Lotus knowledge petals.	16	Thyroid	Earth, Saturn
Heart	Buddhic, higher Mental Planes. Lotus love petals.	12	Thymus	Sun, Jupiter (Neptune)
Solar Plx	Astral plane, the astral body, and astral centres.	10	Pancreas	Mars, Neptune (Moon)
Sacral	Physical etheric plane and the etheric body.	6	Gonads	Uranus (Mars)
Base	Physical dense plane and body, and Mother Nature.	4	Adrenals	Pluto (Saturn)

Planes: Esoteric Healing, 45. *Planets: Esoteric Astrology 517; brackets - from other sources*

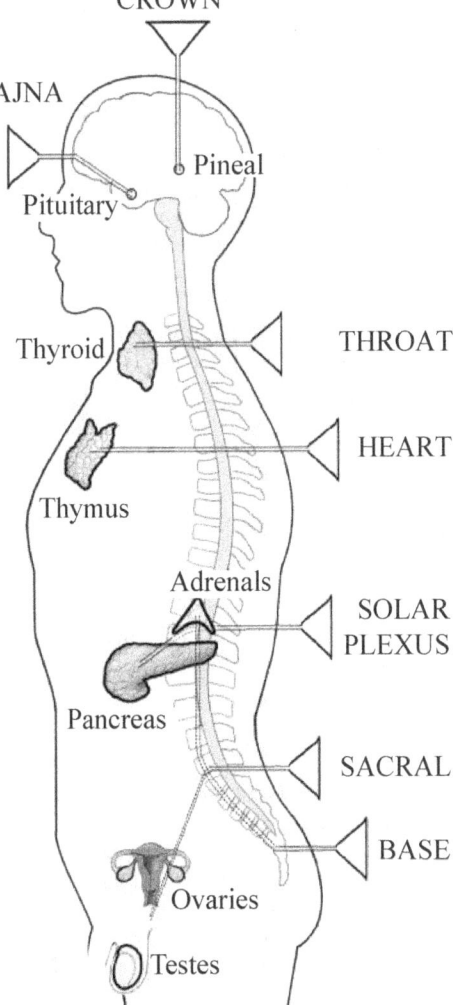

- The soul body/ egoic lotus, is on the higher Mental Plane. It has 9 petals. They represent knowledge, love and sacrifice, and unfold as we develop these qualities. 3 inner petals open when consciousness aligns with spirit, to reveal 'the jewel in the lotus'.

- The chakras anchor in the seven glands of the endocrine system. The chart shows the chakra - gland relationship.

- Each chakra has a different number of petals. The higher the plane that energises a chakra, the faster are the energies and the more numerous the petals.

- As energy pours through a chakra, it vitalises the associated endocrine gland which in response, releases hormones into the bloodstream.

- Congestion in a chakra occurs when force flowing through a centre is disrupted. If force is blocked as it pours into the centre, then the energy is thrown back upon its originating source - either the astral or mental body, resulting in a psychological disturbance. When the blockage is in the outlet into the physical body, the gland is either overstimulated or undernourished, destabilising its secretion, resulting finally in disease. A major cause of chakra congestion and blockages occurs when we use our wills to repress a natural body impulse, such as sexual desire.

Three etheric spinal channels

Within the etheric spine are three nadis (*pingala, sushumna, ida*), which are related to consciousness development. Material life pours through Pingala. Soul energy flows via Ida. Sushumna, the central thread, is the path for pure spirit. As consciousness unfolds, energy flow via the nadis increases, until at a very advanced stage spiritual force utilises fully the central thread. The chakras connect into these channels.

1. The Crown (Sahasrara) Chakra

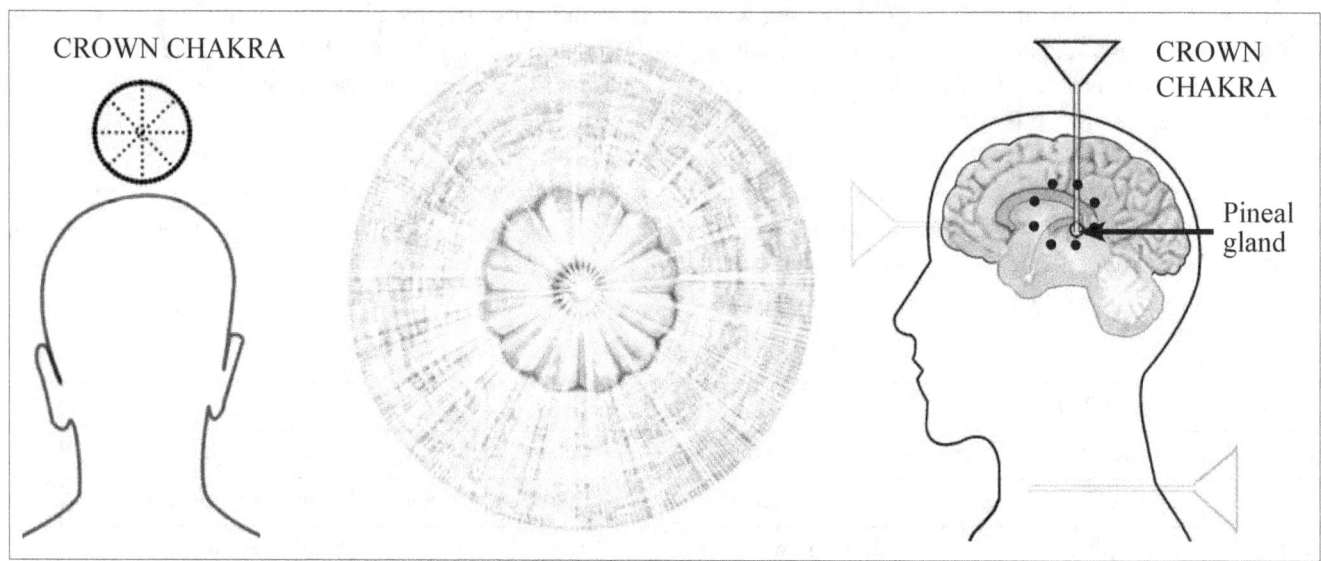

- The crown enters the body through the top of the head. At its centre is a 12-petalled lotus of white and gold. This is the higher correspondence of the heart centre. Around these are 960 secondary petals. [1]
- The crown is vitalised from the Logoic, Monadic and Atmic Planes; from the Logos, the monad, from atma, and from the egoic lotus on the Mental Plane.
- The crown is an entry portal for Ray 1 of Will and Power. Ray 7 works with this centre. [2]
- The crown chakra enters the body in the Aries ruled region.
- The planet rulers of the crown are Pluto, Vulcan and Uranus.

1. Psychology

The function of the crown chakra (and its physical anchorage - the pineal gland), is to provide a grounding, entry point for our spiritual nature. The pineal is called the seat of the soul, and when the soul is in control of the life, it guides affairs and controls the body through that gland. However, the crown chakra is not open in the average person because consciousness is still firmly grounded in the lower self and the lower chakras. At this stage, the crown can be likened to an unoccupied space at the top of a corporate office building, that one day will be the pent-house suite for the Chief Executive Officer. When fully awake, the crown chakra is the organ of spiritual glory.

Ray 1 of Will and Power flows through this centre when it is open, demonstrating as the will-to-good. People who are consciously working at this level are powerful forces for good in the world. Otherwise, before the centre opens, this force pours down and out through the base chakra. There it manifests via Pluto as selfish, personal will, the force that drives dictators.

2. Body

a. The pineal gland. The crown chakra anchors in the pineal gland. Light activates the pineal to produce *serotonin*, the neurotransmitter responsible for mood levels. Sunlight helps us feel better. Then at night, the absence of light stimulates the production of *melatonin*, which with the light–dark cycle, co-ordinates our internal clock, the 24-hour circadian rhythm. Through melatonin, the pineal maintains and regulates homeostasis during sleep by fine tuning body functions such as sleep, blood pressure and hormone levels.

b. The brain and the upper brain. The crown chakra generally rules the cerebrum and specifically rules a region around the pineal gland. [3] This is the higher brain region, the seat of the intuition [4] and of the soul when intuitive cells around the pineal gland come alive. It is "the entire brain area around the pineal gland, wherein the spiritual man assumes control". [5]

---

1 The chakra drawings in this section are based on clairvoyant investigations by Charles Leadbeater 1854 - 1934.
2 Bailey, Alice: Esoteric Psychology II, 622.
3 Bailey, Alice A; Esoteric Healing, 45.
4 Bailey, Alice A; From Intellect to Intuition, 211.
5 Bailey, Alice A; Esoteric Psychology II, 581.

Body substance generally is ruled by the 3rd ray of matter via the base chakra. Saturn and the Moon carry the 3rd ray (the latter via its sign Cancer), and they rule brain substance. This means that may be involved in diseases that affect brain tissue such as dementia.

c. The consciousness thread (antahkarana). This stream of lighted energy connects the soul to the brain, in the region of the pineal gland. This region in the head is the seat of consciousness, the seat of the soul. From there, the soul's job is to control human consciousness via the brain and nervous system. But this level of higher soul control takes many lives to achieve. Driven by the ego, in average man, consciousness is centred in one of the lower chakras.

d. The right eye of buddhi. The crown chakra governs the right eye, and in those who are conscious on the Buddhic Plane, it distributes love and wisdom from that level - through the right eye.

e. Sleep and death. The crown also governs the sleep-death processes via the consciousness thread. Every night in the hours of sleep, the consciousness thread withdraws from the crown chakra and we die to the Physical Plane and function on the Astral Plane. The process of sleep and death are identical, excepting that in sleep the life-thread remains intact so that consciousness can return to the body. In death this thread snaps.

3. Disease

- Diseases, injuries that affect the organs and systems governed by the crown chakra - the head and brain generally.
- Disturbed sleep rhythm.

a. Trouble via the 1st ray. Sometimes 1st ray force registers in the brain precipitately. If so, it inflames brain cells and may cause the breaking down of the cellular structure of the brain, tumours in the brain, abscesses and meningitis. This can also happen if a person has a powerful and explosive will and temper, or if kundalini fire rises from the base chakra too soon, caused by unwise spiritual practices. For these conditions, look for afflictions to 1st ray planets Pluto, Saturn or Uranus, or to planets afflicted in Aries.

The first aspect (1st ray) when not functioning properly, produces death, insanity and some of the diseases of the brain. [1]

b. Troubled sleep. Prolonged night use of electronic apparatus that relies on artificial light such as TV, computers and cell-phones damages the eyes and melatonin absorption, degrading sleep quality. Shallow or broken sleep patterns interfere with recuperative processes, which normally take place at night. For instance, blood pressure drops by up to 20 percent, easing stress upon the cardiovascular system. If this cycle is disturbed it increases the risk of high blood pressure and disorders such as anxiety, mood disorders and depression.

c. Trouble with the consciousness thread. Possession or obsession can happen if the life-thread is attached to the original owner of the body but the consciousness thread is not. Having become disconnected, the thread is snapped up by a discarnate person or entity. Reasons for disconnection: the thread may just be loose, a shock or disaster may sever it, or a person just may have great dislike for physical incarnation and withdraws persistently inwards.

SIDS babies - sudden death infant syndrome, this occurs when both the consciousness thread and the life-thread are snapped. Whether this is part of the design of the soul or occurs for some other reason is not clear.

▲ **Psychology**
The powerful and assertive will of the spiritually advanced person. Selfish wilfulness is the effect of the base chakra.

▲ **Body**
Antahkarana.
Blood pressure.
Brain, upper.
Cerebrum.
Circadian rhythm.
Consciousness thread.
Head.
Melatonin.
Neocortex.
Pineal gland.
Self consciousness.
Serotonin.
Sleep.

▲ **Problems affecting the Crown's organs**
Alzheimer's.
Ataxia.
Blood pressure high, pineal cause.
Brain cells. overactive: cancer, tumour, abscess.
Brain congenital disorders.
Brain haemorrhage, inflammation.
Brain lesion.
Cerebral-spinal meningitis.
Comas.
Concussion: head injuries.
Convulsions.
Dementia.
Encephalitis.
Head injuries.
Huntington's disease.
Hydrocephalus
Hypertension, pineal cause.
Insanity, idiocy.
Insomnia.
Lewy body dementia.
Lunacy.
Multiple personalities.
Possession.
Senile decay.
SIDS: sudden death infant syndrome.
Stroke.

---
1 Bailey, Alice A; Esoteric Healing, 108.

2. The Brow (Ajna) Chakra

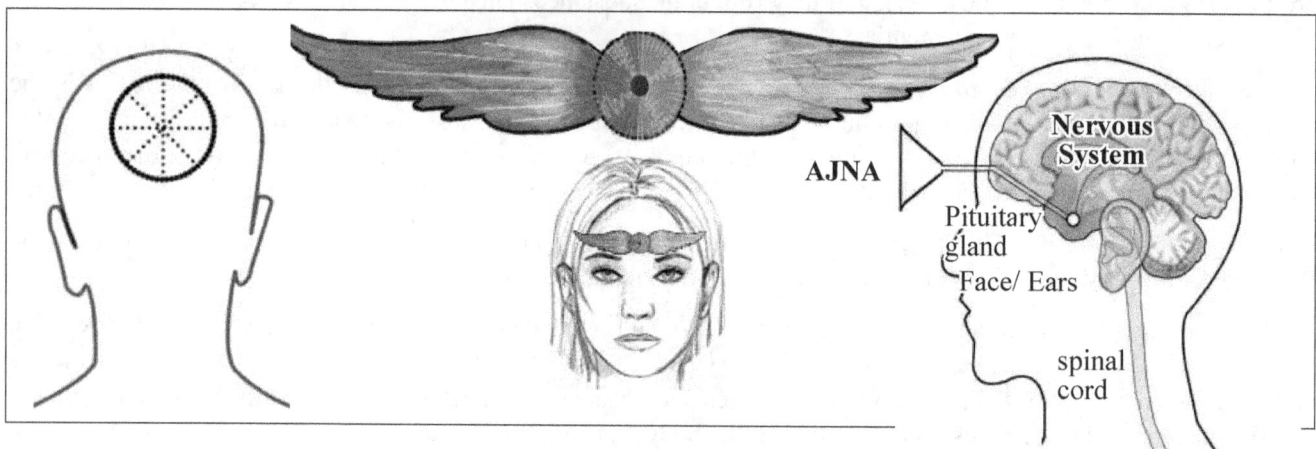

- The ajna enters the body through the brow just above the eyebrows, anchoring in the pituitary gland. 96 petals spread out like two wings of an aeroplane.
- The ajna is vitalised from the Monadic, Buddhic and higher Mental Planes, and sacrifice petals of the egoic lotus.
- The ajna is the main entry portal for ray 5 of Concrete Mind. Also associated with this centre is ray 4 via Mercury - one of the ajna's rulers, and ray 2 of consciousness [1].
- The ajna is in the Aries ruled part of the body, but Venus and Mercury govern the ajna.

1. Psychology

The function of the ajna (and its anchorage the pituitary gland), is to focalise the forces of the personality. When developed, the personality is the force of the advanced, intelligent and fully integrated human being who dominates the environment with his/ her dynamic power, intelligent organising skills and visionary imagination. Ray 5 of Concrete Mind and Science flows through the ajna, giving those conscious at this level, their acute and dominant mentality. Before soul wisdom is developed, they are mentally aloof, detached and judgemental. But when the forces of the soul flow through the ajna and therefore through the personality, the higher Venus qualities of intelligent love are expressed.

The ajna rules the face, revealing to the world, character, self-awareness and intelligence. A large number of human beings are not fully developed at this level. They have the concentration of their force in a lower chakra. However, through widespread education, the ajna is rapidly awakening en masse.

2. Body

a. The Pituitary gland. Venus rules the pituitary gland and the influence of its balancing sign Libra is evident. The hormones of the pituitary maintain homeostasis, balance and stability in the body. Scientists say the pituitary body is the master gland, because it appears to direct most endocrine activities. This role is taken over by the pineal when the crown chakra awakens and the spiritual man emerges. Problems in the pituitary can cause inferior moral and intellectual development, excessive growth or dwarfism and abnormal function of ovaries and testes.

b. The lower brain and "lower" faculties. The ajna is related to the "lower brain", which is located in the region around the pituitary gland. "Lower faculties" refers to the concrete mind and the emotional (limbic) brain:

> In the region of the pituitary body, we have the seat of the lower faculties, when co-ordinated in the higher type of human being - here are to be found the emotions and the more concrete aspects of the mind (growing out of racial habits and inherited instincts, and, hence, calling for no exercise of the creative or higher mind). [2]

---

1 Bailey, Alice A; Esoteric Healing, 187-188.
2 Bailey, Alice A; From Intellect to Intuition, 212.

c. The central nervous system (CNS). Consists of the brain and spinal cord, the complex of nerve tissues that controls the activities of the body and interacts with the outer world via the 5 senses. The CNS can be likened to a computer - the brain to the operating system, and the messaging function of the NS to the application programs - managed by the operating system. The crown rules the brain, while the ajna rules the messaging system.

Although the nervous system is ruled by the ajna chakra, some of its parts can be influenced by other centres. For example, the nerves of the sympathetic nervous system that govern the "fight or flight reaction", emerge from the spinal cord in the solar plexus region and its reactions are largely controlled by the emotions, or instinct.

d. The Third Eye. This is the etheric correspondence of the pineal gland. It is the eye of the soul and when activated, through right spiritual living and a vegetarian diet, the soul can see into the physical world and we into higher spiritual realms.

e. Front of the head, eyes, ears and nose. The ajna chakra vitalises all frontal areas of the head including the face, eyes and nose. It shares rulership of the ears with the throat chakra. These sense organs are vital for the development of personality consciousness, which is associated with the ajna.

f. Left eye of manas. Once the personality and soul are aligned, the eyes become distributing channels for higher energies. The crown and the right-eye distribute soul love and wisdom, while the ajna and the left-eye distribute the mental energies of the personality.

3. Disease

- Modern psychological disorders involving dissociation, separativeness, egomania.
- Diseases of the pituitary gland and of the nervous system.
- Injuries or diseases of the face, eyes, ears and nose.
- Headaches, migraine, epilepsy and seizures.

The nervous system is ruled by Gemini, Mercury, Venus. Uranus and Aquarius are related. Nervous disorders will have at least one of these planets involved in a Health Triangle, or a planet in one of these signs.

▲ **Negative psychology**
Asperger's.
Autism.
Dogmatism. [1]
Egomania.
Imbecilities.
Insanities.
Megalomania.
Psychological troubles.
Selfishness. [2]

▲ **Body/ functions**
Balance, equilibrium.
Brain, lower.
Brow.
Central nervous system.
Cerebral cortex.
Cognition.

Dopamine.
Ears.
Eyes and all its parts.
Face.
Hearing.
Homeostasis.
Hypothalamus.
Intelligent self-consciousness.
Lacrimal glands.
Nerve synapses.
Neurons.
Nose.
Pituitary gland.
Pupils.
Regulation, balance.
Self-consciousness.
Senses, the 5.
Sentiency.
Sight.
Smell.
Spinal cord.
Synapses .

Taste.
Thalamus.
Touch.
Vision.

▲ **Problems affecting the Ajna's organs**
Eyes, vision.
Astigmatism.
Blindness.
Cataracts.
Conjunctivitis.
Glaucoma.
Keratitis.
Myopia.
Short sighted.
Pituitary malfunction:
Acromegaly.
Gigantism.
Growth stunted.
Hypopituitarism
Simmond's disease.

Nervous system.
ALS/ Lou Gehrig's/ motor neurone disease.
Bells palsy.
Cerebral palsy.
Epilepsy.
Guillain-Barre syndrome.
Labyrinthitis.
Multiple sclerosis.
Nerve spasms.
Neuralgia.
Neuro-degenerative diseases.
Paralysis.
Palsy.
Parkinson's disease.
Seizures.
Spasms, nerves.
Spasticity.
Tourette's syndrome.
Tremors.

Twitching, tics.

Balance problems.
Deafness.
Headaches.
Meniere's disease.
Middle ear problems.
Migraine.
Shingles.
Tinnitus.
Vertigo.

---
1 Bailey, Alice: Esoteric Healing, 51.
2 Ibid.

3. The Throat (Vishuddha) Chakra

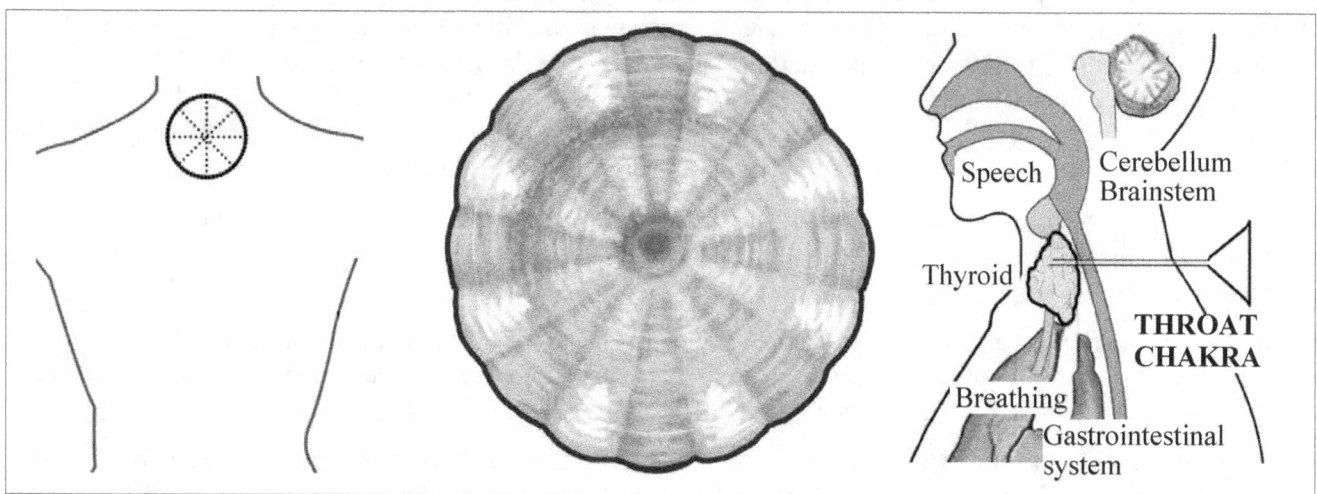

- The throat chakra enters the spine at the base of the neck, between C7 and T1, anchoring in the thyroid gland. Its 16 petals of blue and silver look like moonlight on rippling water.
- The throat is vitalised from the Atmic and lower Mental Planes, the knowledge petals of the egoic lotus, and from the mental body and the mental chakras.
- The throat is an entry portal for Ray 3 of Intelligent Activity and ray 7 for [1] disciples.
- Taurus and Gemini rule the throat chakra, so do their rulers Venus and Mercury. The Earth and Saturn are the ray 3 rulers of the throat centre.

1. Psychology

The function of the throat chakra (and its anchorage in the body - the thyroid gland), is to represent the powers and faculties of lower mind. Only when it is active can we truly identify as a "self", as an "I". Ray 3 of Intelligent Activity flows through the throat and it teaches us to think and speak intelligently. One of the throat chakra's names is "the great organ of creation through sound". [2] When we speak, we create. As we become more confident intellectually, voicing our opinions more coherently and effectively, we start to influence the world around us because of the power of our thoughts and voice. We become true creators, magicians in a sense.

The throat and sacral chakras are partners in that they are the creative centres in the body. But before the throat becomes active, the sacral is the dominant centre and creative power flows straight through the throat down to the sacral to feed the sexual appetites. But once the mind starts to find artistic or scientific subjects attractive, this flow is arrested at the throat and it pours into the creative areas of the brain.

2. Body

a. The thyroid gland. The throat chakra anchors in the thyroid gland, which is the "keystone of the endocrine system". [3] A keystone is the central principle that locks all together. When this system is healthy, the glands work together like clock-work, dispensing hormones to maintain homeostasis and keep the body balanced. A disturbed thyroid can cause a whole range of problems. For example, wrong hormone dispensing and disturbed metabolism. [4]

b. Lower brain. The lower brain is co-ruled by the throat chakra. [5] Gemini is related to this centre and the cerebellum. They are all involved with upper body movement via the shoulders, arms, hands and fingers.

c. Respiration and the bronchial tree. Respiration supplies the blood with life-giving oxygen. Oxygen inhaled into the lungs via the bronchi (vitalised by the throat chakra), clings to red blood cells and is distributed throughout the body by the arteries.

---

1 Bailey, Alice A; Telepathy and the Etheric Vehicle, 137.
2 Bailey, Alice A; Initiation, Human and Solar, 98.
3 Bailey, Alice A; The Soul and its Mechanism, 46.
4 Bailey, Alice A; The Soul and its Mechanism, 47.
5 Bailey, Alice A; Treatise on White Magic, 284.

d. Speech. The throat chakra vitalises the organs of speech.

e. Gastrointestinal tract (GI), digestion. The throat chakra governs the GI as a whole. The mid-region part of the GI - the stomach, pancreas, liver and gallbladder; are governed by the solar plexus chakra.

f. The lymphatic system. This is the sewerage system of the body, relating it to the gastrointestinal tract, which excretes waste from the body. Both are ruled by the 3rd ray via the throat chakra. The lymphatic system is responsible for the removal of interstitial fluid from tissues. When it is sluggish, or when the throat and chest organs are attacked by pathogens, the lymphatic system becomes congested and the tonsils and lymph nodes swell, proof the immune system is doing its job.

3. Disease

- Problems with the thyroid gland and metabolism.
- Psychological trouble due to mental hyper-activity or manipulative tendencies.
- Infectious diseases especially those that affect breathing. Also, disorders of the lymphatic system.
- Diseases affecting the mouth and throat, the vocal cords, speech and ears.

Trouble with breathing, speech impediments or any problems associated with articulating words are related to this centre and the organs it rules. Airborne infectious diseases belong here. Bailey said they are related to the mental nature. [1] This suggests that Physical Plane infectious diseases are a manifestation or reflection of our collective, irritable, angry, toxic thoughts and words.

▲ **Negative Psychology**
ADD, ADHD: attention deficit hyperactivity disorder.
Con-men.
Psychopaths.
Tricksters.

▲ **Body/ functions**
Breathing/ respiration
Airways.
Alveoli.
Bronchial tree.
Diaphragm.
Lungs.
Trachea.
Windpipe.
Digestion/ gastro-intestinal tract:
Anus.
Appendix.
Appetite.
Colon.
Defecation.
Esophagus.
Intestines.
Mouth.
Rectum.
Stomach.
Salivary glands.

Lower brain:
Brain-stem.
Cerebellum.
Limbic system.
Medulla oblongata.
Pons.
Reptilian brain.
Lymphatic system:
Adenoids.
Lymph nodes.
Peristalsis.
Thoracic duct.
Throat/ pharynx/ neck:
Adam's apple.
Carotid gland, carotid arteries.
Jugular vein.
Larynx.
Parathyroids.
Sinuses.
Thyroid, thyroxine.
Tongue.
Tonsils.
Uvula.
Vocal cords.

Ears.
Enteric NS.
Hearing.

Lips.
Metabolism.
Taste.

▲ **Problems affecting the Throat's organs**
Thyroid:
Grave's disease.
Hashimoto's disease.
Brain/ speech:
Aphasia.
Dyslexia.
Learning difficulties.
Gastro-intestinal:
Anal fissure.
Appendicitis.
Choking.
Celiac disease.
Colic.
Colitis.
Constipation.
Crohn's disease.
Flatulence.
Hemorrhoids.
Irritable bowel syn.
Infection/ allergies:
Air-borne infections.
Allergies caused by breathing.
Asthma.

Bronchitis.
Catarrh.
Chicken pox.
Cholera.
Common cold.
Croup.
Dengue fever.
Diarrhea.
Diphtheria.
Diverticulitis
Dysentery.
Enteritis.
Epstein–Barr virus, mononucleosis.
Glandular fever, swellings.
Goitre.
Influenza.
Labyrinthitis.
Laryngitis.
Measles.
Mumps.
Pneumonia.
Pulmonary tuberculosis.
Rubella.
Scarlet fever.
Smallpox.
Pleurisy.
Sinusitis.
Tonsillitis.
Toothache.

Typhoid fever.

Asphyxia.
Bad breath, halitosis.
Carpal tunnel syn.
Cervical osteoarthritis.
Cystic fibrosis.
Deafness.
Dental problems.
Drowns, drowning.
Emphysema.
Fatigue - thyroid.
Goitre.
Hodgkin's disease.
Hormonal trouble.
Lymphoma.
Meniere's disease.
Sleep apnoea.
Snoring.
Strangulation.
Speech impediments
Suffocation.
Thyroid imbalance.
Tinnitus.
Weight gain or loss, thyroid cause.

---
1 Bailey, Alice A; Esoteric Healing, 312.

4. The Heart (Anahata) Chakra

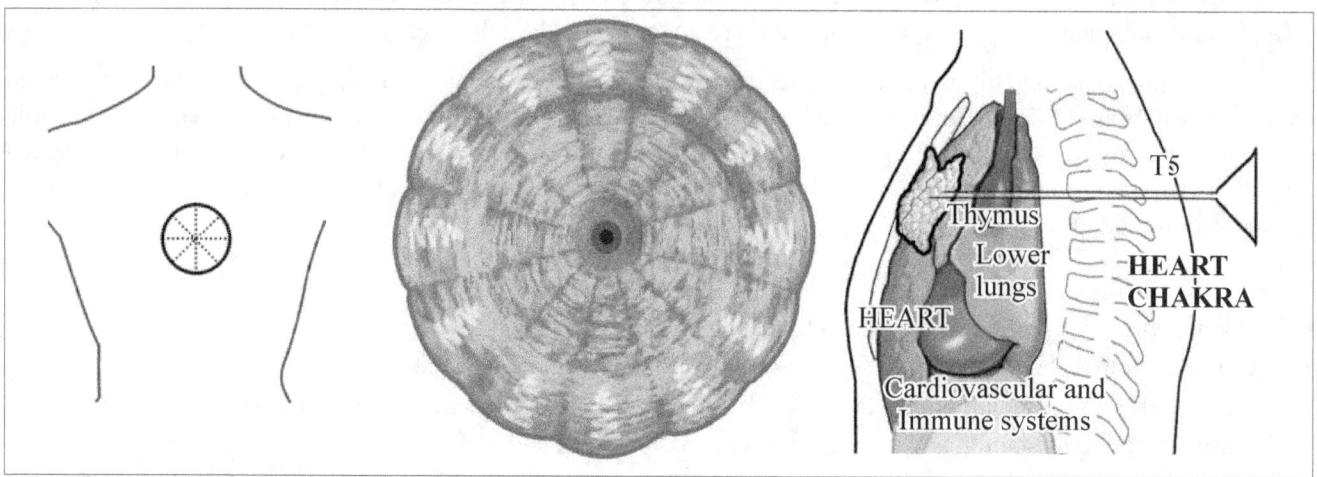

- The heart chakra enters the spine between the shoulder blades, around T5, and anchors in the thymus gland. It has 12 petals coloured with a golden hue.
- The heart is vitalised from the Buddhic and higher Mental Planes, and from the love petals of the egoic lotus.
- The heart centre is an entry portal for Ray 2 of Love and Wisdom.
- The forces of Leo and the Sun flow through the heart chakra, while Jupiter is influential in disciples.

1. Psychology

The function of the heart chakra (and its anchorage in the body the thymus gland), is to channel Ray 2 of Love and Wisdom. This chakra is the organ of spiritual love. It comes alive in the higher sense as we purify the astral nature, transmute lower desire into inclusive love and begin to work cooperatively in groups for world good.

Located at the centre of the crown chakra is a higher heart centre - a replica of the 12-petalled lotus found on the spine. As the lower heart centre unfolds due to a growing sense of inclusiveness, group relations and the expression of goodwill, it brings the higher centre alive. When the higher heart portal is functioning, it indicates that divine will-to-good is being expressed.

Unmodified by human emotions, soul love is never personal, selfish and conditional. These are ray 6 emotional, selfish solar plexus traits. St. Paul's verses from the Bible, Corinthians 13:4-7 describe soul love in action.

> Love is patient, love is kind. It does not envy, it does not boast, it is not proud. It does not dishonour others, it is not self-seeking, it is not easily angered, it keeps no record of wrongs. Love does not delight in evil but rejoices with the truth. It always protects, always trusts, always hopes, always perseveres.

The earliest opening of the heart is not necessarily an altruistic affair. Material and selfish leaders at the heart of an organisation open this chakra. The years from 28 to 35 are particularly conducive to heart chakra unfoldment. With the adolescent and youthful years lying behind, with struggles and disappointments softening up the ego, if the heart is not already open, it is more difficult to achieve in later years.

2. Body

a. Thymus gland and the immune system. The heart chakra anchors in the thymus, relating Leo and the Sun to the gland in its connection with the immune system. It is an organ of defence. Killer T-cells of the immune system mature in this gland. In most people around puberty, the thymus starts to shrink. This, however, does not happen in spiritually advanced people who have opened the heart chakra. The gland starts functioning at a new and higher level, which means immune protection is heightened.

b. Life force. A stream or thread of life energy known as the sutratma originates from the Monad, our highest spiritual source, and anchors in the heart centre and physical heart. From there it uses the spleen, bloodstream, arteries, veins and lungs to give life to the entire organism. The soul utilises the sutratma to hold the body coherently together during life. When death takes place, when the soul snaps the life-thread, the atoms disperse and the body falls apart.

c. Heart, cardiovascular system and vitalisation of the body. The heart chakra and heart organ are governed by the Sun. Just as the Sun holds the planets of the solar system together and nourishes them with solar fire, so does the heart chakra operate in the body. Working through the heart organ and channelling inpouring life-force and prana and sending this force out through the cardiovascular system, it maintains the health of the cells of the body, vitalising and nourishing them. The heart chakra rules cell life. [1] Metabolism (conversion of calories to energy) is part of the vitalisation process.

d. Vagus nerve. It allows the brain to monitor and receive information about several of the body's different functions. The heart and base chakras are connected with the vagus nerve. When the soul, functioning through the head brings these two centres under control - when the head, heart and base centre are in a magnetic rapport; the final work of merging the fires of the body, of raising the kundalini fire from the base chakra to merge with the fire of spirit in the crown is undertaken. It is through the stimulation and the control of the vagus nerve that this is accomplished. It swings the entire nervous system into a special form of rhythmic activity and responsiveness, which initiates the process. After this event takes place, the soul is in control of the entire lower nature and its influence - through the purified personality, is profoundly effective for world good.

3. Disease

- Diseases affecting the heart chakra organs, the heart, the blood, the cardiovascular system as a whole.

Thousands of people in the world are having their heart chakra's stimulated, as they move from being emotionally and selfishly focused (the solar plexus chakra), up to being inclusive and group conscious. This puts a strain on the heart with subsequent trouble in that organ.

> The transference of all the accumulated energies in the solar plexus centre into the heart centre will cause difficulty, very frequently of a serious nature; this is the reason why today so many advanced people die of heart disease. [2] For a period, this can result in increased emotionalism. [3]

The Sun rules cell life and the cardiovascular system nourishes all cells in the body with blood. A very interesting point to note is that germs are living organisms that find their way into the body through the medium of the life-force. As this force flows into the heart and bloodstream, so do the invaders. Once in, if they are not stopped, they wreak havoc; attacking cell-life and disrupting the entire organism.

▲ **Negative Psychology**

Group oriented in a greedy material, immoral, selfish way.

▲ **Body/ functions**

Aorta.
Arteries.
Blood.
Bloodstream.
Blood cells.
Capillaries.
Cardiovascular system.
Cell life.
Constitution
Haemoglobin
Heart.
Immune system.
Iron in the blood.
Leukocytes.
Life-force, soul energy.
Life-thread/ stream, sutratma, silver cord.
Metabolism.
Oxygen, oxygenation.
Pericardium.
Plasma.
Prana.
Pulmonary circulation.
Recuperative power.
Spleen.
Stem cells.
Sternum.
Thymus.
Vagus nerve.
Valves - heart.
Veins.
Vena cava.
Venous system.
Vitality.
Vitamin D3, sunshine vitamin.

▲ **Problems affecting the Heart's organs**

Anaemia.
Aneurism.
Angina.
Arrhythmia.
Arteriosclerosis.
Atrial fibrillation.
Autoimmune diseases, immune system attacks.
Blood circulation, bloodstream problems.
Blood disorders, blood cancer, blood poisoned.
Bruises.
Cardiomyopathy.
Cholesterol.
Congenital heart problems.
Deep vein thrombosis.
Devitalisation.
Heart attack, heart disease, heart fibrillation, all heart trouble.
Fainting.
Fevers.
High blood pressure, hypertension.
High temperature.
Hypotension
Immunity low.
Inflammation.
Leukaemia, blood cancer.
Myocarditis.
Palpitations.
Raynaud's disease.
Shock.
Varicose veins.

---

1 Bailey, Alice A; Treatise on White Magic, 284.
2 Bailey, Alice A; Esoteric Healing, 175.
3 Bailey, Alice; Esoteric Psychology II, 595.

5. The Solar Plexus (Manipura) Chakra

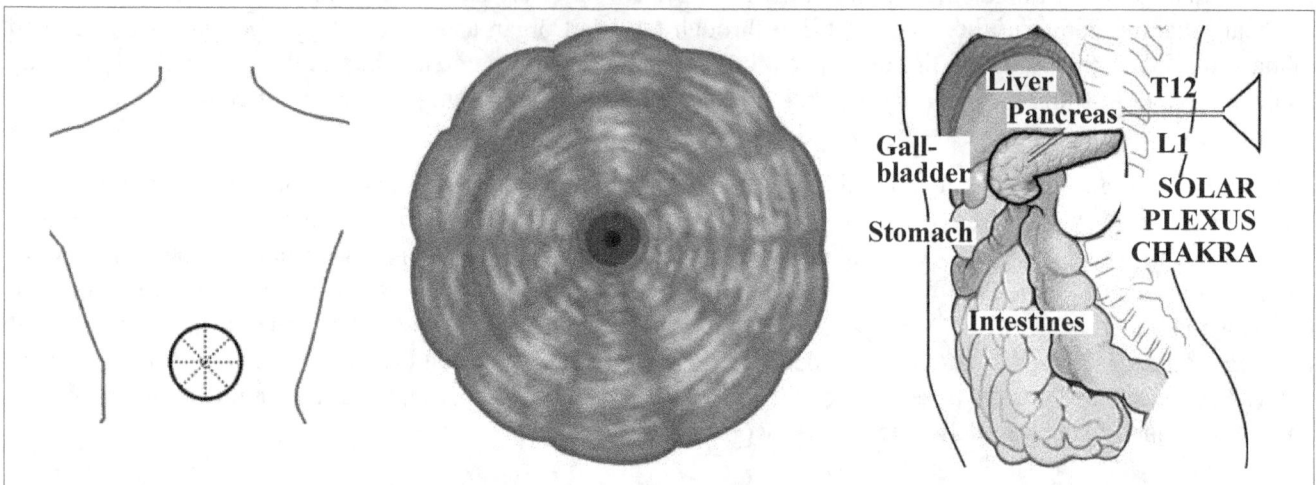

- The solar plexus enters the spine around T12 and L1, anchoring in the pancreas gland. It has 10 petals. The colour is described as rosy with a mixture of green.
- The solar plexus is vitalised from the astral body and the astral chakras.
- The solar plexus chakra is the main entry portal for ray 6. Ray 2, the ray 3 - the 3rd aspect [1]; they are also associated with this centre.
- Cancer traditionally rules digestion. Planet rulers of the solar plexus chakra are Mars, Neptune and the Moon via Cancer.

1. Psychology

The psychological function of the solar plexus chakra is to give expression to our emotions. The solar plexus is the doorway to the Astral Plane and the entry portal into the body for the 6th emotional ray. This force dominates the average person, which makes it and the solar plexus chakra very potent.

Our emotions and desires constantly yearn for happiness and pleasure. If they are denied, if we are rejected it registers in the solar plexus. Even if we get what we want, this centre is not satisfied for long. It thirsts for new satisfactions. The forces of emotion and desire keep those under their control swinging between the opposites of pleasure and pain. Getting off this treadmill requires the transmuting of desire into an aspiration for something higher and finer - moving focus from the solar plexus up to the inclusive heart chakra. The reward for those who achieve this is emotional peace and serenity.

From age seven to fourteen, the soul tries to grip the astral body, to balance the emotions and to bring them under its control. Parents can help their children in this period by teaching them to express their emotions in a healthy way.

2. Body

a. The Pancreas. The solar plexus chakra anchors in the pancreas, working particularly through the endocrine parts of the gland - the islets of Langerhans. They secrete insulin and glycogen to control blood sugar levels.

b. Mid-region digestion. The throat chakra rules the gastrointestinal or alimentary tract. [2] However, the solar plexus is the primary ruler of the stomach, liver, gallbladder and pancreas. The digestive process begins at the throat (Taurus), proceeds through the central digestion organs (Cancer), and ends at the anus and excretion of solid waste (Scorpio).

c. The Sympathetic Nervous System (SNS). It is immediately affected by solar plexus activity. Nerves that signal through the sympathetic system originate from the spinal cord in the solar plexus region.

---

1 Bailey, Alice A; Esoteric Healing, 107.
2 Bailey, Alice: Esoteric Healing, 45.

3. Disease

- The many psychological and nervous disorders caused by unstable emotions.
- Indigestion and diseases of the digestive organs, the pancreas and intestinal disorders.
- Trouble with the bloodstream: sepsis, blood poisoning, skin eruptions.

Troubled 6th ray force causing emotional disturbances and etheric/ chakra congestion, lies behind most health problems. Nervous and gastric disorders are warning signs the body is unable to handle the toxicity being produced. The heart and solar plexus centres are closely allied and problems with blood quality can arise from a solar plexus disturbance. Insidiously, a troubled solar plexus can infect energetically, any other chakra or body organ that has a weakness, causing trouble in their organs.

Cancer, the disease: it is ancient and the seeds of this trouble lie within our DNA, within the emotional body.

> The roots of cancer "are deep-seated in the emotional or desire nature, and are grounded in the astral body." [1]

Cancer is primarily a disease of inhibition, [2] of repression - of emotion and desire. This triggers a reaction from the will-to-live aspect of the 1st ray (that senses the survival of the body is at risk), with consequent overactivity and growth of cells [3] (a reaction of the 2nd ray). This in turn creates congestion and overactivity in a centre, [4] and consequent increased energy pouring into the cells and organs ruled by that chakra. The result is the disease cancer.

Chronic repression of emotion, of desire (1st ray), will result in cancer/ cell overbuilding (2nd ray).

In the natal chart, the pattern to look for is: a hard aspect between a ruler of the emotions (Moon, Mars, Neptune), to a planet that carries the 1st ray (Saturn and Pluto); with a link to Jupiter (ray 2).

The home of the emotional life - the solar plexus chakra, is the main centre of infection. But this can spread to any other chakra or part of the body that is debilitated. For instance, cancer may appear in the throat if we are afraid to talk about a serious abuse, in our bones if we suppress a fear of life, or in the genitals through forced celibacy.

> Fear, emotionalism and inertia, are the great predisposing factors (for cancer). [5]

We can help to avoid cancer by keeping our systems free-flowing and happy, by avoiding repressions of any sort and by finding alternative means to express force if a normal outlet is not available. Meditation to achieve inner serenity and the practice of harmlessness and kindness are super-preventatives. But as we age and the soul begins to withdraw, the body breaks down and we can contract any disease - even cancer.

▲ **Negative Psychology**
Addictions.
Alcoholism.
Anorexia.
Anxiety, worry.
Astral maniac.
Bipolar.
Bulimia.
Cuts, cutting.
Delirium, delusion.
Depression.
Dreams, troubled.
Drug, substance abuse.
Emotional trouble, all.
Fear.
Glamour.
Hallucination.
Hysteria.
Manic depression.
Mood swings.
Neuroses.
Obsessive compulsive.
Panic attacks.
Paranoia.
Phobias.
PTSD.
Schizophrenia
Self-harm, self-injury.
Sleep-walking.

▲ **Body/ functions**
Abdomen.
Bile.
Chyle.
Gallbladder.
Insulin.
Islets of Langerhans.
Liver.
Nutrition.
Pancreas.
Stomach.
Sympathetic NS.

▲ **Problems affecting the solar plexus organs**
Acid reflux.
Acidosis.
Allergies, digestive.
Cancer: pancreatic, stomach, liver, gallbladder.
Diabetes.
Dyspepsia.
Eating disorders.
Fatty stomach.
Food allergies.
Food poisoning.
Gallstones.
Gastric disorders.
Gastroenteritis.
Heartburn.
Hepatitis.
Hyperglycemia.
Hypoglycaemia.
Indigestion.
Jaundice.
Liver disease, cirrhosis.
Malnutrition.
Nausea.
Nightmares.
Obesity.
Pancreatitis.
Parasites, stomach.
Peritonitis.
Reflux.
Scurvy.
Starvation.
Ulcers, stomach.
Vomiting.

---

1 Bailey, Alice; Esoteric Healing, 58.
2 Bailey, Alice; Esoteric Healing, 59.
3 Bailey, Alice; Esoteric Healing, 383.
4 Bailey, Alice A; Esoteric Healing, 239.
5 Bailey, Alice; Esoteric Healing 315.

6. The Sacral (Svadhisthana) Chakra

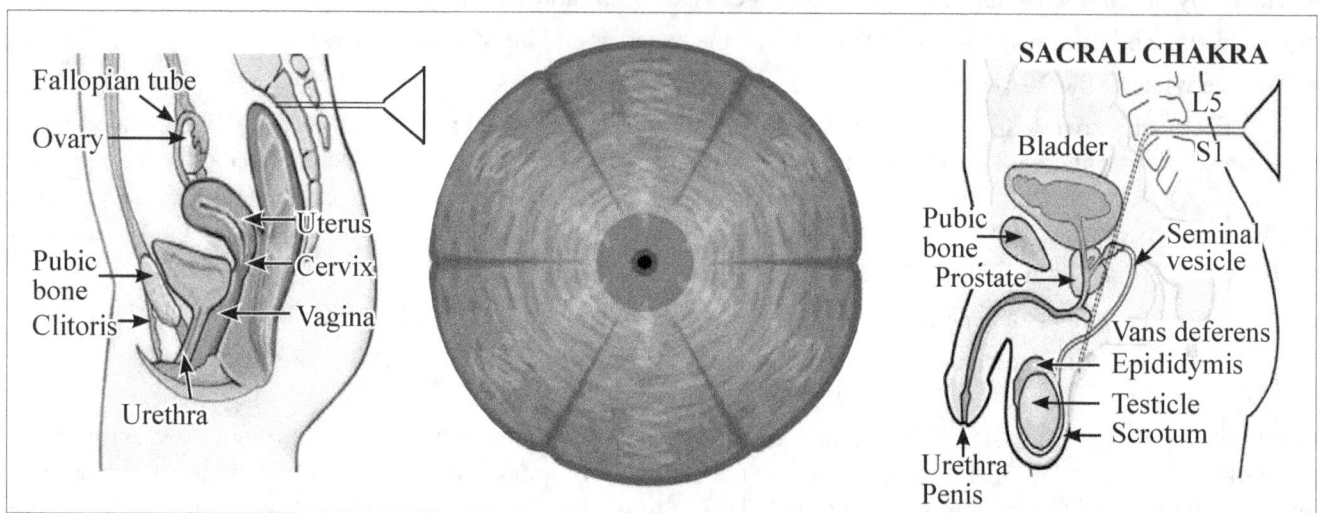

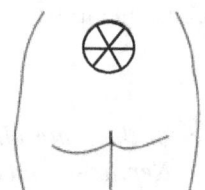

- The sacral enters the spine around L5 and S1, anchoring in the reproductive organs – the testes in males and the ovaries in women. It has six petals and the colour is described as being vermilion.

- The sacral is the main entry portal for Ray 7 of Ceremony, Order and Magic. But other rays play through it as well, such as ray 3. Another important ray that plays through the sacral centre is ray 6.[1] This is the ray of desire and the sacral chakra houses or harbours lower desire. The Astral Plane works creatively through this centre.

- Scorpio and Mars are the traditional rulers of sex and reproduction. So is Venus, which relates it to this centre. However, Cancer is also a prime ruler of reproduction, especially in women. Uranus that carries the 7th ray governs sexual attitudes and the building of forms for reproduction. Sagittarius governs the sacral chakra which provides the energy for the use of the creative powers of the physical life.[2]

1. Psychology

The function of the sacral chakra is to give expression to sexual and material desire. The desire to be rich and have a luxurious life or a desire for comfort or security (economic, social or religious), these are sacral chakra expressions. The 6th ray of desire influences this centre. Although most people on earth are focused in a higher centre, the sacral remains powerful because the lower appetites still drive most people. If the sacral is overemphasised, people can become obsessed and unstoppable in their urge to satisfy their sexual cravings - such as sexual, criminal deviants.

The sacral and throat centres are opposite poles. A great evolutionary change occurs when the focus of desire rises to the throat. This occurs as sexual-desire transforms into an aspiration for higher intellectual, artistic or spiritual pursuits. Desire does not disappear, it simply mutates into a higher form. The 7th ray that flows through the sacral assists this process. It transforms our sex attitudes into higher forms of expression.

2. Body

a. Etheric web. This vitalising body on which the dense physical body is constructed, is related to the sacral.[3]

b. Sex, reproduction - the gonads. The sacral chakra is the sex organ whose function is to govern the sexual act right to its intended final result - reproduction. It rules the male and female reproductive systems in their entirety.[4] The gonads are the endocrine reproductive glands - in males they are the testes, in females the ovaries. The female reproductive system consisting of the uterus or womb, fallopian tubes and ovaries are ruled primarily by Cancer and the Moon. Cancer carries two rays that rule sex and reproduction, rays 3 and 7. They also rule pregnancy, birth, babies, nursing and motherhood. However, the vagina, clitoris, pubis, vulva and labia - these sexual reproductive organs are primarily ruled by Venus and Mars.

---

1 Bailey, Alice A; Esoteric Psychology I, 420.
2 Bailey, Alice A; Esoteric Astrology, 191.
3 Bailey, Alice A; Esoteric Healing, 45.
4 Ibid, 202.

The male reproduction system consists of the penis, testicles, scrotum, epididymis, vas deferens, prostate, Cowper and seminal glands. Scorpio and Mars rule these organs and male sexuality.

c. DNA, foetal development, congenital and genetic disorders. The basic energy pattern of the physical body is recorded in the physical permanent atom, which is etheric in nature, and in our DNA. In early foetal development, genes give out the instructions that tell the body how to build and grow. This work takes place via the sacral chakra organs.

The sacral centre, controls the sex life and the building of forms of expression.[1]

When the soul is ready to reincarnate, it sounds its note and the vibration attracts to the physical-etheric permanent atom, appropriate substance from which the etheric body develops. On this etheric form - with the assistance of the base chakra, the dense physical body of the foetus develops.

d. Vital, animal, physical energy. The rude energy of life that drives the physical-etheric body, enters the form via the sacral centre.[2]

3. Disease

- Genetic or congenital diseases.
- Problems or diseases concerning sex or reproduction.

Trouble in this region is often due to suppressed desire or through the misuse of sexual force. On a higher level, another cause is due to the transfer of desire from the sacral to the throat centre, an important evolutionary development. In such a case, disease may arise in the organs ruled by either centre until energy flux evens out.

Ray 7 and the sacral are involved when things go wrong during conception and pregnancy. This is shown in the chart by afflictions to 7th ray Uranus or to the Moon that carries the 7th ray via Cancer, or to planets in Cancer. The Moon is the mother of form and is linked again to the sacral chakra by the "lunar lords" (nature's builders) which work through this centre.

A congenital defect occurs when the foetus develops an abnormality in the womb. This may be due to a genetic disorder that is caused by an abnormality in DNA, passed on by parents who have the condition or who are healthy carriers of the mutated gene. Or, the abnormality may occur due to an aberration in the womb, for instance as cells divide.

▲ **Negative Psychology**
Frigidity
Immorality
Sexual: addiction, rape, paedophilia, sadism, perversions, sexually based murders, promiscuity.

▲ **Body/ functions**
Physical power and strength.
DNA
Chromosomes
Etheric body.
Genes, genetics.
Physical permanent atom.
Reproduction
Birth
Cervix
Clitoris.
Conception.
Cowper's glands.
Egg ovum.
Embryo.
Epididymis.
Estrogen.
Fallopian tubes.
Fertility.
Genitals.
Gestation.
Labia.
Menstruation.
Ovaries.
Penis.
Periods.
Placenta.
Pregnancy.
Procreation.
Progesterone.
Prostate gland.
Puberty.
Scrotum.
Semen.
Seminal vesicle.
Sex hormones, organs.
Sigmoid flexure.
Sperm.
Testes.
Testicles.
Testosterone.
Urethra, for semen.
Urge to self-perpetuate.
Uterus.
Vagina.
Vans deferens.
Vulva.
Womb.
Sex
Libido.
Sexual development.
Sexual power.
Sex relations.

▲ **Problems affecting the Sacral's organs**
DNA
Gene mutations.
Genetic diseases.
Hereditary diseases.
Reproduction problems.
Abortion.
Barrenness.
Castration.
Congenital diseases.
Endometriosis.
Fibroids in womb.
Impotency, physical cause.
Infertility.
Miscarriages.
Prostate trouble.
Sterility.
Thrush, vaginal.
Uterine troubles.
Social diseases
Chlamydia.
Genital disorders, warts.
Gonorrhea.
Herpes, genital.
Pubic, crabs.
STD: sexually transmitted diseases.
Syphilis.
Venereal disease.

---
1 Bailey, Alice A; Esoteric Psychology I, 261.
2 Bailey, Alice; Esoteric Healing 45.

7. The Base (Muladhara) Chakra

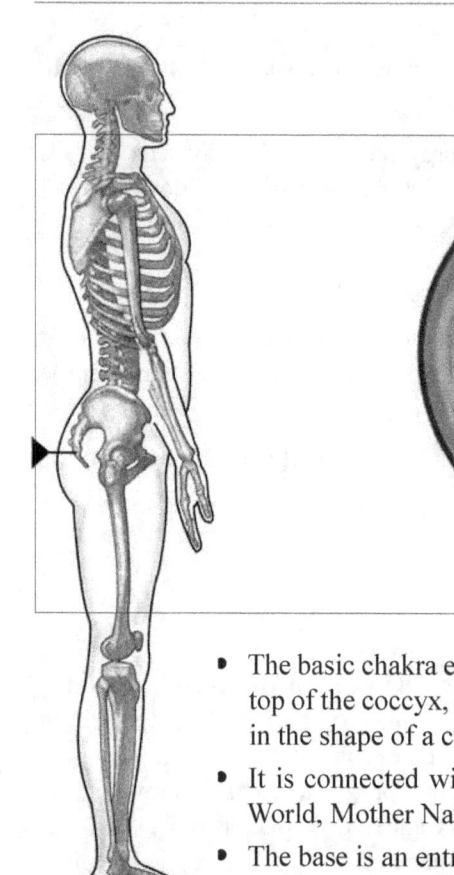
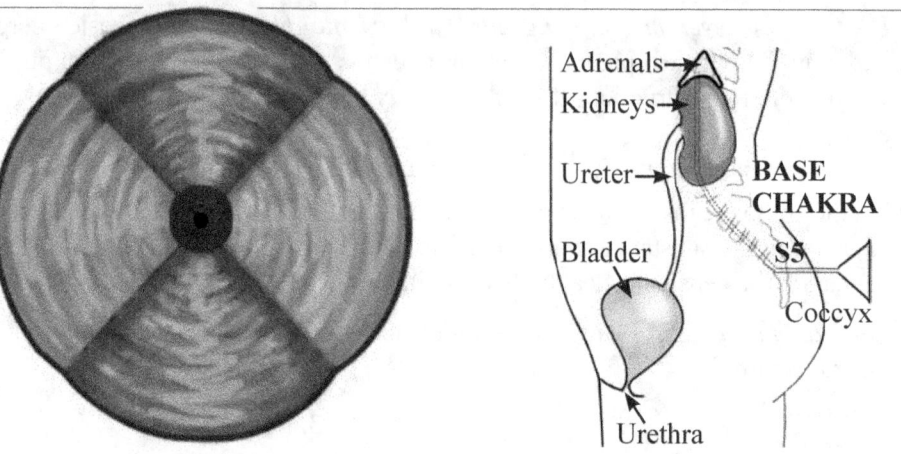
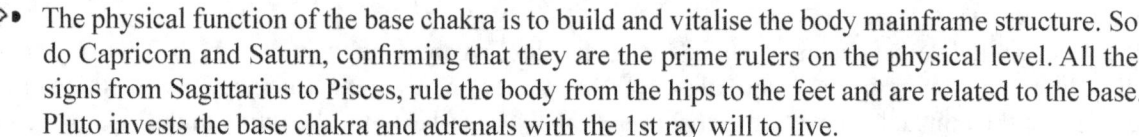

- The basic chakra enters the spine at the base of the spine around S5 and the top of the coccyx, anchoring in the adrenal glands. It has 4 petals, arranged in the shape of a cross that radiates orange fire.
- It is connected with the life-force, and is vitalised by the Mother of the World, Mother Nature. The kundalini fire is housed in this chakra.
- The base is an entry portal for ray 1, and ray 3.[1] Other associated rays are 4 and 7.
- The physical function of the base chakra is to build and vitalise the body mainframe structure. So do Capricorn and Saturn, confirming that they are the prime rulers on the physical level. All the signs from Sagittarius to Pisces, rule the body from the hips to the feet and are related to the base. Pluto invests the base chakra and adrenals with the 1st ray will to live.

1. Psychology

The function of the base chakra is to ground the animal impulse to live and to survive. It is also the organ of personal will, and dictators who have very strong and selfish personal wills use the 1st ray power of this chakra. For example, Adolf Hitler - he was a highly intelligent and evil man, with an extraordinary will. The tone he set in the world was base and materialistic, indicating that he drew upon the power of the basic material centre. Such people are materialists who try to rule the world through war, fear and cruelty.

2. Body

a. The adrenal glands. These glands are located at the top of each kidney. They anchor the base chakra. The inner part of the gland, the adrenal-medulla, produces adrenaline, a hormone involved in the fight or flight syndrome. This is a 1st ray via Pluto and Scorpio instinct, which when playing through the base gives the animal nature the "will to survive". Libra and Venus rule the outer part of the gland, the adrenal-cortex. It helps regulate metabolism and salt-water balance in the blood.

b. Kidneys and urine elimination. The kidneys are the major organs of the urinary tract and are vitalised by the base chakra.[2] Other components are the ureters, bladder and urethra. The kidneys filter out liquid waste, which then passes to the ureters and bladder to be disposed of as urine. Libra rules the kidneys, Scorpio the removal of waste.

c. The dense physical body, vertebral column and kundalini. This chakra vitalises tissue throughout the entire body, excepting for those main organs governed by the six higher chakras. This rulership also covers the skeleton and the entire "spinal column".[3] Located at the bottom of the spine, this centre functions like a basement boiler in an apartment block, whose job is to keep all higher levels of the building warm and pleasant for residents. This heat is provided by kundalini, the fire of matter, which is housed in this centre.

---

1 Bailey, Alice A; The Destiny of the Nations, 117-8.
2 Bailey, Alice: Light of the Soul, 309.
3 Bailey, Alice A; Esoteric Healing, 202.

For the first four years in life, the base is the dominant chakra, vitalising rapid body growth. In these early years, the soul hovers over its physical form. Then from age four to seven (earlier in souls who are advanced), the soul tries to grip the body and get it under its control via the nervous system. If this process is disrupted because of accident or abuse, soul-body control may not be completed or be inadequate. The result would be an under-functioning base chakra and an inadequately earthed or grounded physical body, physical weakness, disease and illness.

3. Disease

- Problems with the body structure, including the skeleton, spine, bones, tissue, muscles and skin.
- Diseases of the adrenals, of the urinary tract - the kidneys and bladder.
- Problems with physical body vitalisation.

The base chakra in most people is only partially open, just enough to do its job of vitalising the physical form. It is the last centre to open fully. This occurs when spiritual union with the soul takes place in consciousness. Then kundalini rises up the spine to merge with spiritual force in the crown. If kundalini rises prematurely through unwise spiritual practices, tissue is burnt which can result in insanity, even death.

▲ **Negative Psychology**
Black Magic, Esoteric Healing, 51.
Egomania.
Megalomania.
Pure selfishness.

▲ **Body/ functions**
Adrenals
Bladder.
Cortisol.
Fight or flight.
Survival instinct.
Will to live.
Will to exist.
Kidneys
Urea.
Ureters.
Urethra.
Urinary tract.
Urine.
Mainframe structure of the body.
This chakra rules all bones, joints and tissue in the body generally. However, bones and tissue in the close vicinity of a higher chakra, are also influenced by that higher chakra.
Body containers, sheaths.
Body warmth.
Bone marrow.
Calcium.
Cartilage, connective tissue.
Cells of the physical body.
Enamel.
Feet.
Flesh.
Hair.
Integumentary system
Kundalini.
Ligaments.
Limbs, lower.
Matter. This basic centre is the one through which the life of matter itself works. Esoteric Healing, 209.
Membranes.
Muscles.
Nails.
Physical body, foetal body development.
Pleurae.
Skeleton.
Skin.
Skull.
Spinal column.
Substance.
Teeth.
Tendons.
Thighs.
Tissue.
Vertebrae, all.

▲ **Problems affecting the Base's organs**
Adrenal trouble
Addison's disease.
Cushing's syndrome.
Fatigue: adrenal overload.
Kidney trouble
Hyperuricaemia.
Kidney infection.
Kidney stones.
Nephritis.
Urinary tract infections.
Mainframe structure
Ankle problems.
Ankylosis spondylosis.
Arthritis.
Back pain.
Birthmark.
Bone fractures.
Bone deformities.
Bunions.
Bursitis.
Cervical osteoarthritis.
Cramps.
Crippled.
Cystitis.
Dysplasia of the hip.
Feet problems.
Fractures, bones.
Gingivitis, pyorrhea.
Hardening, stiffening.
Hernia.
Hip disease.
Joints stiff.
Knee problems.
Limping.
Lumbago.
Melanoma.
Osteoarthritis.
Osteoporosis.
Paget's disease.
Physical body deformities.
Rheumatic fever.
Rheumatism.
Rheumatoid arthritis.
Rickets.
Scleroderma.
Sclerosis.
Scoliosis.
Skull: injuries.
Spina bifida.
Spinal fractures.
Vertebrae. degeneration.
Warts.

NB. Obviously there are many more parts for the mainframe body structure than are listed here. This is an overview.

ASTROLOGY - CHAKRA DIVISIONS

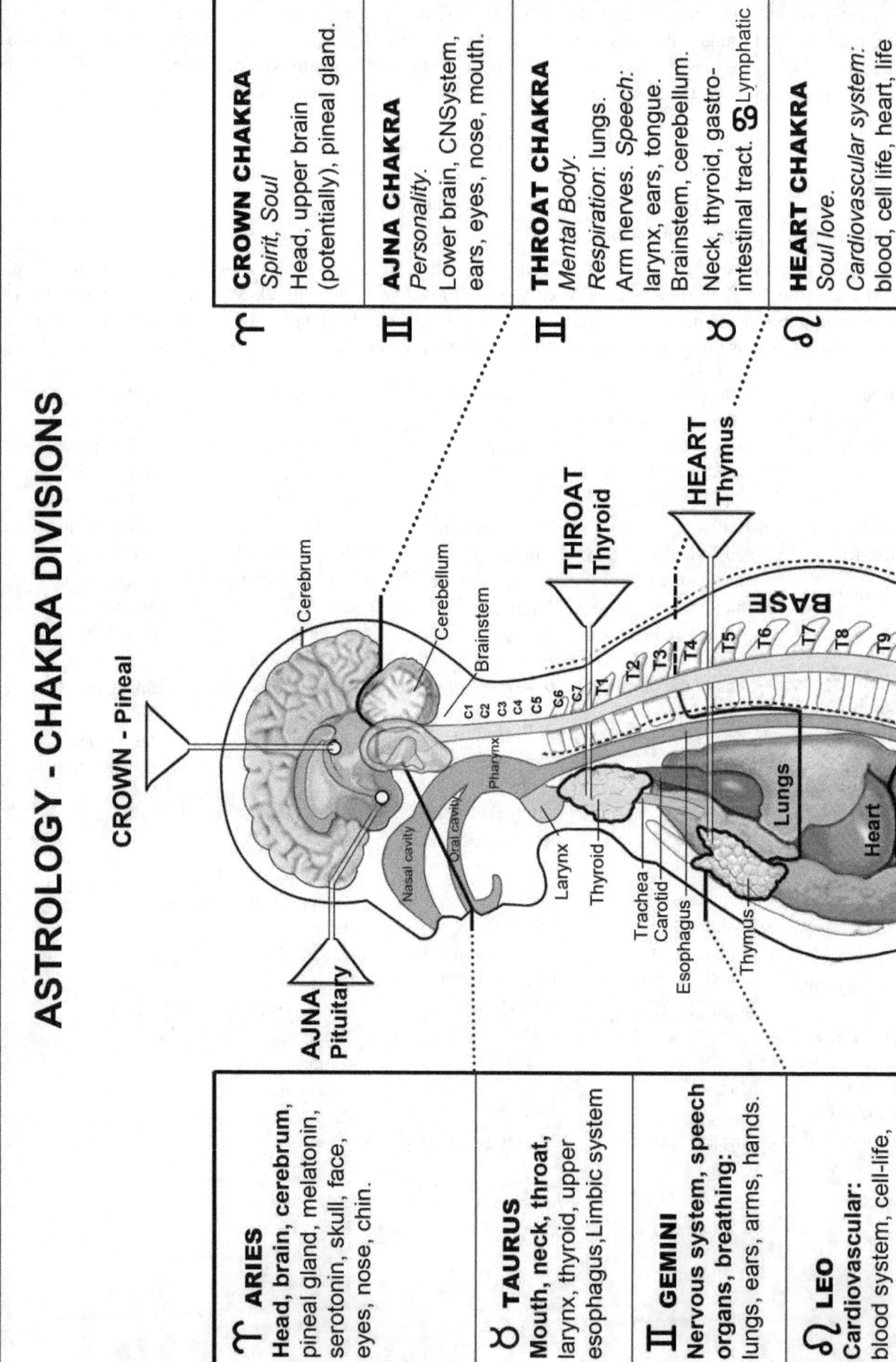

♈ CROWN CHAKRA
Spirit, Soul
Head, upper brain (potentially), pineal gland.

♊ AJNA CHAKRA
Personality.
Lower brain, CNSystem, ears, eyes, nose, mouth.

♊ THROAT CHAKRA
Mental Body.
Respiration: lungs. Arm nerves. Speech: larynx, ears, tongue. Brainstem, cerebellum. Neck, thyroid, gastro-intestinal tract. ♋ Lymphatic

♌ HEART CHAKRA
Soul love.
Cardiovascular system: blood, cell life, heart, life

♈ ARIES
Head, brain, cerebrum, pineal gland, melatonin, serotonin, skull, face, eyes, nose, chin.

♉ TAURUS
Mouth, neck, throat, larynx, thyroid, upper esophagus, Limbic system

♊ GEMINI
Nervous system, speech organs, breathing: lungs, ears, arms, hands.

♌ LEO
Cardiovascular: blood system, cell-life,

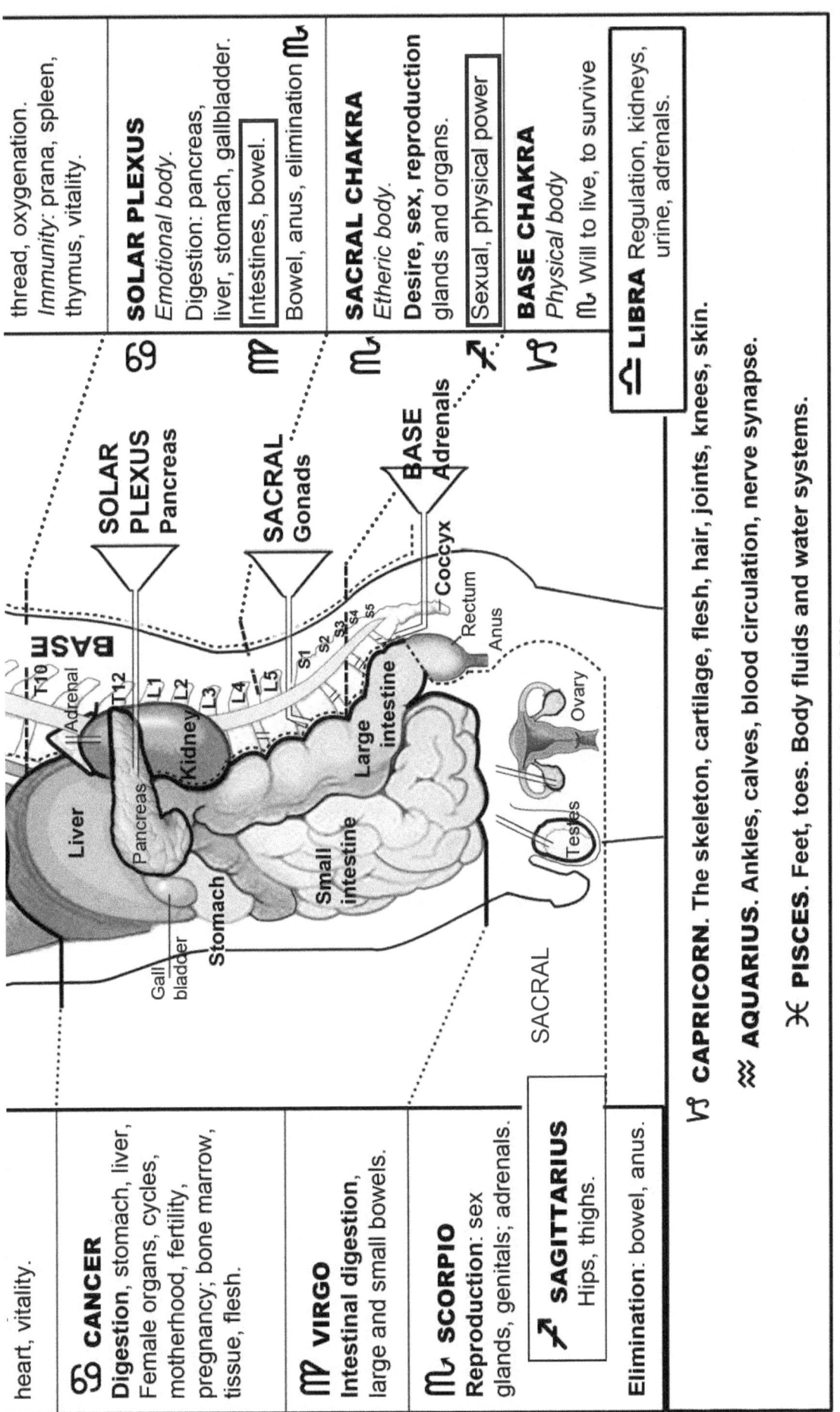

© Leoni Hodgson 2018.

3. DISEASE, DIAGNOSING, COUNSELLING.

A. Disease and its cause - it is simply the misuse of energy

In a general sense the cause of disease is simple - disharmony with life. Clashing energies and conflicts cause disease. In man, the immediate problem is disharmony with his soul.

> All disease is the result of inhibited soul life, and that is true of all forms in all kingdoms. [1]

This means that prior to enlightenment, which is that advanced state when soul-personality illumination occurs and the flow of soul energy through the form is full and free; illness is inevitable. The bodies we inherit from past lives are imperfect, the consequence of our actions in previous lives. The good news is that, each life offers us a new opportunity to build a healthier and stronger body through right-living. But even so, healthy or unhealthy, at some stage the body will begin to break down. In earlier years - due to disease. Or in later years, due to the soul making preparations to end the incarnation (allowing the body to die). Disease is simply nature's way of letting us know that its flow is blocked and that an adjustment or easing of that blockage is required. Consequently, its effect is purificatory. The final act of adjustment, release and purification that we go through on earth, is the death of the physical body. This allows the soul to pick up a new and healthier body in the next incarnation, through which to continue its journey to enlightenment.

1. The emotional body is the primary cause of disease

> Disease is simply the misuse of the forces of the etheric, the astral and of the dense physical levels.

The physical body is an animal form and when it has no inherited weaknesses and vitality flows freely, it is resistant to germs and infection. Primitive man had this type of body and excellent physical health, but when the emotional nature and later the mind started to unfold, trouble started. Their misuse distorts energy flow as these steps show:

a. The mind thinks, it plans, it idealises and has ambitions.
b. The thoughts it creates descend to the Astral Plane where they blend with astral force. When disappointments and frustrations set in because things don't go the way we would like them to or because we cannot get what we want, bitterness sets in. Then disease follows according to the weaknesses we have inherited in the physical body - as shown in the natal chart.

Ninety per cent of the causes of disease are to be found originating in troubled astral and etheric bodies; [2] wrong use of mental energy and misapplied desire are major contributing factors. This is because most people are still emotional in consciousness.

The mind is not usually a causal factor of disease. Bailey said that only 5 percent of all modern disease originates in the mental body. Even then, the accompanying emotional reaction causes the problem. For instance, a person may think that he is a superior person, but it is only when that thought is taken over by negative emotions such as hatred or dislike for others, that trouble arises. Unstable and erratic emotions generate toxic chemical reactions in the physical body and if left unresolved they manifest as a physical illness.

Trouble can arise in the mental body when we are mentally aloof and live in a world of our own. In such a case our thoughts are not put into action in our physical life, but remain on the Mental Plane and in the mind body, building a wall between its owner and others. This is a problem of cleavage covered in the Ray 5 section.

From an esoteric perspective, disease is the working out into manifestation of undesirable, subjective conditions - mental, emotional and etheric. In the future, as the race becomes more intellectual, the percentages given above will change.

> **In summary, if our thoughts and emotions are violent, disturbed or repressed, this causes disruption in the etheric body and the glandular release of toxic chemicals in the physical that eventually lead to disease. The drawing on the following page - "Disrupted Energy Flow resulting in Disease" depicts this process.**
>
> **If our thoughts and emotions are positive and filled with joy, then energy flow will be smoother and the result will be more wholesome and health benefiting. So, the good news is we can do something to improve the body we are stuck with, by improving energy flow through the mind, emotions and the physical body.**

---

1 Bailey, Alice A; Esoteric Healing, 5.
2 Bailey, Alice A; Esoteric Healing, 112.

Chapter 3. Disease, Diagnosing, Counselling ▲ 99

Chart 5: Disrupted Energy Flow resulting in Disease

Planes	Etheric chakras	Nervous system	Endocrine system	Bloodstream	Body organs, bones

Mental force — Ajna, Throat

Astral energy — Solar plexus

Etheric energy — Sacral

Dense physical force — Base

Endocrine: Pituitary, Thyroid, Pancreas, Adrenals, Gonads

Force flows in from the planes of nature to our > *chakras* > *nervous system* > *endocrine system* > *into the bloodstream* > *into the entire body.*

Depending upon the health of the chakras, energy flows easily and smoothly, or is degraded in some way. When there are mental and emotional issues, the energy disturbance causes a disruptive domino effect down the line.

The drawing depicts an emotional disturbance that ends up affecting organs ruled by the solar plexus chakra. What we do as a consequence of the emotion, determines which organ will be affected and the type of diseases we get. For instance, if we drink alcohol excessively, the liver is the target and cirrhosis is the likely result. Or, the consumption of rich and sugary foods could upset the pancreas function so we get diabetes.

2. Clear thoughts and clear emotions are the key to good health

When we are able to carry our thoughts - undamaged or unchanged to the physical brain and from there use them to direct our life-actions; it usually results in good health. Here is how the Tibetan puts it:

> When the thought can be carried through to the physical brain and there becomes a directing agent of the life force, you will usually have a condition of good health.. whether the individual thought has been good or bad, rightly motivated or wrongly oriented. It is simply the effect of integration, because saints and sinners, the selfish and the unselfish and all kinds of people, can achieve integration and a thought-directed life. [1]

If the thoughts behind our actions are not corrupted or interrupted by an astral disturbance it benefits health. This is because good health is a consequence of good energy flow. The Tibetan points out that both good and bad people can do this. However, wrong intention and bad thoughts will attract karmic retribution at some point in time.

Ultimately though, good health occurs when we are able to express the harmonious, holistic and inclusive rhythms of the soul. These energies straighten out any kinks in our energy streams, benefiting health. Taking this a step further, if we are able to carry soul energy on the wings of our thought life and express these with good intent, we become natural healers, of ourselves and of others.

> **Soul energy, expressed through right thinking, can cure diseases to which man is prone.** [2]

This happens whether we are in the healing professions or not. Many of us have had the experience when in the presence of a really good and compassionate person, we find ourselves feeling uplifted, energised and inspired by the contact. This is evidence of the healing power of the love and wisdom of the soul. Many of us who are practising spiritual disciplines such as meditation and are expressing goodwill are becoming natural healers or already are.

> Meditation on spiritual matters and to improve character, is the prime method used through the ages to transform an earth-bound consciousness into one that is enlightened.

3. The primary cause of personal disease is karmic

a. Personal karma.

During the life span of the physical body, just as a motor car wears out and starts to break down, so does the physical body. But some people have better bodies than others and enjoy better health. The reason for this is karmic. Karma is the universal law of cause and effect, whatever we do has consequences. Karma determines the type of body we are born with and the type of diseases to which we are susceptible. We carry karma from life to life. All that we are at the end of one life is recorded in "memory cells" called permanent atoms, which are located on the mental, emotional and physical levels. This is replicated in our DNA (deoxyribonucleic acid) in the next incarnation. The karmic pay-off is that, if we abuse our bodies through vice, drugs, alcohol, laziness, etc., then we inherit a weakened physical body in the next. Similarly, on emotional and mental levels; if we are driven by abusive thoughts and uncontrolled emotionalism when we die, we are fated to inherit that type of psychological pattern in our next incarnation.

The good news is, it is possible to reverse or minimise many karmic and physical impairments. By harmonising thoughts, acting with compassion and kindness and practising moderation in the way we live; we can build healthier bodies. Or, if a disease's progression is too advanced, reap a better body in the next life.

b. Collective karma and disease.

We also inherit diseases that are a result of collective karma, that arise due to the racial, religious, cultural or family group into which we are born. Additionally, all physical bodies carry the seeds of three ancient illness passed down from our forefathers through our DNA - these "indigenous" diseases are syphilis, cancer and tuberculosis. Bailey divides the diseases we inherit into five major groups:

1. Tuberculosis (an indigenous disease).
2. Syphilitic or sexually transmitted diseases (an indigenous disease).
3. Cancer (an indigenous disease).
4. Heart difficulties.
5. Nervous diseases. [3]

---

1 Bailey, Alice A; Esoteric Healing, 96.
2 Ibid, 94.
3 Ibid, 55.

Heart and nervous difficulties are afflictions that are more recent. This is due to the mass opening of the heart and ajna chakras in modern man. Heart difficulties are due to group work, the bonding together of individuals towards a common goal that may be spiritual or material. Heart disease is a consequence of giving our heart life-blood metaphorically, to the group or to the organisation we belong to. The 'group' may be our family, or the football club we belong to, or a business we own which has several employees. Brain and nervous difficulties are a consequence of wide-spread modern education, which is stimulating the latent mental faculties of the masses into life. If soul and mental force pouring in is too much for the existing equipment to handle, brain and nerve cells are overstimulated.

4. Other causes of disease

a. Accidents: those that are true accidents and those due to our own karma.

Surprisingly, personal karma causes most so-called accidents. They are generated by the unkind thoughts and critical words of those involved in the accident. Hatred, jealousy or vindictiveness generates explosions of force that rebound on their owners like a boomerang.

Apart from this, it is possible to be accidentally in the wrong place at the wrong time and to be the victim of a catastrophe or catch a disease to which we have no karmic link. True accidents do happen. A car crash or succumbing to an epidemic or contagious disease could just simply - be an accident.

b. Problems of Mystics and Disciples.

People who are transforming spiritually through meditation and other spiritual disciplines get the same diseases as everyone else. But the cause may differ. For instance, in average man disease in the solar plexus region is caused by emotional trouble. In aspirants and disciples, it is caused as the solar plexus refines and energies start moving upwards to the selfless heart. Generally, more advanced people tend to get diseases in the upper part of the body while those still focused in the lower chakras have trouble there.

There are other problems that belong peculiarly to this group of people as a consequence of being impressed with soul illumination. When soul light pours through, those who have not yet stabilised their mental and emotional equipment and who have not yet developed discrimination; they can have the astral nature over-stimulated. This can result in paranoia, glamour and delusion, or lower psychic powers shared with animals may be brought to life again. Visions may be seen of holy ones and beloved teachers that are astral distortions stemming from the wish life. The powerful yearning to be one with God can become so compelling, the physical body is starved of energy.

The remedy is to stop all spiritual practices for the rest of the life, and to pursue mental projects and physical exercise. This will build up the mental and brain equipment so that a more stable reaction to soul energy can occur next life.

5. Death is a natural process

We have died many times before. More correctly, the physical body has repeatedly died, not consciousness, which continues to evolve and grow through the bodies it picks up and then discards each life, until enlightenment is reached.

**Death releases the soul from a body
that can no longer serve its need to evolve.**

In the normal course of events in our final years, the soul prepares to release the physical form and the consequent lowering of vitality means that the body may succumb to any germ or illness. The actual death process is initiated by the soul who withdraws the etheric and subtle bodies from the dense form, the consciousness thread from the brain and the life-thread from the heart. This completely disrupts the body, reducing it to its essential elements - chemical, mineral and inorganic substances which can be absorbed into the soil of the planet. The atoms disperse, to be regenerated and refreshed until called upon again by the soul to form a new body in the next incarnation.

The fear of death, which has ridden mankind for aeons is beginning to lose its power. This is because many more men and women every day are realising that their true Self is the soul, not the body. As part of this, the belief in a devil and the horror of going to hell is also fading.

> It is interesting to note that the work of the Devil, the imprisoner of souls, is beginning to lose its power, for the race is on the verge of understanding that true death is immersion in form, and that matter is but a part of the divine whole. [1]

---

[1] Bailey, Alice A; A Treatise on White Magic, 240.

B. Diagnosing Health and Disease in the Chart.

The planets represent man on all levels - spiritual, psychological, and physical. They also represent the universal forces that pour through the signs and planets to us. The planets are receivers, conductors and distributors of energy on all levels. The signs govern different parts of the body and the planets that govern each sign, also govern those same body parts. Every body organ, every process, every function is represented by at least one planet, sometimes more. Ill health is found in the natal chart by examining the planets, the patterns they make and their location in the signs and houses.

One of the first steps in medical astrology is to assess the strength of each planet, especially the strength of the personal planets, Sun, Moon, Mercury, Venus and Mars. This is because they are the primary rulers of our mental, emotional and physical states.

> The Sun: the personality consciousness.
>
> The Moon: emotional patterns and the physical form.
>
> Mercury: the mind.
>
> Venus: expression of personal love and affection.
>
> Mars: expression of desire, passion, sex.

This will reveal the health or otherwise of the organs and parts that each planet rules. A well aspected planet is conducive to good health; a poorly aspected or afflicted planet points to the potential for malfunction and disease.

A planet is considered "afflicted" if it is in a sign hostile to its force, if it has many hard aspects, is unaspected or retrograde. Healthwise, a planet is also considered potentially afflicted if it is located in the 12th house of hospitals or in the 6th house of health.

All planets can represent a disease, but the outer planets more so. In traditional, pre-psychological astrology, Mars and Saturn were viewed as "malefic" (Uranus, Neptune and Pluto were added later); because it was thought they had an evil effect. This concept remains valid today where health is concerned for the simple reason that they each represent ways the body breaks down in serious ways and succumbs to disease. Mars inflames, Saturn blocks, Uranus causes aberrations, Neptune perverts and Pluto destroys. Of the others: the Sun inflames, the Moon and Mercury debilitate, Venus weakens and Jupiter causes cell over-growth.

An afflicted planet in the chart does not necessarily mean that disease will follow. Everyone has them. An examination of the charts of highly successful people shows planet afflictions everywhere. What makes the difference is how we deal with stress. If we learn from our disappointments and challenges to be wiser and make better choices in the future, if we go forward with positivity rather than succumb to bitterness; metaphorically, we transmute our "squares" into "trines". For instance, Saturn square Mercury can manifest as a fear of speaking out and if this eventuates, can lead to throat problems. Overcoming the fear and speaking courageously transmutes the negative force into a positive character attribute, easing and even eliminating the potential for throat trouble.

<u>**Basic steps when diagnosing health and disease.**</u>

1. Examine the Sun - how strong is this person's will, heart and vitality?
   Sometimes the Ascendant sign and 1H can also be consulted.
2. Examine the Moon, Mars or Neptune - how is emotional expression?
3. Examine the planets. Are their energies healthy or afflicted?
4. Examine the 6th and 12 "health" houses.
5. Look for a major health warning pattern in the chart.
6. Look for a health-warning triangle in the chart.

1. Examine the Sun - how strong is this person's will, heart and vitality?

A well placed and well aspected Sun in the natal chart indicates a cardiovascular system that absorbs prana (solar energy) easily, vitalising cell life and boosting the immune system. It gives the power and the will to throw off disease and to recover quickly from illness. Solar power increases in Aries and Leo, signs in which the Sun is most compatible; and in Sagittarius, another fire sign. Easy aspects from Mars and Jupiter to the Sun boost vitality. These planets when located in Leo, the Sun's sign, will have a similar vitalising effect. Even hard aspects from Mars and Jupiter are better than none. In this case, energy is available, though if misused will lead to burn-out and inflammation. An afflicted Sun shows potential trouble in the heart chakra, the heart organ and cardiovascular system.

John Howard (26 July 1939, 02:21 Earlwood Australia).

Howard was the Australian PM from 1996-2007. The Sun in its dignity in Leo conjunct 1st ray Pluto, gives Howard a very strong personality and will. It also gives a strong heart action and potentially good vitality. This is accentuated with the trine to expansive Jupiter in Aries, and opposition to Mars. The Sun-Mars opposition does indicate potential heart trouble at some time; but Howard's excellent health and vitality served him well. He was in politics for 40 years, the longest serving Australian PM whose 'heart' held his party and the country together for many years. He retired when he lost the support of the people and his seat in the 2007 elections.

Henry Fonda (16 May 1905, 14:00, Grand Island NE).

Fonda died of heart disease on 12 August 1982. His Sun is weak when compared with Howard's. Taurus can give a strong, "bullish" constitution and there is a trine to the ascendant, which is helpful. But that is as good as it gets. The Sun is located in the cadent 9th house (9H), which is not physically energising. Its inconjunct to the Moon in Libra indicates a troubled connection with the etheric body causing debilitation. Psychologically, Sun square Saturn in the 6H of health represents difficulty in 'giving from the heart'. This manifested physically as poor circulation and heart disease. Readers who remember Fonda may recall he moved languidly, as if he was conserving energy.

Sometimes the Ascendant sign and 1H can be consulted.

The ascendant sign represents variously: our appearance, a new incarnation, the head, and with the 1H, the physical body. The body parts ruled by the ascendant sign, may be susceptible to health problems.

Questions to answer:
1. What sign is on the ascendant cusp? (Capricorn).
2. What parts of the body does that sign rule? (Knees, joints, mainframe bony structure, skin, ligaments, teeth).
3. Are there hard aspects to the asc? (No, which is fortunate for health).
4. What planet rules the asc? (Saturn in Scorpio on MC).
5. Is it afflicted? Yes, being retrograde and by aspect. (T-square with Mars, Jupiter in Aquarius 1H; and with Neptune in Leo 7H).
6. Does Saturn have easy aspects? (Yes, sextile ascendant, trine to Uranus).

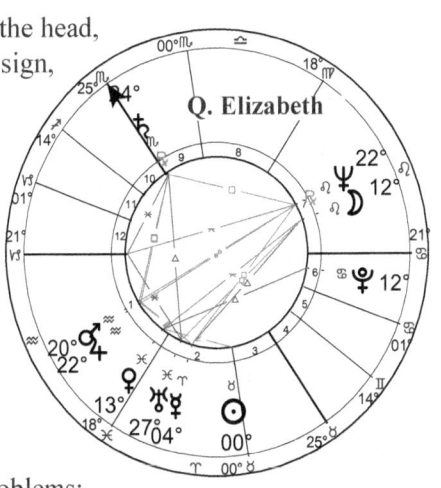

From this data we know the Queen was susceptible to knee, back and feet problems; the consequence of many hours standing as she went about her duties. However, modern or alternative medical techniques such as physiotherapy or naturopathy would benefit her.

2. Examine the Moon, Mars or Neptune - how is emotional expression?

The Moon and Mars are the primary representatives of emotions in most people and Neptune in the more advanced. Since disturbed emotions cause most diseases, their influence in the chart should be carefully studied. The Moon is potentially a contagious point. Its force indicates that which is past, the baggage we hold on to and the habits we fall back on when we are in fear or confusion. Esoterically, it shows where the "prison of the soul is to be found". [1]

> The Moon carries Ray 4 of Harmony through Conflict, which debilitates and exhausts if we are besieged with inner conflict. This then can make us susceptible to the indigenous diseases of the planet, which are cancer, tuberculosis and sexual diseases.

The following brief statements have been drawn up specifically for the Moon and Mars in the twelve signs. For each, they link psychological - emotional reactions to diseases. Included also are lower and higher keynotes for each sign.

- *Aries*: emotions are hot, powerful and volatile. Fiery upsets affect the brain and head. There could be inflammatory brain explosions such as a stroke or accidents because of angry and impulsive actions. The lower note is "Let form again be sought", meaning, powerful desires rule the mind. The higher note is "I come forth and from the plane of mind - I rule". The intelligent mind should rule all actions.

- *Taurus*: emotions and desires are powerful and intense. The Moon is exalted so its effect on health is more benign than with Mars, which falls in this sign. However, they both cause emotional instability and conflict, trouble in the throat, thyroid and reproductive area via Mars. The lower note is, "Let struggle be undismayed", meaning, inner conflict is a real problem. The higher note, "I see and when the eye is opened, all is light", refers to self-observation and self-understanding; which when adopted will bring emotional stability.

- *Gemini*: emotions are rationalised (Moon), or there is mental irritation (Mars). In both, there is a tendency to split the mind off from the emotions so that emotional trouble or trauma may not be recognised until nervous disorders arise or inflammation or phlegm affects the airways and lungs. The lower note is "Let instability do its work", meaning, mental - emotional instability is a problem. Balance and insight will bring forth wisdom and better health - "I see my other self, and in the waning of that self, I grow and glow".

- *Cancer:* the lower note is "Let isolation be the rule and yet the crowd exists"; emotions are highly defensive, conflicted, warlike and tend to be repressed. Mars falls in this sign. This upsets digestion and body fluids, creating phlegm and trouble in digestion and reproduction. Emotional refinement will strengthen the body and improve intimate relationships - "I build a lighted house and therein dwell".

- *Leo*: the lower note "Let other forms exist, I rule", tells us that pride and arrogance is this sign's downfall. Fiery, volcanic emotions and explosions lead to inflammatory conditions of the heart, its valves, walls and sepsis of the blood. An orientation towards a higher life demonstration represented by the higher note, "I am That, and That am I", will strengthen the heart and life.

- *Virgo*: emotions are tight and desire for perfection can lead to their repression by the fussy and critical mind. If so, trouble will seep out unhealthily in the intestinal and bowel region. The lower note is "Let matter reign"; meaning, materialism is fine in its place but can entrap the soul. The aspirational goal is to reach for something finer, represented by the phrase, "I am the mother and the child, I God, I matter am".

- *Libra*: the lower note is "Let choice be made", referring to the oscillating mind of the Libran who is stuck in indecision. If upset emotions are flicked aside to avoid facing the truth or from hurting people; "pissed off" feelings that affect the kidneys will be left behind. This is especially true of Mars, which is in detriment in this sign. The development goal is to be decisive and to move straight forwards with confidence - "I choose the way which lies between the two great lines of force".

- *Scorpio*: the lower note is "Let maya flourish and let deception rule". Holding on to grievances, dark and poisonous emotions, harbouring revenge and thoughts of attack, results in strokes, blood disorders and festering infections in the gut and reproduction organs. Scorpio's have to fight to free their minds from delusion and emotionalism. The war-cry, which will help them reach victory, is "Warrior I am, and from the battle I emerge triumphant".

- *Sagittarius*: Over-indulgence is a problem, the lower note is "Let food again be sought". Sometimes this refers to a dark, predatory side and criminal activities. Loss of faith stiffens hips, thighs and mobility generally. Aspiring to

---
1 Bailey, Alice A; Esoteric Astrology, 19.

the heights is the goal for Sagittarian's - "I see the goal, I reach that goal, and then I see another". This will help them move forwards in the right direction.

- *Capricorn*: "Let ambition rule and let the door stand wide"; selfish, greedy ambition (Mars) and emotional repression (Moon in detriment), leads to crystallisation and stiffness, particularly the knee joints. Using all one's power and resources for the greater good is the goal - "Lost am I in light supernal, yet on that light I turn my back". Having seen the "light", one carries it to those who suffer.

- *Aquarius*: powerful and selfish desires ("Let desire in form be ruler"), coupled with mental separativeness disrupts energy flow between the mind and emotions. A psychic barrier is erected that impairs blood circulation and blood quality. Stiffness and crystallisation in the lower leg region and ankles especially, affects mobility. The higher note, "Water of life am I, poured forth for thirsty men" directs Aquarius people to assist those who are in need.

- *Pisces*: the lower note of Pisces, "Go forth into matter" directs the Piscean person who is still focused in the solar plexus chakra, to continue swimming in the waters of emotional life. This leads to devitalisation, eventually upsets the watery systems of the body and causes swelling and various other problems with the feet that affect mobility. The aspirational note of Pisces is, "I leave my Father's house, and turning back, I save".

Liza Minnelli (12 March 1946, 07:58, LA, CA).

American singer and actress, the daughter of fabulous Judy Garland. Both mother and daughter had great difficulty with emotional expression and problems with alcohol and drug abuse. Of Minnelli, a writer said, "Her life has been a Big Dipper ride in which manifestations of her talent alternate with displays of self-destruction"; which is a creative but accurate description.

She is inhibited emotionally. Mars and the Moon are in Cancer, conjunct the great "repressor", Saturn. The lower note for Cancer gives us insight into her emotions - "Let isolation be the rule and yet the crowd exists". Amongst fame and glory, she feels alone and unloved. The problem lies within her - she is afraid to open up and trust at a deep and intimate level because she fears she cannot handle rejection.

Queen Elizabeth II (21 April 1926, 02:40 London UK).

The Queen's whole life demonstration, how she attended her public duties, is one of remarkable graciousness and kindness. This indicates that she was spiritually advanced and that Neptune is the primary indicator of her emotional expression.

Neptune is in Leo, in a t-square with Saturn at the hub and Mars-Jupiter. From one angle, this tells us that the Queen burned with zeal to meet her royal duties (Neptune in Leo), steadfastly (Saturn), energetically and wisely (Mars-Jupiter). She dedicated her life to duty (Saturn, conjunct MC, square Neptune and planets in the 1H).

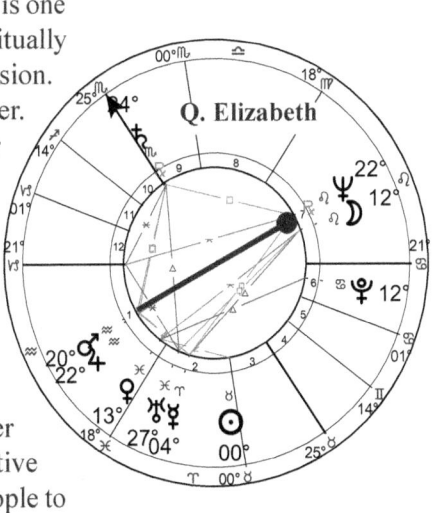

The three rulers of the solar plexus chakra are all connected - Neptune opposes Mars and is in a wide conjunction with the Moon. Neptune is the supreme "refiner" and its contact with these planets is indicative of the Queen's refined emotional vehicle. She has never demonstrated the arrogance of lower Leo, rather, she has been poised and serene in all her public interactions. Her steady, dedicated service to her country is reflective of the higher note of Leo - "I am That, and That am I". It instructs Leo people to identify with the very highest which is in them and to radiate that inner warmth to the world.

The fact the Queen had robust health all her life is evidence her emotional field was balanced. Consequently, it is quite likely she was being used by her soul to help harmonise the world.

3. Examine the planets. Are their energies healthy or afflicted?

1. Afflicted Planets and Stress.

Potential ill health is found in the natal chart by finding and analysing afflicted planets. This because their forces have been compromised in some way. Their vitalising functions have become toxic. The forces may be repressed, may flow too powerfully, or be otherwise expressed in a manner that is undermining health.

> A general rule to remember is that a well aspected planet is conducive to good health; a poorly aspected or *afflicted* planet indicates the potential for malfunction and disease.

When afflicted planets link up with other planets and points in the chart, they form a 'stress pattern', also called a health or disease pattern in this book.

> Generally, a stress pattern consists of 2 or more planets in aspect to each other (usually a hard aspect), especially if it connects to the health houses - the 6th (acute illnesses) and 12th (chronic illnesses).

Stress patterns in the chart represent shortcomings and limitations in our psychology. Unregenerated, they cause inner conflict, and eventually - a physical or mental illness.

Planet stresses and afflictions in a chart do not necessarily mean disease is imminent. Everyone has them. As previously stated, charts of highly successful people have many planet afflictions. What makes the difference is how we deal with stress. If we learn from our disappointments and challenges to be wiser and make better choices in the future, if we make lifestyle changes to alleviate the stress, if we go forward with positivity rather than succumb to bitterness; potentially we can neutralise a potential health crisis. When stress is removed so that energies can flow freely and healthily, it benefits health.

2. Planets afflicted by sign.

A planet is considered afflicted if it is in a sign that is hostile to its force - a sign in which it *falls* or is in *detriment*. When this occurs, its energy is distorted in some way, is misaligned, has become toxic, is inharmonious; which means potential trouble for health. Afflictions by sign are probably the most important indicators of potential health trouble. Note them carefully.

> The following chart shows the signs in which planet forces are positively strengthened, or are distorted and toxic. This information is critical when analysing the inherent health of the body, of body organs and systems.

Chart 6: Planet Dignities, Detriments, Exaltations and Fall.

Signs	Dignified *strengthened*	Detriment *energy distorted*	Exalted *strengthened*	Falls *energy distorted*
Sun	Leo	Aquarius	Aries	Libra
Moon	Cancer	Capricorn	Taurus	Scorpio
Mercury	Gemini-Virgo	Sagittarius-Pisces	Aquarius	Leo
Venus	Taurus-Libra	Scorpio-Aries	Pisces	Virgo
Mars	Aries-Scorpio	Libra-Taurus	Capricorn	Cancer
Jupiter	Sagittarius-Pisces	Gemini-Virgo	Cancer	Capricorn
Saturn	Capricorn-Aquarius	Cancer-Leo	Libra	Aries
Uranus	Aquarius	Leo	Scorpio	Taurus
Neptune	Pisces	Virgo	Cancer	Capricorn
Pluto	Scorpio	Taurus	Aries	Libra

3. Planets afflicted by aspects.

A planet is considered afflicted if it has many *hard* aspects. Such aspects represent disruptive energies - of the nature of the planets involved.

a. The major hard aspects:

They represent the most disruptive forces:
- The square (□, 90°).
- The opposition (☍, 180°).
- The conjunction (☌, 0°) when it is made by a 'malefic' planet to a 'personal planet,' or to the ascendant.
- Midpoints that contain malefics.

b. Minor hard aspects

The forces these aspects represent, are not usually considered to be as disruptive as the major hard aspects. But do not be fooled. A *minor* negative habit in character (which minor aspects supposedly represent), if it endures across the years will turn into a chronic negative attitude and eventually cause havoc with health. While major planet patterns with hard aspects - such as the t-square, tend to predominate with major health issues; minor aspects are also numerous.

These four minor aspects are often implicated:
- The semi-square (∠, 45°).
- The quincunx or inconjunct (⚻, 150°).
- The sesquiquadrate (⚼, 135°).
- The quindecile (qd, 165°).

c. Easy aspects.
- The trine (△, 120°).
- The sextile (✶, 60°).

Do not dismiss easy aspects when looking for disease patterns. Normally considered to be beneficial, technically they simply indicate an easy flow of energy. If a malefic is involved or a planet is afflicted, an easy aspect can represent the easy flow of toxic energy.

Here are 3 examples.
- *Mars is in Taurus, sextile Saturn in Cancer.* Both planets are in detriment which means - though their forces flow relatively well; this force is toxic.
- *Saturn is in Cancer trine the Sun in the 6H.* Saturn is in detriment and the Sun is in the 6H. This easy flow of toxic force from Saturn will potentially affect heart health.
- *Retrograde Mars in Aries, sextile Mercury in Aquarius.* Retrograde planets also indicate an affliction, toxic flow.

Keep this in mind and use the trine or sextile aspects in a disease pattern if it seems appropriate to do so.

4. Planets afflicted in other ways.

a. Unaspected or retrograde planets. They are considered afflicted. Especially retrograde Mercury, Venus and Mars; and the unaspected Sun, Moon, Mercury, Venus and Mars. The latter are not integrated into the psyche and that is a major problem.

b. 6th - 12th houses. Healthwise, a planet is potentially afflicted if it is located in the 12th house of hospitals or in the 6th house of health.

c. Jupiter and Venus. These are considered to be beneficial and helpful planets - and they are. But in a stress pattern, they can also represent disease effects in the body. Venus can corrupt and weaken, and Jupiter represents over-growth and over-building.

d. The Sun, Moon and Mercury are considered neutral planets. But when afflicted their forces can be toxic. The Sun inflames and over-builds, Mercury spreads airborne germs, and the Moon can represent corruption, decay and the breeding of germs.

4. Examine the 6th and 12 "health" houses.

The 6th house traditionally rules health, the 12th house hospitals (chronic health problems). If planets are connected by hard aspect to these houses, it is a red flag warning for health. The sign on the house cusp, the planet ruler and the sign it is in, planets in the house - a planet connected into these; all could represent organs and systems that potentially could develop problems and become diseased.

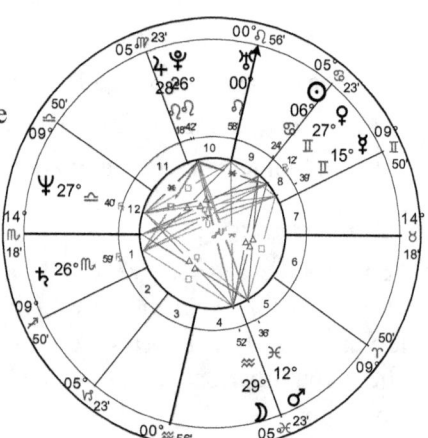

6th House - questions to answer.
1. What sign is on the cusp? (Aries).
2. What parts of the body does that sign rule? Potentially, those parts are susceptible to health problems (skull, head, brain, face, nose, etc).
3. What planet rules the 6H? (Mars in Pisces 5H).
4. Is it afflicted? Yes, by aspect.
   - Square Mercury in Gemini (headaches, nerve pain).
   - Quindecile Jupiter/ Pluto in Leo (serious heart/ arterial blood flow problems).
   - Sesquiquadrate Neptune in Libra 12H (bloodstream, addictions, kidneys).
5. Is there a planet in the 6H? (No).

12th House - questions to answer.
1. What sign is on the cusp? (Libra).
2. What parts of the body does that sign rule? Potentially, those parts are susceptible to chronic health problems (kidneys, urinary tract, bladder; body balance problems).
3. What planet rules the 12H? (Venus in Gemini 8H).
4. Is Venus afflicted? Yes, by aspect.
   - Inconjunct Saturn 1H (depression, kidney disease).
   - Sesquiquadrate Scorpio ascendant (kidney, urinary tract infections, bowel).
5. Is there a planet in 12H? (Neptune in Libra: hidden addictions bloodstream/ lymph, feet; kidney infections).
6. Is Neptune afflicted? Yes, by aspect.
   - Square Uranus in Leo (heart, blood circulation; ankles).
   - Sesquiquadrate Mercury in Gemini 8H (nerves).
   - Sesquiquadrate Mars in Pisces 5H (attacks, inflammation).

Assemble the data.
Nerves, kidneys, the heart and cardiovascular system are emphasised. There may be troubles/ injuries to the head and brain (Aries), and hidden addictions (Neptune, Pisces).

The Health Reading.
Conveying health information to a client or friend is covered more fully in a following section.

Here is an example of a basic reading for a healthy person, when the health component is the third part of a career - love - health reading. It is assembled from data gathered above.

- The Sun. "You have great energy and vitality which will help you fight off disease (well aspected Sun)".
- 6 - 12H. "You are susceptible to headaches and nerve pain. If so, and you resort to smoking, alcohol or drugs to cope, take care to avoid addiction. Long term - and importantly, look after your kidney and heart health. They show potential weaknesses. You can help your heart by avoiding fatty foods, and your kidneys by drinking lots of water." And so on.

Footnote:

The owner of this chart had abundant energy all through the life and excellent health. There were occasional bouts of depression, a smoking addiction and "occasionally could drink too much". In 2022 he had a heart attack. The arteries were blocked. Surgery was successful.

5. Look for a major health warning in the chart.

Major health patterns occur when 3 or more planets are locked together, usually by hard aspect. They are often at the heart of any serious disease, especially if they touch the 12th or 6th houses.

These are the major patterns:

- *T-square:* 2 planets opposite each other and both square a third planet. It represents hard attitudes that if not eased over time, will cause health problems.
- *Grand-cross:* 4 planets in all four quadrants of the chart square and opposing each other. It shows the most serious hardening of attitudes and of potential disease.
- *Easy-opposition:* 2 planets oppose each other, trine and sextile a third planet. The easy aspects promise an easing of the condition, but this is not always the case.
- *Yod:* 2 planets sextile to each other, both inconjunct to a third, which is called "the Finger of God". This is another trouble making pattern. The owner is continually trying to resolve conflicting issues.

Occasionally the astrologer will come across a chart where the health houses do not clearly indicate the part of the body that is diseased. This emphasises the importance of looking outside of a health house if necessary, for a major stress pattern that does represent the trouble. Here are some examples.

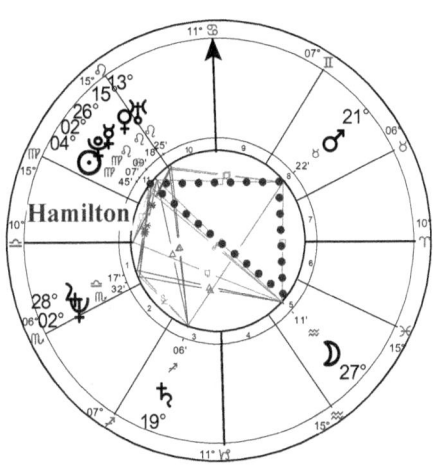

Scott Hamilton (28 August 1958, 09:00 Toledo OH).
Hamilton has had testicular and pituitary cancer. But Scorpio that rules the testes is not on a health house, and Aries, ruler of the pituitary only partially rules the 6th.

The powerful t-square consisting of Mars, Moon and Mercury-Pluto, contains representatives for the pituitary (Mercury) and the testes (Mars and Pluto), and for the troubled cell-life (Moon opp. Pluto). But these planets are not in the health houses.

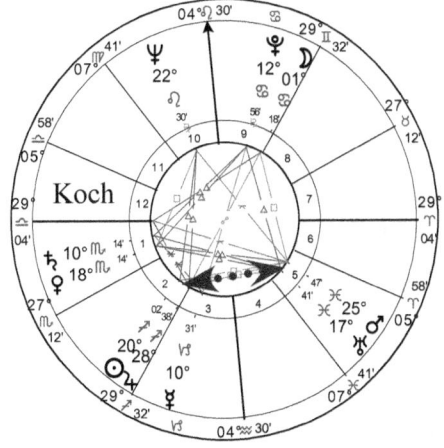

Ed Koch (12 Dec 1924, 03:00, Bronx NY).
Koch was diagnosed with heart arrhythmia in 1991. The only clue we have that there could be heart trouble from the health houses, is because Mars (ruling the 6H), squares the Sun. Things become clearer when the major stress pattern in the chart is examined - four squares bundled together from Sun conjunct Jupiter (rulers of the heart), to Mars and Uranus.

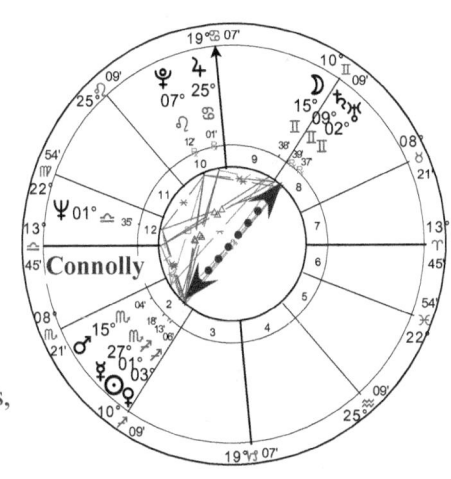

Billy Connolly (24 Nov 1942, 04:30, Glasgow, Scotland).
Connolly was diagnosed with Parkinson's disease - a tremor of the central nervous system. The nerves are ruled primarily by Gemini, also by Aquarius. But these signs are not on the health houses, neither are Mercury, Uranus and Venus (planet rulers of the nerves) in the health houses. The major stress pattern in Connolly's chart is easy to see - the opposition aspects between 5 planets: Mercury - Sun - Venus to the malefics Saturn and Uranus in the 8H of death and transformation. Mercury (the nerves) opposes Uranus (tremors, jerks). This is a signature pattern for Parkinson's.

6. Look for a Health Triangle in the chart.

Triangles in sacred geometry represent balance and harmony. The three-sided shape can be related to the body-mind-spirit Triad, with the upward-facing point indicating the raising of consciousness. Esotericists consider the triangle to be the basic geometric form that underlies the entire fabric of the universe.

> The triangle is the basic geometric form of all manifestation and it is to be seen (by those who have eyes to see) underlying the entire fabric of manifestation, whether it is the manifestation of a solar system, the manifestation of the zodiacal round, the cosmic triplicities or the tiny reflection of this divine triple whole which we call man. [1]

In terms of energy, these 3 points represent:

(1) The force which is pouring in,
(2) the body into which it is pouring, and
(3) the effect.

If the inpouring force is toxic and chronic (eg. chronic negative thinking, ongoing depression, perpetual rage), it causes a chain reaction in the atoms and cells in the body that are affected. In time, the health processes, balances and exchanges of energy will break down and disease will arise.

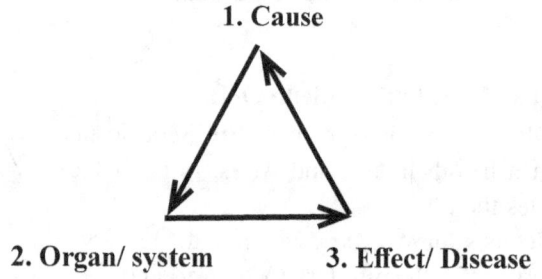

The Health Triangle in a chart is formed by a minimum of three planets in mainly hard aspect, which represent:

(1) The inpouring causal, toxic force,
(2) The organ it is affecting, and
(3) The potential disease.

The triangle/ stress pattern represents:

1. **A psychological or a karmic disturbance.**
2. **... which causes congestion or other trouble in a chakra and an organ.**
3. **... which in turn manifests as a physical disease.**

The astrologer searches the chart to find a minimum of three planets to represent these three factors.

- ▲ **Triangle point 1, the CAUSE (C).** Find the core planet/s that represent the psychological disturbance or karmic-genetic factor that gives birth to the physical disease.
- ▲ **Triangle point 2, the Organ (O).** Find a planet to represent the affected organ, which the disease targets or lodges in.
- ▲ **Triangle point 3, the EFFECT (E).** Find a planet or planets to represent the physical disease and the noticeable impairments that occur in the body and life as a consequence of the disease.

Helpful notes:

- Sometimes it may be best to find the affected organ first. Eg. For heart trouble start with the Sun, for knee trouble start with Saturn. Sometimes starting with the cause planet is preferred. Eg. A stroke, look at Mars; for arthritis start with Saturn. If your chosen planet is afflicted, you have potentially found your candidate.
- When looking for the cause, remember that disease is primarily caused by an emotional disturbance. So, look for a connection from the organ or disease planet, to one of the emotional representatives - the Moon, Mars or Neptune. Or to a planet (or ascendant), in a water sign - Cancer, Scorpio or Pisces, which are related to the emotions. Sometimes, if the cause is karmic or genetic, Saturn or Uranus may represent the cause.

---

1 Bailey, Alice; Esoteric Astrology, 429.

Find a Health Triangle, exercise 1.
Joseph Stalin (18 December 1878), died from a stroke in March 1953.

Time unknown, chart set up at 12 noon, 0 degrees Aries rising. Although the Moon's location in Stalin's chart's is approximate, for the exercise we will work with it as being exact at 12 Libra.

We will search for a Health Triangle to represent the stroke, the affected organ and the psychological cause.

The organ (O) and disease (E) points.
We start by searching for the organ, the brain in this case. The brain in general is ruled by the crown chakra, Aries, and Mars via Aries. The Moon is a ruler of brain tissue.

In Stalin's chart there are no planets in Aries and we see that Mars opposes Pluto, which is sesquiquadrate the Moon, which in turn is semi-square Mars. We have a triangular pattern and these three planets have the ingredients to form the Health Triangle.

Both Mars and the Moon could rule the brain.

Mars rules strokes. It is in the 8H of death, and the stroke killed Stalin. Additionally, Mars opposes Pluto, which carries the 1st ray that "blocks". A stroke is caused by a blocked artery to the brain.

Mars (with Pluto), can be placed at the (E) effect point. This leaves the Moon to represent the brain, the (O) point.

The (C) cause point.
Now our search turns to the emotional/ psychological/ karmic cause behind the stroke.

The Moon and Mars both rule the emotions. Although they have already been used - because we so far have three planets in the pattern; either could be used again for the cause.

While the Moon in Libra does not suit Stalin's personality, Mars in Scorpio opposing Pluto does. In the "emotional expression" list in the previous section we read for Scorpio:

> Holding on to grievances, dark and poisonous emotions, harbouring revenge and thoughts of attack, results in strokes.

Mars opposite Pluto can be placed at the psychological (C) cause point. This means it appears twice in the formula. Consequently, the Health Triangle is written like this.

▲ (C) Mars (opposite Pluto). (O) Moon. (E) Mars, Pluto.

A quick interpretation for this triangle pattern is:

> "A blockage (Pluto carrying ray 1 that blocks), stopped blood flow (Mars) to the brain (Moon), causing a stroke (Mars), that killed him (Pluto, and Mars in the 8H of death)."

Other planets could be linked into the disease effects by following aspects from triangle planets. For instance:
- Pluto is sesquiquadrate Mercury - the stroke paralysed his nervous system.
- Mars is quindecile Neptune which rules the bloodstream. Because it was a blood blockage, we could have included Neptune as an (O) organ planet.
- Pluto is inconjunct the Sun, the stroke killed him.

The black dot always represents the organ

Find a Health Triangle, exercise 2:
Scott Hamilton (28 August 1958, 09:00, Toledo OH), cancer/ tumours in the testes and brain.

Find a Health Triangle for testicular cancer.

Scott Hamilton, a retired American figure skater and 1984 Olympic gold medallist, was diagnosed with testicular cancer in 1997.

The (O) organ point.
The sacral chakra rules the sex organs and Mars is a ruler of the testes. In Hamilton's chart, Mars stands out. It is the dominant point of a T-square and falls in Taurus. Mars is our (O) organ candidate.

The (C) cause point.
Mars squares the Moon. Both these planets rule the emotions. Hamilton was a Virgo Sun perfectionist who rationalised his emotions/ desires and clamped down on them. Suppression of force lies at the root of cancer. This suppression is shown by Moon opposite Pluto, and Mars inconjunct Saturn. Both the Moon and Mars can be placed at the (C) causal point of the triangle. Saturn and Pluto (the indicators of suppression), can be included. This means Mars appears twice.

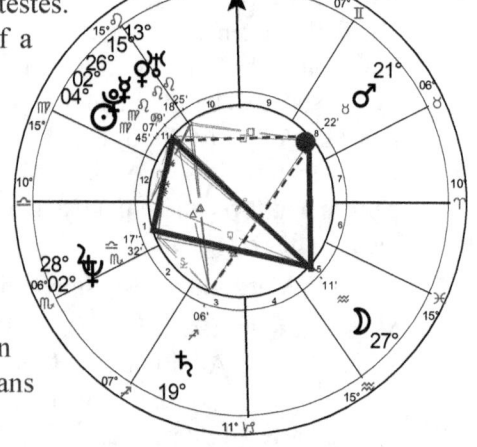

The (E) disease point.
Jupiter is the prime ruler of the force that over-builds. It is in an easy-opposition aspect with the Moon and Pluto. Since Pluto represents dangerous cell malignancies, it can be added.

▲ (C) Moon, Mars (Saturn, Pluto). (O) Mars. (E) Jupiter (Pluto).

Find a Health Triangle for malignant pituitary cancer/ tumours.

Hamilton was first diagnosed with pituitary cancer in 2004. They returned in 2010 and 2016.

The (C) cause and (E) effect points.
The cause and effect points in the previous triangle are re-used, which leaves the organ point.

The (O) organ point.
Venus, as the prime ruler of the ajna chakra, is the prime ruler of the pituitary gland. Mercury - as ruler of Gemini, is a substitute ruler for the gland. They both link into the combination of forces we are working with, as follows.

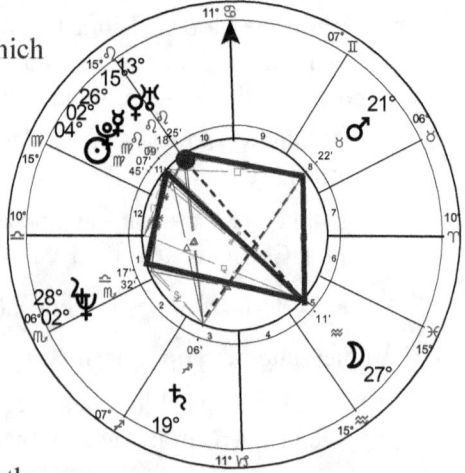

i. Mercury (conjunct Pluto), is in the t-square with Moon and Mars; and is sextile Jupiter.

ii. Venus squares Mars, and is indirectly linked to the Moon:
  - Moon-Venus are related via their respective squares to Mars.
  - Mars is exactly midpoint Venus and the Moon, relating them both.
  - Uranus conjunct Venus, disposits the Moon, forming another link.

Venus does not have a direct aspect to Jupiter. But it is in the second decanate of Leo, which is ruled by Jupiter, Sagittarius.

▲ (C) Moon, Mars (Saturn, Pluto). (O) Venus, Mercury. (E) Jupiter (Pluto).

> *When we include doubled-up planets, we have seven planets for the trouble with the testes, and eight for the pituitary trouble. They all generally slot into one or more of the Cause, Organ and Effect points of the Health Triangle.*

In this section, transits, directions and progressions are used to show readers the method used to examine prevailing astrological conditions for the appearance of a disease. The chart is set for 2016.

Hamilton's Solar-arc Directions, June 2016

The tumours appeared in 2004, 2010 and 2016.

- 2004. The Moon by solar-arc was on the decendant, opposing the ascendant, and all were squared by transit Saturn in Cancer, which formed a t-square. The tumours appeared.
- 2010. Solar-arc Venus was in the 12H at 6 Libra applying to the ascendant. Transit Uranus was in the 6H representing aberrant pituitary growths.
- 2016: (the chart). Solar-arc Uranus and Venus were at 10-11 Libra, sitting on the ascendant. Solar-arc Mars at 18 Cancer was being opposed by transit Pluto from 17-18 Capricorn. Solar-arc Moon and transit Uranus were conjunct at 23 Aries. The whole Health Triangle/ the disease, was active.

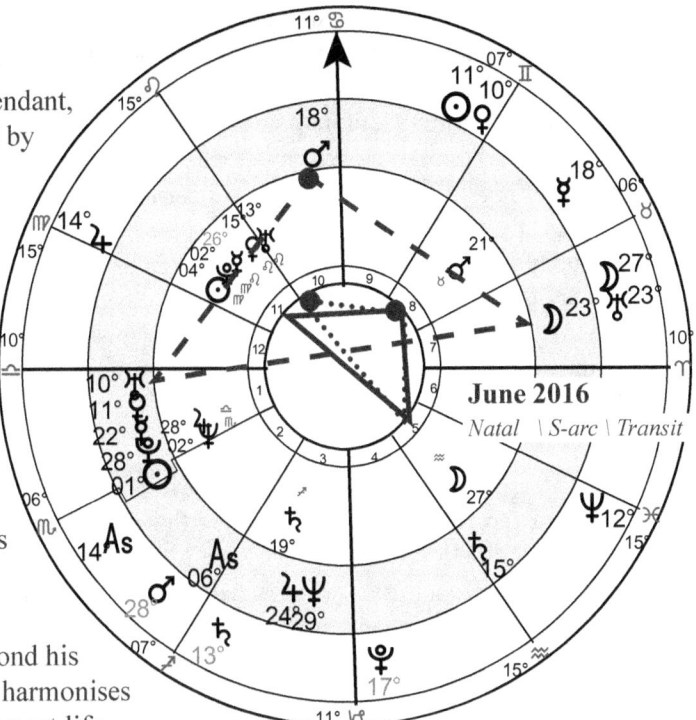

Hamilton is married and says he is blessed beyond his wildest imagination. If he does the inner work, harmonises his stress triangles, the trouble should not recur next life.

Tips to help find links between planets

a. Widen the traditional orbs or rules.

- Widen aspect orbs, especially with the Sun or Moon. Eminent astrologer from early last century, Alan Leo, used orbs up to 15 degrees for the Sun and Moon.
- If you have two favoured planets that are a few degrees beyond an aspect and there are no other suitable candidates, and you are sure that you have not overlooked another more suitable pattern, then extend the orbs. If the disease exists, so does the pattern.
- Planets in opposite signs, even if not in a traditional orb, can be considered hostile to each other. Taking this a step further, consider planets in the same mode (cardinal, fixed or mutable), as being hostile to planets in a different mode.

b. Accept that you have a triangle, even if two of the three planets are not aspecting each other. For example, planet A squares planets B and C, but B and C are not in aspect to each other. Even so, you have three planets to form a triangle and if this is your best option, go with it.

c. Consider dispositorship. A planet disposits all planets located in its sign. Eg. (i). Saturn disposits Mercury in Capricorn, and this creates a link between Mercury and Saturn. (ii). Mercury disposits and is connected to any planet located in its signs - Gemini and Virgo.

d. Consider the decanates. Each sign has three decanates, which are ruled by the signs and ruling planets of the same element.

- If for example, you are looking for a link between Saturn and Mercury, and Mercury is located in the third decanate of Taurus, ruled by Capricorn and Saturn; this creates a link between them.

e. Consider the midpoints. They are a very valuable means of finding non-obvious links between planets. The midpoint degree is a dynamic point where the forces of two planets meet. If for instance, Mercury lies at the midpoint between Saturn and say the Moon, a triangle is formed between the three planets.

Find a Health Triangle, exercise 3:
Jacqueline Du Pre (26 Jan 1945, 11:30, Oxford, UK), multiple sclerosis (MS).

Du Pre was a musical prodigy, a cellist with a brilliant talent. A passionate person (Moon opposite Mars), she released her inner tension through her music and the fiery intensity of her virtuosity brought her fame. MS brought this all to a crashing halt in the early 1970's.

In MS, the immune system attacks the brain and spinal cord relentlessly, never letting up. This is how 1st ray diseases work. MS causes damage to the myelin sheath, the protective covering that surrounds nerve cells. Control of the body is consequently lost as nerve signals slow down then stop. There is a scarring, general atrophying of the body and restriction of movement. The body becomes paralysed. Paralysis is a ray 1 problem.

At the root of autoimmune disease is misuse of the power of thought. Negative thoughts such as self-hatred and self-anger, are directed at the self with such intensity and fervour; the immune system thinks the body is under attack and it reacts. Mars is the primary representative for an immune attack.

Two Health Triangles to investigate.

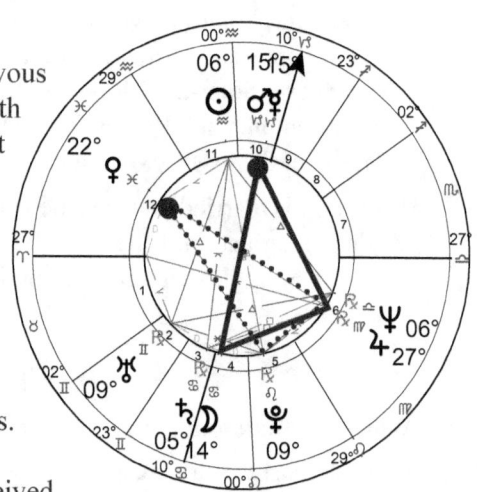

In this exercise, Mercury and Venus that both represent the nervous system will be investigated. They are in different triangles, and both represent the condition. This is being done to show readers that causes behind the emergence of a disease can vary, and they can show up in more than one place in the chart.

Triangle 1.

The (O) organ points. Mercury, the nervous system.

The (C) causal point. Du Pre was emotionally inhibited (the Moon has a wide conjunction to Saturn, which is heavily afflicted in Cancer), a consequence of her own karma and repressive parents. She was also her harshest critic (Mars conjunct Mercury opposing Saturn-Moon), attacking herself with vicious self-talk for her perceived shortcomings. Moon-Mars (with Saturn and Mercury), represent the cause behind the disease.

The (E) effect point. Mars is the first choice for the attacking immune system. Saturn squares Neptune and Jupiter in the 6H of health. These three planets represent the weakening, crippling and paralysing effects of MS. Jupiter also corules the 12H of hospitals and the 8H of death - MS eventually killed Du Pre. Jupiter, Neptune and Saturn can be added to Mars in the (E) point.

Here is the triangle 1.

▲ (C) Moon, Mars, Saturn, Mercury. (O) Mercury. (E) Mars, Saturn, Jupiter, Neptune.

Triangle 2.

The (O) organ points. Venus, the nervous system.

The (C) causal point. Du Pre had deep seated emotional issues. Venus is in Pisces (a sign that rules the emotions), in the 12H, which rules the unconscious. In this hidden part of the mind, negative core beliefs are stored and from there they emerge when triggered. Venus sesquiquadrate Pluto in the 5H of romance, shows a negative belief that love will always die, or that love will destroy you. This inhibited her emotional expression. Venus in Pisces and Pluto represent the cause behind the disease.

The (E) effect point. Pluto is in Leo. Both carry the 1st ray that atrophies, hardens and paralyses - the action of MS. The disease impairs mobility (Jupiter 6H, opposing Venus, square Saturn). Pluto and Jupiter represent the disease effect point.

Here is the triangle 2.

▲ (C) Venus in Pisces (Pluto). (O) Venus. (E) Pluto, Jupiter (Saturn).

Both triangles show the causal factor behind the disease is emotional inhibition (Moon conjunct Saturn, and Venus in Pisces sesquiquadrate Pluto). Moon in the 4H, indicates a pattern inherited from the mother/ from the family. Venus in the 12H, the pattern was already embedded in the unconscious.

Both triangles are valid. But when the disease first struck, the triangle with Mercury was more potent by solar-arc directions. It is wise to test a hypothetical Health Triangle. If the triangle planets are correct, they will make dynamic connections to the natal/ progressed/ directed planets at the time the problem emerges.

Experiment with the triangles. As this exercise has shown,
they can be drawn different ways and with more than three planets.

Disease appearance

The disease began to affect Du Pre in 1971 when she started to lose control of her fingers. Diagnosed in 1973, she stopped playing when she could no longer judge the weight of the bow in her hands. Diseases such as MS are active before symptoms show and Triangle 1 shows the likely activation date is around 1968

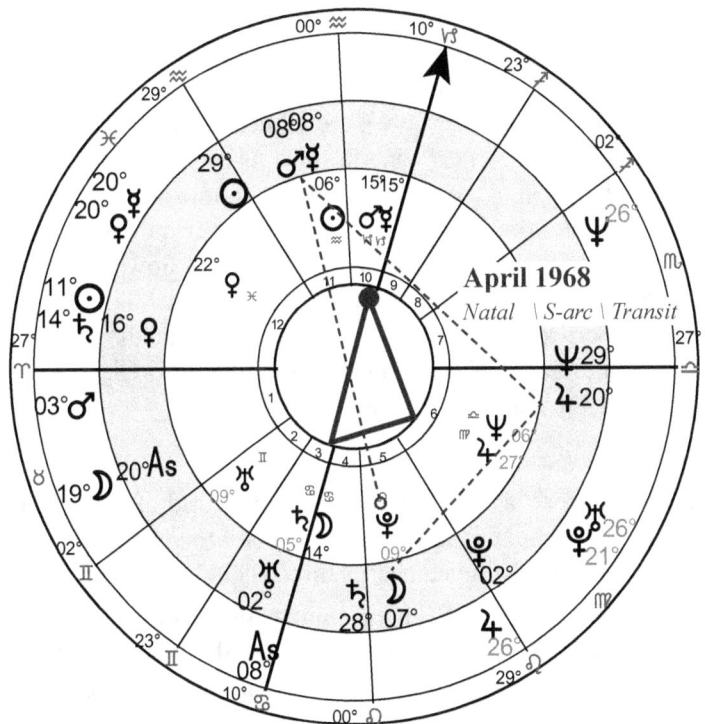

Solar-arc Directions April 1968

- 1968-1970: the Moon by solar-arc was at 7 Leo, moving towards natal Pluto; and solar-arc Mars-Mercury at 8 Aquarius opposed it. The disease was seeded. It must have been accompanied by devastating emotional distress due to the breakdown of her marriage (Pluto co-rules the 7H of marriage.

- Although the Moon had cleared Pluto by 1971, solar-arc Saturn was still moving towards Pluto, marking the relentless progression of the disease.

- During this period, the solar-arc Jupiter point progressed through the 6H and was at 20 Libra, inconjunct natal Venus, linking the two (Mercury and Venus) triangles and marking the onset of the loss of feeling in her hands.

- Mars-Mercury were travelling by solar-arc with the midheaven. Her physical devastation was played out in public adding extra stress.

Du Pre lived for another 17 years, dying on 19 October 1987. Benevolent Jupiter was moving over her ascendant. It is a blessing for the soul to be freed from a seriously impaired body.

This completes this section on finding Health Triangles. Study the three steps involved then work with charts to familiarise yourself with them. Often when you look at a chart, a triangle stands out and each point simply slots into place. Other times, a little more effort is required to put the three points together. Remember to think in terms of energy, and that the problem is due to the misuse of energy.

C. Remedial Advice

1. Counselling.

Once the astrology data has been assembled, the astrologer is ready to counsel. Counselling or psychotherapy is a 3rd ray art that heals through words of wisdom sent forth on the wings of love. The goal is to help people make healthy adjustments in the way they see themselves and their place in the world.

> **Central to the esoteric counselling approach is the concept of the soul. The counsellor's task is to shift the person's identification from the lower troubled self, from the diseased or broken down part of the body, up to the soul. This is the true self, the light-filled, radiant wisdom part of the nature. When this is achieved, the soul has a clearer pathway through the etheric body for healing.**

Using the astrology chart as the reference point, through skilled manipulation with words, energies and subtle suggestions, the astrologer (either consciously or unconsciously) impresses his soul charged personality onto the weakened energies of the client. This helps to draw together the many frayed threads in the person's psyche, and to weave them into a new life-tapestry with the person/ the soul, cast as the central figure. The story of the life and the onset of the disease is retold from a different perspective, bringing into the light the positive side of the experience. Clarity is given, about the higher purpose of the incarnation and how to move positively into the future. That there will be future opportunities and incarnations in which to write a new life story. Any sense of guilt or sin should be eliminated. The notion that we are all here to learn and so-called "mistakes" or "failures" are a normal and natural part of the process of growing in spirit, is emphasised.

In other words, the person's life is reframed, giving it a higher and more meaningful interpretation. This helps to free people from any negative patterns they may be embedded in, so they can move forward. Bringing about an alignment with the soul allows healing light to flow through the mind into the body to facilitate the healing process.

While the counselling work is progressing, while the energies remain quiet and calm between the healer and the client, a vortex of whirling force is created around the two. Energetically, the client is being lifted out of the stagnant pool of energies in which he or she has become mired. By bringing in new and higher forces, the astrologer promotes a condition to support the healing process.

The world of energies.

To do this work, astrologers look into the world of energies represented by astrology. The goal is to find blockages to energy (hard planet aspects) in the chart/ the client's psyche, and give advice on how to remove them/ heal them/ straighten the misaligned energy threads out.

> **Human beings are energy units functioning in a world of energies, blockages within the mental, emotional and etheric bodies hinder the life-sustaining forces pouring in from the soul and Sun so that parts of the physical body become under-nourished. This results in disease.**

The astrologer identifies these blockages, where they lie, what is causing them and how to get rid of them. This is the core part of astrological work that no other professional group can match - in terms of the preciseness and detail which the astrologer can bring to bear to suit the individual client.

As a Master said:

> Astrology is essentially the purest presentation of occult truth in the world at this time, because it is the science which deals with those conditioning and governing energies and forces which play through and upon the whole field of space and all that is found within that field. [1]

To emphasise the points that have been made - the prime work is to adjust misaligned energies, to straighten out and harmonise the psychological forces.

Note. You do not have to be a professional to offer counselling advice. Just approach each session as a helpful friend would, one who has the best interests of the person at heart. Skill grows with practice.

---

[1] Bailey, Alice A; Esoteric Astrology, 5.

1a. Three types of clients.
Broadly, people are at three different levels of evolutionary development in the way they perceive and approach life, and the counselling approach is adjusted to the client's level. Here is an over-view of these three levels, remembering that individuals are complex and cannot be so easily type-cast.

i. *The emotional client.* The solar plexus chakra is dominant. Although the mind is awake, the emotions are more powerful and control decision making and the way life is viewed. Such people are often beset by negative emotions, fear and depression. So, care must be taken because one negative word could drown out a hundred positives. Because personality will has not yet been developed (it requires a determined and dominant mind), those in this group usually find it hard to stick to a healing program. This type of client wants emotional healing.

ii. *The intelligent, non-spiritual client.* He or she is working through the throat and ajna chakras. Intellectually alive, the will is strong, but the client has not yet consciously awakened to the higher spiritual realities. Such intellectuals are often quick to dismiss astrology as nonscientific. Which means that those who consult an astrologer will likely be open to the notion of the psychology-disease effect, the power of the mind and positive thinking, the notion of soul, karma etc. Recommend a meditation that will facilitate healing, explaining how it will help, the effects of positive visualisation. This type of client is seeking knowledge and has the will to put what is learnt into action. They will stick to a healing program if they think it will benefit them.

iii. *A client 'on the Path' - mystics and disciples.* The crown and heart chakras are activated. This intelligent person has awakened to the higher spiritual realities in an esoteric, not a fundamentalist religious sense. He or she is actively seeking contact with the soul and higher realities through spiritual practices such as meditation. Consciousness is developed and informed, and those in this group are comfortable with all psychological, spiritual, esoteric, life-death discussions. They are seeking information.

1b. Introducing the link between psychology and disease.
Traditional medicine is slowly making the link between psychology and disease, between our mental and emotional states and the many disorders that plague us. For instance, there is a general acceptance that unrelieved mental and emotional stress contributes to high blood pressure and that depression weakens the effectiveness of the immune system. But generally, medicine still looks to external factors as a cause of disease.

> The esoteric view is that most complaints in individual average man are based upon an emotional cause or a clearly defined desire. These compel people to act in ways or do things that result in disease. For instance, emotional anxiety may compel people to take drugs to alleviate anxiety, so they become addicted. Unresolved anger may cause people to rant and rave so they have a stroke or an accident.

Well-established emotional and mental attitudes, habits and preferences that produce disease, stem from previous incarnations. Until expunged, they follow us karmically from life to life in our genetic make-up, showing up in our natal chart.

Astrologers are esotericists and medical astrologers lead the way in making the link between psychology and disease. In the future, astrology will have a respected part to play in mainstream psychology. Negative patterns that could potentially result in a disease, or patterns that are related to a disease that has already manifested - these will be identified, and mental-physical exercises will be given to balance these warring forces. Djwhal Khul said:

> The Science of the Centres, the Science of the Rays and the Science of Astrology. These three sciences will constitute the three major departments of the Science of Psychology in the New Age. [1]

The link between psychology and disease can be introduced simply. For example:

> When health is good. "You are fortunate to have good health. To maintain this, it is important to ensure your outlook on life is positive because the way we think and feel - in time, has a direct impact on health. Negative thoughts and emotions are detrimental to good health. Positive thoughts and feelings are healing".

> When a health issue has manifested: "You can greatly benefit your physical health by attending to your inner health. Your condition is a combination of stress and negative thinking. It is the same for all of us. Negative thoughts and emotions are detrimental to good health. Positive thoughts and emotions are beneficial".

---

[1] Bailey, Alice; Esoteric Psychology II, 479.

2. Giving remedial advice from the chart.

In health counselling, because disruptive emotions are most often the root cause of the manifested trouble, advice will almost always focus on balancing and harmonising the emotions. In life, this is usually achieved through maturity. By 'growing up'. By developing the mind and using the knowledge and experience it contains to apply the exercises and disciplines necessary to make better life choices. This process - developing maturity and wisdom through experience, will most often form the basis of counselling advice. The following points will help achieve this:

a. Identify the emotions and the planet, at the root of the health problem. (Call this planet C, for 'causal' planet).

b. Give remedial advice, based on the house and sign that planet C is located in, and its aspects.

c. Examine the esoteric planet that rules C's sign. The development of its higher qualities and those of its sign, and their healthy expression through the house it is in; these will help to heal the toxicity causing the trouble. Since the esoteric planets represent the energies of the soul and its intentions, this advice is crucially important for healing.

d. At times, it may be appropriate to give development advice for the ascendant sign, which represents the 'purpose of the soul' in the current incarnation (in terms of spiritual growth). This will help heal all parts of the life.

Remedial advice, example 1. Jacqueline Du Pre.

The following suggestions are brief, but they give the idea.

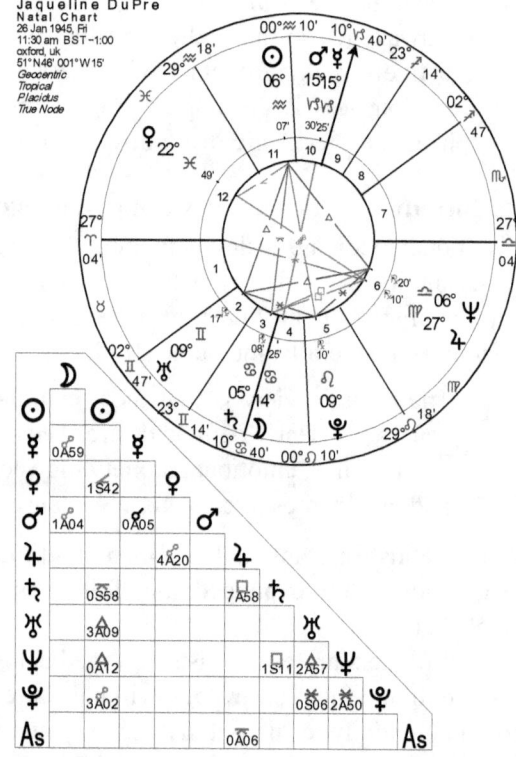

a. Identify the emotions and the planet at the root of the health problem. *Moon in Cancer 4H; is the problem planet.*

Du Pre's problematic emotions are represented by the Moon in Cancer conjunct Saturn in Cancer - fear of rejection, and the erection of protective psychological barriers that stifle emotional expression and health. These difficulties are family inherited.

b. Advice, based on the house and sign the Moon is located in, and its aspects. *Moon is in Cancer in the 4H, conjunct Saturn, and opposed to Mars-Mercury in the 10H.*

There are no easy aspects to the Moon. Easy aspects represent easy, even pleasurable things to do, to help heal difficulties. Hard aspects indicate hard work, hard effort and discipline.

Her difficulty is family inherited (4H). With Aries rising, she must strive to free herself from family negativity and be independent. With Mercury-Mars in 10, make efforts to develop a positive self-image, and to be assertive in her projection and speech - especially in career and family matters.

c. Advice, based on the esoteric planet ruler of the Moon sign (Cancer). *Neptune in Libra 6H, is the esoteric ruler of Cancer.*

The esoteric ruler of the Moon sign - Cancer, is Neptune in Libra. This means its location (6H) and situation, is key to the inner development work which is required, to free the soul from emotional negativity.

Refinement and balance in relationships is being demanded. Working hard (Neptune square Saturn), to develop her musical skills, her artistry, her interactions with her co-workers etc (6H); these would contribute to this refinement and healing. Her achievements would increase her self-confidence and self-value (trine Sun and Uranus 2H). So would, metaphysical study and spiritual healing which Neptune also represents.

d. Advice from the ascendant sign, and the esoteric ruler of that sign.

With Aries rising, Mercury in Capricorn 10H, is the esoteric ruler of the chart, of the life.

With Aries rising, soul purpose is to be assertive, a leader of her own life and that of others. To learn to communicate assertively (Mercury), regarding issues related to her career. This makes Mercury's message doubly important.

Note. The fact that MS developed, informs us that Du Pre was unable to overcome her stifling fear and defensive wall-building. This is not unusual. It can take more than one life to fully heal a negative pattern deeply embedded in the unconscious. Du Pre will have another opportunity next life to make further corrections.

Remedial advice, example 2. Digestive trouble.

a. Identify the emotions and the planet at the root of the health problem.
Moon in Scorpio, 4/5H, is the problem planet.

The owner of this chart has had digestion problems since childhood, chronic pain and inflammation. Difficulty digesting food is related to difficulty digesting life.

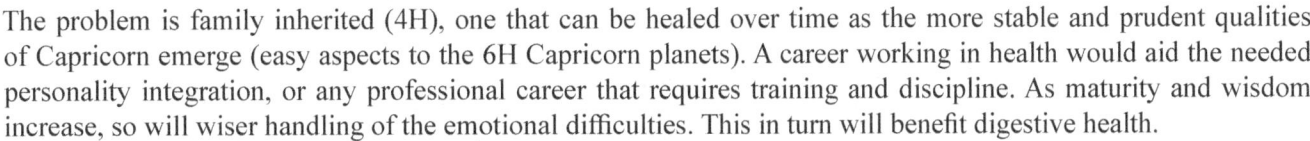

The Moon, which rules the stomach, digestion and the emotions; is heavily afflicted in Scorpio, conjunct Pluto. This indicates very intense, churning emotions, drama, wanting to control circumstances in order to feel safe, resorting to anger and stubbornness as a defence (quindecile Mars in Taurus). This is mirrored in the digestive system. The difficulty is exacerbated by a liking for fatty and sweet foods (Moon square Jupiter and Venus). Common sense advice would include dietary information.

b. Advice, based on the house and sign the Moon is located in, and its aspects. *Moon is sextile the Sun, Neptune, Uranus in Capricorn, in the 6H of health and work.*

The problem is family inherited (4H), one that can be healed over time as the more stable and prudent qualities of Capricorn emerge (easy aspects to the 6H Capricorn planets). A career working in health would aid the needed personality integration, or any professional career that requires training and discipline. As maturity and wisdom increase, so will wiser handling of the emotional difficulties. This in turn will benefit digestive health.

Additionally, the problem could be assisted by spiritual healing (Moon sextile Neptune) and/ or by following the advice of a professional natural therapist (sextile Uranus in Capricorn).

c. Advice, based on the esoteric planet ruler of the Moon sign (Scorpio).

The esoteric ruler of the Moon sign - Scorpio, is Mars. This means its location and situation is key to the inner development work which is required, to free the soul from the binding 'prison of the soul' (Moon) pattern that limits its creativity and expression. Mars is afflicted in Taurus, and a hard quindecile aspect to the Moon indicates the pattern is deeply ingrained and ongoing effort will be required to overcome the habit. But because Mars *is* the esoteric ruler of the Moon, this must be done to free this person from negative emotions and thinking.

Because Mars is located in the 11H, interaction with friends, groups, and organizations will bring the drama-filled reactions to the surface (aggressively causing trouble, arguments, conflict). The incentive to change, to become a valued team-player and member, will be driven by a desire not to lose valued friends, or to be expelled from important groups the person is deeply invested in. This information is carefully explained to the person receiving the reading.

d. Advice from the ascendant sign, and the esoteric ruler of that sign.
With Cancer rising, the esoteric ruler of the chart is Neptune, 6H.

With Cancer rising - and Neptune being the esoteric ruler of the ascendant sign, of the chart and of the life; refinement of emotional expression in relationships, is the paramount developmental life goal. Neptune is afflicted by sign - as are the other two emotional rulers, Mars and the Moon. This repeats the message that emotional expression is in great need of refinement, healing, balancing.

Additionally - with Neptune conjunct the Sun and Uranus, the person could be encouraged to undertake a serious study of spiritual and esoteric teachings, to practice spiritual disciplines such as meditation. The wisdom and knowledge gained would strengthen the personality, help the emotional work, and this in turn would benefit the digestive problems. All this is carefully explained.

Note. The esoteric forces combine with the orthodox planets and do not negate their influence. They supplement and dominate them. The man is thereby enriched and his consciousness expanded by the new energies... the new influences will condition and motivate gradually and steadily all his activities. [1]

---

1 Bailey, Alice; Esoteric Astrology, 139-140.

Remedial advice, example 3. Obsessive Compulsive Disorder.

a. Identify the emotions and the planets at the root of the health problem. *Moon - Mars in Taurus 12H, are the problem planets.*

The owner of this chart was a diagnosed with OCD. The condition is characterized by being driven by compelling emotions/ desires to perform repeated rituals (ray 7, Uranus), in order to stave off an imagined disaster.

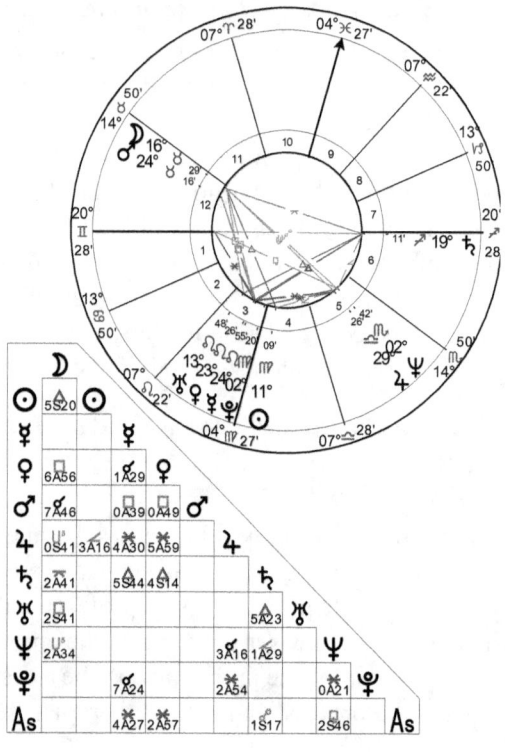

The source of the problem is the Moon-Mars conjunction in Taurus - the sign of desire. Because they are in the 12H, the impulse driving the trouble is embedded very deeply in the unconscious and will be a challenge to change. Since we know that the soul is on a journey to enlightenment, we also know that everything changes in time, even the deepest, buried, negative beliefs. The chart indicates forced change will begin in this incarnation.

The compelling urge to perform rituals is represented by Uranus (square the Moon). Since Uranus is located in the 3H of lower mind, it suggests a cycling pattern of negative and chaotic thinking underlies the trouble.

b. Advice, based on the house and sign Moon-Mars are located in, and their aspects. *Moon-Mars sextile the Sun in Virgo, 4H.*

There is one easy aspect to the Moon, a trine to the Virgo Sun in the 4H. Easy aspects are preferred to hard aspects, because their energies make it easier to make the desired changes. They represent activities that are easier, more pleasurable.

In this case, the person could be encouraged to draw on wise and discriminating assistance from parents/ family, while in therapy. Additionally or alternatively, to build and create her own healthy and stable family base and be very discriminating about who she admits into her inner sanctum.

c. Advice, based on the esoteric planet ruler of the Moon sign. *Vulcan in Virgo, 4H.*

The esoteric ruler of the Moon sign - Taurus, is Vulcan. It is located within 8 degrees of the Sun, between the Sun and Mercury (so somewhere within the range of 3 to 11 degrees of Virgo, placing it most likely in the 4H). So, everything said in the previous (Sun in the 4H) statement is accentuated. Vulcan's outstanding function is purification. Its location in the 4H suggests there may be unhealthy dynamics within the family that need pruning, even cutting away. This level of advice could centre around that.

d. Advice from the ascendant sign, and the esoteric ruler of that sign.

With Gemini rising, Venus in Leo 3H; is the esoteric ruler of the chart.

Becoming a wise messenger, and distributing words of beauty and wisdom into the local environment is the important life task (soul purpose), for this person. An avenue through which this could be achieved is to teach children (Venus rules the 5H), or to write books (3H), which would help to enhance and beautify people's lives.

In relation to OCD, since Venus' higher task is to beautify the mind and thought life, if this is attended to, it would help heal or overwrite the negative self-talk which is at the root of the problem. The real task is to learn to focus the mind and keep in the present moment, not let it drift back to the past and into unhealthy imaginings. This is only achieved through self-training. Mindfulness meditation could be recommended.

Note. In psychology, the ascendant sign represents the soul and its purpose in the incarnation. The Sun represents the personality, the conscious self, individual power, autonomy and control. The Moon represents the unconscious self, the prison of the soul pattern - our past emotional, unresolved baggage. In terms of development, to overcome the negatives of the Moon sign, development of the Sun and ascendant sign qualities are preferred. Development of the ascendant sign qualities will balance and heal all Sun and Moon sign negatives.

3. Suggested remedial meditations/ exercises.

1. Better health though diet/ lifestyle.
A moderate and balanced lifestyle with adequate exercise, bathing, fresh air, sunlight, and a diet based largely upon clear water, fresh fruit and vegetables, nuts and grains will result in better assimilation of the pranic fluids, improving the vitality of the etheric body and physical organs. Salt sea bathing is beneficial - water absorbed through the skin and by the mouth helps to prevent disease. Minimal consumption of meat is recommended, especially when one is sick. Vegetarianism is preferred. On the sexual level, promiscuity or wrong techniques introduce germs into the body. Balance, moderation and cleanliness is required throughout.

2. Meditation.
When energies are blocked due to negative psychological patterns, the application of a suitable spiritual discipline such as meditation is recommended. Meditation is calming and balancing and it contributes to emotional healing and balancing. As we meditate on topics like the love and wisdom of God and the beauty of Mother Nature, consciousness fills with beneficial energies and this is beneficial. There are many books that will teach the basic principles of meditation. If practiced daily and across time, the habitual patterns of thought that are the problem can be overwritten by the new and positive patterns of thought. Here are some simple but very effective meditations.

a. A Garden Meditation
In your mind's eye, find a beautiful spot in nature and imaginatively create a garden. Select flowers, shrubs and trees, add rocks or water features to maximise its beauty. Each day return to your garden in meditation. Tidy it, do weeding if necessary, replanting and reconstructing if you wish to. But mainly, drink in the beauty, serenity, and healing energies of the garden. Imagine as you breathe in the fragrant beauty of your garden that every cell in your body is being filled with light. Finally, send a blessing of peace and love to the world.

b. A simple meditation on Light.
Place your consciousness in the middle of your head and endeavour to hold it there.
Silently and slowly say each line, visualising that line as you go.

> There is only one supreme Life.
> That great Being is the source of all Light and Love in the world.
> I am a ray of Light emanating from that great Life
> All souls on earth are rays of light, emanating from that Life.
> I am one with all those rays of Light.
> I am one with that source of Light.
> I am that Light, that Self am I.

c. Invoking love and light - the 'noon mantra'.
This mantra is to be sounded (silently or out loud), every day at noon. It brings the energy fields into alignment with the stream of love emanating from the heart of God. It removes energy blocks, and opens the heart chakra.

Think of all the suffering in the world and feel compassion begin to flow from your heart.
Visualise the Sun as Deity, the source of all Life, shining love and goodness all over the earth.
Connect to the sun with a line of light. Then say -

> "O Lord of Light and Love I know about the need;
> Touch my heart anew with love,
> that I too may love and give." OM

See the light of the Sun shine through your heart, out into the world for healing.

3. Positive thinking - "Think an opposite thought."
This technique trains the mind to think positively, but it requires continuous effort to be successful. Whenever you catch yourself thinking critically about someone or something, think an opposite positive/ kind/ compassionate thought. Find something admirable in the person and acknowledge that. Alternatively, imaginatively hold the person in the light and love of their soul or God.

When successfully applied this technique improves health because it removes negative emotional-mental habits that cause most of our diseases. It also accelerates spiritual growth, because when we remove impediments to soul flow, increased light and wisdom flows through the mind and heart.

4. Cultivate positive qualities to benefit health.
a. Develop *goodwill*. Sending goodwill to all people in the world heals respiratory tract, lung and throat diseases. This positive force stabilises brain cells, cures insanities and obsessions, establishes equilibrium, rhythm and leads to greater life longevity. [1]

b. Develop *harmlessness*. Strive to be inclusive, kind and harmless. This allows higher energies to flow in and these have the power to arrest the progression of a disease. [2] Whenever a harmful thought appears in the mind, immediately practise the "think an opposite thought" technique.

5. Exercises, visualisations to increase vitality.
Sedentary and lazy lifestyle habits make the whole system sluggish, so that vitalisation of the body and circulation of nourishing life and prana to all cells in the body is diminished. This is related to a variety of diseases including dementia. Brain cells do not receive adequate vitalisation.

a. Daily moderate exercise such as walking will keep circulation moving healthily.

b. Visualising prana 1: One technique is to visualise golden prana surrounding the spleen - not the physical organ, but the etheric area surrounding it and picture it as bathed in pure golden prana.

c. Visualising prana 2: Another technique is to visualise solar prana flowing into the pranic triangle (which includes the etheric spleen), and circulating around it three times before being transmitted to all parts of the etheric vehicle and from then to the dense physical body.

d. A third technique is to bare the back to the sun for a few minutes daily. This makes it easier for prana to be absorbed.

Pranic Triangle between shoulder blades above diaphragm Spleen

6. Clearing, vitalising the chakras.
Balance and tone up the chakras by breathing colour energy through them.
Visualise your etheric body and the chakras. Then starting from the base chakra and working upwards:

Breathe in, visualise a colour. On the out-breath, imagine an energy stream of that colour is washing through the chakra - flushing, balancing and healing. Gradually fade the colour to pure white. Simultaneously - while you are doing that, sound an OM through the chakra. Finally, see the chakra healthy and vibrant. Do the same for all the chakras.

Recommended colours - or use your own colours. Base - red. Sacral - orange. Solar plexus - pale blue. Heart - gold. Throat - electric blue. Brow - indigo blue. Crown - violet or white.

7. Colour therapy.
Wear these colours, or bathe yourself in coloured light.
- Violet and orange help the etheric body. Orange stimulates the action of the etheric body and the chakras, removes congestion and increases the flow of prana.
- Gold strengthens the etheric web and its flow.
- Rose improves the nervous system, removes depression and its symptoms and increases the will to live.
- Green being the colour of nature has a general healing effect, especially on the dense physical body. It helps ease inflammation and fever.

Note. These are just a few suggestions. They are easy to apply, but are very effective in making changes to how energy flows into and through the body.

---

1 Bailey, Alice A; Esoteric Healing, 108.
2 Ibid, 40.

4. HEALTH READINGS.

The healer must understand also how to radiate, for the radiation of the soul will stimulate to activity the soul of the one to be healed and the healing process will be set in motion; the radiation of his mind will illumine the other mind and polarise the will of the patient; the radiation of his astral body, controlled and selfless, will impose a rhythm upon the agitation of the patient's astral body, and so enable the patient to take right action, whilst the radiation of the vital body, working through the splenic centre, will aid in organising the patient's force-body and so facilitate the work of healing. Therefore, the healer has the duty of rendering himself effective, and according to what he is, so will be the effect upon the patient. When a healer works magnetically and radiates his soul force to the patient, that patient is enabled more easily to achieve the end desired—which may be complete healing, or it may be the establishing of a state of mind which will enable the patient to live with himself and with his complaint, unhandicapped by the karmic limitations of the body. Or it may be enabling the patient to achieve (with joy and facility) the right liberation from the body and, through the portal of death, to pass to complete health. [1]

---

[1] Bailey, Alice A; Esoteric Healing, 7-8.

Helpful charts

Chart 7 ||. This is an important chart. It describes the pathology of the 7 RAYS when their forces become toxic, and gives examples of the types of diseases they are responsible for.

Chart 7: RAYS: Psychology - Disease - Astrology

	Ray pathology.	*Diseases by Ray.*	*Astrology.*
Ray 1	Abstracts, ages, atrophies, contracts, hardens, crystallises, stiffens, kills.	When imperfect, this energy crystallises, hardens, restricts, blocks, reduces, atrophies, paralyses, and ages. It is relentless and unstoppable, and when chronic, its diseases move inexorably towards death - whether rapid or lingering. Alzheimer's, arthritis, arteriosclerosis, clots, comas, cripples, heart disease via ageing, osteoporosis.	Pluto, Saturn. Aries, Leo, Capricorn.
Ray 2	The building-growth ray. Over-develops, causes uncontrolled growth, too many atoms, excess.	When imperfect, R2 overstimulates. Excess energy pours in, more than the body can handle. The result is multiplication of atoms, inappropriate growths such as tumours and cancer, and extra body parts. Amyloidosis, arteriosclerosis, bloating, cancer, cholesterol (high), congestion, gigantism, gluttony.	Sun, Jupiter. Gemini, Virgo, Pisces.
Ray 3	Mental force that twists, turns; the mind is misused to steal, lie.	When malfunctioning, the intelligent functioning of body systems can go awry. Eg. endocrine malfunction. There may be excessive energy and smothering in one direction, and energy-starvation in another. Dyslexia, dyspepsia, fatigue - thyroid, gastric disorders, STDs, endocrine dispensing wrong hormones.	Saturn, Earth. Cancer, Libra, Capricorn.
Ray 4	Mental force in constant conflict, upsets emotions, debilitates.	The combative force of ray 4, is responsible for devitalisation, emotional swings, allergic reactions, mucous build up - and on a global level, epidemics and pandemics. Abscesses, allergic reactions, asthma, bronchitis, chronic fatigue, colds, flu, excess mucous.	Moon, Mercury. Taurus, Scorpio, Sagittarius.
Ray 5	Mental force that divides, separates, alienates.	Causes many modern psychological disorders. Nervous system troubles. Eg. Brain lesions, migraine, diseases caused by wrong thinking, pituitary cancers/ tumours.	Venus. Leo, Sagittarius, Aquarius.
Ray 6	Emotional force, volatile or repressed.	This energy when virulent via Mars, is acidic and burns. Eg. Accidents, fevers, autoimmune diseases/ attacks, blood poisoning, rashes, ulcers, murders. When virulent via Neptune, diseases are obscure, hard to see, find and treat. Escapism, drug/ alcohol abuse, sexual perversions.	Mars, Neptune. Virgo, Sagittarius, Pisces.
Ray 7	Causes aberrations, cell promiscuity, mutations.	When awry, fosters the activity of germs, infections, and bacteria within the medium which best nurtures them. Infections and contagious diseases. Electrical system malfunctions. Eg. Via Uranus, arrhythmia, seizures, spasms, wild and uncontrolled growth. Problems with circulation and blood quality.	Uranus. Aries, Cancer, Capricorn.

Chart 8 ||. As consciousness rises through the chakras, our psychology expands, becomes wiser, more intelligent. This CHAKRAS chart can be used to diagnose disease by chakra development pathology.

Chart 8: CHAKRAS: Body - Disease - Astrology.

Chakra	*Negative psychology by chakra.*	*Body parts and systems ruled by the chakras.*	*Diseases in the chakra regions.*	*Astrology.*
Crown	Wilfulness, wanting to dominate. (Force pours down into the base chakra).	Pineal gland. Head, brain, cerebrum, consciousness thread, right eye, sleep, sutratma.	Pineal trouble. Aneurisms, brain diseases, cerebral palsy, dementia, insanity, meningitis, strokes.	Pluto, Vulcan, Uranus. *Aries.*
Ajna	Anti-social, aloofness, separativeness, divisiveness, cold and clinical analysis without heart or feeling. Sectarianism.	Pituitary gland. Face, ears, eyes, lower brain, mental comprehension, nervous system, nose, vision.	Pituitary trouble. Epilepsy, eye-ear troubles, headache, insanity, mental problems, migraine, nervous disorders.	Venus, Mercury. *Gemini.*
Throat	Mental dishonesty, trickery, lying, manipulation, fraud, theft, white collar crimes. Psychopathic.	Thyroid gland. Airways, Breath, breathing, lower brain, ears, mouth, palate, sinuses, speech organs, teeth. Neck: larynx, trachea, carotid gland. Endocrine system, gastrointestinal tract - intestines, lymphatic system.	Thyroid trouble, goitre. Asthma, breathing and gastric problems, speech difficulties. Lymphatic trouble, excess phlegm.	Venus, Mercury, Saturn. *Taurus. Virgo for intestines, Scorpio for elimination.*
Heart	Giving too much care and concern. Naivety, fear and anxiety. Group work for material gain.	Thymus gland. Blood, cardiovascular system, cell-life, heart, immune system, lower lungs, prana, spleen, vitality.	Thymus trouble. Heart, blood, cardiovascular, circulation troubles. AIDS, autoimmune diseases, tuberculosis.	Sun, Jupiter. *Leo/ Aquarius.*
Solar plexus	Emotionalism: reactive, volatile, repressed. Fearfulness, anger, cruelty. Sociopathic.	Pancreas gland. Emotions. Abdominal area, digestion - gallbladder, liver, stomach. Sympathetic nervous system.	Pancreas trouble. Diabetes, digestive trouble, nervous trouble caused through emotionalism.	Moon, Mars, Neptune. *Cancer.*
Sacral	Misuse of sex, sexual perversions, sadism. Driven by powerful desires.	Gonads. Etheric, sex life. DNA, Etheric body, foetal development, gestation, reproduction, sex life and organs.	Reproductive organs and sex problems. Foetal abnormalities, genetic disorders, venereal diseases.	Uranus, Mars. *Scorpio, Sagittarius.*
Base	Wilfulness, aggression, hardness, bullying, inflexible, crystallised attitudes.	Adrenals, fight or flight, flesh, substance, integumentary system, skeleton, spinal column, kidneys, urinary tract. Kundalini fire.	Adrenal trouble. Crystallisation, hardening of tissue, inflamed meninges, kidney - urine infections/ diseases. Spine, joint, bone problems.	Pluto, Saturn. *Libra, Capricorn, Aquarius, Pisces.*

Chart 9 ||. This chart features the SIGNS. It is most useful for identifying the sign that rules any part of the body. It also includes types of diseases each sign is responsible for, when its force goes awry.

Chart 9: SIGNS: body parts ruled and disease.

Signs	Chakras/ body parts signs rule/ are related to.	Diseases the signs cause.
Aries	Crown chakra, pineal. Skull, head, the brain, face, nose, upper jaw.	Aries fire strikes suddenly - strokes, brain meningitis, head injuries.
Taurus	Throat chakra, thyroid. The neck and all within it including the tonsils, the upper digestive tract.	Fosters unregulated desire, gluttony that can lead to weight gain and diseases like diabetes.
Gemini	Ajna, throat chakras, pituitary, thymus. Nervous system. Brainstem, pons, medulla oblongata, cerebellum. Ears, speech, bronchi, oxygenation. Shoulders, arms, hands, fingers.	Promotes the rapid spread of air-borne pathogens and pollutants that can evolve into epidemics such as influenza.
Cancer	Solar plexus, pancreas. Digestion, stomach, gallbladder, liver. The physical form, tissue, flesh. Stem cells. Reproduction: pregnancy, gestation, birth, female reproduction cycles. Body containers: breasts, womb. White body fluids, lymphatic sys.	Causes seepy, watery, damp, infectious, lethargic and devitalising diseases. With the Moon, troubled emotions that are the cause of most individual diseases. Diseases we inherit genetically, through our family line.
Leo	Heart chakra, thymus. The heart/ cardiovascular, vitalisation, vitality of the immune system. Spinal column and vertebrae.	As an afflictor, Leo burns and inflames.
Virgo	Throat, solar plexus. The intestines, intestinal digestion.	Promotes criticalness, worry, fretfulness, peevishness, all of which can lead to niggling problems with the bowels.
Libra	Ajna, solar plexus, sacral, base. Balancing, regulating. Pancreas: Islets of Langerhans. Adrenals, kidneys: urinary tract, bladder. Sexual relationships.	Diseases that are adaptive, acute and may strike suddenly - like cystitis.
Scorpio	Throat chakra: elimination. Sacral: sex, reproduction. Base chakra: adrenal medulla 'fight or flight' reaction. Also rules death.	Sluggish, damp conditions that are slow-moving, chronic. Thick body fluids - phlegm. Anger poisons the blood - nasty skin conditions, ulcers. Inner conflict grinds down vitality, undermining immunity.
Sagittarius	Sacral. Physical power, hips, thighs, buttocks, mobility, locomotion.	Problems of excess, obesity and associated problems that impair the liver or mobility. Horse-riding accidents.
Capricorn	Base chakra. The main-frame rigid skeleton, bones, bony structure, joints (especially knees), tendons, ligaments, cartilage that tie the body together. Skin, teeth, hair.	With its ruler Saturn, its force chills, it hardens and ages.
Aquarius	Heart, sacral, base. Lower legs, calves, ankles. Electrochemical activity of the nervous system via Uranus. Blood circulation/ quality. Etheric body, DNA.	Upsets the nervous system/ messaging. EG, neural pathways may atrophy (autism). Interference in the energy play between the pineal and pituitary glands (migraine).
Pisces	Throat, heart, base. Feet. Body fluids, lymphatic sys, bloodstream. Governs sleep with Neptune.	Overstimulation of cells - fatness, tumours and cancer. Excess fluid. Troubled waterways. Obscure diseases. Drug/ alcohol abuse, addictions.

Chart 10 ||. PLANETS are the prime indicators of energy - healthy and toxic. This chart matches planets to the rays they carry, to the chakras they work through, to the body parts that the planets and chakras rule; and to problems and diseases the planet causes when its force has turned toxic.

Chart 10: PLANETS: body parts ruled and disease.

Planets.	Body parts ruled.	When causing disease/ problems.
The Sun. R2, the building ray.	Heart chakra, thymus. Heart/ cardiovascular, spine, the eyes, vision; the constitution, vitalisation, spleen, immune system, cell-life.	Burns, scalds, causes high temperatures, fevers, autoimmune attacks. Via, R2 overstimulates, overgrowth.
The Moon. R4 harmony through conflict.	Solar plexus, pancreas. Flesh, tissue (brain tissue), body fluids, body cycles, lymphatic system, reproduction, pregnancy, birth, ovaries, uterus, babies. The eyes. Via Cancer, digestion.	Excess damp/ water, corrupts - toxic thick liquids, pus, excess mucous/ phlegm. Allergic reactions. Trouble with pregnancy, birth.
Mercury. R4 harmony through conflict.	Ajna, throat, pituitary, thyroid. Nerves, speech, consciousness thread, hearing; shoulders, arms, hands. Respiration, airways, oxygenation, bronchi, upper lungs. Intestines. All body tubes that transport information/ matter.	Wrong connections, wrong messaging. Rapid spread of germs through the air to cause epidemics such as colds, influenza, Covid-19.
Venus. R5 of concrete mind.	Ajna, throat chakra, pituitary, thyroid, pancreas. Nervous sys, venous sys, kidneys, bladder, urinary tract. Insulin, glucose levels. Sex relationships. Balance, homeostasis via Libra.	Weakens, cause prolapses. Strengthens desire for 'sweet things' that can result in physical disease. Via R5, psychological disorders.
Mars. R6 of idealism, devotion, emotion, passion/ desire, anger, war.	Solar plexus, sacral, pancreas, gonads. Via Aries: brain, skull. Muscles, sex. Sympathetic NS, fight-flight, adrenals, adrenaline. Blood, haemoglobin, energy, vitalisation.	Hot, infectious diseases, fevers, inflammation, autoimmune attacks, ulcers, acidic, skin eruptions, rashes, poisoned blood. Attacks, accidents, strokes, murders, sexual misuse.
Jupiter. R2, the building ray.	Heart chakra, thymus. Arteries, arterial blood, heart. Liver, sciatic nerve, hips, thighs, physical strength, locomotion. Growth.	Overstimulates, over-produces atoms - growths, tumours, cancer, congestion, organs too big, too many etc.
Saturn. R3 intelligent substance. R1 the life-death force.	Throat, base, thyroid. Dense physical structure: bones, skeleton, joints, spine, skin, hair, teeth, ligaments.	Chills, deprives, hardens, colds, crystallises, atrophies, ages, calcifies, congests, dries, contracts, stiffens. Slow forming, chronic, enduring diseases.
Uranus. R7, the manifesting ray, rules the ethers.	Sacral, crown. DNA, body electricity, nervous energy, nerve synapses, genes. Via Aquarius: blood circulation/ quality, calves, ankles.	Abnormalities, arrhythmia, spasms, cramps, asymmetry. Shocks, shatters, acute infectious diseases that strike suddenly. Virulent germs, bacterial infections, contagious diseases.
Neptune. R6, force of subtle emotions.	Solar plexus. Body secretions, fluids. The circular fluid highways (bloodstream, lymphatic). Feet, toes via Pisces. Sleep.	Weakens, dilutes, subtly undermines, distorts, insidious and unhealthy changes. Diseases that are obscure, hard to detect or to diagnose. Viruses. Drug/ alcohol abuse, addictions.
Pluto. R1, the life and death force.	Crown: sleep and death. Base: adrenals, fight-flight, survival instinct, atomic life.	Destroys, hardens, crystallises, atrophies, ages, calcifies, blocks, dries, contracts, stiffens, kills. Malevolent, life-threatening diseases, cell malignancies. Death.

A. Basic Health Reading, when Health is Good.

This is a general type of health reading for a client who has good health - it is basic and condensed. It typically forms the fourth part of a life reading, being preceded by character, love and career. These three topics are usually more important for a young and healthy client. Confirm with the client, the status of the health before the reading.

Method.

Preparatory work

Gather health details.
Print out the natal, transit and progressed charts.

1. Examine the Sun for vitality and potential disease.

2. Examine the Moon/ Mars or Neptune for emotional expression.

3a. Examine the 6th and 12 "health" houses.

3b. Alternatively, you see a major warning pattern in the chart that is not - or is only peripherally, connected to the health houses.

4. From the transit/ progression charts - find important dates moving forwards.

The live consultation.

1. Introduce the link between psychology and disease and the importance of changing the psychology in order to harmonise energy flow into the body.

2. Give remedial advice - based on aspects related to the health houses, or to a major health warning in the chart.

3. Give health advice from the transits, progressions and directions analysis.

Quotes on 'good health.'

The goal of meditation is to bring about the free play of all the incoming forces so that there is no impediment offered at any point to the incoming energy of the soul; so that no obstruction and congestion is permitted and no lack of power—physical, psychic, mental and spiritual—is to be found in any part of the body. This will mean not only good health and the full and free use of all the faculties (higher and lower) but direct contact with the soul. It will produce that constant renewing of the body which is characteristic of the life expression of the initiate and the Master, as well as of the disciple, only in a lesser degree. It will produce rhythmic expression of the divine life in form. [1]

Freedom from self-centredness is one of the first laws of good health. [2]

As the focus of racial attention shifts into the region of the higher values the physical vehicle will gain enormously, and good health—through right rhythmic living, plus correct thinking and soul contact—will become permanently established. [3]

---

1 Bailey, Alice; Esoteric Psychology II, 593.
2 Bailey, Alice; From Bethlehem to Calvary, 121.
3 Bailey, Alice; Esoteric Healing, 90.

Here is an example for this type of simple reading.

<h3 style="text-align:center">Henry Fonda - Born 16 May 1905, 14:00, Grand Island, Nebraska, USA.</h3>

i. Pre-counsel information gathering stage and analysis of chart.

Henry Fonda was an American actor who was born and raised in Nebraska. He made his mark early as a Broadway actor and made his Hollywood film debut in 1935. Fonda was married five times and had three children, one of them adopted. Imagine it is 1940.

Fonda's star is rising and he asks for an astrology life reading, with emphasis on his career. He confirms that he has good health (always ask).

1. Examine the Taurus Sun for vitality, and for potential disease.

Sun square Saturn in Pisces 6H.

Assemble the data. Eg., from Sun-Saturn: repression of feelings, vitality easily exhausted, potential heart disease. (Sun in Taurus), throat, thyroid problems.

2. Examine the Moon (Libra) for emotional expression. *Moon opposite retrograde Venus, afflicted in Aries.*

He values relationship harmony. But is selfish, difficult in love and this creates conflict.

3. A major health warning involving the 6H.

Saturn in Pisces in 6H, square Sun. Aquarius on the cusp, Uranus opposite Neptune, sesquiquadrate Jupiter.

Trouble with blood circulation, arteries. Blockages to bloodstream, heart disease.

4. Transits and progressions.

a. *Check Mars.* For a healthy person, unforeseen accidents usually hold the greatest risk. So, check Mars - ruler of accidents, carefully. Look to see if: transit Mars is making hard aspects to the natal or progressed chart, if natal Mars is being aspected by a malefic, or if progressed or

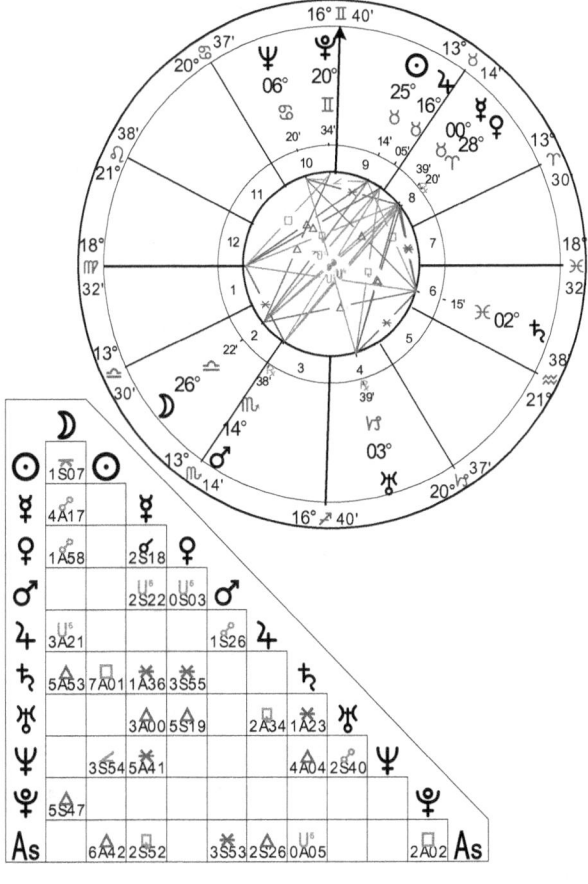

directed Mars are forming hard aspects. Such aspects could foretell an accident.

b. Check to see what the outer transit planets are doing.

c. Whether a solar eclipse will hit the Sun, angles or any planets connected with the health houses. Such eclipses
can give a health warning.

d. Finally, look for positive health indicators.

e. The outstanding events in 1940, 1941 for Fonda were:

   i. Solar-arc Mars was squaring the ascendant.

   ii. Transit Neptune was moving through the 1st house.

   iii. Transit Jupiter would return to its natal position.

ii. The live consultation

The astrologers goal: Give advice designed to maintain good health and to avoid potential health problems from manifesting in the future. (In this example, advice is written in the second person).

1. Introduce the link between psychology and disease.

- Eg: "You are fortunate to have good health. To maintain this, try to keep your outlook on life positive because the way we think and feel - in time, has a direct impact on health. Negative thoughts and emotions are detrimental to good health".

2. Give remedial advice: re the major health warning (Sun square Saturn 6H).

i. Eg. "You have a Taurus Sun, which means you are susceptible to throat and thyroid troubles. It also means you can be stubborn when difficulties arise - in the home (Sun inconjunct Moon [1]), with your children (Saturn rules the 5H of children), or at work (6H). Do you identify with this?"

Interaction with a client and requesting feedback will ensure you and the client are in harmony with the analysis. It will also give the client an opportunity to express emotion, part of the healing-effect of a health reading.

ii. "While it is important to stand your ground where important principles (9H) are concerned, try to be flexible in smaller matters. Rigidity hinders life-giving energy from flowing freely through the heart and circulation system.
It is also very advisable to get in touch with your emotions and to express how you feel (Moon opposite Mercury, Venus); rather than to deny injured feelings exist. Endeavour to be more heart-open, and heart-expressive. Remember this, because it is important for your long term health."

Thus, addressing in a benign way, the primary health warning seen in the chart - chronic heart disease. Reports said that Fonda was stand-offish and had difficulty expressing his emotions. In an interview in 2022, Fonda's daughter Jane, spoke about her attempts to connect more deeply with her father.

> Fonda said she wasn't able to achieve everything she wanted in her relationship with her father before he died. "You don't become somebody that you've never been at the end of your life," she said. "My dad was not a communicative person. He just didn't know how."

3. Give health advice from transits, progressions and directions - how to move forwards positively.

The following aspects were outstanding for Fonda through 1940 and 1941.

i. (Solar-arc Mars was squaring the ascendant for several months). "You have been in an accident-prone phase for a few months and this will continue until September 1941. During this period, you may find you are more reactive than usual, more impulsive. So, take care with machinery and cars to avoid an accident. If you are annoyed with someone, try to think before you speak to avoid saying things you may later regret."

ii. (Transit Neptune was moving through the 1st house). "The mystical planet Neptune is connecting with you for several years, making you very sensitive psychologically and physically. It is an excellent time to explore your spiritual side if that is something that interests you. Physically, your energy levels may be low and you may be susceptible to viruses and other complaints you could normally shrug off. So, look after yourself and your health. Ensure that you get adequate rest and time out to recoup your energy, etc."

iii. (Transit Jupiter would return to its natal position - 16 Taurus). "The period from September until mid-1941 is beneficial for your health, and this will assist you with your energy levels. This transit can be beneficial for all areas of your life. You are in a very fortunate phase of your career and your star is rising, etc."

4. Summarise the reading, ending on a positive note.

Re-address the major negative aspect or pattern detrimental to health.

> "It is important that you to learn to get in touch with your emotions and deal with issues rather than deny they exist. Try to be more heart-open, and heart-expressive. This will help ensure that the good health you currently experience will extend way into your senior years. In the meantime, your star is rising and you have abundant good health. Go forwards and enjoy your life".

---

1 The words in brackets are informational only and are not verbalised or said to a client.

B. Health Readings when a Disease has been Diagnosed.

These are stand-alone health readings, which are usually requested when a serious health issue has been diagnosed.

Method

Preparatory work

Gather health details.
Print out the natal, transit, directed and progressed charts.

1. Examine the Sun for vitality and potential disease.

2. Find a Health Triangle for the disease.

Gather data for remedial advice:

3. Look for easy natal chart aspects, to any of the Health Triangle planets.

4. Find and examine the esoteric ruler of the Cause planet (sign, location, aspects). The development of its higher qualities, and those of its sign, their healthy expression through the house it is in. These will help heal the toxicity causing the trouble.

5. Examine the transit/ progressed/ directed charts for a year or two ahead. List any major aspects that are being made - hard aspects for health warnings, and easy aspects which usually benefit health. Note the dates when these occur.

    - Study what the progressed/ directed Health Triangle is doing.
    - Study the Sun, hits to the natal Sun, and what is happening with the progressed Sun.
    - Other points of interest: asc/ progressed Moon/ 6th-12th houses, other major happenings.

The live consultation.

1. Introduce the link between psychology and disease and the importance of changing how we think and feel in order to harmonise energy flow into the body.

2. Address the Health Triangle. Relate the troubled psychology and the disease.

Give remedial/ helpful advice:

3. Advice from natal chart aspects to Health Triangle planets.

4. Advice related to the esoteric ruler of the Cause planet.

5. Advice from transit/ progressed/ directed charts for a few years ahead.

    (Include advice based on the astrologer's acquired wisdom. If appropriate, also include advice based on the esoteric planet ruler of the ascendant/ of the chart).

6. a. For diseases which are not immediately life-threatening, summarise any important points and end on a positive note.

    b. For life-threatening diseases, end the consultation with a spiritual discussion on "things to do" as we approach the final stretch of life.

B1. Health Reading for a chronic disease that is not immediately life-threatening.

Such as diabetes, arthritis and osteoporosis.

A chronic disease is: "A health problem that requires ongoing management over a period of years or decades and is one that cannot currently be cured but can be controlled with the use of medication and/or other therapies."

> **The astrologer's goal: To convey good news. To boost the spirits. This will facilitate positive energy inflow that will assist health. Convey to the client, the link between the troubled psychology and the disease. Guide the client into a therapy program that will be health-benefitting. Give helpful advice to help change/ transmute/ heal the troubled negative attitudes, so that vital healing energies can flow through.**

Example: James Coburn (31 Aug 1928, 20:15, Laurel, NE), rheumatoid arthritis.

i. Pre-counsel information gathering stage and analysis of chart.

Imagine it is 1979, and American actor Coburn asked for a consultation regarding his arthritis problem. Ask questions like: "What has been diagnosed? Exactly when? What are your symptoms? When did they start? Before diagnosis, what was your health like? Is this a family pattern"? If you want to introduce a metaphysical element into the reading, ask, "Do you believe in the existence of the soul and future lives"?

1. Examine the natal Sun for vitality and potential disease.
Although the Sun is in a health house, it has a very powerful vitalising aspect to Jupiter in the 1H of the physical body. It also has a square to Mars. Although the latter indicates a potential heart-attack, in a healthy person it is energising. Altogether - in the immediate, it means Coburn has good vitality and the power to throw off disease.

2. Find a Health Triangle for the disease.
In rheumatoid arthritis, the immune system attacks the joints and joint linings. By 1990, Coburn could barely walk.

    Point 1. Cause. Moon in Pisces, 12H, square Mars. These are the 'causal' planets. They connect into a Grand Cross pattern if orbs are widened. Coburn was a critical, aggressive perfectionist, (Mars square Sun); who harboured angry, bitter, resentment (Mars opp. Saturn); and buried grief, unresolved emotional pain (Moon 12). This pattern poisoned his system, affecting health.

    Point 2. Organ. Saturn for joints.

    Point 3. Effect. Mars, Saturn. Inflammatory (Mars) attacks on joints, impairing mobility (Saturn in Sagittarius).

Gather data for remedial advice:

3. Data from natal chart aspects to the Health Triangle planets.
Mars is sextile the ascendant. Saturn which rules the joints, trines Uranus and the ascendant, promising improvements if alternative/ radically advanced modern treatments are applied.

4. Data related to the esoteric ruler of the Cause planet. (There are two Cause planets - Moon in Pisces, Mars in Gemini. The esoteric ruler of Pisces is Pluto, the esoteric ruler of Gemini is Venus).

a. Pluto in Cancer 4H, trine the Moon. Healing for his emotional pain and loss as a child could be found by privately sharing what happened with sympathetic family members, and/ or private therapy sessions with a spiritual counsellor.

b. Venus, afflicted in Virgo 6H, opp. the Moon. The beauty of Venus (appreciation of people/ life/ the self), has been impaired by criticism, small-mindedness. Therapy to help see the self as worthy, and deserving of love and good things in life could be recommended.

5. Data from transit/ progressed/ directed charts for a year or two ahead.

a. For late 1979, the Health Triangle was studied. It was triggered in 1979 as Saturn moved through the 6H, and over the natal Sun. It is likely Coburn was under intense pressure at work and was repressing angry emotions. This was the catalyst that triggered the latent disease. As part of therapy, this period could be discussed.

b. The natal Sun and progressed Sun were studied. Good vitality represented by the Sun, is essential for healing and a sense of well-being. In 1979/, 1980, the progressed Sun was in the final degrees of Libra and in mid - 1981, it moved into Scorpio. Vitality is at a low point when the Sun moves through the final degrees of a sign. There is energy renewal as it moves into the new sign.

c. Look for other important 'hits' from transits, progressions, directions.

    i. For 2 years (mid 1979 onwards), the progressed Moon moved through the 11H.

    ii. Until 1982, Saturn transited the 6H.

ii. The live consultation

1. Introduce the link between psychology and disease and the importance of changing how one thinks/ feels in order to harmonise energy flow into the body.

    Eg: "We are energy beings, and there is a direct link between the energies created when we think and feel, and what happens with the body. Negative thoughts and emotions disrupt energy flow. Positive thoughts and emotions are beneficial for good health. There is a pattern in your birth chart that shows a direct link between the way you think and your joint trouble".

2. Address the Health Triangle. Relate the troubled psychology and the disease.

    "You are a perfectionist where your work is concerned. Not only are you critical when others do things wrong, you criticise yourself when your work does not measure up to your high standards (Sun Virgo). The result is angry resentment (square Mars, Saturn), a psychological poison that in time has affected your body - the inflammatory attacks (Mars) on your joints and impaired mobility (Saturn in Sagittarius).

    Driving this behaviour is unresolved emotional pain, anger and grief, due to physical and psychological abuse you received as a child, and which crippled you emotionally. Do you relate to this?"

Always check when suggestions like these are put to the client. This will ensure you are both in harmony with the direction of the reading. If the answer is yes, let the client talk it through.

Give remedial advice:

3. Advice based on natal chart aspects to Health Triangle planets.

a. (Mars sextile Aries ascendant). "Redirecting your energy into new and interesting physical projects and adventures, which are physically and mentally challenging, where you can take the lead and use your initiative - this will help your overall sense of wellbeing".

b. (Natal Sun 6, trine Jupiter). "You have a warm, sunny and generous side to your nature. People see this in you and are attracted by your magnetism. If your use your fame and success to help people who are in need, this in turn will benefit your health. Selflessness and service to others is a spiritual tonic."

c. (Saturn trine Uranus and the Aries ascendant). "Your joint health could be greatly improved by consulting a natural therapist and by using natural or pioneering therapeutic techniques. Massage and other physical techniques such as physiotherapy would also be beneficial." (Mars, ruler of Aries, for physical therapies).

In 1998, Coburn began an intense natural treatment plan which combined fasting, deep tissue massage, electromagnetic treatments, and natural supplements. It enabled him to return to work. If he had consulted an astrologer in 1979 and was referred to a natural therapist, it would have saved him years of pain.

d. (Returning to the aspect Sun 6H, trine Jupiter 1H). "It will also benefit you to look after your heart health. (Sun square Mars, ruler 8H of death). Take time out from your busy schedule to relax and enjoy life. Study wise teachings and apply spiritual disciplines such as meditation." (Jupiter rules the 9H of wisdom, spirituality).

4. **Advice related to the esoteric ruler of the Cause planet. Include the esoteric ruler of the chart if relevant.**

    Eg. Mercury is the esoteric ruler of the chart with Aries rising. Mercury is in Virgo in the 6H, indicating that the acquiring of mental discrimination and being able to talk freely about trauma suffered in the home (Mercury sextile Pluto 4H); is vital for his healing and soul growth. This information is included in this section.

    a. *Pluto in Cancer 4H, trine Moon.* "It is important for your spiritual and physical health, that you seek counselling to bring up and heal the emotional pain associated with the abuse you suffered growing up. It will also help if you have deep and meaningful discussions with key family members who knew what was happening. How do you feel about bringing this up with your mother, who witnessed the abuse from your father?" And so on.

    b. *Venus, afflicted in Virgo 6H, opp. the Moon.* "Appreciation of your worthiness to be loved, has been impaired by negative self-talk. Therapy to help see yourself as being worthy and deserving of love is recommended".

5. **Advice based on the astrologer's acquired wisdom.**

    Psychological and spiritual exercises designed to correct wrong-thinking and train the mind to think positively, are recommended. Here is a suggestion.

    "This detachment meditation exercise gives insight and better control over our thought processes and emotional reactions. It will help you become more aware of your negative thought processes and the power to change and transmute them. It also invokes positive light-filled energy which is beneficial for health".

    "Close the eyes, turn within, breathe quietly and steadily. Steadily affirm:
    I have a body, but I am not that body.
    I have emotions, but I am not those emotions.
    I have a mind, but I am not that mind.
    I am the Divine Self. Immortal. Eternal. Radiant with Spiritual Light.
    I am that Self of Light, that Self am I.
    Imagine yourself filled with light".

6. **Advice from transit/ progressed/ directed charts for a few years ahead.**

    a. (Sun moving from Libra to Scorpio). "Until mid-1981, you are in an end of cycle period, one in which your task is to tidy up loose ends and deal with unfinished business from the past 30 years. It is not a time to begin new projects, but rather a time of inner reflection and planning for the future. This makes it a good time to plan your therapeutic treatments and how you will adjust your career and outer life to support the changes happening in your body. Plan to start actively moving forwards again, or start new projects in April 1981 (when the Sun moves into Scorpio)".

    "With your Sun moving from Libra to Scorpio, your personality is changing and evolving. You will find yourself wanting to delve more deeply into matters that interest you. This makes it a good time to begin spiritual practices such as the meditation given previously. Read spiritual esoteric literature, what it says about the mind and how our thoughts influence our lives and bodies". (And so on).

    b. (Progressed Moon moving from the 10H to 11). "You have also begun a 2-year period, where you will be more interested in deepening your group and friendship connections, rather than to give all you have to your career. You may for instance find it beneficial to join a group or organisation, which is investigating alternative treatments for rheumatoid arthritis (progressed Moon currently in Aquarius, natal Uranus trine Saturn)".

    c. "The planet Saturn that rules both the joints in the body and the disease arthritis, entered your house of health around the time you were diagnosed. It leaves in late 1981, 1982, and that will be helpful for health improvement. In the meantime, use the time to reflect upon you and your life and what you need to change/ to modify, so that your life is better balanced".

7. **Summarise any important points and end on a positive note.**

    Something simple like:

    "Remember, if you train yourself to think and speak kindly to yourself and to others, you will remove inner friction that is impacting your health. You will have more vitality and positive energy available to heal your body. You have many more wonderful years ahead of you to enjoy life and these changes will help you maximise your enjoyment."

B2: Health reading for a chronic disease that is life-threatening.

Such as heart disease, cancer, a stroke.

A client has been diagnosed with a serious and life-threatening disease that is being managed with appropriate treatment and medication. A terminal diagnosis has not been given. Such people seek a consultation because they want to hear good news. They want to know if the condition can be managed and that they have many more years ahead of them to live. In case of children, the parents or carers may request an astrology reading.

> **The astrologer's goal: To convey good news. To boost the spirits. This will facilitate positive energy inflow that will assist healing if that is meant to be, or an extended period of grace before death occurs. Convey to the client, the link between the troubled psychology and the disease. Then guide the client into a therapy program that will be health-benefitting. Give helpful advice to help change/ transmute/ heal the troubled negative attitudes, so that vital healing energies can flow through. Include a section that is philosophical about life, that prepares the person for the end of this incarnation. This is done in a subtle, non-threatening, and inspiring way.**

Example: Henry Fonda - heart disease.
i. Pre-counsel information gathering stage and analysis of chart.

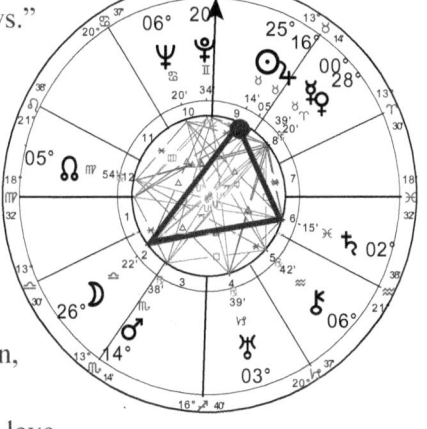

Imagine it is late 1974. The actor Henry Fonda is 69. He contacts you and says, "I have been diagnosed with heart disease and I would like to know what my chart says."

1. Examine the Sun for vitality and potential disease.
Because the Sun is square debilitating Saturn from the 6H of health, and inconjunct the Moon; vitality is not as strong as it could be.

2. Find a Health Triangle for the disease.
As previously noted, Sun square Saturn represents the heart problem. This combination is a classic ruler of chronic heart disease as a result of old age. Saturn's location in the 6H, confirms this. They form the foundation for the Health Triangle. The third point is the Moon, which has an inconjunct to the Sun, and an out-of-sign trine to Saturn. The Health Triangle is:

    Point 1. Cause. Moon in Libra, 2H (opp. Venus). Can be selfish, difficult in love and this creates conflict.
    Point 2. Organ. The Sun (the heart).
    Point 3. Effect. The disease. Saturn in Pisces 6H. Chronic heart disease.

Gather data for remedial advice:

3. Data from natal chart aspects to Health Triangle planets.
The Sun is trine the Virgo ascendant. Saturn is well aspected with sextiles to Venus, Mercury and Uranus and a trine to Neptune in the 10H.

4. Data from the esoteric ruler of the Cause planet (Moon in Libra).
Uranus in Capricorn in the 4H, is the esoteric ruler of Libra. Uranus is the awakener, which demands a totally new and radical change in the way Fonda manages his emotional and family (4H) dynamics.

5. Data from transit/ progressed/ directed charts for a year or two ahead.
Look for beneficial aspects to the natal/ progressed Sun. Also study the ascendant, which represents the body and the incarnation. If Pluto is involved when a serious diagnosis has been given to an aged person, then potentially, that disease (or one related), will cause death. The speed at which this happens depends upon whether there are positive aspects (which may extend life), upon the quality of life (poor quality, a person may will themselves to death), and whether the person has a strong will and wants to live. If the astrologer sees that relentless and hard Pluto hits are involved, preparing the client for death becomes more urgent.

Negative aspects

[74 and 75] The solar-arc Moon in the Health Triangle, was moving over natal/ progressed Uranus, the ruler of the 6H.
- Transit Saturn (10H) was opposing the Moon/ Uranus connection.
- Progressed Sun (11H) in the Health Triangle, was forming a Yod with the Moon/ Uranus connection on one leg, and natal/ progressed Saturn on the other.

Positive aspects

[73 to 2002] Progressed Sun was making no beneficial long-term aspects. But it had just progressed into its own sign Leo, which is beneficial for healing vitality.

[74] Transit Jupiter is sextile natal Jupiter.

[75 Mar to Nov 1977] Progressed Moon moved into and through the 9H.

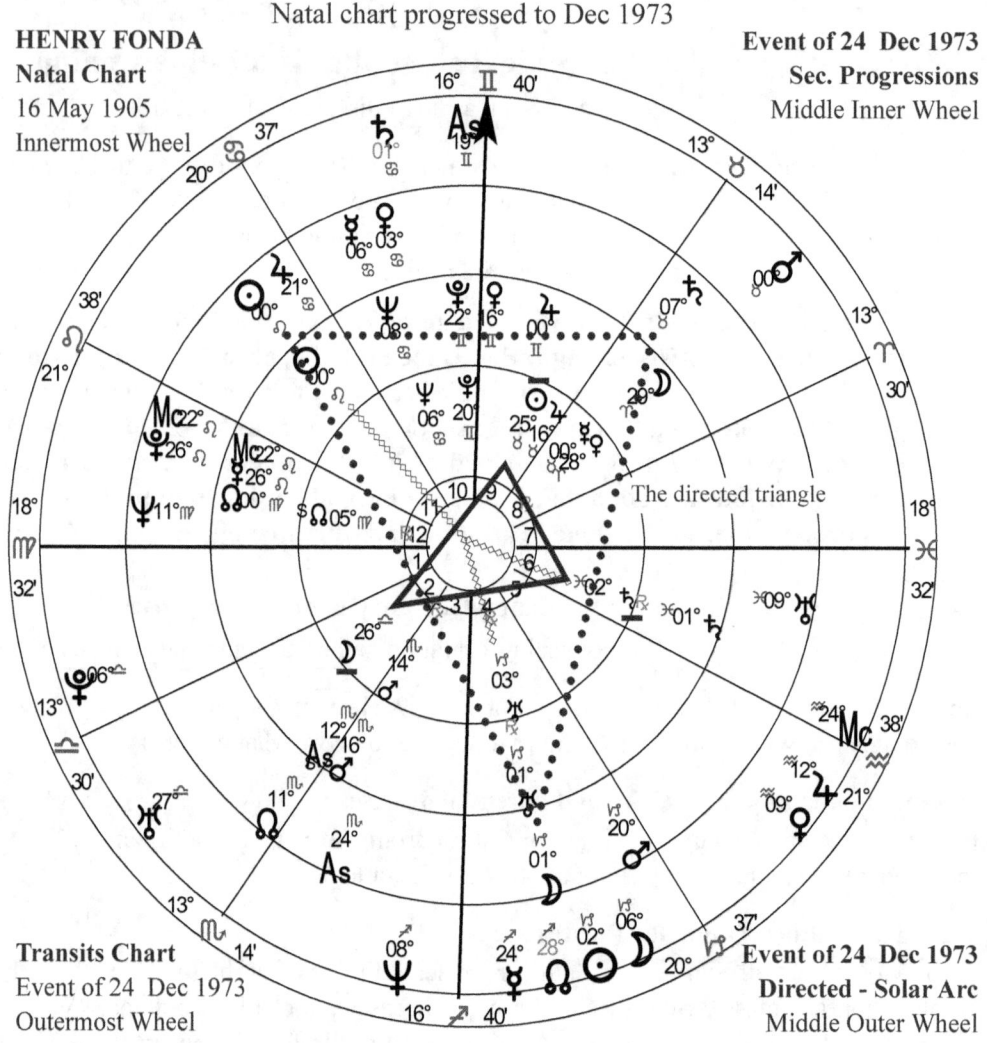

ii. The live consultation.

1. **Introduce the link between psychology and health.**

   After sympathetic introductory remarks: "What I can help you with today, is to use your chart to make the link between your psychology and the disease which has manifested. We are energy beings and thoughts and emotions are energies. Negative expressions are detrimental to good health. Positive thoughts and emotions are beneficial. Identifying your negative patterns gives you the power to make inner changes in your self-expression, so you increase beneficial health-giving energies flowing through your body. This empowers the disease-fighting properties in your body".

2. **Address the Health Triangle. Relate the troubled psychology and the disease.**

   "Difficulty with emotional expression is related to your health trouble. You are afraid of rejection, of being judged, criticised, devalued. To protect yourself, you can repress your feelings, disconnect from them, rationalise them. Do you identify with this"?

   "Blocking energy circulation like this over the years, isolating your feelings to protect yourself; this has had a negative effect on your heart. Now you are aware of this, you can do something about it."

Give remedial advice:

3. **Advice based on natal chart aspects to Health Triangle planets.**

   "Learn to feel and acknowledge your emotions, to express them, talk about them and learn to value yourself for who you are (Moon 2H). Go into therapy for your fear of rejection (Sun square Saturn 6H). I know this will be difficult, but you have everything to gain and nothing to lose."

4. Advice related to the esoteric ruler of the Cause planet (Moon in Libra).

(The esoteric ruler of Libra is Uranus, which is in Capricorn, 4H). "It is important for your spiritual and physical health, and emotional healing, that you restructure your family dynamics along totally new and open lines. It will be very healing for both you and your children, if you can connect with them at an emotional level, and let them know how much they mean to you." (Saturn 6H, ruler of the 5H of children, trine Moon).

5. Advice based on the astrologer's acquired wisdom.

Eg. "This mantram is excellent for opening up the energies of the heart. Sound it every day at noon".

"O Lord of Light and Love I know about the need;
Touch my heart anew with love,
that I too may love and give."

6. Advice from transit/ progressed/ directed charts for a few years ahead.

a. "Now and until the end of 1975, adhere carefully to the treatment - exercise plan you have been given. This will help stabilise your health." (He still had many hard aspects targeting the Health Triangle and the Sun).

b. (The Sun). "You have positive energies supporting you. The Sun that rules the heart has moved into its own sign Leo and it will be there for 30 odd years. This is most beneficial for your heart-health. Leo is a sign that gives abundant energy and this will greatly support your body in its healing efforts."

c. (Transit Jupiter and progressed Moon). "Now until the end of 1977, focus on your inner, spiritual health. Travel far - physically or spiritually, in a search for wisdom and understanding. It is a good time to deepen your connection with God with the natural flow of nature (choosing words that suit your client). You will benefit greatly by talking to people who are insightful and wise."

7. For life-threatening diseases, end the consultation with a spiritual discussion on "things to do" as we approach the final stretch of life. (Make this an interactive session, inviting the client to share his or her thoughts at every stage of the reading).

Eg. "You have lived an amazing life. Now you are in your senior years there is another important task which I highly recommend. That is, to make peace with yourself, and with others. You are an 'immortal' soul, a child of God, here on earth to gain wisdom and to learn to be kind. In the process, because we are still imperfect, we make mistakes. We hurt people. But that is normal. If we are not making mistakes, we are not learning, we are not growing wiser. Our task is to learn from every situation and aim do better next time. If you are harbouring any guilt, let it go. Forgive yourself and try to do better next time.

If there are alienations with people close to you, this is a good time to begin make peace with them. If you reach out and you are rejected, that is fine. You will know in your heart you offered the hand of reconciliation and forgiveness. If there is someone who hurt you badly and you do not wish to have contact, then try to forgive them their actions. Remember, they are evolving souls and will eventually be held accountable by God/ by karma. By healing damaged or disruptive relationships - or alternatively, being able to forgive and move on; this will free up blocked force, which will benefit this period of your life.

By doing this work, when your time comes in the distant future to cross-over to the next level of your soul journey; you can do so lightly, peacefully. Each new incarnation is filled with brand new opportunities and it helps to start with a clean slate. In the meantime, celebrate who you are now, the challenges you overcame and your achievements."

Be creative in the way you address death. If your client expresses interest, then expand the conversation on the topic. Ensure that the last things you say are positive and supportive.

Fonda died of heart disease in 1982, at age 77. This was 8 years after diagnosis.

C. Conversations with people diagnosed as terminally ill.

These are not "astrology readings" per se. Rather, they are conversations in which the astrologer uses all acquired knowledge and wisdom to help the person navigate the death/ dying process. Because needs may differ from person to person, there is no set format. The astrologer collects information, then responds as best he or she can in the moment.

Method.

Preparatory work

Gather health details.
Print out the natal, transit and progressed charts.

1. Find a Health Triangle for the disease, and/ or identify where emotional difficulties lie. These may come up for discussion.

2. Gather information for remedial advice:
    a. Examine the esoteric planet ruler of the chart/ of the incarnation. It may be an appropriate point for discussion:
    b. Examine the transit/ progressed/ directed charts for a year or two ahead. This information may be useful.

The live consultation.

1. Unobtrusively, the astrologer makes soul alignment, then enfolds the person with his/ her lighted aura. Asks for soul-assistance to help speak words of wisdom that will be helpful. With quiet and general conversation, sets the person at ease prior to the deeper conversation.

2. Important points to address if possible:
    a. Relate the person's soul and personality.
    b. Address unresolved hurts.
    c. Eliminate any sense of guilt and sin.
    d. Address the cross-over process.
    e. If appropriate, discuss the life purpose of the soul.

Death, the final act of life, holds great fears for many, and usually the news is received with shock and disbelief. Then follows five stages - denial and isolation, anger, bargaining, depression, and finally acceptance. These five steps were formulated by doctor/ psychiatrist Elisabeth Kubler-Ross in her book, 'On Death and Dying'.

Sometimes the astrologer becomes involved, and is asked for advice or to counsel a dying person. Or the astrologer has a close relationship with the dying person, and wanting to help, initiates a conversation. In all cases, it is important that the astrologer is comfortable with the death and dying process, to avoid passing on fear. There is also a need to be sensitive to - and supportive of, wherever the person is in the five stages.

> **The astrologer's goal: Help the person make peace within, with others and with the past. Tidy up loose end and, navigate the great cross-over process without fear and with a lighter heart.**

All astrology jargon should be eliminated. Rather, a friendly conversation designed to meet the needs of the person involved should be the goal. Here are some points which can be included, remembering that because the conversation is often guided by the person's need at that moment, not all these points may be addressed

a. Relate the person's soul and personality. Use words appropriate for the person's belief, but the goal is to help the person identify as a living, vital and beautiful soul, rather than as a diseased body which will soon die. (Eg. "You are a child of God," "An immortal soul"). To see the journey of the soul/ of consciousness, as a continuum. ("After a rest period, we are born again to continue our journey to enlightenment. A new life starts with a clean slate and holds future opportunities to learn and achieve"). These two latter points are usually inspiring in this type of conversation.

b. Address unresolved hurts. Regrets make the cross-over more difficult than it needs to be. They keep the soul bound to the Wheel of Life, forcing it back into incarnation to resolve them. Ask questions like, "Do you have any regrets, any unresolved wounds or hurts? Is there anything you have not completed in this life that you have regrets about? Is there anyone you have not been able to forgive? Is there anyone you have hurt that you would like forgiveness from?" If the person shares in this manner, then giving further advice may be helpful. For instance, ("You don't have to contact that person. A simple healing-type/ forgiveness meditation is very effective").

c. Eliminate any sense of guilt and sin. This is a very important point.

> Eg. "We are all souls, children of God. Our goal - while we are here on earth, is to gain wisdom and learn to develop loving relationships. In the process, because we are still imperfect, we make mistakes. Do wrong things. We hurt people, while we ourselves are hurt. But that is a normal part of the process. If we are not making mistakes, we are not learning. Our higher task is to learn from our mistakes and try to do better next time."

d. Address the cross-over process. Many people hold deep fears about what will happen when they die. This quote from the Master Djwhal Khul gives an Eastern spiritual perspective on death.

> Death, is one of our most practised activities. We have died many times and shall die again and again. Death is essentially a matter of consciousness. We are conscious one moment on the Physical Plane, and a moment later we have withdrawn into another plane and are actively conscious there. Just as long as our consciousness is identified with the form aspect, death will hold for us its ancient terror. Just as soon as we know ourselves to be souls, and find that we are capable of focusing our consciousness or sense of awareness in any forms or on any plane at will, or in any direction within the form of God, we will no longer know death. [1]

Ask a question like, "Would you like to know what I believe happens when we cross to the next life?" Then say something like: "It is a simple process. The body simply feels very tired. We fall asleep, only to wake up to find ourselves moving towards a bright light, a doorway. At that light we find waiting, friends and loved ones who have gone before us. They are there to greet us, and to show us what to do next. There is no need to worry."

e. Celebrate achievements connected with the soul purpose:

The purpose of the soul is to develop and express the higher qualities of the ascendant sign, and of the esoteric ruler of that sign. Then to use the developed qualities to forge a higher path in life and to help people. In their hearts, most people sense this purpose, and a discussion related to matters connected with the ascendant sign and its ruler, can be uplifting. It is an opportunity to help the client celebrate his/ her important life achievements.

> For example, if Aquarius rises, the soul purpose is to develop and express the humanitarian principles of universal brotherliness and equality. The esoteric ruler of Aquarius is Jupiter, and a conversation could be initiated like this:

---

[1] Bailey, Alice: A Treatise on White Magic, 494.

"You worked extensively with children in your teaching career, helping them grow into confident and wise adults. You must feel very satisfied with your achievements, how you contributed to the betterment of so many young lives?".

Example 1. Carole - bowel cancer.

Born 29 November 1946, time rectified to 18:00. Carole had health symptoms for a year or so, and medical misdiagnosis meant that when the diagnosis for bowel cancer was finally made, it was terminal. The cancer had metastasized.

Carole always seemed serene and unruffled. However, the development of bowel cancer indicates the opposite was true. The root cause of cancer is emotional repression and her Moon had a classic pattern:

> Point 1. Cause. Moon opposite Saturn/ Pluto (emotional repression).
> Point 2. Organ. Pluto, rules the bowel via Scorpio.
> Point 3. Effect. Jupiter in Scorpio, overbuilding of bowel cells, hence cancer.

The author was a relative. Because metaphysical philosophy had never been discussed between the two before, the author was careful about how to begin. The visit began with casual catch-up type conversation. Then, "Would you like to hear about what happens when we cross-over and meet those we love on the other side"? Carole said "Yes," making it clear from her heightened interest and body language that such a discussion would be welcome. The essence of the conversation followed the advice given previously: "It is a simple process. We just fall asleep as we usually do (and so on)."

> Carole's interest was at its most intense when mention was made of loved ones waiting for her on the other side, and that the next life would hold future opportunities to further her interests and ambitions.

With an intention to release any residual Moon opposite Saturn-Pluto emotional issues, the author turned the conversation towards Carole's husband. He had died three years previously, leaving her emotionally traumatised. It was known that some in the family had not thought well of him, causing her sadness.

His thoughtful and kind nature was discussed. That he was a wonderful father, who helped her raise fine, drug-free children who had good jobs and lives. This opened the flood-gates. Words poured out of Carole - the hurt she experienced over the family's attitude towards her husband. She appeared to grow lighter as she spoke of her feelings. After about 45 minutes the conversation was over. From her demeanour, the light in her face and smile, the author knew the conversation had been helpful.

That was the last intimate conversation between the two. Relatives gave positive feedback, said that Carole had enjoyed the discussion. She passed a few weeks later.

Example 2. Mary - cancer.

An acquaintance made contact with the author on behalf of a friend (Mary), who was dying from cancer. She said that Mary seemed troubled. She definitely was not at peace. Because she loved her friend and wanted her final weeks to be more peaceful, she asked if there was anything in her friend's chart that might indicate the source of the discontent. She wanted to get her friend talking in the hope that whatever was causing her unease could at the least be eased, at the best healed and dissipated.

> The chart showed a very afflicted Mars in the 4H and the possibility of sexual assault within the family. Afflictions from Saturn indicated unresolved emotional pain and silence associated with the assault, in order to preserve family harmony.

The author advised that this be raised with the dying woman ("did you suffer abuse growing up"?). If she was responsive, to discuss it with her.

This eventuated. Mary shared with her friend that she had suffered a sexual violation in the home, which had been hidden and never discussed. Over days she talked about the experience. The author advised the inclusion of the Garden Meditation (in the Remedial Advice section), which could include imagined discussions with relevant people involved in the family incident.

The friend said Mary seemed to be emptying herself of grief and other powerful emotions during these conversations and meditations. When she died shortly after, she appeared to be at peace.

Example 3. Professional astrologer Jeanni - amyloidosis.
Jeanni (22 June 1949, 05:11, Bulawayo, Zimbabwe), was a close friend of the author. Jeanni was deeply interested in esoteric subjects and spiritual growth. She used this understanding to heal herself of rheumatoid arthritis in 1988, through healing meditations and visualisations. When she was diagnosed with amyloidosis in February 2020, Jeanni was determined to heal herself again using metaphysical techniques.

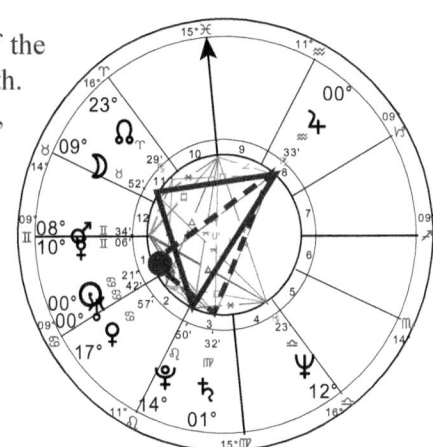

Amyloidosis is caused by abnormal protein deposits, which are usually produced in bone marrow. They gather on the heart, kidney or other organs causing blockages and malfunction. There is currently no cure though treatment can help clear deposits before they build up again.

The pathology of the disease in the chart.

Jeanni's Health Triangle was added to by a Yod planet configuration, which consists of two planets sextile each other, both inconjunct a third planet. The Yod represents change. The introduction of a new - either exciting or confronting challenge (the forces of the third inconjunct planet), which forces change upon the existing life (the sextile planets). The new situation often demands that a choice be made between competing interests. Something has to be cut away to make room for the new. Self-initiated change is welcome. Forced change is not, and trouble arises when it causes deep resentment and unhappiness.

Jeanni's change planet was Jupiter in Aquarius 8H. She welcomed the compelling urge to search for Aquarian-age occult knowledge and wisdom which it represented. But forced change in intimate relationships (Jupiter rules the 7H), caused deep unhappiness and sometimes an emotional shut-down (Jupiter quindecile Pluto, square Moon). Because Jupiter also corules the 6H of health (with Sagittarius sharing the cusp), this had health consequences. Jupiter also represents cell over-building. The Health Triangle is:

Point 1. Psychological cause. Moon square Pluto, Sun in Cancer semi-square Pluto (emotional repression).

Point 2. Organs affected. Sun (the heart), and Venus in Cancer (kidneys).

Point 3. Effect. Jupiter inconjunct Saturn. Cell over-building causing blockages, malfunction.

Amyloidosis was diagnosed in 2018, when transit Pluto connected with Jupiter (retrograde progressed to 22 Capricorn). Ominously, the transit would last for 5-6 years before Pluto would finally leave its conjunction with natal and progressed Jupiter (the end of 2024).

One of the important decisions Jeanni had to make was whether to follow professional (Saturn) advice and supplement her inner work with chemotherapy, or to heal herself only through herbs and meditation as she had done before (the Sun-Uranus leg of the Yod). She opted for a combination of both. She tried chemotherapy for several months, then stopped, opting instead for dialysis treatments. Her primary work was inner healing meditations.

During this process, the author simply supported all the decisions Jeanni made. The astrology was often consulted and discussed together. The prime focus was to try to understand the psychology of the Yod and of Jupiter's role in particular. From the spiritual perspective, a conclusion made was that - no matter the outcome, the wisdom Jeanni gained as a result of the experience would be of great benefit to her and to her astrology service work in her next incarnation. Nothing is lost in the fullness of soul-time. With Pluto driving it, the disease proved unstoppable. It is likely this was simply Jeanni's time.

> In later years due to aging (Jeanni was in her 70's), the soul begins to separate itself from its earthly vestures in preparation for the great transition. As a consequence, the physical body begins to break down and a disease potential in the chart will manifest as a reality.

Remaining joyful and positive, Jeanni never gave up until heart damage became so advanced, it began to fail. Then she faced the inevitable with her characteristic joy and the end came swiftly (in July 2023).

> Jeanni's soul purpose was represented by Gemini rising, and Venus in Cancer. Jeanni's purpose was to become a wise-woman messenger, and help people find their way through earthly life with her words of wisdom - a wisdom gained by being insightful through her own emotional suffering (Venus square Neptune). Jeanni achieved these goals.

Jeanni was a wise woman who died surrounded by love.

5. CASE STUDIES.

Esoteric Healing - Rule Three

Let the healer train himself to know the inner stage of thought or of desire of the one who seeks his help. He can thereby know the source from whence the trouble comes. Let him relate the cause and the effect, and know the point exact through which the help must come.

Bailey, Alice A; Esoteric Healing, page 134-135.

1. Crown Chakra Diseases

The crown chakra rules the pineal gland, the brain, sleep and death. It receives energy from Ray 1, Aries, Pluto, Vulcan, Uranus.

1a. The Brain

a. Aneurysm in the brain

An aneurysm is a weak spot in the wall of a blood vessel that balloons out and fills with blood. The weakness can be present at birth or be the result of other health conditions. Sudden death can occur if an aneurysm haemorrhages. The inner cause is related to repressed anger/ rage so that pressure builds until there is an explosion - in a blood vessel in the case of a haemorrhage.

Cacilda Becker (6 April 1921 09:25, Pirassununga Brazil)
Latino stage and film actress who achieved success in her natal Brazil. She was volatile and passionate, marrying three times. During a performance on stage on May 6 1969, she collapsed - she had suffered a brain aneurysm that resulted in a stroke. Although she was immediately rushed to the hospital, she died a few weeks later on 14th June 1969.

Cause: emotional. Becker found it difficult to express her emotions, to release anger. She would brood on her hurts, hide them away and hold them in. This built up tension and stress that is linked to her brain trouble. (Mars is in detriment in the 12H of hidden things).

Organ: crown. Mars for the brain, head and blood; the arteries Jupiter.

Effect: aneurysm. Becker developed high blood pressure (Mars). Artery walls weakened and an aneurysm developed (trine Jupiter afflicted in Virgo, conjunct retrograde Venus). It ruptured suddenly, killing her (easy-opposition pattern; Mars, Uranus and Jupiter that rules the 8H of death).

▲ (C) Mars. (O) Mars, Jupiter. (E) Mars, Venus, Uranus.

Joe Biden (20 November 1942 08:30, Scranton PA)
American politician, the 47th Vice President of the United States serving with the first black President of the US, Barack Obama. He survived a brain aneurysm at age 45, which required two operations to correct.

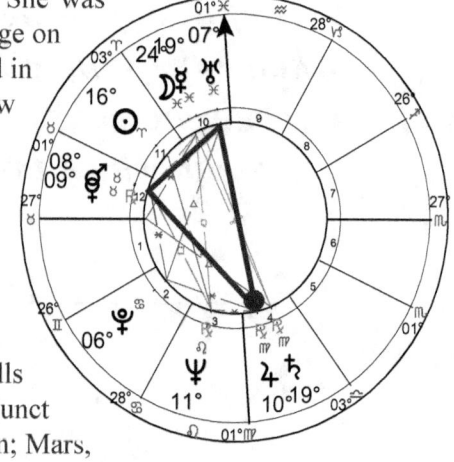

Cause: emotional. Biden has a volcanic temper (Pluto in Leo square Mars), is exceedingly stubborn and suppresses his emotions until he is like a pressure-cooker about to explode (Moon in Taurus square Jupiter in Cancer). These patterns are related to his aneurysm.

Organ: crown - brain mass the Moon; the arteries Jupiter.

Effect: aneurysm. Repression of force caused high blood pressure (Pluto > Mars). Artery walls weakened and he developed a cerebral aneurysm (Jupiter trine Venus that weakens, inconjunct the Moon). He was lucky to have beneficial Jupiter on his side (trine the Sun, Venus and ascendant). His hospital treatment was successful and he evaded death.

▲ (C) Mars, Pluto, Moon. (O) Moon, Jupiter. (E) Pluto, Mars, Venus.

Biden's line-up of planets in the 12H of hospitals is a warning that potentially, his own actions (the 12th is the house of self-undoing), could undermine his health and bring him down. But he has thrived in the cut and thrust world of modern politics (Uranus opposite the Sun and Venus, trine Neptune in the 10th house of government). He is helped by his Sun trine Jupiter, which gives him great vitality and a lot of luck.

b. Brain cancer, tumours

Ray 2 that overbuilds governs cancer. But the 1st ray when used to stifle force is a major cause. It causes congestion in the chakras, affecting related body tissue. Then if cells start to multiply (ray 2) cancer will appear and grow.

George Gershwin (26 September 1898 11:09, Brooklyn NY).
American composer famous for works such as 'Rhapsody in Blue'. A fast growing tumour in his temporal lobe killed him, 11 July 1937.
Cause: emotional. Gershwin was stubborn and strong willed (Saturn-Uranus on the ascendant). He would stifle his feelings of hurt and anger rather than deal with them directly and this caused congestion in the brain region (sesquiquadrate Mars, which falls in Cancer).
Organ: crown - brain mass, Mars in Cancer.
Effect: tumour. Cells began to multiply rapidly and a fast growing tumour suddenly emerged (Jupiter square Mars > Uranus).
- ▲ (C) Mars, Saturn, Uranus. (O) Mars. (E) Mars, Uranus, Jupiter.
- In December 1936, ten months before his death, the progressed Moon moved into the 8H of death and crossed natal Mars. In that month, there was also an eclipse on Mars, showing an acceleration of trouble in the brain.

[There is a second pattern: cancerous cells (the Sun carrying the second ray, falls in Libra), in the temporal region (semi-square Venus ruling the pituitary gland), of the brain (Venus trine Mars in Cancer; square Moon)].

Yves Saint-Laurent (1 August 1936 19:45, Oran Algeria)
Famous French fashion designer Saint-Laurent was diagnosed with a brain tumour just 2 weeks before he died on June 1 2008.
Cause: emotional. A friend said of Yves said "he was an unhappy person, depression ran deep". We see this with the Moon, the emotions, in detriment in chilly and arid Capricorn. He also had a volatile and angry side that he repressed and that simmered away underneath (Moon opposing Mars in Cancer, conjunct Pluto). The seeds of his brain trouble are rooted here.
Organ: crown - brain Mars in Cancer, brain mass the Moon.
Effect: tumour. Consequently, carcinogenic changes (Neptune) occurred in brain tissue (trine the Moon on the cusp of the 12H of hospitals; septile Mars in the 6H of health). The tumour developed and grew (Neptune square Jupiter).
- ▲ (C) Moon, Mars, Pluto. (O) Mars, Moon. (E) Neptune, Jupiter.

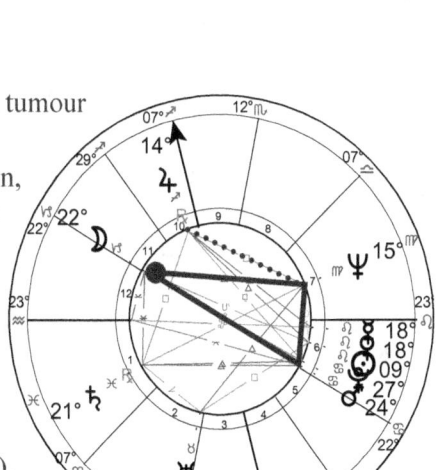

c. Brain trauma, died

Sonny Bono (16 February 1935, 21:21, Detroit, MI)
American entertainer who was killed on 5 January 1998, in a skiing accident. He hit a tree, dying instantly from brain trauma.
Cause: emotional. Most accidents are self-inflicted, caused by chronic anger. Bono had such a pattern: a t-square with three volatile planets fighting each other (Pluto, Uranus and Mars). This bred emotional toxicity that rebounded on him like a boomerang.
Organ: crown - brain and head, Mars in the 1H.
Effect: brain trauma. While skiing (Uranus rules the 5H of recreation), he suffered a massive blow to the head and died (Pluto-Mars > Uranus in Aries, which is located on the cusp of the 8H of death).
- ▲ (C) Mars, Pluto, Uranus. (O) Mars. (E) Mars, Pluto, Uranus.
- On the day Bono died, the Mars wing of the t-square by solar-arc, had progressed to 26 Sagittarius, the midpoint of Mars-Saturn. The event was karmic.

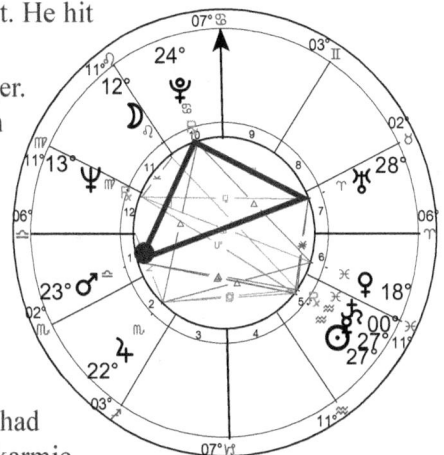

Ennis Cosby (15 April 1969, 00:28 Los Angeles CA)

Son of Bill and Camille Cosby. On 16 January 1997, while repairing his car tire, he was shot in the head during a robbery.

Cause: emotional. Cosby was hot-headed with a temper that could rapidly erupt (Moon in Aries - trine Mars, opposite Uranus). This type of force attracts "accidents".

Organ: crown - brain mass, the Moon in Aries.

Effect: brain trauma. Cosby was shot (Mars), in the brain (Moon in Aries), and died (Uranus in the 8th house of death).

▲ (C) Mars, Moon. (O) Moon. (E) Mars, Uranus.

- On the day Cosby was shot, solar-arc Mars (guns and violence), had progressed to 13 Capricorn and was on the ascendant, which is related to the head.

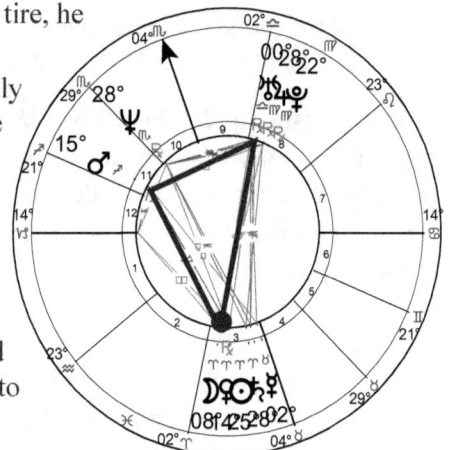

Abraham Lincoln (12 February 1809, 06:54 Hodgenville KY)

Lincoln, the 16th President of the United States was a disciple. People at this level are able to release tension positively through service activities. This means that the cause of death that occurred on April 14 1865 was not caused by his anger or negativity. His goodness attracted fanatics.

Cause: karmic. Lincoln was stalked and attacked by a fanatic who opposed him ideologically and the core values he stood for (Mars, ruler of the 2H of values, semi-square Neptune). The fanatic belonged to a secret organisation (Neptune septile Moon in Capricorn in the 12H of hidden things). With Saturn conjunct Neptune, karma was involved.

Organ: crown - head, Mars, brain mass the Moon.

Effect: brain trauma. The fanatic shot Lincoln in the brain (Mars square Moon), and he died (Mars in the 8H of death).

▲ (C) Saturn, Neptune. (O) Mars, Moon. (E) Mars.

- On the fatal day, transit Mars was at 7 Cancer, square natal Venus at 7 Aries, the ruler of the 8H of death. Additionally, transit Saturn, ruler of the 12H of hidden enemies, was moving over natal Mars. The killer was an agent of his political and ideological foes.

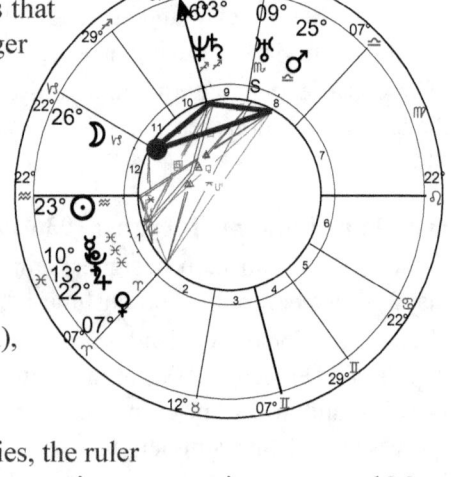

d. Hydrocephalus

Congenital hydrocephalus is caused by a brain malformation, a structural defect in the brain present at birth, which causes excessive cerebrospinal fluid to accumulate in brain cavities. The brain mass and structure are ruled by the 3rd ray, carried by Cancer, Capricorn and their rulers Saturn and the Moon.

Linda Martel (21 August 1956, 03.30 BST, Guernsey UK)

British child born with spina bifida and hydrocephalus. A prodigy, Martel healed some 2000 people before she died at age 5. An advanced soul, she may have returned briefly to work off personal karma to do with parenting and children (Saturn is in the 5H of children).

Cause: karmic-genetic. Defective DNA, a karmic implication from a past life (Moon in Aquarius, in the 8H of inheritances, square Saturn), caused a deformity in the brain structure and serious abnormalities in the spine (opposite Sun-Pluto in Leo; a t-square).

Organ: crown - brain mass the Moon, the spine Leo.

Effect: hydrocephalus. Brain malformations let fluid to leak into brain cavities (Moon > Saturn).

▲ (C) Saturn, Moon. (O) Moon, Leo. (E) Saturn, Pluto.

- Martel died at 5. The Moon by solar-arc had moved to 28 Aquarius, exactly opposite the natal Sun and Pluto that rules death.

e. Meningitis

The meninges membranes (Moon or Saturn), that cover the central nervous system become inflamed due to a bacterial infection (Uranus), a fungus (Moon), or virus (Neptune). It is life-threatening, especially if Pluto is involved in the Health Triangle.

Alexander Eben (11 December 1953, 02.42 am, Charlotte NC)

Eben is an American neurosurgeon and author of 'Proof of Heaven' in which he describes his 2008 near-death experience while in a meningitis-induced coma. He has a 'Kite' planetary pattern with Pluto as the focal point. Pluto is a ruler of the crown chakra and brain, and Eben is a neurosurgeon, which fits Eben's profession.

Cause: emotional. A volatile and explosive temper is behind the trouble. His fiery displays invited inflammatory attacks like meningitis (Mars, co-ruler of the 6H of health with Aries sharing the cusp, square Uranus).

Organ: crown - brain mass and meninges, Cancer and the Moon.

Effect: meningitis. Reports say Eben had a bacterial infection. This is helpful, because from the chart it is hard to tell whether a virus (Neptune) or bacteria (Uranus), caused his attack. Both these planets aspect Mars. The brain infection caused seizures (Uranus square Mars, the Moon disposits Uranus).

▲ (C) Mars, Uranus. (O) Cancer, Moon. (E) Uranus, Mars.

- In 2008, the Kite pattern had rotated by solar-arc, so that the Pluto wing was at 20 Libra and stationed on the ascendant. Eben contracted meningitis and nearly died. The ascendant represents soul purpose. Eben changed. Now he uses his experience to help others.

Oscar Wilde (16 October 1854, 03:00, Dublin Ireland)

Irish playwright and poet, Wilde died lonely, broke and disease-ravaged from acute meningitis on 30 November 1900. The Moon represents the "prison of the soul". It is in luxury loving Leo, in close proximity to the 12H cusp. He lived an extravagant lifestyle, which contributed to his self-undoing.

Cause: misuse of sexual force. The cause of the disease is reported as being syphilis related (Uranus). Though married, he was promiscuous and had affairs (Uranus, the ruler of the sexual sacral chakra falls in Taurus, the sign of desire).

Organ: crown - brain meninges the Moon, nervous system Mercury.

Effect: meningitis. The trouble is shown by a t-square. Wilde picked up a bacterial infection (Uranus), which attacked the meninges (Moon) of the nervous system (Mercury). There were seizures and he died (Uranus - Mercury in Scorpio, the natural ruler of the 8H of death).

▲ (C) Uranus. (O) Moon, Mercury. (E) Uranus.

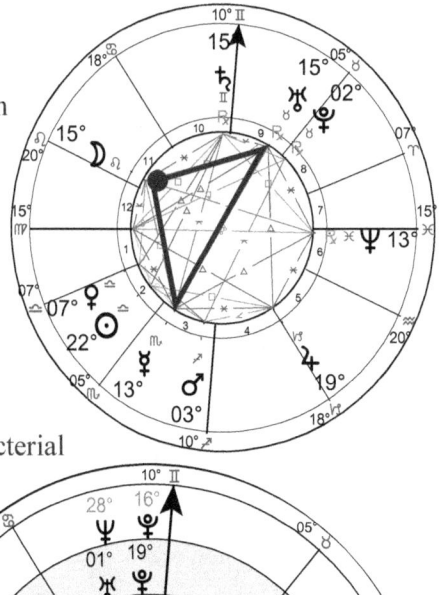

Chart for 30 November 1900: inner chart natal, middle chart solar-arc directions, outer chart transits.

- When Wilde died, the progressed Moon was in the 8H, moving towards Pluto.

- At the same time, the t-square had rotated by solar-arc, so that all three planets aspected natal Pluto. Solar-arc Moon was in the 1st house, inconjunct Pluto; solar-arc Uranus was at 1 Cancer sextile Pluto; solar-arc Saturn was at 1 Leo square Pluto. The dying process for Wilde was not easy.

f. Sleep disorders

Sleep is governed by the 1st ray and the crown chakra. Melatonin produced by the pineal gland affects the circadian rhythm, which keeps us in harmony with the 24-hour day.

Astro.com 12077 (29 January 1952, 15:30) - narcolepsy

American male with narcolepsy, a disorder where there is excessive daytime sleepiness and uncontrollable, sudden, falling asleep. He was the grandson and son of two narcoleptic women.

Cause: emotional. This condition can occur with people whose Physical Plane grounding is very weak, who are astral in consciousness and are focused in the solar plexus. This enables them to slip away easily to the Astral Plane.

Organ: crown - sleep, represented by 1st ray Pluto, Neptune governs the sleep state.

Effect: narcolepsy. The Moon in Pisces represents the trouble. It is the "finger" of God point in a Yod planetary pattern, with the two planets associated with sleep - Neptune and Pluto, the prongs. Developmentally, our subject was being asked to ground himself securely in his physical body (earth-sign Virgo is opposite the "finger point"). This would close the easy-access door to the Astral Plane, restoring balance to his sleep patterns (Moon in Pisces inconjunct Neptune in Libra sextile Pluto).

▲ (C) Moon, Neptune. (O) Pluto, Neptune. (E) Pisces, Neptune.

Linda Ronstadt (15 July 1946, 17:39, Tucson AZ) - sleep apnoea

American singer of country, folk, ballads and rock who had obstructive sleep apnoea, a problem associated with obesity.

Cause: emotional. Disturbed emotions dominated Ronstadt's life (Moon, the handle of a "bucket" pattern, standing alone on one side of the chart). To offset anxiety she would mentally detach from her feelings (Mercury opposite the Moon in Aquarius), and comfort-eat fatty and sugary foods (Mercury in Leo, ruler of 6H of diet; Moon trine Jupiter in Libra).

Organ: throat - airways, Mercury.

Effect: sleep apnoea. As a consequence of diet, a fatty-tissue blockage formed in the airways (Jupiter sextile Mercury). This interrupted breathing during sleep (Pluto conjunct Mercury). It is a dangerous condition that can result in death.

▲ (C) Moon. (O) Mercury. (E) Jupiter, Pluto.

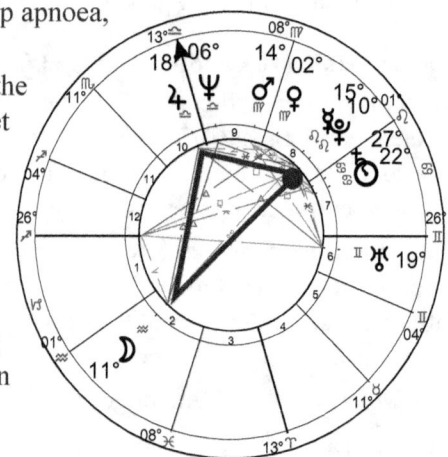

Billy Martin (16 May 1928 15:43, Berkeley CA) - insomnia

American baseball player who had treatment for insomnia and acute melancholia following a divorce in 1955.

Cause: emotional. Martin was very intense emotionally and was powerfully invested in his marriage (Pluto in Cancer square the Moon in the 7H of marriage). Consequently, when his marriage broke apart he was so distressed he had a temporary mental break-down. Pluto in Cancer is the primary instigator of the trouble.

Organ: crown - sleep, 1st ray Pluto.

Effect: insomnia, depression. Martin suffered from insomnia his disturbed emotions just would not let his brain rest (Pluto square Moon in Aries conjunct Jupiter; ruler of Aries - Mars, conjunct Uranus). Exhausted, he went into deep depression (Pluto inconjunct Saturn, trine the Moon).

▲ (C) Moon, Pluto. (O) Pluto. (E) Moon in Aries, Saturn.

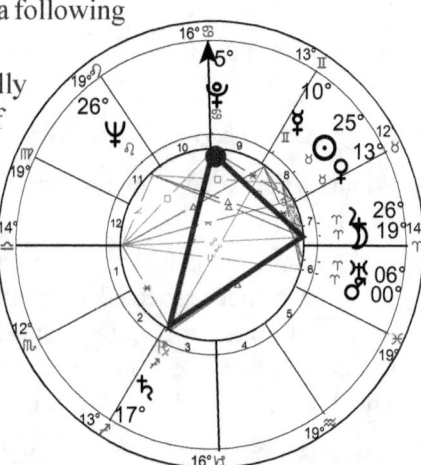

g. Stroke

A stroke occurs when the arteries block or rupture so that life-giving blood does not reach the brain and cells die from lack of oxygen. Stroke is a 1st ray disease, carried by Pluto, Mars via Aries, Uranus and Saturn. Jupiter rules arteries and Saturn is the major "blocker".

John Quincy Adams (11 July 1767, 11:00, Quincy Neck MA)

Adams was an American statesman and the 6th President of the United States. He had a paralytic stroke in Boston in 1847, and died 23 February 1848.

Cause: emotional. Adams was a sensitive and emotional Cancer Sun person and being President of the US placed great strain upon him. There was tremendous frustration and pressure in both his professional and family life (Cancer-Capricorn opposition across the 10th - 4th houses). Matters were not helped by his volatile temper, which caused pressure to build (Mars in Leo square Uranus, which is sesquiquadrate Jupiter in the 12H of self-undoing. Jupiter rules the 6H of health with Pisces on the cusp). This latter pattern is related to his eventual stroke.

Organ: crown - brain, Mars.

Effect: stroke. Quincy was 81 when he had his stroke so his body was ageing and stiffening. Finally it was all too much. High blood pressure caused a paralysing stroke and he died (Mars > Jupiter and Uranus that is in the 8H of death).

▲ (C) Mars, Uranus. (O) Mars. (E) Mars, Uranus, Jupiter.

- When Adams died, the Sun > Pluto-Moon aspect, had rotated by solar-arc so that it straddled the decendant - ascendant axis, rendering the head and brain (the ascendant) vulnerable to trouble.

Hilda Doolittle (10 September 1886, 12:35, Bethlehem PA)

Doolittle was an American poet and novelist who become known for her association with early 20th century avant-garde poets. She was very independent for her time and an individualist (Moon in Aquarius, handle of a "bucket" planet pattern). She suffered a stroke in July 1961 and died two months later.

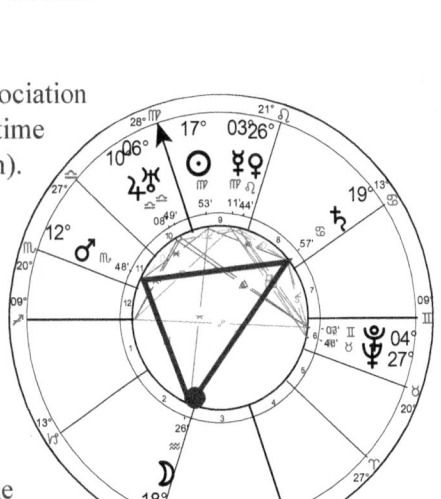

Cause: emotional. Saturn in Cancer is emotionally debilitating. People like Doolittle who have it, wall off their emotions because they are unable to deal with hurt feelings that follow rejection. This was easy for Doolittle, because with the Moon in cerebral Aquarius, she rationalised how she felt. But she also harboured revengeful anger, which she vented on friends or those in her group (Mars in Scorpio in the 11H of friends, square the Moon). This anger and repression of emotions, built up stress.

Additionally, a love of rich, sweet foods (Venus in Leo is the ruler of the 6H of diet with greedy Taurus on the cusp), and alcohol (square Neptune in the 6H of health); contributed to fatty build up in the arteries (Venus semi-square Jupiter).

Organ: crown - brain mass the Moon.

Effect: stroke. Eventually, a blockage (Saturn), to blood flow (inconjunct Moon in Aquarius), brought on a stroke (Moon square Mars), which eventually killed her (Saturn in the 8H of death).

▲ (C) Saturn in Cancer, Moon, Mars. (O) Moon. (E) Saturn, Mars.

- In the month Doolittle had her stroke (July 1961), Mars by solar-arc was at 27 Capricorn, with transit Saturn sitting on top of it, representing loss of blood supply and the stroke.
- Venus represents the nervous system and also the cardiovascular system because of its natal location in Leo. By solar-arc it had rotated to natal Mars. The stroke occurred, and these systems were damaged.
- Progressed Moon, the ruler of the 8H of death was at 16 Scorpio, still 2 degrees out from the exact square to the natal Moon at 18 Aquarius. She withstood death for 2 more months before the soul freed itself.

1b. The Brain - Dementia

Dementia is the breakdown of the cellular structure of the brain so that consciousness is unable to work through the nervous system. The result is fading cognition. The brain mass is governed by ray 3, carried by the Moon via Cancer, and Saturn. Sometimes Mars via Aries represents the brain. Damage causing brain shrinkage is a 1st ray effect, brought on primarily by Saturn and Pluto. Nervous system rulers (Mercury, Venus, Uranus and planets in Gemini), represent cognition. There are three main types of dementia.

- The most common is *Alzheimer's* (50-70% of dementia cases). Nerve cells die, forming plaques and tangles that impair brain function. There is tissue loss, the cortex shrinks and atrophies. Pluto and Saturn are the danger planets.
- In *vascular dementia* (VCD - 25%), a part of the brain dies because it does not get enough blood due to damaged brain blood-vessels, typically caused through small strokes. Look particularly at Mars for strokes and alternatively, Uranus.
- *Lewy body dementia* (LBD - 15%). There are visual hallucinations and Parkinson-like movements. Abnormal protein deposits in the brain cause problems with thinking, movement and moods. Uranus may be involved.

a. Alzheimer's

Harold Wilson (11 March 1916, 10:45, Huddersfield UK)
Ex-British Prime Minister renowned for his razor like intellect. In April 1976, when he resigned, commentators say he was showing the symptoms of intellectual decline. He died in May 1995.

Cause: emotional. Wilson used his formidable will to suppress his emotions and this served him well in his career where he demonstrated powerful self-resolve (Saturn-Pluto in Cancer on the ascendant, Pluto trine MC).

Organ: crown - brain mass, the Moon.

Effect: Alzheimer's. But Wilson's habit of blocking force caused congestion in the crown chakra (Pluto), wreaking havoc with brain tissue (Moon), causing the disease. Pluto and Saturn are midpoint the Moon and Neptune, representing brain tissue destruction and descent into oblivion (Neptune).

▲ (C) Pluto and Saturn in Cancer. (O) Moon. (E) Pluto, Saturn, Neptune.

- In 1974-75, two years before he retired, Wilson went through his second Saturn return and at the same time, the Sun progressed into the 12H, symbolising consciousness going into obscuration. Astrologically, this could pinpoint the start of his mental decline.

Ronald Reagan (6 February 1911, 04:16, Tampico, IL)
American movie star and US President. Publicly, he was diagnosed in 1994, though symptoms were already showing in 1984.

Cause: emotional. Reagan was an intelligent Aquarian Sun person with a stubborn Taurus Moon, which he hid this under a benevolent Sagittarius appearance (ascendant). The combination - with good looks, brought him popularity in film and politics. But stubbornness and a tendency to fester over slights is related to the disease (Moon semi-square Pluto in Gemini that rules the 7H of "others"; Pluto inconjunct Uranus-Mercury).

Organ: crown - brain mass the Moon, cognition Mercury.

Effect: Alzheimer's. By the time he reached 70, his habit of blocking force plus the deteriorating effects of age caused damage to brain cells (Pluto in the 6H of health > Moon). Cognition was gradually destroyed (Pluto in Gemini > Uranus-Mercury in ageing Capricorn). Side-effects of the disease eventually killed him (Mercury co-rules the 8H of death with Virgo sharing the cusp).

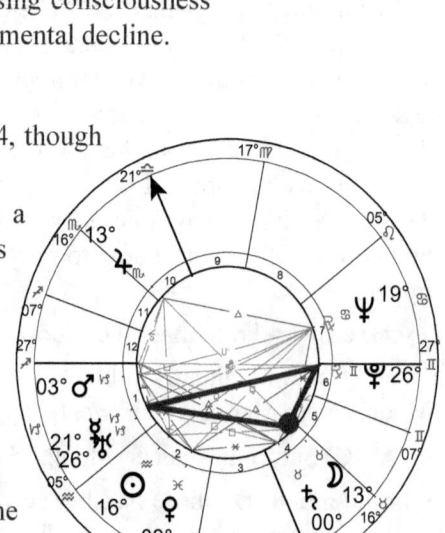

▲ (C) Moon, Pluto. (O) Moon, Mercury. (E) Pluto, Uranus.

b. Alzheimer's caused by a syphilitic gene

A cause of dementia is the syphilitic gene which most of us have inherited from our fore-fathers. The sacral chakra rulers - Mars and Uranus may be implicated.

> [Dementia] due to the breaking down of the brain tissue. Far more of these are definitely syphilitic in origin.. for the physical sex organs are a lower correspondence of the negative-positive relation existing in the brain between the two head centres and the pituitary and pineal glands. [1]

Glen Campbell (22 April 1936, 20:14, Delight, AR)

American country music singer, known for a series of hit songs in the 1960's and 70's. He had many tumultuous affairs and married four times.

Cause: sexual misuse. With the influence of sensuous Taurus powerfully embedded in his nature and romantic Venus afflicted in aggressive and lusty Aries, we see that Campbell had a powerful sex drive and was inclined to promiscuity. It is likely with this line up on planets and their influence in the 6H of health that he caught STD's.

Organ: crown - brain Mars, consciousness Uranus.

Effect: Alzheimer's. Campbell inherited the syphilitic gene (Mars wide conjunction to Uranus). Brain tissue was damaged as brain fluid atrophied (Mars in an easy-opposition pattern with Saturn in Pisces and Neptune afflicted in Virgo). Consequently, consciousness disappeared into oblivion.

▲ (C) Taurus, Mars. (O) Mars, Uranus. (E) Mars, Saturn, Neptune.

• Loss of memory probably started as early as 2001 when the Taurus stellium by solar-arc started to move over natal Pluto. Serious trouble started in 2009-2010 when Mercury crossed, then Mars in 2009-2010. Campbell went public in June 2011 with the news that he had Alzheimer's. He became a patient at an Alzheimer's long-term care and treatment facility in 2014 and died of the disease on August 8 2017.

c. Huntington's Disease

Huntington's that leads to dementia is genetic (Uranus). Accompanying symptoms are mood swings (Moon) and jerky movements (Uranus). Because it is inherited, examine the Moon or Uranus from a psychological angle to try to uncover toxic attitudes being passed down the family line.

Sophie Daumier (24 November 1934, 05:30; Boulongne sur Mer, France)

French film actress who inherited and died from Huntington's. So did her son.

Cause: genetic. The defective gene is shown by Uranus, retrograde in the 6H of health. Uranus rules the 4H of family, so its location tells us that there is a history of chronic ill health in the family arising from this DNA legacy (Uranus square destructive Pluto in Cancer, and dispositing Saturn).

Daumier's family life was not easy, with disciplinarian Saturn standing guard over the family on the 4H cusp, ready to deal out biting criticism and public shaming for any mistakes she made (Saturn inconjunct Mars-Neptune in the 10th house of status). The passing on of this horrendous disease is due to family karma.

Organ: crown - brain mass Pluto in Cancer, cognition Uranus.

Effect: Huntington's. The gene caused the destruction of brain tissue and brain neurons (Uranus in Aries square Pluto in Cancer), resulting in the loss of cognition so that consciousness slipped into oblivion (Uranus sesquiquadrate Neptune, which in turn is semi-square Pluto).

▲ (C) Uranus. (O) Pluto in Cancer, Uranus. (E) Pluto, Neptune.

---

[1] Bailey, Alice A; Esoteric Healing, 316.

Woody Guthrie (14 July 1912, Okemah, OK).
Unknown time, 12 PM midday used and the 0 degrees Aries House System.
American singer-songwriter who died from complications of Huntington's disease on 19 November 2015.
Cause: genetic. Potential trouble is quickly seen - the defective gene (Uranus) opposes a Cancer stellium that includes the Moon, which rules the brain mass. The unhealthy family pattern being passed down the family line points to hidden abuse (Uranus opposite Neptune, the natural ruler of the 12H).
Organ: crown - brain mass the Moon, cognition Uranus and Mercury.
Effect: Huntington's. The gene (Uranus) caused aberrations in brain tissue that resulted in mood swings (Cancer planets and the Moon). As damage proceeded, there was a loss of cognition as consciousness disappeared into oblivion (Uranus quindecile Mercury, opposite Neptune).

▲ (C) Uranus, Cancer. (O) Moon, Uranus, Mercury. (E) Uranus, Neptune.

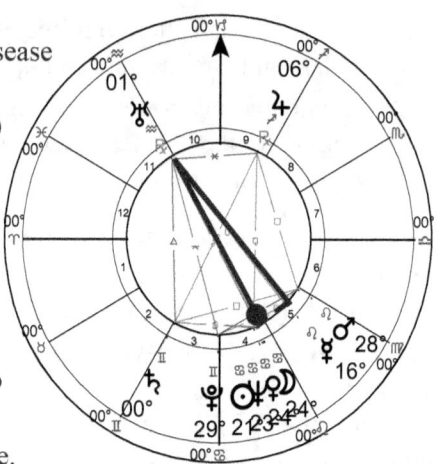

d. Lewy Body Dementia (LBD)

LBD differs from Alzheimer's because it incorporates a form of Parkinsonism, resulting in tremors (Uranus), visual hallucinations (Moon-Neptune), mood swings and depression (Saturn).

Robin Williams (21 July 1951, 13:34, Chicago IL)
American actor who became famous in the TV series Mork and Mindy. He hung himself on 11 August 2014. Afterwards it was revealed he had LBD.
Cause: genetic-emotional. Behind his funny, joke-quipping facade, Williams was deeply troubled. He was very sensitive emotionally (Moon in Pisces), but also explosively angry (Mars conjunct Uranus), and would brood over slights. He released tension through his film work, but there was a manic, unstable aspect (Mars-Uranus in Cancer). This was the root cause of the trouble, since Mars rules the 6H of health.
Organ: crown - brain mass, Mars in Cancer and Jupiter in Aries.
Effect: LBD. Damage to brain cells manifested rapidly in 2013. There was inflammation (Mars and Jupiter in Aries), chemical disturbances and mutations in brain neurons (Uranus). As his cognitive function dissolved, he hallucinated (Uranus square Neptune on the cusp of the 12H of the mysterious and unknown).

▲ (C) Mars, Uranus. (O) Mars in Cancer, Aries. (E) Mars, Uranus, Neptune.

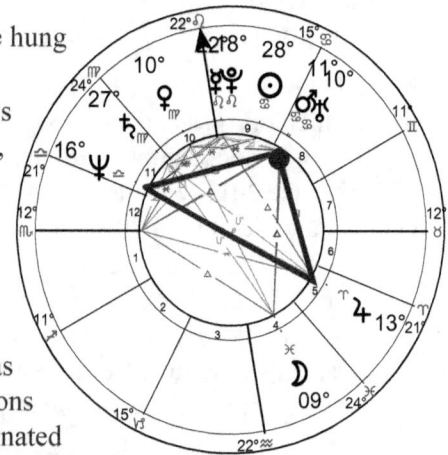

- Trouble started around November 2013, when there was an eclipse on the ascendant, a warning of the serious brain and nervous system trouble that was unfolding.
- At the same time, transit Pluto was in Capricorn, moving opposite natal Uranus-Mars at the hub of the t-square. 1st ray fire attacked, triggering the neurological trouble. Williams was lucid one minute then a minute later was lost in confusion - classic symptoms of LBD.
- When Williams hung himself on 11 August 2014, Pluto was still in this position, opposing Mars in the 8th house of death. Additionally, transit Mars was on his Scorpio ascendant, a sign that rules suffocation.

|| NB. SUICIDE. No one is expected to suffer the rigours of a broken or diseased body. The sage Djwhal Khul said: *"Lives are preserved in form (frequently an unconscious invalid, an old person whose response apparatus of contact and response is imperfect, or a baby who is not normal) that could be well permitted liberation. They serve no useful purpose and cause much pain and suffering to forms which nature (left to herself) would extinguish.* **Through our overemphasis on the value of form life and through the universal fear of death.. we arrest the natural processes and hold the life, which is struggling to be free.***"* [1]

Suicide is not sanctioned, but the releasing of the soul from a seriously damaged body is within the "law" if there is no quality of life and the body is being unnaturally preserved by modern medicine and technology.

---

[1] Bailey, Alice A; Esoteric Healing, 350-1.

e. Vascular Dementia (VCD)

In VCD, look for evidence of strokes (Aries, Mars, Uranus), and deprivation (Saturn, Pluto) of blood (Mars, Uranus, Neptune, perhaps the Sun and Leo) to the brain. Brain explosions such as strokes are manifestations of emotional explosions caused by unresolved anger and hatred.

Margaret Thatcher (13 October 1925, 09:00, Grantham UK)

Thatcher was a long serving Prime Minister of the United Kingdom from 1979 to 1990. She made some hard economic decisions that earned her the approval of some and hatred from others. A neurologist said that Thatcher had a series of small strokes over many years that went unnoticed until her legendary memory started to slip. The public was informed she had dementia in 2005.

Cause: emotional. Thatcher had dreams of greatness (Moon-Neptune in Leo conjunct the MC), which she realised. She was called the Iron Lady because of the toughness she displayed in pushing through her conservative economic reforms and policies. We see this force coming from the grand-trine of 1st ray planets (Saturn on the Scorpio ascendant, trine Pluto and Uranus) and it brought her political success.

Thatcher was fine when things were going her way (the grand-trine, but she could be explosive when she was crossed (Pluto in a t-square with Mars and Jupiter). This latter pattern underlies her trouble, since Mars rules the 6H of health.

Organ: crown - brain mass Pluto in Cancer, cognition Uranus.

Effect: dementia. Arteries hardened (Jupiter in Capricorn), and she had a series of small strokes that destroyed brain tissue (Mars). The consequence was loss of cognition and disengagement from reality at the end of life (Uranus in Pisces in the 4H of life endings).

▲ (C) Mars, Pluto. (O) Pluto in Cancer, Uranus. (E) Jupiter, Mars, Uranus.

Andrew Sachs (7 April 1930, 09:00, Berlin Germany)

British actor born in Berlin, his family immigrated to London in 1938 to escape Nazi persecution. Diagnosed with VCD in 2012, it eventually left him unable to speak and move without a wheelchair. He died on 23 November 2016, aged 86.

Cause: emotional. Sachs was tough and hard (t-square with three 1st ray planets - Uranus, Pluto, Saturn), and had difficulty processing his emotions in a healthy way. Defensive and protective he would repress injured feelings (Pluto in the 1H in Cancer opposite Saturn; Moon in Cancer quindecile Saturn); then would explode in a volcanic rage when he could no longer hold this force in (the t-square forces).

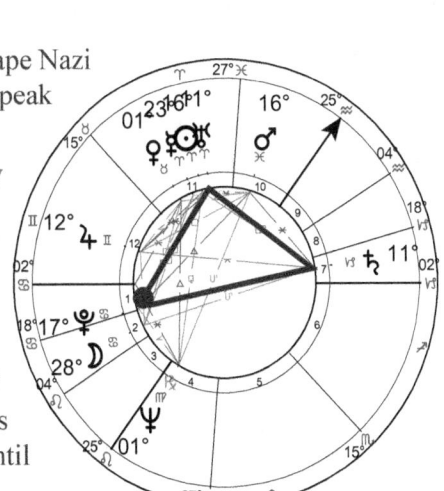

Although this pattern is related to his disease (Pluto rules the 6H of health), it did not manifest until he was in his 80's. This tells us that Sachs managed to achieve a state of relative harmony and balance in his life until common ageing took its toll.

Organ: crown - brain mass Pluto in Cancer; nervous system and cognition Uranus in Aries.

Effect: dementia. In later life as blood vessels hardened and stress built (the t-square), Sachs had a series of small strokes, which restricted blood flow to the brain (Uranus in Aries > Pluto in Cancer), so that brain tissue and cognition were gradually destroyed. Sachs lived on several years after the disease began to incapacitate him, destroying his quality of life and mobility so that he was wheelchair bound (Saturn inconjunct Jupiter in the 12H of major illnesses and hospitals).

▲ (C) Pluto in Cancer in the 1H. (O) Cancer, Uranus (E) Saturn, Uranus, Pluto.

- The condition struck him as the Uranus point of the Health Triangle by solar-arc, approached and moved over the ascendant.

2. Ajna Chakra Diseases

The ajna rules the pituitary gland, the nervous system, the senses and the eyes, ears, nose and face. It receives energy from Rays 5 and 4, Aries and Gemini, Venus and Mercury.

2a. Ears

When hearing is impaired, sound waves or nerve electrical impulses are not passed to the brain. The most common cause is disease or damage to the auditory nerves through injuries or noise explosions. Defective genes that affect hearing can be passed down to children - estimated to be around 60% to 65% of cases. A foetus may incur damage if mother has a disease such as rubella, or again if a child itself has rubella or other virulent infection. The ears are ruled by the ajna (Mercury, Venus and Gemini) and also the throat chakra (Mercury). The psychology underlying deafness is related to an unwillingness to hear bad news. Saturn, which blocks, is the primary indicator of deafness.

a. Congenital deafness

Astro.com 13842 (13 January 1963, 10:05, London)
A British man, deaf from birth.
Cause: genetic-karmic. Hypothetically, there is a karmic backlash for misusing speech in a previous life (Saturn conjunct Mercury in the 12H).
Organ: ajna - ear nerves Mercury and Venus.
Effect: deafness. A bacterial infection (Uranus), which the mother contracted while pregnant (conjunct Moon in the 6H of health), damaged nerve cells (square Venus, inconjunct Mercury), resulting in shrivelled auditory nerves and deafness (Mercury conjunct Saturn).
▲ (C) Uranus, Saturn. (O) Mercury, Venus. (E) Uranus, Saturn.

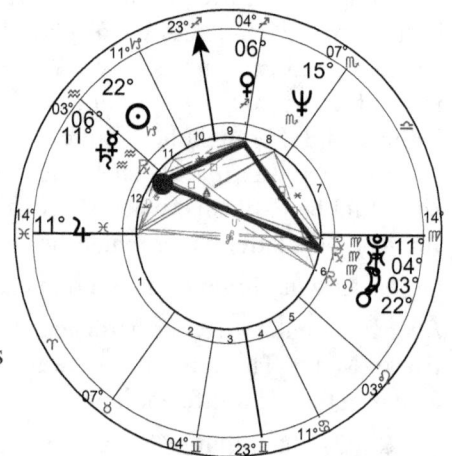

Astro.com 12561 (14 January 1954 06:58, Berwyn Il).
American male with congenital deafness, unknown cause.
Cause: congenital. The cause of his deafness was probably a virus (Neptune), contracted by the mother during pregnancy (square Uranus in Cancer, Neptune inconjunct the Moon). The virus targeted the organs of hearing (Neptune square Venus and Mercury, a t-square).
Organ: ajna - ear nerves Mercury and Venus.
Effect: deafness. He was left deaf (Venus-Mercury in Capricorn).
▲ (C) Uranus in Cancer. (O) Mercury, Venus. (E) Neptune, Capricorn.

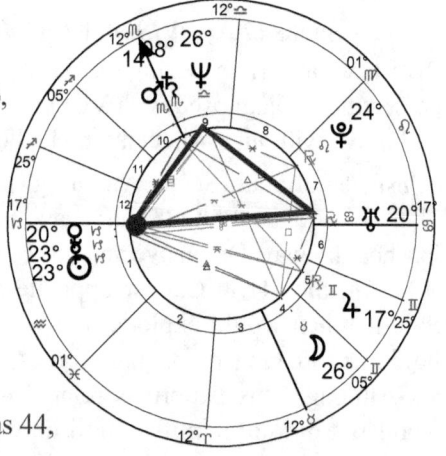

Ludwig van Beethoven (16 December 1770, 03:40, Bonn Germany).
Brilliant musician, who began to lose his hearing at age 26. By the time he was 44, he was almost completely deaf.
Cause: congenital. Beethoven was born with a susceptibility to ear infections (Mercury in detriment in Sagittarius, conjunct the Moon, square Neptune, opposite Mars in Gemini. Mars rules the 6H of health).
Organ: ajna - ear nerves, Mercury.
Effect: deafness. By the time he reached his middle twenties, his ear nerves were damaged to the point he had difficulty hearing.
▲ (C) Moon. (O) Mercury. (E) Mars, Neptune.

- In 1796 when he was 26, Neptune was transiting backwards and forwards over the natal ascendant, exacerbating his trouble.
- Additionally, solar-arc Mercury (ear nerves) had progressed to malevolent Pluto in Capricorn, indicating nerve damage.

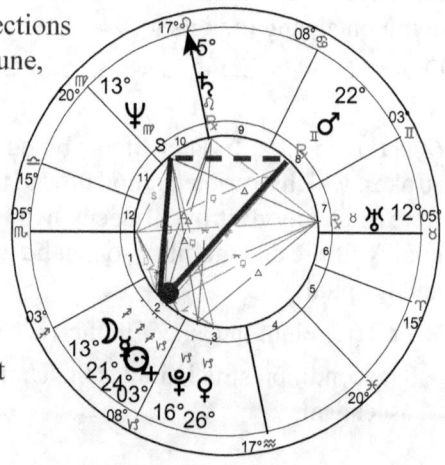

b. Deafness caused by Measles/ Rubella

Charles Eyck (24 March 1897, 11:00, Meerssen, Holland).
Dutch visual artist who had several gallery and museum exhibitions. At age 11, he became deaf after contracting rubella.

Cause: emotional. Eyck was born with a pattern that shows an unwillingness to hear bad news (Mercury square Neptune in the 12H of hidden things), which would explain why he was born with a congenital weakness in his ear nerves (Moon in the 6H of health square Mercury in detriment in Pisces). He was also susceptible to ear damage from viral infections. Mercury and Neptune are in a hostile mutual reception, are in each other's signs, which in this case is detrimental to auditory health.

Organ: ajna - ear nerves, Mercury and Gemini.

Effect: deafness. A viral attack (Neptune), destroyed ear nerves causing deafness (Mercury square Neptune that is in turn conjunct Pluto in Gemini).

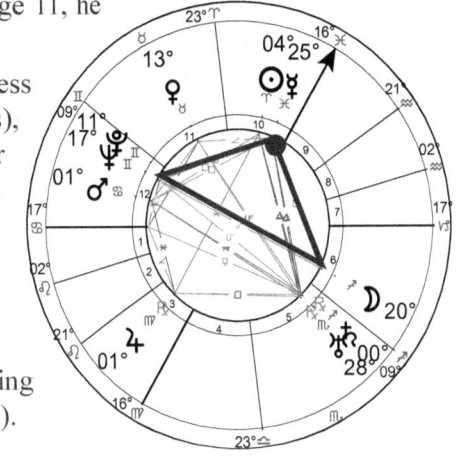

▲ (C) Moon. (O) Mercury, Gemini. (E) Neptune, Pluto.

• In 1908, transit Neptune moved over his ascendant, indicating the viral attack.

Astro.com 14115 (20 November 1965, 16:47, Chester PA).
This American child was given a measles vaccine at age one. Two days later he had terrible nerve pain in his ears. a high fever and he lost his hearing.

Cause: karmic. Our subject had lessons to learn about the misuse of speech (Saturn square Mercury). It seems this karma came via a vaccine (opposite Uranus) that may have been contaminated (Uranus conjunct Pluto). Pluto co-rules the 6H of health with Scorpio sharing the cusp.

Organ: ajna - ear nerves, Mercury.

Effect: deafness. A violent reaction to the vaccine left the child deaf (Mercury in detriment in Sagittarius in a t-square with Uranus, Pluto and Saturn). If the child's astrology chart had been consulted the parents would have been alerted to the dangers of "modern" (Uranus) medicine.

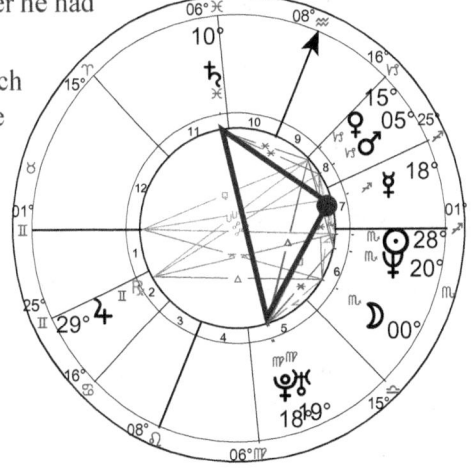

▲ (C) Saturn. (O) Mercury. (E) Uranus, Pluto, Saturn.

c. Deafness caused by Otosclerosis

Dame Kathleen Ollerenshaw (1 October 1912, 07:00, Manchester UK)
British mathematician and politician who was Lord Mayor of Manchester from 1975 to 1976 and an advisor on educational matters to Margaret Thatcher's government in the 1980s.

Cause: karmic-emotional. Ollerenshaw inherited a hearing problem from her father's side (the Moon co-rules the 10H of the father with Cancer sharing the cusp, in Gemini; conjunct Saturn, in the 8H of inheritances). Mercury is buried in the 12H of hidden matters, a classic placement for a person who does not want to hear bad news, a psychological pattern related to deafness.

Organ: ajna - ear nerves, Mercury, Venus and Gemini.

Effect: deafness. Ollerenshaw was born partially deaf due to otosclerosis, a condition where middle ear bones fuse, preventing normal transmission of sound from the eardrum into the inner ear (Moon-Saturn in Gemini). Then when she was 8, a viral infection (Neptune ruling the 6H of health) further damaged ear nerves, leaving her almost completely deaf (septile Gemini planets, square Venus afflicted in Scorpio; Saturn inconjunct Venus).

▲ (C) Saturn, Moon. (O) Mercury, Venus, Gemini. (E) Saturn, Neptune.

2b. Eyes

Vision depends upon the ability of the eye to receive and focus light rays and transfer this information to the occipital lobe of the brain for processing. The key element is *light*. The physical eye came into being in response to the light of the Sun. The Sun rules the eyes, particularly the right eye. The Moon reflects the light of the Sun and co-rules the eyes, particularly the left eye. Light rays enter the eye through the cornea, which bends the light rays so they pass freely through the pupil and eye lens, which in turn focuses the light ray onto the retina. The bringing in, carrying and transporting of light messages through the eye is a Mercury function. The cells in the retina absorb and convert the light to electrochemical impulses, which are transferred along the optic nerve to the brain. This is a Mercury-Uranus function.

Certain points in the zodiac have a detrimental effect on sight, especially when the Sun or Moon is located here. These are the Pleiades at 29 Taurus, the Ascelli at Leo 6 and Antares at Sagittarius 8.

When vision is lost through disease, it suggests on a psychological level, that what is seen is not liked and that by closing the eyes we can block out reality. Babies with a vision handicap at birth or in early childhood, have a karmic carry-over from a previous life that may belong to them personally or to the family.

a. Congenital Blindness

Stevie Wonder (13 May 1950, 16:15, Saginaw MI).
Wonder is a blind African-American musician and singer. Neptune on the ascendant was both a blessing and a curse - he inherited magical music talent, but strange events related to his birth left him blind.

Cause: congenital. Wonder was born with a pattern of obscuring reality (Neptune on the ascendant) when he did not want to face the truth or see unpleasantness (opposite Venus afflicted in Aries, conjunct the Moon). Neptune carries the 6th ray and in its lower aspect is a symbol for racial bigotry and fanaticism. Its place on the ascendant that represents life perception, suggests Wonder's blindness and suffering is connected to racial abuse in a past life.

Organ: ajna - eyesight the Sun and Moon, eye nerves Mercury, Venus and Uranus.

Effect: blindness. Born prematurely (Moon in Aries), eye nerves were undeveloped (Moon > Neptune, Venus square Uranus); causing the retinas (Uranus) to detach.

The Sun and Mercury are conjunct the "dangerous to sight degree" of 29 Taurus. When oxygen was inappropriately pumped into the incubator, eye nerves were destroyed causing permanent blindness. Sun-Mercury (oxygen) are midpoint Uranus (incubator) and Venus (eye nerves).

▲ (C) Neptune. (O) Sun, Moon, Mercury, Venus, Uranus. (E) Neptune, Uranus.

The Roles Triplets (25 May 1975, 10:20, Sydney Australia).
The cause of blindness in these Australian triplets was the same as for Stevie Wonder. Born prematurely, they were given oxygen that damaged their eyes.

Cause: karmic-congenital. The birth was premature and foetal development was incomplete (the Moon is sesquiquadrate Saturn and Venus in Cancer). With Saturn's inclusion, we know the trouble is karmic.

Organ: ajna - eyesight the Sun and Moon, eye nerves Venus.

Effect: blindness. Blood vessels in the eyes were undeveloped and shrivelled (Saturn conjunct Venus; Sun opposite Neptune, which rules the bloodstream). The babies were left blind when they were given oxygen in their incubators (Sun in Gemini > Neptune, which is conjunct the Sagittarius 8th degree that is dangerous for eyesight).

▲ (C) Saturn, Moon. (O) Sun, Moon, Venus. (E) Saturn, Neptune.

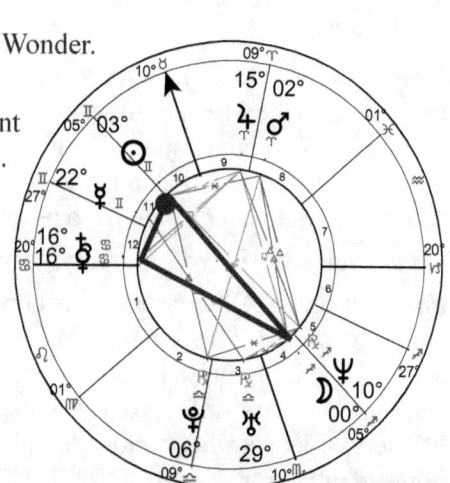

b. Blinded by Injuries

Georgie Borkowski (13 January 1950, 19:25, Medford Oregon).
American astrologer and student of religious philosophy, Borkowski's sight was destroyed in a bungled caesarean birth.

Cause: emotional. The Moon (eyes) is afflicted. It falls in Scorpio and opposes the 29 Taurus "dangerous to sight" degree. The injury may be karmically linked to serious past life family transgressions, with Pluto on the ascendant, the doorway into life, square the Moon in the 4H of family.

Organ: ajna - eye nerves Venus, sight the Moon.

Effect: blindness. Instruments (Uranus), used with roughness and lack of care at birth (semi-square Pluto on the ascendant), destroyed eye nerves (Pluto opposes Venus that is retrograde in Aquarius. Venus is sesquiquadrate Uranus). The result was blindness.

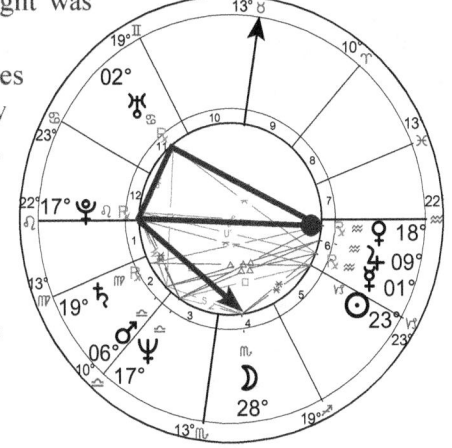

▲ (C) Moon. (O) Venus, Moon. (E) Uranus, Pluto

Vincent Humbert (3 February 1981, 10:32, Evreux France).
A car accident on 24 September 2000, left this youth blind, mute and quadriplegic.

Cause: emotional. Humbert was an explosively angry youth (Mars square Uranus), a pattern that lies behind many so-called accidents. It is a dangerous pattern because Uranus is in the 8H of death. Although the accident did not kill him, he was left in a condition where he wanted to die. He could only move his fingers.

Organ: ajna - eye nerves Mercury and Uranus.

Effect: blindness. The accident severed spinal nerves (Mars in Aquarius sesquiquadrate Saturn in the 6H of health. Uranus is septile Saturn), and damaged eye nerves (Mars conjunct Mercury, square Uranus). Uranus opposes the "dangerous to sight degree" of 29 Taurus.

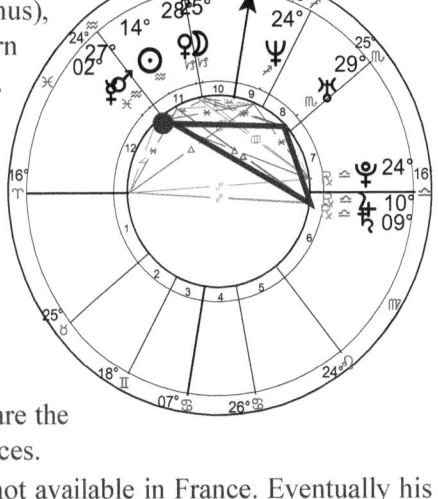

▲ (C) Mars, Uranus. (O) Mercury, Uranus. (E) Mars, Uranus, Saturn.

- On the day of the accident, solar-arc Pluto at 14 Scorpio was exactly square the natal Sun, and transit Mars at 4 Virgo opposed the progressed Sun at 4 Pisces.
- Unhappy with his situation, Humbert begged to die, but euthanasia was not available in France. Eventually his mother, with the assistance of a doctor, helped him die on 26 September 2003. The progressed Moon was in Scorpio, in the 8H of death conjunct Uranus.

Mel B, Melanie Brown (29 May 1975, 17:59, Leeds UK).
English singer who was a member of the Spice Girls pop group. She was left blind in her left eye after botched laser eye surgery sometime around 1999.

Cause: emotional. When she is afraid, Mel B has great difficulty facing and dealing with life without a huge emotional reaction (Uranus on the ascendant, square the Moon and Venus in Cancer). There is an unconscious fear that something shocking (Uranus) will happen and this underlies the trouble.

Organ: ajna - eye nerves Venus, left eye the Moon.

Effect: blindness. Laser surgery (Uranus) damaged nerves in the left eye (the Moon), causing blindness (Moon quindecile Saturn). With this pattern and Uranus in the 12H of major illnesses, Brown should be very careful in the future of ultra-modern medicine, especially of an experimental nature. She should also deal with her anger (Uranus inconjunct Mars) to avoid any "accidents" in the future.

▲ (C) Moon. (O) Moon, Venus. (E) Uranus, Saturn.

- In 1999, transit Mars moved over Uranus and ascendant from January to July. It is very likely the botched operation took part during that period.

Timothy Knatchbull (18 November 1964, 16:00, London UK).

Knatchbull was blinded by an IRA terrorist bombing while on holiday.

Cause: karmic. The attack targeted the aristocracy to which Knatchbull belonged, indicating family or group karma (Saturn rules 10H of royalty, with Capricorn on the cusp). Terrorists planted the bomb (the malefic planet group in Virgo, which carries the fanatical 6th ray). The attack occurred while Knatchbull was on holiday (malefics in the 5H of recreation). It killed his grandfather, Lord Louis Mountbatten and his identical twin.

Organ: ajna - eyesight the Sun, eye nerves Mercury, Uranus.

Effect: blindness. An ominous sign for eye health, is Knatchbull's ascendant which conjuncts the Pleiades at the "dangerous to sight" 29 Taurus degree - opposed by the Sun at 26 Scorpio. The bomb-damaged eye nerves (Mars conjunct Uranus square Mercury), destroying vision (Mars disposits the Sun; Saturn square the Sun; Mercury square Pluto). Mercury rules the 6H of health.

▲ (C) Saturn. (O) Sun, Mercury, Uranus. (E) Mars, Saturn.

Chart set for 27 August 1979: inner chart - natal, middle chart - secondary progressions, outer chart - transits.

- The bomb exploded on 27 August 1979. The Sun had progressed to 11 Sagittarius, conjunct Antares at 8 Sagittarius, a "dangerous for sight" region.
- Mars (the bomb), by progression, it was within 1 degree of the conjunction to Uranus. By transit, it was at 12 Cancer, inconjunct the progressed Sun (the eyes) and Antares.
- Saturn was transiting over Mars-Uranus-Pluto, highlighting the karmic factor.

Later, Knatchbull forgave Martin McGuinness, the man who most likely sanctioned the attack. When the Queen met McGuinness as her deputy First Minister of Northern Ireland in 2012, Knatchbull reportedly said, "We should be grateful to him for having changed".

c. Blinded through a Virus (unidentified)

Helen Keller (27 June 1880, 16:02, Tuscumbia Alabama)

American Keller contracted an illness when she was a child, which left her deaf and blind. The story of how she learned to communicate was made into a film called 'The Miracle Worker'. Keller blossomed and was the first deaf-blind person to earn a Bachelor of Arts degree.

Cause: karmic. Serious childhood diseases will usually be due to karma and Keller's chart shows potential damage to vision. Malefic Pluto is conjunct the "dangerous to sight" point - 29 Taurus, opposing the ascendant that is related to birth, the head and eyes.

Organ: ajna - eyesight the Sun, eye nerves Venus.

Effect: blindness. Keller was fine at birth, and then at 19 months in December 1881 she caught a virus, which damaged the eye nerves. Pluto is midpoint Venus (nerves) and Saturn in Aries (blindness). Neptune in the 6H of health represents the virus and its attack on eye nerves (semi-square Venus conjunct the Sun. Neptune is midpoint Pluto and Saturn, indicating a virulent and dangerous virus).

▲ (C) Saturn. (O) Sun, Venus. (E) Neptune, Saturn, Pluto

- Advancing the natal chart by 1 and a half to 2 degrees (for 19 months of age), solar-arc Pluto is now exactly on the fatal 29 Taurus degree. Solar-arc Neptune (the virus) is exactly square natal Mars, and the ascendant (the body and eyes) is almost within 1 degree exactly opposite Pluto. Keller was left blind and deaf.

d. Eye disease - Cataracts

Most cataracts develop through ageing or injury. Tissue that makes up the eye's lens become less flexible, less transparent and thicker. Psychologically, being unable to see any hope in the future is related to the problem.

James Cheek (4 December 1932, 14:30, Roanoke Rapids, NC).

Cheek is an African American academic who has received many honours. He was born with a severe congenital, cataract condition.

Cause: congenital. Cheek inherited his condition (Sun and Mercury retrograde in the 8H of inheritances, square the Moon that rules "the past"). It is possible the problem arose because of a family history of racial abuse, bigotry and violence (Moon opposite Mars and Neptune that carry the fanatical 6th ray). Closing one's eyes to what is occurring and blotting out the sight of lynching's etc. either way, is a means to cope emotionally.

Organ: ajna - eyesight the Sun and Moon, eye nerves Mercury.

Effect: cataracts. Both the Sun and Moon are afflicted in a t-square with Neptune - cataracts developed, clouding and distorting vision.

▲ (C) Moon. (O) Sun, Moon, Mercury (E) Neptune.

Larry King (19 November 1933, 10:38, Brooklyn NY)

American TV personality Larry King, developed cataracts in his 70's.

Cause: ageing. King's eyes had a weakness and he wore glasses (Mercury retrograde), but the main problem was due to ageing.

Organ: ajna - eyesight the Sun, eye nerves Mercury.

Effect: cataracts. King developed age-related cataracts. The Sun and Mercury that represent vision and eye nerves are midpoint the malefics that most commonly represent age-related clouding of vision - Saturn and Neptune. Mercury rules the 6H of health.

▲ (C) Saturn. (O) Sun, Mercury. (E) Saturn, Neptune.

• In 2006-7 just before the trouble, solar-arc Neptune moved over the Mercury-Sun point, while solar-arc Saturn made an inconjunct aspect. This accelerated the damage and clouding of vision. He had cataract surgery in 2009.

e. Eye disease - Glaucoma

Glaucoma is caused by an imbalance in eye fluid that puts pressure on the eye, destroying the optic nerve. Emotional stress and pressure so that life is hard to look at, seems related to this disorder.

Andrea Bocelli (22 September 1958, 05:15, Pisa Italy).

Popular Italian singer of opera and romantic ballads who is blind.

Cause: karmic, emotional. Bocelli was born with hereditary glaucoma, which suggests his family has a history of emotional suppression (Saturn is in the 4H of family, semi-square Neptune; and the Moon in Capricorn).

Organ: ajna - eye nerves, Mercury and Venus.

Effect: glaucoma. An imbalance in eye fluid (Mercury-Venus semi-square Neptune), put pressure on the eye (square Saturn), resulting in glaucoma, damage and loss of vision.

▲ (C) Saturn, Neptune. (O) Mercury, Venus. (E) Neptune, Saturn.

• Bocelli went completely blind at 12 when he was hit by a ball. Solar-arc Pluto was conjunct Venus and transit Pluto was on the natal Sun.

Jose Feliciano (10 September 1945, 10:00, Lares Puerto Rica)

Puerto Rican singer known for hit songs such as 'Feliz Navidad', who has been blind from birth because of congenital glaucoma.

Cause: congenital. Feliciano has great difficulty with emotional expression (the Moon is in detriment in Scorpio and Saturn is in detriment in Cancer). The Moon is related to eye problems, so there is a link between these afflictions and his trouble. Further, mother (the Moon) may have caught a bacterial infection that caused the trouble (sesquiquadrate Uranus).

Organ: ajna - eyesight the Sun and Moon.

Effect: glaucoma. Fluid imbalance and consequent pressure in the eye (Moon), caused damage to the optic nerve (Uranus), destroying sight (Uranus squares the Sun, while the Moon is semi-square to the Sun).

▲ (C) Moon, Saturn in Cancer. (O) Sun, Moon. (E) Scorpio, Uranus.

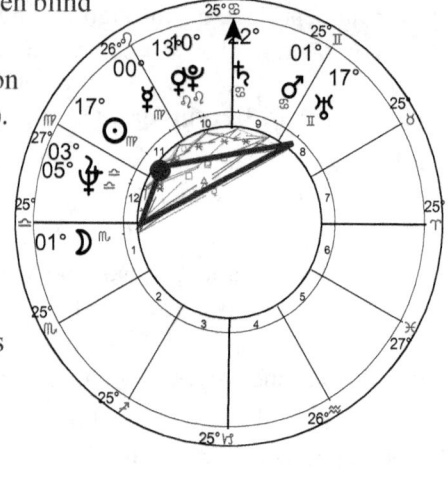

f. Eye disease - Macular degeneration

The macula is a small area at the centre of the retina responsible for seeing straight ahead and fine details. When diseased there is blindness at the centre of vision. 'Dry' macular degeneration is age-related; 'wet' degeneration occurs when blood vessels under the retina haemorrhage. The disease is related to a combination of heredity and environmental factors such as smoking and diet.

Colleen McCullough (1 June 1937, 19:30, Wellington Australia).

Australian author, famous for her novel 'The Thorn Birds'.

Cause: genetic, emotional. McCullough inherited the eye disorder from her mother (Mars that rules the 4H of mother opposes Mercury. Mercury in turn is conjunct Uranus and semi-square Saturn in the 4H in Aries, a sign related to the eyes. Uranus is afflicted in Taurus).

Organ: ajna - eyesight the Moon, eye nerves Mercury and Uranus.

Effect: macular degeneration. In 2003, McCullough suddenly lost sight in the left eye (Moon) due to a haemorrhage (Mars and Uranus). The macular was destroyed (Mercury conjunct Uranus, and Uranus semi-square Saturn).

▲ (C) Uranus, Moon. (O) Moon, Mercury, Uranus. (E) Mars.

- The Moon-Mars aspect was triggered in June 2003, when transit Uranus and Mars came together at 0 degrees Pisces, and crossed the natal Moon simultaneously.

Stephen King (21 September 1947, 01:30, Portland Maine).

American writer of supernatural stories, King was diagnosed with macular degeneration at 49 and is gradually going blind.

Cause: genetic. King inherited an eye weakness (the Sun is square Uranus in Gemini, ruler of the 8H of inheritances with Aquarius on the cusp), and a pattern that showed premature ageing of his vision (the Sun is semi-square Pluto conjunct Saturn - two 1st ray ageing planets).

Organ: ajna - eyesight the Sun, eye nerves Venus and Uranus.

Effect: macular degeneration. Deterioration of the macular began relatively early for King, at 49 in 1996. He is now legally blind.

▲ (C) Uranus. (O) Sun, Venus, Uranus. (E) Saturn, Pluto.

- Timing for the trouble in his 49th year is shown by Uranus. By solar-arc it had rotated to 14 Leo, conjunct natal Pluto, triggering the age-related damage.

- Simultaneously solar-arc Pluto and Saturn were at 2-6 Libra, sitting on natal Venus and Neptune representing vision being gradually destroyed.

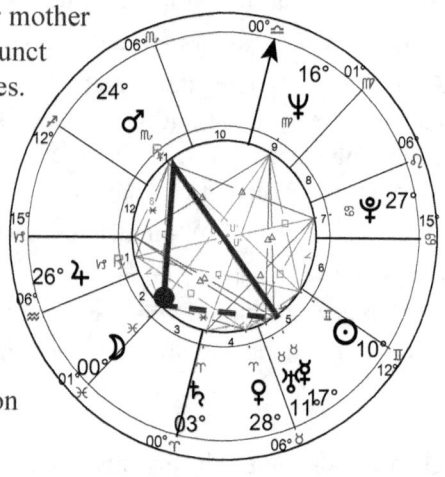

2c. The Nose

The ajna - and therefore Venus and Mercury, govern the senses and organs for smelling. Aries and Mars govern the nose, especially if trouble is caused by an accident.

a. Sinusitis

Sinusitis is inflammation or swelling of the tissue lining the sinuses (the Moon), causing blockages that allow bacteria (Uranus) to breed, resulting in swelling and pain. Psychologically, something has "got up one's nose".

Stephen Fry (24 August 1957, 06:00, Hampstead UK).
English comedian, actor and TV presenter, suffered painful bouts of sinusitis. He wrote, "Awoke with satanically painful sinusitis, wanted to wrench my left eye out. Work, pseudoephedrine!"
Cause: emotional. What "gets up Fry's nose"? Hidden family hypocrisy (Mars, the nose, squares Saturn in the 4H of family). However, it is Fry's own tendency to criticise himself (Mercury semi-square the Moon), that is behind his sinus trouble and pain.
Organ: ajna - sinuses the Moon, nerves Mercury.
Effect: sinusitis. The linings (Moon) of his breathing passages became inflamed (conjunct Uranus in Leo), and congested (Saturn). Bacteria bred (Uranus), causing excruciating nerve pain (Uranus semi-square Mercury). He would take medicine (Uranus trine Saturn) and retire to bed.

▲ (C) Moon. (O) Moon, Mercury. (E) Uranus, Saturn.

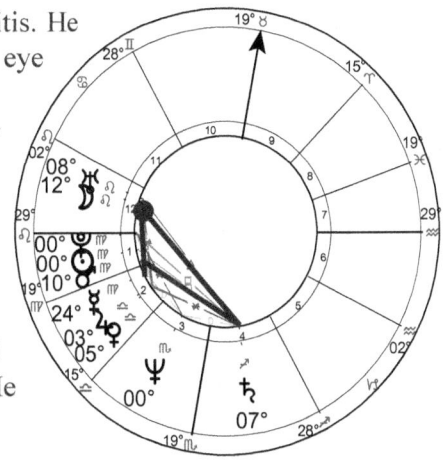

b. Broken nose

Silvio Berlusconi (29 September 1936, 05:40 Milan Italy)
Italy's 54th Prime Minister was attacked and his nose broken when he was addressing a public rally on 13 December 2009.
Cause: karmic. Berlusconi liked bizarre sex (Mars trine Uranus afflicted in Taurus in the 8H of sex), and partied with prostitutes (sextile Venus in Scorpio, in the 2H of money). Karma (Saturn), due to the misuse of sexual force triggered the attack. His improprieties (Mars-Uranus) raised the ire of the conservative public (Mars quindecile Saturn, which is conjunct the Moon in the 6H of health), attracting anger towards him and health issues.
Organ: ajna - nose Mars, and bones Saturn.
Effect: sinusitis. Someone from the public (Moon) attacked him (Mars, Uranus), fracturing his nose and breaking his teeth (Saturn).

▲ (C) Saturn. (O) Mars, Saturn. (E) Moon, Mars, Uranus.

- When he was attacked, solar-arc Saturn was at 1 Gemini, squaring natal Mars. It was karmic.

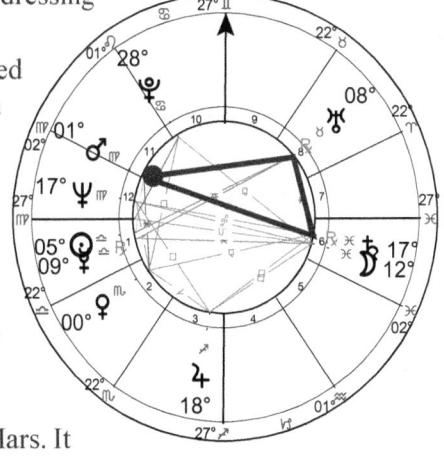

c. Cocaine damage to the septum

Stevie Nicks (26 May 1948, 03:02, Phoenix Arizona).
Singing star of Fleetwood Mac, a popular 70's group. Nick has been called the Queen of Rock and Roll. For 10 years she sniffed cocaine, burning a hole through the cartilage of her nose.
Cause: emotional. Nicks had a yearning for love (Neptune square Venus) that manifested as a drug addiction. This is seen in a t-square: a habit (Moon), of loving (Venus), drugs (Neptune).
Organ: ajna - nose cartilage, Moon in Capricorn.
Effect: cartilage. Nicks self-indulged (Venus) in a cocaine habit (Neptune) that dissolved the cartilage in her nose (square Moon).

▲ (C) Moon, Neptune. (O) Moon. (E) Venus, Neptune.

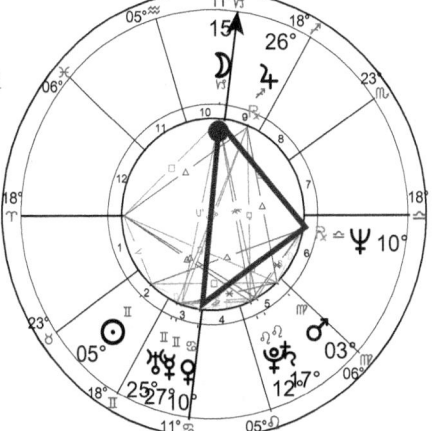

2d. The Nervous System

The ajna chakra rules the nervous system, the means through which consciousness interacts with the environment. Impressions flow along the millions of nerve pathways to the brain. Here they transform into information and in response, outward travelling nerve impulses galvanise us into action. In emotional man, the solar plexus chakra dominates consciousness via the sympathetic nervous system.

a. Amyotrophic lateral sclerosis, Motor Neurone Disease (ALS)

ALS is a fatal and progressive neurological disease, which is characterized by progressive muscle weakness. Researchers believe it is an autoimmune disease. Sufferers become gradually immobile, developing a "locked-in" state. The nature of the disease suggests the inner child is angry but feels inadequate and powerless to deal with whatever is happening and curls inwards to avoid further punishment or emotional pain.

Stephen Hawking (8 Jan 1942, Oxford, UK).
Unknown time, 12 PM midday used and the 0 degrees Aries House System.
One of the most famous scientists of the 20th Century, Hawking was diagnosed with ALS in 1963 when he was 21.

Cause: emotional. Hawking was easy-going (grand-trines: Sun-Moon-Saturn; Mercury-Neptune-Uranus), but he had an explosive, angry side (t-square: Mars-Mercury-Pluto), which he would vent with cutting thoughts and words. Because the disease manifested, we know he turned this toxic force relentlessly upon himself, triggering an autoimmune attack.

Organ: ajna - the nervous system Mercury.

Effect: ALS. While a first year doctoral student at Cambridge University, Hawking was assigned a supervisor beneath his talents. He must have felt deeply enraged as well as helpless, because the immune-system (Mars) attacked the motor nerves (Mercury), and gradually muscles compressed (Pluto). He has become locked-in physically.

▲ (C) Mars, Pluto. (O) Mercury. (E) Mars, Pluto.

- In 1963 by solar-arc, the Mars point of the Health Triangle had reached Saturn, showing that lesions on nerve cells had reached the point that muscles were affected. Simultaneously, the Pluto point was square natal Uranus showing serious damage to nerve cells.

b. Cerebral Palsy

Cerebral palsy is caused by damage to the developing brain either during pregnancy or shortly after birth. Most people are born with it. Nerves fire but muscles spasm (Uranus), causing jerky movements. The fundamental psychological pattern is great fear and hesitation in moving forward in life, in taking action.

Fred Berry (20 December 1949, 23:36, Salem Massachusetts)
American politician born with cerebral palsy. In spite of his infirmity, he became a Massachusetts State Senator, serving for 30 years.

Cause: congenital. Measles can cause cerebral palsy and it is possible that Berry's mother caught the virus and this caused his infirmity (Moon in the 4H of mother, square Neptune, the ruler of the 6H of health). The same Moon in Capricorn - Neptune aspect shows Berry's fear and hesitancy in moving forward in life.

Organ: ajna - the nervous system, Mercury.

Effect: cerebral palsy. He was born with palsy (Moon conjunct Mercury square Neptune) that caused muscle spasms (Mercury disposits Mars that squares Uranus; Mercury is conjunct the Moon that disposits Uranus).

▲ (C) Moon. (O) Mercury. (E) Neptune, Mars, Uranus.

c. Epilepsy

An epileptic seizure occurs when large numbers of brain cells fire uncontrollably. One cause of epilepsy is due to a loose consciousness thread,[1] an attack occurs when the thread temporarily withdraws. Other causes are head injuries and strokes. Uranus governs electrical signalling and is often central to the disorder.

Dionne Quintuplets (28 May 1934, 03:56, Corbeil Canada).

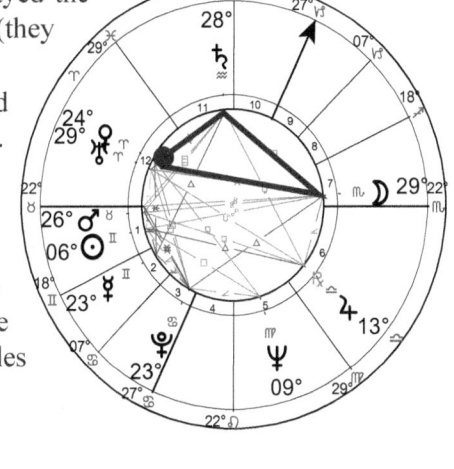

Canadian quintuplets born two months premature. The government displayed the babies in a theme park called Quintland. But when the public lost interest (they were 14), they were given back to the parents.

Cause: karmic, congenital. The experience was due to family karma and misuse of power in a previous life (Saturn ruler of the 10H square the Moon).

Organ: ajna - the consciousness thread, Venus.

Effect: epilepsy. Born prematurely (the Moon is inconjunct Uranus in 12H of hospitals), building work on the nervous system was incomplete (Uranus is conjunct Venus and the Moon squares Saturn in Aquarius). The consciousness thread (Venus) was not securely grounded (inconjunct the Moon), resulting in epilepsy (Uranus) whenever it loosened. Venus co-rules the 6H of health with Libra sharing the cusp.

▲ (C) Saturn, Moon. (O) Venus. (E) Uranus, Saturn.

Afonso Pedro (23 February 1845 13:35, Rio de Janiero Brazil)

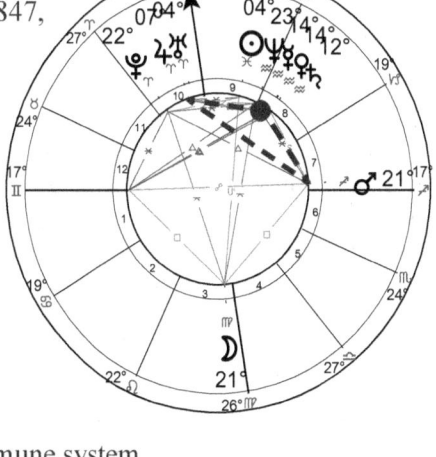

The 2 year old child of Emperor Dom Pedro II of Brazil died on 11 June 1847, from an epilepsy seizure.

Cause: genetic. Afonso was born sickly and with low vitality (Sun in Pisces in the cadent 9H, inconjunct the Moon); a genetic condition related to inbreeding (Mars square the Moon in fussy Virgo and dispositing Uranus).

Organ: ajna - the consciousness thread, Mercury.

Effect: epilepsy. An epileptic attack occurred whenever the consciousness thread in the brain loosened (Mercury is midpoint Mars ruler of the 6H of health and Uranus in Aries).

▲ (C) Uranus. (O) Mercury. (E) Uranus, Mars.

d. Guillain-Barre Syndrome (GBS)

An autoimmune disorder, where the peripheral nerves are attacked by the immune system (water signs and rulers).

Anita Cortesi (1 October 1955, 17:45, Zurich Switzerland)

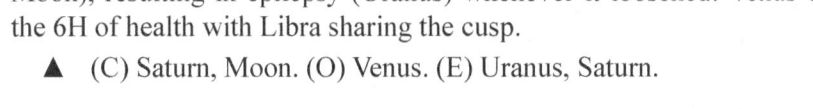

Swiss professional astrologer. In 2010, she caught GBS and was from then on confined to a wheelchair.

Cause: emotional. Cortesi is an easy going Libra personality who is dominated by a fiery emotional body (the Moon is in Aries in the 1H of self, opposite the Sun). This showy anger is the outer display of hurt and frustration hidden within; Mars, the dispositor of the Moon is in hypercritical Virgo. This is the root cause of the trouble because Mars is in the 6H of health. The fact that Cortesi developed an autoimmune disease tells us that she turned the force of stinging criticism on herself (Mars is opposite the ascendant).

Organ: ajna - the nervous system Mercury and Uranus.

Effect: GBS. Continual self-criticism provoked a reaction from the immune system (Mars) and it attacked the peripheral nerves (Mars is conjunct the midpoint between Mercury and Uranus). The damage caused paralysis (Mercury is conjunct Neptune, and 1st ray Pluto afflicts Jupiter (movement) in the 6H of health.

▲ (C) Mars. (O) Mercury, Uranus. (E) Mars, Neptune, Pluto.

---

1 Bailey, Alice A; Esoteric Psychology II, 418.

e. Multiple Sclerosis (MS)

An example of multiple sclerosis was given previously in the coverage of Jacqueline du Pre. The immune system attacks nerve cells, damaging the myelin sheath covering so that nerve signals are not passed on.

At the root of autoimmune diseases is a self-hatred pattern arising from persistent negative thoughts such as being "stupid, dumb, naive" etc. In time, the immune system responds and attacks the body. Connect nervous system rulers (Mercury, Venus and Uranus) with immune system rulers (water signs and their planet rulers).

L1001. (30 August 1959, 19:55, St. Louis, Missouri)

An intelligent American lady with a modest Virgo personality, who studies trans-Himalayan and other esoteric modalities. This point is important because contact with soul energy through meditation keeps ill health at bay. She was relatively healthy prior to the onset of MS. After twenty years and three children, in 1999 her marriage dissolved. Becoming re-established over the coming years took its toll. Symptoms started in 2003; she was diagnosed in 2004 and unable to work since 2010.

Cause: emotional. Our subject had a habit of criticising herself (Virgo planets with Venus in Virgo opposite the ascendant); and finding herself coming up short when she measured herself against her important values and principles. The disease cause lies here. The 6th house has a five planet stellium within it, showing a lot of energy being poured into work and duty. But since the disease developed this focus has turned to the care and management of her condition.

Organ: ajna - the nervous system, Venus, Mercury and Uranus.

Effect: MS. In response to her negative thoughts, the immune system attacked the nervous system (Pluto conjunct Venus. The disease causes scarring of nerve cells (Mars square Saturn), so that nerve signalling is gradually inhibited (Saturn is sesquiquadrate Uranus, which in turn is conjunct Mercury).

▲ (C) Mars in Virgo. (O) Venus, Mercury, Uranus. (E) Sun, Mars, Saturn.

- Trouble always starts before symptoms appear. In 1999, Mars, a representative of the immune system, had rotated by solar-arc to conjunct natal Neptune at 4 Scorpio. The marriage dissolved.

- Simultaneously, solar-arc Uranus was conjunct natal Mars at 26 Virgo, triggering self-recrimination and beginning the manifestation of the disease.

From 2014, there have been exacerbations (flare-up of symptoms). The client notices that these occur when planets transit through Virgo and her 6th house. Severely weakened during those times, she still walks, even if just for short distances. By 2017, lesions had spread to her brain and spinal cord.

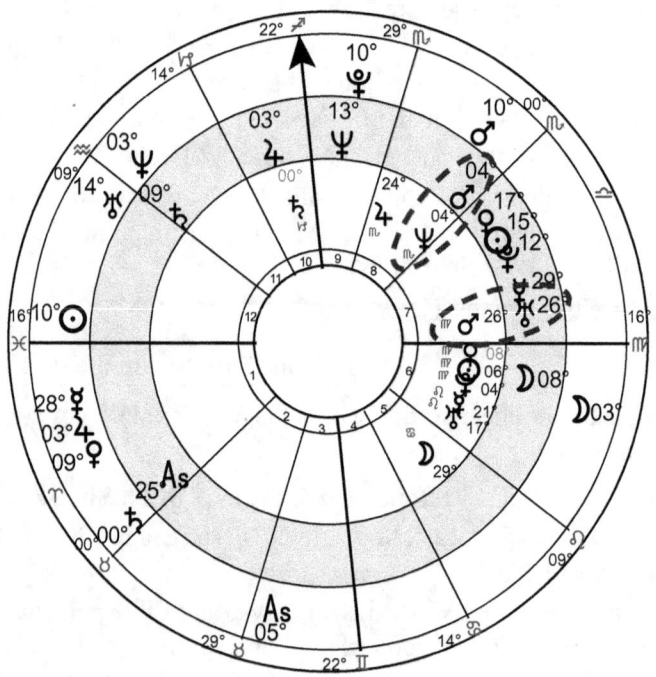

Chart set for May 1999. Inner chart Natal, middle chart solar-arc, outer chart transits

This student of the Wisdom Teachings understands the effect our psychology has upon our health and combines allopathic medicine with alternative and complementary healing modalities, including meditation and her spiritual studies, to try to alleviate symptoms. She does not take MS medications that help slow the disease, or go on a special diet, finding these do not work for her. She believes that her practice of "gratitude" has positive effects on her health.

She does not "look sick" (in 2017) and is grateful she has retained her independence, is able to live by herself and take care of things with the appropriate modifications. She maintains hope that her condition will improve, at least to where she does not have exacerbations all the time.

f. Quadriplegia

Christopher Reeves (25 September 1952, 03:12, Manhattan NY).
American actor who became quadriplegic after being thrown from a horse.
Cause: emotional. Reeves' anger erupted would arise suddenly in temper ((Uranus in Cancer inconjunct Mars). This pattern is related to the accident.
Organ: ajna - the spine Saturn; nerves Uranus.
Effect: quadriplegia. Through a horse-riding accident (Mars in Sagittarius), he suffered terrible injuries. Spinal nerves (Uranus sitting on the 12H of hospitals) were severed (inconjunct Mars), and he was paralysed, immobilised (Mars sextile Saturn that squares Uranus).

▲ (C) Mars, Uranus. (O) Saturn, Uranus. (E) Mars, Uranus, Saturn.
The accident happened on May 27 1995.

- Transit Mars was at 0 Virgo, exactly conjunct solar-arc Uranus at the same degree. Spinal nerves were severed.
- Transit Uranus was at 0 Aquarius, conjunct solar-arc Mars in the 6H of health, indicating the accident.
- Solar-arc Jupiter was at 2 Cancer, square natal Sun and Mercury - the spinal injuries inhibiting movement.

g. Polio

The polio virus multiplies in the intestines then enters the bloodstream to paralyse the central nervous system.

Franklin D. Roosevelt (30 January 1882, 20:45, Hyde Park, NY)
FDR served as the 32nd President of the US. In 1921, he contracted polio and was left with permanent paralysis from the waist down.
Cause: emotional. FDR prized freedom (Uranus on the ascendant). Married in 1905, within years he wanted to leave the marriage for a mistress but was forced to remain for political reasons. He felt trapped (Saturn, the jailer, conjunct Neptune that rules the 7H of marriage with Pisces on the cusp; square the Sun and Venus in the 5H of romance). When wife Eleanor discovered his infidelity in 1918, he was beset with guilt. This sapped his vitality, opening his system up to disease.
Organ: ajna - the nervous system, Venus and Uranus.

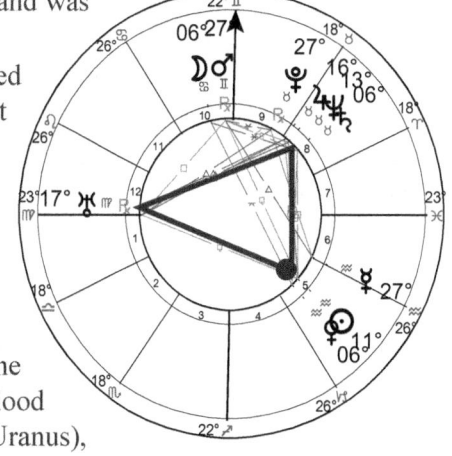

Effect: polio. In 1921 the polio virus (Neptune) invaded the intestines (trine Uranus in Virgo), perverting cell life it spread through the body via blood circulation (the Sun in Aquarius). It attacked the nervous system (Venus, Uranus), paralysing him (Saturn > Venus-Sun; also Pluto square Mercury in the 6H of health).

▲ (C) Neptune, Saturn. (O) Venus, Uranus. (E) Neptune, Saturn.

- In 1921, transit Neptune was in Leo moving opposite the natal Sun-Venus conjunction and forming a t-square with its natal position in Taurus. At that time, he was susceptible to viral attacks.
- Solar-arc Neptune was moving towards natal Mars at 27 Gemini, representing the viral attack.

h. Parkinson's disease

Parkinson's affects nerve cells. They fire but muscles can't respond properly, resulting in spasms, tremors.

Muhammad Ali (17 January 1942, 18:35, Louisville, Kentucky).
American champion boxer. Parkinson's symptoms began in 1978 as vocal stutters and trembling hands. He died on June 3 2016.

Cause: emotional. Growing up in racist Kentucky, Ali learned to hide his rage (Mars square Pluto in the 12H of hidden things), because open defiance would bring dangerous repercussions. This contributed to his health disorder.

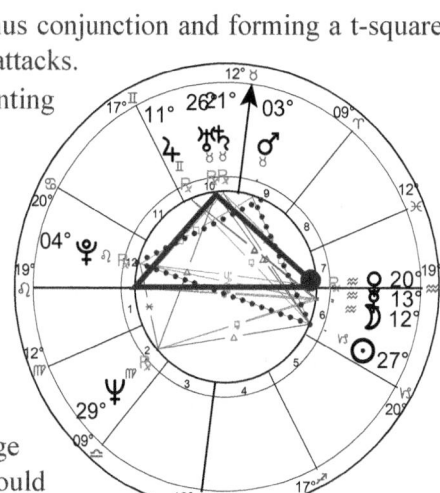

Organ: ajna - the nervous system, Mercury, Venus, Uranus; the body, the ascendant.

Effect: Parkinson's. The battering to Ali's head eventually affected the nervous system (Mars is in detriment in Taurus and is disposited by Venus in Aquarius). Scarring and damage to neurons occurred (Saturn-Uranus). Parkinson's developed - the misfiring of synapses and jerky, rigid, movements (t-square: Venus, Saturn-Uranus and the ascendant).

▲ (C) Mars, Pluto. (O) Mercury, Venus, Uranus; the ascendant. (E) Mars, Saturn, Uranus.

- Trouble started in 1975 when progressed Mars began moving over natal Saturn-Uranus (a nine year period) triggering the Health Triangle. Ali fought 14 times in this period and any of these matches potentially started and contributed to the trouble.

i. Nerves - Shingles

Shingles is caused by the same virus that causes chickenpox. It can strike nerves and skin anywhere in the body, causing intense nerve pain.

David Letterman (12 April 1947 06:00, Indianapolis IN)

American talk show host in late night TV. In February 2003, he suffered a painful bout of shingles.

Cause: emotional. Letterman has a busy active mind, which is sharp and witty and can be biting and caustic (Mars in Aries conjunct Mercury). It helped to make him famous, but it also affected his health - Mercury rules the 6H of health.

Organ: ajna - the nervous system Mercury and Uranus; the skin Saturn.

Effect: shingles. Letterman's nerves are susceptible to a viral attack (Mercury in detriment in Pisces), and an attack of shingles struck in February 2003, raising a painful rash on his skin (Mars conjunct Mercury and trine Saturn; Mercury square Uranus that is in turn semi-square Saturn).

▲ (C) Mars. (O) Mercury, Uranus, Saturn. (E) Pisces, Mars, Saturn.

- When the attack occurred, transit Mars was around 25 Sagittarius, square natal Mars and Mercury.

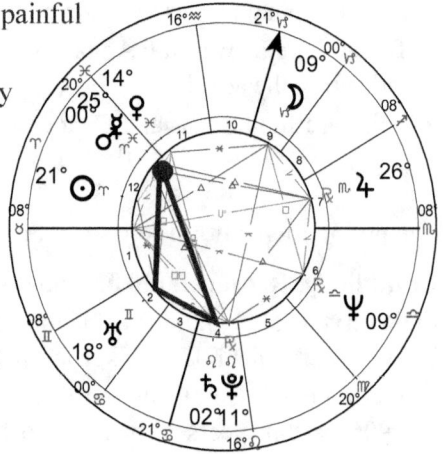

j. Tourette's syndrome

Tourette syndrome causes repeated, involuntary physical movements and vocal outbursts. It is the most severe kind of tic syndrome, a reaction to serious, unresolved emotional trauma buried in the unconscious.

Jim Eisenreich (18 April 1959 16:19, St. Cloud Minnesota)

Eisenreich played American major league baseball. Since age 6 he had tics, jerks and his eyes would blink uncontrollably. Sometimes he had to come off the field because he could not control muscle spasms. In 1984, he retired to seek a cure. Later, he returned and had a few more years of success.

Cause: emotional. People with Tourette's have experienced serious trauma in childhood. Eisenreich's home life was especially harsh with mental and physical abuse (t-square, Mars and Mercury with Saturn located in the 4H of family). The appearance of Tourette's testifies to the fact he was emotionally traumatised and scarred.

Organ: ajna - the nervous system, Mercury.

Effect: Tourette's. Mercury in the t-square represents the trembling nervous system and its reaction to trauma buried in the unconscious (Mercury rules the 12H of the unconscious), and the flinching, eye blinking and muscular contractions.

▲ (C) Mars, Saturn. (O) Mercury. (E) Mars.

- In 1984 when he had treatment, solar-arc Mercury was moving over the natal Sun, bringing the buried trauma into the light of the conscious mind so he could see his trauma and deal with it.

2e. The Pituitary Gland

a. Acromegaly (gigantism)

Anthony Robbins (29 February 1960, 20:10, Los Angeles CA)

Successful American life-coach, Robbins grew almost 10 inches in his junior year. When he was 31, he was told he had a pituitary tumour and acromegaly. Since his growth had stabilised, he refused surgery.

Cause: emotional. The pattern representing the disease is a t-square with Neptune at the hub and Venus and Uranus. The psychological cause hypothetically, is confusion and anxiety over being abandoned in some way when young (Uranus opposite Venus in the 4H of family).

Organ: ajna - pituitary Venus; muscles Mars.

Effect: acromegaly. In his teen years, aberrations in cells (Uranus in Leo) in the pituitary (Venus) occurred and a tumour grew (Neptune carries the 2nd ray via Pisces). Body-muscular over-growth occurred (Mars conjunct Venus).

▲ (C) Neptune. (O) Venus, Mars. (E) Uranus, Neptune.

• Venus in Robbins' chart governs the 8H of transformation. The same triangle that represented the disease also represents his ability to change the way he thinks. He demonstrates how a latent disease, even if it should be triggered, may not progress to a morbid stage. Robbins teaches a form of positive thinking, which is a modern off-shoot of Raja Yoga, the kingly science of mind. This science teaches us how to transform negative thoughts and forces we inherit into positive thoughts and life expressions.

b. Dwarfism: Proportionate, Growth Hormone Deficiency (GHD)

Charles Stratton (4 January 1838, Bridgeport CT).

Unknown time, 12 PM used and the 0 degrees Aries House System for both charts.

Stratton achieved great fame as "General Tom Thumb", in P. T. Barnum's Circus. Normal at birth, he reached 25 inches tall at six months and then suddenly stopped growing in height. He was perfectly proportioned.

Cause: genetic. Uranus, ruler of genetics is conjunct Venus - pituitary malfunction. (NB. These studies would fit in the Sacral-genetics section).

Organ: ajna - pituitary Venus, cells the Sun.

Effect: dwarfism. An abnormality (Uranus) in pituitary cells (conjunct Venus semi-square the Sun), resulted in GHD, a diminished body size (Venus square Saturn).

▲ (C) Uranus. (O) Venus, Sun. (E) Saturn.

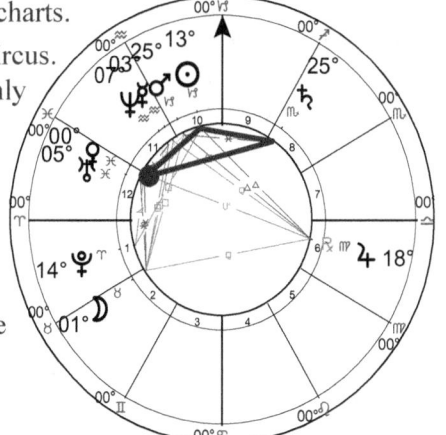

Lavinia Warren (31 October 1842, Middleboro MA).

Lavinia Warren came from a genteel New England family. Normal at birth, healthy and well-proportioned, she reached 2.6 feet. She joined show business where she met and married Charles Stratton. They were reality celebrities of their day, becoming famous and wealthy.

Cause: genetic. Family (Moon), karma (square Saturn), was responsible for the genetic abnormality (Venus, the pituitary, disposits the Moon).

Organ: ajna - pituitary, Venus.

Effect: dwarfism. Warren inherited a genetic (Uranus) form of GHD (square Venus), a consequence of in-breeding, because sexual partners (Venus) were drawn from a too narrow breeding pool (square Mars in fussy Virgo in the 6H of health). Growth was stunted (Jupiter conjunct Saturn).

▲ (C) Uranus. (O) Venus. (E) Mars, Jupiter, Saturn.

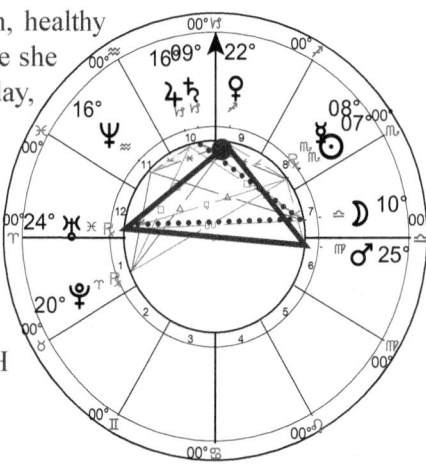

c. Migraine

A painful migraine is a severe headache, often accompanied by nausea, vomiting and sensitivity to light and sound. It can last for days. Researchers say migraines are linked to heightened neurovascular reactivity in response to stress caused by something not liked in the environment. This fits with two causes given by Bailey: firstly that migraines are related to heightened activity in the ajna; secondly, being separative in attitude (a ray 5 trait) causes a lack of relation between the pituitary and pineal glands [1] that can lead to migraine. The charts on this page have inhibiting Saturn in 5th ray Aquarius.

Charlotte Bronte (21 April 1816, 14:41, Thornton, UK).

The oldest of three talented sisters, Bronte became famous for her novel Jane Eyre. She suffered from migraines.

Cause: emotional. Bronte is reported as being bossy and controlling. She was also exceedingly cool, reserved and isolative emotionally (Moon and Saturn in Aquarius, semi-square Venus in detriment in Aries). This latter pattern is linked to her migraine trouble.

Organ: ajna - pituitary, Venus.

Effect: migraine. Stress and the tendency to distance herself from others emotionally (Saturn-Moon), disturbed neurovascular balance, increasing activity around the pituitary that resulted in migraines (Venus square Mars, Mars trine Moon-Saturn).

▲ (C) Moon in Aquarius. (O) Venus. (E) Saturn, Mars.

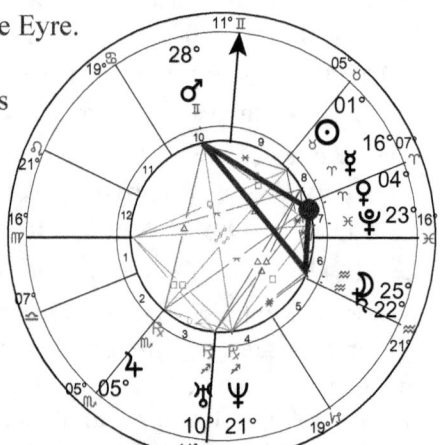

Loretta Lynn (14 April 1932, 16:00, Van Lear Kentucky).

American Country and Western singer Lynn said her father suffered from migraines and so had she since age 17. They were so severe sometimes she lost consciousness when she had an attack.

Cause: emotional. Lynn was fiery (Aries Sun) and dismissed and walled out people she did not like (Leo Moon opposite Saturn in Aquarius).

Organ: ajna - pituitary, Mercury.

Effect: migraine. Divisive attitudes can cause brain trouble. When Lynn was tired and stressed (Moon > Saturn that squares Mars in Aries), severe migraines would occur (Mercury the pituitary, square Pluto the pineal). Sometimes she lost consciousness (Uranus sesquiquadrate Neptune in the 12H of the unconscious).

▲ (C) Moon, Saturn in Aquarius. (O) Mercury. (E) Mars, Pluto.

Lisa Kudrow (30 July 1963, 04:37, Encino Ca).

American actress, star of the popular TV show, Friends. Kudrow inherited migraines from her father and had excruciating attacks as a child.

Cause: emotional. Kudrow adored her father. She inherited his susceptibility to migraines, which means she inherited his attitudes - compartmentalising her feelings and building walls between her and people she dislikes (the Moon square Saturn in Aquarius).

Organ: ajna - pituitary, Mercury.

Effect: migraine. Mental walls cause trouble, a dissonance between the pituitary (Mercury) and pineal glands (opposite 1st ray Saturn representing the pineal). This tendency plus stress and tiredness (t-square: Saturn-Moon-Mercury) resulted in migraines. Kudrow must be developing more inclusive attitudes because her attacks have diminished over the years.

▲ (C) Moon in Aquarius, Saturn. (O) Mercury. (E) Saturn.

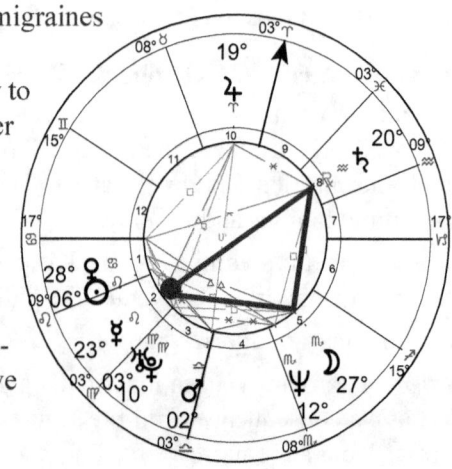

---

[1] Bailey, Alice A; Esoteric Healing, 302.

2f. 5th Ray Psychological Disorders

The activity of the 5th ray flowing through the ajna, is responsible for many dissociative / cleavage type mental disorders. A cleavage is best described as being torn in two directions. When it occurs within the personality, causing one part of the nature to be out of touch with another, serious mental health issues arise.

a. Autism Spectrum Disorder (ASD): Autism and Asperger's

ASD is defined as a serious developmental problem characterized by great difficulty in communicating and forming relationships because of avoidance and dissociation tendencies. These are 5th ray "cleavage" traits - one part of the nature is out of touch with another, bringing ASD under its auspices. Here is a quote.

> In the activity of [the 5th ray] will be found eventually the source of many psychological disorders and mental trouble. Cleavage is the outstanding characteristic—within the individual or between the individual and his group, rendering him anti-social. Other results are certain forms of insanities, brain lesions and *those gaps in the relation of the physical body to the subtle bodies which show as imbecilities and psychological troubles.* [1]

In ASD, brain and nervous system function is impaired. Scientists who have studied autism say there are fewer alpha and beta waves, which points to under-connectivity especially in important strategic areas that have to do with the emotions and relating. Some now believe autism is a genetic disorder. This fits with the esoteric understanding that individual disease is mostly karmic and therefore comes through an inherited gene. It is also possible we are dealing with souls who greatly dislike physical incarnation and who try to avoid it and this creates the cleavage. Look for communication problems that translate into brainwave and nervous system under-connectivity - afflictions to Mercury and Venus, or to planets in Gemini and Aquarius.

Autism

Tagtrug Mukpo (9 March 1971, 18:50, Boulder Colorado)

Tibetan-American, the son of Chogyam Trungpa Rinpoche and his wife, Lady Diana Mukpo. Severely autistic, Mukpo requires 24-hour supervision. Over the years and with ongoing care and attention, his condition is reported as having improved.

Cause: ray 5 cleavage. Tagtrug's case is intriguing. He was born to spiritually advanced parents and it is possible the karma is theirs. Lord of Karma, Saturn, is in the 8H of inheritances and co-rules the 4H of the mother with Capricorn sharing the cusp. Saturn is in Taurus, the sign of desire.

Organ: ajna - the mind and nervous system Mercury; senses Mars.

Effect: psychological. The serious communication difficulty is shown by the condition of Mercury, the mind. It is afflicted in Pisces, which suggests a mind that resides primarily on the Astral Plane because its access through the brain is seriously impeded. This impediment is a cleavage between the mind and the brain, shown by 5th ray Venus in Aquarius, which is midpoint Mercury square Mars. This also suggests an atrophying of the sense perceptions or *vrittis* (as the father of Raja Yoga, Patanjali called them), since Mars rules the five senses.

The serious obstruction is shown by Pluto, which rules the crown chakra that vitalises the brain. It sits on the ascendant, which is a representative of the head and the brain. Its opposition to Mercury suggests serious damage or limitation in connectivity with the nervous system and strategic parts of the brain.

Mukpo's case is severe, indicating also a possible disruption with the consciousness thread, which is governed by Mercury. In any event, the mind is unable to work through the brain in any intelligent way, hence the trouble.

▲ (C) Venus in Aquarius. (O) Mercury, Mars. (E) Pluto.

---

1 Bailey, Alice A; Esoteric Healing, 302.

Jett Travolta (13 April 1992, 00:33, Daytona Beach Florida)

Son of American actor John Travolta, was a high-functioning autistic. He died 2 January 2009, from a head injury sustained during a seizure.

Cause: ray 5 cleavage. Saturn in 5th ray Aquarius is central to Travolta's trouble. It suggests a history of living exclusively in his thought life, to the detriment of the physical body.

Organ: ajna - the mind Mercury, Venus; brain the ascendant.

Effect: psychological. Trouble with the mind and its ability to communicate effectively via the nervous system is immediately seen with both its rulers afflicted - Venus in Aries and Mercury in Pisces. The gap in the relation between the mind and the brain that is causing the trouble is represented by Saturn in Aquarius. It is midpoint the ascendant, the brain; and Mercury, the mind. Travolta also suffered from seizures, which suggests that he may have had a loose consciousness thread (Mercury) connection which is a cause of that malady.

▲ (C) Saturn in Aquarius. (O) Mercury, Venus; ascendant. (E) Saturn.

Asperger's

Asperger's people are less introverted emotionally than those with autism. There are more left brain connections and a higher IQ, but they still have communication difficulties. Autistic savants seem to fit in this group. An evolutionary advancement that nature has not perfected yet, may account for talented savants like Negro.

Andrea Negro (25 August 2001, 17:00, Nice, Fr)

A prodigy with Asperger's, he got a Bachelor in Science for maths at age 13.

Cause: ray 5 cleavage. Though lacking social skills, Negro has mathematical brilliance. Perhaps he lived too exclusively on the Mental Plane in his last life and his condition is a karmic consequence (Saturn in Gemini, in the 6H of health, semi-square Venus).

Organ: ajna - the mind, Mercury.

Effect: psychological. The mind/ Mercury is strong in Virgo, but its ability to communicate through the brain and nervous system is impaired by a cleavage, represented by Uranus in Aquarius, which is inconjunct Mercury. Negro struggles to communicate with the world generally (Mercury square Saturn in Gemini, ruler of the ascendant).

Negro's mathematical genius suggests he was using the higher abstract mind. Mercury represents both the concrete and abstract minds. [1]

▲ (C) Uranus in Aquarius. (O) Mercury. (E) Saturn.

Susan Boyle (1 April 1961, 09:50, Blackburn Scotland)

Scottish singer who became famous for her beautiful voice after she appeared on the TV programme Britain's Got Talent in 2009.

Cause: ray 5 cleavage. Boyle's Asperger's was diagnosed as being caused by brain damage as a child. If so, it was karmic (Venus square Saturn).

Organ: ajna - the mind and nervous system, Mercury, Venus.

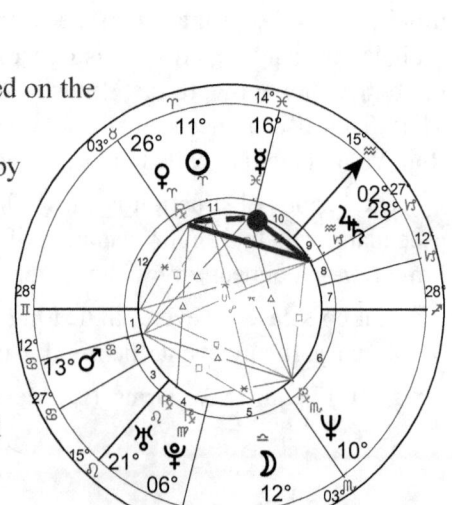

Effect: psychological. Communication difficulties are highlighted (the rulers of the nervous system are afflicted - Venus in Aries, Mercury in Pisces). The cleavage related to brainwave under-connectivity is represented by 5th ray and retrograde Venus, which squares Saturn; and Mercury semi-square to Saturn. Mercury rules the ascendant, highlighting her social and communication difficulties.

▲ (C) Venus. (O) Mercury, Venus. (E) Saturn.

---

1 Bailey, Alice A; Esoteric Astrology 281.

b. Insanity as a consequence of narrow crystallised thinking and partisan devotion

Anders Breivik (13 February 1979, 12:50, Oslo Norway).
Far-right, racist Norwegian who killed over 70 people on 22 July 2011. He is diagnosed with a narcissistic personality disorder (Venus opposite the ascendant) but is quite insane. His trouble arises from intense mental activity and devotion to his narrow belief that he is part of a white master race that needs to kill to maintain superiority in the world. These thoughtforms now control him. Here is an esoteric description of the malady.

> A thought form of such potency is built, it holds the man mentally and emotionally. There is no sense of balance, no sense of proportion and no sense of humour. He has become a victim of the thought form, it holds him and controls him. "Such people are the violent partisans in any group, in any church, order or government. They are frequently sadistic.. and willing to sacrifice or to damage anyone who seems to them inimical to their fixed idea of what is right and true. The men who engineered the Spanish Inquisition.. are samples of the worst forms of this line of thought and development... People tainted with this psychological trouble of blind adherence to ideas and of personality devotions are found [everywhere].. the trouble from which they suffer is contagious. They are a menace.. [1]

Cause: desire and lower-will. Breivik is a cold, critical, humourless fanatic and bigot (the Moon conjunct Saturn in Virgo). The thoughtforms that drive him are represented by the Mercury, Sun and Mars group in separative Aquarius, clustered on the MC. He has delusions of White Supremacy greatness, to be achieved through mass murder (Mars trine Pluto), and revolution (square Uranus). Killing people for his political goals was a sport to him, they were fair game (Uranus in the 5H of pleasure and sport).

Organ: ajna - the mind, Mercury.

Effect: mental. Driven forth by the delusory thought life which controlled him, he committed mass murder.

▲ (C) Mars, Saturn, Uranus. (O) Mercury. (E) Mars, Pluto.

• On the day of the slaughter, solar-arc Mars had reached 21 Pisces, trine his natal Uranus in the sign of death, Scorpio. Simultaneously, solar-arc Pluto was conjunct natal Uranus. We all get patterns like this during life but most of us use the experience as a stepping stone to improve psychological health and quality of life.

Charles Manson (12 November 1934, 16:40, Cincinnati Ohio).
American leader of the 'Manson Family', a cult that committed a series of murders in 1969, notably that of pregnant actress Sharon Tate.

Cause: desire and lower-will. Manson was born with past-life delusional fantasies of greatness (Moon in separative Aquarius in the 10th house of status). He had a powerful will (Uranus in Aries) and was an intelligent personality working through the ajna. He was also insane, being controlled by thoughts and desires of world domination and control - a grand-cross pattern anchored by destructive Pluto on Cancer. It showed he was torn by internal conflicts and tried to control the world around him in an attempt to bring order to his inner life.

Organ: ajna - mind, Mercury.

Effect: mental. Manson was a murderous and sadistic thug (Mars conjunct Neptune) who manipulated his group of followers to commit mayhem (Uranus sesquiquadrate Mars). The grand-cross pattern seems to represent the burning cross of warped fanatics like Manson and the Ku Klux Klan.

▲ (C) Uranus, Pluto. (O) Mercury. (E) Pluto, Uranus.

---
1 Bailey, Alice A; Esoteric Psychology II, 455-456..

3. Throat Chakra Diseases

The throat chakra rules the thyroid gland, respiration, speech, hearing, digestion and the lower brain. It receives energy from rays 3 and 7, Taurus and Gemini, Saturn and Mercury

Throat and chest disorders arise from congestion in the throat chakra, a consequence of emotionalism. Phlegm is a manifestation of emotional congestion. Aspirants who are transmuting sexual sacral force, raising and expressing it through the throat chakra can also have throat trouble.

3a. Breathing Problems

a. Asthma

Asthma is a respiratory condition marked by attacks or spasms in the bronchi that causes difficulty breathing. The underlying psychological pattern is emotional shock, being in terror for one's life.

Theodore Roosevelt (27 October 1858 19:4 5, New York NY)
American statesman, soldier, reformer who served as the 26th President of the United States. His asthma problems began in early childhood.

Cause: emotional. Roosevelt was sensitive emotionally (Moon in Cancer). But he harboured anger (Moon opposite Mars), perhaps as a consequence of hidden physical and verbal abuse that would strike suddenly and unexpectedly (Mars sesquiquadrate Uranus in Gemini in the 12H of hidden things). This pattern is related to his breathing difficulties.

Organ: - airways, Uranus in Gemini.

Effect: asthma. Anxiety that he might be hurt caused the spasms (Moon > Mars > Uranus in the 12H. Mars rules the 6H of health).

▲ (C) Moon, Mars. (O) Gemini. (E) Mars, Uranus.

b. Bronchitis

Bronchitis is inflammation of the lining of the bronchial tubes. Heavy phlegm (Moon, Mars, Neptune) is coughed up. It can be caused by a virus (Neptune), a bacterial infection (Uranus) or air-borne contaminants.

Dixie Lee Ray (3 September 1914, 01:00, Tacoma WA).
Marine biologist who served as a governor of Washington State. She died in 1994, having suffered from a severe bronchial condition for several months.

Cause: ageing. Immediately we see the dangerous 1st ray planets Pluto and Saturn in emotional Cancer, in the 12H of major illnesses. It indicates emotional repression, phlegm and bronchial trouble that could migrate into a serious health condition if not appropriately dealt with. This was not easy for Ray, a scientist who felt more comfortable mentally disconnecting from her feelings (Moon in Aquarius). However, she had reasonable health most of her life, dying at 80, which tells us that she found emotional balance (Saturn-Pluto are in a grand-trine with Venus and the Moon).

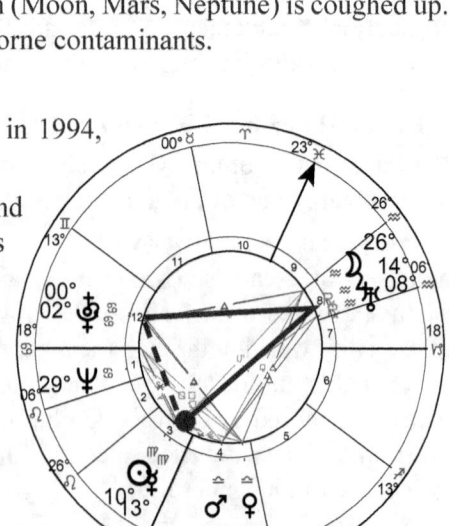

Organ: throat - airways, Mercury.

Effect: bronchitis. Towards the end of her life a virulent bacterial infection invaded Rays' airways and lungs (Uranus-Jupiter inconjunct Mercury). There was a rapid build-up of phlegm (Jupiter sesquiquadrate Pluto-Saturn in Cancer in the 12H of hospitals). Ray could not shake off the infection and she died (Aquarius planets in the 8H of death).

▲ (C) Saturn. (O) Mercury. (E) Pluto, Jupiter-Uranus.

• When Ray died on 2 January 1994, transit Pluto was on her progressed Sun at 28 Scorpio. Pluto carries the 1st ray and rules death.

c. Croup

A viral infection of the throat and windpipe that causes noisy breathing, a hoarse voice and a barking cough.

Amy Rodden (23 November 1949, 00:45, Palo Alto CA)

American musician who at age 2, contracted croup which ended up as pneumonia.

Cause: emotional. A lung-phlegm related disease signifies that emotionally we are drowning in emotional tides. In Rodden's case, her Moon in Capricorn shows a paucity of nurturing (real or imagined), resulting in grief and sorrow (the Moon square Neptune). It is very interesting because mother was famed astrologer Lois Rodden. From the chart we see that Amy felt abandoned, thought that her mother's professional life was more important to her mother than she (Moon opposing Uranus - the astrologer, in the 10H).

Organ: throat - airways, Mercury.

Effect: croup. There is susceptibility to chestiness and phlegm, spasms and coughing (Mercury afflicted in Sagittarius, inconjunct Uranus in Cancer, ruler of the 6H of health). She developed croup that migrated into pneumonia (Mercury > Uranus in Cancer; Jupiter disposits Mercury).

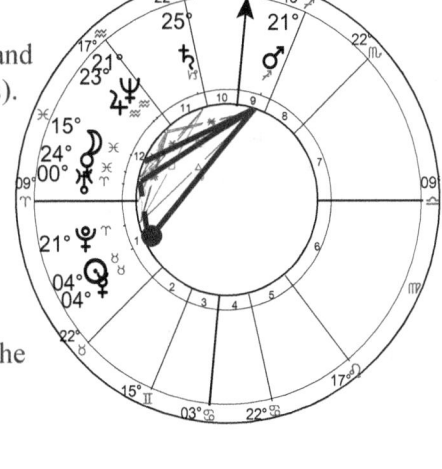

▲ (C) Moon, Neptune. (O) Mercury. (E) Uranus.

• Solar-arc Mercury was exactly inconjunct Uranus when Rodden caught croup.

d. Diphtheria (various body parts)

A serious bacterial infection that causes fever and a thick coating in the nose and airways.

Princess Alice (25 April 1843, 04:05, London UK).

Queen Victoria's third child. She married Prince Louis of Hesse in 1862 and died of diphtheria on 14 December 1878. She was aged 35.

Cause: emotional. Alice would hide her feelings, her emotional pain and disappointments (the Moon is in the 12H of hidden things, square Mars). Emotionally congested, she was susceptible to chest complaints.

Organ: throat - airways, Mercury.

Effect: diphtheria. Alice caught diphtheria (Uranus) and the infection (Mars) invaded her airways and lungs (Mars sesquiquadrate the Sun and Mercury, the planets that rule the 6H of health).

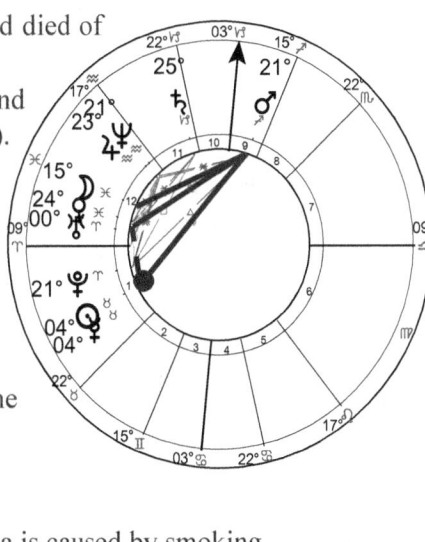

▲ (C) Moon. (O) Mercury, (E) Mars, Uranus.

• When she died, solar-arc Uranus (the bacterial infection), was conjunct the natal Sun-Mercury point in Taurus and so was transit Neptune.

e. Emphysema

Damage to air sacs results in shortness of breath. 85% of the time emphysema is caused by smoking.

Dean Martin (7 June 1917 23:55, Steubenville OH).

Italian-American singer and actor who smoked and died of emphysema.

Cause: emotional. Martin had difficulty expressing his emotions in a healthy way. He repressed them (Saturn in Cancer, Moon in Capricorn), and self-medicated with alcohol and smoking (Neptune conjunct Saturn that is semi-square the Sun, the ruler of the 6H of health).

Organ: throat - airways, Mercury, Sun (for lower lungs).

Effect: emphysema. Smoking damaged the air sacs in the lungs (semi-square the Sun in Gemini, sextile Mercury), causing shortness of breath (Uranus in Aquarius square Mercury). It was made worse by chronic bronchitis (Mercury conjunct Jupiter and Mars, sextile Saturn in Cancer). Mars rules the 8H of death - he died from the effects of emphysema on 25 December 1995.

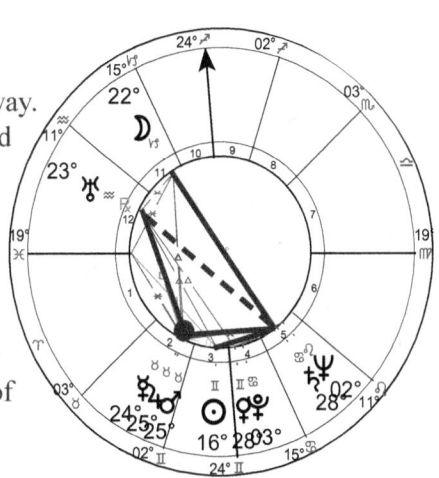

▲ (C) Saturn, Moon. (O) Mercury, Sun. (E) Neptune, Saturn, Uranus.

f. Hay fever

Air-borne contaminants cause hay fever, resulting in itchy, watery eyes and sneezing.

Astro.com 3118 (13 March, 1884, 03:34, New Orleans, LA)

American hay fever victim who suffered for many years from seasonal attacks. She moved often in an effort to find a congenial environment

Cause: emotional. As a child she suffered abuse (malefics in the 4H of family). As an adult, fear and constant vigilance that bad things would continue to happen manifested as hay fever (Saturn square Mercury). Our subject constantly moved house, but when emotional damage from abuse is not dealt with the consequences follow us no matter where we go.

Organ: throat - airways, Mercury.

Effect: hay fever. Air-borne contaminants (Saturn in Gemini) caused an exaggerated reaction from the immune system (sextile Mars in Leo conjunct Jupiter). It caused watery eyes and sneezing (Mercury afflicted in Pisces, sesquiquadrate retrograde Jupiter in Cancer in the 6H of health, conjunct Mars).

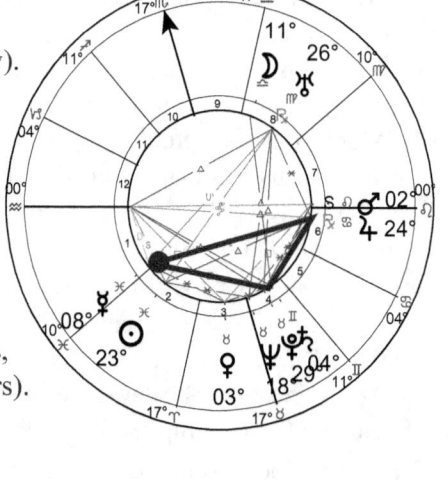

▲ (C) Mars, Saturn. (O) Mercury. (E) Saturn, Mars.

g. Influenza

A highly contagious viral infection of the respiratory tract causing fever and phlegm.

Inayat Khan (5 July 1882, 23:28, Baroda India)

Khan came to the West as an Indian classical musician and founded the Sufi Order in 1914. He died from influenza on 5 February 1927, aged 44.

Cause: discipleship work. Khan was a spiritual teacher whose mission took him amongst the masses (Moon in Pisces in the 12H of universal sacrifice).

Organ: throat - airways, Gemini, Mercury.

Effect: influenza. Khan's airways were susceptible to viral infections (Mercury is retrograde in phlegm-producing Cancer, semi-square Neptune that disposits the Moon in Pisces). He was caught up in an influenza epidemic (Moon opposite Uranus that carries the 4th and 7th epidemic producing forces). His lungs flooded with cell debris (Jupiter in Gemini square the Moon in Pisces), and he literally drowned.

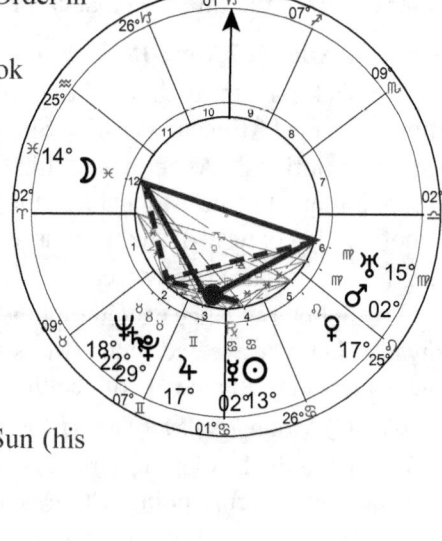

▲ (C) Pisces. (O) Gemini, Mercury. (E) Neptune, Jupiter, Uranus.

- When Khan died, transit Neptune (the flu virus) was on the progressed Sun (his life and vitality), on the cusp of the 6H of health, at 26 Leo.

h. Pneumonia

In pneumonia, lungs become inflamed, the air sacs fill with pus and other liquid, making breathing impossible.

Lorne Greene (12 February 1915 20:30, Ottawa Canada)

Canadian actor who starred as Ben Cartwright in the TV show Bonanza. He caught pneumonia in hospital, dying 11 September 1987, at age 72.

Cause: ageing. Greene's death was age related (Saturn), which means he lived a relatively moderate and balanced life.

Organ: throat - airways, Mercury and Gemini.

Effect: pneumonia. While recovering in hospital from ulcer surgery Greene caught a bacterial infection that migrated into pneumonia (Uranus conjunct the Moon, sesquiquadrate Saturn in Gemini; Saturn conjunct Pluto in Cancer; Pluto trine Mercury in Pisces in the 6H of health). There was a rapid build-up of fluid in the lungs (Mercury conjunct Jupiter in Pisces).

▲ (C) Saturn. (O) Mercury, Gemini. (E) Uranus, Pluto, Saturn, Jupiter.

- When Greene caught pneumonia, solar-arc Saturn and Pluto were at 7-12 degrees of Virgo in the 12H of major illnesses, inconjunct natal Mars and Uranus.

i. Pulmonary Tuberculosis (TB)

An infectious bacterial disease characterised by the growth of nodules (tubercles) in lung tissue.

Princess Mathilde (17 August 1877 21:00, Munich Germany)
Bavarian princess, who died of tuberculosis on 6 August 1906, aged 29.
Cause: emotional. Mathilde yearned to be free but felt imprisoned by her royal status (Moon in Sagittarius, conjunct Jupiter, square Saturn ruling the 10H of royalty, in the obscure 12H). Her unhappiness manifested as constant illnesses (t-square the 6th-12th health houses).
Organ: throat - airways, Mercury.
Effect: TB. Mathilde was prone to infections in the airways (Mars in Pisces, opposite Mercury in the 6H of health), and she developed pulmonary tuberculosis (square Jupiter).

▲ (C) Moon, Saturn. (O) Mercury. (E) Mars, Jupiter.

- When Mathilde died, solar-arc Pluto was at 23 Gemini opposite Jupiter. Both Pluto via Scorpio, and Jupiter via Sagittarius, rule the 8H of death.

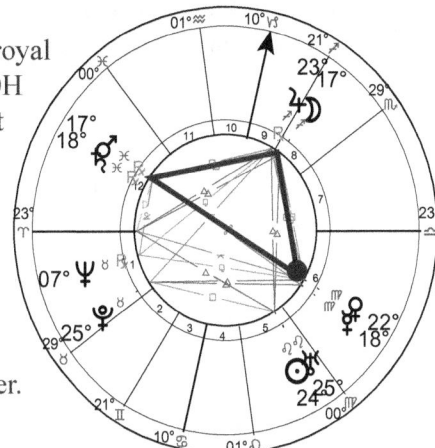

j. Smallpox

Smallpox spreads mainly through the air and launches its attack on the entire body from the respiratory organs. It cripples the immune system, breeds its toxicity in the body, shown by a skin rash with small blisters.

Abraham Lincoln (12 February 1809 06:54, Hodgenville KY)
President of the United States, he caught and recovered from smallpox.
Cause: epidemic. Although his vitality is good with the Sun on the ascendant trine Mars, these planets are in their detriment. His responsibilities could quickly debilitate his energies, rendering him susceptible to illnesses (Saturn conjunct Neptune on the MC, and Neptune semi-square Mars). He was also prone to depression (the Moon is afflicted in the 12H, rules the 6H of health).
Organ: throat - airways, Mercury.
Effect: smallpox. Just after the Gettysburg Address in November 1863, he was caught up in a smallpox epidemic (the Moon carrying the 4th ray). The virus (Neptune), invaded his airways (square Mercury). He recovered. It was not his destiny to die at that time.

▲ (C) Moon. (O) Mercury. (E) Neptune.

- When Lincoln caught smallpox, solar-arc Moon was at 22 Pisces moving over progressed Mercury and natal Jupiter.

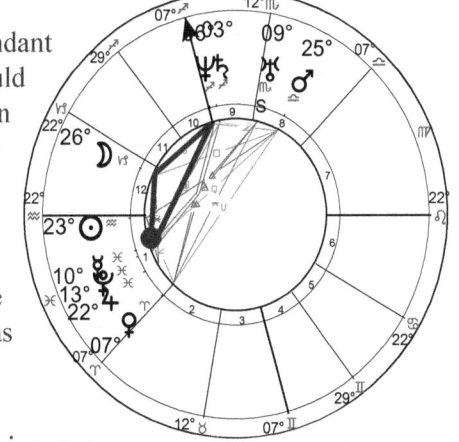

Mary Stuart (14 November 1631 04:00, London UK)
Eldest daughter of King Charles I of England-Scotland-Ireland. She died from smallpox on 24 December 1660, aged 29.
Cause: emotional. Stuart was an emotionally intense (4 planets in Scorpio), a pattern that made her susceptible to breathing and chest infections because Mercury and Neptune in Scorpio rule the 12th and 6th health houses.
Organ: throat - airways, Mercury.
Effect: smallpox. Stuart was caught in a smallpox (Neptune) epidemic (semi-square Uranus) that quickly spread through the masses (trine Pluto). The virus was lethal. It attacked her airways (Neptune conjunct retrograde Mercury) and she died (Mercury quindecile Pluto in the 8H of death).

▲ (C) Neptune. (O) Mercury. (E) Neptune, Uranus, Pluto.

- When Mary Stuart died, solar-arc Sun had reached natal Venus, the ruler of the 8H of death; and solar-arc Pluto was opposing Venus from 22 Gemini.

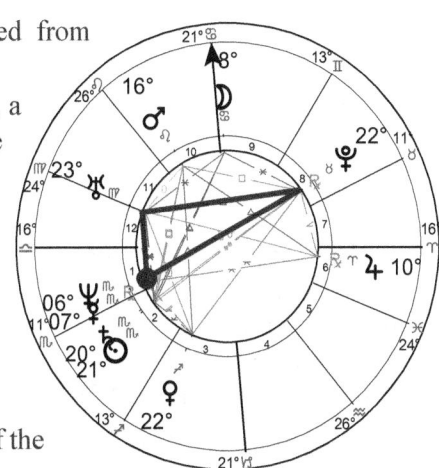

3b. Thyroid Disorders

The thyroid gland is the physical anchorage of the throat chakra. Its hormonal functions include the regulation of metabolism, breathing and heart rate, etc. Thyroid disorders are often caused by emotional hyper-activity.

> [an over-developed and over-stimulated] astral body, leading to over-sensitivity of the solar plexus centre or of the throat centre. Much of the thyroid instability of the present time is based upon this. [1]

a. Grave's Disease (GD)

Graves' disease is an autoimmune disorder that causes the thyroid to over-produce hormones. It disturbs moods, behaviour and judgement. Racing anxiety is a psychological cause.

President George H. W. Bush (12 June 1924, 10:30, Milton MA)
Bush was the 41st President of the United States from 1989 to 1993 and father of the 43rd President George W. Bush. In 1991, he was diagnosed with GD.

Cause: emotional. Bush represses his emotions and moderates what he says (Saturn conjunct Moon in Libra in the 3H of communications). This is to present himself in the best possible light (Sun in the 10H of status, Leo on the ascendant). If he fails, if he does the wrong thing, he may mentally or even physically attack himself (Saturn trine Mars in Aquarius opposite the ascendant).

Organ: throat - thyroid, Venus.

Effect: GD. In response to his negative impulses, the immune system (Mars) attacked the thyroid causing over-activity in hormone production (sesquiquadrate retrograde Venus); dangerously so if not treated (Pluto-Venus).

▲ (C) Moon, Saturn. (O) Venus, Mercury. (E) Mars, Pluto.

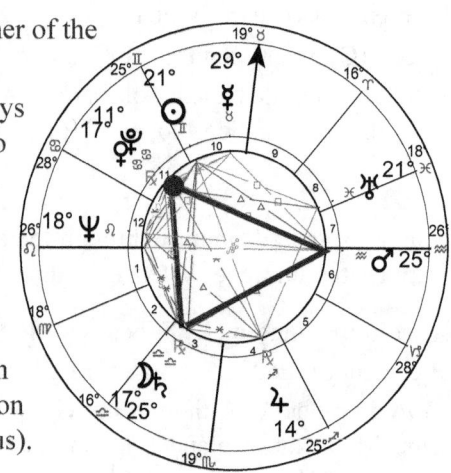

b. Hashimoto's Disease

The thyroid is underactive. The autoimmune system attacks the gland causing chronic inflammation and its eventual failure. There is tiredness and lethargy.

Oprah Winfrey (29 January 1954 04:30, Kosciusko MS)
Talk-show host Winfrey, in 2007, exhausted and gaining weight she was diagnosed with a thyroid disease. There are two patterns that link into 1st ray Pluto.

Cause: emotional. Winfrey was born with low self-esteem (Sun conjunct Venus square Saturn), quite likely a consequence of growing up as an impoverished black girl in the racist Southern States. She felt devalued and attacked (Aquarius planet group in the 2H of values, Mercury square Mars). Negative self-talk and self-attack when she failed to meet her own high expectations is behind the thyroid trouble (Mercury rules the 6H of health). The positive side of this is that Winfrey felt motivated to succeed in life in spite of the obstacles placed in her way (Sun square Saturn in the 10H of professional success).

Organ: throat - thyroid, Venus and Mercury.

Effect: Hashimoto's. The thyroid was attacked by the immune system (Venus quindecile Pluto in Leo, Mercury in a t-square with Mars and Pluto), impairing and inhibiting (Saturn and Pluto) hormone production.

Depression and verbal attacks were followed by comfort eating (Venus trine Jupiter in the 6H of food habits). Coupled with a slow metabolism, she gained weight.

▲ (C) Mars. (O) Venus, Mercury. (E) Mars, Pluto, Saturn.

---

[1] Bailey, Alice A; Esoteric Psychology II, 315.

3c. Cancer in Throat Chakra Organs

a. Lymphatic cancer

Lymphatic cancer or lymphoma strikes the lymphocytes, disease infection-fighting white cells that cycle within the lymphatic system. The most common type of lymphoma is non-Hodgkin. In Hodgkin's disease, different white cells are affected.

Richard Harris (1 October 1930 11:20, Limerick Ireland)

Irish actor and singer described as a "hell-raiser", "half man, half maniac", with a love of booze. He was diagnosed with Hodgkin's disease in August 2002 and died on the 25th of October of that year.

Cause: emotional. Harris' chart shows he suffered enormous emotional conflict and pain in his childhood and family life (Moon in Capricorn opposite Mars and Pluto in Cancer). To cope, he repressed his emotions, a dangerous habit where health is concerned. He also drank excessively (Mars conjunct Jupiter in Cancer, semi-square Neptune), and had a wild, partying lifestyle (square Uranus in the 5H of recreation), which brought its own set of health problems (Mars rules the 6H of health).

Organ: throat - lymphatic system, the Moon, Neptune.

Effect: cancer. The Moon and Cancer are rulers of the lymphatic system, and the Health Triangle is based on this polarity. Due to stress and congestion in the body, lymphocytes (the Moon), became perverted (6th ray Mars), malignant (Pluto) and cancerous (Jupiter). The square from the Cancer planets to Uranus indicates that his wild and undisciplined life-style contributed to the onset of the disease and to the aberrant behaviour of cells (Uranus opposite the Sun).

▲ (C) Cancer planets, Moon. (O) Moon, Neptune. (E) Mars, Pluto, Jupiter, Uranus.

- When Harris was diagnosed in 2002, the solar-arc ascendant had reached 27 Capricorn and was passing over the natal Moon, representing the trouble occurring in body tissue. Simultaneously, the other ruler of the lymphatic system - Neptune, by solar-arc it had reached 16 Scorpio and was conjunct the ascendant. The cancer grew and spread via the bloodstream, which Neptune rules.
- On the day he died, the transit Moon entered the 8H of death.

Charles Harvey (22 June 1940 09:16, Little Bookham UK)

British astrologer. In 1999, Harvey contracted a form of lymphatic cancer. After a heavy treatment of chemotherapy, he died on 22 February 2000.

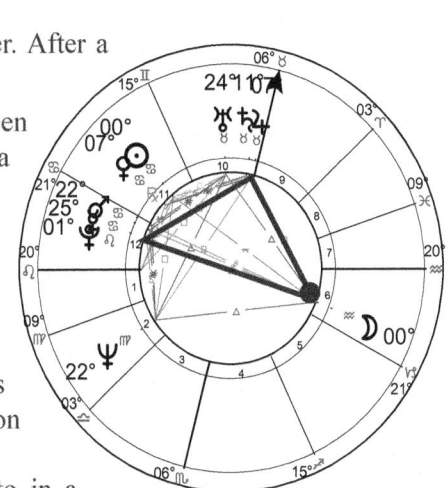

Cause: emotional. Serious trouble affecting the fluids of the body can be seen with Cancer dominating the 12H of hospitals. Cancer the disease becomes a candidate when we see that Harvey had a habit of repressing his thoughts and feelings (Pluto conjunct Mercury and Mars in Cancer). This caused congestion in the throat chakra, the ruler of the lymphatic system.

Organ: throat - lymphatic system, the Moon and Cancer.

Effect: cancer. White blood cells (the Moon opposite Mars in Cancer) became malignant (Pluto) and cancerous (square Jupiter). Blood quality was seriously degraded (the Moon in Aquarius > Mars), inhibiting oxygenation (Mercury) and the nourishing of blood cells.

Chemotherapy (Pluto) could not stop the march of the disease (Pluto in a t-square with Jupiter and the Moon), and the cancer eventually killed him. Jupiter rules the 8H of death with Pisces on the cusp.

▲ (C) Moon, Mars. (O) Moon, Cancer. (E) Pluto, Jupiter.

- When Harvey was diagnosed in 1999, the progressed Moon was moving through the 8H of death and was still there when he died in 2000.

b. Mouth and Jaw Cancer

Gordon MacRae (12 March 1921, 07:15, East Orange NJ)

American actor and singer, who was best known from his Rodgers and Hammerstein musical films, Oklahoma (1955) and Carousel (1956). On January 24 1986 at the age of 64, he died of pneumonia, the result of complications from cancer of the mouth and jaw.

Cause: emotional. MacRae was emotionally reactive and fiery (Moon-Mars in Aries), which clashed with his down-to-earth perfectionist tendencies where his craft was concerned (inconjunct Saturn in Virgo in the 6H of work). He worked exceedingly hard and was hyper-critical of his and other people's performances if he thought they fell below par. He could not let go of disappointments and frustrations and would worry about them, undermining his health (Saturn quindecile Mercury in detriment in Pisces, opposite the Sun in the 12H of self-undoing).

Organ: throat - mouth, jaw Mars in Aries, Venus in Taurus.

Effect: cancer. Congestion and trouble in the throat chakra (Saturn retrograde in the 6H of health), caused carcinogenic changes (quindecile Uranus in Pisces in the 12H of major illnesses), in tissue in the mouth and jaw (inconjunct Mars-Moon in Aries in the 1H; sesquiquadrate Venus). Cancer grew (Saturn conjunct Jupiter).

▲ (C) Moon, Mars, Saturn. (O) Mars, Venus. (E) Uranus, Jupiter.

- When he died in 1986, solar-arc Venus was at 7 Cancer, conjunct malignant Pluto in Cancer. This represented the final onslaught of the disease in his throat that caused his death - Pluto rules the 8H of death.
- He died of pneumonia due to a build-up of phlegm and cell debris in his lungs (Pluto in Cancer trine afflicted Mercury in Pisces in the 12H).

c. Throat Cancer

Medical experts tell us the human papilloma virus (HPV) is a leading cause of throat cancer and may spread from person to person via oral sex. Astrologically, it fits. Venus, which rules the throat, also rules sex.

Michael Douglas (25 September 1944 10:30, New Brunswick NJ).

American actor and son of actor Kirk Douglas. In mid-August 2010, he announced he had stage four throat cancer and that oral sex was a cause. Though he later retracted this, it probably is the truth - many sexually active people have the HPV virus and his chart shows he was susceptible. After successful treatment, Douglas returned to his acting career.

Cause: karmic - sexual. Douglas is a Libran who inhibits his emotions (Saturn in Cancer in a t-square with the Moon in Capricorn, and Neptune), in order to try to create peace and equilibrium around him. But this creates congestion and trouble in the solar plexus chakra, which in the long term leads to overall debilitation and susceptibility to viruses and disease generally.

Organ: throat, Venus.

Effect: cancer. Oral sex (Venus conjunct Mars), although it is generally accepted as being a normal part of sexual expression, health-wise it is a misuse of the sexual function because it spreads the HPV virus. In Douglas' case, the virus (Mars, ruler of the 6H of health with Aries on the cusp), attacked the throat and mouth (Venus). Tissue became carcinogenic (square Saturn in Cancer) and cancer eventually developed (semi-square Jupiter afflicted in Virgo).

▲ (C) Saturn, Mars. (O) Venus. (E) Mars, Saturn, Jupiter.

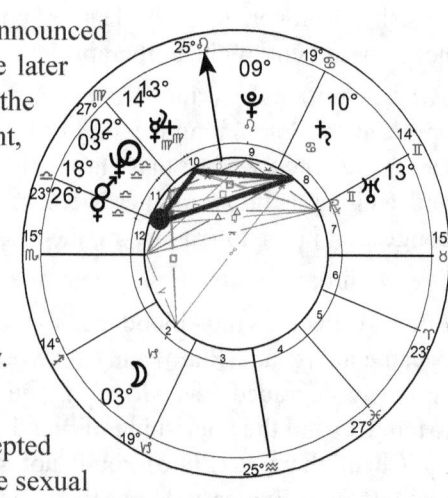

d. Lung Cancer

Although the lungs are part of the respiratory system governed by the throat chakra, the heart chakra shares rulership of the lungs, particularly the lower lobes. The following quote helps to clarify the differences.

> If the patient should be suffering from difficulty in the heart or the lungs the healer will use the heart centre, employing the throat centre for diseases of the bronchial tract... [1]

That aside here are two examples of lung cancer, both most likely caused by smoking. That may have been the outer cause, but as we know, there is always an inner cause for most personal diseases.

Brian Keith (14 November 1921 02:00, Bayonne NJ)

American film and television actor who worked successfully in the industry for 60 years. During the latter part of his life, Keith suffered from emphysema and lung cancer, despite having quit smoking ten years earlier. Ironically, he had appeared in an endorsement campaign for Camel cigarettes in 1955. On June 24 1997, he shot himself to avoid suffering a cancer death.

Cause: emotional. Keith was highly disciplined (Scorpio Sun semi-square Saturn rising), and repressed his emotions (Saturn conjunct Mars in Libra) to maintain a semblance of balance in his life. He smoked (Neptune square the Sun) to help relieve tension and obviously did not know at that time, that smoking was carcinogenic and was going to affect his health (Neptune co-rules the 6H of health with Pisces sharing the cusp).

Organ: heart - the lungs, the Sun.

Effect: lung cancer. A combination of emotional repression and smoking caused carcinogenic cell changes in the lungs (Neptune > Sun), which led to lung cancer (the Sun semi-square Jupiter). Not wanting to face the suffering of a slow death that cancer brings, he shot himself (Mars rules guns, and the 8H of death with Aries on the cusp).

▲ (C) Mars, Saturn, Neptune. (O) The Sun. (E) Jupiter.

- When Keith shot himself, transit Mars was in the 1st house that rules the head, and was beginning to move over natal Saturn and Mars. He took action to avoid having to go through the prolonged pain and suffering that accompanies cancer.

Rosemary Clooney (23 May 1928 02:30, Maysville KY).

American singer who came to prominence in the early 1950's with songs such as 'Come On-a My House'. A long-time smoker, Clooney was diagnosed with lung cancer at the end of 2001. Despite surgery, she died six months later on June 29 2002. Her nephew, George Clooney was a pallbearer at her funeral, which was attended by numerous stars.

Cause: emotional. A bubbling Gemini Sun person, underneath Clooney was very sensitive and suffered anxiety attacks (the Sun square Neptune in Leo). Smoking helped relieve the tension, but exacerbated health problems.

Organ: heart - the lungs, the Sun.

Effect: lung cancer. Smoking was dangerous for Clooney's health because Neptune, which rules smoking, is located in the 6H of health. It also co-rules the 12H of hospitals with Pisces sharing rulership of the cusp. Smoking had a malignant effect on the lungs, causing carcinogenic changes in cells (Neptune > Sun in Gemini) that resulted in malignant cancerous growth (Pluto and the Moon in Cancer, midpoint the Sun and Neptune). It killed her (Pluto rules the 8H of death).

▲ (C) Neptune. (O) Sun. (E) Neptune, Moon-Pluto in Cancer.

---

1 Bailey, Alice A; Esoteric Healing, 602.

e. Bowel/ Colorectal and Rectal Cancer

The throat chakra governs the alimentary canal.[1]

Robin Gibb (22 December 1949, 03:15, Douglas, Man of Isle)

Born in England and raised in Australia, Gibb was a member of the very successful pop group, the Bee Gees. He died 20 May 2012, from liver and kidney failure brought on by colorectal cancer.

Cause: emotional. Mars in Virgo is a classic symbol for holding onto one's "shit" because of an anal/ narrow/ critical view of the world. This pattern underlies Gibb's trouble. Mars rules the 6H of health, with Aries located on its cusp.

Organ: solar plexus - colon, Mars.

Effect: colon cancer. T-square: colon (Mars) cells (Sun), turned aberrant (opposite Uranus), began to rapidly multiply (Sun in Sagittarius), and he died from cancer (Sun semi-square Venus, ruler of the 8H of death).

▲ (C) Mars. (O) Mars. (E) Sun, Uranus.

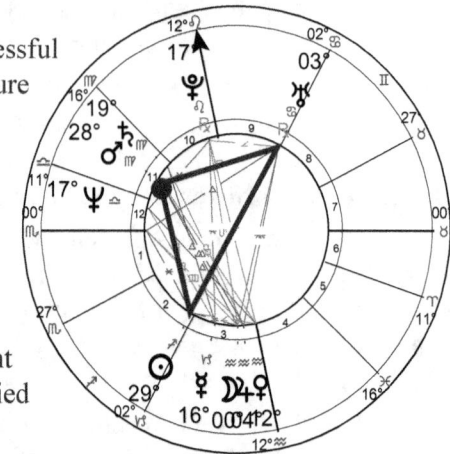

Tammy Bakker (7 March 1942, 03:27, International Falls MN)

Bakker, an American Christian evangelist, formed a very successful online televangelist show with her husband Jim Bakker - until he was imprisoned for fraud and conspiracy. This would have had an impact upon her health. She had rectal surgery for cancer on 6 March 1996.

Cause: emotional. Bakker held onto the rage she felt when her when husband was convicted of fraud in 1989 - and accused of sexual indiscretion (Moon square Pluto in Leo in the 8H of sex).

Organ: solar plexus - colon, Moon in Scorpio and Pluto.

Effect: colon cancer. Emotional conflict congested the solar plexus, causing carcinogenic changes in tissue in the rectum (Moon in Scorpio > Pluto), causing cancer (inconjunct Jupiter 6H). She had surgery and lived for another 8 years, dying July 20 2007.

▲ (C) Moon, Pluto. (O) Moon in Scorpio, Pluto. (E) Pluto, Jupiter.

Ada Phillips (4 May 1908 16:30, Brighton UK)

British astrologer, who was a founding member and long term supporter of the British Astrological Association. She died 9 December 1996, from rectum cancer.

Cause: emotional. The 5-planet stellium can be read as a group conjunction. In the 9H of higher mind we get the sense of mental congestion (3 planets are in Gemini), and emotional repression (Moon square Saturn in the 6H of health). With the rulers of the bowel involved (Mars, Pluto and the Moon), congestion occurred, causing cellular trouble in that region.

Organ: solar plexus - rectum, Pluto and Mars.

Effect: rectum cancer. Carcinogenic changes in bowel tissue (Pluto-Mars, Saturn square the Moon), migrated into rectal cancer (Jupiter semi-square Pluto, trine Saturn).

▲ (C) Moon, Saturn. (O) Pluto, Mars. (E) Jupiter.

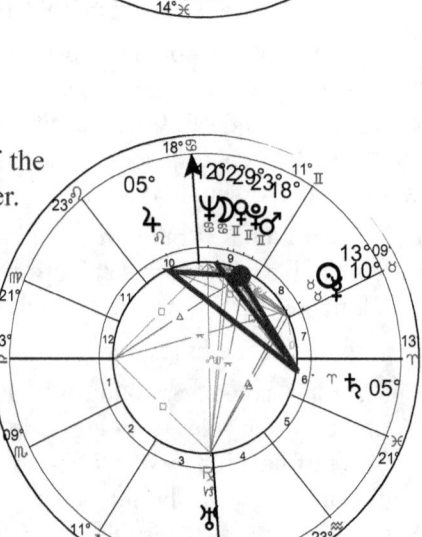

---

1 Bailey, Alice; Esoteric Healing, 45.

3d. Intestinal, Bowel Trouble

a. Colitis

The autoimmune system attacks the inner lining of the colon.

John F. Kennedy (29 May 1917 15:00, Brookline MA)
Charismatic USA president, Kennedy was diagnosed with colitis in 1934.

Cause: emotional. Kennedy was born with a self-criticising pattern (a Virgo Moon), which caused the trouble. He felt unloved by his father (the Moon rules the 10H, and is semi-square Neptune, which conjuncts Saturn), and resented having to enter politics to further his family's political (Uranus) ambitions (Mercury conjunct Mars square Uranus in the 4H of family).

Organ: solar plexus - colon, Mercury and Mars.

Effect: colitis. In response to his inner unhappiness, the immune system turned rogue (Mars in detriment in Taurus), and attacked the bowel (conjunct Mercury), causing diarrhea, abdominal cramping and spasms (Mars > Uranus).

▲ (C) Moon. (O) Mercury, Mars. (E) Mars, Uranus.

b. Crohn's disease

A chronic inflammatory bowel disease of the digestive tract lining. An abnormal response from the immune system is the possible cause. Anal retention, holding onto one's "shit" is the psychological cause.

Mary Ann Mobley (17 February 1937, 16:00, Biloxi MS)
American beauty queen, diagnosed with Crohn's disease in 1962.

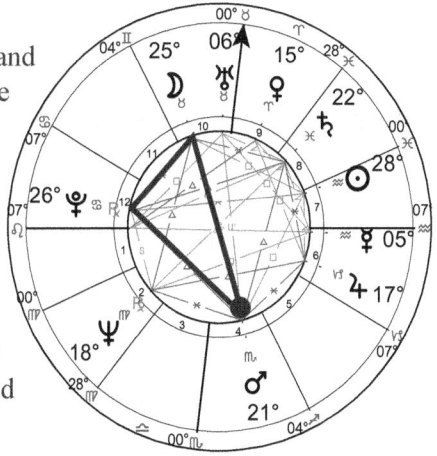

Cause: emotional. Mobley's instinctual impulse is to stand stubbornly firm and not give in - she has a Taurus Moon. While she needed inner strength to rise above secret family abuse (easy-opposition Moon-Mars-Pluto, touching the 4th and 10th family houses and the secretive 12th); it also meant she would hold onto the trauma of her experiences and find it hard to move on. This pattern underlies her bowel trouble. She holds onto her "shit".

Organ: solar plexus - bowel, Mars, Pluto.

Effect: Crohn's disease. Like so many victims, Mobley blamed and attacked herself for her family traumas, triggering an immune attack (Mars). Her inner pattern manifested as an attack on the walls of the bowel (Moon > Pluto and Mars), causing inflammation and diarrhea.

▲ (C) Moon. (O) Mars, Pluto. (E) Mars, Pluto.

c. Diverticulitis

Constipation, small sacs or blisters in the lining of the colon. If they are infected, it's called diverticulitis, causing pain and disturbed bowel function.

Jack Nicklaus (21 January 1940, 03:10, Columbus OH)
Golf great Jack Nicklaus was hospitalized in October 2010 for severe abdominal pain and was diagnosed as having diverticulitis.

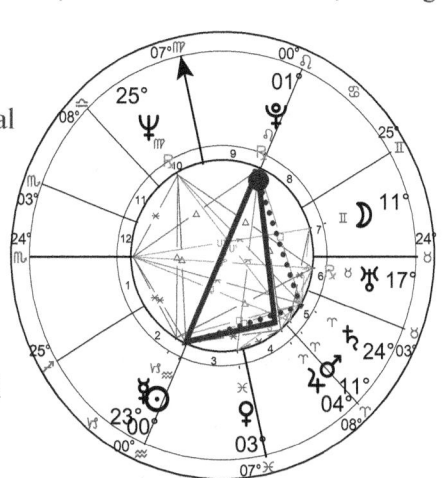

Cause: emotional. With Scorpio rising and Pluto in a t-square with Saturn, the Sun and Mercury, Nicklaus faces life defensively. He stubbornly holds on to issues and absorbs anger and this is related to his bowel trouble.

Organ: solar plexus - bowel, Pluto.

Effect: diverticulitis. Stubbornness translated into constipation. Diverticula blisters developed in bowel walls (Pluto trines Jupiter and Mars in Aries) and became infected (Jupiter semi-squares Uranus).

▲ (C) Scorpio ascendant. (O) Pluto. (E) Saturn, Sun, Mars.

d. Hemorrhoids

Hemorrhoids are swollen or bulging veins around the anus. They can develop from straining during bowel movements, particularly as we age.

Karl Marx (5 May 1818, 02:00, Trier Germany)

Prussian-German revolutionary socialist, Marx had hemorrhoids. Writing to his friend Friedrich Engels he said, "To finish 'Das Kapital' I must at least be able to sit down. I hope the bourgeoisie will remember my carbuncles."

Cause: emotional. Marx was a fighting idealist (Mars in Cancer), a stubborn Taurus personality who was angry about the injustices suffered by the masses (Mars opposite Jupiter in the 11H of social affairs). Through his writings (semi-square Mercury, he argued for social change, for greater fairness and equality (Mars is septile Venus).

Organ: solar plexus - veins Venus, anus Mars.

Effect: hemorrhoids. Marx's stubbornness caused high blood pressure (Saturn-Pluto in Pisces square Uranus-Neptune), and congestion in the lower digestive region (Mars in Cancer). He developed inflamed hemorrhoids (opposite Jupiter), in veins (septile Venus) around the anus (Mars for Scorpio).

▲ (C) Mars in Cancer. (O) Venus, Mars. (E) Mars, Jupiter.

e. Cholera

Cholera is an infectious disease caused by consuming food and water contaminated by the faeces of people infected with the bacteria (Uranus). It strikes the gut causing severe diarrhea (Mars) and dehydration (Saturn).

President Zachary Taylor (24 November 1784 10:57, Barboursville VI)

American politician who was the 12th President of the United States of America. After 16 months in office he died suddenly on 9 July 1850, from cholera

Cause: karmic. It was likely that the epidemic which claimed Taylor was group karma rather than individual. Lord of Karma, Saturn, is in the 12H of the masses, opposite Uranus in Cancer a sign that is also related to the masses. He picked it up while attending to his political responsibilities.

Organ: solar plexus - intestines, Mercury.

Effect: cholera. Taylor caught cholera (Uranus), spread through contaminated food and water (in Cancer, in the 6H of diet and health). It attacked his intestines (sesquiquadrate Mercury). Dehydrated (Saturn), and suffering with diarrhea (Uranus in Cancer), he died (Mercury rules the 8H of death with Virgo on the cusp).

▲ (C) Saturn. (O) Mercury. (E) Saturn, Uranus.

Victor Jaquemont (8 August 1801 23:00, Paris FR)

French botanist and geologist who went to India in 1828. He died of cholera in Bombay on 8 December 1832.

Cause: epidemic. Jaquemont's work took him to places and amongst people where viruses and epidemics flourished (Neptune in the 6H of work semi-square Uranus).

Organ: solar plexus - intestines, Mercury.

Effect: cholera. He caught cholera, a bacterial infection of the gut (Uranus in Virgo), by drinking water (semi-square Neptune in the 6H of health), contaminated by faeces (Neptune in Scorpio). The infection killed him (Neptune square Jupiter, ruler of 8H of death).

▲ (C) Uranus. (O) Mercury. (E) Uranus, Neptune.

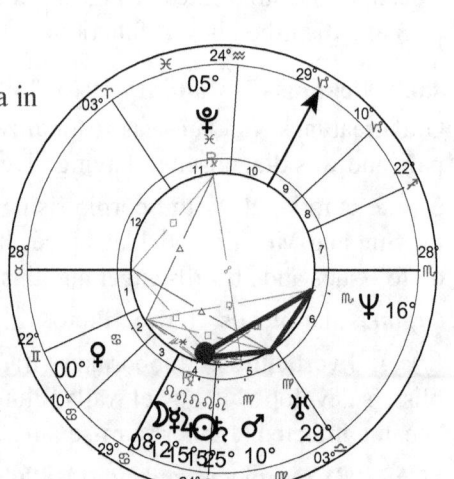

4. Heart Chakra Diseases

Diseases of the Cardiovascular System.

The heart rules the thymus gland, vitality and the cardiovascular, immune and lymphatic systems. It receives energy from ray 2, from Leo, the Sun and Jupiter.

4a. Problems with the Blood

The cardiovascular system overall is ruled by the Sun and Leo. Blood is ruled primarily by Mars, arterial blood by Jupiter, and venous blood by Venus. Blood circulation is governed by Aquarius and the bloodstream by Neptune. The 7th ray is usually involved when there are problems with the blood, primarily through Uranus.

<u>a. Anaemia - Aplastic</u>

Bone marrow fails to produce enough blood cells.

Marie Curie (7 November 1867 12:00, Warsaw Poland)
French physicist and chemist, who pioneered research on radioactivity, but years of exposure resulted in aplastic anaemia. She died on 4 July 1934.
Cause: discipleship. Curie was a disciple who focused in the higher chakras, quite likely the crown chakra since it is ruled by Pluto, a planet that rules radiation. The Sun on the MC opposing Pluto, suggests that the 12-petalled heart lotus at the centre of the crown chakra was coming alive and in response, kundalini (Pluto) was rising. The cause of the disease was due to radiation poisoning, an accidental by-product of her discipleship work.
Organ: heart - cell life and health, the Sun.
Effect: anaemia. Radiation poisoning (Pluto afflicted in Taurus), impairs the body's ability to produce healthy cells from bone marrow (sextile Uranus retrograde in Cancer), and destroys the health of cell life and blood (opposite the Sun). Life was leached from blood cells (Uranus in Cancer), draining away the life-force (Sun).

▲ (C) Pluto. (O) The Sun. (E) Pluto, Uranus.

<u>b. Anaemia - Pernicious (PA)</u>

Vitamin B12, which is needed to make healthy red blood cells, is destroyed by the immune system.

Robert Peary (6 May 1856 12:04, Cresson PA)
American explorer who died of pernicious anaemia on 20 February 1920.
Cause: emotional. Because an autoimmune disease arose, we know Peary attacked himself psychologically. He had an authoritative "parent voice" playing in his head chastising him for his unworthiness (Saturn in Gemini square Mars in the 2H of self-worth). It was quite likely imprinted on his consciousness by a bullying patriarchal figure in whose presence he felt helpless (Mars afflicted in Libra and retrograde). This is at the root of the disorder.
Organ: heart - red blood cells and B12, Mars.
Effect: anaemia. The immune system attacked and destroyed B12 preventing the production of healthy red blood cells so that the blood was leached of its vitalising life (t-square: Mars > Saturn, opposite Jupiter in Pisces representing the impaired blood quality). Peary became anaemic (Saturn) and died (Jupiter in the 8H of death).

▲ (C) Mars. (O) Mars. (E) Mars, Saturn, Jupiter.

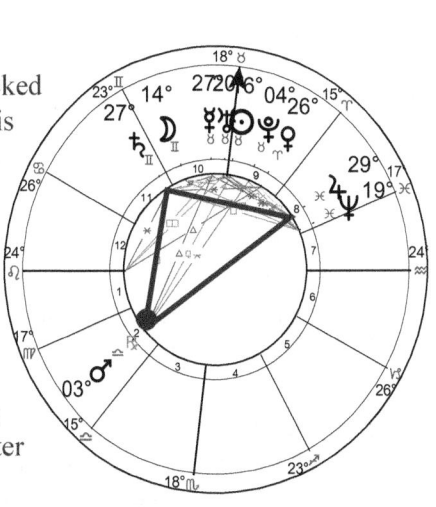

- When Peary died, solar-arc Saturn was in the 1st house at 29 Leo, inconjunct natal Jupiter at 29 Pisces, representing the devitalisation taking place in the blood. Solar-arc Mars was at 4 Sagittarius, inconjunct natal Pluto at 4 Taurus, representing the destruction of the body's ability to produce healthy red blood cells.

c. Anaemia - Sickle Cell

Red blood cells take a sickle shape and die early, leaving a shortage of healthy red blood cells. Diseased cells block blood flow, causing pain. It is a genetic disorder.

Tionne Watkins (26 April 1970, 18:55, Des Moines IA)
American singer of hip hop girl-group TLC. As a child, Watkins was diagnosed with sickle-cell anaemia and since the age of seven has been in and out of hospital. Many African-Americans have the disease.

Cause: genetic, emotional. Although this is a genetic (Uranus) disorder, Watkins' emotional disturbances are connected. This is because Mars, which rules red blood cells is also a ruler of the solar plexus and Watkins' emotions are powerful. They swamp her (Neptune opposite Mars), and she tries to repress them (Moon in Capricorn). This caused trouble.

Organ: heart - red blood cells, Mars.

Effect: anaemia. Watkins inherited a gene (Uranus) that perverts (sextile Neptune) red blood cells (Neptune opposite Mars), so that oxygenation and vitalisation of the body is severely impaired (Mars in Gemini).

▲ (C) Uranus, Mars. (O) Mars. (E) Neptune.

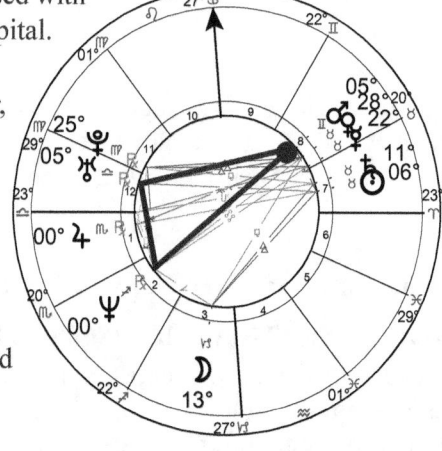

d. Haemophilia

An inherited genetic disease, where blood does not clot leading to prolonged bleeding. Queen Victoria was a carrier and passed it on to several royal houses.

Queen Victoria (24 May 1819, 04:15, London UK)
Queen Victoria did not inherit the gene haemophilia. The mutation was spontaneous and her passing on the "royal disease" cursed many royal houses in Europe. Females only have mild symptoms if any at all while male children inherit the full disease.

Cause: karmic. We are entering into the Aquarian Age of universal brotherhood and the time for autocratic royal houses is over. Perhaps the Lord of Karma was making this point with the gene mutation.

Organ: heart - bloodstream Neptune and Pisces; genes, Uranus.

Effect: haemophilia. The gene (Uranus) that clots blood (square Saturn), was corrupted (Pluto conjunct Saturn, Neptune conjunct Uranus). This meant blood flow would not clot (Jupiter in Aquarius that rules blood circulation, is midpoint Saturn in Pisces, and Neptune). The gene was passed to her descendants (Uranus on the cusp of the 8H of inheritances, sesquiquadrate Mercury, co-ruler of the 5H of children with Virgo sharing the cusp).

▲ (C) Saturn. (O) Neptune, Pisces, Uranus. (E) Pluto, Neptune, Jupiter.

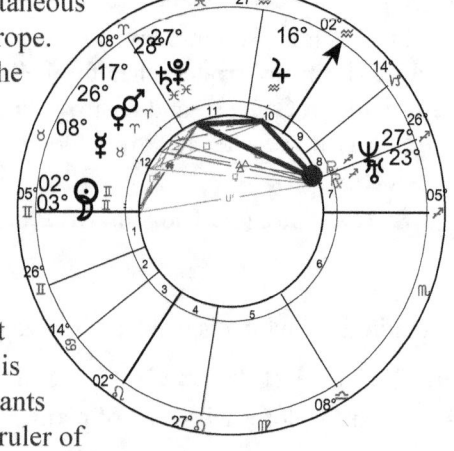

Prince Alexei (12 August 1904 01:15 pm, Petrodvorec Russia).
Alexei was the great-grandson of Victoria and heir to the Russian throne. He was murdered with his family by the Bolsheviks.

Cause: genetic. Alexei inherited the defective gene (Uranus) from his mother and the royal line (trine the Moon conjunct the MC).

Organ: heart - blood, Mars.

Effect: haemophilia. The gene prevented the blood from clotting (Uranus inconjunct Mars square Jupiter in the 6H of health; Jupiter trines Uranus).

▲ (C) Uranus. (O) Mars. (E) Jupiter.

- Alexei was murdered with his family by the Bolsheviks around the 16th or 17th July 1918. Solar-arc Mars was at 12 Leo symbolising the dominant "Red" Army that took his life (square the ascendant).

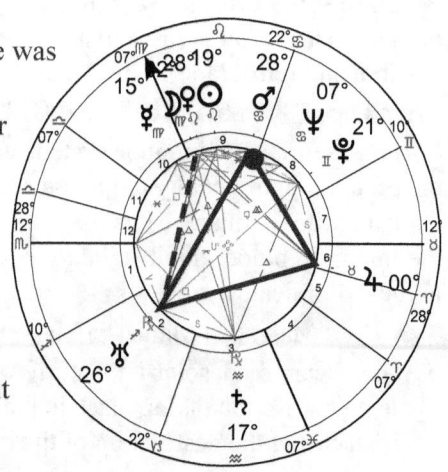

e. Angina

Inadequate blood supply to the heart results in severe chest pain that may spread to the shoulders, arms and neck.

Sir Ernest Shackleton (15 February 1874, 05:00, Kilkea Ireland)

British explorer who examined sections of Antarctica.

Cause: emotional. Shackleton was emotionally detached and could repress his feelings, a habit that affects circulation (the Moon-Saturn conjunction in Aquarius).

Organ: heart - blood circulation Uranus in Leo, arteries Jupiter.

Effect: angina. Consequently, circulation became restricted as arteries hardened (Saturn in Aquarius opposite Uranus in Leo, trine retrograde Jupiter). He developed painful angina and eventually the disease killed him (Jupiter in the 8H of death).

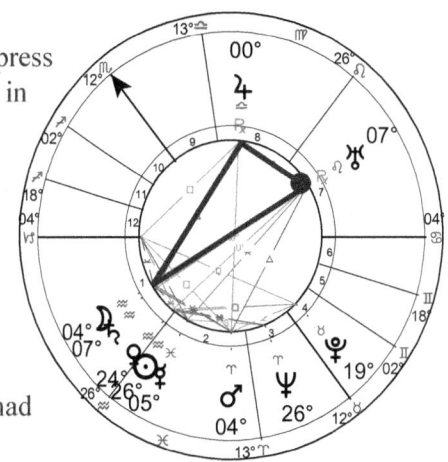

▲ (C) Moon, Saturn. (O) Uranus, Jupiter. (E) Saturn, Uranus.

- When Shackleton died on January 5 1922, solar-arc Jupiter (the arteries) had progressed to 18 Scorpio, moving opposite natal Pluto at 19 Taurus.

f. Deep Vein Thrombosis (DVT)

DVT is a blood clot that forms in the veins of the leg, that then breaks loose and travels through the blood until it lodges in an organ - for instance in the lungs. It causes serious damage, even death.

Charles Chaplin Jr. (5 May 1925 06:10, Los Angeles CA)

Son of legendary actor-comic Charles Chaplin and Lita Gray. He died of a pulmonary embolism on 20 March 1968, aged 42. In the previous week he broke his leg and it seems this trouble contributed to the formation of the dangerous blood clot.

Cause: karmic. Psychologically, a blood clot suggests that there is interference to the flow of life, a loss of joy and being cut off from an important love. With Venus in the 12H of hidden things opposite Saturn, Chaplin was inclined to be fearful and guarded about love and relationships. These two planets, Venus and Saturn, are included in the Health Triangle. Saturn in the 6H of health indicates karma.

Organ: heart - the veins Venus, blood Mars, lungs the Sun.

Effect: heart - blood clot. The clot (Saturn) formed. It travelled through the blood (Mars) and veins (Venus), lodging in the lungs (Mars in Gemini, Saturn opposes the Sun in the 12H of major illnesses). Blood flow blocked and he died (Saturn co-rules the 8H of death).

▲ (C) Saturn in Scorpio. (O) Venus, Mars, Sun. (E) Saturn.

- When Chaplin died, solar-arc Sun and Venus were at 25-28 Gemini, straddling natal Mars; simultaneously, solar-arc Saturn was at 22 Sagittarius opposing natal Mars. The blockage occurred.

The Racial Problem and Veins.

> The only solution to the racial problem is the basic recognition that all men are brothers; that one blood pours through *human veins*; that we are all the children of the one Father and that our failure to recognise this fact is simply an indication of man's stupidity. Historical backgrounds, climatic conditions and widespread intermarriage have made the different races what they are today. Essentially, however, humanity is one—the heir of the ages, the product of many fusions, conditioned by circumstances and enriched by the processes of evolutionary development. This basic unity must now be recognised. [1]

---

[1] Bailey, Alice; Externalisation of the Hierarchy, 194.

g. Leukaemia

Leukaemia is cancer of the immune system, a malignant progressive disease in which the bone marrow and other blood-forming organs produce increased numbers of immature or abnormal leucocytes (white blood cells). These suppress the production of normal blood cells, leading to anaemia and other symptoms. It is thought to be a genetic disease but not inherited. The psychology associated with it is a sense of being smothered by a myriad of events that one has no control over.

L1003 (3 July 1963, 12:50, Melbourne Australia.

Australian female scientist who worked in a fulfilling job and led an active and healthy lifestyle. The year before diagnosis, at age 50, there were a series of events that were upsetting to her. She lost her job, broke her left foot, had an unpleasant confrontation with a close friend and suffered deeply with a friend who had a miscarriage.

Cause: emotional. Our subject is a kind and easy-going Cancerian. But underneath, she has a heightened sense of survival (the Moon is afflicted in Scorpio), a sense that she has to continually fight to maintain order in her life if she is going to survive (square Saturn and Uranus-Pluto). This operated at a subliminal level and it exhausted her health reserves.

Organ: heart - immune system, Mars.

Effect: leukaemia. All the incidents previously mentioned tapped into fears connected with the Scorpio Moon - anxiety she has about friendships (Moon square Uranus) and her career (Cancer on the 10th house cusp).

Within 6 months she developed a chest infection that would not go away and heavy sweating. Diagnosed in February 2014, her leukaemia is of the type where a "genetic switch" occurs. It happened around November 2013. A gene went aberrant (Uranus) and when it "switched", abnormal leucocytes (lymphoblast) cells began to be produced from bone marrow (square the Moon afflicted in Scorpio), in large numbers (conjunct Pluto). Gradually the fighting power of the immune system was destroyed (Pluto conjunct Mars) and blood quality corrupted (Moon square Saturn in Aquarius; Pluto quindecile Saturn).

▲ (C) Moon, Saturn, Pluto. (O) Mars. (E) Uranus-Pluto, Saturn.

The chart is set for November 2013, the date when the specialist told our subject the genetic-switch occurred.

- By solar-arc (SA), the Health Triangle had rotated so that the stellium consisting of Mars, Pluto (Lord of Death), and Uranus was on the ascendant; the point in the chart that represents "birth." Together these planets represent the astounding radical change and transformational set of circumstances that cause a genetic switch or mutation.
- SA Moon (the form), is at the bottom of the chart. The Moon rules bone marrow, and the subject received new DNA with a bone marrow transplant on 1 August 2014.
- SA Saturn, another ruler of bone marrow, is in the 6H of health. Uranus, which rules DNA and brings radical change, is transiting over Saturn; symbolising the genetic switch.
- Jupiter, which brings luck and good fortune, was powerful in the midheaven.

Nine years later in 2023, our subject is off medication and immunosuppression and "the donor cells are making blood and marrow beautifully".

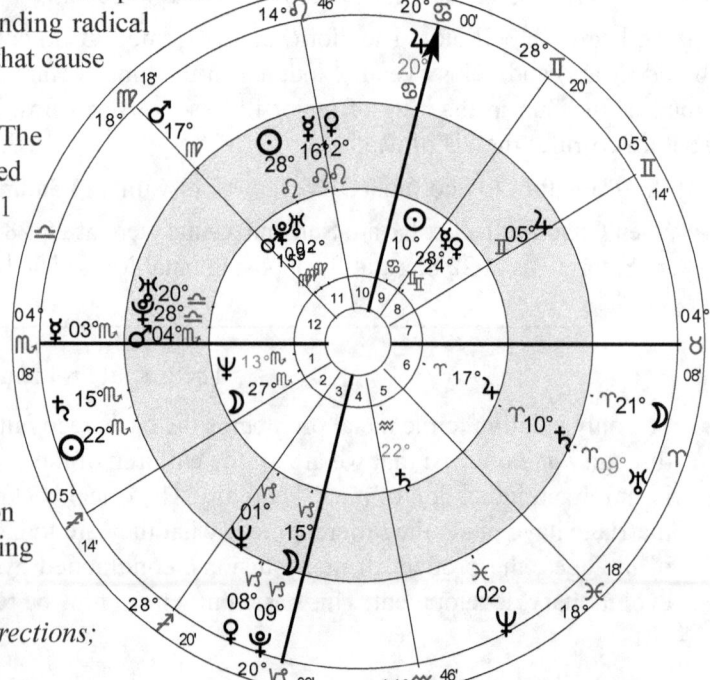

Inner chart - natal; middle chart - solar-arc directions; outer chart - transits.

4b. Problems with Blood vessels

See also "Stroke', in the Crown Chakra 'Brain' section.

a. Aortic Aneurysm

An aneurysm is a weak spot in the wall of a blood vessel that balloons out and fills with blood. Life is under threat if the aneurysm bursts. High blood pressure is often a cause.

Joe Louis (13 May 1914, 08:00, Lafayette, AL)

African-American professional boxer, world heavyweight champion from 1937 to 1949. In October 1977, he had an aortic aneurysm.

Cause: emotional. Louis's body took a battering, which contributed to his health issues. Psychologically, he had hidden and unexpressed anger (Mars semi-square Saturn in the 12H), which builds up stress in the cardiovascular system so that problems like aneurysms arise.

Organ: heart - arteries, Jupiter.

Effect: aneurysm. Stress (Saturn) caused high blood pressure (semi-square Mars in Leo), and an aneurysm (Venus trine Jupiter symbolises the weakening and the swelling aneurysm), developed in an aortic artery.

▲ (C) Mars, Saturn. (O) Jupiter. (E) Saturn, Mars, Venus.

• Louis died of a heart attack on 12 April 1981.

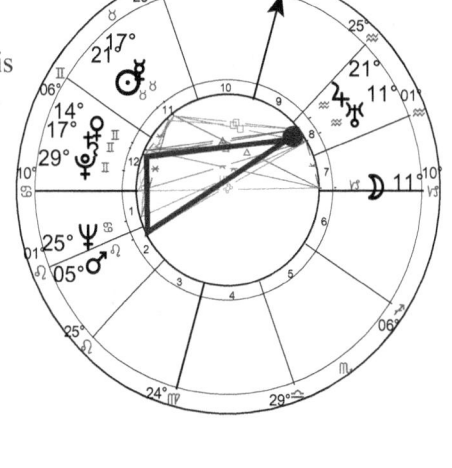

b. Arteriosclerosis - Artherosclerosis

Artery walls harden and thicken, restricting blood flow to organs.

Evangeline Booth (25 December 1865, 15:00, London UK)

British theologian and 4th General of The Salvation Army from 1934 to 1939. She died 17 July 1950, from the effects of arteriosclerosis.

Cause: emotional. There was a hard-hearted side to Booth (Sun conjunct Jupiter afflicted in Capricorn), a lack of compassion (square Neptune conjunct the Moon in bossy Aries), which is related to the trouble.

Organ: heart - arteries, Jupiter.

Effect: arteriosclerosis. The walls of the arteries thickened and hardened (Uranus in Cancer opposite Jupiter conjunct the Sun), restricting blood flow (Uranus and Neptune are connected with circulation).

▲ (C) Moon. (O) Jupiter. (E) Uranus.

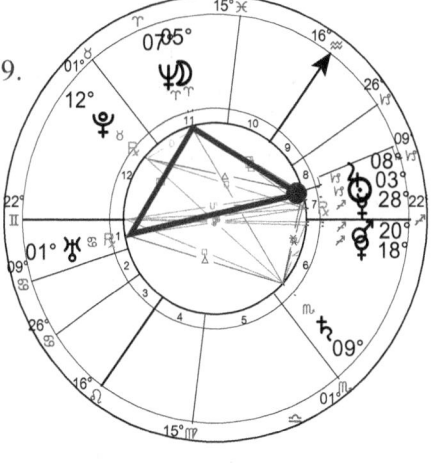

c. High Blood Pressure, Hypertension (HBP)

HBP - most commonly caused by plaque buildup in the arteries; causes the heart to work harder and can lead to complications such as a heart attack and stroke.

Barry White (12 September 1944, 16:42, Galveston TX)

American R&B singer, who had HBP for years, contributing to kidney failure in 1995. He died 4 July 2003, from his problems and a low-grade infection.

Cause: emotional. White grew up feeling emotionally deprived (Saturn in Cancer). He ate and drank rich foods and alcohol to fill an emotional void, because he felt unloved (Saturn in the 6H of diet square Venus).

Organ: heart - blood pressure, Mars.

Effect: heart failure. Cholesterol build-up in the arteries (Saturn in Cancer in the 6H of health, sextile Jupiter afflicted in Virgo), obstructed blood flow (Saturn square Mars).

▲ (C) Saturn in Cancer. (O) Mars. (E) Jupiter, Saturn.

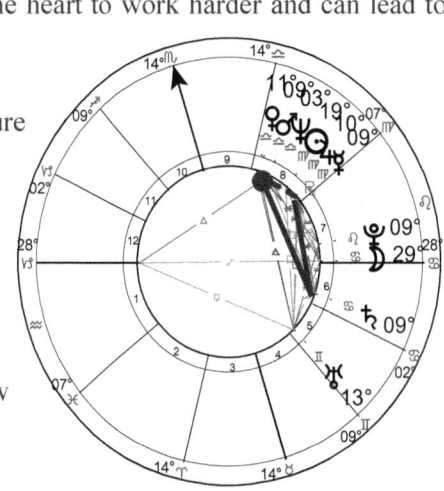

4c. Problems with the Heart

a. Heart Disease - Congenital

Congenital heart problems are structural defects present at birth. For example, holes in the heart, leaking valves, problems with the heart muscle or walls and bad connections between blood vessels. Such defects can lead to heart failure because the heart pumps inefficiently. In practice, look for afflictions to the Sun or to a planet in Leo and build on that; Saturn and/ or the Moon for congenital conditions. Mars for a hole and Neptune for a leak.

L1002 (14 November 1956 07:56, Philadelphia PA)
American male, a lawyer who represented individuals with disabilities and toddlers who had been sexually and physically abused. Retiring after 20 years, he is now a licensed Acupuncturist.

He was born with a block in the intestines - pyloric stenosis and almost died during corrective surgery. Virgo rules the intestines and the life-threatening problem is shown by Pluto in Virgo square to Mercury (tubes), and Saturn (a blockage), and the Sun (life threatening).

Dangerous conditions like these in babies are a karmic carry-over from a previous life. Great difficulty in digesting life is at the root of this condition because of hidden abuse, likely in a religious setting (Pluto in the 9H of religion). He had a speech impediment that was corrected, but was bullied for this by a nun teacher (Pluto > Saturn representing the hard, religious disciplinarian).

Cause: discipleship. Physical heart problems are related to hard-heartedness in the average person, or to the development of an inclusive spirit in the more advanced. This latter involves the transference of energy from the selfish, emotional solar plexus chakra (Mars), up to the inclusive heart centre (opposing Jupiter). Our subject has dedicated his life to helping others, so is in the latter category. Consequently, his heart should be stronger and healthier in his next incarnation. It is interesting to note however that Jupiter, the higher ruler of the heart chakra, is afflicted in Virgo and opposes Mars pointing to a deep heart wounding being incurred in a previous life. This is related to the trouble.

Organ: heart - the heart organ, the Sun; the arteries Jupiter.

Effect: congenital heart problem. From the teens onwards, he had heart pain but was told all was well. Then in 2009 at age 53, the pain became serious and he had a mild heart attack. Cardiologists discovered that the main coronary artery (left anterior descending) "goes up instead of down, eventually became buried in the heart muscle and winding up between the main vessels at the top of the heart".

The Sun in the 12H of hospitalisation can point to an inherited heart defect, because the prognosis is that one day an inherent heart condition will require hospitalisation and therefore serious treatment. The 12th house also represents 'hidden things' and consequently, the condition was not discovered until he was in his 50's, most likely due to his living a healthy lifestyle. His heart was very strong, with no plaque. The positive aspects between the Sun (heart and vitality), Jupiter (expansive) and Mars (energy), show an otherwise healthy body with good energy flow, which helped the heart do its job in spite of the physical defect.

The congenital condition was inherited (Sun sesquiquadrate Moon in the 4H of family, Moon trine Uranus in Leo in the 8H of inheritances). The defect lies buried in the family DNA (Uranus). A perversion occurred to the construction of the foetal heart within the 1st month (Neptune in the first degree of Scorpio, square Uranus). The result was an aberration in artery placement (Jupiter, the arteries, is midpoint the Sun and Uranus). Jupiter rules the arteries and the problem of the artery going in the wrong direction is shown by Jupiter being afflicted in Virgo, opposite Mars in Pisces representing trouble with the plumbing configuration.

He had heart bypass surgery but reports that the fix was worse than the problem. "I go through periods of vagus nerve issues, like the congestive heart failure and other annoying symptoms. I self-medicate".

▲ (C) Jupiter. (O) Sun, Jupiter. (E) Uranus.

- In 2009, transit Saturn was moving back and forth over natal Jupiter, crystallising the arterial defect so he had physical pain and discomfort. Additionally, transit Uranus was in Pisces, moving opposite Jupiter, representing modern science's attempt to fix the problem.

b. Heart Attack

This occurs when the heart is suddenly deprived of blood due to an artery blockage.

Peter Sellers (8 September 1925 06:00, Southsea UK)
English film actor and comedian who suffered his first heart attack in 1964 and died following a third heart attack on 24 July 1980.

Cause: emotional. Sellers was born with a healthy heart, but there were latent problems that were exacerbated by his attitudes. He was known for being "flawed, spiteful and selfish" (Sun conjunct Mars in Virgo, opposing Uranus). Hard-heartedness causes the heart muscle to harden (the Sun-Mars conjunction is midpoint Saturn and Pluto).

Organ: heart - the heart organ, the Sun.

Effect: heart attack.

▲ (C) Mars, Uranus. (O) Sun. (E) Pluto, Saturn.

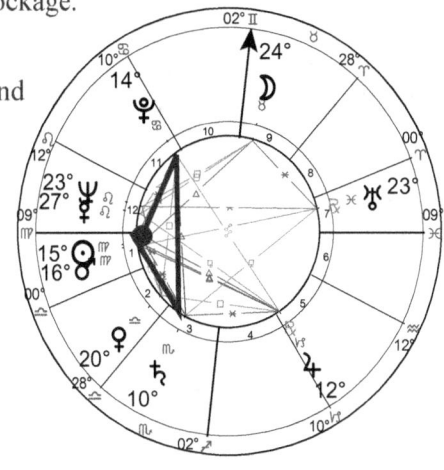

c. Heart Failure

Heart failure occurs when the heart fails to pump blood around the system. The cause may be due to a birth defect, a heart attack, high blood pressure or just from ageing. Mars represents the pumping action.

Elizabeth Taylor (27 February 1932 02:30, London UK)
British-American actress, renowned for her great beauty. She suffered from congestive heart failure in her later years, dying from it on March 23 2011.

Cause: emotional. Taylor was 79 when she died, pointing to ageing and lifestyle as contributing to heart failure. She had a good appetite (Taurus on the 6H of food habits), loved rich food and lots of it (Venus trine Jupiter in Leo), and alcohol (the Sun in Pisces opposite Neptune).

Organ: heart - the heart organ the Sun.

Effect: heart failure. Due to her age, diet and sedentary lifestyle the heart muscle gradually, weakened and failed to do its work (the Sun conjunct Mars in Pisces, and Mars semi-square Venus).

▲ (C) Venus, Jupiter. (O) Sun. (E) Venus, Mars in Pisces.

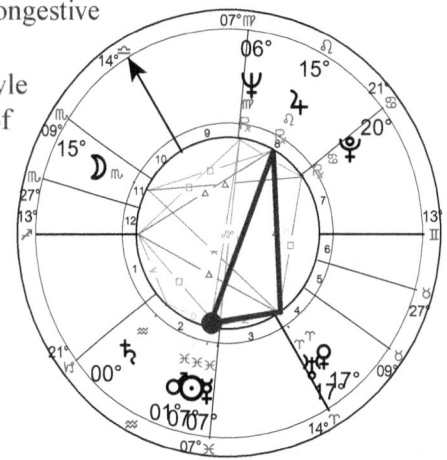

d. Heart fibrillation, arrhythmia,

Heart arrhythmia or atrial fibrillation is an irregular and often rapid heart rate that occurs when the two upper chambers of the heart experience chaotic electrical signals.

Elton John (25 March 1947 15:28, Pinner UK)
English singer collapsed on a plane as he flew to sing at the wedding of Posh Spice and David Beckham in y 1999. He was fitted with a heart pacemaker.

Cause: emotional. The heart is a muscle, so Mars, which rules all muscles in the body is of interested psychologically when heart trouble occurs. Mars squares Uranus in Gemini, pointing to emotional verbal tirades. Mars is also in Pisces, which is related to drug use via Neptune. John has confessed to being a drug addict for a great period of his life, and this would have contributed to the fibrillation trouble.

Organ: heart - the heart muscle, Mars.

Effect: heart fibrillation. Drug use (Mars in Pisces), contributed to John's fibrillation trouble (square Uranus), but it was not the only cause. The chart shows he was born with a latent weakness in the heart (Saturn and Pluto are in Leo that rules the heart, in the 12H of hidden things. Uranus is semi-square Saturn in Leo; and Saturn is sesquiquadrate Mars).

▲ (C) Mars in Pisces. (O) Mars. (E) Uranus, Saturn, Pluto.

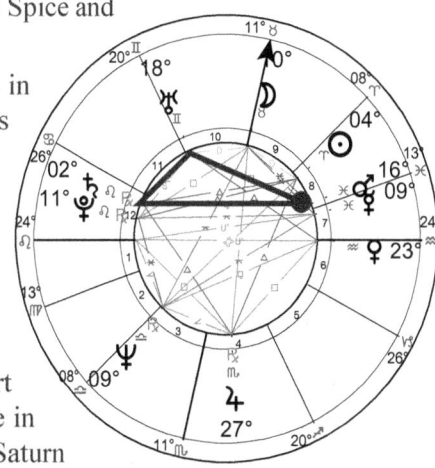

4d. Immune System

a. Acquired immune deficiency syndrome (AIDS)

The HIV (human immunodeficiency virus), attacks the immune system, destroying immunity. In the final stages when immune cell count is very low and viral cells predominate, the disease has progressed to AIDS.

Rudolph Nureyev (17 March 1938 13:00, Irkutsk Russia)

Nureyev, regarded as one of ballet's most gifted male dancers, died from AIDS on 6 January 1993, age 54.

Cause: emotional. Emotionally very intense (Sun in Pisces trine Pluto in Cancer), Nureyev tried to find relief, happiness and self-understanding through deep and serious sexual encounters (Pluto in the 1H square Mars).

Organ: heart - immune system, Mars.

Effect: AIDS. He caught the virus (Neptune septile Pluto in Cancer), which attacked the immune system and gradually but persistently destroyed it (Neptune opposite Sun, sesquiquadrate Mars; Pluto trine the Sun and square Mars). We do not know what psychological changes Nureyev went through as the disease progressed. But with Pluto in the personal 1st house, changes would have been deep and profound.

▲ (C) Pisces. (O) The Sun, Mars. (E) Neptune, Pluto.

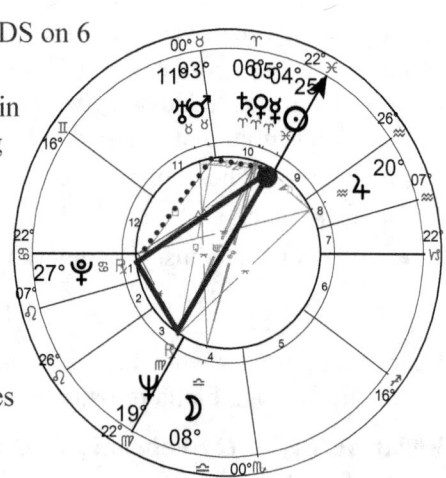

b. Immune deficient

David Vetter (21 September 1971, 07:00, Houston TX)

American child known as "Boy in the Bubble." His body could not produce T and B lymphocytes due to defective DNA - a fatal disease without treatment. To keep alive, he lived in a germ-free bubble for 12 years. His last 15 days were spent out of the bubble, in hospital undergoing corrective surgery. It failed and he died 22 February 1984, aged 13.

Cause: Karmic. Saturn dominates the chart from the 9H of moral judgements. This was a karmic, teaching/ learning experience.

Organ: heart - immune system Mars; white cells the Moon.

Effect: immune deficiency. The body's ability to produce immune-fighting cells (Moon) was subverted (conjunct Uranus that rules the 6H of health). This destroyed the fighting power of the immune system (Pluto conjunct the Sun, and sesquiquadrate Mars), leaving the body defenceless against invading pathogens (Saturn). Vetter was kept isolated from the world to save his life, in an oxygen bubble (Mercury, ruler of the ascendant is in the 12H of isolation). Mercury and Gemini rule oxygenation.

▲ (C) Saturn. (O) Mars, Moon. (E) Uranus, Pluto, Saturn.

Astro.com 7221 (20 March 1933, 05:50, Tacoma WA)

American child, immune deficient, requiring constant hospital treatment.

Cause: karmic. The Moon in Capricorn represents a karmic cause.

Organ: heart - immune system, Mars.

Effect: immune deficiency. The body was unable to produce white immune blood cells from bone marrow (the Moon is afflicted in Capricorn, and opposes Pluto in Cancer. The result was an immune system (the Sun and Mars) that was rendered useless (Neptune that is afflicted in Virgo is conjunct Mars and disposits the Sun; it is sesquiquadrate the Moon and semi-square Pluto). The body was left defenceless against invading pathogens.

▲ (C) Moon in Capricorn. (O) Mars. (E) Pluto, Neptune.

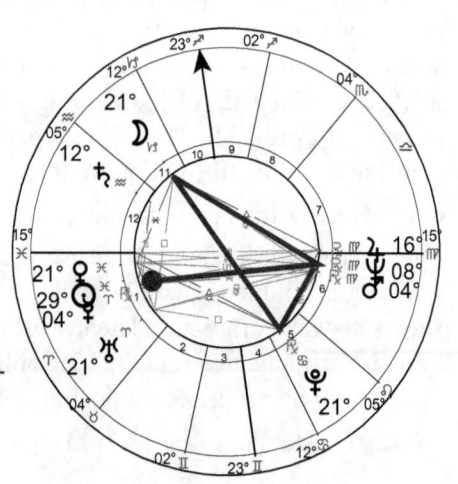

c. Chronic Fatigue Syndrome (CFS), Myalgic Encephalomyelitis (ME)

Chronic fatigue syndrome is extreme fatigue that cannot be explained by any underlying medical condition. A primary cause is incessant anxiety and worry, 4th ray negatives carried by the Moon and Mercury. This wears down and debilitates the immune system.

Michael Crawford (19 January 1942, 06:00, Salisbury UK).

British actor and singing star of 'The Phantom of the Opera'. In 2004, he was working in a show when he began to feel unwell. His tiredness became so extreme he had to pull out. He was diagnosed with CFS.

Cause: emotional. Prior to his illness, living a conflict-filled life was normal for Crawford. Aggressive and sexual Mars was strong in his nature (t-square: Mars in detriment in Taurus, square the Sun and Pluto). The source of stress came from his home and family life (Mars in the 4H of family). There were reports of his affairs and infidelity.

Organ: heart - vitality, the Sun.

Effect: CFS. Continuous conflict (Mars in 4th ray Taurus), grinds down (Pluto) vitality (the Sun). It triggers the fight-flight system (Mars), depleting adrenal reserves, adding to the trouble. Debilitated and exhausted, in 2004 he developed CFS. He may also have had an underactive thyroid; Saturn is in Taurus that rules the thyroid and the 6H of health.

▲ (C) Mars. (O) The Sun. (E) Pluto.

- In 2003-4, the progressed Sun reached 29 Pisces, opposite natal Neptune. His energy levels melted away, he had no reserves left.

- By getting in touch with his feelings and harmonising his inner conflict, Crawford restored his vitality levels to normal within 4 years.

Ebola virus

Ebola is a deadly virus, placed in this chakra section because its primary attack comes through the cardiovascular system. It is caught by contact with body fluids of an infected person, including sweat, blood etc. It damages the immune system and organs and inhibits blood-clotting so that uncontrollable bleeding occurs.

Ameyo Adadevoh (27 October 1956, Lagos Nigeria)

Unknown time, 12 PM midday used and the 0 degrees Aries House System. Female Nigerian physician who died of ebola on 19 August 2014.

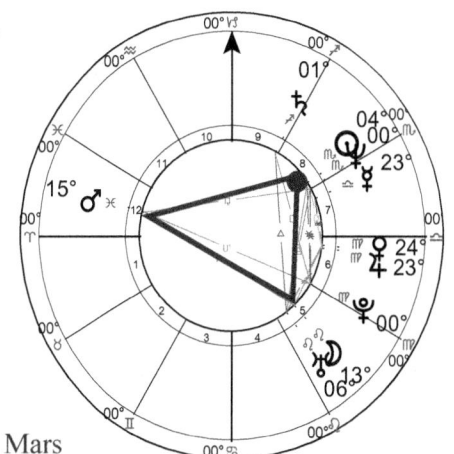

Cause: epidemic. Adadevoh harboured emotional tension and conflict that was debilitating (the Sun square Uranus-Moon), rendering her susceptible to viral attacks (the Sun conjunct Neptune) and epidemics (Uranus-Moon).

Organ: heart - cardiovascular organs, the Sun, Leo.

Effect: ebola. The virus attacked blood cells and spread through the body via the bloodstream (the Neptune-Sun point is sesquiquadrate Mars), damaging cardiovascular organs (square Uranus in Leo). There was massive haemorrhaging (Mars inconjunct the Moon, which is conjunct Uranus).

▲ (C) Moon, Uranus. (O) Sun. (E) Neptune, Mars, Uranus.

- The attack of the virus on the body in August 2014 is shown by solar-arc Mars that had reached 13 Taurus, square the Moon at 13 Leo. When she died, transit Mars had joined them to form a t-square from 14 Scorpio.

5. Solar Plexus Chakra Diseases

The solar plexus chakra rules the pancreas glands, mid-region digestion and the emotions. It causes trouble in all other chakras and many examples of this have been included in this section. The solar plexus receives energy from ray 6 primarily, and also from Cancer, Virgo, Mars, Neptune and the Moon.

5a. Allergies

An allergy is a hypersensitive response to a substance that is normally harmless. The immune system over-reacts, producing antibodies that cause cells to release too many chemicals, causing the reaction. The condition is related to the fight or flight syndrome, governed by the sympathetic nervous system, which is in turn governed by the solar plexus chakra. Fear, fright and frustration are emotions associated with allergies.

a. Allergic to anaesthetics

Jean-Pierre Chevenement (9 March 1939 23:00, Belfort FR)
A French politician in the 80's and 90's. On 2 September 1998, he suffered a heart attack after an allergic reaction to an anaesthetic administered for gallbladder surgery. It left him in a coma for eight days.
Cause: emotional. Chevenement was intensely sensitive and emotionally reactive to things he disliked. This affected his immune system response, making it also super-sensitive (Sun in Pisces opposite Neptune).
Organ: heart - the immune system, the Sun.
Effect: allergic reaction. Chevenement's immune system (the Sun) reacted suddenly and violently and his body went into shock (sextile Uranus afflicted in Taurus), when given an anaesthetic. He went into a coma (Neptune).

▲ (C) Pisces, Neptune. (O) Sun. (E) Uranus, Neptune.

- In September 1998, when he had his violent reaction, solar-arc Neptune was stationed on the ascendant at 20 Scorpio, rendering his whole organism super-sensitive generally and to drugs in particular.
- The progressed Sun was in the 6H of health at 17 Taurus, conjunct progressed Uranus at 17 Taurus. The shock of his body's reaction caused the heart attack.
- Jupiter, the "lucky" planet, was transiting back and forth over 20 Pisces during 1998, conjunct his natal Sun and trine solar-arc Neptune and ascendant. While this contributed to the over-reaction, it also helped him to survive.

b. Anaphylaxis - allergic to bee stings

Anaphylaxis is a severe, potentially life-threatening allergic reaction.

Karen, Astro.com (16 July 1945, 01:35, Cleveland OH)
American female seriously allergic to bee stings so that she must treat herself immediately or she could die.
Cause: emotional. Extreme emotional sensitivity and reactivity (Moon conjunct Neptune and sesquiquadrate Mars), due to a fear of being hurt (Moon squares Saturn and is septile Mars); underlies Karen's reaction to bee stings (Mars).
Organ: heart - the immune system, the Sun.
Effect: allergic reaction. Mars, a ruler of the solar plexus chakra, the immune system and of insect attacks, is in the 1st house that rules the physical organism as a whole. It is in detriment in Taurus indicating that her physical and emotional reactions can be extreme (Mars > Saturn, which is conjunct the Sun). Her violent reaction to bee stings is a physical equivalent to how she felt emotionally when she was traumatised as a child (Saturn conjunct the Sun on the 4H of family cusp).

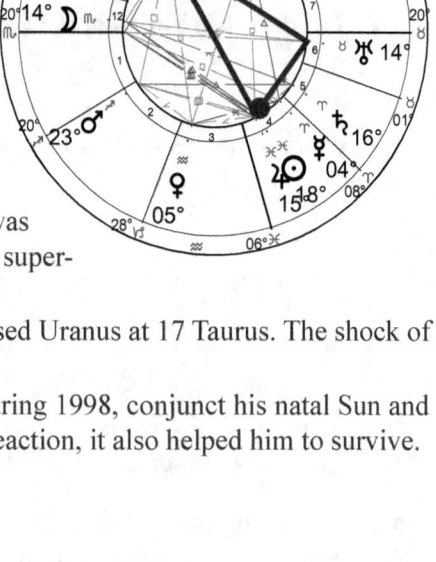

▲ (C) Moon, Neptune, Mars, Saturn. (O) Sun. (E) Mars.

c. Allergic to gluten - celiac/ coelic disease

Celiac disease is an autoimmune condition triggered by consuming gluten. Some symptoms are diarrhea and bloating. An inability to digest life at some level is related to allergic reactions to food.

Jane Swift (24 February 1965, 07:48, North Adams MA)
First female Governor of Massachusetts had many medical examinations before being diagnosed with celiac disease.
Cause: emotional. Any autoimmune attack is triggered by a self-attack at some level. Swift had high ideals (Moon in Sagittarius in the 9H of morals), and criticised herself when she fell short of her idea of perfection (square Mars in Virgo). This had health repercussions in the gut (Virgo in the 6H of health).
Organ: solar plexus - intestines, Virgo.
Effect: allergic reaction. Self-criticism caused the immune system to attack the intestines causing diarrhea (Mars in Virgo), and bloating (Moon inconjunct Jupiter).
▲ (C) Moon, Mars. (O) Virgo planets. (E) Mars, Jupiter.

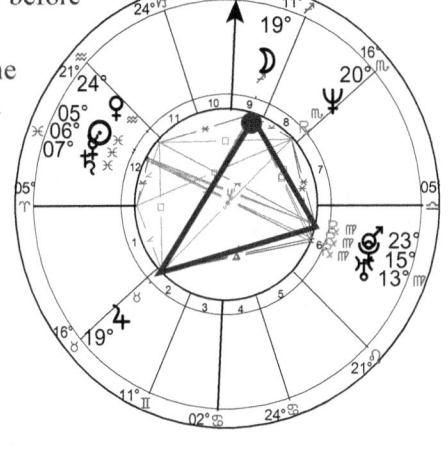

d. Allergic to milk

Astro.com 6814 (18 October 1930 10:00; 41n27, 79w40)
American infant, normal at birth, who died suddenly at six weeks of age on 28 November 1930, of milk poisoning.
Cause: karmic. There are 3 planets in Cancer, which rules digestion, in the 8H of inheritances, opposed by karmic Saturn (by sign). Psychologically, the pattern points to difficulty giving and receiving emotional nourishment. This occurred in a previous life, the Moon rules the past. In the current life, it manifested as repudiation by the body for the most basic source of nourishment for babies - mother's milk (Moon).
Organ: solar plexus - digestion the Moon, intestines Virgo.
Effect: allergic reaction. Milk was toxic to this child (Moon conjunct Neptune in detriment in Virgo, semi-square Mars and Pluto in Cancer), and the intestines would not absorb it (Virgo).
▲ (C) Moon, Neptune, Saturn. (O) Moon, Virgo. (E) Saturn, Pluto, Neptune.

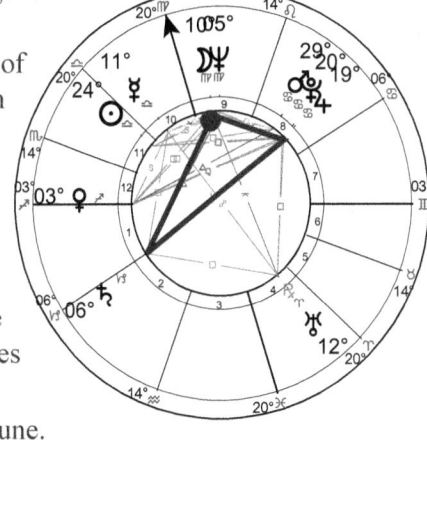

e. Lyme Disease

Lyme disease (borreliosis) is an inflammatory bacterial infection caused by a tick bite that can affect multiple organ systems. It is placed in this section because Mars, which rules insect bites, rules the solar plexus chakra.

Yolanda Hadid (11 January 1964, Papendrecht, Netherlands)
Unknown time, 12 PM midday used and the 0 degrees Aries House System.
US "reality" star in the TV show the 'The Real Housewives of Beverly Hills'. Hadid was diagnosed with lyme disease in 2012 and suffers debilitating exhaustion.
Cause: emotional. Deep exhaustion is a 4th ray problem, the result of chronic inner conflict. Hadid's inner child is constantly trying to flee and be free of (Moon in Sagittarius), a critical, menacing presence (square Pluto-Uranus in Virgo). This is an after-shock of a childhood trauma. The Moon's location is approximate, but it squared the 2 malefics throughout the day.
Organ: heart - vitality, Mars.
Effect: lyme disease and exhaustion. She was bitten by a tick (Mars), causing a bacterial infection (sesquiquadrate Pluto-Uranus). But the true cause of her exhaustion is emotional. Hadid's unresolved issues keep gnawing away at her "guts" (Virgo), cannibalising her energies.
▲ (C) Moon, Pluto, Uranus, (O) Mars. (E) Pluto.

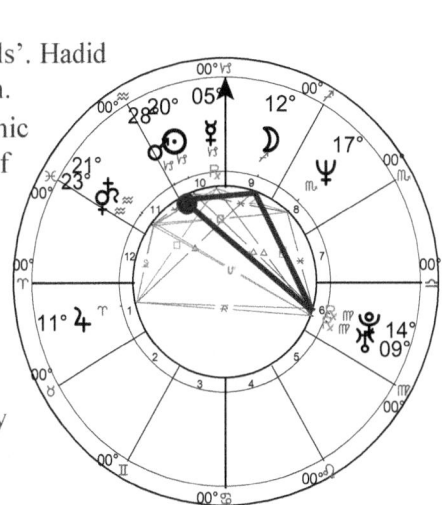

5b. Gallbladder and Stomach

a. Acid Reflux

Mark Spitz (10 February 1950, 17:45, Modesta CA)

Cause: emotional. Olympic swimming champion Spitz had acid reflux. Competition (Moon in Sagittarius, the sign ruling the 5H), caused nervousness that affected his digestive system (semi-square Mercury).

Organ: solar plexus - digestion, the Moon and Mercury.

Effect: digestive. The muscles (Mars) that should keep acid in the stomach (Moon) were weak (Mars in detriment in Libra, trine retrograde Venus) and were not doing their job. A liking for alcohol (Neptune conjunct Mars), sweet, fatty and fast-foods (trine Jupiter and Venus in the 6H of diet) contributed to his acid reflux problem (Mars > Jupiter).

▲ (C) Moon. (O) Moon, Mercury. (E) Mars, Jupiter.

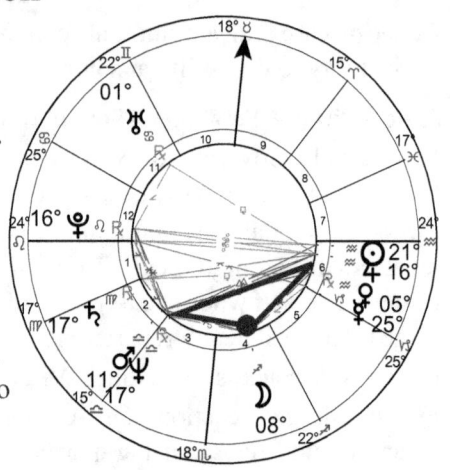

b. Food poisoning

Harry Shaw (7 May 1916 03:00, Port Bannatyne Scotland)

80 year old Scottish pensioner, who died from food poisoning (E-coli).

Cause: emotional. Shaw had violent emotional reactions (Mars) to things he did not like (opposite Uranus) and this disturbed his digestive system (Mars, ruler of the solar plexus chakra in the 6H of health).

Organ: solar plexus - digestion, Cancer.

Effect: digestive. At a social lunch (Venus in Cancer), virulent bacteria lurked in the food (conjunct Pluto sesquiquadrate Uranus). It attacked the bowel (Pluto semi-square Mars), putting Shaw into hospital (Mars > Uranus 12H), where he died.

▲ (C) Mars, Uranus. (O) Cancer. (E) Uranus, Pluto

- On 26 November 1996 when Shaw died, the natal pattern was triggered by transit Uranus. It was in the 12H at 1 Aquarius, inconjunct Pluto at 1 Cancer.

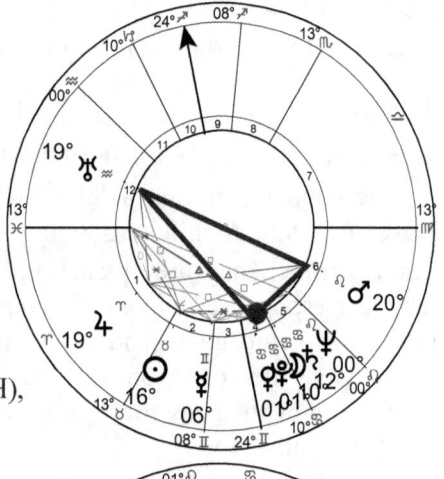

c. Gallstones

Eric Clapton (30 March 1945, 20:45, Ripley UK)

English rock and blues guitarist, singer, and songwriter had surgery in October 2009 to remove gallstones.

Cause: emotional. Trouble is shown in a t-square: he repressed his emotions (Saturn in Cancer) to avoid grief (Neptune) and pain (the Sun in Aries in the 6H of health).

Organ: solar plexus - gallbladder, Saturn in Cancer.

Effect: gallstones. His repression caused gallstones.

▲ (C) Saturn in Cancer, Neptune. (O) Saturn in Cancer. (E) Saturn, Sun.

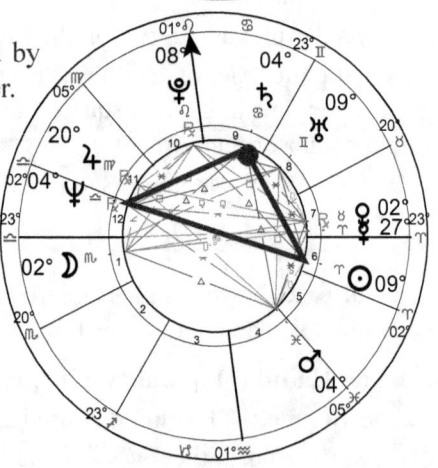

d. Stomach Ulcers

Nat King Cole (17 March 1919 03:00, Montgomery AL)

Cole collapsed from stomach ulcers in 1953.

Cause: emotional. In confrontations, Cole's natural instinct was to keep the peace (Moon in Libra). To do so he repressed his anger (t-square: Moon, Mars, Pluto), backing up emotional toxicity that caused trouble later.

Organ: solar plexus - stomach, the Moon.

Effect: ulcer. Repressed anger manifested as corrosive acid that burnt its way through the stomach lining (Mars > Pluto in Cancer in the 6H of health).

▲ (C) Moon, Mars, Pluto. (O) Moon. (E) Pluto in Cancer

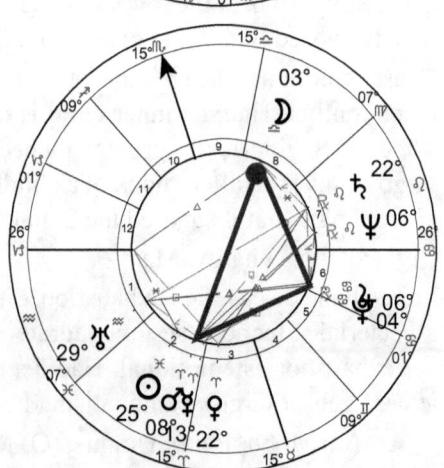

5c. Liver

a. Cirrhosis

In cirrhosis of the liver, healthy cells are replaced by scar tissue, impairing liver function. Excessive alcohol consumption is a primary cause of liver cirrhosis, but it can also occur through hepatitis or fatty liver disease.

Billie Holiday (7 April 1915, 02:30, Philadelphia PA)
American jazz singer. She suffered from long term drug and alcohol abuse, developing cirrhosis of the liver and dying of the disease on July 17 1959.
Cause: emotional. Holiday was an insecure and emotional Negro woman growing up in racist America (Moon in detriment in Capricorn, opposite Neptune in Cancer, the sign ruling the USA). She self-medicated with alcohol to alleviate anxiety (Neptune 6H of health).
Organ: solar plexus - liver, Jupiter.
Effect: cirrhosis. Alcohol and drug abuse (Neptune), damaged Holiday's liver beyond repair (sesquiquadrate Jupiter; the Moon is in the 12H of serious illnesses septile Jupiter), and she died of liver disease.
▲ (C) Moon, Neptune. (O) Jupiter. (E) Neptune.

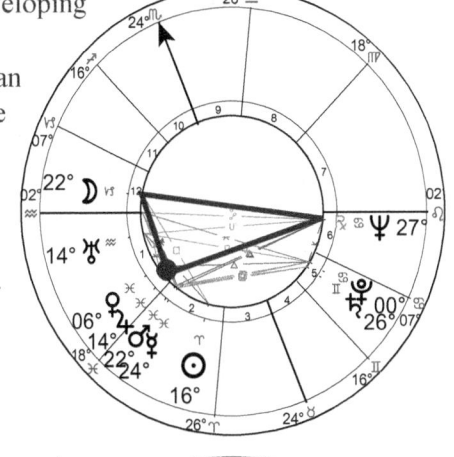

Florence Aadland (20 September 1914 23:50, Salt Lake City UT)
American mother of teenage ingénue Beverly Aadland, who had an affair with ageing actor Errol Flynn. An alcoholic, she started bleeding internally from cirrhosis of the liver and died 10 May 1965.
Cause: emotional. With a Libran Moon and ruler Venus in the 5H of pleasure, partying and drinking helped Aadland overcome her emotional insecurities (Saturn and Pluto in Cancer in the 12H of hidden things).
Organ: solar plexus - liver, Jupiter.
Effect: cirrhosis. Excessive alcohol consumption damaged the liver (Jupiter that rules the 6H of health squares Venus, and is inconjunct the ascendant, which in turn is conjunct Pluto and Saturn). Cirrhosis developed, the liver haemorrhaged and she died (Jupiter is conjunct Uranus in the 8H of death).
▲ (C) Moon, Saturn-Pluto in Cancer. (O) Jupiter. (E) Neptune, Uranus.

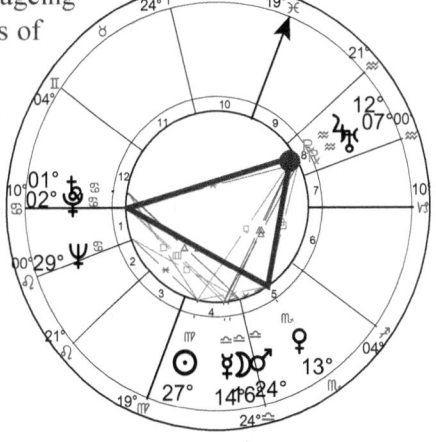

b. Hepatitis A

The Hepatitis A virus is spread when traces of faeces containing the virus is ingested through food or water. The liver becomes inflamed, there may be nausea, vomiting and fatigue, but its effect is usually short lived.

L1004 (30 June 1944, 14:04, Gisborne NZ)
New Zealand woman from a large family that lived in a rural, farm setting, caught hepatitis-A as a child.
Cause: emotional. An emotional Cancer stellium person who preferred to hide away from the world (Moon in the 12H of hidden things). She was hypersensitive, defensive and susceptible to viruses (Cancer planets square Neptune).
Organ: solar plexus - liver, Jupiter.
Effect: hepatitis. The Hep-A virus was picked up through eating contaminated food (Neptune square the Cancer planets). The liver was infected (the Cancer planets semi-square Jupiter) and she was sick for a few months.
▲ (C) Cancer planets. (O) Jupiter. (E) Neptune.

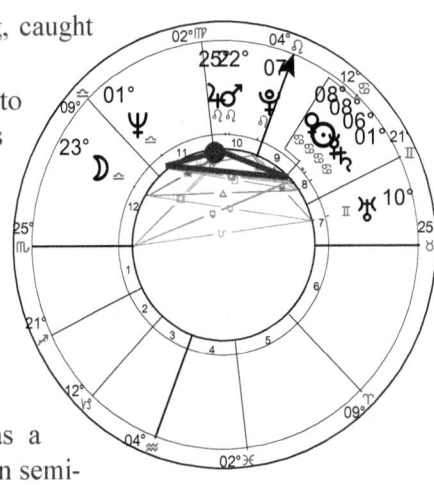

In later life, the subject developed a fatty-liver condition most likely as a consequence of eating dairy foods - especially milk, in large quantities (Moon semi-square the Cancer planets).

c. Hepatitis C

The Hepatitis C virus is most commonly spread through contact with infected blood. It is dangerous. About 85% of hepatitis C infections lead to chronic liver disease, cirrhosis of the liver or liver cancer.

L1005 (7 October 1953, 1:28)
Australian male who contracted the Hep-C virus through intravenous drug use in the late 1970's and early 80's, before he finally broke the habit in 1984. In 2013, he had chemotherapy to kill the virus.

Cause: emotional. Jupiter is in detriment in Gemini, which indicates the liver is not as robust as it could be. Psychologically, the negative force generated by self-criticism (Moon in Virgo, square Jupiter), and unresolved emotional issues (the Moon rules the 12H of self-undoing), will lodge in the organ.

The addictive pattern is Moon square Jupiter (a habit of excess). The Moon is in the third, Taurus decanate, the sign related to the desire pleasure centres in the brain.

Organ: solar plexus - liver, Jupiter.

Effect: hepatitis. The Hep-C virus (Neptune), entered the body through contact with contaminated blood (sextile Pluto in Leo), lodging in the liver (trine Jupiter).

▲ (C) Moon. (O) Jupiter. (E) Neptune, Pluto.

- 1979-1983. The drug addiction phase began in 1979. Solar-arc Jupiter (excess), conjunct Uranus at 22 Cancer (excessive experimentation), and squared natal Neptune at 23 Libra (with drugs). Simultaneously, solar-arc Moon moved over Neptune (becoming addicted).

  During 1980-81, this was followed by transit Neptune in the 5H of pleasure at 22 Sagittarius, inconjunct solar-arc Jupiter and natal Uranus at 22 Cancer.

  Then in 1982-83, transit Neptune moved back and forth opposite natal and progressed Jupiter at 25-26 Gemini. During this period of his addiction, he caught the Hep-C virus.

- 1984. He "went cold turkey" on 21 January 1984. The ascendant, "soul purpose", had just progressed into Virgo and the 2nd house - it was time to begin a new phase in life, develop a new and higher set of Christ values to live by. He had the will to do it - Saturn, ruler of the 6H of health and of healing, was transiting over the progressed Sun at 13 Scorpio. He persevered and broke the addiction.

- In 2012, tests showed the liver was close to developing cirrhosis. By now, solar-arc Pluto had reached natal Neptune at 23 Libra, triggering the infection in a malignant way. Simultaneously, solar-arc Jupiter (the liver) was moving over natal Pluto (potential cirrhosis); and solar-arc Neptune was at 22 Sagittarius inconjunct natal Uranus (energising the virus).

- In 2013, February, he started 7 months of chemotherapy. Pluto rules death and it killed the virus. The natal aspect (Pluto in Leo {which rules cell life}, sextile Jupiter), promised treatment would go well and that his liver could be "reborn" and it has. During this period, he went through his second Saturn return - a new cycle started. He also had a Jupiter return which boosted his liver health.

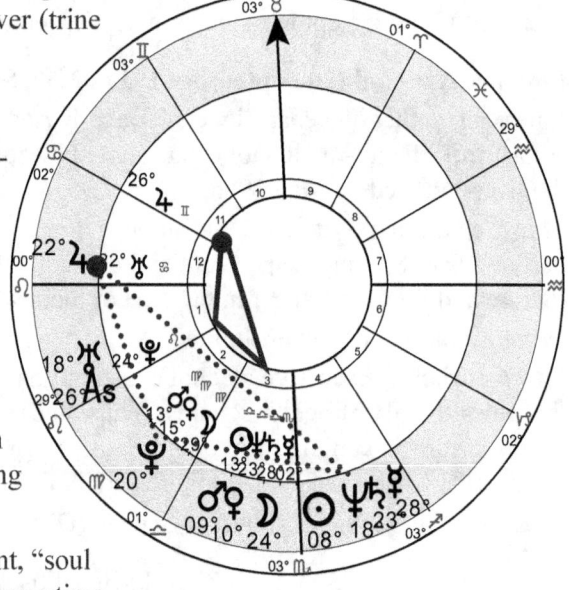

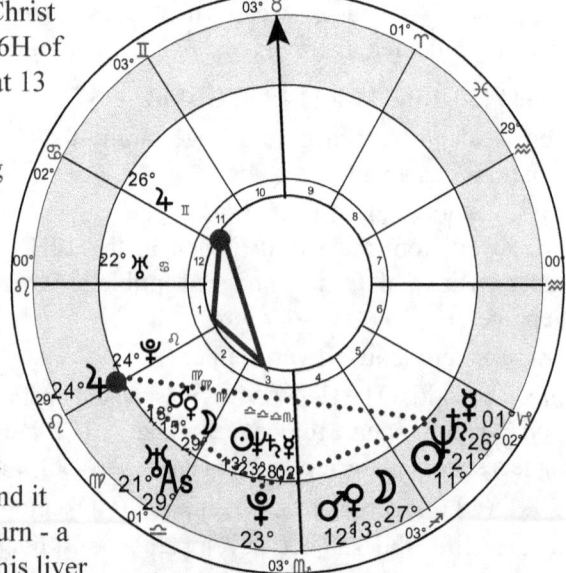

Higher chart, natal; outer solar-arc directions
1st chart 1979, lower chart 2012.

5d. Pancreas

a. Diabetes

Common type-2 diabetes is commonly linked to a diet high in fats or sugars so that the body's ability to use insulin to regulate blood sugar levels is impaired. However, Djwhal Khul said that "diabetes is more definitely the result of wrong inner desires and is not so definitely the result of wrong outer desires". [1] This means it is the inner desire and craving for love or other form of inner satisfaction, which then usually manifests as eating "comfort" food that is the cause of common diabetes. Khul goes on to say that "Cancer and diabetes are more definitely in the class of diseases which are connected with inner emotional desires and the violent suppressed wish-life". [2] This seems to fit type-1 diabetes where the immune system violently attacks and destroys insulin-producing cells.

Linda Goodman (9 April 1925, 06:05, Morgantown WV).

Goodman was the astrology author of 'Sun Signs', which sold paperback rights for a record-breaking $225 million. But she was bankrupt when she died on October 21 1995, from complications of diabetes.

Cause: emotional. Goodman's Moon is in Libra, in the 7H of intimate relationships. She was paranoid about her relationships (opposite Venus in Aries, in the 12H of hidden things. Venus squares Pluto). Friends said she would ask them to spend the night so that she did not have to be alone.

The fact Goodman died bankrupt and developed diabetes tells us she did not value herself as being worthy for love. Money, love, values and diabetes are all ruled by Venus. Perhaps a lover abandoned her, reinforcing a negative belief about being unlovable and triggering a violent suppression of her wish/ love life (Pluto in Cancer square Venus). This, and the foods she ate, contributed to the development of diabetes. People who feel deprived of love often seek comfort by eating foods high in sugar and carbohydrates, which Venus rules.

Organ: solar plexus - pancreas the Moon, insulin by Venus.

Effect: diabetes. At some stage, the cells in the pancreas were unable to absorb insulin (Venus), because of serious trouble (square Pluto) in the regulating function (Moon in Libra opposite Venus), and diabetes developed.

▲ (C) Moon. (O) Moon, Venus. (E) Pluto in Cancer.

Halle Berry (14 August 1966, 23:59, Cleveland OH) Type 1

Beautiful African-American actress has type-1 diabetes. During the taping of the TV series 'Living Dolls' in 1989, she lapsed into a diabetic coma. Shortly afterwards she was diagnosed and is insulin-dependent.

Cause: emotional. With the Moon in Leo, Berry was born with a natural self-confidence. But virulent criticisms directed at her in her childhood left their mark on her psyche (Moon in the 4H of family, semi-square Uranus and Pluto in Virgo), to resurface later as an autoimmune attack.

Organ: solar plexus - pancreas the Moon, insulin Venus.

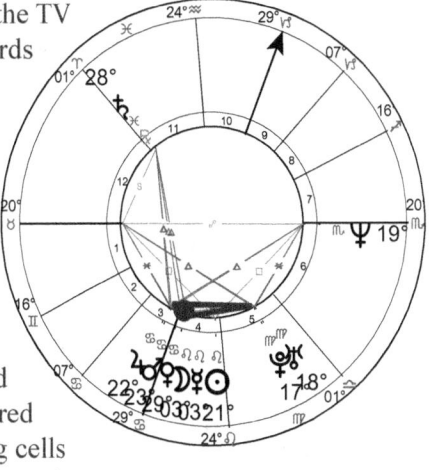

Effect: diabetes. The disease appeared when she was an adult - perhaps a lover (planets in the 5H of romance), repeated the abuse that occurred when she was a child, triggering a negative core belief that she was unworthy and unlovable (Moon-Venus > Pluto-Uranus). The subliminal self-attack triggered an autoimmune attack (Mars) that targeted the pancreas and insulin producing cells (Mars is in Cancer, conjunct Venus and the Moon). Diabetes developed (Venus rules the 6H of health with Libra on the cusp).

▲ (C) Moon, Virgo. (O) Moon, Venus. (E) Mars, Uranus, Pluto.

• In 1988 and early 1989, solar-arc Venus had moved onto the natal Sun at 21 Leo, triggering her emotional and self-hate issues. This is when diabetes surfaced.

---

1 Bailey, Alice A; Esoteric Healing, 311.
2 Bailey, Alice A; Esoteric Healing, 312.

b. Hypoglycaemia

Nicole Richie (21 September 1981 04:10, Berkeley CA)
American TV personality diagnosed with hypoglycaemia while filming the reality show The Simple Life in early 2007. The condition occurs when sugar levels are too low. She has been treated for drug addiction, which is a known cause.

Cause: emotional. Richie is super-sensitive emotionally (a Cancer Moon that is quindecile Neptune) and insecure in love (Neptune semi-squares Venus). Her childhood was very unstable (Uranus in the 4H), and there could have been hidden abuse (Mars that rules the 4H, is in the 12H of hidden things square Venus). Life stabilised and became more exciting, when pop-star Lionel Richie adopted her (Uranus sextile the Sun).

Organ: solar plexus - pancreas, Venus and the Moon.

Effect: hypoglycaemia. Richie self-medicated with drugs and alcohol (Moon > Neptune) and developed hypoglycaemia (Moon trine Venus that is afflicted in Scorpio).

▲ (C) Moon, Neptune. (O) Moon, Venus. (E) Neptune.

c. Pancreatitis

Pancreatitis is severe pain caused by an inflamed pancreas. Heavy alcohol consumption is a known cause of the trouble. Anger over the loss of love or sweetness in life is related.

Ernst, Prince of Hanover (26 February 1954 07:22, Hanover Germany)
Husband of Princess Caroline of Monaco, Ernst has been described as "a drunken, thuggish brawler". In April 2005, he suffered acute pancreatitis.

Cause: emotional. With the Moon in Sagittarius conjunct Mars, Ernst' natural impulse when he feels threatened is to strike out, to get others before they get him, and this is at the root of his problem. He is a sensitive Pisces personality who drinks alcohol to relieve anxiety and fear; who strikes out at life to protect himself.

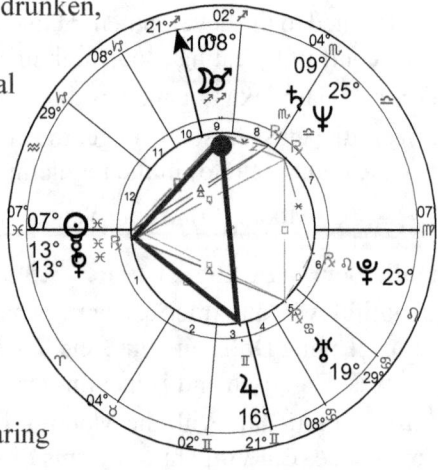

Organ: solar plexus - pancreas, the Moon.

Effect: pancreatitis. Anxiety contributes to excessive drinking (Mars opposite Jupiter), which inflames (Mars) the pancreas (Moon).

▲ (C) Moon, Mars. (O) Moon. (E) Mars, Jupiter.

- When Ernst collapsed in 2005, solar-arc Uranus had reached 10 Virgo, squaring the natal Moon, symbolising the attack on the pancreas.

Freddie King (3 September 1934 12:00, Gilmer TX)
Freddie King was an American blues guitarist and singer, one of the "Three Kings" of electric blues guitar, along with Albert and B. B. King. Described as "living hard and drinking copiously", he died on December 28 1976, from acute pancreatitis.

Cause: emotional. King was a hyper-sensitive Cancer Moon person who masked his insecurities with alcohol (the Moon is sextile Neptune, and Mars is conjunct Pluto in Cancer).

Organ: solar plexus - pancreas, Venus.

Effect: pancreatitis. Alcoholic poisoning (Neptune in Virgo), seriously damaged his pancreas (Venus that rules the 6H of health, is midpoint Neptune and Pluto in Cancer). It put him into hospital, where he died (Pluto rules the 12H of hospitals and is in the 8H of death).

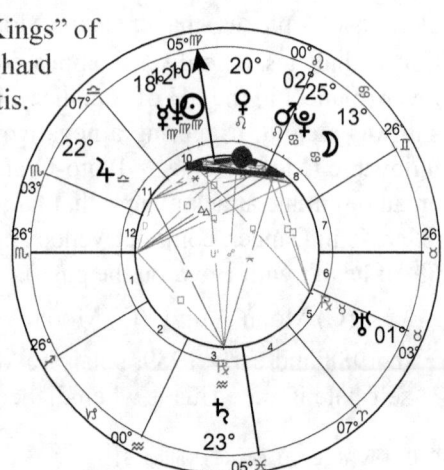

▲ (C) Moon, Mars. (O) Venus. (E) Neptune, Pluto

5e. Cancer in the Solar Plexus Organs

a. Breast cancer

Breast cancer primarily affects women, but men can get it too. Associated negative core beliefs are those of a belief in being unlovable, of not being worthy to receive love or emotional nourishment.

Jill Ireland (24 April 1936 19:00, Hounslow UK)

Ireland was a British actress who was diagnosed with breast cancer in 1984 and died of the disease on 18 May 1990.

Cause: emotional. Ireland suppressed her emotions (t-square: the Moon squares Saturn and Neptune), and rationalised her feelings (the Moon is in cerebral Gemini), to avoid a negative belief that she was unlovable (Neptune inconjunct Venus afflicted in Aries). This pattern underlies her illness.

Organ: solar plexus - breasts, the Moon and Venus.

Effect: breast cancer. Congestion (Saturn) in the solar plexus chakra (in Pisces), caused carcinogenic changes (opposite Neptune) in breast tissue (Moon, Venus in the 6H of health). She developed cancer, which killed her (the Moon is in the 8H of death).

▲ (C) Moon, Saturn, Neptune. (O) Moon, Venus. (E) Neptune.

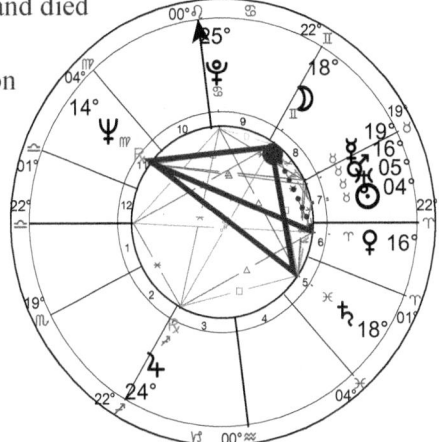

Linda McCartney (24 September 1941 10:00, New York NY)

Married to rock star Paul McCartney, Linda was diagnosed with breast cancer in 1995. It quickly spread to the liver and she died 17 April 1998.

Cause: emotional. McCartney was very intense emotionally (the Moon conjunct Venus in Scorpio), and her chart shows she harboured a negative belief about love causing emotional pain and destruction (Venus square Pluto). In spite of a happy marriage, the fact that she developed breast cancer shows that she repressed this fear rather than healed it.

Organ: solar plexus - breasts, the Moon and Venus.

Effect: breast cancer. Carcinogenic (Neptune) changes occurred in breast tissue (semi-square Venus and septile the Moon, both of which are afflicted in Scorpio). It resulted in malignant cell growth and cancer (Neptune and Pluto in Leo. Venus rules the 12H of major illnesses).

▲ (C) Moon, Pluto. (O) Moon, Venus. (E) Pluto, Neptune.

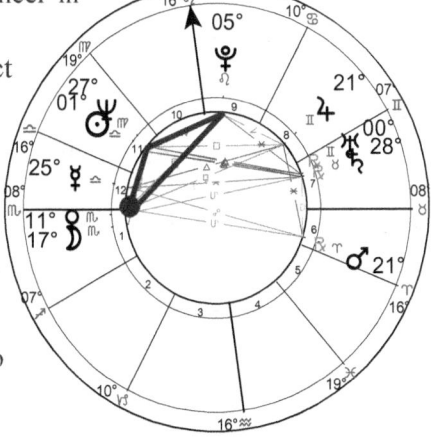

Olivia Newton John (26 September 1948 06:00, Cambridge UK)

Pop star and movie actress, John was successfully treated for breast cancer in July 1992, which included a mastectomy. In May 2017 it was announced she had stage 4 breast cancer that had spread to her lower spine.

Cause: emotional. Emotionally fragile (the Moon conjuncts Uranus in Cancer), John was (is) terrified that she would lose love, and if love died or left her, she could not survive the hurt (the Venus-Pluto conjunction is midpoint the Moon and Uranus on one wing and Neptune on the other).

Organ: solar plexus - breasts, the Moon and Venus.

Effect: breast cancer. Disruption in the solar plexus chakra (Uranus-Moon in Cancer > Neptune), caused carcinogenic changes (Neptune) in breast tissue (Moon in Cancer), and a malignant cancerous growth formed (Pluto, Neptune).

▲ (C) Moon, Uranus. (O) Moon, Venus. (E) Pluto, Uranus, Neptune.

- The onset of cancer in 1992 is shown by solar-arc Moon moving over natal Pluto at 15 Leo. Jupiter transiting through the 12th and 1st houses in this period helped her heal.

- In 2017, the solar-arc Moon-Uranus point had reached 9-11 Virgo, midpoint Venus-Pluto and the Sun. This re-energised the disease pattern. The Sun rules the spine, to which cancer has spread.

b. Pancreatic Cancer

Pancreatic cancer is highly dangerous because there are often no symptoms until it is advanced. It kills most people by spreading to the liver, which then fails.

Donna Reed (27 January 1921 14:00, Denison Iowa)

American movie actress, Reed was diagnosed with pancreatic cancer in 1985, dying a few weeks later of the disease on January 14 1986.

Cause: emotional. The arc of trouble in Reed's chart is the 5-planet opposition group from the 10th to the 4th houses. It contains two rulers of the pancreas (Moon and Venus). Repression of emotion was the cause of the trouble (Saturn conjunct the Moon, and both opposing Venus in Cancer).

Organ: solar plexus - pancreas, the Moon and Venus.

Effect: pancreatic cancer. Congestion in the solar plexus caused carcinogenic changes in pancreatic cells (the Moon opposing Venus in Pisces); causing cell over-growth and cancer (Venus opposes Jupiter that is afflicted in Virgo, and semi-squares the Sun that carries the "over-building" ray 2).

▲ (C) Moon, Saturn. (O) Moon, Venus. (E) The Sun, Jupiter.

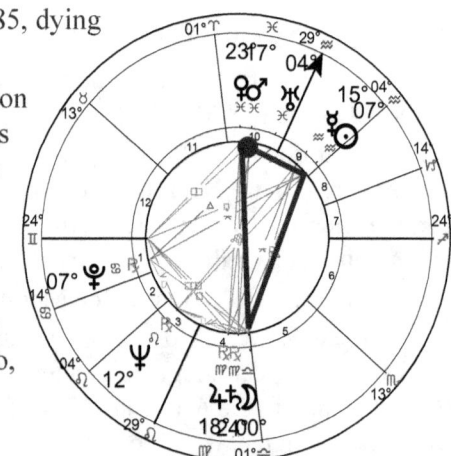

c. Liver cancer

Michael Landon (31 October 1936, 12:12, Jamaica NY)

American star of the TV programme 'The Little House on the Prairie'. In February 1991 he was told he had inoperable pancreatic cancer, which had metastasized to his liver and lymph nodes. He died 1 July 1991.

Cause: emotional. Self-criticism and repression of anger (t-square: Jupiter square Neptune-Mars and Saturn), caused trouble in the abdominal organs (Mars and Neptune in Virgo).

Organ: solar plexus - liver, Jupiter.

Effect: liver cancer. Repression coupled with heavy drinking, caused carcinogenic changes (Mars conjunct Neptune) in liver cells that migrated into cancer (square Jupiter). The cancer had metastasized from the pancreas (Venus square Neptune), spreading also into the lymph nodes (Neptune).

▲ (C) Mars, Saturn. (O) Jupiter. (E) Jupiter, Neptune.

d. Stomach Cancer

George Santayana (16 December 1863, 21:00, Madrid Spain)

Spanish-American philosopher and poet who died of stomach cancer in September 1952. He had a lifelong, unrequited passion for a straight man.

Cause: emotional. Santayana was a homosexual (Uranus), who hid his sexual preference from the public (square the Moon that rules the 12H of hidden things). This and his unsatisfied desire for the man he loved caused the trouble.

Organ: solar plexus - stomach, the Moon.

Effect: stomach cancer. Emotional-sexual repression and frustration for not being able to slake his sexual appetite for the one he desired (Uranus > Moon in the 8H of sex, inconjunct Saturn); manifested as carcinogenic tissue growth in the stomach and cancer (Moon in Pisces). It killed him (the Moon is in the 8H of death).

▲ (C) Moon, Saturn. (O) Moon. (E) Uranus, Pisces.

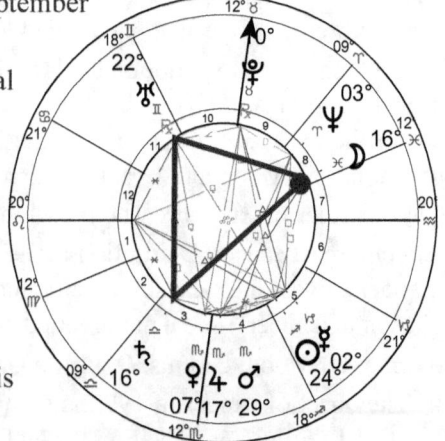

5f. Psychological-Emotional Disorders

The nervous system is controlled principally today from the astral body, via the etheric, and the basis of all nervous trouble lies hidden in the emotional body. [1]

a. Anorexia Nervosa

The psychological problem associated with anorexia is "glamour", a condition where troubled emotions distort perception. When we have a glamour problem, we see and believe whatever we want to see and believe. In anorexia, body-image is distorted. The anorexic person has an obsessive desire to lose weight and achieves this by refusing to eat. It is an unhealthy way of trying to cope with emotional problems.

Karen Carpenter (2 March 1950 11:45, New Haven CT).

American member of the Carpenters singing duo in the 1970's, Karen developed anorexia and died from heart failure caused by complications related to the illness on 4 February 1983.

Cause: emotional. Carpenter was deeply emotional and intense and because she developed terminal anorexia, we know was also deeply troubled (menacing Pluto sitting on the Moon). We do not know the circumstances but there may have been abuse in the family (retrograde Mars is in the 4H of family, in detriment in Libra, square Uranus). Emotional trauma connected with her childhood lay at the root of her anorexia trouble (Moon > Pluto).

Organ: solar plexus - emotions, the Moon.

Effect: anorexia. As part of her disorder, Carpenter's self-worth was tied to her appearance, her body image (Moon, ruler of the 2H of values, semi-square the ascendant). She wanted to lose weight to look better, to gain people's approval so that she would be loved. To this end she used her will to suppress her appetite (Pluto that rules the 6H of health and diet, is conjunct the Moon).

▲ (C) Moon, Pluto, Mars. (O) Moon. (E) Pluto, Uranus, Mars.

Carpenter's heart was damaged (Pluto in Leo, Saturn opposite the Sun) and she died. Saturn rules the 8H of death.

Gelsey Kirkland (29 December 1952 09:36, Fountain Hill PA).

American ballerina who was top of the ballet world in the mid-70's. It ended with emotional problems, anorexia and addiction to cocaine. Trouble started at age 8, when she was unfavourably compared to her sister. She said "It made me withdraw. I developed a lot of inhibitions, complexes about my eyes, my nose, my complexion".

Cause: emotional. Kirkland intellectualised her emotions (Moon in Gemini). She brushed aside hurt feelings and determined to work as hard as she could to ensure people would think she was as pretty and talented as her sister (the Moon trines Venus and Mars in the 1H of appearances).

Organ: solar plexus - emotions, the Moon.

Effect: anorexia. Obsessed with her "unattractive" looks (Pluto opposite Venus in the 1H), she had cosmetic surgery (Mars in the 1H of appearances), she took drugs (Mars trine Neptune), and stopped eating (Pluto > Moon and Cancer on the 6H of diet and health). Controlling what she ate helped her feel she was in control of her life.

▲ (C) Moon, Pluto. (O) Moon. (E) Mars, Pluto.

Kirkland made peace with herself and in 2017 was in a happy relationship and back in New York running a successful ballet school.

---

[1] Bailey, Alice A; Esoteric Healing, 107

b. Attention-deficit/hyperactivity disorder (ADHD)

ADHD is a combination of problems such as inattention, hyperactivity and impulsive behaviour

Russell Brand (4 June 1975, 0:00, Grays UK).

British comedian and actor who was diagnosed with ADHD and bipolar. In his earlier years he drank excessively and took drugs.

Cause: emotional. Chronic hyperactivity stems from emotional instability and volatility (Moon-Mars in Aries, Mars is quindecile Uranus). His energies were chaotic and needed grounding. Brand has no natal planets in earth signs and drugs made things worse (the Aries planets trine Neptune).

Organ: ajna - the nervous system, Mercury.

Effect: ADHD. Brand's over-stimulated nervous system kept his body hyper-active and on constant over-drive. His liking for sugary foods (Venus in Cancer, the sign ruling the 6H of diet), exacerbated the problem.

▲ (C) Moon, Mars, Uranus. (O) Mercury. (E) Uranus.

Brand says he has quietened down and is trying to live a decent, spiritual life. He is guided by Neptune in the 10H, a sort of North Star influence that continually encourages him to refine his energies and life expression. Additionally, five of his planets by solar-arc are slowly moving through earth signs, providing a counterbalance of stability to his fire-air, yang force.

c. Alcohol and Substance Abuse

Richard Burton (10 November 1925 15:00, Pontrhydfendigaid Wales)

Celebrated British actor who was a long term alcoholic.

Cause: emotional. Burton had a tough childhood. He was the twelfth child of an impoverished coal-miner and lost his mother when he was two years old (Pluto in the 4H). Criticised and bullied, he was unable to grieve his loss (the Sun-Saturn conjunction squaring Neptune). There was no soft place for him to fall and no kind words to encourage him (Mercury square the Moon). Consequently, he grew up with unresolved emotional trauma that was never attended to.

Organ: solar plexus - emotions, Neptune.

Effect: alcoholism. Burton self-medicated with alcohol (Neptune in the 6H), seeking oblivion from life's hardships (square the Saturn-Sun point), and painful emotions (inconjunct Uranus in Pisces in the 12H of hidden things).

▲ (C) Neptune, Saturn. (O) Neptune. (E) Sun-Saturn, Uranus.

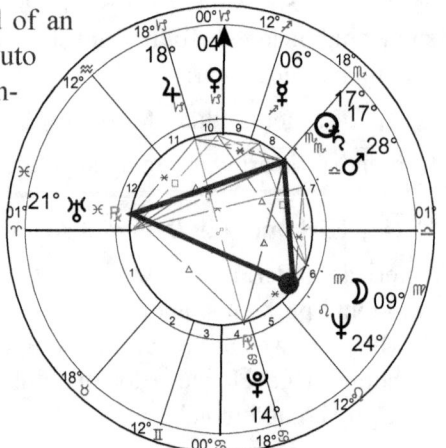

d. Bipolar (manic depression, mood swings)

Mood-swing disorders arise when the 4th Ray of Conflict, goes awry.

Vivien Leigh (5 November 1913, 17:16, Darjeeling India).

English actress best known for her Oscar-winning role as Scarlett O'Hara in the classic film 'Gone with the Wind'. Mild symptoms of bipolar were evident when she was at school in the 1920's. At 39, while filming 'Elephant Walk', she had a full breakdown.

Cause: emotional. Leigh was emotionally unstable and insecure (Moon conjunct Uranus) quite likely an inherited family pattern (quindecile the Mars-Neptune point in Cancer, which conjunct the 4H family cusp). The fact that she descended into insanity is an indication she was unable to find inner stability.

Organ: ajna - nervous system, Mercury.

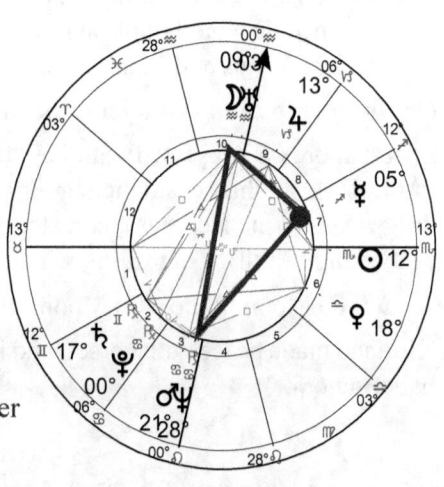

Effect: solar plexus. As her star rose, Leigh's fragile grip on reality frayed. She sparkled with brilliance and wit when things were going well (Moon-Uranus on the MC, sextile Mercury), but would swing into depression when they were not and throw violent rages (Mars-Neptune). When Mercury and the Moon, which both carry ray 4 are involved in a conflict pattern, it exacerbates mood swings in emotionally susceptible people.

▲ (C) Moon-Uranus opposing Mars-Neptune. (O) Mercury. (E) Moon.

e. Bulimia Nervosa

A cycle of and purging that can become an obsession if it is used to handle emotional distress.

Princess Diana 1 July 1961 19:45, Sandringham UK)

Princess Diana said in an interview, "I had bulimia for a number of years. You inflict it upon yourself because your self-esteem is at a low ebb, and you don't think you're worthy or valuable. You fill your stomach up four or five times a day - and it gives you a feeling of comfort."

Cause: emotional. Diana's troubles can be traced to her childhood. It is likely she never recovered from her mother's "abandonment" of her (Moon opposite Uranus), when she divorced Diana's father and remarried. Though she was a very emotional person (Sun in Cancer), to cope, she could split off from her feelings, compartmentalising those she did not want to deal with and lock them away (the Moon is in Aquarius, which carries the 5th ray that dissociates). But repressed emotions prevent us from developing healthy emotional expression and Diana was very shy and immature when she married sophisticated Charles. As we know now, it was a total mismatch (Jupiter, ruler of Diana's ascendant is inconjunct the 7H ruler of marriage, Mercury).

Organ: solar plexus - emotions, the Moon.

Effect: bulimia. The emotional hurts she stuffed away came up anyway - via her food. Diana would eat for comfort, then vomit it all up (Uranus > Moon; the Moon disposits Mercury that rules the 6H of diet and is inconjunct Jupiter).

▲ (C) Moon, Uranus. (O) Moon. (E) Sun, Mercury, Uranus.

When Diana died in the infamous car crash in Paris on 31 August 1997, progressed Mercury, one of the rulers of the 8H of death, was in the 8th house at 5 Leo. Mercury rules transport and the suddenness of the accident is shown by transit Uranus at 5 Aquarius, opposing Mercury.

f. Cutting

Self-injury is an unhealthy way to cope with emotional pain, anger and frustration.

Amy Winehouse (14 September 1983 22:25, Enfield UK)

Talented English rocker and soul singer who had "criss-cross scars and scratches" up and down her left arm, 'People' magazine reported. A video showed her scratching her exposed midriff with a shard from a broken mirror.

Cause: emotional. Winehouse's feelings of emotional deprivation, of being without comfort, are shown by the Moon's location in the cold and icy realm of Capricorn. She felt lost (conjunct Neptune), unloved and abandoned (the Moon and Neptune square the Sun-Mercury point in Virgo in the 5H of romance). She perpetuated the problem with negative self-talk and criticism.

Organ: solar plexus - emotions, the Moon.

Effect: self-harm. Winehouse self-medicated with alcohol and drugs (Neptune); and cut herself because it felt good (trine Mars conjunct Venus).

▲ (C) Moon, Neptune. (O) Moon. (E) Mercury, Neptune, Mars

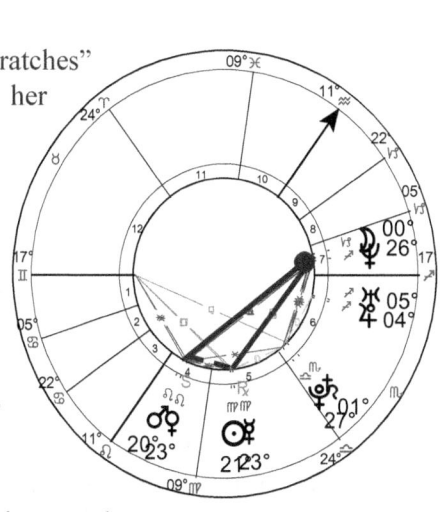

When Winehouse died in 23 July 2011, her progressed Moon was at 6 Capricorn and had just entered the 8H of death and transformation. Simultaneously, Saturn, the ruler of the 8H of death, had transited to 11 Libra in the 5th house of "pleasure". She died of an overdose while seeking "a high".

g. Obsessive compulsive disorder (OCD)

OCD is an anxiety disorder. Sufferers feel compelled to take certain actions, to repeatedly do something to avoid something bad happening. This helps to alleviate anxiety.

Astro.com 37914 (26 August 1958 14:30, 37S55, 145E Australia)
Australian female with OCD. "She has sought professional help over a period of many years from a variety of medical and alternative practitioners and is becoming suicidal in her desperation to find a cure or satisfactory means of controlling her disorder, a sad and desperate woman."
Cause: emotional. The Moon/ the astral nature, dominates perception (the Moon is conjunct the ascendant). She sees life through a prism of negativity, pessimism and despair (the Moon is in detriment in Capricorn). This is at the root of the problem - the Moon co-rules the 6H of health.
Organ: solar plexus - emotions, the Moon.
Effect: OCD. Driven by an anxiety disorder (Moon square Neptune), she is compelled to take action (trine Mars), to avoid something bad happening (Mars inconjunct Saturn on the 12H cusp of the unknown).
▲ (C) Moon, Neptune. (O) Moon. (E) Mars.

Stabilising the emotional nature. This woman is captive to her neurotic thoughts and feelings and needs help to break the negative cycle. Cognitive therapy or esoteric counselling from a kind and skilled practitioner to help expose untruths she believes about herself or unresolved emotional wounds that require healing, would help relieve tension and stabilise the nature. An active physical life with outdoor walks, swims and gentle Sun exposure will strengthen the etheric body and vitality. The home should be kept clean, bright and airy with beautiful music played. If marked improvement is made, then a simple meditation like building a beautiful garden would help restore emotional balance and bring inner quietness.

h. Panic-attack - Agoraphobia

A panic attack is a sudden overwhelming feeling of acute and disabling anxiety. Accompanying physical symptoms are sweating and a racing heart.

Susan, Astro.com 44645 (13 December 1958, 23:05, Scunthorpe UK)
British woman who has panic attacks that last for minutes. After an attack, she is afraid to go out for several days. Her symptoms began after her son was born and she suffered post-partum depression. By 1996, her attacks became too overwhelming for her to handle even with medication.
Cause: emotional. Susan disconnects from her emotions, from her deeper feelings (Moon in Aquarius square Neptune), and trauma (inconjunct Pluto in the 12H of self-undoing). This means she drags these unresolved emotions around like baggage. It is possible that her pregnancy triggered a past life memory of pain and suffering connected with childbirth (the Moon is in the 5H of children, inconjunct Pluto), hence her reaction.
Organ: solar plexus - emotions, the Moon.
Effect: panic attack. Until Susan gets in touch with her deeper feelings and heals them, she will continue to suffer from panic attacks.
▲ (C) Moon, Neptune, Pluto. (O) Moon. (E) Pluto.

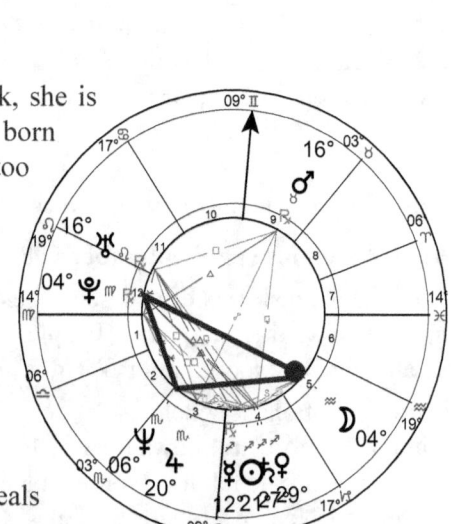

- During 1994 and 1995, solar-arc Neptune was passing over natal Mercury at 12 Sagittarius. This indicates the power of the astral nature over the mind, clouding rationality and enhancing emotionalism.
- Solar-arc Pluto had reached 10 Libra, conjunct the progressed ascendant at 11 Libra, and for a few years they travelled forward together. This added serious paranoia to her perception and accentuated her belief she was in serious physical and psychological danger.
- By 2002 as solar-arc Pluto moved away from the progressed ascendant, things should have started to improve, her perceptions of life had a chance to stabilise.

i. Post-traumatic stress disorder (PTSD)

PTSD is triggered by a terrifying event, with symptoms that may include flashbacks, nightmares and severe anxiety about the event. During an episode, researchers have found that the amygdala part of the brain that is key to the normal expression of emotions - especially fear, is highly active. At the same time the rationalising part seems ineffective.

John Mulligan (2 June 1950, 05:00 BST, Kirkintilloch UK).
Scottish-American ex-soldier who wrote about the horrors he witnessed in Vietnam. He came away with severe post-traumatic stress disorder.

Cause: emotional. Mulligan was born with a depressive pattern (Moon in Capricorn) and emotions that react violently to trauma (opposite Uranus in Cancer). So it is not surprising he suffered from PTSD as a consequence of his experiences in the Vietnam War.

Organ: solar plexus - emotions the Moon; ajna - mind Mercury.

Effect: PTSD. During an attack, the emotion producing amygdala (the Moon), becomes highly active (opposite Uranus). Simultaneously, the rationalising mind is rendered ineffective, neutered by the emotions (Mercury in the 12H of hidden things is sesquiquadrate the Moon and semi-square Uranus).

▲ (C) Moon, Uranus. (O) Moon, Mercury. (E) Uranus.

- In the first few years Mulligan was in Vietnam, the solar-arc ascendant was in Cancer, moving over natal and progressed Uranus and opposite natal Moon. This emphasises the shattering effect that the horrors he was experiencing had on his psyche.

- In the final months in Vietnam, his progressed Sun had reached Uranus, indicating the complete change in his personality due to his war experiences.

j. Schizophrenia and Psychosis

Schizophrenia involves a breakdown between thought, emotion and behaviour. The result is a withdrawal into delusion. It usually appears in teenage years or early adulthood.

Vincent Van Gogh (30 March 1853 11:00, Zundert Netherlands)
Brilliantly talented Dutch artist, Van Gogh lived his brief life in misery and poverty. Disappointed in love and religion, he was intense, difficult and unhappy. In October 1889, he was put in an asylum. His doctor encouraged him to keep painting and flying into a creative frenzy he completed 70 canvases in 70 days. Six months later, while painting in a wheat field, he shot himself and died two days later on 29 July, 1890.

Cause: emotional. Van Gogh's violent and unstable emotional body (Moon in Sagittarius conjunct Jupiter, square Mars in Pisces) dominated his nature and his approach to life (the Moon carries the 4th ray of conflict and it rules the ascendant). The personality was not integrated or developed (an unaspected Sun), which means his personal will was not strong enough, nor was his intellect, to bring a moderating influence to his emotional swings and excesses.

Organ: solar plexus - emotions the Moon and Mars; ajna - mind Mercury.

Effect: schizophrenia. Dominated by his emotional life, it was easy for Van Gogh to believe that the dark, phantom images rising from his unfettered imagination (Pluto is conjunct Mercury, the ruler of the 12H of self-undoing), were real. He lived in delusion.

▲ (C) Moon, Mars. (O) Moon, Mars, Mercury. (E) Pluto.

- When Van Gogh shot himself, he could no longer cope with his inner demons. His progressed Moon was at zero degrees Taurus, conjunct natal Pluto.

6. Sacral Chakra Diseases

The sacral chakra rules the reproductive glands, sex and reproduction. It receives energy primarily from rays 7 and 6, also ray 3. Sagittarius, Scorpio, Mars and Uranus are the main rulers while the Moon and Venus are influential for female reproduction and sex.

6a. Genetic Diseases

A genetic disorder is caused by an abnormality in DNA, especially a condition that is present from birth (congenital). DNA is the genetic or karmic map on which the foetus is modelled. It reflects any diseases or defects being passed on by parents. Ray 7 that flows via Uranus, rules DNA.

a. Achondroplasia: disproportionate dwarfism

Dwarfism (usually with abnormally short legs), accounts for about 75% of all dwarfism. Cartilage does not convert to bone in this genetic bone disorder.

Peter Dinklage (June 11 1969, 01:37 Point Pleasure NJ)
American actor who has lately been acclaimed for his portrayal of Tyrion Lannister in the TV series 'Game of Thrones'.
Cause: genetic-emotional. Jupiter that represents growth is afflicted in Virgo. This suggests that in a previous life, Dinklage was emotionally stifled and stunted due to virulent and demeaning criticism (Moon conjunct Saturn).
Organ: ajna - growth hormone Venus; heart - growth, the Sun, Jupiter.
Effect: dwarfism. His physical growth was affected. A corrupted gene (Pluto conjunct Uranus), inhibited the pituitary growth hormone (sesquiquadrate Venus that is conjunct Saturn). Consequently bone (Saturn) growth was stunted (semi-square the Sun; Pluto is conjunct Jupiter and squares the Sun).
▲ (C) Uranus; Moon-Saturn. (O) Venus, Sun, Jupiter. (E) Pluto, Saturn.

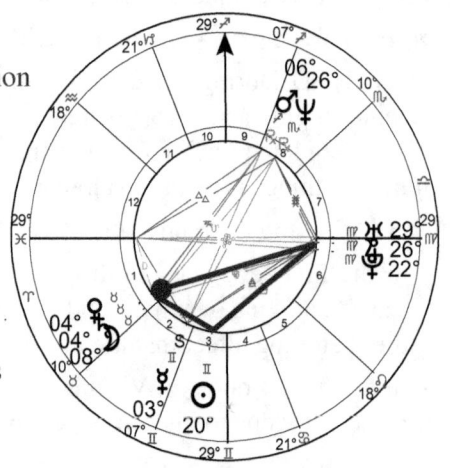

b. Cystic Fibrosis

A protein that controls how salt and water move through cells is flawed. Thick mucous clogs organs and airways. There are constant respiratory infections.

Annie Tulcin (14 June 1953 17:36, New York NY).
American woman born with cystic fibrosis.
Cause: genetic-emotional. Impaired water movement in the body suggests emotional congestion that drowns (Saturn-Neptune).
Organ: throat - airways, represented by Mercury and Gemini.
Effect: cystic fibrosis. The protein that controls salt-water balance was perverted, mucous was too thick (Neptune conjunct Saturn in Libra, sesquiquadrate Jupiter), clogging the airways (Jupiter in Gemini; and the Saturn-Neptune point squares Mercury in Cancer).
▲ (C) Uranus, Saturn-Neptune. (O) Mercury, Gemini. (E) Saturn-Neptune, Jupiter.

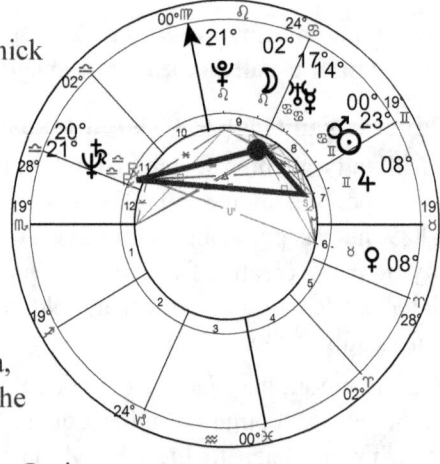

Greg Lemarchal (13 May 1983 05:08, La Tronche France).
French singer who won a TV competition. Born with cystic fibrosis, in 2007 he died while waiting for a lung transplant.
Cause: genetic. Emotional congestion (Moon conjunct Mars, inconjunct Pluto conjunct Saturn), underlies the problem.
Organ: throat - lungs, Mercury; heart - the Sun.
Effect: cystic fibrosis. A flawed salt-water regulating protein (Saturn-Pluto in Libra), thickened body fluids (Moon-Mars in Taurus) and produced mucous that clogged the lungs (Moon conjunct Sun-Mercury quindecile, Uranus-Jupiter).
▲ (C) Uranus, Moon-Mars. (O) Sun, Mercury. (E) Saturn-Pluto, Jupiter.

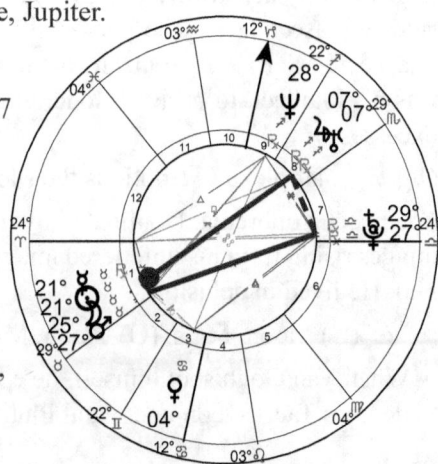

c. Down's Syndrome

A gene is composed of tiny chromosomes, each of which determines a particular characteristic. There is an extra chromosome in Down's syndrome. There may be mental disability, atypical facial structure and physical defects. Look for connections between Uranus (DNA) and Jupiter (extra). Here is a search over several Astro.com charts.

- 10068 (13 November 1945 22:01) Uranus trine Jupiter.
- 12437 (10 June 1953 02:30) Uranus semi-square Moon conjunct Jupiter
- 12768 (2 December 1954 08:22) Uranus conjunct Jupiter.
- 13234 (11 December 1957 06:14) Uranus trine Sun in Sagittarius.
- 13650 (20 March 1961 08:05) Jupiter in Aquarius.
- 13748 (4 February 1962 13:38) Jupiter in Aquarius.

Baby Doe (9 April 1982 20:18, Bloomington IL)

Cause: genetic. Uranus in Sagittarius represents the extra chromosome.

Organ: ajna - consciousness, the Sun and Mercury.

Effect: Down's. Because of the mutation, consciousness (Mercury conjunct the Sun) could not work effectively through the brain (opposite Saturn).

▲ (C) Uranus. (O) Sun-Mercury. (E) Saturn.

The baby was born with a throat fistula that blocked the alimentary tract so it could not eat. Instead of making a surgical correction, a hard-hearted hospital obstetrician advised the parents to let the baby die because its life was "not valuable". They let the baby starve to death.

d. Muscular Dystrophy (Duchenne)

It is caused by a faulty gene, which inhibits an essential protein for muscle growth so that muscles waste away.

Rona Barrett (8 October 1936, 04:15, New York NY)

American gossip columnist and businesswoman. As a child, she had muscular dystrophy and wore leg braces.

Cause: genetic-emotional. Uranus falls in Taurus, representing the mutated gene. It is trine Mars, the muscles, located in the 12H of self-undoing. On an emotional level this suggests a belief in being unable to cope with life. This is reinforced by the Moon-Pluto conjunction that is semi-square Mars.

Organ: base - muscles Mars.

Effect: muscular dystrophy. The gene inhibits a protein (Saturn in a t-square, in the 6H of health), so that movement is restricted (Jupiter) because muscles waste away (Neptune, wide conjunct to Mars).

▲ (C) Uranus, Mars. (O) Mars. (E) Saturn, Jupiter, Neptune.

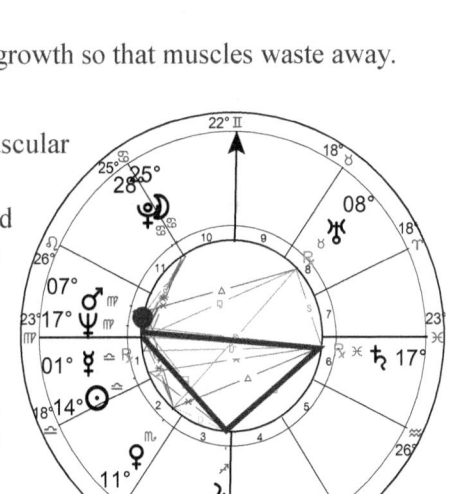

e. Progeria

Progeria is caused by a gene mutation that makes the nucleus of cells unstable, leading to premature ageing.

Peedie Snipes (10 May 1977 17:15, Burlington NC)

Snipes' hair began to fall out at age 1, he had age spots and cataracts at 3, arthritis at 13 and died of old age at 14, on 8 March 1992.

Cause: karmic: Saturn is the most exalted planet in the chart. It represents ageing and is in Leo that rules cells, square Uranus - the defective gene.

Organ: heart - cell life, the Sun, Leo.

Effect: progeria. Cell life is represented by the Sun, but it is unaspected, indicating a lack of nurturing from the life aspect. Perhaps this has something to do with the fact that it is conjunct the "evil" star Algol, the head of the Medusa at 26 Taurus. To look on it would turn the observer to stone.

Venus disposits the Sun. Afflicted in hasty Aries, trine Saturn and opposed by 1st ray Pluto; it represents the unnaturally accelerated life-span of cells.

▲ (C) Saturn. (O) Sun, Leo. (E) Venus, Pluto, Saturn.

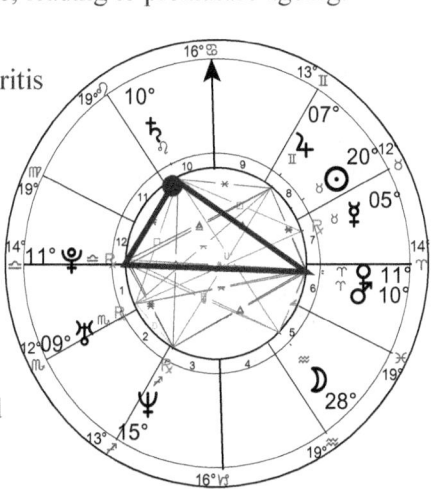

6b. Reproduction Problems

a. Abortion

Anais Nin (21 February 1903, 20:25, Paris France)
French female activist who had an abortion (August 21 1940), because financial circumstances were unfavourable. She was 3 months pregnant.
Cause: the mind. Although Nin was a Pisces Sun personality, her emotions were ruled by her intellect and expediency. She was non-maternal (the Moon is in chilly Capricorn conjunct individualistic Uranus).
Organ: sacral - foetus, the Moon.
Effect: abortion. The foetus was aborted (Moon conjunct Uranus opposite Pluto. Uranus rules the 5H of children). It was a clinical decision for financial reasons (Uranus square Venus that rules the 2H of money).
  ▲ (C) Venus. (O) Moon. (E) Venus, Uranus, Pluto.
- On the day of the abortion, transit Mars (the abortion), was at 1 Virgo, opposite natal Jupiter-Sun in the 5H of children.

b. Ectopic Pregnancy

The most common reason for an ectopic pregnancy is a damaged fallopian tube, causing a blockage or narrowing which prevents the egg from reaching its destination. Instead, it settles in the tube wall.

Sophie Rhys-Jones (20 January 1965, 12:46, Oxford UK)
Wife of Prince Edward, the son of Queen Elizabeth. On 6 December 2001, Sophie miscarried a two-month ectopic pregnancy.
Cause: karmic. It is difficult for Rhys-Jones to conceive or carry a baby full term. She has karma involving children - there are three malefics in the 5H of children, all crowding the maternal Moon.
Organ: sacral - fallopian tubes, the Moon, Mercury.
Effect: ectopic pregnancy. A blocked and diseased fallopian tube (Mercury in Capricorn, septile Neptune in Scorpio), caused the embryo to attach to the tube wall. It miscarried (trine Moon conjunct Uranus and Pluto). Luckily, the Moon is in a grand-trine with Jupiter. With assistance and care she now has two children.
  ▲ (C) Capricorn. (O) Moon, Mercury. (E) Neptune, Uranus, Pluto.

c. Endometriosis

The endometrium (inner tissue-surface of the uterus) grows outside the uterine cavity. Irregular menstrual blood flow is given as the likely cause. It results in painful periods and fertility problems.

Dolly Parton (19 January 1946, 20:25, Sevierville TN)
American singer-songwriter and actress. In 1982, Parton had a partial hysterectomy due to endometriosis.
Cause: emotional. Parton rejected her maternal side, said she was too selfish to have children (the Moon is in hyper-critical Virgo, and Saturn is in Cancer). Her attitude had a physical effect.
Organ: sacral - uterus the Moon, periods Venus.
Effect: endometriosis. Parton had very painful menstrual cycles (the Moon disposits Mars conjunct Saturn in Cancer; and Saturn opposes Venus). To remedy the problem she had a partial hysterectomy.
  ▲ (C) Moon. (O) Moon, Venus. (E) Mars, Saturn.
- In 1982, solar-arc Uranus had reach 20 Cancer and was on the natal Saturn-Mars point. This was when she had the partial hysterectomy.

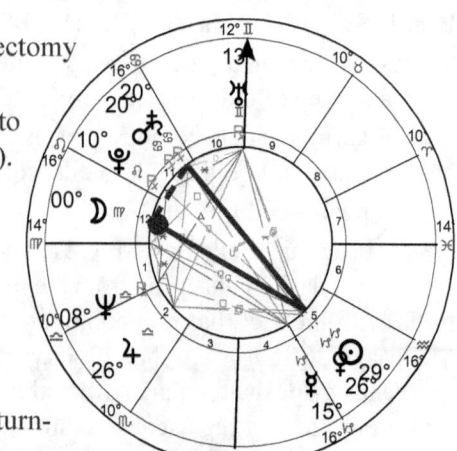

d. Hysterectomy

Althea Flynt (6 November 1953, 17:45, Marietta OH)
American publisher of Hustler magazine with her husband Larry Flynt. In 1982, she had a hysterectomy.

Cause: emotional. Flynt had deep emotional problems, a consequence of abuse suffered in her early years (the Moon is afflicted in Scorpio, in the 6H of health, square Pluto in the 4H of home). The same pattern showed serious obstacles for Flynt's hopes of motherhood.

Organ: sacral - womb, the Moon.

Effect: hysterectomy. All was not well with Flynt's uterus (Moon > Pluto), and eventually she was forced to have it removed (surgical Mars in the 5H of children, semi-squares the Moon).

▲ (C) Moon, Pluto. (O) Moon. (E) Pluto, Mars.

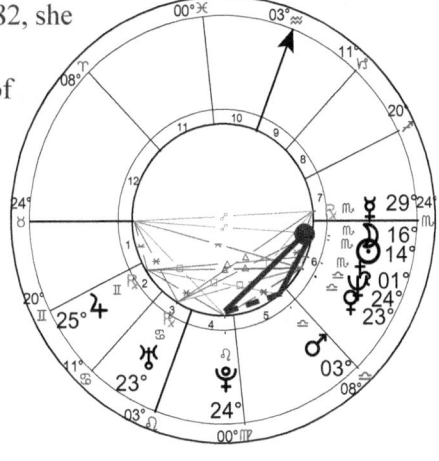

e. Infertility

Soraya (22 June 1932, 22:30, Isfahan Iran)
The second wife of the Shah of Iran. Her childless plight and divorce so the Shah could have children captured the attention of the world in the 1950's.

Cause: emotional. Conception requires a healthy and happy Moon, especially since in Soraya's chart it sits on the ascendant, a point that is also related to birth. Soraya was cool emotionally (Moon in Aquarius) and may also have been cool to the idea of having children (the Moon rules the 5H of children). Cancer planets located there include Pluto, which is hostile to children.

Organ: sacral - reproduction, the Moon.

Effect: infertile. The fallopian tubes (Mercury in Cancer), were blocked or irreparably damaged (conjunct Pluto), so that eggs (Moon), could not travel to the uterus (Moon sesquiquadrate Mercury) to be fertilised (square Mars).

▲ (C) Moon. (O) Moon. (E) Cancer planets, Mars.

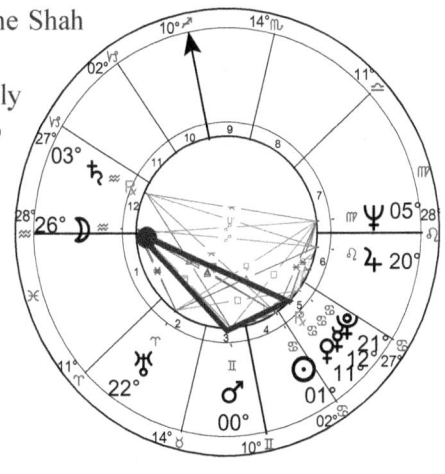

f. Miscarriage

Sophia Loren (20 September 1934, 14:10, Rome Italy)
Loren said "Always, in the third month, I was losing my babies—I had a lack of estrogen. Losing two babies made me feel such a failure as a woman".

Cause: emotional. Loren's maternal problems are linked to the Moon-Saturn conjunction versus Mars polarity in the chart.

Loren was illegitimate and the family impoverished, causing great hardship when she was growing up (Moon conjunct Saturn in the 2H of values). She fought her way to a better standard of living and towards respectability. But planet Mars, which represents this ability to fight hard, is also related to her miscarriages.

Organ: sacral - female sex hormone, the Moon.

Effect: miscarriage. Estrogen, the female sex hormone, is essential for the growth and delivery of a healthy baby. But Loren had a deficiency (Moon > Saturn), and this is given as the cause of her many miscarriages.

From her chart, it appears her testosterone levels were too high (Mars in Leo, sextile Jupiter). This destabilised and weakened the natal processes, causing irregularities (sextile Mercury ruling the 6H of health, opposite the Moon) and is linked to miscarriage and recurrent incidents of miscarriage.

▲ (C) Moon, Saturn. (O) Moon. (E) Saturn, Mars, Mercury.

g. Ovarian Cyst

Anne Elliot (7 July 1946 07:00, Melbourne Australia)
Australian astrologer. In October 1978 she required surgery for a ruptured ovarian cyst.
Cause: emotional. Elliot is a sensitive Cancer personality who tries to keep the peace and get on with everyone (Sun square Moon conjunct Jupiter in Libra). But she also tends to nurse hurts and disappointments from the past (the Moon squares Saturn in Cancer), which builds up emotional congestion. An ovarian cyst is a manifestation of this.
Organ: sacral - ovaries, the Moon.
Effect: ovarian cyst. A cyst, a fluid filled sac (Moon-Jupiter), developed in an ovary when an aberration (Uranus) occurred during egg release. It ruptured, requiring surgery (Mars semi-square Moon)

▲ (C) Moon, Saturn. (O) Moon. (E) Jupiter, Uranus, Mars.

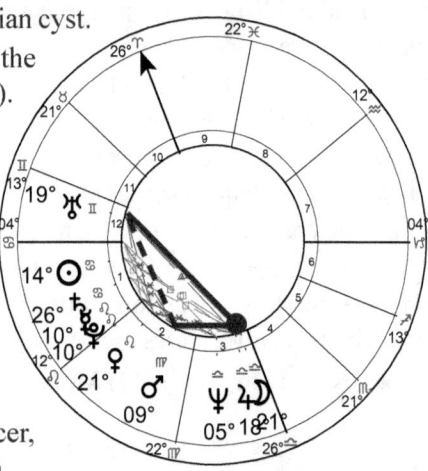

- The rupture and surgery occurred when solar-arc Uranus reached 20 Cancer, square natal Moon and inconjunct the progressed Moon in the 6H of health.

h. Conjoined Twins

The condition is not genetic but occurs randomly. Trouble occurs very shortly after a single embryo has been fertilised. It does not properly split, so that instead of two identical twins being born, the twins are attached. The etheric web is the model upon which the physical body is constructed, so the problem lies there. It does not divide correctly. Look for afflictions to the signs that rule the etheric - Gemini and Aquarius.

Nolan Twins (3 May 2001, 09:43, Brisbane Australia)
Australian craniopagic twin sisters Alyssa and Bethany Nolan were born joined at the top of their heads. They had separate brains, but shared cranial draining vessels - veins that drain blood from the brain, emptying into the jugular vein. In addition, Alyssa was born with one kidney; Bethany had no kidney and no bladder. In less than a month, Bethany's health suddenly deteriorated and on 26 May 2001 doctors tried to separate them and Bethany died. Alyssa survived but has continuing health complications including 40 operations by age 8.
Cause: karmic. Uranus, ruling aberrations, is in the 8H of inheritances, square Saturn. This indicates that karma was involved in the condition.
Organ: sacral - etheric web, Gemini and Aquarius.
Effect: conjoined twins. A mutation occurred during the form-building process. Division of the etheric web upon which the physical body is constructed, was incomplete - Uranus in Aquarius governs the etheric and also the sacral chakra that

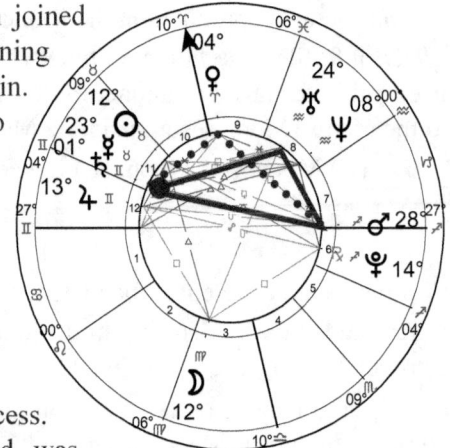

manages the building of the form. It squares Saturn in Gemini that governs twins. Building work by the nature elementals went awry in the head (Mars inconjunct Saturn, sextile Uranus). Mars rules the lunar elementals that build the body [1] and it also rules the head via Aries. With a flawed design, the completed physical structures were also flawed - joined at the head (Mars quindecile Jupiter that "fuses").

The specific trouble involves Venus' function. It carries deoxygenated blood back to the heart via the cranial veins to the jugular veins. The twins shared these veins. Lower in the body via Libra, Venus governs the kidneys (and is related to the bladder), which Bethany lacked. Impairment in these functions is shown by afflicted Venus in the sign ruling the head - Aries, forming an easy-opposition with Saturn and Mars.

▲ (C) Saturn, Uranus. (O) Gemini, Aquarius. (E) Saturn, Uranus, Mars, Venus.

At 13, Alyssa was attending high school and although more operations were scheduled, photos taken of her in that period show her to be a happy teenager.

---

[1] Bailey, Alice A; Esoteric Astrology, 186.

6c. Sexually Transmitted Diseases (STD's)

a. Syphilis

Randolph Churchill (13 February 1849, 00:01, Oxfordshire, UK)
British peer, who entered Parliament in 1874 and was the father of Sir Winston. He is reported as dying of syphilis on 24 January 1895.

Cause: sexual karma. With the Moon in Scorpio, Churchill had sexual issues from a past life to deal with. He was a sensual man with powerful carnal habits (Mars is exalted in Capricorn).

Organ: sacral - sex organs, Mars and Uranus.

Effect: syphilis. Churchill caught syphilis (Mars square Pluto and Uranus in the 6H of health). The opposition from Pluto to the Moon in Scorpio in the 12H of hidden things, points to the point of infection coming from a back-street assignation or brothel, possibly in a foreign country (the Moon rules the 9H of foreign countries). Mars and Pluto disposit the Moon. After a lengthy fight against the disease he died in 1895 (the Moon co-rules the 8H of death).

▲ (C) Moon, Pluto. (O) Mars, Uranus. (E) Uranus, Pluto.

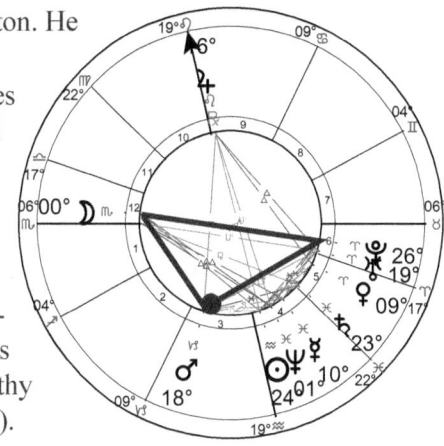

b. Gonorrhea

Laurie (24 February 1961, 08:47, Portland Maine)
(From Millard 'Case notes of a Medical Astrologer' page 109). Raised in religious family, Laurie was diagnosed with gonorrhea at 13, had a baby at 15 and a year later became sterile through another bout of gonorrhea.

Cause: emotional. Laurie was a malleable and emotional Pisces Sun and Cancer Moon girl, who was preyed upon sexually by predators from her church or cult at a young age (Mars conjunct the Moon; Saturn - and Jupiter that rules the 9H of religion, both square Venus in the 12H of hidden things). Consequently, Laurie grew up with loose morals and values (Venus afflicted) and poor sexual hygiene (Venus sesquiquadrate Pluto in Virgo).

Organ: sacral - sex organs, Venus.

Effect: gonorrhea. The result was several STD's (Venus, which is in detriment in Aries and co-rules the 6H of health, is trine Uranus). In turn, Uranus rules the sacral chakra and bacterial infections. Her reproductive organs were damaged and she was rendered sterile (Uranus in Leo, the sign ruling children, is in the 5H of children, septile the Moon).

▲ (C) Moon, Mars. (O) Venus. (E) Uranus.

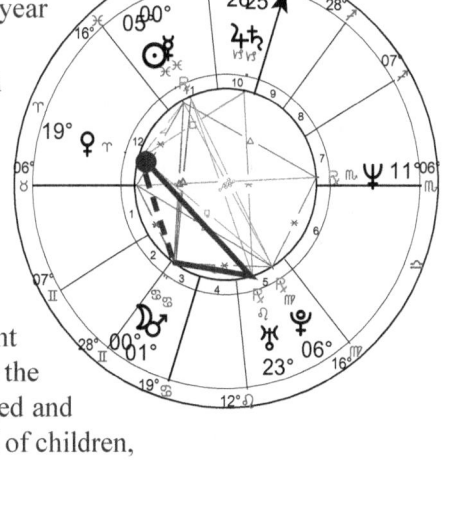

c. Herpes

Astro.com 5976 (30 June 1925, 07:00, Canton OH).
American insurance credit counsellor, married four times. She had a hysterectomy at an early age, breast cysts and herpes - a virus causing contagious sores, most often around the mouth or on the genitals

Cause: emotional. Our subject was an emotionally needy woman (a Cancer stellium in the 12H), who sought happiness through a succession of relationships and affairs (the Moon in Libra squares Venus that is conjunct Mars on the ascendant). Her sexual escapades contributed to health problems (Venus opposite Jupiter in the 6H of health), and the break-down of important intimate relationships.

Organ: sacral - sex organs, Mars and Venus.

Effect: herpes. She caught genital herpes (Mars-Venus > Jupiter inconjunct Neptune), causing blistering on her genitals (Mars-Venus).

▲ (C) Moon. (O) Venus, Mars. (E) Jupiter, Neptune, Mars.

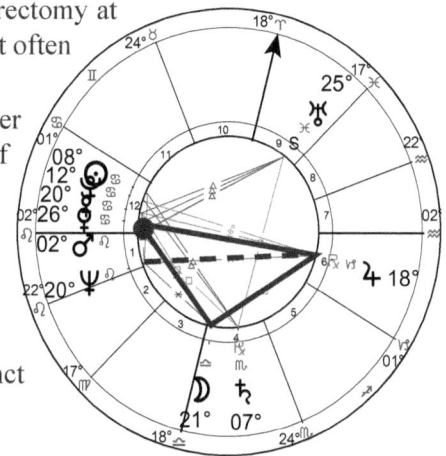

6d. Cancer in the Sacral Chakra Organs

a. Cancer of the Cervix and Uterus

Mirka Mora (18 March 1928 15:00, Paris France)

French-Australian artist, who led a bohemian and unconventional lifestyle. In 1993 she had a hysterectomy because of cancer in the cervix and uterus.

Cause: emotional. Mora was a sexually liberated woman (Mars in Aquarius), and likely caught the human papilloma virus, which causes most cases of cervical cancer through casual sex (Mars semi-square the Sun that is inconjunct Neptune on the ascendant. Neptune rules the 8H of sex).

Organ: sacral - the uterus and cervix, the Moon.

Effect: cancer. The HPV virus (Neptune), caused malignant changes in uterus and cervix tissue (semi-square Pluto in Cancer; Pluto is inconjunct the Moon and Mars), and cancerous cells developed. It required a hysterectomy (Mars conjunct the Moon in the 6H of health).

▲ (C) Moon, Mars. (O) Moon. (E) Mars, Neptune, Pluto.

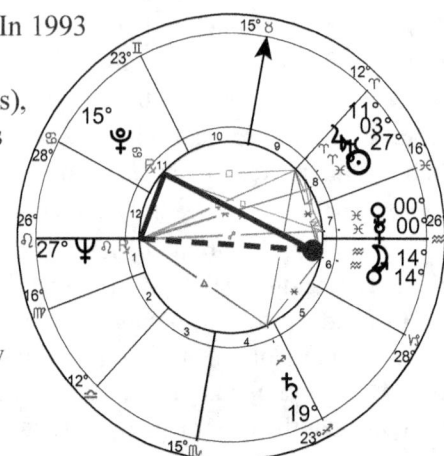

b. Ovarian Cancer

Patsy Ramsey (29 December 1956 14:00, Parkersburg WV)

Mother of JonBenet Ramsey, the child beauty pageant queen murdered in 1996. Diagnosed with ovarian cancer in 1993, she died from it on June 24 2006.

Cause: emotional. The unexplained murder of JonBenet is shown by Pluto (death) in the 5H of children, sesquiquadrate Mars (murder) in the 12H of hidden things. Psychologically, Ramsey was a very disciplined Capricorn personality who liked to keep her emotions controlled (Saturn conjunct Moon), and this repression as we have seen, so often leads to cancer.

Organ: sacral - ovaries, the Moon and Venus.

Effect: cancer. Carcinogenic changes (Neptune in the 6H of health), in ovarian tissue (semi-square the Moon), led to the development of ovarian cancer (Neptune is midpoint the Venus-Moon point and Jupiter). It caused her death (Jupiter rules the 8H of death). Grief over the tragedy surrounding her daughter contributed greatly to her illness (Neptune in Scorpio, sextile Pluto).

▲ (C) Moon, Saturn. (O) Moon, Venus. (E) Jupiter, Neptune.

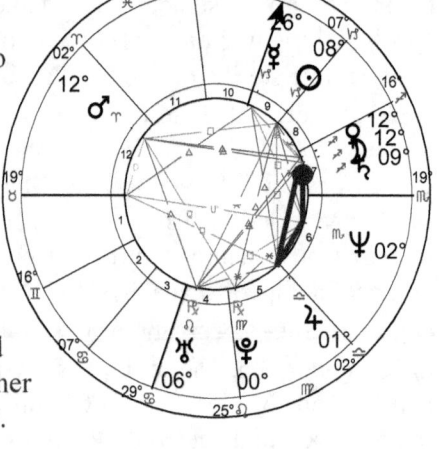

c. Prostate Cancer

Harry Secombe (8 September 1921, 12:00, Swansea UK)

Welsh comedian famous from the British radio comedy programme 'The Goon Show'. He died on April 11 2001, of prostate cancer.

Cause: ageing. Secombe's disease was age related - he got it in his late 70's. Body resilience and immunity wind down as we age. Secombe's Moon is in Sagittarius, the sign that rules the sacral chakra, pointing to potential trouble at some time in the sex organs.

Organ: sacral - prostate, Mars.

Effect: cancer. Tissue malignancies occurred in the prostate (Moon inconjunct Pluto in Cancer, semi-square Mars, the ruler 6H of health). It migrated into full blown cancer that killed him (the Moon is in Sagittarius that expands inconjunct Pluto in the 8H of death).

▲ (C) Moon, Pluto. (O) Mars. (E) Moon in Sagittarius, Pluto.

• Solar-arc Moon moved through 22 - 23 Aquarius, opposite natal Mars during 1997 to 1999, triggering the disease. When he died, solar-arc Mars was passing over the ascendant.

7. Base Chakra Diseases

The base rules the adrenal glands, urinary system, physical body tissue generally and the skeleton. It receives energy primarily from rays 1 and 3, from Capricorn, Aquarius, Pisces, Pluto and Saturn.

7a. Adrenal Glands

a. Addison's disease (underproduction of hormones)

Addison's is caused mainly by an autoimmune attack upon the adrenals, impairing hormones that deal with stress (cortisol) and salt-water regulation (aldosterone). Symptoms include fatigue, nausea and dizziness.

John F. Kennedy (29 May 1917 15:00, Brookline MA)
Popular US President, in 1947 he was diagnosed with Addison's disease.
Cause: emotional. In this chart, the adrenals are represented by Mars, which is afflicted in Taurus. Since Kennedy was born with the aspect, we know he had a latent weakness in his adrenals, which emerged as a disease just after his brother died and he was elected into congress.

Self-attack is always involved in an autoimmune disease and his chart shows that he felt threatened from affairs at home (Uranus in the 4H of family). He felt emasculated; perhaps felt attacked or attacked himself (square Mars) for not being able to measure up to his father's political aspirations. This may explain his promiscuity - trying to prove he was a man by having sex with many women.
Organ: base - adrenals, Mars and Venus.
Effect: Addison's disease. The immune system attacked (Mars) the adrenals and the salt-water regulating function was unbalanced (Venus disposits Mars). Mars represents the adrenals, the immune system and the attack on the adrenals and co-rules the 6H of health.

▲ (C) Mars. (O) Mars, Venus. (E) Uranus.

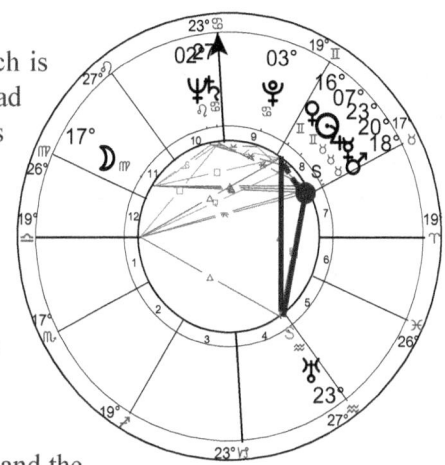

b. Adrenal disease

Dane Rudhyar (23 March 1895 01:00, Paris France)
Famed astrologer Rudhyar, his youth was marred by ill health. In 1908 when he was just 13 years of age, he had a life-threatening operation that removed his left kidney and adrenal gland.
Cause: emotional. Rudhyar had a busy and active mind (planets in Gemini) and could lose himself in his world of thought (Aquarius Moon), which could be negative and self-critical. This contributed to ongoing ory trouble when he was young (Mercury is afflicted in the 2H of values, and squares Mars and Pluto in the 6H of health).
Organ: base - adrenals, Mars and Venus.
Effect: adrenal disease. Malefics in Gemini, the sign that rules oxygenation, indicates difficulty with this function and consequent toxicity in the blood (Mars, the blood, conjunct Neptune, the bloodstream). Inflammation and an infection (Mars) occurred in the left-hand side upper urinary tract, in the ureters (square Mercury). It resulted in the left kidney and adrenal gland becoming diseased (Venus is afflicted in Aries and is semi-square Mars, Pluto and Neptune), requiring their surgical removal (Mars).

▲ (C) Mars. (O) Mars, Venus. (E) Mercury, Pluto, Neptune.

- In 1908, progressed Mars was at 19 Gemini, inconjunct natal Uranus in Scorpio. This represents the onset of the bacterial infection that struck the left side urinary tract and adrenal gland. Solar-arc Saturn, which is a ruler of the base chakra via the 3rd ray, was at 19 Scorpio conjunct natal Uranus. The disease was chronic and eventually the organ failed.

7b. Bladder, Kidney problems

a. Bladder infection and kidney stone

Una Chiodini (21 November 1936 10:58, Chicago IL)

American numerologist, palmist and astrologer. On 3 June 1993, she had a bladder infection and passed a kidney stone, starting after 1:30 PM.

Cause: emotional. Chiodini is an intense Scorpio, but when she gets angry or "pissed off", her natural impulse is to hold onto the aggravation and brood over things (ruler Mars that is emasculated in Libra, squares Venus in Capricorn in the 12H of hidden things). This breeds inner toxicity.

Organ: base - kidneys, bladder, Venus and Mars.

Effect: bladder infection. Chiodini is susceptible to urinary tract infections (Venus > Mars sextile Pluto in Cancer, the sign ruling the 6H of health).

- The infection she caught on June 3, occurred when solar-arc Mars was at 1 Sagittarius, conjunct natal Mercury, square the Moon. It triggered the natal infection-breeding circumstances. The transit Moon passed over these two points between 8 am and 12 noon, indicating the fertile period for the infection.

- Venus in crystallising Capricorn symbolises the kidney stone. Solar-arc Venus was at 3 Pisces, inconjunct Mars at 4 Libra, when the stone passed in 1993.

  ▲ (C) Mars. (O) Venus, Mars. (E) Pluto.

b. Kidney stone

Billy Joel (9 May 1949 09:30, Bronx NY)

American singer and writer of popular ballads. He went to a New York Hospital on 24 September 1989, for the removal of kidney stones.

Cause: emotional. Joel's instinct is to keep the peace and avoid conflict (Moon conjunct Neptune in Libra). He would rather gloss over problems than deal with them head on, something he learned at home (the Moon in the 4H of family rules the ascendant). But this built up inner tension and stress and led to health problems (the Moon is sesquiquadrate Venus, which in turn squares Saturn, the co-ruler of the 6H of health with Capricorn sharing the cusp).

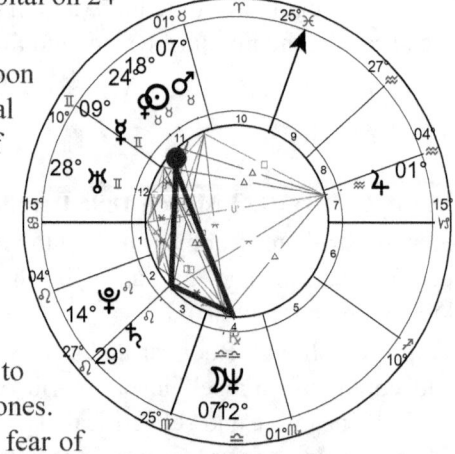

Organ: base - kidneys, Venus.

Effect: kidney stones. Joel developed kidney stones during his marriage to model Christie Brinkley. Venus square Saturn is a classic aspect for these stones. The marriage supposedly failed because of his drinking and infidelity. But fear of rejection and insecurity - the Venus > Saturn factor; really did the damage.

  ▲ (C) Moon. (O) Venus. (E) Saturn.

- On the day of surgery, transit Mars was at 3 Libra, square solar-arc Venus in the 12H of hospitals at 3 Cancer.

c. Kidney failure

Sarah Bernhardt (23 October 1844 20:00, Paris France)

French stage actress, the star of her day, who had a "larger than life personality". She was riddled with ill health from childhood into adulthood and died of kidney failure on March 26, 1923.

Cause: emotional. Bernhardt was emotional, volatile and expressive as actors tend to be (t-square: Cancer ascendant square the Moon and Uranus in Aries and Mars in Libra). This contributed to her ongoing health problems.

Organ: base - kidneys, Mars.

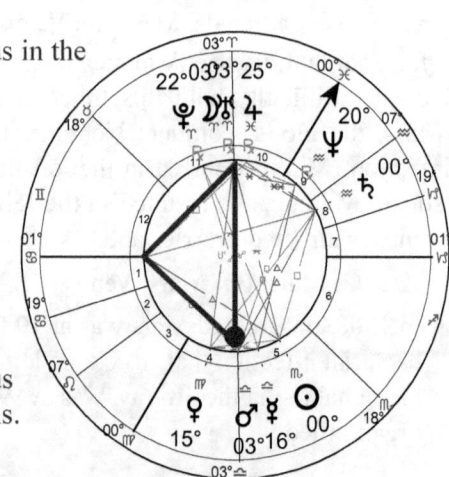

Effect: kidney failure. Kidneys are the cleansers of our system and Bernhardt's had a weakness (Mars afflicted in Libra opposite Uranus and the Moon). As her body started to age, they could no longer cope. Blood quality deteriorated affecting kidney health and a serious infection developed (Uranus > Mars that rules the 6H of health). The kidneys became diseased, they failed and she died (Mars trine Saturn in the 8H of death.

▲ (C) Moon, Uranus. (O) Mars. (E) Ascendant, Uranus.

- When she died, solar-arc Saturn, ruler of the 8H of death, was at 20 Aries moving over progressed Pluto (Lord of Death), at 21 Aries.

d. Kidney disease (Bright's disease, nephritis)

The kidneys become inflamed. It can lead to kidney failure if left untreated.

Georges Vallerey (21 October 1927 03:30, Amiens France)
French champion swimmer. In 1950 he was diagnosed with nephritis (inflammation of the kidneys). After four years of very painful treatments, he died on October 4 1954. He was just 27.

Cause: emotional. Mars and Venus rule the kidneys and they are both afflicted by sign, indicating both psychological and physical problems. Vallerey had low self-esteem. He was self-critical and tended to dwell on his problems, holding tension and stress in rather than releasing it (Venus in Virgo, ruling the 2H of values, in the 12H of self-undoing). This generated toxins in the blood (Venus semi-square Mars in Libra) making it harder for the kidneys to do their job.

Organ: base - kidneys, Venus and Mars.

Effect: Nephritis. The kidneys picked up a bacterial infection and because of their poor condition it spread rapidly (Venus quindecile Uranus; Mars inconjunct Jupiter that rules the 6H of health). He died (Mars rules the 8H of death).

▲ (C) Mars. (O) Venus, Mars. (E) Uranus, Jupiter.

- In 1950, solar-arc Moon reached 0 Libra opposite Uranus at 0 Aries and the disease took hold.
- In 1953, solar-arc Uranus was in the 8H of death at 26 Aries, moving opposite natal Mars at 26 Libra. In this period the kidneys were irreparably damaged.
- In 1954 when he died, solar-arc Moon had reached 4 Libra, the midpoint between natal Venus > Mars. This was the virulent core of the disease pattern. Transit Uranus was at 27 Cancer, square solar-arc Uranus at 27 Aries, in the 8H of death.

Astro.com 14834 (16 February 1982 10:45, Redmond WA).
American baby born with a severe kidney defect. We do not know if the child survived.

Cause: karmic. The danger to the kidneys is shown by three malefic planets in Libra that rules the kidneys, in the 6H of health that is also ruled by Libra. Saturn is one of the planets, pointing to kidney trouble in a previous life caused by the person's own choices and actions. All chronic illnesses in babies are karmic (Saturn conjunct Mars in this case). Parents who will pass the condition onto the child via their DNA are carefully chosen by the soul with this end in mind. These learning experiences teach us to take better care of the body.

Organ: base - kidneys, Venus and Mars.

Effect: kidney disease. The kidneys could not do their task of filtering urine due to a chronic defect in the organ (Venus in Capricorn square the planets in Libra). He was susceptible to kidney infections (Uranus septile Venus, semi-square Mars).

▲ (C) Saturn. (O) Venus, Mars. (E) Libra afflictions, Uranus.

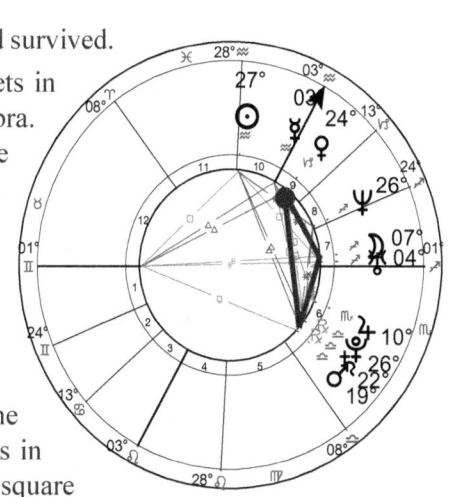

7c. Skeletal, Spine, Joint, Muscle Diseases

a. Arthritis - Osteoarthritis

Psychological friction that translates into physical friction can cause early onset osteoarthritis. In most cases, simple ageing is the cause. Cartilage wears away as bone rubs against bone.

Carole Hemstreet (6 July 1938, 06:21, Los Angeles CA)
American woman who in her 40's began to develop early onset osteoarthritis.
Cause: emotional. Difficulty with joints, especially when it occurs at a relatively early age (mid- 40's), suggests rigidity in attitude. Hemstreet was an emotional Cancerian who repressed her feelings (Cancer planets in the 12H of self-undoing square Saturn). She could be fixed and stubborn and this pattern underlies her arthritic condition. Saturn rules the 6H of health.
Organ: base - cartilage, bones, Saturn.
Effect: arthritis. Over time, cartilage (Saturn) wore away through friction (square Mars), and arthritis set in, restricting movement (Saturn semi-square Jupiter, and Mars sesquiquadrate Jupiter).
▲ (C) Mars, Saturn. (O) Saturn. (E) Saturn, Jupiter.

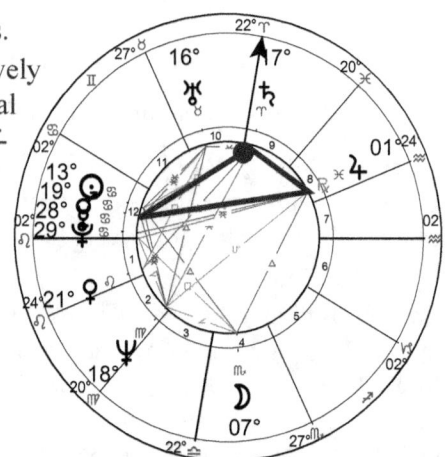

b. Bone - Osteoporosis

Sally Field (6 November 1946 04:23, Pasadena CA)
Popular American TV/ film actress, diagnosed with osteoporosis.
Cause: ageing. Trouble did not manifest until Field approached her 60th birthday indicating an age-related disease. She could be tough when she needed to be (Saturn-Pluto in Leo square Sun-Jupiter in Scorpio in the 1H), but she had an easy way about her that helped good energy flow in the body overall (grand-trine configuration - Saturn, Moon and Mercury-Venus).
Organ: base - bones, Saturn.
Effect: osteoporosis. 1st ray Saturn and Pluto in 1st ray Leo points to skeletal rigidity at some point in time (as well as future heart trouble). As she aged, minerals were leached from the bones (Uranus semi-square Saturn) and they became dry and brittle, impairing her mobility (sesquiquadrate Jupiter).
▲ (C) Saturn. (O) Saturn. (E) Uranus, Pluto, Jupiter.

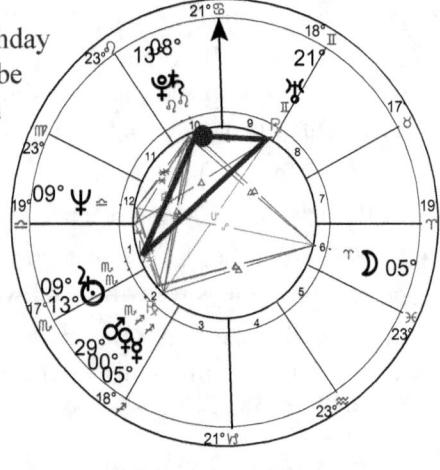

c. Arthritis - Rheumatoid Arthritis

In rheumatoid arthritis, the immune system attacks the joints, resulting in painful deformity and immobility.

Elsie Wheeler (3 September 1887 21:45, Norris City IL)
American spiritualist psychic who worked with Marc Edmund Jones to create the Sabian symbols - impressions for each degree of the zodiac. Wheeler was an astral psychic who worked through her solar plexus chakra (Moon in Pisces).
Cause: karmic-emotional. Crippled with arthritis and wheelchair bound from age 3, Wheeler was born with a powerful and destructive psychological pattern brought through from a previous life. The nature of her illness suggests she hated her body and thought it ugly (the Sun in critical Virgo squares the ascendant that governs the appearance).
Organ: base - bones and joints, Saturn.
Effect: rheumatoid arthritis. The toxicity generated by her negativity, triggered the immune system (Mars in Leo). It attacked the bones and joints (Saturn), twisting the body until it matched her thoughts and she was immobilised (square Jupiter in the 6H, and Jupiter inconjunct the ascendant).
▲ (C) Saturn, Mars. (O) Saturn. (C) Ascendant, Jupiter.

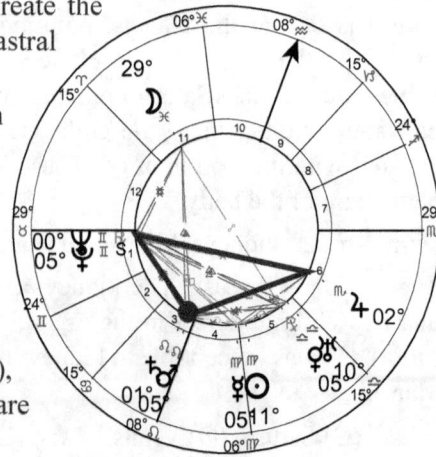

Jeanni (22 June 1949, 05:11, Bulawayo Zimbabwe)

Australian woman who contracted rheumatoid arthritis in 1988 and became partially crippled. But she managed to heal herself.

Cause: emotional. At the root of an autoimmune disease is a self-attack pattern and finding that pattern in the chart is vital.

> **Saturn is the key. It is the primary planet symbol of arthritis and its situation in the chart should reveal the attack pattern behind Jeanni's affliction. Saturn squares Mars - a classic pattern for arthritis.**

Jeanni can be her own harshest critic (Mars-Mercury square Saturn in Virgo), something she learned from her mother (Mercury rules the 4H of mother with Virgo on the cusp). Her inner child just accepted the verbal abuse and repeated it to herself because she was "bad and deserved to be punished." This pattern and Mars rose to the forefront in the late 1980's when she went through a crisis in a personal relationship.

Organ: base - bones and joints, Saturn.

Effect: rheumatoid arthritis. The immune system attacked her joints (Mars square Saturn), crippling and impairing her movement (Saturn inconjunct Jupiter in Aquarius). Mars rules the 6H of health.

▲ (C) Mars, Saturn. (O) Saturn. (E) Saturn, Jupiter.

Two important factors to consider:

1. Healing the self-attack pattern was an important spiritual goal for Jeanni. This is because Mars and Mercury are parked on the ascendant and the ascendant sign (Gemini in this case) and its higher esoteric ruler (Venus), represent the purpose of the soul in the current incarnation. Venus in Cancer tells us that healing the pattern will release Jeanni from deep grief concerning betrayal by loved ones (square to Neptune), and help restore her self-worth and self-esteem (in the 2nd house of values).

2. Saturn is a wing in a Yod pattern (Jupiter is at the apex of the Yod, inconjunct Sun-Uranus and Saturn). A Yod highlights the need for a change of perception so that an inner integration can be achieved. The message from Jupiter in Aquarius in the 8H, is for Jeanni to study the wisdom philosophies, develop a more inclusive and spiritually oriented perception of life; then use what she has learnt to free her from the self-judging pattern.

Chart set for March 1989.

By 1988, Jeanni was ready. She had obtained a degree in psychology and wrote a thesis on psychosomatic illnesses. She was also exploring alternative and spiritual healing approaches.

- A crisis was initiated by her soul when solar-arc Mars and the ascendant made conjunctions to natal Venus.

- Transit Pluto moved into the 6H of health - which it rules with Scorpio on the cusp and squared its natal position; initiating a midlife crisis connected with health.

- At the same time, solar-arc Jupiter reached 8 Pisces (square natal Mars at 8 Gemini). This brought the 2 patterns - the Health Triangle and the Yod, into a collision.

- Jupiter rules the 7H and Jeanni's important relationship was in trouble. Up came the attack pattern and arthritis struck. At the worst of it, she could only walk with assistance.

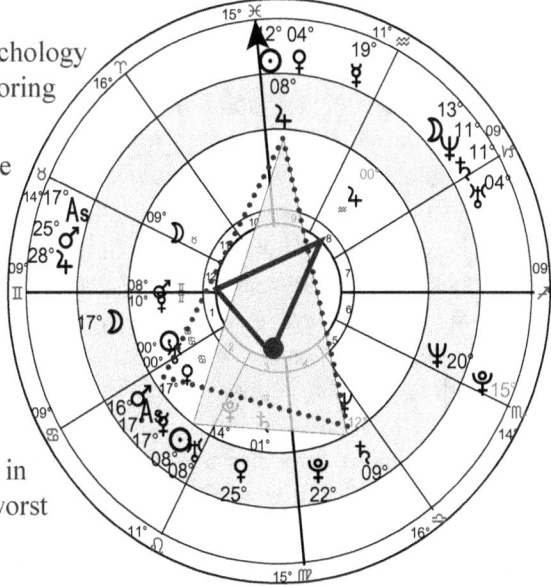

What did she do? Jeanni who is an astrologer, tells her story:

"A specialist told me I could end up in a wheel chair, but I refused to accept this and set out to heal myself. A deep tissue massage therapist would ask me to go into the physical pain in my body to retrieve painful emotional memories. As I recalled unhappy incidents, I cried a lot, releasing painful emotions through my tears. My naturopath put me on a cleansing program including juice fasting and I followed Jane Fonda's exercise video."

But the most important part of what I did was to meditate. I followed a taped, guided meditation where I visualised healing light and love flowing to my joints, restoring them to good health. In April 1990, the progressed Moon entered the 6H of health, allowing me to heal hidden issues with my mother and to work on the emotional body in a deeply purging way. In May 1990 the progressed Moon conjuncted transit Pluto. This was the catalyst for the healing. Within a year my body healed quite radically and I was walking normally, even running with joy on the beach again with my children."

d. Bursitis

Barry Manilow (17 June 1943 09:00, Brooklyn NY)

Popular singer and songwriter had surgery for bursitis (inflamed bursa) in his hips. Bursa are sacs of fluid around joints that provide cushioning.

Cause: emotional. One side of Manilow wants to be free to enjoy life (the Moon is in Sagittarius in the 5H of pleasure); but another side fears moving forward in life in case something bad happens or he gets attacked and is hurt (an easy-opposition pattern with Mars, Saturn).

Organ: base - the bursa, the Moon.

Effect: bursitis. The stress this inner conflict generated accentuated normal wear and tear on the body (Saturn). Friction (Mars) in the hip bursa (the Moon in Sagittarius), resulted in inflammation and pain (Mars).

▲ (C) Moon, Saturn. (O) Moon. (E) Saturn, Mars.

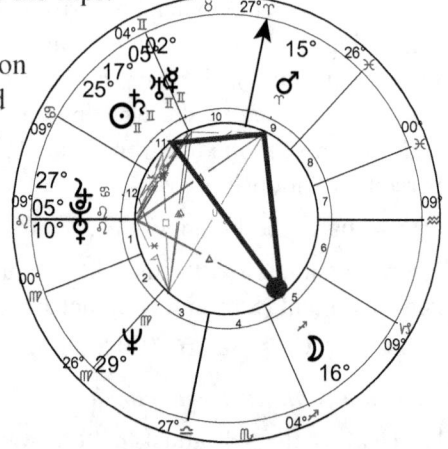

e. Spina Bifida

Spina bifida is incomplete closure of the vertebra around the spinal canal, leaving nerves exposed. Severe forms of the condition are accompanied by nerve defects and damage that impairs mobility, bowel and bladder function. The Sun, Leo and Saturn rule the spine.

Samuel Reynolds (22 November 1967 13:20, Buffalo NY)

American male, born with spina bifida, he endured 25 surgeries before age 21. The pain and suffering he experienced caused him to seek spiritual answers for his life. This is not surprising, mystical Neptune is conjunct his Sun. At age 12, he became a minister of his church and preached his first sermon in 1980. Then in 1990, after receiving counselling from an astrologer, he studied the science and became a dedicated student and teacher of astrology (Sun sextile Uranus).

- At that time in 1990, solar-arc ascendant had reached 28 Pisces and solar-arc Jupiter 27 Virgo. They made contact with the astrologer's planet Uranus at natal 28 Virgo. This encouraged him to make astrology his profession - Jupiter rules the 10H of career.

Cause: karmic. Saturn dominates the chart from the point of view it is the handle of a "bucket" planetary pattern. This makes its message powerful. It is afflicted, falling in Aries, retrograde and in an easy-opposition pattern with Uranus and the Moon in Leo in the 6H of health. On a physical level, the pattern represents the unfinished (Saturn) state of the spine and nerve endings. But on a metaphysical level, Saturn informs us that this affliction is karmic and provides opportunities to overcome adversity and make progress in life. With his achievements, he can show others (Saturn is in the 1H of the appearance), how they too can rise above their disabilities. He may have a physically damaged spine, but his psychic spine is dignified and erect (Saturn is in a grand-trine with the Sun and Moon in Leo).

Organ: base - spine, Leo and Saturn.

Effect: spina bifida. There was a serious aberration in the pattern of the etheric web (Uranus conjunct Pluto). Spinal closure work was incomplete and nerves were left exposed (easy-opposition pattern). Consequently, in his early years he spent a lot of time in hospital (Uranus rules the 12H of hospitals with Aquarius on the cusp), to fix the spine, nerves and associated health complications.

▲ (C) Saturn. (O) Leo, Saturn. (E) Uranus, Pluto.

f. Scoliosis

Rowena Wallace (23 August 1947 08:10, Coventry UK)
Australian actress of TV and theatre. At 19, she was diagnosed with scoliosis, a curve of the spine. She has required painkillers almost continuously since.
Cause: emotional. A stellium of 5 planets in Leo draws attention to the spine, which Leo rules. Positively, Leo represents our ability to stand erect and strong in life. The fact that the spine weakened indicates that Wallace wilted due to painful incidences in her teens. She was born with a morose and suspicious side (Moon falling in Scorpio). Perhaps she was bullied at school (Sun square Moon the 3H of formal education) and this started the damage.
Organ: base - spine, the Sun and Leo.
Effect: scoliosis. The spine (Sun in Leo), weakened (conjunct Venus), and became distorted, deviated from the norm (square the Moon in Scorpio and sextile Uranus). Scoliosis developed.

▲ (C) Moon. (O) The Sun, Leo. (E) Venus, Uranus.

- In the year prior to diagnosis, trouble started. The progressed Sun was in the 12H of hidden things at 16 Virgo, when transit Uranus and Pluto crossed it.
- Solar-arc ascendant was at 9 Libra, moving over natal Neptune. On a psychological level, it shows she was feeling vulnerable, weak and unsupported at that time in her life. The inherited weakness in the spine manifested.

Miscellaneous: muscle wall - Hernia

L1010 (8 September 1947 01:55 BST, Hawkwell UK)
Australian car mechanic who had an operation in 2009 to repair a stomach hernia - intestines had protruded through the abdomen lining.
Cause: emotional. Our subject was struggling to deal with the weight of emotional problems in his marriage at the time the hernia occurred. On a physical level, lifting heavy objects caused the problem.
Organ: base - intestines and the abdomen, Mercury and Virgo.
Effect: hernia. There was a weakness in the wall of the abdomen (Venus that weakens, is afflicted in Virgo, conjunct Mercury). Pressure (the Saturn-Pluto, aspect is midpoint Mars and Venus), caused a tear (Mars) and the intestines protruded through. It required corrective surgery and a short hospital stay (Mars in the 12H of hospitals). He has had many auto accidents in his life.

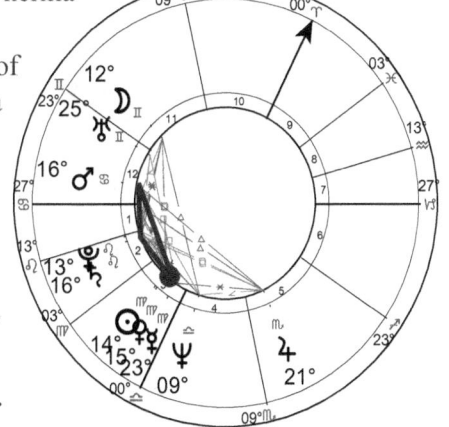

▲ (C) Mars, Saturn. (O) Mercury, Virgo. (E) Venus, Saturn-Pluto, Mars.

Miscellaneous: nerves at the base of the spine - Sciatica

Jeannie Longo (31 October 1958 15:00, Annecy France)
World champion French racing cyclist, who was plagued with sciatic nerve pain while racing in August 2008.
Cause: emotional. Longo thrives on mental and emotional tension. It helped make her a champion athlete (Mars opposite Mercury).
Organ: ajna - sciatic nerve, Mercury.
Effect: sciatica. During strenuous competition in 2008, Longo experienced excruciating pain in the sciatic nerve (Mercury opposite Mars and square Uranus in the 6H of health. Uranus squares Jupiter).

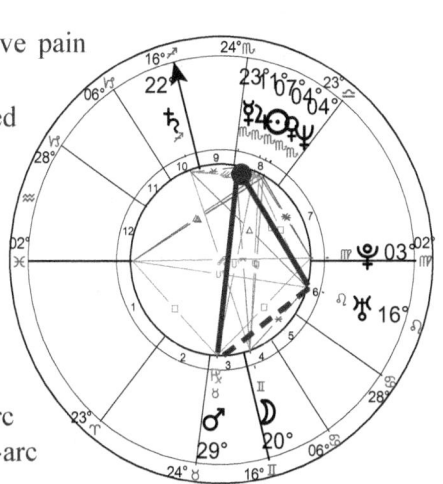

▲ (C) Mars. (O) Mercury. (E) Uranus, Jupiter.

- When the trouble happened in August 2008, transit Jupiter (which is related to the sciatic nerve), was at 12-13 Capricorn, moving over solar-arc Mercury at 13 Capricorn. At the same time transit Mars moved over solar-arc Uranus at 6 Libra.

7d. Skin and Hair

> Violent emotion.. If suppressed .. results in the poisons which.. find their outlet in certain cases of septic poisoning, in skin diseases.. [1]

a. Alopecia areata

Alopecia areata is hair loss that occurs when the immune system mistakenly attacks hair follicles.

L1006 (6 April 1951, 13:51, London UK)
Australian woman whose hair fell out at age 7 - shortly "after I fell off a swing". At 14 it grew back, only to fall out again at 21, then grew back at 28. Since then, only occasional patches fall. Saturn, which every 7 years makes a challenging aspect to its natal position, is involved.

Cause: emotional. Our subject can quickly fly into a panic when something unfortunate happens or she is criticised (the Moon and Sun are in Aries quindecile Saturn in Virgo; and Mars is in Aries inconjunct Saturn). The fact that she got alopecia, which drastically affects the appearance, suggests sensitivity about her appearance - the Sun rules the Leo ascendant.

Our subject confirmed that before age 7, she came to believe she was unloved because she was unattractive. She recalls vividly her mother telling her she was going to be adopted, and her uncle calling her "tubs". Falling off a swing was a metaphor for her feeling that she was unsupported.

Organ: base - the hair, Aries and Saturn.

Effect: alopecia areata. Unhappiness and self-criticism about her appearance sets off a panic attack (Uranus in Cancer that is disposited by the Moon). This in turn caused an autoimmune attack (the Sun and Mars) on hair follicles (Aries), and her hair fell out (Mars inconjunct Saturn).

▲ (C) Moon. (O) Aries, Saturn. (E) Mars, Uranus.

- At age 7, transit Saturn squared its natal position. This forced her to confront the "truth" she had formed about herself "that she was unattractive", and believing it, her hair fell out.
- At age 14, transit Saturn opposed its natal position and the Sun progressed into Taurus - a stabilising and maturing period for our subject. She felt stronger and more confident and her hair grew back.
- At age 21, transit Saturn squared its natal position. A failed relationship caused the negative belief to surface again. Solar-arc Mars had reached 19 Taurus and was moving over Venus. The immune system attacked and her hair fell out.
- At age 28-29, Saturn returned to its natal position. This is a maturing period, when a serious assessment of the life is made. With Saturn in the 2nd house, our subject learned to appreciate and value herself for the fine and accomplished woman she is and the problem virtually disappeared.

b. Eczema

Skin becomes rough and inflamed with blisters, causing itching and bleeding.

Jean Didier Wolfromm (21 May 1941 21:00, Paris France)
French novelist and literary critic who had chronic eczema.

Cause: emotional. Eczema is caused by an emotional disturbance. Wolfromm had fiery and irritable emotions, bubbling resentment and anger (Moon in Aries semi-square Uranus; Mars square Uranus).

Organ: base - skin, Saturn.

Effect: eczema. Emotional toxicity poisoned the blood (Mars in Pisces > Uranus), causing his eczema, skin eruptions and bleeding (Uranus conjunct Saturn that is in the 6H of health). Consequently, his appearance was marred (Saturn-Uranus opposite the ascendant).

▲ (C) Moon, Mars. (O) Saturn. (E) Uranus, ascendant.

---

[1] Bailey, Alice A; Letters on Occult Meditation, 159.

c. Leprosy

Leprosy is a bacterial infection that damages nerve endings causing numbness. Scaly white skin crustaceans make sufferers look like corpses. It is caught after repeated contact with a carrier of the disease.

Leprosy - case study (19 March 1896 19:50, Calcutta India)

This case is from Max Heindel's 'Astro-Diagnosis' page 305. He put the cause of leprosy in this case as "moral depravity".

Cause: karmic. Our subject had karma associated with the misuse of sex (Saturn in Scorpio: conjunct Uranus the ruler of the sacral chakra, square Mars, and opposite the Moon in Taurus in the 8H of sex).

Organ: ajna - nerves Uranus, Gemini and Aquarius; base - the skin Saturn.

Effect: leprosy. The leprosy bacteria (Uranus), infected the subject during sexual contact (Mars co-rules the 6H of health with Aries sharing the cusp). Nerve endings were damaged (Saturn conjunct Uranus, Neptune-Pluto in Gemini, and Pluto quindecile Uranus). White crustaceans covered the skin - the Moon's colour is white and it rules soft tissue.

▲ (C) Saturn, Mars. (O) Aquarius, Gemini; Saturn. (E) Mars, Uranus, Pluto.

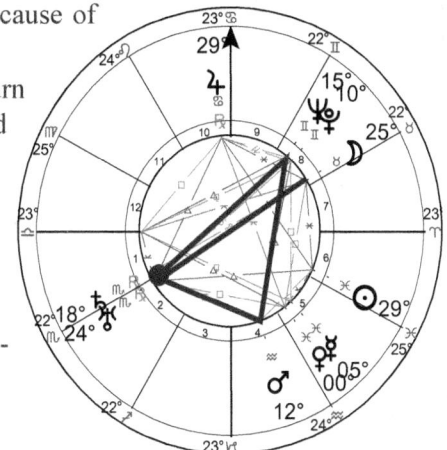

Father Damien (3 January 1840, 12:30, Tremelo Belgium)

Roman Catholic priest. He caught leprosy after sixteen years of working in a Hawaiian leper colony and died from the disease 15 April 1889.

Cause: karmic. Damien had karma to do with sex and hygiene. (Saturn in the 8H of sex is conjunct Mercury that rules hygiene and the 6H of health. Mercury is afflicted in Sagittarius, is sextile Mars and square Uranus). Perhaps he thought he was immune to the disease because for years he never caught it.

Organ: ajna - nervous system Mercury, base - the skin Saturn.

Effect: leprosy. Damien was infected with the leprosy bacteria (Uranus), which damaged nerve endings (square Mercury), causing numbness (Mercury-Saturn). Eventually his skin became covered with unsightly white crustaceans (Saturn and Mercury, conjunct the Moon).

▲ (C) Saturn. (O) Mercury, Saturn. (E) Uranus.

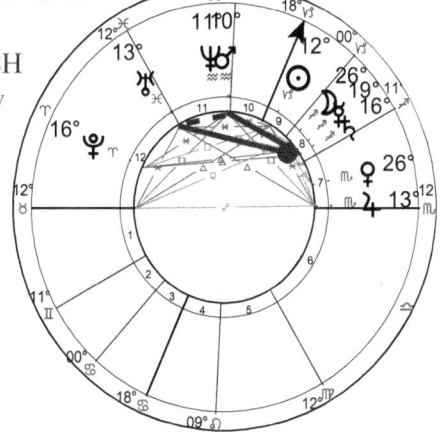

d. Lupus

Seal (19 February 1963 15:34, London UK)

English singer of African descent, Seal has extreme scarring on his face, the result of a cutaneous lupus that attacks the skin. He had it as a teenager. Lupus is an autoimmune attack that can affect any part of the body.

Cause: emotional. Seal's self-attack pattern is represented by a t-square, headed by Mars on the ascendant. This shows anger, simmering closely on the surface, caused by strange and unstable home-life conditions (square Neptune in the 4H), also cruelty and hardship (opposite Saturn, ruler of the 6H of health). Perhaps he was told that he was ugly or unworthy and believing it triggered the autoimmune attack on the face.

Organ: base - skin, Saturn.

Effect: lupus. The immune system attacked his face (Mars conjunct ascendant), causing scarring (Saturn).

▲ (C) Mars, Saturn. (O) Saturn (E) Mars, Saturn, Neptune.

- When he was 14, solar-arc Saturn was at 0 degrees Pisces, conjunct the natal Sun, the immune system. This is either the start of the attack or an acceleration of its attack on the body. Solar-arc Neptune was at 0 degrees Sagittarius, square the Sun.

e. Proteus Syndrome

A rare congenital disorder that causes skin overgrowth and atypical bone development, often accompanied by tumours over half the body.

Joseph Merrick, "Elephant Man" (5 August 1862 Leicester UK)
Unknown time, 12 PM midday used and the 0 degrees Aries House System. Born normal, Merrick's skin became thick and lumpy during the first few years of his life until he was grossly deformed with skin hanging off his head. He spent time in a workhouse, then as a professional "freak" in side-shows, called "the Elephant Man".

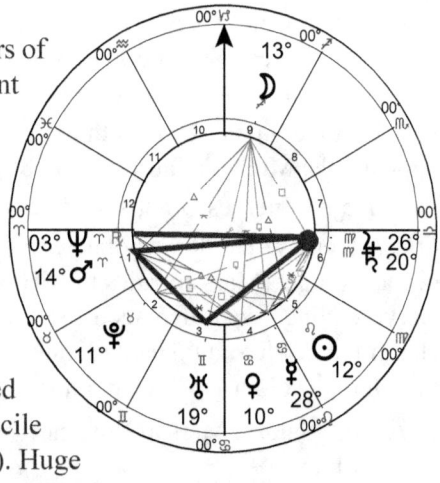

Cause: karmic. We do not have a birth time so cannot use the ascendant, the appearance, to help us find the disease pattern. Merrick had karma (Saturn) to do with sexual excess (conjunct Jupiter, square Uranus that rules the sexual, sacral chakra). Saturn is in Virgo, the natural ruler of the 6H of health.

Organ: base - skin Saturn, cells the Sun.

Effect: proteus syndrome. The growth factor (Jupiter) in the body was subverted (Jupiter afflicted in Virgo, conjunct Saturn, opposing Neptune, and quindecile Mars), so that cell-building (semi-square the Sun) went wild (square Uranus). Huge and freakish protuberances appeared on his head (Aries planets > Jupiter > Uranus; sesquiquadrate to Pluto). He went into a trade as a freak (Uranus is in Gemini and in the 3rd house that rules trade).

▲ (C) Saturn. (O) Saturn, Sun. (E) Jupiter, Uranus, Neptune, Pluto.

• Merrick's karma was exhausted before he died. He was befriended by a surgeon who was sympathetic to his plight and from 1886 until his death in 1890, lived quietly in a London Hospital with his friend.

f. Scleroderma

Scleroderma results from an overproduction of collagen in body tissues, caused by an autoimmune malfunction. There is chronic hardening and contraction of the skin and connective tissue throughout the body.

Alice Lon (23 November 1926 10:00, Kilgore TX)
American singer and dancer on The Lawrence Welk Show during its early years on television. She died "after a long battle" with scleroderma, on 24 April 1981.

Cause: emotional. Saturn rules the professional life and the disease surfaced sometime after Lon was fired from the Lawrence Welk show and had a vitriolic, public brawl with him. Lon must have been deeply embittered (Saturn in unforgiving Scorpio), because the disease appeared. Saturn rules the skin, scarring and hardening and co-rules the base chakra. It is central to the trouble.

Lon's Health Triangle includes the Moon, which always represents the "prison of the soul" pattern, or in modern psychological terminology, a negative core belief. Moon conjunct Pluto suggests a belief such as "I am bad and deserve to die"; opposite the ascendant - "Dangerous people want to hurt me". The public death (Moon-Pluto), of her employment (Pluto sesquiquadrate Saturn), was simply the proof that her beliefs about herself were true.

Organ: base - collagen, Saturn; connective tissue Mercury.

Effect: scleroderma. The immune system attacked (Mars afflicted in Taurus and retrograde) the body's collagen and connective tissue (inconjunct retrograde Mercury that is in detriment in Sagittarius. Mercury in turn conjuncts Saturn and rules the 6H of health, with Gemini on the cusp). Gradually hardened and scarred tissue (Moon-Pluto > Saturn), formed a tightened prison around organs and she died (the Sun rules the 8H of death with Leo on the cusp).

▲ (C) Moon, Pluto. (O) Saturn, Mercury. (E) Mars, Saturn, Pluto.

7e. Cancer in the Base chakra Organs

a. Adrenal Cancer

Gary Betty (4 March 1957, Atlanta Georgia)

Unknown time, 12 PM midday used and the 0 degrees Aries House System.

President and CEO of internet provider EarthLink, who was diagnosed with adrenal cortical cancer late 2006, dying January 3 2007.

Cause: emotional. Betty would hold in his frustration and anger until he exploded (Mars afflicted in Taurus, square Pluto). This pattern impacted negatively on his relationships (Pluto opposite Venus) and health.

Organ: base - adrenals, Mars.

Effect: cancer. Trouble in the solar plexus (Mars) and base (Pluto) chakras affected cells (Pluto in Leo) in the adrenals (Mars). Dangerous carcinogenic changes (ray 6 via Mars), led to adrenal cancer (Mars trine Jupiter afflicted in Virgo, the natural ruler of the 6H). He died - Pluto rules death.

▲ (C) Mars. (O) Mars. (E) Pluto.

- In late 2006 when the cancer made its rapid appearance, solar-arc Neptune, was at 21 Sagittarius inconjunct natal Mars, ruler of the adrenals. The cancer grew vigorously.

b. Bone Cancer

George Estregan (10 July 1939 12:25, Manila Philippines)

Filipino film actor and younger brother of former Philippine President Joseph Estrada. He died on 8 August 1988 of bone cancer.

Cause: emotional - karmic. Bone cancer indicates deep seated anger an emotional pain from the past that is held onto and not released. Saturn rules the skeleton and it is in a grand-cross. Estregan was bullied at home (Mars in the 4H of family), by carers (square Saturn, opposing Pluto in the 10H of father). Unable to fight back against his all-powerful tormentors (Pluto), he suppressed his rage and despair (Saturn square Mars) and it settled in his bones (Saturn).

Organ: base - bones, Saturn.

Effect: cancer. Homoeostasis (Libra ascendant) was destroyed (Saturn, Pluto). Bone (Saturn) cells turned malignant (square Pluto in Leo), and began to rapidly overbuild (Jupiter forms an easy-opposition pattern with Mars and Pluto). Within 8 months of diagnosis, he was dead (Jupiter square Venus, ruler of the 8H of death).

▲ (C) Mars, Saturn. (O) Saturn. (E) Pluto, Jupiter.

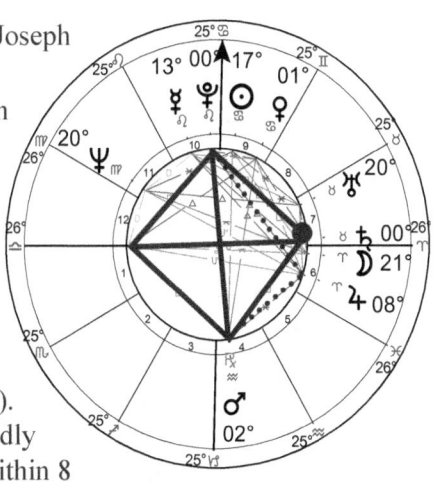

c. Bladder Cancer

Jon Hall (26 February 1915 22:00, Fresno CA)

Handsome Tahitian actor, who had surgery for bladder cancer in February of 1979, but shot himself on the 13th December 1979.

Cause: emotional. Mars rules the bladder (Venus is related), and both are in triangles that indicate the trouble. Hall may have felt "pissed off" (Moon opposite Mars) and guilty (conjunct Neptune), because of "sexual" things he did to further his career (Venus is in the business sign Capricorn, in the bartering 3H, opposite Neptune conjunct the MC).

Organ: base - the bladder, Venus and Libra.

Effect: cancer. There were carcinogenic (Neptune, Moon) changes in bladder cells (Venus, Mars), and surgery left him impotent and incontinent (Mars rules the 6H of health; Venus rules the 8H of sex and death); which would explain why he killed himself a year later, being unable to deal with the infirmity.

▲ (C) Moon. (O) Venus, Mars. (E) Neptune, ascendant.

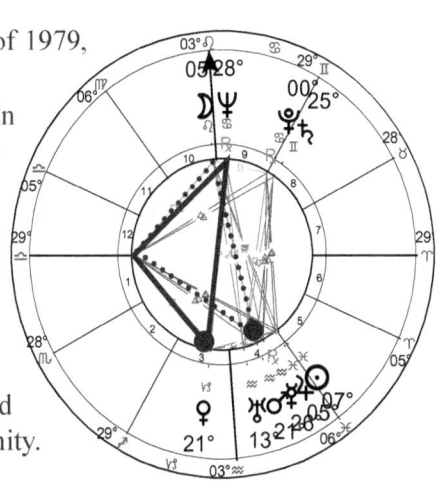

d. Melanoma (Skin)

John McCain (29 August 1936, 18:25, Colon Panama)

American politician and Senator from Arizona. He has had melanomas, on his back (1993), arm (2000), and nose (2002). In 2017, he was diagnosed with a glioblastoma, an aggressive brain cancer.

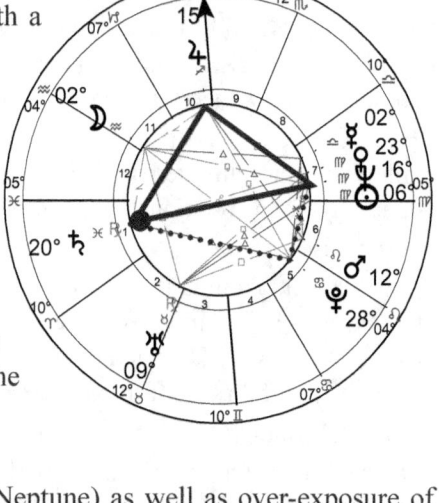

Cause: emotional. Saturn represents the skin. It is located in the 1st house that governs the body generally, and in Pisces that carries the 2nd ray that causes cell over-building. Further, it is in a stressful t-square, opposing Neptune (in detriment in Virgo), which represents potential carcinogenicity. We have the base arm of the Health Triangle.

Psychologically, the aspect represents a disciplined (Saturn), clamping down on any form of inner vulnerability or weakness (Neptune), in order to survive life challenges (Jupiter in Sagittarius). He grew a "tough skin". This helped him through his war years, but repression is a recipe for disease in the long term.

Organ: base - skin, Saturn.

Effect: cancer. Repression of emotional sensitivity and unexpressed grief (Neptune) as well as over-exposure of skin to the Sun (opposite ascendant), led to insidious cell changes (Neptune), and skin cancer developed (t-square: Saturn-Neptune-Jupiter).

▲ (C) Neptune. (O) Saturn. (E) Jupiter, Neptune.

- In 2017, McCain announced he had an aggressive brain cancer. The transference of malignancy from the base to the crown chakra brings Pluto into play - see the lower triangle in the chart. It is in Cancer, which rules the brain mass. At the announcement - by solar-arc, Pluto was at 18 Libra in the 8H of death.

Colin Bloomfield (22 February 1982 19:30, Montford Bridge UK)

English radio personality and sports commentator. In 2001, a malignant melanoma was removed from his leg. But it returned in 2013 and metastasized into his lungs. He died 25 April 2015.

Cause: emotional. There are two candidates for the skin - Saturn and Venus because it is in Capricorn. They are in mutual reception and square each other. Psychologically, Venus-Capricorn-Saturn people are very cautious in love. They fear showing their feelings, because to do so would expose them to rejection and emotional pain. Repression of affection has health repercussions.

Organ: base - skin, Saturn.

Effect: cancer. Scorching of the skin (Sun sesquiquadrate Saturn), caused aberrant (square Uranus) cell conditions in the skin of his thigh (Uranus in Sagittarius), which became cancerous (the Sun that carries the 2nd over-building ray, is in the 6H of health).

▲ (C) Pisces. (O) Saturn. (E) Sun, Uranus.

- In 2000, overexposure of the skin to the Sun triggered the malignant skin cells (the progressed Sun was at 21 Pisces inconjunct natal Saturn at 21 Libra.
- In 2012, the melanoma reappeared (progressed Sun was at 4 Aries, trine natal Uranus at 4 Sagittarius), and cancerous cells metastasized (Neptune, ruler of the bloodstream and lymph system, which spreads cells, was in Pisces transiting over the Sun). Cancer appeared in his lungs (the Sun co-rules the lungs).

Final words

We are all trying to live happy and successful lives and the breakdown of health cuts across that like a lightning bolt felling a tree. But often it is unnecessary. A moderate lifestyle, an adjustment in our nature to ease energy flow, a more positive life-outlook, the concentrated practice of harmlessness - this may be all that is required to keep disease at bay. At least in the earlier stages.

If a condition has progressed too far, so that a restoral of good health is not possible; such adjustments will ease the process of crossing over to the next life.

Either way, by giving people the information they need in a helpful and supportive context so they can begin to move forward positively again in time and space; is the task of the medical astrologer.

APPENDIX
Glossary

Antahkarana	A bridge of mental essence between the higher and lower minds, that serves as a medium of communication between the two.
Aspirant	Those who are aspiring to something higher and finer than ordinary material life.
Aura	Subtle invisible essence or energy that emanates from all living beings.
Buddhi	The Universal Soul. Spiritual love, whose faculty is the intuition. This level of consciousness is located at the Buddhic Plane level.
Chakras	Where many nadis/ energy strands cross in the etheric web, energy vortexes form. These are the etheric reception and distribution centres for energy, the chakras.
Consciousness	There are two levels of consciousness: self-consciousness that uses the ajna, and soul or higher consciousness that uses the crown.
Consciousness	- Thread: the thread of intelligence that comes directly from the soul and anchors in the head in the region of the pineal gland. There is the seat of "soul" consciousness.
Devas	The eastern equivalent of angels. Nature's builders.
Disciple	One who is pledged to a Master and who co-operates with the plans of the Masters as best he may. The personal task is to transform the nature, thereby taking initiation and become enlightened.
Djwhal Khul	Tibetan Master of the Wisdom, who worked telepathically with Alice Bailey (1880 - 1949), to dictate the content of most books published under her name.
Egoic Lotus	The Causal Body. It is the centre of human or soul consciousness and is formed from the conjunction of Buddhic and mental essence. All knowledge and wisdom accumulated throughout our incarnations is stored in the lotus, in its petals. Each petal in the lotus represents a quality. There are nine petals surrounding an inner bud, which is called the jewel in the lotus. Spiritual essence connects with that inner point. The lotus shatters at the 4th initiation when we become spiritually aware.
Enlightenment	In Bailey's work, enlightenment is associated with the 3rd initiation of Transfiguration, symbolised by Jesus on the mountaintop when he was flooded with spiritual light. In Buddhism, it seems to equal Monadic awareness, or esoterically, the 6th Initiation.
Esoteric	The words "esoteric" and "occult" signify "that which is hidden". They indicate that which lies behind the outer, the inner world of energies that produce the outer appearance and effects. In this book, 'esoteric' means more than this. It refers to the presence and influence of the soul in the life of the human personality. To understand esoterically, means to take into consideration the presence, the life, the energies, and the effects - of the soul, as it journeys through a series of incarnations towards enlightenment.
Esoteric Healing	Concerns the area in which the disease is to be found, its controlling etheric centre and its higher correspondence, and the energies coming from the soul. The remainder of his work involves the use the creative imagination and ability to move and direct energy currents. [1]
Etheric body	The energy framework/ blueprint upon which the dense physical body is constructed and with which it conforms. Underlying and interpenetrating the entire organism, the web gives the physical body quality, energy and life.
Indigenous disease	Three diseases (tuberculosis, cancer and syphilis) that are indigenous to our planet and to the matter from which our physical bodies are constructed. This means they are in our physical body DNA.
Initiates	Higher than a disciple in consciousness, but beneath a Master. One in whom soul and personality have fused, and who rules the human worlds. He is a spiritual man, a blend of scientific and religious training, who is guided by the Monad.
Initiation	An expansion of consciousness. Each initiation enables us to function consciously on a higher

---
[1] Bailey, Alice: Bailey, Alice: Esoteric Healing, 574-575.

	level than before, and to express a greater proportion of wisdom.
Karma	The law of cause and effect. It is the power that controls the behaviour of all things.
Kundalini	The power of physical life, the fire of matter. It is centred in the base chakra and rises up the spine when man connects consciously with his spiritual nature.
Life-thread	Synonyms are sutratma, silver cord and thread soul. It originates from the Monad and via the soul, it anchors in the heart. Life force streams along the life-thread.
Logos	Gk: the word of God, in some cases it can represent God. The divine Life behind the sun is the solar Logos. This level of God-consciousness is located at the Logoic Plane level.
Manas	Spiritual mind.
Master	A Master of the Wisdom has expanded His centre of consciousness to include the plane of spirit.
Monad	It is the spiritual Spark, the God aspect in our nature anchored in the pineal gland.
Mystic	One who senses divine realities from the heights of aspiration. Who contacts the mystical vision through prayer, adoration and worship, then longs ceaselessly for the constant repetition of the achieved ecstatic state. The mystic must eventually become an occultist.
Occult	See "Esoteric".
OM	A sacred word, sound or vibration. When we sound an OM with positive intent, the vibration purifies our nature and brings us into alignment with the soul.
Path (the)	An abbreviated term for the Path of Spiritual Development, also called the Path of Discipleship. We step onto the Path when we begin to aspire to something higher and finer than ordinary material life. It is the call or influence of the soul, of our spiritual nature that awakens this desire within us.
Permanent atom	There are five, one on each of the five planes of human evolution. The Monad appropriates them for the purposes of manifestation. Around them the various sheaths or bodies are built. They are small force centres that carry the "DNA" of a person's bodies from life to life.
Planet pattern	A recognised arrangement of planets that represent patterns of energy flow. Some such as a grand-trine represent an easy flow of energy, others such as the t-square represent blockages and disruptions.
Prana	The Life Principle, the breath of Life.
Raja Yoga	The Royal Science of the Mind, or union with the Divine through mind. It involves the exercise, regulation and concentration of thought.
Ray	One of the seven fundamental energy streams of force in the universe, a ray of energy.
Rayology work	7 Ray Personality Profiling is a stand-alone science and is not included in this book. The technique is comprehensive; consciousness is examined at the soul, personality, mental, emotional and physical levels. There is a slight similarity with Myers-Briggs Type Indicator.
Shamballa	The seat of world spiritual government, headed by Sanat Kumara.
Soul	The consciousness aspect in all living things. The human soul (egoic lotus or causal body) is the storehouse of man's expanding soul knowledge, love and wisdom. The Solar Angel mentors the human soul.
Souls old, young	From one angle, old soul/ young soul refers to the time period we have been cycling through incarnation on the Path of Evolution. Older souls started before younger souls. However, from another angle - since some souls travel faster on the Path because they make a greater effort, it refers to wisdom. Older souls have a more expanded consciousness, are wiser, more intelligent and compassionate than younger souls.

BIBLIOGRAPHY

Bailey, Alice. A. *A Treatise on Cosmic Fire.* Lucis Press, London, fifteenth printing 1999.

Bailey, Alice. A. *A Treatise on White Magic.* Lucis Press, London, nineteenth printing 2001.

Bailey, Alice. A. *Destiny of the Nations.* Lucis Press, London, third printing 1968

Bailey, Alice. A. *Discipleship in the New Age I.* Lucis Press, London,

Bailey, Alice. A. *Discipleship in the New Age II.* Lucis Press, London, fifth printing 1979.

Bailey, Alice. A. *Esoteric Astrology.* Lucis Press, London, eighteenth printing 2016.

Bailey, Alice. A. *Esoteric Healing.* Lucis Press, London, eighth printing 1977.

Bailey, Alice. A. *Esoteric Psychology I.* Lucis Press, London, ninth printing 1979

Bailey, Alice. A. *Esoteric Psychology II.* Lucis Press, London, eighth printing 1981.

Bailey, Alice. A. *Externalisation of the Hierarchy.* Lucis Press, London, seventh printing 1982.

Bailey, Alice. A. *From Intellect to Intuition.* Lucis Press, London, sixth printing 1965.

Bailey, Alice. A. *Glamour: A World Problem.* Lucis Press, London, third printing 1967.

Bailey, Alice. A. *Initiation, Human and Solar.* Lucis Press, London, sixth edition 1951.

Bailey, Alice. A. *Letters on Occult Meditation.* Lucis Press, London, eleventh printing 1973.

Bailey, Alice. A. *The Soul and its Mechanism.* Lucis Press, London, fifth printing 1971.

Bailey, Alice. A. *Telepathy.* Lucis Press, London, sixth printing 1971.

Carter, C.E.O. *An Encyclopaedia of Psychological Astrology,* Theosophical Publishing House London, 1963

Cornell, H. L., M.D. *The Encyclopaedia of Medical Astrology.* third edition, 1972.

Cramer, Diane. L. Dictionary of Medical Astrology. American Fed. Astrologers, 2003.

Daath, Heinrich. *Medical Astrology.* Cosimo Classics, NY. 2005.

Hay, Louise. L. *Heal your Body.* Published by Louise L. Hay. Revised edition 1984.

Heindel, Max. *Astro-Diagnosis. A Guide to Healing.* Rosicrucian Fellowship, tenth edition, 2011.

Hodgson, Leoni, Ph.D. *Journey of the Soul.* Kindle Direct Publishing, seventh edition 2018.

Hodgson, Leoni, Ph.D. *Astrology of Spirit, Soul & Body.* Kindle Direct Publishing, 2018.

Hodgson, Leoni, Ph.D. *Encyclopaedia of Medical & Psychological Astrology.* Kindle Direct Publishing, 2023.

Jacka, Judy. N.D. *Synthesis in Healing.* Hamptons Roads Publishing Company, Inc. 2003

Jacka, Judy. N.D. *Esoteric Healing workbooks 1-4.* Published by Judy Jacka.

Jansky, Robert. C. *Modern Medical Astrology.* Astro-Analytics Pub. CA., second revision 1978.

Lansdowne, Zachary, F. Ph.D. *The Chakras and Esoteric Healing.* Samuel Weiser, Inc. 1986.

Millard, Margaret. M.D. *Casenotes of a Medical Astrologer.* Samuel Weiser, Inc. 1984.

Tansley, David. V. D.C. *Radionics and the Subtle Anatomy of Man.* Penguin Random House. 1972.

Tansley, David. V. D.C. *Chakras - Rays and Radionics.* C.W. Daniel Co. Second impression 1985.

Tyl, Noel. *Astrological Timing of Critical Illness.* Llewellyn Publications. First edition 1998.

INDEX

Symbols

1 Charts
    Chart 1: Planet rulers of the Signs 6
    Chart 2: Seven Rays and Astrology 13
    Chart 3: Sign rulerships in the Body 29
    Chart 4: the 7 Major Chakras 79
    Chart 5: Disrupted Energy Flow resulting in Disease 99
    Chart 6: Planet Dignities, Detriments, Exaltations and Fall 106
    Chart 7: RAYS: Psychology - Disease - Astrology 124
    Chart 8: CHAKRAS: Body - Disease - Astrology 125
    Chart 9: SIGNS: body parts ruled and disease 126
    Chart 10: PLANETS: body parts ruled and disease. 127

2 Diagrams
    Astrology - Chakra Divisions 94–95
    Chakras 78
    Chakras and the Glands 79
    Pranic Triangle 122
    Rays in the solar system 12
    Seven Rays and Astrology 13
    Spirit, Soul, Body 2
    The 7 Rays in our system 12
    The Path and Consciousness 3

A

Aadland, Florence 195
Abortion 45, 59, 65, 75, 91
    case study 208
Abscess, abscesses 21, 25–26, 31, 37, 59, 65, 81, 89, 124
Accident, accidents, accidental 25, 31, 47, 65, 93, 101, 104, 117, 127, 130
    case studies 161
        car accident 157, 203
        horse-riding accident 165
        skiing accident 145
    defined 101
    how to check for potential accidents 129–130
Achondroplasia (dwarfism) 27, 71, 91
    case study 206
Acidic, acidosis 25, 65, 89, 124, 127
Acid reflux 25, 37, 59, 65, 89
    case study 194
Acne 25, 31, 65, 89
Acromegaly 63, 67, 71, 83
    case studies 167
Adadevoh, Ameyo 191
Adams, John Quincy 149
Addict, addiction, addictions, addictive 24–25, 33, 36–37, 45–47, 52–53, 59, 66, 72–73, 91, 126–127
    case studies
        cocaine addiction 161, 201
        drug addiction 189, 196, 198
        smoking, drinking 108

Addison's disease 43, 93
    case study 213
Adenoids 19, 33, 53–54, 63, 85
ADHD: attention deficit (hyperactivity) disorder 19, 61, 65, 71, 85
    case study 202
Adrenaline 15, 45, 64–65, 75, 92, 127
Adrenals 14–15, 42–45, 63–65, 68, 74–75, 79, 92–93, 99, 125–127
    case studies
        adrenal cancer 223
        adrenal disease 213
        chronic fatigue 191
Ages, aging 49, 124, 126–127
    soul begins to separate itself 141
AIDS 25, 27, 39, 57, 65, 73, 75, 125
    case study 190
Airways 21, 35, 60–61, 85, 104, 125, 127
    case studies
        breathing problems 172–175
        cystic fibrosis 206
        sleep apnoea 148
AJNA Chakra
    0-overview 82–83
    case studies
        Acromegaly 167
        ALS: motor neurone disease 162
        Asperger's 170
        Autism 169–170
        Blinded - Injuries 157–158
        Blinded - virus 158
        Cerebral palsy 162
        Congenital blindness 156
        Congenital deafness 154
        Deafness - measles 155
        Deafness - otosclerosis 155
        Dwarfism 167
        Epilepsy 163
        Glaucoma 159–160
        Guillain-Barre Syndrome 163
        Insanity - crystallised thinking 171
        Migraine 168
        Multiple sclerosis 164
        Nose - broken 161
        Nose - cocaine damage 161
        Parkinson's disease 165–166
        Pituitary tumours 109
        Polio 165
        Quadriplegia 165
        Shingles 166
        Sinusitis 161
        Tourette's syndrome 166
Alcoholism 12, 25, 65, 73, 89, 124, 126–127
    case studies 202
Alimentary canal 33, 41, 60, 180
Ali, Muhammad 165
Allergies, allergic 21, 35, 37, 59, 85, 89, 124, 127
    case studies
        anaesthetics 192
        bee stings 192
        gluten 193
        milk 193
Alopecia 31, 89
    case study 220

ALS: amyotrophic lateral sclerosis 35, 47, 61, 65, 71, 83
    case study 162
Alta-major 19, 35, 61, 69
Alveoli 19, 35, 61, 85
Alzheimer's 53, 73, 75, 81, 124
    case studies 150–151
Amputates, amputation 65
Amyloidosis 17, 124, 141
Anaemia 27, 39, 51, 71, 87
    case studies 186
        aplastic 183
        pernicious 183
        sickle cell 184
Anal fissure 25, 45, 65, 75, 85
Anaphylaxis shock 25, 65, 71
    case study 192
Aneurysm 73, 87, 125
    case studies 144, 187
Anger (see Emotions) 182
Angina 39, 51, 87
    case study 185
Ankles 29, 50–51, 70–71, 93, 105, 108, 126–127
Ankylosis spondylosis 25, 39, 69, 93
Anorexia 25, 37, 89
    case study 201
Anus 19, 40, 45, 61, 74–75, 85, 88
    case study - hemorrhoids 182
Anxiety 5, 21, 25, 37, 58–59, 72, 81, 89, 117, 125
    in case studies 148, 167, 172, 176, 179, 186, 191, 195, 198, 204–205
Aorta 39, 56–57, 67, 87
Aphasia 35, 61, 85
Appendicitis 25, 41, 61, 85
Appendix 19, 41, 53–54, 61, 85, 126
AQUARIUS - overview 50–51
ARIES - overview 30–31
Arms, arm 29, 34–35, 40, 60–62, 84, 126–127
    in case studies 185
        cutting 203
        melanomas 224
Arrested development 57, 67
Arrhythmia 27, 39, 71, 87, 109, 124, 127
    case study 189
Arteries 14, 32–33, 39, 51, 57, 66–67, 72, 84, 86, 108, 127, 129
    and the Path of Outgoing 57
    in case studies 144, 149, 153, 185, 187–189
Arteriosclerosis 51, 67, 87, 124
    case study 187
Arthritis 33, 47, 49, 67, 69, 85, 93, 110, 124
    case studies 141, 207
        osteoarthritis 216–217
        osteoporosis 216
        rheumatoid arthritis 132–134, 216–217
Asperger's 23, 51, 61, 63, 83
    case studies 169–170

Asphyxia 35, 45, 61, 75, 85
Assassinates, assassination 15, 65, 75
Asthma 21, 35, 85, 124–125
    case studies 172
Astigmatism 27, 31, 83
Astral maniac 25, 65, 89
Astro.com case study charts
    3118 174
    5976 211
    6814 193
    7221 190
    10068 207
    12077 148
    12437 207
    12768 207
    13234 207
    13650 207
    13748 207
    13842 154
    14115 155
    14834 215
    37914 204
    44645 204
    Karen 192
Ataxia 35, 43, 47, 61, 67, 81
Athlete's foot 37, 53, 59, 73
Atrial fibrillation 27, 39, 71, 87
    case studies 189
Autism 23, 51, 61, 63, 83, 126
    case studies 169–170
Autoimmune disorders 25, 39, 65, 87, 124–125, 127
    case studies
        Addison's dis. 213
        alopecia areata 220
        ALS 162
        celiac dis. 193
        colitis 181
        Graves' dis. 176
        Guillain-Barre Syndrome 163
        hashimoto's dis. 176
        lupus 221
        multiple sclerosis 164
        pernicious anaemia 183
        rheumatoid arthritis 217
        scleroderma 222
        type-1 diabetes 197
    cause of 114

B

Baby, babies 36–37, 58–59, 90, 127, 152
    case studies 156, 163, 188, 193, 207–209, 211, 215
Baby Doe 207
Back pain 39, 49, 69, 93
Bacterial infection 27, 31, 70–71, 124, 127
    case studies 147, 154, 160, 172–174, 182, 193, 211, 213, 215, 221
Bad breath 61, 85
Bakker, Tammy 180
Baldness 31
Barrenness 37, 59, 91
Barrett, Rona 207
BASE chakra

0-overview 92–93
case studies
    Addison's disease 213
    Adrenal disease 213
    Alopecia 220
    Bladder infection 214
    Bursitis 218
    Cancer - adrenal 223
    Cancer - bladder 223
    Cancer - bone 223
    Cancer - melanoma 224
    Eczema 220
    Hernia 219
    Kidney disease 215
    Kidney failure 214
    Kidney stone 214
    Leprosy 221
    Lupus 221
    Osteoarthritis 216
    Proteus syndrome 222
    Rheumatoid arthritis 216–217
    Sciatica 219
    Scleroderma 222
    Scoliosis 219
    Spina Bifida 218
Becker, Cacilda 144
Beethoven, Ludwig van 154
Bells Palsy 35, 61, 83
Berlusconi, Silvio 161
Bernhardt, Sarah 214
Berry, Fred 162
Berry, Halle 197
Betty, Gary 223
Biden, Joe 144
Bile 19, 37, 66, 69, 89
Bipolar 21, 37, 61, 71, 89
    case studies 202
Birth 14, 36, 40, 90, 110, 126–127, 133
    in a case study 144, 146, 154, 156–158, 160, 162, 167, 186, 188–189, 193, 206, 209
Birthmark 49, 93
Bladder 18–19, 43–45, 65, 74–75, 92–93, 108, 126–127
    case studies
        bladder infection 214
        cancer 223
        no bladder 210
        spina bifida 218
Blind, blindness vi, 24, 31, 59, 83
    case studies 156–160, 171
Bloats, bloating 37, 41, 59, 67, 124
    case studies 193
BLOOD, bloodstream 14–18, 24–25, 27, 35, 38–39, 43, 51–53, 56–62, 64–67, 70–71, 81, 87–88, 124–127
    blood cells
        red 64, 84, 183–184
        white 36, 39, 53, 56, 58, 177, 186–187
    blood pressure
        high 189
    case studies
        anaemia, aplastic 183
        anaemia, pernicious 183

        anaemia, sickle cell 184
        aneurysm 144
        angina 185
        arteriosclerosis 187
        deep vein thrombosis 185
        ebola 191
        haemophilia 184
        hypertension 187
        leukaemia 186
        polio 165
        stroke 111, 149
        vascular dementia 153
    oxygenation, oxygenated 34, 60, 62, 66, 84
    pressure 43, 80–81, 117
        high 144, 149, 182, 187
    the heart fails to pump 189
Bloomfield, Colin 224
Bocelli, Andrea 159
Body fluids 21, 36, 45, 52–53, 58, 72, 104, 126–127
    in case studies 191, 206
    white body fluids 36, 59, 126
Boils 21, 25, 65, 71
Bone marrow 36–37, 49, 53, 59, 93
    problems 141, 183, 186–187
Bones 14–15, 19, 26, 31–32, 35, 48–50, 52–53, 63, 68–69, 89, 93, 99, 125–127
    cartilage problems 206, 216
    case studies
        achondroplasia 206
        bone cancer 223
        broken nose 161
        bursitis 218
        osteoarthritis 216
        osteoporosis 216
        otosclerosis 155
        rheumatoid arthritis 216–217
        scoliosis 219
        spina bifida 218
Bono, Sonny 145
Booth, Evangeline 187
Borderline personality disorder 25, 57
Borkowski, Georgie 157
Bowel, bowels 19, 25, 41, 45, 65, 75, 85, 104, 108, 126
    case studies 218
        bowel cancer 140, 180
        cholera 182
        colitis 181
        crohn's disease 181
        diverticulitis 181
        food poisoning 194
        hemorrhoids 182
Boyle, Susan 170
Brain 7, 14–15, 18–23, 30–31, 33, 36, 49, 53, 58–65, 69, 73, 80–83, 104, 108, 124–126
    brain higher 80
    brain lower 82, 84–85, 125, 172
    case studies
        aneurysm 144
        Asperger's 170
        autism 169
        brain cancer 145, 224

brain trauma 145–146
cerebral palsy 162
dementia 150–153
down's syndrome 207
hydrocephalus 146
meningitis 147
migraine 168
multiple sclerosis 114, 164
PTSD 205
stroke 111, 149
goodwill stabilises 122
Brainstem 35, 61, 126
Brand, Russell 202
Breasts 19, 29, 37, 59, 126
case studies - cancer 199
Breath, breathing 14–15, 18, 31–32, 35, 61, 85, 125, 228
case studies: impaired breathing 161, 176
asthma 172
bronchitis 172
croup 173
diphtheria 173
emphysema 173, 179
hay fever 174
influenza 174
pneumonia 174
sleep apnoea 148
tuberculosis 175
exercises 121–122, 134
Breivik, Anders 171
Bright's disease - see nephritis 215
Bronchial tree/ tract 18–19, 34–35, 60–61, 84–85, 126–127
case studies 172, 179
Bronchitis 21, 35, 37, 59, 61, 85, 124
case studies 172–173
Bronte, Charlotte 168
Brown, Melanie 157
Bruises 65, 87
Bubonic plague 71
Bulimia 25, 37, 89
case study 203
Burns 17, 25, 49, 57, 65, 124, 126–127
Bursitis 49, 69, 93
case study 218
Burton, Richard 202
Bush, George 176

C

Calcium 49, 68–69, 93
Calf, calves 50–51, 70–71, 126–127
Campbell, Glen 151
Cancer (disease) 15, 17, 53, 57, 59, 67, 75, 81, 89, 100, 104, 124, 126–127, 135, 196
case studies 140
adrenal 223
bladder 223
bone 223
bowel 140, 180
brain 145
breast 199
cervical 212

hodgkin's 177
leukaemia 186
liver 200
lung 179
lymphatic 177
melanoma 224
mouth and jaw 178
ovarian 212
pancreatic 200
pituitary 109, 112
prostate 212
stomach 200
testicular 112
throat 178
cause of 15, 17, 37, 89
defined 89
indigenous disease 37, 59, 100, 104, 227
to find in the chart 15, 89
CANCER (sign) - overview 36–37
Candida 21, 25, 37, 59
CAPRICORN - overview 48–49
Carbohydrates 43, 62–63, 197
Carcinogenic 21, 53, 73, 75
defined 21
in case studies 145, 178–180, 199–200, 212, 223
Cardiomyopathy 39, 65, 87
Cardiovascular system 16–17, 38–39, 56–57, 62, 66, 81, 87, 103, 108
2nd ray uses 16
cause of its diseases 39
immune system is a subset of 56
in case studies 149, 183–191
nourishes all cells in the body with blood. 87
organs of 57
vessel for vitalisation 87
Carole - bowel cancer 140
Carotid glands, arteries 19, 32–33, 63, 85, 125
Carpal tunnel 27, 35, 61, 85
Carpenter, Karen 201
Cartilage 48–49, 68–69, 93, 126
in case studies 161, 206, 216
Castration 45, 65, 75, 91
Cataracts 31, 59, 83
case studies 159, 207
Catarrh 21, 35, 37, 59, 85
Celiac/ coelic disease 21, 41, 61, 85
case studies 193
Cells
cell-life 57, 73, 87, 109, 125, 127
physical body cells ruled by ray 3 19
red blood cells 39, 64–65, 84
in case studies 183–184
Mars rules 64
stem cells 19, 37, 59, 87, 126
white blood cells 36–37, 39, 53, 56, 58–59
Cancer, Moon rule 58
in case studies 177, 186
Central nervous system - see Nerves 18
Cerebellum 19, 31, 35, 61, 67, 84–85, 126
Cerebral cortex 19, 31, 81, 83

case study 144
Cerebral palsy 27, 31, 35, 61, 71, 83, 125
case study 162
Cerebrum 31, 80–81, 81, 125
Cervical vertebrae 33, 69
cervical osteoarthritis 33, 85, 93
Cervix 19, 36–37, 59, 90–91
case studies - cancer 212
CHAKRAS (see individual Chakras)
0-overview 77–93
Chart 2: The Seven Rays and Astrology 13
Chart 8: Chakras. Body - Disease - Astrology. 125
clearing, vitalising chakras 122
congestion 16, 79, 89, 110
in a case study 145, 150, 172, 177–178, 200, 206
defined 13, 79, 227
visualise the chakras in the spinal column 79
Chaplin, Charles 185
Cheek, James 159
Chemotherapy 15, 71, 75
in a case study 141, 177, 196
Chevenement, Jean-Pierre 192
Chicken pox 25, 27, 73, 85
Chills 127
Chin 32–33
Chiodini, Una 214
Chlamydia 25, 27, 45, 91
Cholera 27, 41, 61, 65, 71, 85
case studies 182
Cholesterol 67, 87, 124
in a case study 187
Chromosome 51
in a case study 207
Chronic disease 49
defined 132
health readings 135–137
Chronic fatigue (see fatigue) 191
Churchill, Randolph 211
Chyle 37, 41, 59, 89
Circadian rhythm 80–81
in a case study 148
Circulation 4, 27, 35, 51, 53, 57–59, 61, 70–71, 76, 78, 87, 105, 122, 124–127
in case studies 103, 108, 129–130, 136, 165, 183–185, 187
Cirrhosis, liver 37, 67, 89, 99
case study 195–196
Clapton, Eric 194
Clavicle 35
Cleavage (psychological) 98
defined 22–23, 51, 169
in a case study 169–170
Clients, 3 types 117
Clitoris 19, 45, 63, 90–91
Clooney, Rosemary 179
Clot, clots, clotting (blood) 67, 124
in case studies 184–185, 191
Coburn, James 132–133

Cocaine - case study 161
Coccyx - tailbone 44, 47–48, 48, 67, 69, 92
Cold, common 25, 27, 53, 73, 85, 124, 127
Cold, in character 16, 23, 48, 62, 68, 125
    in a case study 171, 203
Cole, Nat King 194
Colic 19, 41, 61, 85
Colon 19, 41, 45, 65, 74–75, 85
    case studies
        colitis 181
        colon cancer 180
        diverticulitis 181
Colour therapy 122
Coma 31, 61, 81, 124
    in case studies 147, 192, 197
Conception 19, 37, 45, 58–59, 65, 91
    case studies - infertility 209
Concussion 31, 65, 81
Confusion 104
    in case studies 152, 167
Congenital 81, 91
    case studies 162–163
        blindness 156
        cataracts 159
        deafness 154–155
        glaucoma 160
        heart disease 188
        hydrocephalus 146
        proteus syndrome 222
    defined 91, 206
Congests, congestion, congestive 21, 36, 85, 110, 122, 124, 127
    case studies 145, 161, 177, 180, 182, 188–189
    chakras, etheric 16, 37, 78–79, 89, 110
        case studies 145, 150, 172, 177–178, 199–201
    emotions, emotional 21, 37
        case studies 172–173, 180, 206, 210
    removes congestion 122
Conjoined twins 210
Conjunctivitis 25, 27, 31, 71, 83
Connolly, Billy 109
Consciousness 56
    0 - Evolution of 2–7
    defined 16, 34, 48
    development of 60
    does not die 101
    Pluto never destroys 74
    thread 16–17, 60–61, 74, 125, 127
        defined 81, 227
        in case studies 163, 169–170
        withdraws at death 101
Constipation 41, 45, 85
    in a case study 181
Constitution (body performance) vi, 39, 57, 67, 87, 127
    in a case study 103
Contagious diseases/ infections 21, 27, 37, 59, 61, 70, 73, 101, 104, 124, 127, 158
    case studies
        affecting airways 172–175

cholera 182
ebola 191
hepatitis 195–196
leprosy 221
measles 155
polio 165
psychological contagion 171
STD's 211
Convulsions 27, 65, 71, 81
Cornea 61, 156
Corpses, cadavers 69
Cortesi, Anita 163
Cortisol 15, 43, 45, 63, 93, 213
Cosby, Ennis 146
COUNSELLING overview 116–118
Covid-19 21, 25, 27, 37, 59, 73, 127
Crabs, pubic 25, 27, 45, 91
Cramps, cramping 27, 65, 71, 93, 127
    in a case study 181
Cranium 30–31, 65
Crawford, Michael 191
Cripples, crippled, crippling 47, 49, 67, 93, 124, 133
    in case studies 114, 175, 216–217
Crohn's disease 25, 41, 45, 65, 75, 85
    case study 181
Croup 21, 33, 35, 59, 61, 85
    case studies 173
CROWN chakra
    0-overview 80–81
    case studies
        Alzheimer's 150–151
        Aneurysm in the brain 144
        Brain cancer, tumours 145
        Brain trauma, died 145
        Huntington's Disease 151
        Hydrocephalus 146
        Lewy Body Dementia 152
        Meningitis 147
        Sleep disorders 148
        Stroke 149
        Vascular Dementia 153
Cruel, cruelty 14, 22–25, 38, 45, 48, 64, 74, 92, 125
    case study 221
Crystallises, crystallised, crystallisation 14–15, 26, 32, 49, 69, 105, 124–125, 127
    in case studies 171, 188, 214
Curie, Marie 183
Cushing's syndrome 43, 63, 93
Cuts, cutting 25, 45, 65, 89
Cyber: bully, crime, stalker, troll 18, 61
Cyst, cysts 37, 73
    case studies
        breast 211
        ovarian 210
Cystic fibrosis 21, 37, 59, 85
    case studies 206
Cystitis 27, 43, 45, 65, 75, 93, 126

D

Daumier, Sophie 151

Deaf, deafness 61, 83, 85
    case studies 154–155, 158
Death 14–15, 45, 74–75, 81, 86, 93, 98, 124, 126–127
    8H of death 109, 111, 114, 133, 144–147, 149–150, 157, 172–173, 175, 177–180, 182–183, 185, 195, 198–201, 203, 211–212, 215, 222–224
    in case studies 144–149, 152, 171–172, 174, 178–179, 185–186, 196, 207, 212, 222–223
    thoughts on death 98, 101, 117, 123, 135, 137–139
Debilitation, debilitates, debility 21, 35, 37, 44, 59, 61, 89, 102, 104, 124
    in case studies 103, 135, 149, 175, 178, 191, 193
Decay 21, 37, 59
    dental decay 27, 69
    Moon can represent 107
    senile decay 31, 81
Deep vein thrombosis 63, 87
    case study 185
Defecation 45, 69, 75, 85
Deformed, deformity 49, 69, 93
    case studies 146, 216, 222
Delirium, delusory, delusion 24–25, 37, 44, 52–53, 72–73, 89, 101, 104
    in case studies 171, 205
Dementia 31, 37, 45, 53, 59, 73, 75, 81, 122, 125
    case studies
        alzheimer's 150–151
        huntington's disease 151
        lewy body dementia 152
        vascular dementia 153
Dengue fever 25, 27, 73, 85
Dental problems 27, 69, 71, 85
Depression 20–21, 25, 61, 69, 81, 89, 110, 117
    case studies 108, 145, 148, 152, 175–176
        manic depression 202–203
        postpartum 204
    five stages 139
    in an emotional client 117
    the colour rose improves 122
Desire - defined 24
Devitalising, devitalisation 21, 37, 60–61, 76, 87, 105, 124, 126
    in a case study 183
Diabetes 25, 33, 37, 43, 62–63, 89, 99, 125–126, 132
    case studies 197
DIAGNOSING DISEASE in the Chart 102–115
    1. Examine the Sun 102–103, 128–129, 131–132, 135
    2. Examine Moon, Mars, Neptune 102, 104–105
    3. Examine the planets. 102, 106–107
    4. Examine the 6th and 12 "health" houses. 102, 108
    5. Look for a major health warning pattern in the chart 102, 109
    6. Look for a health-warning triangle in the chart 102, 110

examine the ascendant 103
Diarrhea 25, 41, 45, 65, 73, 75, 85
    case studies 181–182, 193
Digestion, digestive 18–20, 25, 32, 35–37, 41, 52, 58–59, 61–62, 66–67, 69, 85, 88–89, 104, 125–127, 172
    case studies 119, 181–182, 188, 192–194
Dinklage, Peter 206
Dionne Quintuplets 163
Diphtheria 33, 35, 61, 85
    case studies 173
DISEASE & ITS CAUSE 98–101
Dissociative disorder 23, 51
    case study 169
Diverticulitis 25, 41, 45, 65, 75, 85
    case study 181
DNA (deoxyribonucleic acid) 26–27, 33, 45, 50–51, 70–71, 89, 91, 100, 126–127, 227–228
    in case studies 146, 151, 186, 188, 190, 206–207, 215
Doolittle, Hilda 149
Douglas, Michael 178
Drugs - abuse, addiction 25, 53, 73, 89, 100, 108, 117, 124, 126–127
    in case studies 105, 140, 189, 192, 195–196, 198, 201–203
        cocaine addiction 161
        drug sensitivity 192
        medical 23, 71
        to alleviate anxiety 117
Du Pre, Jacqueline 114–115, 118, 164
Dwarfism 27, 63, 71, 82–83, 91
    case studies 167, 206
Dysentery 25, 41, 45, 65, 75, 85
Dyslexia 19, 35, 61, 85, 124
Dyspepsia 19, 37, 41, 59, 89, 124
Dysplasia 47, 67, 93

E

Ears 19, 31, 34–35, 43, 61, 82–83, 85, 125–126
    case studies - deafness 154–155
EARTH - overview 76
Eating disorders 25, 59, 89
    case studies
        Anorexia Nervosa 201
        Bulimia Nervosa 203
Eben, Alexander 147
Ebola virus - case study 191
Eczema 25, 49, 65, 69
    case study 220
Egg ovum 19, 37, 47, 59, 91
Egoic lotus 2, 2–3, 80, 82, 84, 86, 228
    defined 79
Egomania 15, 56–57, 75, 83, 93
Einstein, Albert 18
Eisenreich, Jim 166
Elbow 35, 61
Electric, electrical 15, 51, 70, 81, 122, 124, 126–127

electric shock 7, 71
    in case studies 133, 154, 156, 163, 189
Elliot, Ann 210
Embryo 19, 37, 59, 91
    in case studies 208, 210
EMOTION, EMOTIONS 24, 36, 52–53, 58–59, 89, 100, 104–107, 125
    anger, angry, volatile emotions 5, 14, 24, 30, 44–45, 85, 104, 117, 124–125, 144–145, 147, 149, 214
        in a case study 114, 119, 132–133, 139, 144–146, 149, 152–154, 157, 161–163, 165, 172, 181–182, 187, 194, 198, 200, 203, 214, 220–221, 223
        Mars represents anger 64–65
    congestion 21, 37
    defined 4–5
    detrimental to health 117, 130
    emotional healing 117–118, 121, 137
    examine for emotional expression 128–129
    lie behind most diseases 25
    mood/ emotional swings 20–21, 61, 124, 151–152, 205
        case study - bipolar 202–203
    primary cause of disease 98, 126
    R6, force of human emotion 24–25
    repressed, repress, repression, suppression of emotions 79, 89, 98, 104–106, 136, 149, 203
        1st ray represses 89, 172
        Capricorn represses 73, 105, 173, 177, 184, 224
        cause of cancer 37, 89, 140–141
        Pluto represses 75, 140–141, 144–145, 153, 172, 177, 194, 199
        Saturn represses 15, 69, 129, 133, 140, 149, 153, 172–173, 176, 179–180, 185, 194, 200, 212, 216, 224
    root trouble of psychological disorders 23
    rulers of the emotions
        Mars 64–65
        Moon 58–59
        Neptune 64–65
    the emotional client 117
Emphysema 25, 35, 61, 85
    case studies 173, 179
Encephalitis 25, 31, 65, 81
Endocrine system (see individual glands) vi–vii, 34–35, 43, 51, 61, 79, 82, 88, 99, 124–125
    18–21, 19, 68, 68–69
    defined 18
    function 20–21, 79
    malfunction 19, 23, 51, 124
    the chakras anchor in the endocrine glands of 18, 79
    the glands are ductless 18
    thyroid gland is the keystone of 20, 68, 84
Endometriosis 27, 37, 59, 91
    case study 208
Enlightenment 4, 74, 101, 120, 139, 227
    defined 3, 48, 98
    many cycles around the zodiac to reach 46

Enteric nervous system 18–19, 41, 61, 85
Enteritis 27, 41, 61, 85
Epidemics 21, 27, 35, 37, 59, 60–61, 70–71, 78, 101, 124, 126–127
    case studies
        cholera 182
        ebola 191
        influenza 174–175
Epilepsy 27, 31, 35, 61, 71, 78, 83, 125
    case study 163
Epstein-Barr virus 25, 27
Esoteric
    defined 227
    esoteric astrology iii, vi, 4, 6
    esoteric forces combine with the orthodox planets 119
    esoteric rulers, planets 131–132, 134–135, 137–138, 138, 217
        development of its higher qualities 131
        location, situation is key to inner development work 118, 119
        of the asc, represents the paramount developmental life goal 119
        represent the energies of the soul 118
        ruler of the chart 6, 118–120, 134, 138
Estregan, George 223
Estrogen 19, 37, 59, 91
    in a case study 209
Etheric web 4, 26–27, 35, 50–51, 58–59, 61, 70–71, 76, 90–91, 98–99, 121–122, 124–126
    0-overview 77–94
    basis of good physical health 16
    case studies
        conjoined Twins 210
        spina bifida 218
    death and the web 101
    defined 13, 78, 227
    determines our health 78
    disease and the web 98–99
    how to strengthen the etheric 121–122, 204
        visualisations 122
    problems in the etheric 16, 59, 78–79, 89, 98, 103, 116, 210, 218
    unhindered flow of prana 16
Excretion 19, 45, 52, 88
Exhaustion - case studies 193
Exocrine glands 49, 69
    defined 18
Extra body parts 67, 124
Eyck, Charles 155
Eye, eyes, eyesight 17, 19, 30–31, 34–35, 56–57, 61, 71, 78, 81–83, 104, 110, 125–126, 127, 154
    case studies 161, 166, 174, 201
        blindness 156–158
        cataracts 159
        glaucoma 159
        macular degeneration 160
    mind's eye 121
    one-eyed 22, 52, 64

F

Face 19, 30–31, 64, 82–83, 125–126, 154
    in case studies 108, 140, 221
        not want to face 156, 179
Faeces 18–19, 45, 69
    in a case study 182, 195
Fainting 39, 87
Fallopian tubes 19, 35, 37, 59–60, 90–91
    in case studies 208–209
Fat, fatty, fatness 17, 52–53, 66–67, 89, 126
    fatty food 43, 66, 108
        in case studies 119, 148, 194
    in case studies 149, 195
Father Damien 221
Fatigue 21, 61
    adrenal 45, 65, 75, 93
    chronic fatigue 21, 124
        case study 191
    in case studies 168, 195, 213
    thyroid 19, 85, 93, 124
        hashimoto's dis 176
Fear, fearfulness 4, 21, 24, 47, 74, 89, 92, 101–102, 104, 117–118, 125, 136
    in case studies 139, 152, 157, 162, 174, 192, 198–199, 205, 214, 224
Feet 29, 52–53, 72–73, 92–93, 105, 126–127
    in a case study 103, 108
Feliciano, Jose 160
Female organs, cycles, reproduction, sex 36, 43, 45, 58–59, 63, 90, 126, 206
    case studies 184
        abortion 208
        miscarriage 209
Fertile, fertility, fertilised 19, 40, 47, 58–59, 63, 65, 91
    case studies 208–210, 214
    degrading effect 47
    infertile 37, 45, 59, 91
        case studies 209
Fever, fevers 21, 25, 27, 31, 39, 57, 65, 87, 122, 124, 127
    case studies 155, 173–174
    colour green eases fever 122
    dengue 25, 27, 73, 85
    glandular 25, 27, 73, 85
    hay fever 21, 61
        case study 174
    rheumatic 67, 69, 93
    scarlet 35, 61, 71, 85
    typhoid 27, 37, 41, 59, 71, 85
    yellow 27, 43
Fibroids, uterine 37, 59, 67, 91
Field, Sally 216
Fight or flight 15, 45, 64, 75, 83, 92–93, 125–127
    in a case study 191–192
Fingers 34–35, 60–61, 84, 126
    in case studies 115, 157
Flabbiness 67
Flatulence 19, 25, 37, 41, 59, 61, 85
Flesh 37, 49, 59, 93, 127
Fluid waterways 53, 72
Flynt, Althea 209
Foetus, foetal 26–27, 91, 93, 125
    in a case study 154, 156, 188, 206, 208
Fonda, Henry 103, 129–130, 135–137
Frigidity 91
Fry, Stephen 161

G

Gallbladder 19, 36–37, 41, 66, 69, 85, 88–89, 125–126
    in a case study 192, 194
Gallstones 37, 89
    case studies 194
Gambling addiction 46–47, 66–67
Gangrene 37
Gastric disorders 18–19, 25, 37, 41–42, 49, 59, 89, 124–125
    juices 41
Gastroenteritis 25, 89
Gastrointestinal 18, 32, 41, 85, 88, 125
GEMINI - overview 34–35
Genes, genetics 26–27, 33, 37, 50–51, 69–71, 91, 110, 117, 125–127
    case studies
        congenital deafness 154
        cystic fibrosis 206
        down's syndrome 207
        dwarfism 167, 206
        epilepsy 163
        haemophilia 184
        huntington's disease 151–152
        hydrocephalus 146
        lewy body dementia 152
        macular degeneration 160
        muscular dystrophy 207
        progeria 207
        sickle cell anaemia 184
    disease from previous incarnations 117
Genitals 19, 29, 45, 65, 89, 91
    case studies 211
Germs 27, 32, 35, 61, 70–71, 98, 107, 121, 124, 127
    body resistant to germs 98
    contaminated water is a breeding ground for 37
    enter body via the life force 57
    find their way into the body 87
    immune cells destroy 53
    the Sun's energy kills all germs 56
    tonsils trap germs 32
Gershwin, George 145
Gestation 17, 19, 37, 58–59, 91, 125–126
Gibb, Robin 180
Gigantism 63, 67, 71, 83, 124
    case study - acromegaly 167
Gingivitis 27, 69, 71, 93
Glamour 25, 36, 52–53, 64–65, 72–73, 89
    defined 24
    doorway to the astral plane leading to 101
    in a case study 201
Glands - see Endocrine, Exocrine 14
Glandular fever 25, 27, 73, 85
Glaucoma 31, 61, 83
    case study 159–160
Glucose 19, 43, 62–63, 127
Gluttony, gluttonous 16–17, 32–33, 47, 66–67, 89, 124, 126
Goitre 33, 63, 67, 85, 125
Gonads 65, 68, 79, 99, 125, 127
    defined 90
Gonorrhea 25, 27, 45, 65, 91
    case study 211
Goodman, Linda 197
Gout 47, 49, 67
Grave's disease 25, 33, 63, 85
    case study 176
Greene, Lorne 174
Growth 4, 17, 27, 49, 57, 63, 66–67, 82–83, 89, 93, 102, 107, 122, 124, 127, 141
    case studies
        acromegaly 167
        stunted - dwarfism 167, 206
    in case studies 175, 179, 199–200, 207, 209, 222
Growths (see Cancer, Tumours) 17, 57, 67, 124, 127
Guillain-Barre syndrome 25, 35, 61, 83
    case study 163
Guilt, guilty 5, 24, 68, 72, 138–139
    eliminate any sense of 116, 138–139
    in a case study 165, 223
    let it go 137
Gums 33, 63
Guthrie, Woody 152

H

Hadid, Yolanda 193
Haemoglobin 39, 64–65, 87, 127
Haemophilia 65, 73
    case studies 184
Haemorrhage 71
    brain 31, 59, 65, 81
        in a case study 144
    in a case study
        liver 195
        retina 160
Hair 19, 31, 49, 69, 93, 126–127
    case studies 207
        alopecia areata 220
Halitosis 85
Hall, Jon 223
Hallucinations 25, 37, 53, 73, 89
    in case studies 150, 152
Hamilton, Scott 109, 112–113
Hands 26, 29, 34–35, 60–61, 84, 126–127
    in a case study 115, 165
Harmlessness - as an healing agent 89, 122, 225
Harris, Richard 177
Harvey, Charles 177
Hashimoto's disease 25, 63, 85
    case study 176
Hawking, Stephen 162

Hay fever 21, 61
    case study 174
Head 29–32, 47, 60, 64–65, 69, 74, 79, 80–81, 83, 87, 103–104, 125–126, 169, 227
    case studies 108, 144–146, 149, 158, 169, 183, 210, 222
        head injuries 145–146, 163, 166, 170, 179
    head of the Medusa 207
    problems 15, 23, 31, 45, 64, 104
Headaches (see Migraine) 23, 31, 83, 125
    case studies 108
Health, healing
    6H of health 103, 107–109, 113–115, 118–119, 129–130, 132–135, 132–137, 141, 145, 147–155, 157–159, 161–163, 165–167, 170, 177–180, 182, 184–187, 189–199, 201–204, 207, 209–224
    Health Triangles, how to find 110–115
    health warning/s 102, 109, 128–131
    Remedial Advice 100, 116–122
HEALTH READINGS 123–141
    a. when health is good 128–130
    b. diagnosed diseases 131–141
        - life-threatening 135
        - not immediately life-threatening 132–134
    c. terminally ill 138
Hearing 31, 34–35, 60–61, 83, 85, 127, 172
    case studies - deafness 154–155
HEART chakra
    0-overview 86–87
    case studies
        AIDS 190
        Anaemia - aplastic 183
        Anaemia - pernicious 183
        Anaemia - sickle cell 184
        Angina 185
        Arteriosclerosis 187
        Chronic Fatigue 191
        Deep vein thrombosis 185
        Ebola 191
        Haemophilia 184
        Heart attack 189
        Heart disease - congenital 188
        Heart failure 189
        Heart fibrillation 189
        High blood pressure 187
        Immune deficiency 190
        Leukaemia 186
        Lung cancer 179
HEART (organ) 14–17, 25, 32, 38–39, 49–50, 53, 56–57, 62–63, 66, 69, 86–87, 100–102, 107–110, 124, 126–127, 176
    case studies 103, 108–109, 129–130, 133, 141, 179, 183–193, 201, 206–207, 210, 216
        heart attack 108, 187–189, 192
        heart failure 187–189, 201
        heart fibrillation/ arrhythmia 109
    chronic heart problems 69
    difficulties due to the mass opening of the heart 101
    for heart trouble start with the Sun 110
    hard heartedness affects the heart 38–39

heart and circulation problems 57
heart disease 27, 87, 101, 103, 129–130
    case studies 135–137, 188
heart fibrillation/ arrhythmia 87
    case study 189
heart of the Solar Logos 66
heart of the Sun 72
how strong is this person's heart? 102–103
inflammatory conditions of 104
is ray 2's means of distribution 16
life energy anchors in the heart 38
mean-spiritedness affects the heart 49
remedial advice 121–122, 130, 133, 179
sutratma anchors in 14
vitalising of the body 14, 16, 38, 57, 66, 87
Hemorrhoids 25, 45, 63, 75, 85
    case studies 182
Hemstreet, Carole 216
Hepatitis 25, 27, 67, 73, 89
    case studies 195–196
Hereditary diseases 27, 37, 71, 91
    in a case study 159
Hernia 45, 93
    case study 219
Herpes 25, 27, 33, 45, 63, 65, 73, 91
    case study 211
Hidden, obscure 25, 58, 73, 124, 126–127, 140, 227
    12H of hidden things 144, 146, 155, 165, 172–173, 175, 185, 189, 195, 197–198, 200, 202, 205, 211–212, 214, 219
    disorders in case studies 108, 114, 152, 161, 163, 172, 187–188, 198, 201, 218
High blood pressure 67, 81, 87, 117
    in case studies 144, 149, 182, 187, 189
Higher mind 82, 180
Hips 29, 46–47, 66–67, 92, 104, 126–127
    case studies 218
Hitler, Adolf 92
Hodgkin's disease 37, 53, 73, 85
    case studies 177
Holiday, Billie 195
Homeostasis 19, 42–43, 63, 80, 82–84, 127
Hormone, hormonal 18–19, 23, 32, 34, 43, 45, 63, 79–80, 82, 84–85, 91–92, 124
    case studies 167, 176, 206, 209, 213
    growth hormone deficiency 167
Horse riding accident 47, 67, 126
    case study 165
Howard, John 103
Humbert, Vincent 157
Huntington's disease 31, 75, 81
    case studies 151–152
Hydrocephalus 25, 31, 73, 81
    case study 146
Hyperglycemia 63, 89
Hypochondria 41, 49, 69
Hypoglycaemia 63, 89
    case studies 198

Hypotension 39, 87

I

Imbecilities 23, 35, 83
    in a case study 169
Immune system 25, 34, 37–39, 53, 56, 59, 85–87, 125–127
    case studies 103, 114, 117, 132, 163–164, 174–176, 181, 183, 186, 190–193, 197, 213, 216–217, 220–222
        AIDS 190
        immune deficient 190
    defined 39, 86
Impetigo 25, 27, 49, 69, 71, 73
Impotent, impotency 45, 65, 91
    in a case study 223
Incest 25, 27, 45, 63
Indigenous diseases 21, 37, 59, 104
    defined 100, 227
Indigestion 19, 25, 37, 41, 59, 89
Infancy, infant 59
    in a case study 193
    SIDS 75, 81
Infectious diseases 21, 25, 27, 61, 65, 85, 127
    case studies 175, 182
Infertile, infertility problems 37, 45, 59, 91
    case study 208–209
Inflammation 25, 31, 39, 65–66, 81, 87, 103–104, 122, 127
    colour green helps inflammation 122
    in a case study 108, 119, 152, 161, 172, 176, 181, 213, 215, 218
Influenza 21, 25, 27, 35, 37, 53, 59, 61, 73, 85, 124, 126–127
    case studies 174
Inherited conditions, diseases, patterns 50, 82, 98
    in case studies 115, 118–120, 151, 155–156, 159–160, 167–169, 184, 188, 202, 219
Initiation
    defined 7
Inner conflict 20–21, 104, 106, 126
    case studies 191, 193, 218
Insane, insanities, insanity 21, 23, 31–32, 35, 61, 81, 83, 93, 125
    case studies 169, 171, 202
    goodwill cures insanities 122
Insomnia 25, 31, 73, 81
    case studies 148
Insulin 19, 43, 62–63, 88–89, 127
    case studies 197
Intestines 19, 29, 41, 60–61, 66, 85, 89, 125–127
    case studies 165, 182, 188, 193, 219
Ireland, Jill 199
Iron in the blood 65, 87
Irritable bowel syndrome 25, 41, 45, 75, 85, 89
Islets of Langerhans 19, 43, 62–63, 88–89, 126
Itches, itchy
    case studies 174, 220

J

Jaquemont, Victor 182
Jaundice 67, 89
Jaw, jaws 30–33, 65, 126
   case study - cancer 178
Jeanni
   amyloidosis 141
   rheumatoid arthritis 217
Jewel in the lotus 79, 227
Joel, Billy 214
John, Elton 189
Joint, joints 47–49, 61, 67–69, 93, 125–127
   case studies 103, 105, 132–134, 216–218
Jugular vein 17, 33, 63, 85
   case studies 210
JUPITER - overview 66–67

K

Karma, karmic 45, 48, 51–52, 62, 68, 100, 117
   collective karma 100
   defined 51, 68, 100, 228
   in a case study 110–111, 114, 137, 145–146, 154–159, 161, 163, 167, 169–170, 178, 182, 184–185, 188, 190, 193, 206–208, 210–211, 215–216, 218, 221–223
   karmic limitations of the body 123
   personal karma 100–101
Keith, Brian 179
Keller, Helen 158
Kennedy, John F 181, 213
Keratitis 25, 31, 83
Keystone of the endocrine system 20, 68, 84
Khan, Inayat 174
Khul, Djwhal 227
Kidneys 18–19, 29, 42–44, 62–63, 65, 74, 92–93, 104, 125–127
   case studies 108, 210
      kidney disease 215
      kidney failure 141, 214–215
      kidney stones 214
King, Freddie 198
King, Larry 159
King, Stephen 160
Kirkland, Gelsey 201
Knatchbull, Timothy 158
Knees 29, 48–49, 68–69, 110, 126
   case studies 103
   Moon in Capricorn effect 105
Koch, Ed 109
Kudrow, Lisa 168
Kundalini 60, 64–65, 81, 87, 92–93, 125
   case studies 183
   defined 18, 228

L

L1001 - case study 164
L1002 - case study 188
L1003 - case study 186
L1004 - case study 195
L1005 - case study 196
L1006 - case study 220
L1010 - case study 219
Labyrinthitis 27, 35, 61, 83, 85
Landon, Michael 200
Laryngitis 25, 33, 35, 61, 63, 85
Larynx 19, 33, 61, 85, 125
Laurie - case study 211
Leg, legs 47, 49, 50–51, 61, 67, 70–71, 105, 126
   case studies 185, 206–207, 224
Leigh, Vivien 202
Lemarchal, Greg 206
LEO - overview 38–39
Leprosy 27, 49, 71, 73
   case study 221
Letterman, David 166
Leukaemia 27, 51, 71, 87
   case studies 186
Lewy body dementia 31, 75, 81, 150
   case study 152
Libido 25, 27, 45, 63, 65, 91
Life force 100, 228
   defined 86
   germs enter the body via 25, 57
   of God and vitality 31
Life thread/ stream/ the sutratma 14–16, 38–39, 56–57, 86–87, 101, 125
   at death 74, 81, 86
   defined 228
Ligaments 48–49, 68–69, 93, 126–127
   in a case study 103
Limbic system 31–33, 62–63, 85
Limping 47, 67, 93
Lincoln, Abraham 50, 146, 175
Link between psychology and disease iii, 12, 117, 128, 130–131, 133, 136
Lips 33, 63, 85
Liver 19, 25, 36–37, 41, 66–67, 85, 88–89, 99, 125–127
   case studies 180
      cirrhosis 195–196
      hepatitis A 195
      hepatitis C 196
      liver cancer 199–200
Locomotion 19, 47, 67, 126–127
Lon, Alice 222
Longo, Jeannie 219
Loren, Sophia 209
Louis, Joe 187
Lumbago 25, 43, 63, 93
Lung, lungs 29, 35, 60–61, 84–86, 104, 122, 125, 127
   case studies 172–175, 178–179, 185, 206
      lung cancer 179, 224
Lupus 25, 57
   case studies 221
Lyme disease 27
   case studies 193
Lymphatic system 18–19, 24, 32, 36–37, 52–53, 58–59, 72–73, 85, 125–127, 183
   case studies - cancer/ lymphoma 177
Lynn, Loretta 168

M

MacLean, Paul D. 30
MacRae, Gordon 178
Macular 61
   case study - macular degeneration 160
Malefic planets defined 102
Malnutrition 41, 59, 89
Manic, manic depression 21, 61, 89
   case studies 152
      manic depression 202
Manilow, Barry 218
Manson, Charles 171
MARS - overview 64–65
Martel, Linda 146
Martin, Billy 148
Martin, Dean 173
Marx, Karl 182
Mary - cancer 140
Masochism 25, 45, 75
Mastectomy 23
   in a case study 199
Maternal, maternity 36, 59
   case studies 208–209
McCain, John 224
McCartney, Linda 199
McCullough, Colleen 160
Measles 25, 27, 73, 85
   case studies 155, 162
Meditation
   for inner work 2, 89, 100–101, 164, 218
   function 100
   recommending meditations 117, 119–122, 133–134, 139–141, 204
Medulla
   adrenal 43, 45, 64–65, 92, 126
   oblongata 19, 35, 61, 85, 126
Megalomania 15, 39, 57, 75, 83, 93
Melanoma 49, 67, 75, 93
   case studies 224
Melatonin 15, 31, 80–81
   in a case study 148
Membranes 37, 49, 59, 69, 93
   case studies 147
Meniere's disease 25, 35, 59, 61, 73, 83, 85
Meninges 125
   in a case study 147
Meningitis 25, 31, 39, 49, 69, 81, 125–126
   case studies 147
Menstruation, menstrual 19, 24, 32, 37, 43, 45, 58–59, 63, 91
   case studies 208

MENTAL attitudes, habits, preferences
   chit-chatter 34
   clinical coldness 22
   conflict 21, 60
   disorders 21, 23, 32
   excessive mental activity 22
   health 22, 61, 69
   hyper-activity 85
   illness 106
   imbalance 43
   in a case study
      abuse 166
      break-down 148
      congestion 180
      decline 150
      disability 207
      disorders 169
      intense mental activity and devotion 171
      tension 219
      walls 168
   indecision 42
   inflexibility 32
   instability 21, 34
   irritation 104
   limitations 16
   negative 42, 122
   rigid 38
   separativeness 105
   stiffness 68
   stress 117
   that produce disease 117
   troubles 63
MERCURY - overview 60–61
Merrick, Joseph 222
Metabolism, metabolic 19, 32, 43, 57, 66, 84–85, 87, 92
   in a case study 176
Metastases, metastasized 17, 67, 73
   case studies 140, 200, 224
Middle ear problems 35, 61, 83
   case studies 155
Migraine 23, 51, 63, 83, 124–126
   case studies 168
Minnelli, Liza 105
Miscarriage 27, 37, 45, 59, 71, 91
   case studies 186, 209
Misdiagnosis 73
   in a case study 140
Mobility, movement 7, 35, 47, 49, 60, 66–68, 84, 104–105, 126
   immobile, immobilised 162, 165, 216
   in case studies 114, 132–133, 150–151, 153, 162–166, 207, 216–218
      immobilised 165
   intellectual 22
   see Paralysed 111
Mobley, Mary Ann 181
Moles (skin) 49, 69
Mood, moods, moody, moodiness 21, 36–37, 61, 80–81, 89
   case studies 150, 176
   swings 20–21, 61
      case studies 151–152, 202–203
MOON - overview 58–59
Mora, Mirka 212

Mother, mothers, motherhood 36–37, 40, 58–59, 78, 90–91, 134
   in a case study 105, 154, 157, 160, 162, 169, 173, 184, 193, 195, 202–203, 209, 212, 217–218, 220
      pattern inherited from 115
   Moon mother of form 58, 91
   mother and the child/ Christ 40, 104
   Mother Earth 76
   Mother Nature 18, 76, 79, 92, 121
Mother Teresa 3
Motor nerves 35, 61, 65
   in a case study 162
Motor neurone disease (see ALS) 83
Mouth 30, 32–33, 41, 62–63, 85, 125
   case studies
      herpes 211
      mouth cancer 178
Mucous 36–37, 58–59
   problems 21, 37, 45, 59, 73, 124, 127
      case study - cystic fibrosis 206
Mukpo, Tagtrug 169
Mulligan, John 205
Mumps 27, 63, 85
Murder, murdered, murderous 24–25, 45, 65, 75, 91, 124, 127
   case studies 171, 184, 212
Muscle, muscles, muscular 4, 26, 32, 35, 41, 46, 48, 49, 50, 53, 64–68, 73, 93
   case studies 167, 194, 216, 219
      muscular dystrophy 207
   heart muscle
      case studies 188–189
   spasms 65
      case studies 162, 165–166
   weak 43, 63, 73
      case studies 162
Myasthenia gravis 25, 35, 61
Myocarditis 25, 39, 87

N

Nails 49, 69, 93
Narcissism, narcissistic 26, 38, 56, 62, 70
   case studies 171
Narcolepsy 25, 73
   case studies 148
Nasal congestion 21, 35, 59
Nausea 19, 25, 37, 89
   in a case study 168, 195, 213
Neck 19, 30, 32–33, 53, 63, 84–85, 125–126
   case studies 185
Negative core beliefs 5, 37, 58–59, 114
   in a case study 120, 197, 199, 222
Negro, Andrea 170
Nephritis (Bright's dis) 43, 63, 93
   case studies 215
NEPTUNE - overview 72–73
NERVES, nervous system 16–21, 34–35, 51, 60–63, 70–71, 100, 124–127
   autonomic 19, 35
   case studies
      ALS 162

      cerebral palsy 162
      epilepsy 163
      guillain-barre syndrome 163
      meningitis 147
      MS 114, 164
      parkinson's 109, 165–166
      polio 165
      quadriplegia 165
      shingles 166
      spina bifida 218
      stroke 111, 149–150
   central nervous 18, 21, 34, 60, 83, 109
      in a case study 114, 147, 165
   colour rose improves 122
   created by the activity of the 3rd ray 18
   enteric 18–19, 35, 41, 61, 85
   peripheral 35
      in a case study 163
   sciatic 25, 35, 47, 61, 67, 127
      case study 219
   sympathetic 19, 24–25, 35, 65, 83, 89, 125, 127
   vagus 19, 35, 61, 87
      in a case study 188
Neuralgia 25, 35, 61, 83
Neurons 35, 41, 61, 71, 83
   case studies 151–152, 166
Neurotic, neuroses 25, 37, 53, 73, 89
   in a case study 204
Newton John, Olivia 199
Nicklaus, Jack 181
Nicks, Stevie 161
Nightmares 25, 72–73, 89
   in a case study 205
Nin, Anais 208
Nolan Twins 210
Nose 19, 30–31, 33, 65, 83, 125–126
   case studies
      broken nose 161
      septum damage 161
      sinusitis 161
   in case studies 108, 154, 173, 201, 224
Nureyev, Rudolph 190
Nutrition 37, 41, 59, 89

O

Obesity 37, 47, 67, 89, 126
   in a case study 148
Obscure (see Hidden) 25
Obsess, obsession, obsessive 15, 41, 81, 90
   goodwill cures 122
   in case studies 201, 203
   obsessive compulsive 25, 65, 73, 75, 89
      case study 120, 204
Oedema 12, 25, 37, 52–53, 59, 72–73
Old age 15, 49, 69
   in a case study 135, 207
Ollerenshaw, Dame Kathleen 155
Osteoarthritis 33, 49, 69, 85, 93
   case studies 216
Osteoporosis 49, 69, 93, 124, 132
   case studies 216
Otosclerosis 69

case studies 155
Ovaries, ovarian 19, 36–37, 43, 58–59, 63, 79, 82, 90–91, 127
   case studies
      cancer 212
      cyst 210
Overbuilds, overbuilding cells 15, 17, 37, 53, 67, 89
   in a case study 140, 145, 223
Overgrowth 67, 127
   case studies 222
Overstimulated, overstimulates 17, 79, 101, 124, 127
Oxygen, oxygenation 34–35, 60–62, 62, 64, 66, 84, 87, 126–127
   case studies 149, 156, 177, 184, 190, 213
   deoxygenated 62, 210

P

Paedophilia 25, 27, 45, 71, 91
Paget's disease 49, 69, 93
Pain 21, 39, 43, 49, 93, 119, 198, 204, 215–219
   and pleasure 4, 88
   case studies 152, 161, 166, 179, 181, 184–185, 188
   emotional pain 15, 53, 132–134, 203, 224
      in case studies 140, 162, 173, 177, 194, 199, 202–203, 223
   menstrual 63
      in case studies 208
   migraine 23, 51, 83
      in case studies 168
   nerve pain 25, 61, 108
      in case studies 155, 161, 166
Palate 19, 32–33, 62–63, 125
Palpitations 71, 87
Pancreas 19, 36–37, 41, 43, 59, 62, 68, 79, 85, 88–89, 99, 125–127
   case studies 192
      diabetes 197
      pancreatic cancer 200
      pancreatitis 198
   function 88
Panic attacks 21, 25, 37, 89
   case study 204
Paralysis, paralyse, paralytic 35, 61, 71, 83, 124
   case studies
      guillain-barre syndrome 163
      MS 114
      polio 165
      quadriplegia 165
      stroke 111, 149
Paranoia 25, 37, 53, 73, 89, 101
   case studies 204
Paraplegia 35, 61, 67, 71
Parasites 19, 41, 61, 75, 89
Parathyroids 19, 33, 63, 68–69, 85
Parkinson's 27, 35, 47, 61, 71, 83
   case studies 109, 165–166
Parton, Dolly 208

Peary, Robert 183
Pedro, Afonso 163
Pelvic girdle 47, 67
Pelvis 45, 47, 67
Penis 19, 45, 65, 91
Peptic ulcer 37, 41, 59, 61
Pericardium 19, 57, 87
Periods 19, 37, 59, 63, 91
   in a case study 208
Peritonitis 27, 37, 41, 59, 89
Permanent atom 27, 51, 69–71
   defined 26, 50, 91, 100, 228
Perverts, perverted, perversions, perverting 25, 27, 45, 65, 72–73, 91, 102, 124–125
   case studies 165, 177, 184, 188, 206
Phillips, Ada 180
Phlegm 21, 36–37, 45, 52–53, 59, 72–73, 104, 125–127
   in case studies 172–174, 178
Phobias 21, 25, 37, 53, 73, 89
Pimples 25
Pineal gland 15, 30, 45, 68, 71, 79, 80–83, 125–126, 144, 227, 228
   blood pressure high 81
   consciousness thread connects 81
   crown chakra anchors in 30, 80
   defined 80
   in case studies
      dementia 151
      migraine 168
      sleep disorders 148
   migraine 23, 51
   sleep cycle 80
   sutratma anchors in 14
PISCES - overview 52–53
Pituitary gland 21, 34, 42, 60–62, 79, 83, 124–127, 154
   ajna anchors in 82
   breaking down of brain tissue 45
   defined 34, 42, 82
   in case studies
      acromegaly 167
      cancer 109, 112–113, 145
      dementia 151
      dwarfism 167, 206
      migraine 168
   migraine 23, 51
   sex function 63
Placenta 19, 37, 59, 91
PLANETS (see individual planets)
   0-overview 55–76
   afflicted by aspects 107
   are the agents of the rays 13
   are the energies healthy or afflicted? 106
   Chart 10: Planets; body parts ruled and disease 127
   how to find links between 113
Pleurisy 25, 35, 61, 85
PLUTO - overview 74–75
Pneumonia 35, 59, 61, 73, 85
   case studies 173–174, 178
Poison, poisoning, poisonous

blood 45, 65, 89, 124, 127
   by viruses 73
   case studies
      alcoholic 198
      blood 220
      emotions 220
      food 194
      milk 193
   emotions 104, 111, 132–134, 220
   food 89
   radiation 75
      in a case study 183
Polio 35, 47, 61, 67, 71
   case study 165
Polyps 67
Possession (multiple personalities)
   how it occurs 78, 81
Postpartum blues 21, 37, 59
Prana 39, 57, 76, 78, 87, 103, 122, 125, 228
   defined 16–17, 38
Predators, predatory 18, 46–47, 104
   in a case study 211
Pregnancy, pregnant 19, 37, 58–59, 90–91, 126–127
   in case studies 154, 162, 171, 204
      abortion 208
      ectopic pregnancy 208
Premature ejaculation 27, 45, 65, 71
Prince Alexei 184
Prince Ernst 198
Princess Alice 173
Princess Diana 203
Princess Mathilde 175
Prison of the soul pattern 20, 104
   defined 5, 58, 222
   in case studies 119–120, 147, 222
Procreation 19, 37, 45, 59, 65, 91
   the will-to-survive is associated 75
Progeria 49, 71
   case study 207
Progesterone 19, 37, 59, 91
Prolapse 43, 45, 93, 127
   defined 43, 63, 73
Prostate 19, 45, 65, 91
   cancer 65
   in a case study 212
Protein, deposits / trouble 17, 64, 67
   case studies
      amyloidosis 141
      cystic fibrosis 206
      dementia 150
      muscular dystrophy 207
Psychological disorders in case studies
   ADD, ADHD 202
   alcohol and substance abuse 202
   anorexia nervosa 201
   autism 169
   bipolar 202
   bulimia nervosa 203
   cutting 203
   dissociative disorder 169
   obsessive compulsive disorder 204
   panic-attack, agoraphobia

204
post-traumatic stress disorder 205
schizophrenia, psychosis 205
Psychopath 19, 85, 125
PTSD 21, 25, 37, 53, 73, 89
   case study 205
Puberty 25, 45, 63, 91
   thymus shrinks 86
Pulmonary
   circulation 35, 61, 87
   embolism case study 185
   obstructive disease (chronic) 35, 61
   tuberculosis 35, 61, 85
     case study 175
Pus 21, 36–37, 59, 73, 127
   in a case study 174

Q

Quadriplegic, quadriplegia 35, 61, 67, 71
   case studies 157, 165
Queen Elizabeth II 103, 105, 208
Queen Victoria 184

R

Ramsey, Patsy 212
Rape 25, 45, 65, 75, 91
Rashes 25, 49, 69, 124, 127
   in case studies 166, 175
Ray, Dixie Lee 172
Raynaud's disease 87
RAYS: the 7, overview 12–13
   Ray 1 overview 14–15
   Ray 2 overview 16–17
   Ray 3 overview 18–19
   Ray 4 overview 20–21
   Ray 5 overview 22–23
   Ray 6 overview 24–25
   Ray 7 overview 26–27
   Rays chart 7: Psychology - Disease - Astrology 124
Reagan, Ronald 150
Rectum, rectal 19, 40, 45, 65, 75, 85
   case studies - cancer 180
Recuperative power 39, 57, 65, 67, 81, 87
Reed, Donna 200
Reeves, Christopher 165
REMEDIAL ADVICE 116–122
   counselling 116–117
   esoteric ruler of asc 118
   esoteric ruler of Moon sign 118–120
   meditations/ visualisations/ exercises 121–122
   Moon: sign, house, aspects 118–119
Repress, repression, repressed, repressive
   cause of cancer 37, 89, 140
   feelings, emotions, desire 37, 59, 69, 73, 75, 79, 98, 104–106, 124–125
     in case studies 129, 133, 136, 140–141, 144–145, 149, 153, 172–173, 176–177, 179–180, 184–185, 194, 199–200, 203, 212, 216, 224
   parents 114

Pluto represses 15
ray 7 standardization 27
the great "repressor", Saturn 105
Reproduction 18–19, 36–37, 43–45, 47, 58–59, 63–65, 90–91, 104, 125–127, 206
   3rd aspect rules sex, reproduction 26
   Cancer (sign), prime ruler of 90
   case studies
     abortion 208
     ectopic pregnancy 208
     endometriosis 208
     hysterectomy 209
     infertility 209
     miscarriage 209
   Moon is the primary ruler of 59
   sacral chakra rules sex, reproduction 206
   Scorpio, Mars traditional rulers 90
Respiration, respiratory problems 14–15, 18, 34–35, 60–61, 84–85, 127
   case studies
     asthma 172
     bronchitis 172
     croup 173
     diphtheria 173
     emphysema 173
     hay fever 174
     influenza 174
     pneumonia 174
     TB 174
   goodwill, heals respiratory tract diseases 122
Retina 61, 71
   in case studies 156, 160
Reynolds, Samuel 218
Rheumatic fever 27, 67, 69, 93
Rheumatism 49, 69, 93
Rheumatoid arthritis 47, 49, 67, 69, 93
   case studies 132–134, 141, 216–217
Rhys-Jones, Sophie 208
Ribs 19, 49, 69
Richie, Nicole 198
Rickets 49, 69, 93
Rigid, rigidity in thought, belief, act 22, 26, 38, 48
Robbins, Anthony 167
Rodden, Amy 173
Roles Triplets 156
Ronstadt, Linda 148
Roosevelt, Franklin 165
Roosevelt, Theodore 172
Rubella 73, 85
   case studies 154–155
Rudhyar, Dane 213

S

Sachs, Andrew 153
SACRAL chakra
   0-Overview 90–91
   case studies
     Abortion 208
     Achondroplasia 206
     Cancer - cervix, uterus 212

Cancer - ovarian 212
Cancer - prostate 212
Conjoined twins 210
Cystic fibrosis 206
Down's syndrome 207
Ectopic Pregnancy 208
Endometriosis 208
Gonorrhea 211
Herpes 211
Hysterectomy 209
Infertility 209
Miscarriage 209
Muscular dystrophy 207
Ovarian cyst 210
Syphilis 211
SAGITTARIUS - overview 46–47
Saint-Laurent, Yves 145
Salivary glands 19, 32–33, 63, 85
Santayana, George 200
SATURN - overview 68–69
Scalds 57, 127
Scarlet fever 35, 61, 71, 85
Scars, scarring
   in case studies 114, 164, 166, 195, 203, 221–222
Schizophrenia 25, 37, 73, 89
   case study 205
Sciatic nerve 47, 61, 67, 127
   sciatica 25, 35, 47, 61, 67
   case study 219
Scleroderma 49, 93
   case studies 222
Scoliosis 27, 39, 49, 69, 93
   case studies 219
SCORPIO - overview 44–45
Scurvy 49, 69, 89
Seal (the artist) 221
Secombe, Harry 212
Seizures 27, 35, 61, 71, 78, 83, 124
   case studies 147, 170
Self-harm, self-injury 25, 65, 89
   in a case study 203
Sellers, Peter 189
Senile 31, 81
Senses, the 16, 18–19, 31–32, 35, 60–61, 83, 154, 161
   in a case study 169
Separative, separateness 22–24, 50–51, 62–63, 83, 105, 124–125
   health issues associated 22–23, 51, 168, 171
Sepsis 27, 51, 71, 73, 89, 104
Sex glands 45, 63
Sex, sexual 19, 26, 33, 43, 45, 47, 62–65, 67, 70–71, 79, 90–91, 102, 125, 206
   diseases 43, 45, 63, 91, 100, 104, 121
   case studies
     gonorrhea 211
     herpes 211
     repression 200
     syphilis 211
   misuse of sex function 25–26, 32, 43, 47, 63, 90–91, 121, 124–125, 127, 140
     in case studies 147, 151, 161, 167,

178, 180, 188, 212–213, 221–223
performance issues 47
relationships 126–127
Ray 7 governs the sex relationship of all forms 26
transmuting 70
Shackleton, Ernest 185
Shaw, Harry 194
Shingles 25, 35, 61, 73, 83
case studies 166
Shoulder, shoulders 32, 34–35, 60–61, 84, 86, 122, 126–127, 185
SIDS: sudden death infant 75, 81
Sight (vision) 17, 35, 57, 61, 83, 125, 127
case studies
blindness 156–158
cataracts 159
glaucoma 159–160
macular degeneration 160
short sighted 31, 59, 83
SIGNS (see individual signs)
0-overview 29–53
Simmond's disease 83
Sinuses, sinusitis 19, 25, 35, 37, 59, 85, 125
case study 161
Skeleton 14–15, 48–49, 68–69, 92–93, 125–127, 213
in a case study 223
Skin 19, 25, 27, 35, 45, 49, 63, 65, 69, 76, 89, 93, 126–127
case studies 103
eczema 220
leprosy 221
lupus 221
melanoma 224
proteus syndrome 222
scleroderma 222
shingles 166
smallpox 175
remedial advice 121
Skull 19, 30–31, 64–65, 69, 93, 108, 126–127
Sleep 14–15, 25–26, 52–53, 72–75, 80–81, 125–127
apnoea 85, 89
case studies 148
case studies 144
narcolepsy 148
retire to the astral plane 72
sleep and death 14, 74, 81, 127, 144
sleep state 52
sleep-walking 25, 73, 89
Smallpox 27, 35, 73, 85
case studies 175
Smell sense 31, 35, 83
Snipes, Peedie 207
Snoring 63, 85
Sociopath 25, 65, 75, 125
SOLAR PLEXUS chakra
0-overview 88–89
case studies 148, 162, 176, 178, 184, 188, 216, 223
Acid reflux 194
ADHD 202

Alcohol abuse 202
Allergic to anaesthetics 192
Allergic to bee stings - anaphylaxis 192
Allergic to gluten - celiac disease 193
Allergic to milk 193
Anorexia nervosa 201
Bipolar 202–203
Bulimia nervosa 203
Cancer - breast 199
Cancer - colorectal, rectal 180
Cancer - liver 200
Cancer - pancreatic 200
Cancer - stomach 200
Cholera 182
Cirrhosis 195
Colitis 181
Crohn's disease 181
Cutting 203
Diabetes 197
Diverticulitis 181
Food poisoning 194
Gallstones 194
Haemorrhoids 182
Hepatitis A 195
Hepatitis C 196
Hypoglycaemia 198
Lyme disease 193
Obsessive compulsive disorder 204
Pancreatitis 198
Panic-attack - agoraphobia 204
PTSD 205
Schizophrenia 205
Stomach ulcers 194
Soraya 209
Sores 25, 27, 65, 73
in a case study 211
SOUL (the)
0-overview 2–7
case studies 146–147, 149, 152, 164, 196, 203, 215, 217, 222
defined 2, 16, 228
prison of 5, 20, 58, 104, 147, 222
soul purpose 120, 138–141, 147, 196
defined 139
is represented by the esoteric planets 6
the ascendant sign represents 118, 147, 196, 217
synonym of soul 2
Spasms 27, 35, 61, 65, 71, 83, 124, 127
case studies 162, 166, 172–173, 181
Spasticity 27, 35, 61, 71, 83
Speech 34–35, 60–61, 85, 125–127, 172
case studies 154–155
impediments 35, 61, 85
in a case study 188
stuttering 19, 35, 61
in a case study 165
throat chakra, the speech centre 60
Spina bifida 27, 69, 93
case studies 146, 218
Spine, spinal column 14, 29, 39, 68–69, 79, 92–93, 125–126, 216, 228
case studies 146, 164, 199
quadriplegia 165
scoliosis 219

spina bifida 218
chakra enters the spine 45, 47–48, 84, 86, 88, 90, 92
five centres lie up the spine 79
problems with 93
within are the three nadis 79
Spirit-Soul-Body overview 2–7
Spiritual practices 81, 93, 101, 117, 121–122, 134
Spitz, Mark 194
Spleen 16–17, 38–39, 53–54, 56–57, 79, 86–87, 122, 125, 127
Stalin, Joseph 111
Starve, starvation, starved 37, 59, 89, 101, 124
in a case study 207
STD's: sexually transmitted diseases 19, 25, 27, 43, 45, 63, 65, 71, 73, 75, 91, 100, 124–125
case studies 151
gonorrhea 211
herpes 211
syphilis 211
Stem cells 19, 37, 59, 87, 126
Sterile, sterility 45, 75
case studies 211
Stomach 19, 29, 36–37, 41, 58–59, 85, 88–89, 125–126
case studies 203
digestive trouble 119
hernia 219
stomach cancer 200
stomach ulcers 194
Stone, stones 49
gallstones 37, 89
case studies 194
kidney stones 43, 63, 93
case studies 214
Strangulation 33, 45, 85
Stratton, Charles 167
Stroke, strokes 12, 31, 81, 104, 110, 117, 125–127, 135
case studies 111, 144, 149, 150, 153, 163, 187
Stuart, Mary 175
Substance abuse 25, 65, 73, 89
case study 202
Suffocation 33, 45, 75, 85, 152
Sugar, sugary 33, 43, 62–63, 66, 88–89, 99
addiction 33, 63
case studies 148, 197–198, 202
Suicide, suicidal 45
a spiritual perspective 152
case studies 204
thoughts 61, 65
Sun (the)
0-overview 56–57
examine for vitality 102–103, 128–129, 131–132, 135
Suppress, suppressed, suppression (see also 'repress')
case studies 112, 186, 197, 201
emotions 12, 15, 91
in case studies 144, 150, 159, 199,

220, 223
fear of life 89
Surgery 65, 71, 108
    case studies 167, 179, 190
        bladder cancer 223
        bursitis 218
        cosmetic 201
        cyst 210
        eye 157, 159
        gallbladder 192
        gallstone 194
        heart 188
        hernia 219
        kidney stone 214
        rectal 180
        ulcer 174
Survival, survival instinct 4, 15, 45, 65, 75, 89, 93, 127
    in a case study 186
Sutratma (see Life thread) 14
Sweats, sweating 18, 59
    in case studies 186, 191, 204
Swells, swollen, swelling 59, 67, 85, 105
    case studies 161, 182, 187
Swift, Jane 193
Sympathetic NS 19, 25, 35, 65, 88–89, 125, 127, 162
    defined 24, 64, 83
    governs fight-flight 192
Syphilis 25, 27, 45, 65, 91
    case studies 147, 211
    indigenous disease 37, 59, 100, 227

T

Tapeworm 41, 61
Taste sense 31, 33, 35, 63, 83, 85
TAURUS - overview 32–33
Taylor, Elizabeth 189
Taylor, President Zachary 182
Tears 18, 37, 59
    in a case study 217
Teeth 30–31, 49, 68–69, 93, 125–127
    case study 103, 161
Testes, testicles 19, 45, 63, 65, 82, 90–91
    in case studies 109, 112
Testosterone 19, 45, 64–65, 91
    in a case study 209
Thatcher, Margaret 153
Thigh, thighs 29, 46–47, 66–67, 93, 104, 126–127
    case studies 224
Think an opposite thought 121–122
Thread of consciousness 18
Throat 29, 32–33, 60, 62–63, 84–85, 88–89, 102, 104, 122, 130, 172
    in case studies 129–130, 172–178, 206
        sleep apnoea 148
        throat cancer 178
        throat fistula 207
THROAT chakra
    0-overview 84–85
    case studies
        Asthma 172

Bronchitis 172
Cancer - lymphatic 177
Cancer - mouth, jaw 178
Cancer - throat 178
Croup 173
Diphtheria 173
Emphysema 173
Graves' disease 176
Hashimoto's disease 176
Hay fever 174
Influenza 174
Pneumonia 174
Pulmonary tuberculosis TB 175
Smallpox 175
Thrush (yeast infection) 21, 25, 37, 59, 73, 91
Thymus gland 35, 38–39, 53, 57, 60, 68, 79, 86–87, 125–127, 183
    atrophies, reactivates 34
    defined 56, 86
    overactive 16, 66
Thyroid gland 18–21, 32–33, 62–63, 68–69, 76, 79, 84–85, 104, 124–127, 172
    case studies 129–130, 191
        grave's disease 176
        hashimoto's disease 176
Tinnitus 27, 35, 61, 83, 85
Toes 52–53, 72–73, 127
Tongue 19, 33, 35, 41, 61, 63, 85
Tonsils, tonsillitis 19, 32–33, 53, 63, 85, 126
Toothache 27, 69, 85
Touch sense 31, 61, 83
Tourette's syndrome 27, 35, 61, 71, 83
    case studies 166
Trauma, traumatic, traumatised, traumatises 21, 71, 75
    case studies 181, 193
        brain trauma 145–146
        PTSD 205
    emotional 45, 104, 140
        case studies 166, 192, 201–202, 204–205
Travolta, Jett 170
Tremors 27, 35, 61, 71, 83
    case studies
        parkinson's 109, 152, 165–166
TRIANGLES (health, disease)
    defined iii, v, vii, 1, 110
    find (how to, examples) 110–115, 131–132, 135, 138
Triune brain 30–31
Tuberculosis, TB 27, 35, 61, 71, 85, 125
    case studies 175
    indigenous disease 100, 104, 227
Tulcin, Annie 206
Tumour, tumours 17, 23, 31, 53, 57, 67, 81, 124, 126–127
    case studies
        brain 112–113, 145
        pituitary 167
        proteus syndrome 222
Twitching, tics 27, 35, 61, 71, 83
    case studies

tourette's syndrome 166
Typhoid fever 27, 37, 41, 59, 71, 85

U

Ulcers, ulcerates 37, 41, 124, 126–127
    gastric 25
    in a case study 174
    peptic/ stomach ulcers 37, 41, 59, 61, 65, 89
    case studies 194
URANUS - overview 70–71
Ureters 19, 45, 92–93
    in a case study 213
Urethra 19, 35, 44–45, 65, 90–93
Uric acid 19, 45, 65
Urinary tract 18–19, 25, 27, 43–45, 65, 71, 75, 92–93, 125–127
    case studies 108, 213
        bladder infection 214
Urine 18–19, 35, 43, 45, 62–63, 92–93, 125
    case studies 215
Uterus, uterine 19, 36–37, 58–59, 90–91, 126–127
    case studies
        cancer of the uterus 212
        ectopic pregnancy 208
        endometriosis 208
        hysterectomy 209
        infertility 209
        miscarriage 209
        ovarian cyst 210
    fibroids 37, 59, 67, 91

V

Vagina 19, 43–45, 63, 90–91
    vaginal candida 21, 91
Vagus nerve 19, 61, 63, 87
    defined 87
    in a case study 188
Vallerey, Georges 215
Valves
    heart valves 51, 71, 87, 104
        case studies 188
    lymphatic 53
    weakened 63
Van Gogh, Vincent 205
Veins 14, 51–53, 57, 62–63, 72, 85–87
    case studies 210
        hemorrhoids 182
    deep vein thrombosis 63, 87
        case studies 185
    jugular vein 33, 52, 63, 85
        in a case study 210
    Path of Return 57, 62
    varicose 63, 87
Vena cava 39, 63, 87
Venereal disease (see STD) 91
Venous system 62–63, 87, 127
    case studies 183
VENUS - overview 62–63
Vertigo 27, 31, 61, 63, 71, 83
Vetter, David 190

Violent, violence, violently 26, 30, 44, 64, 98
   case studies 146, 159, 171
      immune system reacted 192
      reaction to a vaccine 155
   emotions 65
      case studies 194, 197, 203, 205, 220
   mind 12
   thoughts, emotions 98
VIRGO - overview 41–42
Virus, viruses 25, 27, 73, 85, 87, 89, 127, 130
   are of the nature of Neptune 73
   case studies 147, 154, 158, 162, 172, 178, 212
      AIDS 190
      ebola 191
      hepatitis 195–196
      herpes 211
      influenza 174
      measles 162
      polio 165
      shingles 166
      smallpox 175
   Neptune is the primary symbol of 25
Vision - see Sight 156
Vitality, vitalising, vitalisation 20, 31, 38–39, 41, 49, 57, 59, 64–67, 70, 72, 78–80, 82–88, 122, 124–127
   2 major streams of energy 56
   defined 16
   vital life energy flows through 14
Voice, voice box, vocal 19, 84–85
   cords, box 19, 61, 84–85
   in case studies 173, 183
      vocal outbursts 166
      vocal stutters 165
Vomit, vomiting 25, 37, 59, 89
   case studies 168, 195, 203

VULCAN
   0-overview 76
   finding its location 76, 120
   reaches to the very depths 7

W

Wallace, Rowena 219
Warren, Lavinia 167
Warts 19, 25, 45, 49, 67, 73, 91, 93
Watkins, Tionne 184
Wheeler, Elsie 216
White, Barry 187
Wilde, Oscar 147
Williams, Robin 152
Wilson, Harold 150
Windpipe 19, 35, 61, 85
   case studies 173
Winehouse, Amy 203
Winfrey, Oprah 176
Wolfromm, Jean Didier 220
Womb (see Uterus) 37
Wonder, Stevie 156
Wrist 35, 61
Wrong thinking 23, 124

www.ingramcontent.com/pod-product-compliance
Lightning Source LLC
Chambersburg PA
CBHW051209290426
44109CB00021B/2392